4-17-20
CACTUS
SAN Angelo TX

el cAMpo TX- Salt Lake city

c-2019

A Man Absolutely Sure of Himself

A Man Absolutely Sure of Himself

TEXAN GEORGE WASHINGTON
LITTLEFIELD

DAVID B. GRACY II

Foreword by J. PHELPS WHITE III

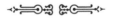

UNIVERSITY OF OKLAHOMA PRESS: NORMAN

LIBRARY OF CONGRESS CATALOGING-IN-PUBLICATION DATA

Names: Gracy, David B., II, 1941– author.

Title: A man absolutely sure of himself : Texan George Washington Littlefield / David B. Gracy II ; foreword by J. Phelps White III.

Other titles: Texan George Washington Littlefield

Description: Norman : University of Oklahoma Press, [2019] | "Appendix A. Littlefield, Nance, Satterwhite, and White Genealogies—Appendix B. Capt. George W. Littlefield's Route over the Chickamauga Battlefield, September 20, 1863— Appendix C. George W. Littlefield's American National Bank Ranching Art: The Murals." | Includes bibliographical references and index.

Identifiers: LCCN 2019014002 | ISBN 978-0-8061-6433-5 (hardcover : alk. paper)

Subjects: LCSH: Littlefield, George W. (George Washington), 1842–1920. | Texas— Biography. | Ranchers—Texas—Biography. | Bankers—Texas—Biography. | Businessmen—Texas—Biography. | Soldiers—Texas—Biography.

Classification: LCC F390 .G73 2019 | DDC 976.4/06092 [B] —dc23

LC record available at https://lccn.loc.gov/2019014002

The paper in this book meets the guidelines for permanence and durability of the Committee on Production Guidelines for Book Longevity of the Council on Library Resources, Inc. ∞

1 2 3 4 5 6 7 8 9 10

To the descendants of
Mildred Terrell Satterwhite White Littlefield

For maintaining the Littlefield-White family bond
that she and her son George Washington Littlefield
nurtured for ninety years

CONTENTS

ILLUSTRATIONS

MAPS

FOREWORD
J. Phelps White III

The author, David B. Gracy II, and I share a common thread with George W. Littlefield, the subject of this book. Littlefield's mother, Mildred Satterwhite White Littlefield, was our great-great-grandmother. The author has placed into the archives of history a magnificent contribution in this epic story of the life of George Littlefield.

Through the years, together and separately, David Gracy and I have visited virtually every site from Texas to Kansas at which George Littlefield played a role. Together we discovered the true location of Mescalero Spring in New Mexico, a well-defined place prominent in Littlefield's ranching career, far off the beaten path today. Together we explored the site of the well-known Bosque Grande on the Pecos, where the LFD Ranch was formed. We also explored the headquarters of the Four Lakes Ranch. In our own time or together, we visited places such as Dodge City, Kansas; the LIT Ranch headquarters; and Old Tascosa and Littlefield, Texas—a community located on the historic Yellow House Ranch, which Gracy's grandfather served as day-to-day operations manager and my grandfather oversaw as ranch and company manager. In addition, Gracy spent untold hours exploring Civil War sites at which Uncle George played a role.

Mescalero Spring deserves special mention. The day we visited this landmark site, it was necessary to hike down an old roadway off the caprock on the Four Lakes Ranch. Upon reaching bottom and looking up behind us, we saw the view depicted by the principal scene on the massive bronze doors George Littlefield commissioned for his American National Bank in Austin. Mescalero Spring represents a milestone in the development of Littlefield's enormous wealth that made possible almost everything that came later.

Regarding that enormous wealth, Gracy recognizes the contributions of Littlefield's trusted nephew Phelps White, my grandfather, and Phelps's brothers, Will and Tom. They formed an extraordinary ranching team. It was Phelps White's devotion to Uncle George that helped Littlefield move forward as an innovative pioneer in the early days of ranching on the plains of eastern New Mexico and West Texas. Gracy and I studied Old Tascosa and the LIT Ranch, where Phelps White and Littlefield personnel brought about the founding of Oldham County, Texas, and the naming of Tascosa as the county seat. It was here on the Canadian River in the Texas Panhandle that Littlefield cattle carried the LIT brand.

Gracy reflects that, as a regent, businessman, banker, and philanthropist, George W. Littlefield had no equal. The University of Texas can look back and thank him not just for his financial support but also for gifts of the Littlefield Fund, the John Henry Wrenn Library, and his home, now the oldest building on the main campus. Downtown Austin was transformed into a metropolitan center, which led to Austin's becoming one of the great American cities of today.

Gracy made several visits to the White family home in Roswell, where he met and enjoyed time with my grandmother, Lou Tomlinson White. I too spent many happy times as a young boy and young adult at this landmark home in Roswell. The home now houses the museum and archives for the Historical Society for Southeast New Mexico.

In these pages the reader will discover George Littlefield's love and support of his family. He truly loved and took care of his wife, Alice, for the many years of their long marriage. He provided financial assistance to many college-bound family members by simply underwriting their expenses or by supplying room and board in his own home. His advice, good morals, discipline, and leadership played positive roles for many young family members. Three generations removed from the close relationship of Uncle George and my grandfather, author David Gracy and I continue to enjoy the camaraderie of our personal family bond begun more than a half century ago.

ACKNOWLEDGMENTS

"On the theory that you will eventually tell the Littlefield Story in full," my mother, Alice Tillar Duggan Gracy (1903–95), wrote on May 11, 1962, telling me of the next phase of genealogical research she was then about to begin on her great uncle, George Washington Littlefield. In fact, she had first delved into his life nearly two decades earlier when she conducted oral history interviews with family members. Despite her longstanding interest in learning the doings of the man she knew as a teenager, writing the story never was her mission. But it could be mine, she must have thought, after she saw my interest in history flare in 1954 during a spur-of-the-moment detour to Shiloh Civil War battlefield. Only twelve years old, I became instantly consumed with reading about and contemplating the events that had occurred on the ground on which I was standing. In 1957 during my sophomore year in Sewanee Military Academy, my interest in Littlefield began to develop when I planned a spring-break trip that took us to sites in the Civil War's Western Theater, including Shiloh, where by then I knew Littlefield had been engaged. Still, her charge in the 1962 letter was optimistic. It came at the end of my junior year in university before I had published my first piece on Littlefield. Now, more than a half century after she wrote, with her extensive genealogical files forming the foundation for my family research enabled by trustworthy electronic sources, and with my master's thesis (developed into a book), doctoral dissertation, and fifteen articles completed on him and on individuals, businesses, and events significant in his life, I am redeeming her trust. Consequently, of all the persons who merit acknowledgment for their contributions to completion of this life's labor of love, she stands foremost.

This book would be a shadow of itself without the fraternity of James Phelps White III. My third half cousin and the grandson of Littlefield's nephew, ranching partner and confidant James Phelps White I, Phelps III served as a partner and confidant for me as his grandfather had been for Littlefield. During more than fifty years, Phelps III made possible multiple visits to Bosque Grande, Mescalero Spring, and the Four Lakes Ranch. From his personal experience in Pecos Valley ranching and in working with the principals, places, and history of ranching and water in New Mexico and Texas, Phelps III greatly extended my knowledge of cattle and of ranching along the river and on the high plains. He introduced me to local historians and to resources that enriched my understanding of the ranching side of Littlefield's life. His enjoyment in studying the role his grandfather played in ranching and the development of eastern New Mexico and in the Littlefield story (in so many ways, the Littlefield-White story) further stimulated my own.

CONTRIBUTIONS OF LITTLEFIELD AND WHITE FAMILY MEMBERS

Without the documents and reminiscences readily shared with me by members of the extended Littlefield and White families (and listed in the bibliography's oral history section), the Littlefield story would be anemic. Lacking space to describe all of the materials, objects, family lore, and other knowledge these dozens of relatives (many now deceased) opened to me during the more than fifty years I have been contacting them, I extend my thanks by listing their names: Cindy and Patrick H. Boone IV, Nancy Buford, Ann Buller, Ann Littlefield Coleman, Nancy White DeYoung, Robert Dowell, Arthur P. Duggan Jr., Campbell J. Duggan, Sarah Harral Duggan, Grace M. Evans, Bonilee Key Garrett, Mary Lou and Wayne Glass, Carla Green, Jennie Walker Harless, Robert and Olivia Harless, Pat G. Iverson, Ruth Key ("Aunt" Ruth earns special thanks for twenty years of conversations in which she shared her knowledge of George and Alice Littlefield from living in the Littlefield Home during the last decade and a half of their years there), Betsy S. Lindstrom, Charles F. Malone, Olivia and Ida McGarity, Norma Maxwell, Elizabeth McCrummen, Kathleen B. Midkiff, Sytha Minter, Susan Wroe Perry, Steven P. Smith, George Littlefield White, Lou Tomlinson (Mrs. James Phelps I) White, James Phelps White Jr., John David White, Elizabeth and James White, W. Walker White, Ruth Gracy Wise, Ed Rhodes Littlefield Wroe Jr., Mary Jo Collie and William A. Wroe Sr., and Dr. William A. Wroe Jr.

OTHER INDIVIDUAL CONTRIBUTIONS

Reminiscences have been a particularly rich resource thanks in part to J. Evetts Haley's interviews conducted for writing his 1943 Littlefield biography. These captured the observations of Littlefield contemporaries on the range, in business, and in politics, most long passed from the scene by the time I began my work. Equally important have been the memories shared with me of the many individuals who knew Littlefield from their positions two or three generations after him.

Two groups have contributed information and research without which this volume would be incomplete. The first is those who assisted with my doctoral dissertation, completed in 1971, on Littlefield's business life and those who contributed documentation and reminiscences. In addition from that period, I also thank R. Sylvan Dunn, Clifford B. Jones, Chester V. Kielman, Mrs. Hood Pitts, and Taylor Pointer.

The second is those who made their contributions during the last forty-seven years of my work on Littlefield: Phelps Anderson, Howard R. Baade, Cherie Baker, T. Lindsay Baker, Lee Bash, Don R. Brownlee, Patricia Cloud, Belle Cook, Ann J. Dolce, Martha Doty Freeman, Ralph Elder, Cora Jane and Norman Farmer, Mark Firmin, Roy Flukinger, Patricia K. Galloway, Emma Gene Gentry, Effie Dean Giles, Jim Gill, Brooks Goldsmith, Jim Harris, Martha A. Hartzog, Tad Hershorn, Harwood and Diana Hinton, Tom Hoover, Andrew Jones, Punch Jones (Debrouilet Ranch), Jacob P. Juba, Lisa M. Kirch, De'Niecechsi C. Layton, Barbara Lightsey, Jennifer C. Madden, Garry L. Nall, W. H. and Alice O'Brien, Mike Pacino, Jana Pankratz and Charlie Palafox, Octavia Rogan, B. Byron Price, Patsy Hill Rahn, Sergio Santos and Brian Morrison, Paul R. Scott, Jimmy M. Skaggs, James F. Springfield, Sledge Taylor, Neal Walker, Scott White, and Elizabeth Whitlow.

The following made extra special and extended contributions: Danny Burger, Brenda S. Gunn, Karl Miller, David J. Murrah, Jim Nicar, David A. Powell, Morris Terry, and Russell Tether.

ARCHIVES AND RECORDS REPOSITORIES AND MUSEUMS

Alexander Architectural Archives, University of Texas at Austin: Nancy L. Sparrow

American Civil War Museum, Richmond, Virginia: Cathy Wright

American Heritage Center, University of Wyoming: Leslie Waggener

Austin History Center, Austin Public Library: Mike Miller and his staff

Blocker History of Medicine Collection, University of Texas Medical Branch: Robert O. Marlin

Chickamauga and Chattanooga National Military Park: Robert Carter

Dolph Briscoe Center for American History, University of Texas at Austin: Don E. Carleton, director, Brenda S. Gunn (then Janey Briscoe Archivist and Director of Research and Collections), Lynn J. Bell, Kathryn E. Kenefick, Stephanie B. Malmros, Director of Research and Collections, and Head of Reference Margaret L. Schlankey

Gonzales County Archives, Gonzales County Clerk: Pat Mosher and Peggie Schultz

Grand Lodge of Texas, A.F. and A.M.: Bruce Mercer and his staff

Nita Stewart Haley Memorial Library, Midland, Texas: J. Pat McDaniel, director, and Librarian Catherine Smith

Harry Ransom Center, University of Texas at Austin: Richard B. Watson

Historical Society for Southeast New Mexico, Museum Archives Center:
    Volunteer Chief Archivist Janice Dunnahoo and John LeMay

Houston Metropolitan Research Center: Joel Draut and Matthew Richardson

Eastern New Mexico University: Steven Gamble and Gene Bundy

Kansas State Historical Society: Benjamin Stone

Panhandle-Plains Historical Museum, Research Center: Warren Stricker

Panola County Courthouse, Sardis, Mississippi: staff

Pennsylvania Hospital: Stacey Peeples

Southwest Collection, Texas Tech University: Monte Monroe, Tai Kreidler,
    and staff

Texas General Land Office: Mark W. Lambert

Texas State Archives: Jelain Chubb, director, Tony Black, Halley Grogan,
    Rebecca Romanchuk, and Tonia Wood

University of Pennsylvania Archives: J. J. Ahern

READERS
Twenty-six individuals from several American states, Australia, and Poland helped
polish the final product by their comments on one or more chapters: Claudia
Chidester, Ann Littlefield Coleman, Sarah Demb, Daniel Doggett, George Dug-
gan, Annette Gracy, Chris Harmon, Lucile Gracy Harmon, Barry Hutcheson,
Sarah Canby Jackson, Lou Harris, Carol Heath, Patricia Garrett Iverson, Betsy
Lindstrom, Susan Perry, Edie Sundby, Morris Terry, Nan Kilkeary, Sallie Duggan
Wier, and Sally Wise. Special thanks go to Tadeusz Bielicki, Robert Coleman,
Benjamin B. Gracy, David J. Murrah, Richard B. McCaslin, and Paul Wilson,
whose comments on the entire manuscript improved the text measurably.

OTHER CONTRIBUTIONS
Contributions from Littlefield Fund for Southern History, administered by the
University of Texas History Department (Chair Jackie Jones) and General Libraries
(Vice Provost and University Librarian Lorraine Haricombe and Deputy to the Vice
Provost Douglas Barnett), made possible color printing of images in the first printing.
    As important as any other assistance has been the backing of my dear wife of
fifty-six years, Laura Lee Baade Gracy. Without her loving support manifested in
unselfish acts accommodating my work, not the least of which has been ensuring
a comfortable home environment in which to work, I could not have brought this
book to culmination.

A Man Absolutely Sure of Himself

INTRODUCTION
A Texan American

For sixty or so years after his birth on June 21, 1842, George Washington Littlefield made news like anyone else—for what he did. From 1871 until his death forty-nine years later on November 10, 1920, Littlefield made money trading cattle and ranching in Texas and New Mexico. His proficiency in both realms earned him a place on the 1892 first list of American millionaires. The several domains over which his cattle, most carrying his LFD brand, ranged in the 1890s constituted a territory larger than the states of Rhode Island and Delaware combined. Eleven years after he bought the 312,000-acre Yellow House Ranch on Texas's South Plains, he founded the town of Littlefield on the portion of the ranch he opened for sale to farmers in 1912.

After settling in Texas's capital city of Austin in 1883, Littlefield played a prominent role in promoting his adopted home. In 1890 he organized and for twenty-eight years headed Austin's highly profitable American National Bank. To house the business, in 1910–11 he built the Littlefield Building, touted as the tallest skyscraper between New Orleans and San Francisco. Unique among the principals in the iconic age of the cattle industry, for the bank's walls and entrance he commissioned murals and a pair of bronze doors depicting scenes on his ranches.

In his last decade and through his will, Littlefield devoted himself to the University of Texas as both a board of regents member and a donor. During his tenure, he offered to underwrite an entire biennium to thwart the governor who sought to take control of the school by vetoing the legislative appropriation. Chief among his benefactions, in 1914 he established the Littlefield Fund for Southern History, which at $25,000 more than doubled the total of all other endowments combined. With a single $225,000 check (equivalent to about two-fifths of the school's annual budget), in 1918 he funded acquisition of the John Henry Wrenn Library of English literature, which vaulted the university to prominence among institutions with rare book collections. The $1.25 million in cash and buildings that Littlefield bequeathed to the university ensured that the school remained on its original campus, across the street from the home he bought to front the institution.

In recognition of his service and gifts, George Littlefield was accorded the extraordinary honor of lying in repose on campus, as of 2018 a respect bestowed only one subsequent time in the 137-year history of the school.

As Littlefield reached his sixties, he had done so much so profitably in so many spheres for so long that the sum of his deeds elevated him from just newsmaker to a man recognized for the breadth of his accomplishments. No wonder. With the drive of a Rockefeller, the vision of a Carnegie, the philanthropic generosity of Texas's George Washington Brackenridge, and the eye for history of Teddy Roosevelt, Littlefield fit his times to an unusual degree.

University of Texas President Robert E. Vinson sensed it. Littlefield, he wrote, "is to be classed with men who carve empires out of the wilderness, who make the desert to rejoice and blossom as the rose, who push against the horizon. Like the chief figure in de Senectute he was busy to the last, always conscious of the generations pressing up behind him, for whom he was making preparation."[1]

America's Gilded Age invited the carving of empires. Expansion into the trans-Mississippi West and a burgeoning population generated phenomenal economic growth. Growth opened opportunities. Opportunities summoned entrepreneurs. Entrepreneurs built empires: Andrew Carnegie in steel, John D. Rockefeller in oil, Gustavus Franklin Swift in meat packing, Cornelius Vanderbilt in railroads, George Pullman in railroad passenger cars, and on the list goes. Looking at their contributions to the rise of American industrial might, some praised this class of businessmen as "captains of industry." Focusing on the costs paid by workers and on the corrupt system from which the businessmen profited, others damned them as "robber barons." Either way, the times clearly roused the ambitious to exploit developments.

Like the magnates, Littlefield lived to do business. As Rockefeller did in his oil company, Littlefield attended to little details, managed the books, and outbargained his counterparts. Like Carnegie, he exhibited a rare capacity for handling large affairs, conducted business at a dizzying pace, and envisioned the future. Carnegie saw that steel would replace iron on railroads and in construction; Littlefield anticipated market movements. But there the parallels end. Neither Littlefield nor any other cattleman followed Rockefeller in using secretive combinations and kickbacks to eliminate competition. And unlike Carnegie and Pullman, Littlefield increased his profits without cutting costs at his workers' expense.[2]

If Littlefield could be accused of robber baron tactics, it would appear to be in appropriating public land for grazing cattle. For use of Texas Panhandle grass, he paid the state not one penny. But it was not because Littlefield dodged anteing up; the state in fact had no mechanism for collecting. With the land unsurveyed, no units existed on which to charge rent. True, beginning in 1879 ranchers as Littlefield were approached about acquiring title, but not by the state. Rather, the agents were entrepreneurs who offered certificates they had bought and, for a profit, would sell the rancher, entitling the holder to locate the amount of acreage allotted by the certificate. Whether or not the rancher bought, the state had collected its due when the speculator paid for the certificates. In New Mexico, for twenty-five years or so, Littlefield used the eastern plains without paying the federal government more than fees for filing on water sources. Again, he was not flouting the law. Like Texas, Congress provided no mechanism for collecting payment. And even had Congress acted, only in the twentieth century did surveyors begin marking LFD range into units on which rent could be levied. Once a mechanism existed and surveying had been completed, George Littlefield paid.

Rather than profiting from taking unethical advantage of Texas or the federal government or his workers or participating in a cabal to control the market, Littlefield's improving fortunes resulted from three qualities that set him apart from the robber barons. One was his uncanny ability to anticipate price fluctuations. In being subject to market movements, cattlemen differed from the likes of Rockefeller and Carnegie, who so dominated their businesses that they controlled their markets. The second was his emphasis on raising a quality product. In the 1880s Littlefield had begun to introduce Hereford bulls on his free-range LIT Ranch, resulting in beefier stock that commonly attracted notice for the higher prices they commanded. The third was the loyalty his fair and respectful treatment stirred in his workers and associates.

One other trait distinguished Littlefield. He appreciated history. "Yes I guess you enjoyed walking around and looking over the old walls of the Alamo," he replied to a great nephew. "Think if they could talk, tell what has transpired within them, of the last acts, and thoughts of those patriots who gave up their lives that Texas might be free."[3] As he reflected on history-changing events and on the qualities that propelled the doers, Littlefield had few counterparts in the leadership of his age. Business leaders weren't known for historical reflection. Rather, the one who stands out is President Theodore Roosevelt, with whom Littlefield worked in the American Defense Society preparing the United States for its role in World War I. Roosevelt wrote history. With an academic endowment, Littlefield encouraged historical study. In scenes of actual events from his ranches immortalized in bronze and on canvas displayed for all to see at Austin's American National Bank, Littlefield encouraged popular appreciation of the period rapidly passing, about which Roosevelt wrote and through which both had lived.

In all this, Littlefield rose above being just a man to know and a figure in history. He became a figure for history—Texas history, southern history, western history, and American history. History professor and subsequent chief historian of the Texas

State Historical Association Walter L. Buenger makes Littlefield's place plain. In "Texas Identity: Alternatives to the Terrible Triplets," Buenger found Littlefield to be the singular illustration of the notion that Texas is not a state distinctly Southern because of its participation in the Confederacy, not a state western for its history with cattle, and not a state exceptional because of its period as an independent nation. Instead it is a state clearly and fully American. In endowing the Littlefield Fund to produce a "true and impartial" history of the South, George Littlefield was a quintessential southerner. Decorating his American National Bank with scenes from his ranching operation accurate down to the LFD brand spread across the right side of every bronze cow identified him as a westerner. The American name for his bank, along with his extraordinary funding in support of America's participation in World War I, left no doubt that, without abandoning either his southern legacy or his ranching heritage, he was American. By linking the Southern and Western contributions to the overarching American character of Texas, Littlefield "demonstrated the importance, mutability, and power of collective memory and culture."[4] In a final confirmation, Littlefield commissioned a memorial gateway for the University of Texas that included statuary of Southern, Texan, and American figures, the whole meant to mark the reunion of North and South in the crucible of World War I.

Buenger portrayed the full magnitude of Littlefield's place in Texas history:

> Take in, then, Littlefield, whose life and works commemorated and enshrined collective memories. As much a gilded age entrepreneur as Andrew Carnegie, he preached sobriety and virtue to his relatives and cowhands. He proudly remembered the South and the Confederacy and wanted others to understand his Lost Cause from his point of view. Yet his bank was an American bank, a national bank, and one decorated with western images. His fountain and accompanying statues mixed American, southern, and Texan prototypes, but the overall drift of Littlefield's life and his legacy was clear. He made Texas American. He rode the leading edge of the economic currents of the nation and the industrialized world toward prosperity. He grew and changed over the course of his life with events like World War I making him even more American. Littlefield stood for Texas and its evolving identity.[5]

Buenger is the last writer so far to consider Littlefield. The first biography of Littlefield was published twenty-three years after his death. No casual undertaking, James Evetts Haley's *George W. Littlefield, Texan* was commissioned by the Littlefield Fund for Southern History. For the job, fund director and professor Eugene C. Barker tapped a former student. Because Barker saw Littlefield primarily as a cattleman active in the most broadly popular age of America's iconic industry, his choice made sense. Haley was a cowman himself. Moreover, he knew Texas cattle history. The thick master's thesis he wrote under Barker, "A Survey of Texas Cattle Drives to the North, 1866–1895," remains a staple source. With a full working knowledge of cattle and ranching and a demonstrated competence in historical research and analysis, Haley was the man then best positioned to discuss Littlefield's cattle and ranching life and to put them into historical context.

As appropriate as he was for the job, Haley recognized the limitations confining a biographer so close in time to his subject. Little documentation was available in archives. In family hands he found only a single cache of Littlefield letters. As thin as that documentation was, fund directors declined to finance research in Littlefield's birth state of Mississippi. In focusing primarily on Littlefield's life in ranching and cattle, Haley ignored non-ranching documentation he could have gotten from family members. Consequently, Haley claimed for his work only "an attempt, through the extensive use of oral sources, to suggest the nature and extent of Littlefield's various and remarkably successful ventures on the ranges of grass." So, for all that Haley's work did tell (and the oral histories are invaluable), it left most of Littlefield's life untold.[6]

Subsequent writers, then, have had a broad field in which to work. Haley contemporary and University of Texas folklorist J. Frank Dobie criticized Littlefield for a political action he took as a university regent. "Bull headed" sums up Dobie's criticisms of Littlefield in the chapter "Having His Own Way" in *Cow People*. Two examples of Dobie's censure beg attention. In one, Dobie reproached Littlefield for saying late in his career with cattle that "the only practical knowledge I have gained in ranching is that a cow will have a calf."[7] Littlefield did not say that at that time. Dobie's only source, University of Texas engineering dean and Littlefield friend T. U. Taylor, wrote that Littlefield "told me one day that [as a cripple after the Civil War] he was at a loss to know how to make a living. He said that the only practical knowledge he had was that a cow would have a calf."[8] Taylor reported Littlefield's description of the knowledge he had *when he began* working with cattle, not the knowledge he had gained from a lifetime as a cowman, cattleman, and rancher. And at that, Littlefield was jesting, just as he was when he said that when he took over the farming operations in 1864, he did not know one kind of plow from another. He had managed family cotton plantations before the war.

Second, Dobie disparages "the ponderous bronze doors to his bank in Austin, Texas, bas-reliefed with cattle, cowboys, chuck wagon and his L F D brand." Calling the doors "indigenous art" of the cattle culture, Haley had answered Dobie before the folklorist penned his criticism. Littlefield "decorated his bank with bronze ropes and brands and western murals before the experts in culture discovered indigenous art," Haley had written. Art unique to and expressive of the cattle kingdom of the Southwest, Dobie of all scholars should have appreciated. In *Life and Literature of the Southwest*, specifically in the chapter "Range Life: Cowboys, Cattle, Sheep," Dobie himself was the first to promote the rich singularity of the literature of the very cattle industry in which Littlefield rose to prominence and which he depicted on the doors.[9]

Historian Fred A. Bailey asserted in "The Best History Money Can Buy: Eugene Campbell Barker, George Washington Littlefield, and the Quest for a Suitable Past," that the 1914 Littlefield Fund for Southern History gift exposed "a darker recess of southern intellectual history. The financing of an archival research depository was, paradoxically, a part of the crusade among southern elites to suppress academic freedom and to impose upon their homeland a version of the past essential to the perpetuation of their power." Bailey's piece constituted one in a series pursuing his thesis.[10] True, Littlefield wanted others to see Southern history as he saw it. Recognizing this, Bailey damned the gift with faint praise, writing that the "happy act of philanthropy remains to this day a boon for those scholars interested in the late Confederacy and the regional culture associated with it." Contrary to Bailey's assertion, the fund from its inception recognized American history as its focus. "It is worth noting with some emphasis," Barker wrote, describing the new gift, "that it is no part of Major Littlefield's purpose to promote the partisan study of history." Littlefield Fund reports document it, and university librarian Ernest William Winkler praised the benefactor for it. "You are willing for the South to be judged by her records," wrote Winkler. "It gives expression to your confidence that when the records are complete they will be to her credit."[11]

The rival stewardship of the University of Texas by regents and benefactors George Littlefield and George Washington Brackenridge has attracted historians' interest for decades. In her *George W. Brackenridge: Maverick Philanthropist*, historian Marilyn McAdams Sibley considered it possible that Brackenridge's reaction to Littlefield's final university benefactions may have hastened Brackenridge's death by thwarting his design to relocate the campus.[12]

The present author took Littlefield as a subject beginning with publication of "With Danger and Honor: George W. Littlefield, 1861–1864," illuminating Littlefield's Civil War experience as revealed in unpublished letters. *Littlefield Lands: Colonization on the Texas Plains, 1912–1920* recounts development of the northeast sixty-four thousand acres of Littlefield's Yellow House Ranch for farming and the founding and early years of the town of Littlefield. "George Washington Littlefield: Portrait of a Cattleman" presents Littlefield's prescription for living as found in letters to the Dowell family. "Business and Books" discusses Littlefield's relationship with libraries, first his service on the Texas Library and Historical Commission that proved to have a bearing on his gift of the Littlefield Fund and second his purchase for the university of the John Henry Wrenn Library. "Mildred Satterwhite Littlefield (1811–1880)" is the most substantial biography of Littlefield's mother. "A Man of Large Heart: George W. Littlefield and the Davis Obelisk" not only recounts Littlefield's engagement with that Kentucky monument but also is one of the few accounts of the movement to raise the world's tallest poured concrete structure. "The Duty of Such As Myself: George W. Littlefield's Ranching and Confederate Art" tells the story of the Confederate paintings and statues that Littlefield ordered for his home and for a memorial gateway to the university. The bronze doors and murals he commissioned for his bank hold a special place in the art of the cattle industry because they depict actual scenes on three Littlefield ranches. "Cows Have Calves: The Hesitant Beginning and Remarkable Career of Cowboy, Cattleman, Rancher George Washington Littlefield" explores Littlefield's three roles in working with cattle. Finally, "The Dowell Family Papers: The Splintering of an Archival Treasure" discusses the challenges raised for telling the Littlefield story, and by extension any historical story, caused by the failure of the family archives' custodian to keep the documentation together.

Contemporaries describe George Washington Littlefield as a man energetic in his step, with a ruddy complexion from his years in the saddle during the Civil War and working cattle on the Texas and New Mexico plains. He weighed in his prime about 180 pounds and stood five feet seven inches tall. Though of average size, he commanded the attention of those to whom he spoke by looking them in the eye. Adults remembered the look as a piercing fixation. Children remembered it as being warmly personal because the important man was addressing them directly (fig. 1).[13]

Both those who knew him personally and those who knew him from his acts alone commented on the absolute integrity with which Littlefield conducted his affairs. "He hated a rogue and a liar worse than anything," said former slave Harrison McClure. "All you had to do was to look at him and know that if he gave you his word in a business transaction that was exactly what he would do," observed a young lawyer. A junior employee in Littlefield's American National Bank, unused to handling financial transactions by word of mouth, suffered the consequences. When the employee encountered an unsigned check in Littlefield's handwriting and asked the bank president to sign it, Littlefield grunted, "It's alright." Being unused to large sums of money being guaranteed so informally, the employee persisted. "But won't you please sign it?" Littlefield looked at him "with eyes like a

rattlesnake and shouted at the teller in the outer office, 'Give Mr. Wells the gold.'"
Concluded the storyteller, "My father had to carry a heavy sack of gold down the
street to the other bank. I guess the Major resented the implication that he might
go back on his verbal agreement to honor the check" (fig. 56).[14]

"He was no hail-fellow-well-met, slap-you-on-the-back somebody," commented
a great niece. "Hospitable" described the experience of former cowhand Jeff
Connolly:

> The last time I was in Austin . . . I went into the American National Bank
> with a friend of mine and I asked the teller of the bank where the Major
> was. He told me he was back in his private office. This friend of mine
> wanted to know why I was asking about Major Littlefield and asked me if
> I knew he was a millionaire? I told him that I knew that, but that I used to
> drive on the old trail for him and was anxious to see him. I went back and
> told the Major who I was and he treated me as fine as any man was ever
> treated. If I had been a millionaire myself he could not have treated me any
> better, and that's what makes us common fellows like him. He is just as
> plain as if he didn't have any more than we have.[15]

No surprise, then, that when former trail riders formed the Old Time Trail Drivers' Association, Littlefield joined and at its first annual meeting in 1916 took a seat
on the board. Talking old times of cowboying, cattle trailing, and life in the West
stirred Littlefield. One afternoon in the lobby of the Hot Springs, Arkansas, Arlington Hotel, Littlefield chanced to hear that W. B. Masterson had arrived. Was this Bat
Masterson, sheriff of Dodge City, Kansas, in the heyday of cattle trailing? Littlefield
asked. Yes. Forty years since the two had last seen each other, Littlefield's rheumatism
and Masterson's neuritis had drawn them to the same spa. Once reunited, "what
an old-time 'fanning' bee they had!'" reported the *Hot Springs Sentinel-Record*. By
the paper's account, Masterson spun the more superlative yarns. "No finer body of
men ever rode herd on the 'long horns' or fought their way from the Panhandle
into Kansas and Nebraska than did the Littlefield men. No outfit ever carried better
Winchesters or could shoot faster and more accurately than the men of that outfit,"
the reporter heard Masterson say. Handling cowboys' exuberant celebrating in town
after two months on the trail keeping the company of a couple of thousand head
of beeves occasioned the situations that had introduced outfit owner Littlefield and
Sheriff Masterson. While such encounters made no news in the 1870s, papers in
Arkansas and Texas, if not beyond, covered the happy reunion in 1919.[16]

As widely known as Littlefield was for his cattle enterprise, his western associations ranged farther and gave him a credibility in speaking about the years through

which he had lived. William F. "Buffalo Bill" Cody called on him for that authority. For a legal case, Cody asked Littlefield to vouch that Buffalo Bill's Wild West Show depicted life as Littlefield had known it on the plains. "He saw my Wild West when it was in its infancy, and knew me before I started it," Cody testified. Cody won.[17] Only reminiscing with his Civil War regimental comrades about the campaigning they shared gave Littlefield more pleasure than reminiscing about the open range days.

Littlefield twice began writing an autobiography. Family conflict drove his father, Fleming, with many of his and wife Mildred's Littlefield and White (from her first marriage) brood, to Texas from Mississippi, where George had spent his first eight years. Upon Fleming's death, Mildred became the extended family's undisputed head. George succeeded her and looked after seven of his nine living siblings and half siblings, their thirty-one living progeny, and the next two generations as they arrived. But despite the depth of his investment in them all, he never wrote or spoke about his ancestry—too busy to look into it, he replied late in life to an inquiring Littlefield family member.[18]

Littlefield enjoyed doing business. No matter how much money he amassed, "he was always working to keep from going broke," said a nephew rancher. In that vein, "When he set in to do anything, he was going to do it one way or another," commented a nephew-by-marriage sugar plantation manager. That included sticking with associates through thick and thin. "He always stood by those he was interested in and never backed up when they needed help," recalled one reviewing their forty-year relationship. "He liked to win," added a niece who played cards with him. "If he didn't, it put him in the worst kind of humor. He wanted to beat, to be ahead."[19]

Children occupied a special place with him. Many he nicknamed. "Rooster" identified the author's mother and another great-niece. "Colonel" designated both a great-niece and former slave Harrison McClure who credited Littlefield with raising him. Littlefield put candy in his pocket to give visiting children, and he allowed neighborhood youth to roller-skate on his ample driveway and walkways.[20]

Littlefield had his habits. When sitting, he commonly cocked a leg over the chair's arm. But the habit most vividly remembered by all who experienced it concerned the wound that ended his military career. Shrapnel from a cannon ball that exploded near him blew away his left hip. While Littlefield lay on the ground taking what his comrades expected to be his last breath, his brigade commander rode up and promoted him to major for gallantry in action. That moment turned the day he almost died into the proudest of his life. He ever enjoyed inviting children, even adults, to feel the void. Remembered one family member: "He would say when as children we visited him 'How many of you children would like to feel where the Yankee cannon ball hit your uncle?' Of course all wanted to feel the hole.

Then he would say, 'Double up your fist and make it as big as possible and stick it in my side.' With eyes as big as dollars we stuck our little fists into his side. Not even with him fully dressed could our little fists fill up the large hole."[21]

As one feature writer saw him, Major Littlefield "is as likable as he is rugged, and he is as optimistic as a youth who knows not the meaning of adversity." Wrote another, "He has hobnobbed with good fortune, but he has not permitted her to rob him of his birthright of human kindliness and human affection." Commented the local paper on the day he died: "Evasiveness was foreign to his nature, and once having reached a conclusion on any public measure, he was as frank in stating it as he was fearless in standing by it."[22] A nephew who boarded in the Littlefield home while attending the University of Texas summed up his uncle's character this way: "He was noble yet hard as nails at times, magnanimous yet unforgiving, generous yet remembering to a penny, a fighter yet he put an overcoat under the head of the man he killed and sent for a doctor. . . . He was a great man and tried to be fair to all."[23]

With reminiscences and descriptions of Littlefield's contemporaries gathered, documentation from archives assembled, an insightful positioning of Littlefield in the fabric of Texas and American history realized, what remains is unfurling a full narrative of George Littlefield's life and of the ways his legacy continues to touch the American state of Texas, the University of Texas, and the city of Austin.

Littlefield steered through life with firm confidence. Family members knew it. Among them his word was law. "'Uncle said . . . ' was all any of them had to hear" to know what they were to do, recalled one. "He always said that he ran his business and that his business didn't run him," testified another. Opponents also knew it. "He was a man absolutely sure of himself," complimented John A. Lomax, who felt Regent Littlefield's weight during the conflict occasioned by Governor James Edward Ferguson's effort to assert control over the University of Texas by vetoing its biennial appropriation. And historian Buenger saw it in Littlefield's leadership of the Americanization of Texas. Wherever he engaged, George Littlefield projected an outsized force: in business and community service, so too in human sensitivity. Freedman Harrison McClure felt Littlefield's magnetism so strongly that he ran away from home to join Littlefield's cattle outfit.[24]

A man known in his lifetime for what he did and who he was, George Washington Littlefield endures as a Texan American significant in our time for both his life and his legacy. The characteristic that above all others distinguished him for contemporaries, for subsequent observers, and for interpreters, John Lomax captured in six words. George Littlefield was a man absolutely sure of himself.

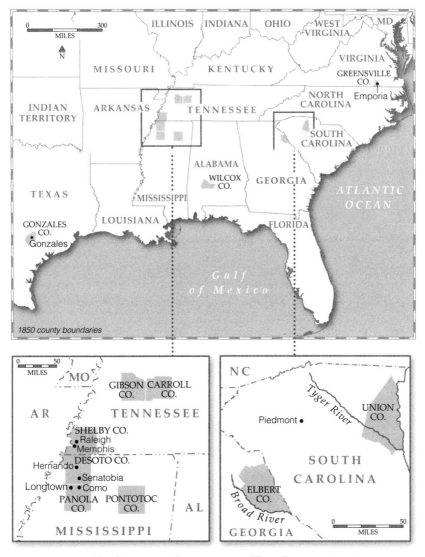

MAP 1. The South of the Littlefield and White Families, 1800–1850.
Map by Carol Zuber-Mallison.

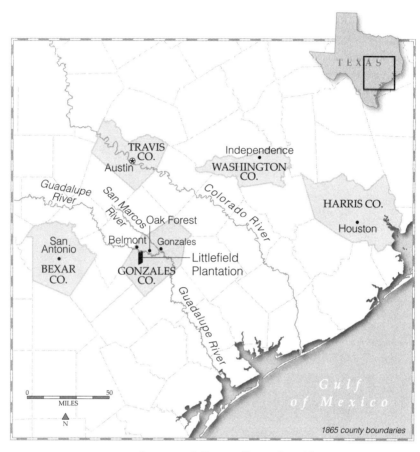

MAP 2. LITTLEFIELD'S CENTRAL TEXAS, 1850–1865.
Map by Carol Zuber-Mallison.

MAP 3. LITTLEFIELD'S CIVIL WAR, 1861–1864.
Map by Carol Zuber-Mallison.

15

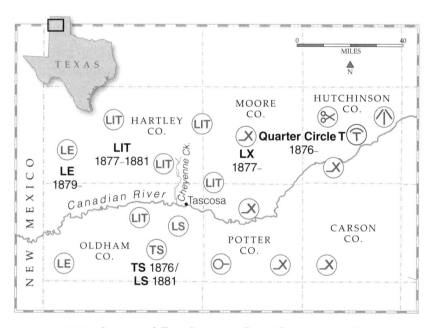

MAP 4. LITTLEFIELD'S TEXAS PANHANDLE CATTLE COUNTRY, 1877–1881.
Map by Carol Zuber-Mallison.

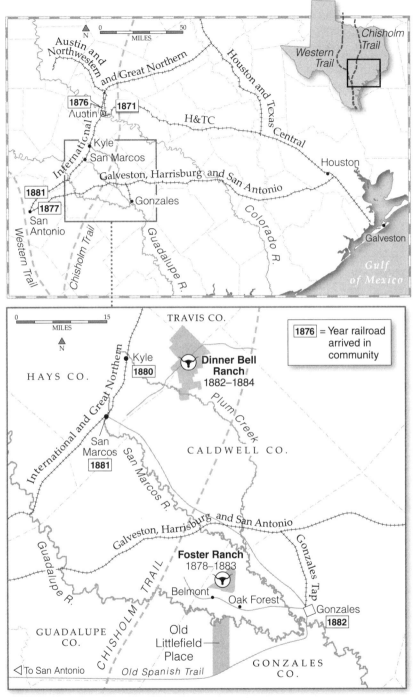

MAP 5. LITTLEFIELD'S CENTRAL TEXAS, 1865–1885.
Map by Carol Zuber-Mallison.

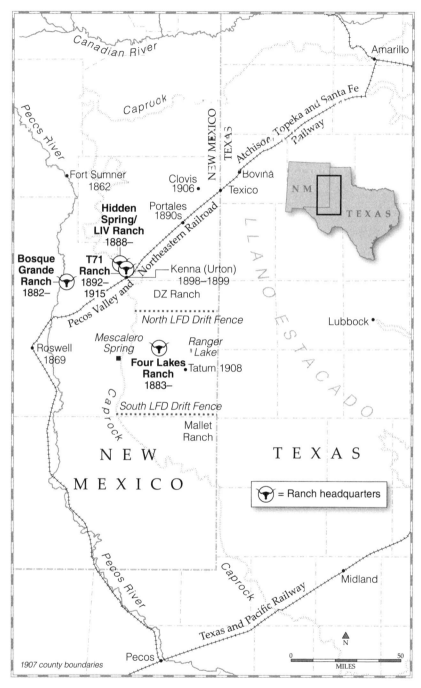

MAP 6. LITTLEFIELD'S NEW MEXICO CATTLE COUNTRY, 1882–1915.
Map by Carol Zuber-Mallison.

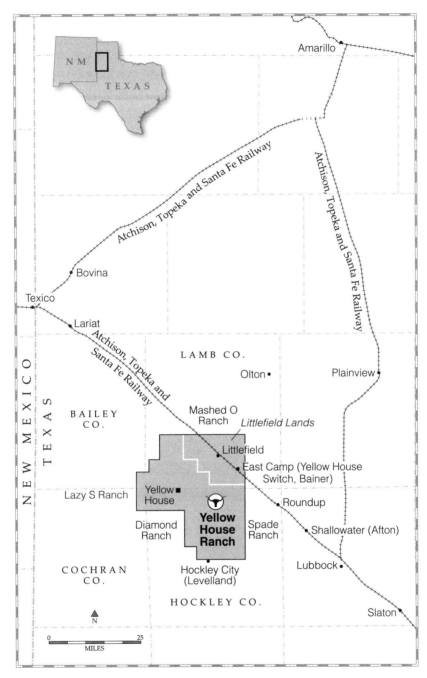

MAP 7. LITTLEFIELD'S YELLOW HOUSE RANCH AND VICINITY, 1901–1920.
Map by Carol Zuber-Mallison.

MAP 8. LITTLEFIELD RANCHES, 1877–1920.
Map by Carol Zuber-Mallison.

1

TROUBLES ENOUGH

George Washington Littlefield thought he had troubles enough on that Sunday in March 1871 before John Watson rode into his cow camp with no good on his mind. Reining in his horse, the intruder announced he had come for Harrison McClure, a young freedman who had taken advantage of emancipation to leave his former master and home. Littlefield was finishing the day's work, preparing to drive 1,100 longhorn cattle to market in Abilene, Kansas, from the camp near his home in south-central Texas's western Gonzales County a full two months' travel north. Never having been on a trail drive, much less bossed one, Littlefield had his mind on ensuring that he overlooked nothing. Along the 750-mile route through open territory, he would have few places to replenish stocks of coffee and other foodstuffs. But overshadowing details of the trip, the drive represented the biggest gamble of his economic life. If it were unprofitable, the consequence was certain to devastate an entire community of his Littlefield, Harral, White, and Dowell kin and the former slaves who stayed on after emancipation to continue farming.

The farming operation was failing. In 1868 drought and worms on the family plantations in the Guadalupe and San Marcos river bottoms left Littlefield with only enough corn for feed and just thirty-five bales of cotton to market—one-fifth of the usual production from five hundred acres. "Another year like this will break us all," he prophesied. July 1869 brought the flood of the century raging down the two streams. "Crops all ruined, washed away several houses, and a great many persons drowned. The water came up above the gin house. You could not look no way but what you would see water," niece Alice M. Dowell described the scene. Littlefield salvaged none of his planting. "No money and very little prospects of getting any," nephew Shelton Clark Dowell summed up the aftermath. To continue, Littlefield had to eliminate expenses, even ones he considered important for the future. "You are well aware that I am not able to [keep] you at Washington College any longer," the former Confederate cavalry captain wrote a month later to nephew John Henry White Dowell studying in Virginia under Confederate idol Robert E. Lee. "When you arrive at home you will see the desperate strait I am reduced to."[1]

Sorrow deepened his desperation when, within days of the great flood, George and his wife, Alice P. Tillar Littlefield, lost their second child, a baby girl, who died so soon after birth that they could not name the lost life. Their first child, a boy, had died two years earlier, in 1867, still a baby only one year old. Then there was the large extended family dependent on Littlefield. In 1868 he had to buy property to rescue his oldest White half brother from bankruptcy. Three months later he shelled out again to rescue his Harral brother-in-law. Beyond the relatives, he had the freed slaves whom he promised to feed, whether or not a crop was made, in thanks for their loyalty in remaining to work the Littlefield land.[2]

Looking beyond his farming and family, the condition of politics and leadership of the state smothered Littlefield's hope for the future. Prewar political leaders who had held civilian and military positions of authority during the Civil War were removed or disqualified from holding office. Chief among them was James Webb Throckmorton, ousted from the governor's chair in July 1867 for failing to implement Reconstruction requirements for readmitting Texas to the American Union—in particular for his unwillingness to accept the Fourteenth Amendment to the United States Constitution, which extended citizenship and equal protection under the law to former slaves. Texas's former Confederate populace embraced no appointed Unionist replacement. Even Elisha Marshall Pease failed to gain favor, though he had fought for Texas's independence from Mexico in 1836, served as governor before the war, and as Throckmorton's successor worked to make the government more accountable to the citizens. Further, men who had been in servitude eight years earlier were not only enfranchised but also elected to seats in the state legislature. "The next four years to come is as full of gloom and despair as our country has ever witnessed," Littlefield wrote his half brother in Mississippi in September 1868. "I fear we have seen our balmyest days, and the great uncertainty[,] death and destruction that's abroad upon the land will remain as it is until the present generation has passed away." He was right. Far from being a new generation, the Radical Reconstruction instituted by Governor Edmund Jackson Davis in 1870 took things from bad to worse in Littlefield's view. Davis packed government and court positions with Republicans of his stripe, centralized power in the executive branch, and, to pay for his programs, raised taxes.[3]

Higher taxes only deepened Littlefield's financial desolation. The losses and expenses he had accumulated already totaled more than Littlefield could absorb by simply eliminating expenditures. He needed seed to continue. Consequently, he had to borrow. Others had to borrow too. The price of borrowing rose. For some loans he had to pay a usurious 24 percent interest.[4] After two years of failed money crops and borrowing, Littlefield was becoming anxious to find something he could do to get himself out of his financial hole until he had cotton to sell.

Fortunately, in Gonzales County, he lived where enterprising risk takers had discovered an undertaking that fit the bill. "Men here are making fortunes in the [cattle] business," he exclaimed a month after he called John Dowell home. "Some have cleared twenty thousand this year in driving to Kansas." However, reluctant to embark without a partner to boss the drive while he remained at home running the plantations, Littlefield decided that while his situation was bad, it could be worse, and he passed up the lucrative 1870 drive to keep on keeping on farming. Before all the drovers returned, he found out he was right. His situation could become worse. A deluge sent the two rivers out of their banks again and swept his year's planting downstream for the second year in a row. Three straight years of losses pushed Littlefield to the brink of economic ruin. As winter gave way to spring in 1871, the twenty-eight-year-old found himself drained—"at a loss," he said later, "to know how to make a living."[5]

His back to the wall, in desperation and uncertainty, Littlefield charted his course. He would continue farming as his mainstay. But the entrepreneur in him determined to do it unconventionally. Rather than changing anything about his agricultural operation, he would bank his future on a venture in the Kansas cattle trade. If prices for Texas longhorns continued their upward trajectory of the previous three years or even just duplicated the $15 to $25 per head profit realized in 1870, Littlefield stood to accomplish his goal. With so much riding on the outcome of the venture, he determined to get a jump on others driving to Kansas by leaving two weeks ahead of the usual start date. Finally, unable to afford an experienced drover at $125 to $150 per month, he would boss the drive himself.

As George Littlefield was completing his preparations on Sunday, March 12, 1871, John H. Watson rode into camp and announced that he had come for Harrison McClure. Five years earlier, in 1866, the ten-year-old boy had seized the opportunity of emancipation to go where he wanted to go and do what he wanted to do. He had run away from home to join Littlefield. "My people wanted me to stay, but I thought a heap of him," McClure reminisced some seventy years later. Littlefield had charisma. He "might meet a hundred little black and white boys, and they'd just take up with him," McClure described Littlefield's magnetism. So it was for McClure from his earliest sight of Littlefield shortly before the Civil War when, as a young boy, he watched the teenager visiting his sweetheart at the home where she boarded while attending Gonzales College.[6]

Stories vary as to whether Watson came for the young man because McClure's mother recanted her permission for her son to leave home or because Watson accused Littlefield of hiring Watson's hands away. Whichever it was, Watson demanded custody. Littlefield refused. Watson left cursing and promising to return the next afternoon with men to take McClure. Preparing for whatever trouble the morrow would bring, Littlefield checked the action of a cap-and-ball six-shooter.

On Monday, when McClure rode into camp from the herd, Watson was waiting.

"Harrison, I guess you're going to leave us this evening," said cook Ben Mucklerath, McClure's uncle by descent or informal adoption.

"Oh, I don't know," McClure answered. "I don't think so."

"What did he say, Ben?" Watson asked.

Upon hearing McClure's reply, twenty-one-year-old Watson flew into a rage and strode over to Littlefield, who was finishing a conversation. Watson demanded to have McClure. Littlefield refused. They argued. As Watson drew his pistol, Littlefield walked to the chuck wagon nearby and retrieved his. Upon his return, a few words passed between them before Watson slapped Littlefield. Littlefield hit him back. If Watson wanted to be able to claim self-defense when he killed Littlefield, the scene was set. Watson fired. A bullet tore through Littlefield's vest. Littlefield raised his gun and pulled the trigger. The pistol jammed. As he worked with it, a bullet pierced his sleeve. Hearing the gunfire and seeing his uncle's plight, Shelton Dowell rode over and handed Uncle his gun. It, too, misfired. As Watson emptied his pistol, to no greater effect than scattering the onlookers, he retreated behind a tree. Cool under fire from his war experience, Littlefield picked up the first six-shooter and adjusted it. Then, when Watson leaned out from behind his protection and taunted him, the veteran raised the old pistol, aimed and fired. The bullet hit Watson square in the chest. He crumpled to the ground dead. However great Littlefield thought his troubles were when the day began, those vexations held no comparison to the murder charge he knew must lie ahead.[7]

Be that as it may, Littlefield had business to attend. He rode into Gonzales, posted bond through his attorney and Civil War comrade James F. Miller, and the next day pushed his animals onto the trail to Abilene. Of the 1,100 or so cattle, Littlefield owned somewhat more than half. The rest he had on credit, further increasing his risk in the venture. In making the drive, he was typical of Texans with cattle to sell in 1871. So many wanted to cash in that the tide of beef surging to Kansas was the largest ever. No fewer than six hundred thousand head, and perhaps as many as one million, reached the shipping pens. Between twenty and twenty-five herds departed Gonzales County alone. All that cattle glutted the market. Prices slumped. Many tens of thousands of animals never changed hands and cost their owners further to winter them in anticipation of the spring market.

Despite his early start, when Littlefield approached Abilene, "that prairie was just lined with cattle for 20 miles," recalled McClure. Even so, Littlefield reached Kansas before the onslaught turned trading tables into a buyer's market. And he made his endeavor pay. Four days after he arrived, Littlefield found a buyer. None too soon for cowboy McClure, who remembered that the herd stampeded the night after the sale. Looking forward, Littlefield was pleased. The transaction gave him enough to satisfy all his debts. On top of that, he reaped a profit of $3,600 with which, he later remarked, "to begin business."[8] Most important of all, he realized what that business should be. As he phrased it in a classic understatement, "he was attracted to the trade."[9] In pursuing a daring bid to revive his farming operation, George Littlefield became a cattleman and found his calling.

He had found his calling, that is, if he were not sent to prison for killing John Watson. On June 22, 1871, the day after his twenty-ninth birthday, a grand jury indicted George Washington Littlefield for murder. Since Littlefield was away with his drive, the trial did not occur until early the next year. Following his policy of relying on family whenever he could for whatever work there was to be done, Littlefield employed his nephew John Dowell, by then qualified before the bar, to defend him. Dowell was not the only one who believed Littlefield innocent of the charge. Among the jurors was a black man who worked Littlefield land on the San Marcos River. For amusement, one of the white jurors needled him, saying: "I'm gonna hold this jury until we convict Mr. Littlefield." The black man retorted that he would die with the man there before he convicted Littlefield. Far short of that, in two days it was over. On the last day of February 1872, the mostly white jury returned its verdict of acquittal.[10]

When Littlefield walked out of the courtroom, the consequence of his shootout and the killing were behind him. He was free to begin business—to turn all of his energies to the cattle trade that he had decided to make his life's work. How different this outcome was from the events twenty-two years earlier, in 1850, when he was eight years old and living on the family plantation in Panola County in northwestern Mississippi.

One day a stranger rode up to the Littlefield home with no good on his mind. He had come to kill George's father, Fleming Littlefield. For years, resentment of Fleming's marriage to the widow Mildred Terrell Satterwhite White had been festering in both her younger brother and a brother of her deceased husband. Conscious of their highborn genealogy, the two despised Fleming with his less distinguished ancestry. Likely even at his tender age, George had overheard conversations and raised voices often enough to comprehend the root of the family strife that brought the gunman that day. Though he never spoke of either the incident or the clashing bloodlines that joined in him, he well understood the consequence of the conflict. It changed his life. And it changed the lives of the Littlefields and the Whites he would come to serve as patriarch.

Unlike his eldest son, Fleming was of a headstrong, hot-blooded disposition (fig. 2). One who lived not far from him on the road to Longtown, Mississippi, said he "was a common rough man of low family," "a Blackguard," and "a d——d rascal." At least that is what family physician Greensville Dowell recalled Col. William H. Carroll saying in warning Dowell "to have no dealings with him." Carroll said that Fleming "had killed a negro for Gov Lynch, was tried and acquitted. He then ran off some negroes to Arkansas for a man who was trying to rob his creditors. He was followed and rumor said he had waylaid his pursuer and shot him."[11] Perhaps events occurred as Colonel Carroll and rumor said; perhaps not. By the time he wrote his autobiography, Dowell had reason to paint Fleming in as dark a light as possible in retaliation for the Littlefield family's ostracizing Dowell in the wake of his failed marriage to Fleming's stepdaughter, Sarah.[12]

Maybe two painful experiences in his early life contributed to Fleming's confrontational nature. Both were rooted in family loss. The first he felt more deeply. On the celebratory day of American Independence in 1822, eight-year-old Flem, as he was called, went swimming with his ten-year-old brother, George Washington, in the pond of the textile mill their father had recently bought. Suddenly, George went under. Flem tried to rescue his brother but failed. George drowned. The brother he lost meant so much to Fleming that a generation later he named his firstborn George Washington for him.[13]

Then, a few years after the drowning, the mill burned. Maybe it was arson. Forty-four-year-old Philip Littlefield had bought the mill to invest in a new line of work for the Littlefields in America—cotton manufacturing, still booming after the War of 1812. His was one of the many cotton mills built along the Tyger River in upland Union County, South Carolina. Where other mill owners were content to produce only a coarse yarn, Philip produced a broadcloth, tradition holds, by pressing rather than by weaving in the customary way. About fifteen months after he began operating the mill, he decided to take a partner. Perhaps Philip needed capital; perhaps he wanted counsel in the manufacture. Though Littlefields had been in cloth manufacture in England, the two generations of his sufficiently prosperous ancestors in America had abandoned textiles for farming. Into the operation he invited John Nance, the brother of his wife of seventeen years. At about the same time, the boom began to wither. Income declined. The partners disagreed ever more vehemently over its division until Littlefield filed suit against Nance for appropriating for himself payments due to the firm. Nance not only quit the

business but retaliated with a perjury charge against Littlefield. If the absence from
the records of a verdict means the case was settled out of court, the settlement did
not allay the family trouble. Fires broke out. Philip's mill burned to the ground,
destroying everything in it. In 1828 Nance was convicted of burning the home,
gin house, and cotton of Philip's daughter-in-law's sister.[14] So much bad blood and
so much loss.[15] Philip did not wait to hear the verdict in Nance's trial. With their
ten children, including Flem in his early teens, Philip and his wife abandoned their
home of more than twenty years. By early 1827 they had established themselves
in Carroll County in northwest Tennessee and put the Appalachian Mountains
and more than five hundred miles between themselves and their South Carolina
in-laws.[16]

In time, likely in his late teens, Flem struck out to establish himself in the
world and, if Dowell is correct, spent much of the decade of the 1830s in central
Mississippi. Though his older brother Zachariah remained behind for several years,
when he finally departed in late 1839 or early 1840, he led the way for four other
Littlefield men with their families. If Zachariah moved to occupy fresh land, he
found what he was looking for about 125 miles to the south in northern Panola
County, Mississippi, in the recently opened Chickasaw Cession. The land was
so rich that "dimes, dollars, and even eagles lie within a foot of [the] surface of
the earth which may be found by the use of proper means." The cash crop that
would produce these riches was cotton. Men looking at land in newly created
Panola County could be assured of that when they learned that the word *ponola* in
Choctaw meant cotton. The attraction was irresistible. Only a few months behind
Zachariah came his older brother William Martin and younger brother Oliver
Hazard Perry (who went by his initials), followed by father Philip in 1841 and
brother Andrew Jackson in 1842.[17]

As fate would have it, O.H.P. chanced to locate near the John Henry White
place (about five miles west of present-day Como) at the same time that the mistress
of the place needed a man like him. On June 28, 1839, a few months before O.H.P.
arrived, John Henry White, in the prime of life, died. His widow, Mildred Terrell
Satterwhite White, who had just turned twenty-eight years old, was left with five
children to rear alone, the oldest, Thomas Jefferson, eleven, the youngest, Charles E.,
a toddler at only sixteen months.[18] Rearing children, along with management of the
household, was woman's work—the only labor allotted the fair sex. Or so men of
the time would have it. Mores of the South, especially for society's upper echelons,
positioned women on pedestals aloof from the trials and tribulations of the workaday
world outside the home. Men reserved to themselves handling the affairs of business.
Mildred chafed at the custom. If she would not be given full charge of the plantation,

she wanted at least a voice in its management. But by court order, John's first cousin, Francis Marion White, a year older than she, was given administration of the place. To manage the twenty-five slaves working the fields, the plantation needed an overseer. In one of those curious, innocent chains of events that shape the course of history, for the job, Mildred hired or convinced her cousin-in-law to hire the recently arrived twenty-four-year-old O.H.P. Littlefield. O.H.P. must have exhibited a powerful presence. His knowledge of plantation management—from directing the toil of slaves to cultivating cotton and food crops and maintaining buildings—had to have been rudimentary. None of his three generations of Littlefield ancestors owned plantations. None owned more than two slaves. He held none. Completing the chain, on an unrecorded occasion O.H.P.'s older brother, Fleming, visited him on the White place and met the "nice pretty looking" widow Mildred White.[19]

Fleming and Mildred liked what they saw in each other. Before long they were talking marriage. Mildred's family, relatives, and friends opposed it to a person. If the resistance redoubled the intentions of the strong-minded woman, her wedding to Fleming on September 16, 1841, likewise steeled the disapproval. Her blood brother James Sanders Satterwhite and brother-in-law Maj. David Shelton White, encouraged by her father, resolved that honor and duty to their ancestry obligated them to sever the union so as to protect the integrity of their community of relations, if not also to rescue Mildred from herself.[20]

For the men, simply put: Mildred was a Satterwhite; her children were Whites; and the Whites and Satterwhites were of a breed and community apart. It was "the most intimate friendly social union ever known among the same number of persons," a contemporary described this group of families that nourished the ideals and styles of the high born. It was that and more. Formed in the Broad River piedmont of northeastern Georgia in the period between the end of the American Revolution and the early years of George Washington's first term as president of the fledgling United States of America, the "Virginian" community, so named for its Old Dominion roots, gained notoriety for the remarkable number of prominent public officials it produced. Four were elected governor of Georgia, two of Alabama, and six had Georgia counties named for them. Central to the community psyche was living up to their heritage. One of Mildred's lines stretched back to Col. John Page, who gave the land and funds for Bruton Parish Church in Williamsburg, Virginia. Another could be traced to Sir Walter de Tirel, who fought with William the Conqueror at the Battle of Hastings in 1066, inaugurating the Norman Conquest of England.[21]

Into this elite society, rich in heritage, wealthy in land and slaves, and confirmed in its superiority by its Old Dominion origin, Mildred "Milly" Terrell Satterwhite was born in Elbert County, Georgia, on June 17, 1811.[22] For eleven years the only child of James Satterwhite and Mildred Wyche, she had ample opportunity to absorb the group's manners and mindset. Marrying her first cousin once removed, Milly kept comfortably within the Virginian circle. In fact, her union with John Henry White on December 19, 1826, joined genealogies already so entangled that the bride shared her two given names with her mother-in-law and a sister-in-law. Only fifteen years old, Mildred married young, even for a time when the customary marrying age for women in the South was eighteen and a half to twenty years.[23]

Marrying so young further complicated the genealogy by blurring generational lines. Milly's first child, Thomas Jefferson White, who went by his initials, T.J., born in 1828 when she was seventeen, was only six years younger than his Satterwhite uncle—her brother, James Sanders Satterwhite (born on March 19, 1822).[24] Six years separated uncle and nephew, while eleven separated brother and sister. Milly's departure from her parents' household when her brother was but four years old no doubt contributed to the siblings' failure to develop a hearty relationship. Rather than to his sister, James S. Satterwhite grew close to her husband's younger brother, David Shelton White Sr., and to her husband, whom both idolized.[25]

As the fertility of the Georgia land declined, the Virginians began to move south and west. Milly's uncle Reuben Satterwhite settled in central Alabama's Wilcox County, where his brothers John and Charles and their sister, Elizabeth, with her husband, Frank McGuire, joined him, establishing a little Satterwhite community. Using a measure of "little" that a large landholding Virginian would appreciate, in 1834 Charles wrote his brother James (Milly's father) still in Georgia: "My settlement is small. It contains but about 3000 acres whitch cost me in settling and all about 7000 Dollars."[26]

However strongly Charles Satterwhite's letter beckoned brother James, it failed to capture the imagination of James's son-in-law. John Henry White fixed his eyes on the cheaper land just then opening farther west and north in the Chickasaw Cession of northern Mississippi. Seeking the freshest land rather than locating in Pontotoc County near his father, Shelton White, with whom as the oldest son he managed family matters in Georgia, thirty-one-year-old John White bought land sixty-five miles west in Panola County. The land he liked in a wilderness populated by fewer than two persons per square mile lay on a broad fertile ridge separating the Tallahatchie and Coldwater River basins. On April 7, 1837, White bought an undivided half interest in two sections of the gently rolling land watered on the east by Arkabutla Creek.[27] Where his grandchildren went, James Satterwhite followed. A widower just shy of sixty years old, he bought the other undivided half interest in the 1,280 acres for himself and his fifteen-year-old son James Sanders Satterwhite.[28]

Once John White selected the land he would develop, the pace of life for his family quickened. Within ten months, he had packed up, moved his family and slaves some 450 miles from upland Georgia to the new home place, and had land cleared, crops planted, and structures erected in time for Milly to give birth on February 26, 1838, to the couple's sixth child. Then a year and four months later, on June 28, 1839, when life had begun settling into a comfortable routine, John Henry White died.[29]

Three years younger than the widow Milly White and the same age as her brother-in-law David White, twenty-six-year-old Fleming Littlefield, if he knew it, could boast a paternal genealogy as solid in England and as long, if not as prominent or wealthy in the New World, as those of the Whites and Satterwhites. Fleming's great-grandfather William had arrived a century earlier with, among other possessions, a dictionary so prized that it still remains with descendants. In the remote Maryland piedmont of Frederick County, he amassed a substantial domain of more than 1,300 acres before taking the Upper Road southwest to Union County in South Carolina's piedmont. William's namesake son served in the South Carolina militia during the American Revolution. His son, Philip, branched out into textile manufacture before moving to Tennessee.[30]

No matter. All that David White and James Sanders Satterwhite needed to know was that Fleming was not a Virginian. In fact, though, that was *not* all. As the relationship between Fleming and Milly blossomed, Flem replaced his brother as her overseer. Professional overseers as a class occupied the bottom rung of the white Southern social scale. To avoid bringing men of this low class onto their places, plantation owners were known to hire sons of plantation owners for the work.[31] (Milly's oldest son, Thomas White, would follow Fleming in the job.) Though Fleming did not come to Mildred as a professional overseer, that he filled the position stoked David's and James Sanders's hostility. They would see that the new couple felt their displeasure in every way they could mete it out.

At the regular monthly meeting of probate court after the wedding, Fleming applied for guardianship of his stepchildren. David White objected. Though common law tradition in the South called for children to be brought up in a home with a male head of household, more important to White was keeping White estate assets out of, as he saw it, the common, rough man's hands. David and estate administrator Francis White petitioned for guardianship also. Before the court had to choose between them, the two sides evidently reached a compromise. Two months later Fleming withdrew his application, and guardianship was awarded to the Whites.

For the next seven years, the guardian Whites in the name of Milly's children bought and sold thousands of dollars' worth of property of various kinds, especially slaves. Milly and Flem surely chafed at having control of neither allocation of nor profit and loss from her children's property. Two groups of slaves—those of Milly and Fleming and those of the children under White control—working the same property no doubt stoked tensions further. In 1844, not three years after reaching the agreement, each man—Littlefield, David White, and James S. Satterwhite— acquired a pistol. If and when a confrontation came, each would be ready.[32]

Maybe it was Fleming's headstrong nature; maybe it was Panola County residents' taking sides; maybe it was nothing more than simple misunderstandings and disagreements. Whatever the causes, court records document a contentious relationship between Fleming on the one hand and his neighbors and those with whom he did business on the other. During the six years from 1843 to 1849, Fleming was party to thirteen suits. Some were simple disputes over payments; some were as complex as suit and counter-suit over the just amount of a doctor's services for three years. Of the five suits he filed, Fleming won three and had two dismissed. Of all thirteen, Fleming prevailed in twice as many as he lost. If a quarrelsome temperament brought Fleming into court, his understanding of the issues sustained him far more often than not.[33]

However upsetting the outside world's contentions might be, life at home proceeded apace. Nine months after they married, on June 21, 1842, Mildred gave birth to her seventh child, Fleming's firstborn, George Washington Littlefield. As was common, the next children followed in two-year intervals: Martha Mildred on February 8, 1844, and Fleming Junior on March 4, 1846. Perhaps in sorrow over the father's namesake living only three months, the parents allowed three years to elapse before Mildred bore her tenth and last child, William Philip, on September 21, 1849.[34]

In the mold of autocratic Southern fathers, Fleming exerted his protective disposition not just over his own brood but also over the White children still living with their mother and him in the house their father built. In Mildred's second child, Sarah Zalinda "Sallie" White, ten years old when George was born, her stepfather took particular interest.[35] "A fairy like creature, open, candid and ingenuous, [she had] beautiful soulful blue eyes, [and] a dazzling complexion. Her hair hung in a profusion of lovely ringlets partially concealing and revealing a neck as fair as untrodden snow," rhapsodized twenty-four-year-old family physician Greensville Dowell over his first sight of her. Fleming wanted this treasure of a girl to marry one of his relatives. Probably he ignored Dowell's affection, thinking it would pass. After all, the doctor fell in love with every pretty girl he saw. "It was easy for me to . . .

transfer my affections from Miss Virginia [of Raleigh, Tennessee] to this darling little [fourteen-year-old] girl," Dowell admitted in his autobiography.[36]

More pressing for Fleming was the opposition from Sallie's uncles. David White tried to keep his niece away from home, either in school in Memphis or visiting her grandfather White in Pontotoc County. Milly's brother thought to have Sallie become engaged to a young man outside the family. James Sanders Satterwhite encouraged one suitor in whom Sallie had expressed an interest to visit her against the wishes of both her stepfather and her mother. Mildred reprimanded her brother so sternly over it that he never entered her house again. The suitor persisted, whereupon Fleming beat him severely to put an end to it. Determined to get away, Sallie made arrangements with Dowell. As for the family doctor nearly twice her age, he could approach the house without arousing suspicion. On the prearranged day, Dowell drove up, and as Littlefield watched, Sallie got into his buggy and rode away to marry him on June 29, 1849.[37]

Later that year, young bachelor James Sanders Satterwhite died. Even in death, he kept the bad blood boiling. He left his property, enriched by his considerable inheritance from his father, to his sister's White children. Not one cent did he allocate for his sister's Littlefield offspring. And in a codicil written a week before he died, he even singled out niece Sarah Dowell for a special bequest of his favorite concubine slave and a gold watch.[38]

With his confederate gone, David White recognized that solving the Fleming Littlefield problem, if it were to be done, was up to him. John Henry White Jr. said that what impelled his Uncle David was learning of Fleming's decision to move his family away from all the unpleasantness. Taking Mildred with him was bad enough, but settling a Virginian Satterwhite White in Texas was unconscionable. White hired a hitman to go to the Littlefield home and spit tobacco juice in Littlefield's face. Then, as Fleming was going for his gun, the man would shoot him. In that scenario, the hired gun could claim self-defense. The plot worked until the shooting began. The assassin spat. Both men grabbed their guns and fired. The assailant's bullet grazed Fleming's ankle. Fleming's shot found its mark. The man fell dead.[39]

Then, as so many did who meant to leave a former life behind, Fleming Littlefield mounted his horse, told Milly to follow with the family, and rode away to Texas, never to return.[40]

$$\rightarrow\!\!\!-\!\!\!=\!\!\!-\!\!\!\circ\!\!\!\circ\quad\mathbf{2}\quad\circ\!\!\!-\!\!\!=\!\!\!-\!\!\!\rightarrow$$

LIKE A MAN

Fleming Littlefield ended his trek from Mississippi when he unsaddled his horse at Robert Hall's place in Gonzales County, Texas, sometime in the latter half of 1850. The Littlefields and Halls had known each other for more than twenty years, since both had lived in the South Carolina piedmont. More than passing acquaintance, two of Philip Littlefield's sisters-in-law had married Halls. Where bad blood had driven the Littlefields to Carroll County in northwestern Tennessee in 1827, sparsely populated country had drawn the Halls the next year to adjacent Gibson County, where fourteen-year-old Bob could spend his days hunting. In the early 1830s, Fleming and Bob each struck out on his own. Whether they went together or separately, each established himself for a time in central Mississippi. If they associated in the Magnolia State, reports of the October 1835 Battle of Gonzales that ignited the Texas Revolution ended that association. Bob Hall departed for the excitement. Independence won, Hall heard that the three prettiest girls in Texas lived in Gonzales County and set his course on marrying one of them. He did. Hall then joined his father-in-law in building a compound at the King place, called Oak Forest, on the north side of the Guadalupe River along the San Antonio–San Felipe road, about nine miles west of the county seat.[1]

In 1850 Gonzales was a Texas county in transition—a good place for a man like Fleming to start anew. Symbolically, the change began on February 19, 1846, when President Anson Jones lowered the flag of the Republic of Texas for the last time and Governor James Pinckney Henderson raised the same banner heralding the state of Texas the twenty-eighth of the United States of America. Joining the American union opened the floodgates of immigration to Texas. In the following four years, some seventy thousand newcomers swelled the population of the Lone Star State by half.

Settlement of the fertile land lying in the alluvial valleys and on the blackland prairies of the San Marcos and Guadalupe River basins that formed Gonzales County, some sixty-five miles east of Texas's oldest and largest town of San Antonio, had begun in 1825, with a grant from the government of Mexico intended to attract American settlers. But Indian troubles and Mexican law discouraged would-be immigrants. The Texas Revolution, which wrested the government of Texas from Mexico, proved to be no catalyst. The war was hard on Gonzales. In what they called the Runaway Scrape, the population fled before the advancing Mexican army, recently victorious at the Alamo. Gonzales, the county seat town, was burned to the ground and was slow to recover. News of the Great Comanche Raid in the summer of 1840, which penetrated settled Texas all the way to the Gulf of Mexico, conveyed no welcome. The decisive engagement with the retreating Indian band occurred in Gonzales County, when an Anglo force scattered the one thousand or so natives in the running Battle of Plum Creek. If the Comanche defeat ended the threat of Indian attack, which residents could not be sure of for some time, it did nothing to deter threats from Mexico. Two years after the Plum Creek fight, a Mexican force captured San Antonio. Well aware of Gonzales's fate the previous time a Mexican army had taken possession of the town, Gonzales residents fled again in the Second Runaway Scrape. Then annexation changed everything. First, the United States Army provided a level of protection unknown during the decade of the republic. Second, immigrants bound for Texas no longer had to leave their country to reach their destination. Gonzales County's share of the tide that poured into Texas between 1846 and 1850 consisted largely of Virginia, Tennessee, and Mississippi planters seeking to establish new plantations on fresh land their slaves could work raising the South's money crop of cotton. As they came and settled, the character of Gonzales County changed markedly.[2]

If Hall saw Gonzales becoming crowded, Littlefield had to have seen it in the opposite light. Gonzales County's 1850 population of slightly fewer than 1,500 souls totaled but one-eighth of the number in Panola County when Littlefield left. In fact he had never known Panola County with as few residents as inhabited Gonzales County. Seen in terms of the country over which the population spread, the difference was even more noticeable. People were packed at more than fifteen per square mile in Panola County, but spread at fewer than two per square mile in Gonzales County. The population mix was different too. Black slaves outnumbered the whites in Panola County in a ratio of 57 to 43 percent, while in Gonzales County, whites and Hispanics outnumbered the slaves by more than two to one.[3]

Littlefield found a quite different geography too. The White and Littlefield home places in Panola County lay on a wide ridge of high ground between two rivers. Settlers in Gonzales County avoided the drier ridges and gravitated to the rivers. Western Gonzales County, where Hall lived, was watered by two substantial streams that joined near the center of the county and flowed thence as one to the Gulf of Mexico. The water courses attracted settlers for the variety of trees along their borders, from hardwood oak, good for building, to pecan, whose nuts fattened hogs nicely. The underbrush included dewberry vines, whose yield made good eating in pies and jams. From river frontage, land owners extended their estates onto the adjacent prairies. Domains of a thousand or so acres were common. The cotton culture the planters brought shortly dominated the county's economy. Still, on the rolling hills beyond the plantations, game and wild cattle roamed freely.[4]

Flem and Bob had not seen each other in at least fourteen years, not since Hall had left Mississippi for Texas. Littlefield's grandson, Victor Harral, who lived for a time in Oak Forest and is the source of the story that Fleming ended his ride at Bob Hall's home, referred to Hall as "Cousin Bob." If the Halls and Littlefields had a blood connection, most likely it is in the Nance genealogy of the men's maternal grandmothers. Perhaps, though, in the way of the South, the two of similar age expressed a particularly close friendship by nicknaming each other "cousin."[5] Whether their paths had crossed as boys in South Carolina, as teenagers in Tennessee, or as young men in Mississippi, the friendship they developed remained strong enough that, nearly a decade and a half after they had last seen each other in the Magnolia State, Littlefield knew the whereabouts and felt the welcome of his "cousin" in Texas.[6]

Maybe it was the new environment in Texas, maybe it was living free of the trouble in Mississippi. Whatever it was, Fleming seemed to be a new man. An entrepreneurial talent blossomed. On a 1,470-acre domain he assembled in June 1851, fronting on the west bank of the Guadalupe River about fifteen miles west of the town of Gonzales, planter Littlefield put more than two dozen slaves to work cultivating cotton and food crops and tending a herd of cattle bearing his FL brand.[7] Entrepreneur Littlefield erected a saw mill and partnered in a gin to separate fiber from seed of the cotton his slaves picked—both available to neighbors who wanted to take advantage of the convenience of the machines. In Gonzales, population three hundred, he put four thousand dollars into partnering with Samuel J. Mays in a mercantile business.[8] Just how pleased and confident Fleming was with his new situation he expressed in the material with which he built his home. Where others put up frame structures, Fleming used brick made on his place by brickmaker Capt. Charles W. Allen, whom he brought from Mississippi for the purpose. And what a home it was for Milly, who arrived in 1851 with her six unmarried children—David, John, and Charles White and George, Martha, and William Littlefield, whose ages ranged from seventeen years old to younger than two.[9] The grand house contained maybe seven rooms (memories vary) with a wide dogtrot hall through the center and an expansive porch. For insulation, the walls were two brick courses thick. For aesthetics, they were covered with plaster on the outside and wall paper on the inside.[10]

Mildred made the house a welcoming home to her relatives all (see fig. 3). "Grandma always liked to have the family around," Ida White Walker recalled. "The more she had, the better she liked it." Ida's brother-in-law Walter agreed, adding that "us boys were just as much at home at Littlefield's as we was at [our] home." By then weighing upwards of two hundred pounds, "too short and thick to be a Southern belle," but "possessed of the most fitting hands for work," according to a grandson and a former slave, Grandma Mildred was easy to be around. Of a tranquil personality, she did not let conflicts and troubles ruffle her. "One of those old-fashioned talking womans," Walter Walker observed, "she would say, 'It couldn't be hoped, and there ain't no use grieving 'bout it. You couldn't hope it.'"[11]

The sentiment likely gave her a strength she needed when history repeated itself. As had happened in Mississippi fifteen years earlier, a little more than a year after she and her family became comfortably settled into their routines on the Texas plantation, her husband died. Fleming Littlefield succumbed to pneumonia on January 8, 1853.[12]

Fifteen years and living under Texas, not Mississippi, law did make a difference, though—a big difference. This time, forty-one-year-old Mildred T. Littlefield (as she signed her name) had complete charge of matters. To the outside world, she had it by legal authority. Fleming appointed her the executrix of his will. On the plantation, she had it by the power of her person. As Harrison McClure put it so colorfully: "Whatever she told you you was going to do, you did it, and whatever she told you was going to become of you, it did."[13]

At last having undisputed charge of business affairs, Mildred had gained what unnumbered women in the South wanted and precious few ever possessed. One Louisiana woman summed it up in a single word—liberty. For Mildred, as for others who attained it, it was a long time coming. In the Virginian circle, whose members conceived of themselves as setting the tone for the Southern social structure and thus needing to act in fullest accord with the Southern ideal, the model of womanhood glistened at its brightest. Girls were taught that women were docile and invested their being in the lives of their husbands. Coupled with being submissive and always sympathetic to the head of the household, the role of women was to bear and rear children. The model did present one significant contradiction, though. Where the ideal cast the woman aloof from day-to-day business activity, reality gave the wife responsibility for managing the house and house servants.[14]

From her birth, Milly Satterwhite met the Virginians' ideal. And if the manner in which she presided over her home in Texas repeated her competence in Georgia and Mississippi, she handled well the business responsibilities allotted to her. With a dozen years' experience when her first husband died, she was ready to assume full responsibility. But society's dictates, imposed through the judicial system, thwarted her.

Whether her second husband meant to enlarge Mildred's role in managing affairs while he was alive, he may have had little option for avoiding it. The majority of their property was hers. She owned more than half of the slaves. The 1850 census of Panola County listed Fleming with forty-six. Mildred was not listed and had not been listed as a slave owner since the 1840 and 1841 Panola County tax rolls when she was last a feme sole. But the inventory of Fleming's estate enumerated twenty-two slaves, not forty-six, as his separate property. Further, except for his interest in the Gonzales store, the remainder of Fleming's estate consisted of his half of the couple's common property.[15] Tangible property aside, it may be that Mildred simply asserted herself beyond her husband's power to resist. After all, she was a woman strong enough to spurn the efforts of relatives intent on forcing the dictates of the Virginian ideal upon her. Whatever the case, once in control, Mildred directed affairs so effectively that one observer, in the vernacular of the time, said in praise that she managed her properties "like a man."[16]

That was saying a lot. Under her wing, she had guardianship of her children and their property. No relative contested her this time. But where the children's property interest in Mississippi had been in a single plantation, Fleming had divided his landed interest four ways, creating separate plantations for Mildred and each of his three children—Martha, George, and William. On the White side, Mildred had to assume control of two other holdings. Her son Charles had lost the mental ability to run his places. If the plantation in Gonzales County would be easy enough to oversee, not so his back in Mississippi.

Fifteen years made one other important difference. Mildred's oldest son had grown of age to help her. Whether or not he had wanted to leave Mississippi, twenty-four-year-old T.J. had accompanied his mother on the move to Texas, saying he could not let her make the long journey by herself.[17] With his mother reunited with her husband, Thomas had returned to Mississippi, married his sweetheart, Martha Elizabeth Phelps, in January 1851, and brought her to Texas to make their home on a property two or three miles from the Littlefield homestead. Mildred's other two White sons who moved with her, David and John Jr., both returned to Panola County. John left the year after Fleming died. David remained only a year or two more. That left the older of her two Littlefield sons, George Washington, ten and a half years old when his father died, as the male on whom she would come to rely. The confluence of all the threads—Mildred's business sense, her positioning to exercise her business acumen unfettered, and George's maturing to the point both of being ready to learn the lessons of life and of subordinating the expectations of the male role in Southern society to hers as parent and mentor—could not have been timed more fortuitously. George worshiped his mother as a mother and as a mentor, and she appreciated the benefit to her of bringing him into partnership in directing family business and handling family personalities.[18]

A partner, of course, had to be grounded in the three Rs of reading, writing, and arithmetic. Fleming had begun George's studies by employing Mary Kaufman, the adopted daughter of the family doctor, to come to the Littlefield Place and in an unoccupied slave home teach lessons to both Littlefield and neighbor children. The year after her husband's death, Mildred changed the venue, sending the twelve-year-old boy and his ten-year-old sister to school in town. If George and Martha Mildred thought that being away from their mother's attentive eye would loosen parental oversight, they were mistaken. "I wish you to take the same control over my children as you do your own," their mother wrote Gonzales Mayor David Sterling Hughes Darst and his wife, Emmeline Zumwalt, who boarded them, "and make them mind you and don't let them go anywhere without your leave and you think proper for them to go."[19]

Two years of study prepared both George and his sister to pass the entrance examinations of the preparatory and female departments of Baylor University. A single difference appears to have promoted Baylor over the nearby four-year-old Gonzales College. It wasn't having a female department in which her daughter could receive education beyond the three Rs that mother Mildred never had an opportunity to obtain. Both schools accepted females. In fact, of the two Gonzales was far more progressive. Its coursework allowed women to earn a four-year bachelor's degree. Not only was Gonzales College the first Texas school to offer women this credential, but it even allowed women to take any course the same as men, just not side by side with them in the classroom. In history, the school stands out as "a forerunner in demonstrating that women were as capable as men in their ability to do college work," credits the historian of higher education in Texas.[20]

Rather, the reason Mildred chose Baylor one hundred miles distant in Independence, Texas, apparently was the institution's Baptist affiliation that accorded with the long-standing Littlefield devotion. Whatever Mildred's reason, at fourteen and thirteen respectively in February 1857, George and Milly required special permission of the university president to enter Baylor, neither having reached the minimum matriculation age of fifteen for young men and fourteen for young women. During the first two years, men studied algebra, geometry, Latin, Greek, and some natural philosophy (the predecessor of modern science). Though George found little value in the traditional curriculum for the life he knew and expected to live, the frame of mind that Baylor nourished shaped him profoundly. Loyalty to Texas and the South were central tenets of the attitude the school endeavored to instill. Students in good disciplinary standing wore "as a badge of distinction, a 'lone star,' and on special occasions may wear a plume, in imitation of the 'Texas Plume.'" With equal fervor, university authorities crusaded against Yankee habits and ideas. "It is the source of regret," Baylor's catalog proclaimed, "to see Texians patronizing Northern or distant colleges, where our youth will imbibe sentiments, habits and tastes antagonistic or alien to ours. . . . A young man, educated in Texas, will have peculiar advantages, not only in forming valuable acquaintances for life while at College, but of learning fully the genius, character and wants [i.e., needs] of the people with whom he is to live and act."[21] When George quit school a month before the end of his sophomore year, he had absorbed into the fiber of his being appreciation of the genius and character of the people of Texas and the South. His devotion to the sentiment never waned and would nearly cost him his life.

While George studied at Baylor, the deteriorating mental condition of his four-years-older half brother, Charles White, caused his mother to conclude that Charles's plantation in Mississippi had to be sold and his assets consolidated in Gonzales County. She called George home in October 1858 and placed the job in his hands. His first business venture would be no small undertaking. Aside from the value of the property he would be handling, the sixteen-year-old would have to make decisions on his own without the benefit of her counsel from seven hundred miles away. And he would be returning to the locale where David White, who hired the would-be assassin of his father, still lived. Nevertheless, whatever she asked of him he would do.

In Mississippi George disposed of the 1858 cotton crop and in March 1859 sold to his brother John White Jr. the half section on which Butterbowl Creek rises. His work done, George bought four wagons to transport Charles's belongings, including his slaves, and set out on a month's journey to Texas.

Half a year after he had left, George arrived home. To his mother he delivered more than two dozen slaves, $6,500 in notes, and $4,500 in gold stuffed into two old leather saddlebags. And he brought important family news. David White had died. Finally clearing the antagonism that had driven her and her family from Panola County nine years earlier, White's passing opened the way for Mildred to return in the spring of 1860 to visit her son John.[22]

In the autobiography he wrote the year before his death, George recalled his pride in successfully completing this first business venture. But the trip back stuck in his memory for something else. "How diferent in after years," he scrawled. "No man would think of bringing such a lot of gold on such a trip, when we camped out every night." Yes, but his recollection of the month spent with the slaves welled up a nostalgia for a way of life lost. He never mentioned the emotion in any other writing. He never spoke of it to any feature writer. And no one within or outside the family interviewed after his death by biographer J. Evetts Haley, by historian Alice Duggan Gracy, or by this author ever hinted at it. The slaves' unquestioning acceptance of being uprooted from Mississippi and moved to Texas embodied, in Littlefield's words, "the confidence existing between the slave owner and the slaves." The two dozen slaves told him so every day on the journey, he believed, by making "the pine forests of Arkansas and East Texas ring with their gleeful songs."[23]

So pleased was Mildred with her son's performance that she gave George a larger job. In his hands she placed management of the family's Gonzales properties—some 2,100 acres belonging to her and to George's brothers Charles White and nine-year-old William Littlefield. Adding his own 350-or-so acres to the total, George had his hands full. His mother's operation on the Littlefield homestead alone, as described in the 1860 census taken the next summer, had 400 acres in cotton and corn, 46 slaves to tend the crops (30 she owned and 16 for whom she was acting as guardian for a Littlefield relative), and hundreds of undeveloped acres on which 250 head of beef cattle and 125 work and saddle horses grazed.[24]

In the summer of 1860, a year after he settled into the work of managing the places, George returned to school, this time in his hometown nondenominational Gonzales College. Among the approximately two dozen colleges in Texas, Gonzales prospered from the moment it opened its doors. A record 276 students, half male, half female, enrolled for the 1859–60 academic year, the school's sixth. If George's mother was behind his return to school and was pleased that he began his class work under college president Alexander A. Brooks, whose job included molding character, George was not. Professor Brooks's fields were languages and belles lettres, neither of which, in George's view, prepared him to better manage a plantation. Consequently, George remained in school for but a short time. "Like a great many young men," he wrote decades later, he quit school "thinking he had education enough." Though the schooling he received likely was little more than what was offered in college preparatory departments of the time, within ten years George Littlefield regretted his decision. "You should prize an education above all things now," he counseled nephew John Dowell a decade later, begging the young man to be frugal with the money Littlefield was sending to keep him in school.[25]

If the class work failed to hold George's interest, a certain third-year student did. George met Alice P. Tillar not long after her stepfather, Whitfield Harral Jr., had settled his family in Gonzales in 1857.[26] Shortly afterward, George went off to Baylor, and Alice's parents enrolled the eleven-year-old in Gonzales College as a finishing school to mature her musical, painting, and literary talents. She blossomed there. But when Harral's business failed to flourish, he moved the family 150 miles east to Houston, then three times more populous, where he could expect a larger clientele. By then, though, the Littlefield and Harral families had bonded. On July 9, 1858, George's fourteen-year-old sister married Whitfield's oldest son, twenty-two-year-old Theophilus Eugene Harral. And George fixed his eyes on Theo's half-sister Alice, happy that her studies ensured she would spend most of the year in Gonzales.[27]

Nearly four full years younger than George, Alice had begun life on April 10, 1846, in the place later named Emporia, the seat of Greensville County, Virginia. More important than the chronological distance between George and Alice, though, was the closeness they shared in the role their mothers played in their lives. Both had lost their fathers. Unlike George, who had had opportunity to know his father, Alice knew little of hers. William Tillar died in 1850, when his daughter was just four years old. Alice's mother, Mildred Williamson Lundy Tillar, provided the only continuity in the young girl's life. After her husband's death, Mildred Tillar moved with her daughter into the home of her father, Joshua C. Lundy Jr., a small slave-owner near Memphis, Tennessee. Five years later, in 1855, the widow Tillar married the non-slave-holding widower and merchant Whitfield Harral Jr. of Hernando, DeSoto County, Mississippi. Two years after that, in 1857, Harral pulled up stakes after more than two decades in Hernando and followed a former partner to Gonzales County, Texas, to establish a mercantile business of his own. In the seven years after William Tillar's death, Alice had lived in two different households in three different communities, her only constant being her mother.[28]

Too, George and Alice had lived in the same part of the country before moving to Texas. Planters of northern Panola County oriented themselves to the trading center of Memphis, Tennessee, forty-some miles to the north. Mildred and Fleming Littlefield sent her daughter Sallie White to school there. Fleming was initiated into and became an officer in the Masonic lodge in Ebenezer, DeSoto County, Mississippi, on the main road through Hernando to Memphis, rather than affiliating with the older lodge south of him in Panola's county seat. Alice had lived in Hernando during the two years before she moved to Texas.[29]

While both George and Alice had grown up with older half siblings, George's were primarily boys—only four, six, and eight years older. During her five years in the Lundy household after her father's death, Alice lived with older girl half siblings in their later teenage years, more than a decade older than her. Living in the Harral household brought a complete reversal. Alice found herself both the only girl in a home with three boys, younger by four years than the youngest of them. While as far back as she could remember, Alice had been the youngest at home, George was the oldest in the Littlefield family. Maybe to satisfy herself of the meaning of those similarities and differences, maybe simply unwilling to marry as quickly as George's sister, who wed about a year after she met Theo Harral, Alice prolonged George's courtship.[30]

As George's relationship with Alice warmed, the bond between his half sister Sallie White and Greensville Dowell, whom she had married so precipitously, weakened. A fine doctor and of good standing as late as 1851 as a partner in a dry goods store in Monthalia, Mississippi, Dowell was a poor money manager. After his father-in-law, Fleming Littlefield, died, Dowell gave in to his wife's entreaties that they move to Texas to have the benefit of mother-in-law Mildred's financial counsel. They moved, but Dowell failed to benefit, Sallie said. Dowell blamed the rancor increasing between him and his wife on Mildred's "wicked and malicious advice." Sallie endured the increasingly unhappy relationship until two days after Christmas in 1856, when she took their three children—John Henry White, Shelton Clark, and Alice—and left. To ensure that she did not lose all of her property, Sallie took her twenty-six slaves too when she abandoned the Brazoria County plantation, which her money had bought and for the operation of which Dowell had borrowed using her slaves as collateral. After a time, Dowell traveled the 150 miles to Gonzales to talk with his wife, who had moved in with her mother, but Sallie refused to go into town to see him. George went. "I met Him in Gonzales and gave Him a terrible abusing. And, Hot Headed Boy like, said to[o] much. But I would of done all I promised the Gentleman Had He not stoped" trying to gain custody of the children, George recalled decades later. Dowell retaliated by filing for divorce and asking for a judgment against Mildred's and Sallie's properties. With Mildred threatening "to scatter things miterly" if Dowell won, eighteen-year-old George accompanied his twenty-eight-year-old half sister to court in September 1860 "as her only protector." Finally, in April 1861, the divorce was granted but without compensation to Dowell.[31]

Mother Mildred had to have been happy. And happy about far more than that her daughter was free of the relationship and that she, Mildred, did not have to carry out her threat. Rather, when George Littlefield defended his White half-sister in words and deeds, Mildred Terrell Satterwhite White Littlefield knew that, of all her children, this son made *her* family—Whites and Littlefields both—*his* family.

Fifty years old and consequently somewhere past the midpoint of her life, she could be comfortable that he would carry forward her role as the head, the patriarch, of the growing clan, seeing after them all.

"Having grown from an eight-year-old boy on a farm in Gonzales Co. Texas under the training of his mother who was a widow," George began his autobiography, he grew and matured fast. By the age of sixteen he had gained all the formal education he would take. By seventeen, he had accomplished the sale of a plantation in Mississippi and moved seven hundred miles to Texas both a large sum in gold and a community of more than two dozen slaves. At seventeen, he accepted from his mother management of multiple plantations. At eighteen, in place of his half sister's full brothers, he took up extracting Sallie from a failed marriage. In all these endeavors, George Littlefield proved his mettle. In proving his mettle, he pleased his mother. In pleasing his mother, he received his fulfillment. At eighteen years of age, his mother could pass on the compliment. Her son George Washington Littlefield was managing like a man.

THE "SISING" OF MINIÉ BALLS

About 1:30 on the brutally hot afternoon of Sunday, July 8, 1860, a fire broke out in Wallace Peak's new drug store on Commerce Street in Dallas, about 250 miles north of Gonzales. Within two hours, Dallas's business district lay in a smoldering ruin. As those flames burned themselves out, fire erupted in Denton, a day's ride northwest. For four days some dozen fires flared out of nowhere in towns and on farms, all within seventy-five miles of Dallas. Alarm over the sudden rash of blazes spread across Texas and the Lower South like the wildfires themselves.

Thoughtful men initially (and correctly) attributed the blazes to "prairie matches," the new and highly unstable phosphorus matches that could ignite spontaneously when subjected to heat. For others, that explanation was too simple, too naïve. Barely one week after the Dallas fire, reports began spreading that something far more sinister lay behind the flames. Newspaper editors such as ultra-Southerner John Marshall of Austin's *Texas State Gazette* followed the lead of the editor of the Dallas paper in singling out slaves incited by abolitionists as the cause of the blazes. These editors, who missed no opportunity to interpret any event possible as a Northern attack on the Southern ethos and in particular on its "peculiar institution," quoted those who had heard it said on what they swore was good authority that these fires were the vanguard of an uprising. Southerners well remembered that only ten months earlier abolitionist John Brown had attacked the Federal arsenal at Harpers Ferry, Virginia, intent on sparking a slave revolt. While no uprising followed the Dallas fires, such a rash of fires erupting in such proximity of time and place gave the "Texas Troubles," as this fright soon came to be called, a heightened reality. Mildred Littlefield felt it in Gonzales. "The incerrection excitement is rageing very high here," she reported on September 1, 1860. "The citizens of Gonzilus Keep guard out all the time for fear of fier."[1]

Though she did not hint at it in her letter, Mildred must have known that she had reason to be apprehensive. Her overseer, Jim Bailey, who had come with the family from Mississippi, had a mean streak in him. "I've got scars all on my back that he put there whipping me with bullwhips," Alf Satterwhite recalled of the two years he labored under Bailey's surveillance. In the slave quarters, Bailey's treatment of Mildred's field hands could not help but temper the maternal concern Mildred expressed for the young slave mothers. The enslaved constituted only 40 percent of Gonzales County's population, but if they got together, three thousand plus could be a considerable force.[2]

As the alarm over the Texas Troubles died down, Mildred's principal worry concerned daughter Sallie's divorce proceeding in Brazoria. Until, that is, the worst happened. On November 6, Abraham Lincoln was elected the sixteenth president of the United States. No Texan voted for him. Southerners opposed the standard-bearer of the Republican Party, who stood on a platform that called for prohibiting the extension of slavery into the territories and denied states' rights, especially the right of secession. "Thire is A great diel of excitement here abou[t] Lincon's election," Sallie Dowell wrote shortly after news of it reached Gonzales. Put in office by the electoral votes of northern states alone, Lincoln's administration, Southerners believed, would usher in an administration hostile to their way of life. Having lost at the ballot box, they could see only one course of action left to them. "I have not A doubt that what we will have A war," Sallie reported the prevailing sentiment. This was no fleeting feeling of a small group. In the statewide referendum on the Ordinance of Secession held three months later in February 1861, in which 76 percent of Texans voted to leave the United States, Gonzales County men approved the referendum by an overwhelming ten-to-one majority, 802 to 80. Littlefield family friend and plantation neighbor across the fence Thomas Neville Waul so actively supported creating the Confederate States of America that the Texas legislature appointed him one of seven delegates to participate in forming the new national government, after which he rose to the rank of brigadier general in the Southern service.[3]

Approving too, eighteen-year-old George Washington Littlefield nevertheless had a decision to make. Did his greater loyalty lie at home with family and the mother of whom he was so fond or in military service in defense of his South? Upon returning home in mid-April from the court session in which Sallie secured her divorce, he thought about joining a Gonzales company to fight Comanche Indians raiding west of San Antonio. But the year's commitment to the frontier was too great. Fighting for the nascent Southern Confederacy, on the other hand, was different. "This may be a chance for all, and all will fight, for I don't think there is a true Southern man but what would rather die like a Souldier before he will submit," Littlefield wrote to brother John White in Mississippi in a long and newsy letter, his earliest to survive. "I have Ma and Sallie to take care of but still if I am needed in the [war] I will go, for I think it would be the noblest deed of our life to fight against Lincolns administration."[4]

Before the letter could reach its destination, George Littlefield offered himself for service in a force Col. Earl Van Dorn was assembling. Shortly after Confederate shelling of Fort Sumter in South Carolina opened the War between the States on April 12, 1861, a call went out in Gonzales for volunteers to ride to the coast to intercept some five hundred Federal soldiers, along with their equipment and supplies, before they could sail for New York. Success on April 25 outfitted the young man with "a regular army . . . Minnie rifle with bayonet bright and keen . . . [and] two good army six-shooters and knife about 14 inches in the blade."[5]

"War harness" in hand, teenage Littlefield was ready to ride into a future he had not planned but which his days at Baylor University primed him to embrace. His mother, as mothers do, knowing that wars leave participants changed in ways they cannot anticipate, tried to dissuade him. "Ma don't want me to go for she don't think it necessary for all of the young men to go and the old ones stay at home," he told his brother. But fueled by the elation of that initial bloodless martial success, infused with high-minded patriotic sentiment, and driven by peer pressure ("Where my brother [David White, who was serving in a Confederate unit in Florida] is now and where my many associates soon will be, Can I stand an[d] be idle. No I cannot!"[6]), propelled George Littlefield forward.

Seeing that nothing she could say would dissuade her son from going to the fight, mother Mildred thought to do the next best thing—send a servant to make his living as comfortable as circumstances would allow. So she summoned Nathan Stokes's mother. George and the young slave Nathan had been close since George's earliest years in Mississippi, where, in the way of the South, white children on the plantation played with black boys and girls. Play was only part of it for Nathan, ten years the older. "Since he wuz a baby," Nathan stated proudly, "I allus laid off to take keer uv him an' I done it."

As Nathan remembered the summer of 1861, "Missis—that's Marse George's Ma—told my mammy that I wuz a-goin' to go 'long with him an' take keer uv him, but she wuzn't ter tell me nothin' 'bout it. I 'member I wuz a-goin' off ter a neighboring plantation on a visit an' my mammy called me to her.

"'Nathan,' sez she. 'If I wuz ter tell you somethin',' would you run off?' 'No, Mammy,' sez I, 'ain't nuthin' gwine ter mek me leave here. Whut is it, Mammy?' sez I.

"'Wal, they'se gwine ter send you to the war with Marse George,' sez she.

"'All right, Mammy,' sez I. 'I'll go enywhere Marse George goes.' I went on an' they sent fer me to come home in a few days. Misses sent fer me an' said ter me:

"'Nathan, I want that you go to war with Marse George.'

"An' I told her, 'All right, I ain't never gwuine to leave him.'"

Mildred asked a commitment only for the war. Nathan honored it for life, and he outlived them all. The bond cemented between the two men during the war—and irrevocably sealed by the explosion of a cannonball—proved to be so remarkable in its strength and endurance that in 1899 Nathan would be declared to be "probably the best cared-for negro in America," and the *New York Times* would honor him by marking his passing.[7]

"Let me have the Guns if you have them," called Capt. Isham G. Jones on the muster roll of the Gonzales Rifles he organized on May 25, 1861, and "I can give any Guarranties you wish." He and his men meant it. "We are all ready and anxious for the trip [to the battleground]. . . . We are going to get into the fight deep," Pvt. George Littlefield reported the sentiments of his one hundred comrades in Jones's unit. Playfully he added in the letter to his brother John that, as his sweetheart asked, he would bring her two pet Yankees. On September 11 in Houston, the Gonzales Rifles were mustered into Confederate service for the duration of the war and grouped with nine other companies to form the Eighth Texas Cavalry Regiment under the command of wealthy plantation owner and signer of Texas's Ordinance of Secession Benjamin Franklin Terry and Texas Revolutionary War veteran Thomas Saltus Lubbock.[8]

Slightly more than a thousand college graduates, professional men, merchants, stockmen, and farmers made up the Eighth Texas, many of them sons of well-to-do families. Important for the service they meant to render, according to Pvt. Lee Giles, they were horsemen. "No Texan walks a yard if he can help it," a British officer noted. Though the Confederate War Department asked Texas for infantry and Captain Jones recruited his company as light infantry—mounted foot soldiers—Terry's regiment joined the Confederate ranks as cavalry. If the men were like Littlefield, they were marksmen as well as horsemen. Littlefield loved to hunt. His oldest surviving possession is a hunting horn inscribed "1858" and "GWL," reminding him of the time when he used the horn as a club to save a favorite hound from being drowned by a raccoon. Hunters like Littlefield were used to living outdoors too, as he had done in camping out every night for a month in bringing the entourage from Mississippi.[9]

The men of the Eighth Texas knew from muster-in that they constituted no ordinary regiment. They were accepted as a ranging unit. With a history dating to 1823 as a force organized by Father of Texas Stephen F. Austin himself, the moniker "Texas Ranger" designated a special service—a tough and agile mounted fighting force used for frontier defense. From his service in the Texas military, capped by two years as secretary of war of the Republic of Texas, Albert Sidney Johnston knew the Rangers' reputation well. Consequently he had the command diverted from the Virginia front to shore up his Army of Tennessee defending the central South between the Mississippi River and the Appalachian Mountains. Terry's men knew the Rangers' reputation too. The designation motivated, if not emboldened them beyond the patriotic fervor that drew them into Confederate ranks. "We started out with the name of Texas Rangers," Henry W. Graber of B Company explained, "with a reputation we had never earned but were called on to sustain." Littlefield's declaration that they meant to get into the fight deep was no mere bluster. The *Houston Telegraph* sensed it when, upon the regiment's organization, it "hazard[ed] nothing in saying that there is an amount of manliness, chivalry, and bravery in the regiment, which cannot be surpassed by any troops in the world." However the editor perceived it even before Terry's Texas Rangers had left for the front, much less seen action, the men indeed took unusual pride in living up to the expectation.[10]

They were "nearly all boys" in their teens and early twenties, as Littlefield characterized them. He wished for some older men to bring military experience to the officer positions. But, always a keen judge of people, he could tell that "when we farely get in to the war then we will make men of ourselves." The men knew that judgment more than age alone qualified a man to lead. True, since the regiment comprised volunteers all, its command was not as authoritarian as that of other units. Many felt as Pvt. Henry W. Graber did that "a private was generally the equal of any officer in command." That said, leaders there must be, and his comrades had seen in Littlefield judgment they could trust. Consequently, following the custom of the time, when the men of Captain Jones's company elected their leaders in Houston, they promoted Littlefield some eight ranks to second sergeant.[11]

Picket duty scouting Federal positions in central Kentucky filled most of the last two months of 1861. Between that routine and being sick for an extended period, Littlefield had little to write about. Oh, brother John in Mississippi sent a large box of ham and bread that Littlefield shared with four or five of the boys. And there was the incongruous beauty of the night flares launched by Union forces trying to illuminate Confederate positions. But the monotony of this cat-and-mouse game of scouting left many, including Littlefield, with time to think about taking a furlough to visit home.

The inactivity ended in the new year, when Union forces advanced on both flanks of Johnston's line. On January 19, 1862, at Mill Spring, Federal forces crushed the Southern right wing in eastern Kentucky. Eighteen days later on the left, Fort Henry fell, opening the broad Tennessee River to Northern gunboats. Fort Donelson nearby on the Cumberland River capitulated on February 16. Within a month, Johnston's defense of Kentucky had been broken, and two water routes into Tennessee, Mississippi, and Alabama provided an avenue beckoning Union advances.[12]

Johnston ordered his troops to withdraw southward. As they evacuated Bowling Green, Kentucky, the Confederates destroyed supplies potentially useful to the approaching Union forces. Littlefield's assignment was to dispose of a stock of whiskey. Small in the grand scheme of the withdrawal, the role demanded more of him than he ever anticipated. On February 14 Gen. Thomas C. Hindman ordered the new second lieutenant, risen to the officer rank by election following the resignation of a senior officer not four weeks earlier, to destroy this stock that a drug store owner had been reportedly selling illegally to soldiers.

On his way, Littlefield learned that an intoxicated Irish Confederate whom the druggist had refused to serve further had concocted the illegal sales story in retribution. When Littlefield met the druggist, rather than a scoundrel, he found "a first class Southern gentleman." And the nineteen-year-old very junior officer confronted the dilemma of leadership. He had orders. But they conflicted with his sense of right and wrong. Obey orders unquestioningly or protect the property of a man on whose behalf he was fighting in the first place—what should he do?

The druggist seemed to have the answer when patriotically he suggested shipping the liquor to the military hospital in Nashville. Littlefield jumped at a course that both solved the problem of inebriation and served his cause. With the dishonorable informant under guard, he started for General Hindman's headquarters. Then he shrank from his resolve. "I am only a Shirttail Lieutenant," he thought, "and General Hindman might not like my suggestions." Rather than find out, he returned to the store and had a barrel of apple brandy brought out and emptied into the street, where it puddled in frozen horse tracks. That had its own consequences when men of Gen. Patrick R. Cleburne's Second Brigade nearby broke ranks, ran to the scene, and began lapping up the free whiskey. If he continued, Littlefield would incapacitate the unit shortly.

When he had the solution, Littlefield took the druggist into the basement and said, "I am only a boy, but I realize if I carry out this unreasonable order brought about by a drunken Irishman, that I make you a poor man." In good conscience he could not do that to a patriotic Southerner. His answer was for them to pound on the casks until everyone outside would think that all of the delicious content had been poured out. To ensure that none of the liquor got to any soldiers before the army evacuated the place the next day, Littlefield held the keys overnight. Commanding the extreme rear guard, he easily completed the mission as he rode out of town.

"One glad man. And one boy Lieutenant made to feel good," Littlefield recalled the incident in his autobiography. "It often happened that some thing good could be done. But for the want of [a] little nerve and forethought it was not. While this order was disobeyed yet the heart always felt good for what was done." Littlefield had exercised the kind of judgment the men of his company had perceived to be in him. It was the kind of nerve and forethought they wanted in their officers. A week later in Nashville, when the company's two senior officers obtained furloughs to return to Texas, 2nd Lt. George Washington Littlefield succeeded to command of I Company, Eighth Texas Cavalry. Whatever wraps the unit would get into, he would have to lead the men through it.[13]

Chaplain Robert Franklin Bunting, who wrote long letters to Texas newspapers informing those at home of the doings of their men, called the withdrawal, first from Kentucky and then from Tennessee, a retreat. "A big run," Littlefield characterized it, dismissing the rosy interpretations in the newspapers he saw. Whether a retreat or a run, "as usual," Bunting wrote, "the Rangers were assigned the post 'of danger and honor,'" protecting the army's rear.[14] But what all wanted to know was where Johnston would stand and fight.

Central in Johnston's planning was protecting the vital Memphis and Charleston Railroad. Completed not five years earlier, it was both the first rail line to stretch between the Atlantic coast and the Mississippi River and the only east-west rail line in the Confederate states. Johnston marshaled 47,000 men at Corinth, Mississippi, astride the M&C Railroad. Meanwhile, Gen. Ulysses S. Grant's force, which had captured Fort Donelson, made its way up the Tennessee River toward northern Mississippi and Alabama. Assuming the Confederates would remain in their position at Corinth, Grant encamped his 49,000 effectives at Pittsburg Landing in southern Tennessee, twenty-two miles north of Johnston, to await the 25,000 men marching from Nashville to reinforce him. After the two armies joined, he would march on Corinth.

General Johnston stole Grant's opportunity. Mindful that the best defense is a good offense and intent on confronting the two armies separately, Johnston attacked. On the first day of the bloody Battle of Shiloh, April 6, 1862, the Confederates time after time broke the Union lines. Over the hilly and wooded ground, passing Shiloh Church, and overwhelming the Hornet's Nest, they advanced. On the Confederate left where Johnston had assigned them, the Rangers were lightly engaged until about four o'clock. Perceiving the enemy's right to be in full retreat, Gen. Pierre Gustave Toutant Beauregard, who had assumed command in the wake of Johnston's death, ordered the Eighth Texas to intercept the fleeing Federals "as he depended upon the Rangers for the final victory of the day. This was all our boys needed," Chaplain Bunting wrote, "and in a gallop they set out for the work." They had gone only a short distance when intense fire from the Thirteenth Iowa Infantry and Battery D of the First Illinois Light Artillery checked their charge. Diverting into protective woods beside the road, I and A Companies led the Rangers' climb of one hundred or so soggy yards out of Tilghman Branch toward the enemy. Thick forest forced the riders to advance single file. Scattered trees on level ground above the stream thwarted commanders who were trying to form the men in line of battle. Unable to effectively return the galling fire, the riders fell back. In the retreat by Littlefield's side, J. D. McClure received a serious wound. "I know now that I will stand the sising of minnie balls," Littlefield wrote fiancée Alice, "but not extremely fond of them, . . . they seemed like they wanted to get right clost to me."[15]

Union reinforcements arriving during the night wrested victory from the Confederates the next day. Between them, the opposing armies reported losses of 23,746 killed, wounded, and missing—just under one-quarter of all engaged. The Rangers lost 66 of 425—nearly 15 percent. During this greatest land battle on the American continent up to that time, Lieutenant Littlefield himself lost only his hat. Two days later he "captured" a Yankee cap to replace it.[16]

Back in Corinth, where the Confederates regrouped and prepared for a Union advance, Littlefield reflected on events. What he saw distressed the idealist in him. In the heat of battle with the enemy on the run on the first day, he had seen Confederate soldiers lose their purpose as they overran the well-supplied Union camps. "I never dreamed that I would see the day when the people of the shivelrous South would lay down there arms on the field and go to plundering. No Mother No *I never thought it once.* But surely it is so." The memory depressed him, even though he wrote another letter on a piece of captured stationery. Worse was the news that the important city of New Orleans had succumbed to Northern gunboats. That meant three things. One, the Federals' superiority on the water gave them virtually unchallenged use of the Mississippi River. Two, the war would have to be won solely by land battles. And three, soldiers like Littlefield from west of the river were cut off from home. "Nothing is more grieving to ones heart than to know that they are separated from there homes." For a moment, Littlefield's fervent patriotic optimism wavered. "Ma, Ma, Ma, I fear the people of the south will not hold out. . . . But Oh Mother *I pray not.* Would that each man of the south would resolve to die or concer [conquer]."[17]

Officers especially should resolve. Too many, he grumbled, were home on furlough rather than fulfilling their military responsibilities. The good news near the end of April was that the two senior officers of I Company returned. But Captain Jones, who had been sick in New Orleans for months, returned only to resign. This presented Lieutenant Littlefield with a problem. Pleased with his leadership, the men of I Company wanted to elect him captain over 1st Lt. Augustus D. Harris, who had missed Shiloh. Preferring older men as officers, Littlefield shrank from being promoted over his fourteen-year elder. To Col. John A. Wharton Littlefield went. Having succeeded the fallen Terry in command of the regiment, Wharton enjoyed a prominence all his own for having been a signer of Texas's secession ordinance and having joined Terry in organizing the unit. Older promotion by rank, Littlefield requested. Wharton refused. Promotion by election was standard practice. But Harris was Wharton's age, I irth fo ld councored, while Littlefield was still a teenager (if by only a month and a half). Wharton refused. Littlefield begged, saying he would take it as a favor if the colonel ordered promotion by rank. Wharton relented, so ordered, and on May 7, 1862, Harris was promoted to captain and Littlefield to first lieutenant.

The worst of luck, Littlefield called it. Two days later, while Littlefield was escorting the brigade wagon train in crossing the Tennessee River, Gus Harris died leading a charge. By Colonel Wharton's order, First Lieutenant Littlefield would rise to captain commanding. Back to Wharton Littlefield went, this time asking the commander to reinstate promotion by election. "It is an office that I did not want. I felt that there was too mutch responsibility in it for me," Littlefield told his sweetheart. Wharton refused, telling Littlefield both that he should not have set aside the normal practice in the first place and that promotion by rank would put Littlefield where Wharton wanted him—in command of the company. Again Littlefield appealed to his commander. Only one man in the entire company was younger than he. Moreover, in the command structure, Littlefield would be the youngest of the regiment's ten captains. Under those circumstances, the lieutenant wanted to know that the men wanted him at their head. Wharton resisted. "Very much affected," Littlefield pleaded. Finally, Wharton gave in. On June 1 the men of I Company—"a good company[,] . . . not as large as some of them. But equally as brave as any of them"—elected Littlefield their captain by acclamation.[18]

After the outnumbered Confederates abandoned Corinth at the end of May, the Eighth Texas joined a brigade assembled by Col. Nathan Bedford Forrest in Chattanooga, Tennessee, 220 miles to the east, for a raid into Middle Tennessee. Half an hour before daybreak on July 13, 1862, Texans leading, the Confederate force fell upon the substantial but unsuspecting and dispersed Union garrison at Murfreesboro, south of the capital at Nashville. Forrest's men overwhelmed the defenders and achieved Forrest's goal of using "active duty as a training scheme and the enemy as a source of supply for needed equipment." The Confederates captured so many supply wagons that to get them away, Forrest had to enlist Union prisoners as teamsters, enticing them with the promise of parole after the wagons had been moved beyond the range of a Union counter-foray.[19]

The engagement was "one of the greatest victories of the war, In which the Rangers were first and foremost," Captain Littlefield trumpeted to his sweetheart. So complete a triumph would lift the spirits of any soldier. Littlefield was exhilarated. For the first time in three months, his letter home did not dwell on mourning the friends he had lost. "My best friends is gone," he had lamented in the same letter in which he had described his election to the captaincy. "You may know my trubles are great from the loss of my Capt. and Jim [1st Sgt. Jim Harris] my best friend on earth. Allice, I cant reflect upon the past without its bringing grief to my heart." Murfreesboro changed that. In place of grief, Littlefield wrote of inspiration and "a nice Silver mounted Sixshooter" to satisfy Alice's request for a battlefield trophy. "It is very small," he told her, "but large enough for you to defend yourself with."[20]

He wanted to take it to her but could hardly think of leaving. After campaigning with the men of I Company for a year and leading them for almost as long, "It is like leaving home to leave them now[,] I have become so mutch attached to them," he wrote in August 1862, during a relaxed period after the Murfreesboro raid. The commanders put those few weeks in camp to good use drilling the regiment. Dismounted skirmish maneuvers in the morning, marching in parade in the afternoon—Littlefield liked it. "I am very fond of discipline," he wrote, and "I would like it if there was more in our Regt."[21] Discipline that welded them as a fighting unit, he understood, would couple with personal tenacity to carry them through brushes and fights with as little loss as possible.

When not drilling, the men had time to meet the people of the country around them. As handsome a young officer as Captain Littlefield attracted women (see fig. 4). "Allice I have found the prettiest little woman here that is anywhere I know. Oh Allice she is so sweet," he wrote his sweetheart in Texas. Maybe he meant to make her jealous. After all, she had written him "of the young man what wants you to remain single until the war is over." If she fell for that young man, then "you will find me with my Tennessee woman. . . . Alice I am allmost temped to love her." But to make sure his words did not push Alice away, two days later he wrote emphatically, "I can't call her mine. No! She is not. For you have given yourself to me and I can claim no other nor would I do it. No! You are my all . . . and you well know my passion for you."[22]

Having restated his love, George described for Alice the East Tennessee mountain people who resembled nothing like he and she had ever seen in Mississippi or Texas. "The people have little log houses with small garden and field, but happy as one can imagine especially the girls. They go it without shoes an bonnet and but few garments of any kind they wear. Some are pretty while others are too ugly to inhabit this or any other world. They go it to the springs without covering to there heads (with the exception of a large bucket whitch is enough to kill anyone to carry it. Great large hands and there feet . . . I won't say what collar) is as large as the feet of two men."[23]

By the time he wrote, Captain Littlefield's days among the mountain people were numbered, and he knew it. Gen. Braxton Bragg, who had been given command of the army Johnston had led out of Kentucky, and Gen. Edmund Kirby-Smith commanding in East Tennessee had laid plans for an offensive. Littlefield thought middle Tennessee was the target, but the commanders in fact meant to drive Union Gen. Don Carlos Buell from Louisville and reestablish the Confederacy's northern boundary at the Ohio River.

From Bardstown, Kentucky, on September 24, 1862, Colonel Wharton sent a detachment of his Eighth Texas "under a good officer," most likely eight companies under Captain Littlefield, to reconnoiter the deployment of Buell's five thousand cavalry in the vicinity of Louisville. Within about four miles of the city, the farthest north the Confederate advance reached, Littlefield's cavalry encountered its Federal counterpart. Falling back after a light engagement, the Texans rejoined the brigade only to have four regiments of Yankee cavalry position themselves between Wharton's men and the rest of the Confederate Army. "Charge!," Wharton shouted. Revolvers blazing and letting loose with the Rebel Yell, the Confederates flung themselves into the Federals. As the Union line gave way, "the mixed up fight," as Littlefield termed it, ensued. In the exhilaration of the chase, he and three Rangers took off after a fleeing group of Ohio cavalry, killing several and capturing the remainder, one of whom was wounded. Rather than impose the hurt man on the Confederate medical staff, the Rangers took the entire group to a nearby house where he could be treated. No sooner had Littlefield and his comrades reached the fence encircling the dwelling than a man ran out, leveling a pistol at them. Instantly, Littlefield drew two of the five revolvers in his belt. The man dropped his gun. But how quickly the fortunes of war change. From behind the house, a host of Yankee cavalry appeared. Abandoning all the prisoners, the Rangers ran for their lives. Littlefield headed for a nearby peach orchard. As his horse jumped a fence, the saddle girth snapped. He clamped his knees against the undulating horse as hard as he could and held on for dear life. While Littlefield managed to save his mount, the five pistols flew every which way. Late that night he reached camp safely to re-arm to fight another day.[24]

The next several days mirrored the ones before—"fight, skirmish and fall back," Littlefield phrased it—until Buell's Army of Ohio "crowded up." In the daylong Battle of Perryville on October 8, 1862, the Rangers maneuvered and fought until dark ended the engagement. The detail Littlefield recorded of the fight was not about his part in the combat but rather about just how good his first meal of the day tasted after the shooting stopped. Parched corn brought momentary relief from the cold and sleet pelting him as he lay on the ground in line of battle, tense in anticipation of the next action. Although General Bragg won a tactical victory at Perryville, he could not sustain his position in Kentucky. The populace had not rallied to the Confederate flag as Southern strategists had expected when they planned the advance into the Bluegrass State. Two days later, on October 10, 1862, Terry's Rangers fell into their usual position guarding the army's rear.[25]

In the little more than a year since the Eighth Texas had joined General Johnston's army in the Western Theater, the some thousand men who arrived ready for duty had dropped to probably half that. Campaigning, fighting, and disease had taken their tolls. The regiment needed recruits. Since units like the companies of the Eighth Texas were raised in specific locales, commanders looked to those places for recruits. In September 1862 Colonel Wharton wrote the Houston newspaper soliciting enlistees. Some came but not enough. He concluded that face-to-face encounters stood to bring in greater numbers. From near Knoxville in November, Wharton dispatched Captain Littlefield and two other officers to Texas on a ninety-day recruiting mission.[26]

In a little more than a year, George Washington Littlefield had grown up in ways he had not expected when he so proudly outfitted himself with war harness of rifle, pistols, knife, and bayonet bright and keen. From an idealist impatient to defend the homeland, he had matured into a tested soldier who would stand the "sising of minnie balls." More significant, he had seasoned into a leader whose men trusted him to steer them skillfully through the most trying situations and whose commander trusted his magnetism to replenish the ranks. What Littlefield trusted as he made his way home was that he could secure a commitment more meaningful for his life than the sum of recruits he could find.

4

THE PROUDEST DAY

Capt. George Littlefield must have known that General Wharton had sent him on a nearly impossible recruiting mission. A large percentage of the thousand or so men of military age in Gonzales County in 1861 had joined the ten companies raised in the initial enthusiasm to fight Lincoln. And recruiters subsequently passing through central Texas had swept up as many as they could of those who had resisted the early enthusiasm that had enveloped the likes of young Littlefield and those who had come of age since the war began. Not even his thirty-five-year-old half brother T.J. White or twenty-six-year-old brother-in-law Theo Harral remained available to the captain. In June 1862 both had enlisted in the Spy Company brigaded in Waul's Legion raised by the Littlefields' neighbor.[1]

Even had men been plentiful, patriotism had cooled in the year since the Eighth Texas had departed for the front. Conscription acts contributed to it by excusing well-to-do slave owners. A rich man's war and a poor man's fight, grumbled many. And men liable for the draft scrambled for medical exemptions. "Rheumatism, which was once dreaded as a torturing fiend, has become as popular as a beautiful coquet," wrote one conscription inspector. "Gout is also much sought after; but in these hard times few families can get above rheumatism."

On top of that, the war was not going so well. It had not turned out to be the glorious romp Southerners had anticipated. Oh, there was news to cheer the spirit. After the defeat at Shiloh, for example, rumor spread through the army of a single triumph in Virginia in which the Yankee losses approximated the number of men in the entire Army of Mississippi. Battle-hardened Littlefield didn't believe it. "I am tired of hearing these big reports. I am getting to believe that the South is more brag than anything else," he wrote in disgust. Yes, victories had been won, as at Murfreesboro in the summer, but they were not knock-out blows. Yes, Gen. Robert E. Lee had saved the capital of Richmond in the Seven Days Battles at the end of June, but his northern advance had been blunted with dreadful loss at Antietam in September. Then in October had followed the miscarriage in Kentucky. "From beginning to end, a brilliant blunder and a magnificent failure," Chaplain Bunting summed up the Rangers' assessment of the grand expedition that cost precious lives. Little wonder, then, that recruiting was no easy assignment.[2]

Duty to country had sent the captain to Gonzales, but a personal mission quickened his step. He wanted to see Alice Tillar. On December 10 from Dull Home in Gonzales, he wrote her in Houston that he wished "to speak with you about the length of our engagement." He wanted to marry before returning to the front. Parents' advice to wait until George came home for good fell on deaf ears. Alice accepted his proposal, and they married in Houston on Tuesday, January 14, 1863. For twelve days the twenty-year-old captain and his sixteen-year-old bride enjoyed the start of their life together.[3] How different the real beginning would be after George returned for good.

The trip to rejoin the Rangers in Tennessee tested Littlefield's determination and ingenuity. It wasn't just trying to sleep on the hard wooden seat of a jolting stagecoach after luxuriating in a bed for more than a month, though he surely missed the bed. It wasn't the inconvenience of the overturned stagecoach that caused him to miss the train from Marshall, Texas, to Shreveport, Louisiana, by five minutes. Nor was it the five hundred extra miles that Union obstacles and available rail lines forced him to travel to rejoin the regiment. Rather, it was water.

Federal movement on the Mississippi River toward the Confederate stronghold of Vicksburg, Mississippi, thwarted his plan of taking the train from the railhead at Monroe, Louisiana, to the west bank of the Mississippi and being ferried across to Vicksburg. In January 1863, at last taking advantage of their June victory in the Battle of Memphis, which eliminated Confederate boats blocking Federal control of the river north of Vicksburg, Union strategists had begun movements to capture the one fortified town that stood between them and cutting the Confederacy in half. A little more than two weeks before Captain Littlefield left Houston, Union boats below Memphis had run up the Arkansas River and captured Arkansas Post. About the time he left, and closer to Vicksburg, men of Union Gen. William T. Sherman's division began digging a canal intended to open passage to the Red River and thence around Vicksburg to the Mississippi below the Confederate position.

At first Captain Littlefield thought of swimming the river on horseback. But flooded fields in Louisiana made even reaching the river problematic. And if he could get to the stream, the stronger-than-usual current resulting from heavy rains upstream discouraged the attempt to swim. "It is my first time that I wanted to go anywhere and could not," he confessed to his new wife. That he was carrying two thousand dollars for the regiment's sick and wounded made his expeditious crossing all the more imperative. Then he hit on the idea of volunteering to serve on a Confederate gunboat headed down the Red River from Alexandria to engage Union craft at the river's mouth. In exchange for his service, he would be deposited in due course on the east bank. But the commanding general forbade it. Perhaps Richard Taylor had learned from the disastrous loss in the Battle of Memphis the folly of manning boats with men unacquainted with sailing and river warfare. Somehow, perhaps by his remaining alternative of finding someone at a friendly plantation to row him across, Littlefield managed to get over the great river. On March 5, 1863, after slightly more than five weeks' travel, he rejoined his regiment and men.[4]

As he traveled, the Confederate officer listened to what people along the way were saying about the war. Having left Texans talking of making peace, he heard Louisianans doubting that the South would win. Mississippians talked as they had from the war's beginning: glorious victories scored within three months would bring independence and peace. He, along with the comrades he joined in the defensive works on the front line in Tennessee, had no illusion about an early peace. Months, maybe years of war remained. But undiscouraged by either that prospect or being undermanned as they knew they were, the men of the Army of Tennessee were ready to fight.[5]

When would the next battle come? they all wondered. The Battle of Stones River, fought at Murfreesboro while Littlefield was in Texas, had been bloody but inconclusive. Since early January the armies had moved little from the positions they took up in its aftermath not that many miles apart. Confederate cavalry scouted, skirmished, and rode on occasional sorties to disrupt Union supply lines. But neither Union Gen. William S. Rosecrans nor Confederate commander Bragg were making moves to initiate the clash.[6]

Spending weeks upon weeks in camp did have the benefit of improving the men's health. When Littlefield described camp conditions, he knew his wife would find it hard to believe that he, or any of them, could be fit. Rain and the resulting mud turned the men into "the dirtiest set you ever saw in your life." More annoying than the mud were lice. "You must not think that it is for the want of respect paid to the body that causes these nasty buggs, for dear Wife, it is impossible to keep them off of you in the army," George explained apologetically. Despite it all, he was pleased to report he was a robust and trim 155 pounds.[7]

Food more varied and better than army rations, he readily admitted, accounted in considerable measure for his good condition. For this luxury he had to thank his mother (though in the letter he didn't), who had sent slave Nathan to war with her son, and Nathan himself, who proved to be an adroit forager. "We are living tolerably hard off of the Government," Littlefield wrote of his rations, "but I send a negro boy out in the country every day and he gets me milk and plenty of nice pies and now and then a chicken or two."[8] What Littlefield did not admit was that Nathan's work was fully as perilous as any soldier's. Nathan decades later well remembered the night he was almost caught. As he told the Littlefields' milkman, in place of a chicken one night, Nathan set his sights on a pig. As he was taking hold of the animal, the door of the house opened, no doubt for the resident to investigate the rustling around outside. Nathan grabbed the pig, froze, and held the animal so tightly, he said, that he all but smothered it. When the coast at last was clear, Nathan returned to camp with his prize. That surely was good pork, Nathan recalled all those years later.[9]

By that time, Littlefield's first mention of him in the surviving letters, Nathan had become essential to his master in more ways than one. He was there to make a good hand. "I wanted to be with the Major, and I was his man, and I had to look after him," Nathan said firmly decades afterward. He did. Once when the captain feared the regimental wagon train might be captured, he sent Nathan to get and protect Alice's photograph and other precious reminders of her affection. And not just Littlefield's dearest mementos. Littlefield trusted Nathan so implicitly that he had him secure good friend John Houston's picture of his wife too.[10]

Just how much Littlefield relied on his servant he documented in the lengthy account he wrote home of the search he made when once Nathan came up missing. "My negro boy Nathan has disappeared, quite strange," Littlefield wrote in the longest passage he devoted to him during the war. On Saturday Littlefield had dispatched Nathan to buy food and pick up the master's washing from the woman to whom Nathan had taken it. When Nathan had not returned the next day, the captain rode out to the farm, where he expected to find him in the slave quarters. Nathan's horse, saddled and bridled, was there. But no Nathan. Nathan had been there the night before, then left, a slave on the place told Littlefield, adding that Nathan's horse had returned riderless that day. Littlefield believed that with the freedom of movement he allowed Nathan while the Rangers' base remained in place, Nathan had found a woman on a nearby farm to whom he had taken a liking. When Nathan had not come in on the second day, Littlefield deduced that either he was hiding out to visit her or he had died at the hands of a jealous rival. Littlefield puzzled: "He can't be run off for he would of taken the horse, and my clothes that was at wash at this negro womans house." Ranger comrades believed the worst had happened. After all, Nathan was cautious around other slaves, but not so much for the reason Littlefield thought. "I was skittish that they might tell [Northern troops of his presence]," Nathan said. "I just didn't have too much to do with them." Nathan's caution saved him from being captured as some other Ranger servants had been. Littlefield never recorded the story's end. Perhaps Nathan's return was enough.[11]

March, April, May, June, July, August—for months little changed. Cavalry continued scouting, sprinting on sorties, and skirmishing. Bragg drilled his troops to high efficiency but sat waiting for Rosecrans to attack his strength in the center

of his line. Smarter than that, Rosecrans outflanked the Confederate Army, forcing Bragg in July to evacuate Tennessee with no more contest than the Rangers'
rearguard fights. In Rome, Georgia, the Rangers once again settled into camp.[12]

Seizing on this return to camp life, chaplains throughout the army called their
flocks to God. "We have a regular revival in our camps," George wrote Alice. "The
meeting has been going on for some twelve days and it still gets better. . . . There
has been several converted and the prospects fine still. It is a *real rousing up of the*
whole *camps*." Tenting only five feet from Chaplain Bunting's preaching, George
heard it all. Even so, whatever he meant by it getting better, Littlefield himself at
first was not roused—did not feel "that conviction that I think a person should
have before going to sutch a place."

Perhaps his strong sense of right and wrong, for which he used the word
"honor," made him feel comfortable in his moral convictions. Every letter he had
written his new wife—every letter—mentioned honor and right living in one
regard or another. Nevertheless, the preaching he could not help hearing made
him reflect on his relationship with his creator. Reflection led to change. "I am a
better man than before and I intend to improve," he wrote Alice on August 2. How
much better he shortly had to declare.

To honor Gen. John Wharton, risen from command of a Ranger company to
leadership of the cavalry division that included the Rangers, the regiment presented
him on August 5, 1863, with as fine a horse as they could find and followed the
ceremony that night with a dance. Sensing that what began as respectable dancing
would end up with lonely men and women together in bed, Littlefield went to
church instead of to the shindig. "It looks too much like a ball," he wrote, respect-
ing his Baptist upbringing. Hearing reports afterward that men and women did
indeed associate with abandon, he could not contain his disgust and disapproval.
Never would he allow "a relation of mine go to sutch a place."[13]

Day by day drawn more to Bunting's preaching, Littlefield presented himself
at the altar late in the month. Chaplain Bunting had converted George Washington Littlefield. True, for most of his life, Littlefield professed no denomination
and darkened few church doors. And even after the war, while Bunting served
for thirteen years in Galveston and was a Mason like Littlefield (who had joined
Terry's Military Lodge, U.D., since its establishment within the regiment a year
earlier), the two men appear to have had little contact. Be that as it may, Littlefield
never forgot the regimental minister who had shown him the way. When a half
century later George Littlefield could see his time on earth ending, to Presbyterians
he would turn. And of two photographs from the war found among Littlefield's
effects, one was of Chaplain Bunting in Confederate uniform.[14]

Very shortly after Littlefield stepped forward, the regiment received orders to obstruct elements of the Union Army crossing the mountains south of Chattanooga, pursuing what General Bragg had led Rosecrans to believe was a demoralized and retreating Confederate force. Having abandoned the important rail junction of Chattanooga without firing a shot, the Confederates were not giving up more territory uncontested. On September 19 the opposing armies collided along West Chickamauga Creek, just south of the Tennessee state line. The fighting in the Battle of Chickamauga was fierce.

"Folkses now don't know nuthin' 'bout no war," Nathan told a reporter for the Austin paper decades later, who relayed as faithfully as he could the old man's recollection of all the engagements he had witnessed, but Chickamauga in particular. "They jes' otter seen them bom shells a'drappin' everywhere. Name o' the Lawd, chile, yo' ain't know whether they gwine to drap on you o' no. Them balls jes' come a-whizzin' an' yo' can't dodge 'em nohow. Look all 'round yo' an' see men wid no legs—men wid no arms—men wid ha'f they head shot off. That wuz war. Folkses now don't know whut war is."[15]

The tide of battle turned in the late morning of September 20 when the Confederates charged through a gap in the center of the Federal line. Only Union Gen. George Thomas's stubborn defensive stand on Horseshoe Ridge and General Bragg's failure to vigorously pursue the Union soldiers and equipment clogging the road through narrow McFarland Gap on their way to Chattanooga averted the destruction of General Rosecrans's shattered army. The loss in dead and wounded from both sides—around 37,000 of some 125,000 engaged, almost one in three—was enormous, second only to the totals sustained in the Battle of Gettysburg three months earlier that ended the Confederates' second and last effort of consequence to carry the war into the North.[16]

Though the extensive patches of thick woods limited cavalry participation in the horrific engagement, the breaching of the Northern line that propelled the Union Army into panicked retreat gave Southern horsemen work mopping up. During the second day's fighting, a Union Twentieth Corps wagon train with a cavalry brigade escort failed to reach its rendezvous at the huge Federal hospital complex at Crawfish Spring on the Union right wing before late afternoon, when the senior sector commander abandoned the hospital. Pushing all the supply wagons and ambulances onto the road north to Chattanooga via the Chattanooga Creek valley, he left the wayward train to its fate. Confederate commanders meant to intercept it and gain its supplies for their men. The train would have to ford upper West Chickamauga Creek somewhere in McLemore's Cove. So, after dark that September 20, Acting Major Littlefield, third in command of the regiment, was detailed at Gen. Joseph Wheeler's cavalry corps headquarters to take six companies from Harrison's brigade and secure Owen's Ford.

This was the sort of duty Littlefield had performed innumerable times in a year and a half of war. But the twelve-mile ride to his post turned out to be unlike any other. His route took him down the Dry Valley Road passing within a couple of hundred yards of the location of the Confederate breakthrough. Fighting there had been intense. Nearby beside the road lay Bloody Pond, the only water of consequence behind the center of the Union line. Wounded who could made their way there to drink, many for the last time. On the ride, Littlefield's every sense was assailed, overwhelmed. Bodies lay everywhere. "We have literally walked on dead men all night," said Fifteenth Texas Dismounted Cavalry Lt. R. M. Collins of the night before. The sight of "ghastly corpses mangled and torn" was hard enough for Littlefield to endure. But shadows cast by moonlight on trees stripped bare—shadows that moved and constantly transformed as a rider made his way—excited the imagination in ways difficult to control. Coupled with the horrid sights, from every direction through the cold blackness rose what one soldier called a storm of shrieks, groans, wails, and cries for help from the wounded, many for a simple drink of water, some for sweet death to relieve their suffering. "Oh, if I could only drown this terrible sound," Alva Griest of the Seventy-Second Indiana, some of whose wounded and dead lay beside Littlefield's route, scribbled in his journal. They could not drown it then or ever. "For God's sake come and help me!"—that ever fainter plea from a fading soldier haunted the Seventy-Second's Sgt. Benjamin F. McGee for the rest of his life. "More horrible and trying to our hearts than was the storm of battle," commented McGee of it, speaking for all. Compounding the hell was the smoke of smoldering brushfires that the heavy cold air held close to the ground, intensifying the acrid smell of bodies barely a day old but already beginning to decompose. "A horrible odor, the battlefield's commentary on war," Terry Ranger Leonidas Banton Giles editorialized forty-eight years later as he remembered a ride of his own that night.[17]

As disciplined as he was, twenty-one-year-old George Washington Littlefield was unprepared for the emotional toll the journey would take on him.

> A dreary ride at the head of the column through that twelve miles of country where the guns of both North and South had mowed the ground like a giant reaper was the most distressing ordeal of my career as a soldier. The moon shone brightly sweet to enjoy, had it not been on one of the hardest fought fields of the war. The screams of the mangled artillery horses made the night hideous with their heart-rending appeals for relief. Everywhere

lay the wounded and dying and the slain of both armies. The prayers of
the conscious, and the death rattle from the throats of those in Blue and
Gray could be heard as they lay mingled on the bloody field awaiting the
ominous visit of the surgeon, or the arrival of the burial parties. The pitiful
moans of those brave fellows who had fought so gallantly through that
dreadful carnage made the tears flow from my eyes, and even to this day I
cannot talk about it without great emotion.[18]

George Littlefield confronted his mortality as he never had before. "The gloom
that clouds one's mind under such circumstances shadows the whole soul," he
described the intense, consuming effect of the ride. Yes, he had lost friends, close
friends, and grieved deeply over their deaths. But the war then was still young. Stirring patriotism and the adrenaline of combat and danger ruled him. He was still
single then and carefree as a young man responsible primarily for himself alone. In
September of 1863, by contrast, he was married. He had a seventeen-year-old wife
to return to, provide for, and take care of. And he had spent much of the previous
month thinking about his relationship with God. Captain Littlefield recognized,
or maybe he admitted as he had not before, that he could be one of those unfortunates pleading for relief to cavalry detachments riding by, ignoring their cries,
focused simply on continuing the fight. He recognized that if the worst happened,
he would have failed in his duty to the woman he longed so much to be with. The
tenor of his letters changed. "Should I die" and "let me exact one promise of you
that is that you meet me in heaven" characterized the tone of his remaining letters
to Alice. "I want to settle up all of Allices and my [affairs] and have every thing in
order that it would be but little trouble if I should happen to be killed," he put it in
business terms to his father-in-law.[19]

For the present, though, fighting remained. With the Union Army regrouping
in Chattanooga, Bragg sent General Wheeler with the pick of the mounted troops,
upwards of four thousand, on a raid around Rosecrans to wreck his supply lines.
The command destroyed railroad tracks, trestles, and bridges and captured wagon
trains, one numbering no fewer than five hundred wagons. By the time the horsemen completed their assignment, Federal troops had closed in and begun harassing
the rear of the column. For once the Texas Rangers, as Littlefield preferred to call
them, had the point rather than the rear. Believing the danger to be behind them,
they rode strung out in two files, unsuspecting of trouble. No sooner had they
entered a cedar break than concealed Federal soldiers unleashed a devastating
barrage. The two regimental commanders were hit. Receiving no support from the
trailing units, to the officers next in seniority fell the job of extracting the Texans.

William R. Jarmon of D Company as acting colonel and George Littlefield of I Company as acting lieutenant colonel led the Rangers out of the ambush, holding the loss to only seventeen other men.[20]

After about three weeks rest from campaigning and combat, the Texas Rangers moved out in the direction of deep East Tennessee. Take Knoxville from the twelve-thousand-man Union garrison, Bragg ordered generals Wheeler and James Longstreet. The move sent Longstreet's infantry corps on a months long campaign that would eventually conclude with the corps' return to Robert E. Lee's Army of Northern Virginia, from which it had been dispatched to support Bragg in confronting Rosecrans.[21]

On November 14 the command approached its objective. The Rangers under Jarmon and Littlefield moved briskly to the front when the men heard the crackle of small arms. Adrenaline pumping, in line of battle the horsemen charged a line of Yankee skirmishers. The line melted. "Onward they go," Chaplain Bunting described the action, "spreading across the field on the left, breaking through the lines of the enemy, and driving him in until our course is checked by a heavy body of infantry which is posted behind a fence." One group, Jarmon and Littlefield in the lead, hurled itself forward still to "within a few yards of their batteries, which were now opening upon us with shot and shell. Our advance had gone up almost to their reserve lines and within one mile of the city of Knoxville." There the charge stalled. "This being a strongly fortified position," Bunting conceded, "it defied our little band, and from necessity we fell back and formed in line of battle in the timber" to await reinforcements. Even with fresh troops, the Confederates simply held their position until nightfall, when they withdrew. So close had they come. Commanders Jarmon and Littlefield, Chaplain Bunting wrote to the home folks, "acted with great coolness and gallantry. They have the honor of leading one of the most brilliant and successful charges which the Rangers have ever made. The distance over which we charged—about three miles—and the speed combined to prevent others from participating with us in either the work or the honor."[22]

For the remainder of November and into early December, the Confederates probed for the weak point in the Federal defense of Knoxville. Engaged daily, the Rangers rejoiced when wounded rejoined their ranks. After Maj. S. Pat Christian returned from convalescence following the cedar breaks ambush a month and a half earlier, Jarmon dropped to acting lieutenant colonel, Littlefield to acting major within the chain of regimental command. Finally, early in December the assault on Knoxville was abandoned. Longstreet's assault on the stronghold of Fort Sanders had failed, and Bragg's defeat at Missionary Ridge freed Union cavalry to ride to Knoxville's relief. In stinging cold, made all the more bitter by dreadfully short rations, by rain-soaked clothes freezing on the backs of some, and by the rear guard being forbidden to kindle fires for heat so as not to alert the enemy to the Rangers' position, the Confederates passed around Knoxville and trudged toward Morristown, some forty miles farther on, to establish winter quarters.[23]

Once concentrated around Morristown, the Confederates found themselves in a struggle less to win national independence and more simply to stay alive. Chaplain Bunting was candid:

> Very soon our front is menaced along Mossy Creek, 12 miles below Morristown. In that direction lies the subsistence which must support both armies. Upon our right is Holston River, but that region is exhausted. Upon our left is Chucky and French Broad, a region rich in provision and stock. From this section the Yankees have been very active in drawing supplies for Knoxville, and they wish to hold it still. Without access to it, Longstreet cannot subsist his army for any length of time. It becomes, therefore, a struggle for life.[24]

As the gravity of the army's circumstance deepened, so too did George Littlefield's despondency, grown from that night ride over the Chickamauga field. Two days before Christmas, he let it out in the most anguished letter he ever wrote.

> Wife there is no possible chance for me to hear from you hereafter and wife I know not that I will ever have another opportunity of writing to you. . . . We are far apart now and know not whether we will ever meet again. This is the 23d now, and soon my friend will leave, but how can I stop writing to you dear Wife, when I know this is my last opportunity. I have said all to you. . . . Wife grieve not over these words for Wife I am in my countrys service and likely to be killed in any little skirmish.[25]

Perhaps Christmas's approach brought George Littlefield's depression to a head. Perhaps he simply reflected the sentiment of his comrades. On Christmas Day, wrote Bunting, they simply had no stomach for a fight. Just perhaps he was having a premonition.[26]

Ready or not, on Saturday morning, December 26, the war resumed. Four times that day the Eighth Texas Cavalry Regiment was ordered to ride forward in cold, sleet, and snow to draw the fire of the Eighteenth Indiana Light Artillery. Four times these four hundred or so Confederates arrayed themselves in line of battle. Four times they sat in formation, unable to defend themselves because the enemy guns fired from positions well beyond the range of the Texans' small arms, and Mossy Creek's deep defile prevented the Confederates from charging the battery and the two brigades of cavalry protecting it. Four times the Eighth Texas dutifully took position.[27]

Shells lobbed at the horsemen exploded here and there, sending shrapnel flying in all directions. If generals took consolation that only four Rangers were hit, they never explained the reason for the sacrifice. Three of the four were wounded so gravely as to end their military service to the Confederacy. Shrapnel mangled the legs of two men. One required amputation. As horrific as they were, these wounds were not seen as mortal. Acting Major Littlefield's injury was different. A piece of a ball exploding to his front tore away his left side from groin to buttock, leaving a gash nine by eleven inches from side to side and so deep that it exposed his hip joint.[28]

As his comrades picked up the stricken officer to take him to safety out of range of the enemy guns, Brig. Gen. Thomas Harrison, former commander of the regiment, rode up and awarded the captain a battlefield promotion "to the rank of Major for gallantry on the field of battle."[29] General Harrison no doubt intended his act, coming clearly at the end of Littlefield's military career and likely his life, as recognition for meritorious service. The advancement never appeared on Littlefield's service record. No matter. The commendation, appreciation, and respect conveyed in the promotion, not the formality of paperwork, would come to mean everything to Littlefield. It would transform the day he nearly died in service to the ideal South that inspired him into the proudest day of his life. None would mistake it. For the last thirty-five or so of his seventy-eight years, George Washington Littlefield would be addressed as Major Littlefield, or just Major.

For nearly seven hours after he was hit in midafternoon, the stricken officer awaited medical attention. Then decisions that determined the quality of the rest of his life happened fast. When about ten o'clock that night the division surgeon finally saw him prostrate on the floor of a house four miles behind the line, the doctor declared the trauma to be fatal, ordered a little morphine to dull the pain of the officer's last hours, and began preparations to amputate the mangled leg of the other Ranger. Soon afterward, Littlefield's former orderly sergeant, William H. Kyle, arrived with a bottle of apple brandy to comfort his commander and friend.

When shortly General Harrison came in covered in sleet and snow, Littlefield invited him to take the chill off with some of the brandy. The general drank a salute to Littlefield's speedy recovery. Littlefield answered with a toast to the division surgeon who had left him to die. Shocked, Harrison corralled the doctor and ordered him to dress the wound. On close inspection, Dr. Holmes concluded that Littlefield's best chance of survival lay in amputating the leg that seemed to be barely attached to his body. Holmes might have begun sawing straightaway but for Edward T. Rhodes, I Company's original fourth sergeant, whom General Harrison detailed to stay with his commander. Rhodes forbade it. So grateful was Littlefield for surviving the night with two legs to use for the rest of his life that in 1866 he named his firstborn Edward Rhodes Littlefield in his protector's honor.[30]

That Littlefield lived was a miracle. First, he survived the seven hours before the doctor assessed his condition. Though no major arteries run through the buttocks, shock could have killed him, as Major Holmes anticipated it would. Perhaps the intense cold staunched the blood flow. On the other hand, if the wound resulted from detonation of percussion caps in the cartridge box on his belt, as Littlefield maintained, then the intense heat of the explosions may have cauterized the bleeders. But the multiple bullets would have mangled the flesh and introduced fragments of clothing into the wound, both greatly increasing the likelihood of infection. Second, he survived without amputation. Sawing off limbs was the preferred treatment for injuries of the magnitude of Littlefield's. One contemporary doctor remarked that more men died from refusing amputation than from enduring it. But two-thirds of those whose legs were amputated at the hip, as surely would have been Littlefield's case, died of the operation.[31]

Close behind the battle line, the wounded got little rest. Before daylight in the face of an enemy advance, they were moved twelve frigid, jolting miles away. The next day fifteen bitter, rough miles more took them to a home where at last they could convalesce, Littlefield tended by Rhodes, Nathan, and the ladies of the place. For what he recalled as three weeks before he entered a military hospital, Littlefield lapsed in and out of consciousness subsisting on little more than morphine and brandy. Rangers who went to see him expected each visit to be the last. So did Dr. J. W. Gulick, the Terry Ranger private raised to brigade surgeon. "What is truly remarkable, he still lives," Gulick exclaimed at the end of the second week, "and I now have strong hopes for his recovery."[32] At the same juncture, Littlefield had Rhodes write Alice in a tone totally different from that last, despairing letter her husband had penned. "As to his condition tis enough to say that he is doing far better than the nature and appearance of the wound at first permitted us to hope for. . . . He says tell his Mother to rest easy, that his wound is not dangerous that he is at a good place and in fine spirits."[33]

Seven weeks after Dr. Holmes had written the captain off for dead, Littlefield had healed to the point that for short times he could sit up in bed. The wound had shrunk by two inches all around. Well out of danger, Littlefield decided that it was time to have his wife and mother receive a firsthand account of his wounding and recovery. One man alone knew the details and could be spared to make the hazardous 1,100-mile trip. Littlefield told Nathan to take a horse and go. Nathan refused. He had promised Mother Littlefield to take care of her son. He would not leave, especially then, when his bedridden charge needed him most. As he remembered events, after Littlefield was wounded, he arranged for the care of their horses, took charge of their possessions, and followed until he caught up with his master. "I found him in a horsepital an' when he wuz able to be moved, I tuk him to Alabamy to Marse Frank McGinnis's [McGuire's] an' thar we stayed 'til he wuz able to come on home. I ain't never lef' him all that time."[34] Nathan's refusal to leave George Littlefield, even for a purpose as important as informing his wife and mother, cemented the relationship between the men into a bond unbreakable for the rest of their lives and into eternity.[35]

After convalescing in central Alabama with his great aunt and uncle, Littlefield went to Atlanta, hoping to find the paperwork from Richmond approving his resignation from the army.[36] While there, on his twenty-second birthday, June 21, 1864, George Littlefield noted that after six months, his wound had healed completely, and he was walking with a crutch and a cane. Still waiting on June 30, he visited a photographer and had his picture taken on "first crutch," still clearly favoring his left side (fig. 5). Not long afterward, the approval arrived, and on borrowed money he and Nathan set out on their three-month horseback journey to Gonzales.[37]

George Littlefield's homecoming was bittersweet. He was conflicted. On the one hand, he had the consuming pleasure of being reunited with his wife after having been away for twenty-one-and-a-half of their twenty-two-month marriage. Never again would he leave her for more than a couple of months at a time during the season for working and trading cattle. On the other hand, so committed was he to the war for Southern independence and so bonded was he with his Terry Ranger comrades that he regretted with equal emotion being unable to return to the fight. But in fact he would return. By then no longer a battle for national independence, the struggle would be, in the vernacular of the sesquicentennial of the Civil War, a battle for hearts and minds. The struggle would be to keep alive for generations to come the Southern consciousness and principles, as he and his fellow veterans remembered and interpreted them, that had called him to arms. And when he returned to the contest, George W. Littlefield—the Major—would have command of the strategy as well as the tactics. But that was for another day.

The struggle before him in the early fall of 1864 was rebuilding the family fortunes that naturally had declined during the war. Taking no more than a very few days to recuperate from the long trip, he began. On October 4, 1864, George Littlefield took charge of a plantation he owned with his brother and "went to work to make the best, as he thought, of a miserable life, having to carry his crutches everywhere."[38]

TO BEGIN BUSINESS

Work and life on the Old Littlefield Place in October 1864 had changed little in the nearly two years since George Washington Littlefield last saw the plantation, or in the three and a half years he had been fighting the Yankees, or since he and his younger brother William had gained a controlling interest in the property in 1859, or, for that matter, since his father had assembled the property in 1851–52. No wonder. Mother Mildred had resumed her competent management of it and the other two Littlefield and White plantations in Gonzales County, awaiting her eldest Littlefield son's return. The work she and the family could see before George that October was simply picking up where he had left off when he rode away to war. And for George, "having grown from an eight-year-old boy on a farm in Gonzales Co," agriculture was the work he knew.[1] What else could he expect to do other than return to farming? But life rarely mirrors expectations for it. The routine into which he was settling could not be the routine of old. Unlike before the war, in 1864 he could get around only with the aid of crutches and canes. He expected this restriction to warp the rest of his life, limiting what he could accomplish. Seven years it took him to realize that only the restrictions he put upon himself limited what he would accomplish.

In Gonzales County, far from the scene of fighting, the Littlefield and White plantations suffered no greater outrage during the war than the theft of a horse and no greater disruption than the loan of slaves for building Fort Waul to protect the county seat from an invasion that never got closer than Galveston Island. Even so, Mildred had her hands full. Some eighty people depended on the production of the plantations—worked by no fewer than ten whites and seventy-two slaves (fifty-seven belonging to Mildred, to three of her children, and to at least one grandchild, and fifteen the property of overseer Bailey). Further demanding her skillful direction, wartime shortages required that, in producing food, clothing, and the other necessities of the three communities, the properties operate as self-sufficiently as they could. She put her hand to the wheel. Literally. She began carding cotton and wool, set up spinning wheels and looms in her house, went into the nearby woods to collect minerals with which to dye the cloth she wove, and produced, as John Dowell remembered, "pretty, rich, soft, firm, strong, comfortable cloth of all kinds and in as many colors as Joseph's coat."[2]

However much running the plantations demanded of Mildred, fifty years old in 1861, it did not satisfy her want to contribute to the war effort. As invested in the Confederate cause as her captain son, Mildred Littlefield needed to make a personal contribution. And so fully did she give of herself and her property that thirty years later her war charities were remembered as "princely." She shared food with needy families of soldiers at the front. Grandson John Dowell fairly carved up the barn doorjambs and windowsills with notches to account for the corn she had him hand out by the bushel. And she sewed. To sewing bees at the nearby Rack schoolhouse she rode, taking teenage son William astride the horse behind her. There with women of the neighborhood she made clothing to send to the fighting men, the Gonzales boys especially, to replace garments tattered and threadbare from constant wear. Trousers were her specialty. "Freely and in great devotion to the cause," she cheerfully secreted coins, some as large as $20 gold pieces, in the pockets. Devoted to his grandmother and eager to hear stories of the benefit of her benevolence, young Dowell asked all the returning soldiers he could meet whether they had received the heartfelt gifts. Not one did. Sadly, John had to "opine the Confederate side of the war was fought from first to last without the aid of any of my poor grandmother's coins, but," he concluded, "there is one consolation. She never knew it unless she has found it out in heaven, which I hope she has not, for the thought of the duty was a great pride and joy to her."[3]

Although life on the Old Littlefield Place had not changed beyond the addition to its routine of Mildred's contribution to the war effort, George's responsibilities for property had. He had married, and his young wife brought property to the marriage. For the most part, during his absence Alice's father managed her slave property, and her mother-in-law handled their common property in Gonzales. Whether or not she had discussed it with George before he left, Alice signaled that she wanted to participate in decisions regarding what was hers. And she had business sense. When the disposition of one of her six slaves arose, she sought her husband's counsel by proposing the way she thought the transaction should be handled. "*I am so mutch pleased with your ideas* in regard to managing property," George praised her, underlining the words to punctuate the magnitude of his pleasure. Appreciating his mother's business acumen, George in his twenties did not stand on the legal and social conventions that directed wives to leave business decisions to their husbands. He did not ask her to worry her pretty little head only with affairs of the home. He did not want a woman aloof and uninformed regarding business. On the contrary, the businessman in him took delight in his wife's interest not just in matters of business but also in the partnership with her husband. "You are so *thoughtful and kind as to ask my opinions,*" he wrote, again emphasizing his words. "How many do we know that have acted differently in managing there affects?" In fact, George would take the difference even further. He determined to keep Alice's property separate for whatever need she might have for it. "It has always been my promise in my own heart to preserve your property and make what I have support us," he wrote from the front, "and yours should be kept and preserved for you should I die that all honest men might say *he was honest.*"[4]

Good intentions aside, property in slaves would be lost if Southern armies could not sustain the fight. And prospects were darkening. The army that Littlefield had seen in camp three or four months before, in June, exuding the unflagging confidence that it would whip the oncoming Yankee horde, had been losing ground slowly but steadily. The news reached Texas about the time Littlefield took charge of the Old Littlefield Place that the army had lost the gateway to the Lower South. Atlanta had fallen. Maybe that was when George accepted finally that the Southern country for which he sacrificed was not to be—and when the businessman took control from the patriot. To protect family assets, the businessman in him determined to sell three slave men. Vigorously his mother protested. "Mother, by George, get some of it into money," he replied and made the sale. "His mother just cried all over the country about him selling those Negroes," said one who saw it all.[5]

Bad news from the front followed bad news. In mid-December Bragg's old army, then under Gen. John Bell Hood, was nearly destroyed in Tennessee. On December 22, Sherman took Charleston, South Carolina, delivering to the North a Christmas present of the city where the war had begun. Finally, in April 1865, the end began cascading toward Texas. Gen. Robert E. Lee surrendered Confederate forces in Virginia on April 9. Gen. Joseph E. Johnston gave up his army, Terry's Texas Rangers with it, in North Carolina on April 18. Gen. Richard Taylor silenced the arms of the forces remaining east of the Mississippi River on May 4. And, finally, Gen. Edmund Kirby-Smith relinquished the Trans-Mississippi Department, which included Texas, on May 26.[6]

However long it took word of the final capitulation to reach Gonzales County, the consequence followed directly on June 19, 1865, with publication of General Order No. 3, abolishing slavery in Texas. Proclaiming Emancipation Day on the Littlefield and White plantations Mildred held to be her duty to all the slaves for whom she was responsible as the matriarch of her family. After the three overseers assembled them all before the long gallery of her house, Mildred Terrell Satterwhite

White Littlefield read the order and told them they were free. "She did not pout, she did not fool about it," John Dowell described his grandmother's demeanor as he watched her from his seat on the porch. "She did not cry. She did not say all was lost. She did not cower. She was not small about it. She did not leave the poor negroes to find out they were free from others. . . . Standing there erect in her greatness of soul, she bid slavery, so far as she was concerned on this earth, a final and complete farewell."[7]

For them all, life as they had known it vanished in that instant. Whatever lay ahead, Mildred had the anchor of property to carry her and her family forward. The freedmen had only the clothes on their backs. "Some of them didn't know which way to go. They never was free before," Harrison McClure recalled the reaction of his fellow former slaves. While George repeated to them that "you are as free as me. You can go anywhere you please and do as you please," he needed at least most of them to stay. The cotton crop still had to be weeded and picked. If what McClure said of the freedmen on the Charles White place was common to the other two plantation properties, as Littlefield's nephew Edgar Harral said it was, "when emancipation came, he [Littlefield] kept them in place as long as they wanted to stay there." He did it, Littlefield said, by giving them a percentage of the crop they would pick. In fact, he did more. For half of what they raised, he provided them teams, allowed them as much land to cultivate for themselves as they could manage, "and then he fed them if they didn't have sufficient stuff to run on. He give them the money to go buy it. He was good to them," McClure told an interviewer long after George Littlefield was dead and gone. No less important, Littlefield protected them. The Littlefield property, testified black preacher Mack Henson, "was one among the best protected from midnight riders and negro terrorizers. No one, however desperate, dared to enter this farm for an evil purpose."[8]

The weather was good to them all in 1865 and produced a bountiful cotton crop. Pleased and hopeful to increase his income, George Littlefield in 1866 expanded the acreage he planted to the fiber. The extent to which this would pay off, though, he could expect to know only in the next picking season. While farming trudged along, as it always did, at the pace of the seasons, Littlefield was impatient to restore the family affluence and reestablish its comfortable way of life.

Maybe the entrepreneurial inspiration to open a store simply came to him. Maybe his father-in-law suggested it. Whitfield Harral Jr. had made his living as a merchant since before he had moved to Texas a decade earlier. And a good living it was. Correspondents reporting on Harral's credit worthiness for the R. G. Dun and Company, America's first credit rating firm, described him in 1859 and 1860 as "a man of Considerable wealth [some twenty thousand dollars]. Owns a fine farm . . .

and works around 20 Negroes." Whatever the source of the spark, while waiting for the 1866 cotton crop to mature, George Littlefield launched a little mercantile business. Prospects appeared good. Farmers had to buy necessities no matter the quality of the crop they brought in. Moreover, the site Littlefield chose did not rely on farmers exclusively. By opening his business on the Littlefield Place beside the Gonzales–San Antonio road, he could serve neighbors and travelers alike. To clerk the enterprise, he engaged Ham Smith and nephew John Dowell. Whether as expedient or policy, in hiring his relative, Littlefield as general manager overseeing multiple ventures instituted the administrative pattern on which he would raise his business empire.[9]

The pattern consisted of two components. One was drawing on his family for managers. For the rest of his life, before considering anyone else to run an operation—whether a store, a ranch, a bank, a hotel, a sugar plantation, a real estate venture, whatever—he looked for a nephew or the husband of a niece to take charge. Of course, business *was* business. As Littlefield wrote nephew rancher Will White once: "While I have all the respect and love for you Will—yet—when I come to deel with you in business, I will talk and do as with an outsider. . . . I simply settle as with any one else." Treating family as anyone else in settlements was only the half of it. "He never fooled with men unless they were making him money," Will contributed. But to encourage conscientious industry and devotion in his managers, Littlefield routinely made them partners with him in the enterprise. "If they had an interest, better profits would be realized," he felt.[10] Only two ever failed him so badly that he turned them out. Consequently, the arrangement had the further benefit of ensuring the family's prosperity.

With the women, it was different. "He didn't think they ought to work. . . . He never wanted the boys to stop, and he never wanted the girls to start," White told an interviewer.[11] Women might rise through circumstances to management positions, as had his mother, to whom he gave credit for mentoring him in business, and wives could advise their husbands. But the honor of the Southern man prescribed that men alone be hired to work. If he was nothing else, George Washington Littlefield was a Southern man to his core.

The other component was George Littlefield's keen mind for business. He thrived on making transactions and overseeing enterprises. Doing business was his recreation, he said rightly. He "was quick in his actions, and he could grasp a proposition as quick as anybody I ever saw—a trade of any kind," Will White marveled at his uncle's facility. "He didn't have to set and study over it. He could take in the situation right now." No detail was too insignificant for Littlefield's attention, either. "He wanted you to keep tab on everything," nephew Charlie

Walker recalled. Land sales manager and nephew by marriage Arthur Pope Duggan echoed Walker when he told a friend, long after the typewriter had come into common use, that Littlefield "is a great . . . [one] to keep everything under his immediate direction, so much that way that he actually writes all of his own letters [by hand], and it is very seldom that he ever requires the services of a stenographer." Keeping records accurately was only the half of it. "He expected you to do everything just right up and not make a mistake," Will White contributed, adding, "which is all wrong. If people didn't make mistakes they wouldn't put rubbers on pencils." As important as his mastery of numbers was Littlefield's uncanny skill at sizing up and, as a result, gaining an edge over those with whom he did business. From fifty years observing Littlefield, Harrison McClure put it the most colorfully when he said that Littlefield "could look in your eye and tell you what you was up to." Will White said that many were simply afraid of him. "I just didn't want to have a fight with him. He said that he and I were the only ones that never had a fight. The rest were so afraid of him, they wouldn't talk back to him."[12] This was the businessman forming when John Dowell went to work for the family mercantile business.

The years 1866 and 1867 came up good for making money in Gonzales County. It rained. Farmers prospered. So did Littlefield's store and plantations. Flush, believing as he had come to do in the value of a good education, and taking his lead as the patriarch of his mother's White and Littlefield family, in 1867 George took sixteen-year-old John Dowell out of the store and sent him to school. Destitute from losing her wealth in her slaves, her health failing, John's mother, Sallie Dowell, could only appreciate that her half brother budgeted five hundred dollars a year to send her son not just to any school but in fact to earn a top-notch education at Washington College in Virginia. Washington was changing from being an academy of classical studies, as was Baylor University, the curriculum of which Littlefield had so disparaged. Two years into his presidency of the Virginia school, Confederate hero and former superintendent of the United States Military Academy Robert E. Lee was shaping the college into a practical and modern university by adding the study of law, business, and journalism to the traditional liberal arts curriculum. Maybe respect for Lee's work as much as for Lee himself attracted Littlefield to the school. The unquestioned Southern influence surely contributed. John's sister, Alice, appreciated it when she wrote that she "didant fancy" the new, northern schoolmistress in her Gonzales school, because the woman "had two much Yankee about her to sute me."[13]

Maybe, though, George invested himself so heavily in his young nephew's schooling as a salve to the sorrow he felt with Alice over the loss of their first child early in 1867. Little Edward Rhodes Littlefield, named for the Terry Ranger who had saved George's leg, had died before reaching his first birthday.[14]

In all of its joy and sadness, 1867 stood out for one occurrence that, only three years earlier, not even George Littlefield thought he would live to see. In July he regained full use of his left leg. His gloomy resignation to a life limited by dependence on crutches had proved unfounded. Not only had he survived the near fatal wound, but he had also confounded all predictions that the injury would leave him permanently disabled. In fact, George's body healed so completely that only those who knew it could see that as he walked he would drop down ever so slightly on his left leg.[15]

Then, a year after Littlefield achieved his new freedom and ability to step into a vigorous future, the forces of nature turned against him. The 1868 cotton crop was devastated by worms; the corn withered in drought. Maybe it was not as bad as the record drought of 1857, when, compounding the misery of crops burned crisp by the sun, a plague of grasshoppers ate some fields "clean of every blade of corn." But the drought of 1868 was bad enough. Half brother T.J. White went broke. George spent $738.50 to save him. "Him and Lizie are both down on me about buying his interest in Charleys Estate. . . . How blind such people to their interest," George wrote in disgust to Tom's brother in Mississippi. "Without *my money* all there property would have gone." Near year's end, $626.25 rescued George's brother-in-law and sister from financial ruin. Too much rain in 1869 compounded the misery. In July his cotton planting on both his farm and his mother's washed away in the flood of the century. With no farm income for the year, Littlefield could not continue to hemorrhage money and called John Dowell home from school, where he was spending double the five hundred dollars budgeted.[16]

To avoid his own financial collapse, George Littlefield looked to the one asset he had on high ground—the store. Keeping it open required his skill as a negotiator. The Confederacy's demise had taken with it the currency that had been circulating for the previous four years. Even a year after war's end, when George opened the store, U.S. greenbacks still were hard to come by in Texas, specie even harder. Barter substituted. Customers offered cattle. At a ratio of six cows to every resident, Texas was overflowing in cattle. And as folklorist J. Frank Dobie said with little exaggeration, all that a man needed to get into the cattle business "was a rope, nerve to use it, and a branding iron." Littlefield accepted payment in cattle as the price of doing business.[17]

Old-timers could have told him that using cattle as currency resurrected a practice of the 1830s in Gonzales, when young heifers and bulls changed hands for five dollars, cows for ten. Though Littlefield took the animals as an expedient, handling them was familiar work. Stock raising was commonplace in Gonzales County before Fleming settled his family on the Guadalupe River. Most of Gonzales County's share of the more than three-quarters of a million cattle in Texas in 1850 ran freely over the rolling hills back from the settled river bottoms. Tending cattle was part of the routine on the Old Littlefield Place. Before father Fleming died a short year and a half after buying the property, he had registered his FL brand and doubtless burned it into the flanks of the three hundred animals in his bunch. Fleming's widow continued the herd. Not two months after Fleming's death, she registered her own brand—FL Over 5. Two years later she added the simpler L5, and three years after that recorded just the number 4. But it was Fleming who, whether or not any of them anticipated it, gave George his start in the cattle business that in time would become his principal life work. Father bequeathed his son fifteen head. In August 1854, when George Littlefield was twelve years old, he became the owner of a herd of cattle.[18]

With slaves to manage the $112.50 worth of beef, and if the date of recording his first brand is a good measure, young George showed little interest in the animals when he received them and for nearly a decade afterward. Four years passed before, at age sixteen, in November 1858, he registered a brand—the Diamond 7. But he didn't stay home to use it. No sooner was the registration completed than he departed for Mississippi on the year-long mission to close out Charles White's interests. Five years passed before cattle came up again. But this time, in the fall of 1863 in a letter to Alice, without elaboration, apropos of nothing else in the letter, and in what survives as his earliest mention of the subject, he wrote firmly that he "should like to have an interest in a stock ranch somewhere in Austin, Texas."[19]

What Littlefield knew of Texas's capital city, located on the Colorado River boundary between blackland prairie to the east and limestone hills to the west, which made it more attractive for stock raising than familiar Gonzales County, must have come from his adventurous, eighty-five-year-old grandfather Philip Bryant Littlefield. If Philip was the inspiration, he could have learned about the Austin country from men driving cattle trails that since the 1840s had converged on river crossings between Austin and Webberville a few miles downstream. However, two short months (considering the time it took mail from Texas to find George at the front in Tennessee) after Philip registered his PL brand in Travis County, George stated his desire.

Perhaps what occasioned this attraction to stock raising over farming was the perception, however vague, of a business opportunity. Failure on the home farms could not have motivated it. Littlefield knew that they continued to be sufficiently productive. Not so farms in the war zone. "One has no idea how it ruins a country to have an army on it[,] that is you that are in Texas," he commented on the devastation he saw as he campaigned in Tennessee, Kentucky, Alabama, and Georgia. During his visit home in the winter of 1862–63, he would have been blind not to see that cattle had multiplied considerably while the stockmen were away at the fight. Settled Texas was fairly overrun with cattle. The three-quarters of a million head enumerated in 1850 had increased five times to somewhere between 4 and 4.7 million in 1860. Free ranging and untended, cattle abounded for the taking. Maybe Littlefield sensed the opportunity that when the war ended, the South would need to restock its herds of cattle and horses too. Money was to be made in supplying the animals.[20]

When George Littlefield returned home from the war in the fall of 1864, though, driving animals eastward was the last thing on his mind. True, cattle continued important enough in the Littlefield operation that mother Mildred responded to the invitation in the *Gonzales Inquirer* newspaper in December 1864 to pay $2.00 to have her Backwards 7 Over Diamond brand included in the *Texas Stock Directory* to facilitate return of stray or stolen animals. But the war dragged on. And even had the veteran wanted to make a drive, he was in no condition to do it. Dependent on crutches to get around and unable to do any physical work as he continued recovering from his wound, George Littlefield could not ride day in and day out rounding up and working cattle.[21]

While Littlefield was accumulating cattle through the store, other men searched for markets for theirs. Some tried shipping by steamboat down the Red and up the Mississippi Rivers to markets in Kentucky and Illinois. Others drove herds overland to eastern Kansas and to the far west.[22] Few of them realized a satisfactory return before 1867, when in mid-season Abilene, Kansas, opened as the first destination offering stock pens, buyers, and rail transportation to Chicago, where the Union Stock Yards, the world's largest complex for trading cattle, hogs, and horses, had become the principal destination of Texas beeves. As word of the Abilene destination spread, the number of cattle arriving there doubled in 1868 and quadrupled in 1869. Still demand outstripped supply. Profits were spectacular. Cattle priced in Texas in 1869 from $2 to $12 a head sold in Abilene for $30 to $45—three times more in the worst case.[23]

Littlefield noticed. "Men here are making fortunes in the [cattle] business," he exclaimed in September 1869. "Some have cleared twenty thousand this year in driving to Kansas." He wanted in on it. But he felt he needed a partner at the market, and he fancied creating that market in the recovering South. "John," he continued to his half brother in Mississippi, "I think you and I are losing money every day by not dealing in stock. I can deliver good Texas beef at [the] mouth of

[the] red river for seventeen $17.00 dollars currency and they can be shipped to some point near you on [the] Miss river for [a] small some. And then you secure pasturage for them and sell in Memphis or any where you can get market. I know and feel that we can make more in one year than in ten at farming."[24]

The arrangement did not materialize. Maybe White, on whom fell the work of finding a market, shrank from dealing with local stock owners who were afraid of Texas Fever, a fatal malady later discovered to be caused by a tick bite to which Texas cattle had become immune. Fear of Texas Fever flared so hot in Illinois the previous year that the legislature had tried to ban Texas cattle from even passing through the state. Perhaps it was a more sober calculation that the return from the venture was likely to be slim on account of the high shipping cost and the deteriorated condition of cattle delivered after being forced to stand in tight quarters on steamboats for several days straight. Whatever the reason, Littlefield was left with no choice but to continue tilling the soil for his livelihood. Planning for his 1870 crop in the day when cotton was valued by variety and location in which grown, Littlefield closed his letter by asking his half brother to ship him 100 to 150 bushels of seed of "the best cotton raised around Memphis."[25]

While Littlefield's proposal for entering the cattle trade was foundering for lack of both a partner and a market, he dispatched a herd of horses and mules to central Alabama. On a trip to settle the estate of Uncle Charles Satterwhite in Wilcox County, he had observed handsome sums being paid for horses and mules. Hurrying home, he dispatched his nineteen-year-old brother William with a bunch. Mirroring the arrangement he tried to fashion with John White, George provided the stock and identified a market. The partner would sell the animals. William could manage a drive. He had brought a herd to Gonzales the year before. Driving was one thing; managing a capital asset was another. George so fervently wanted to get to the Alabama market that he subordinated his misgivings about entrusting the trade to his brother. It was a mistake. William loved life carefree, not business. Hardly had William crossed the Texas line into Louisiana than he "blowed them all in," as one hand worded it, then squandered the proceeds gambling.[26] Clearly having a good partner was as important as having a good market. At a loss for the right combination of the two and believing that things could be worse, George passed up the 1870 driving season.

Maybe the right amount of rain would come at the right time. It didn't. When the heavens opened, a deluge sent the rivers out of their banks for the second year in a row. Littlefield's 1870 planting, and with it his hope for a lucrative year, disappeared in the torrent.[27] He found he had been prophetic. Things had become worse.

To continue working the family farms and stocking the store, Littlefield had to borrow. It wasn't the first time. Borrowing, then borrowing more was propelling him deeper and deeper into debt and toward economic ruin.[28] In the winter of 1870–71 Littlefield faced a question he had not expected when he took over the family farms. Should he keep on keeping on with farming as his mainstay? What he could say of farming was that it was failing him. In six years, half had been good, half bad. But the bad had been worse than the good had been good. After six years, through no fault of his own, farming had driven him into a precarious financial condition.

If not farming, then what? As good as trade had been in the store's first three years, the business mirrored the fortunes of its clientele. The floods that devastated Littlefield ravaged his customers too. Littlefield had to close the once-promising enterprise. What remained were the cattle he had accumulated. What he could say for cattle was what he had proclaimed for two years, that "Texas is and will forever be a stock country. Without our stock we could not live here."[29] Whether others judged the singularity of cattle to life in Texas as he did, men who had the means surely were investing in beef cattle. Through the winter, stockmen, exhilarated by their experience in the 1870 market, crisscrossed Littlefield's part of the state buying cattle and horses to launch toward Kansas around April 1, 1871, when grass along the route would be ready to nourish tens of thousands of beeves grazing steadily northward.[30] To Littlefield's normally entrepreneurial mind, this flurry of activity should have reminded him that, whether on account of hope for the lost cotton crop in 1870 or of failure to arrange his business organization, he had missed a golden opportunity to make money in the bonanza cattle commerce of 1870. It should not only have reminded him; that flurry should have pressed him to decide something.

Weighing it all, George Washington Littlefield reached a surprising verdict. Disregarding his own unequivocal proclamation, he fixed on keeping on keeping on. He concluded, as he had six years earlier, that his future lay in the slower but familiar farming. Yet the entrepreneur in him saw that to stay in farming, he had to venture out of it to raise cash and capital. He had to make money in some other enterprise.

Selling stock where the animals were in demand promised the most expeditious and lucrative return. What had hobbled him in getting into the stock trade was his want of a partner to market the product while he managed affairs at the production end of the business, where the herds were gathered. Twice he had failed to find a partner within his family and then, unwilling to go it alone, held himself out of the 1870 trade, passing up likely handsome profits. Seeing no third family member

near ready to fulfill the partner role, he would have to abandon the business structure to which he had been limiting himself and become his own sales agent. By the
time he accepted this fact in 1871, his dangerously overextended finances forced
him to take on the additional role of trail boss to pilot his herd to market.

Littlefield was completing his preparations for the all-important drive that
March Monday when John Watson returned, demanding that cowhand Harrison
McClure leave Littlefield and return to working for him. After the smoke from the
gunfight cleared, oppressed more by the weight of his obligations to his creditors
than by killing Watson who had picked the fight, Littlefield gave bond to appear in
court and the next morning headed his cattle onto the trail.[31]

Littlefield left no account of the gunfight or of his experience preparing for
the drive or of the drive itself. Perhaps he didn't because, though it was his first
drive (and the only one on which he personally rode), most of the work was second
nature to him. Littlefield knew from the experience of leading his cavalry company
how to manage men and plan movements. He knew from experience, too, the ways
and the art of working cattle.[32]

In no document that has survived did he record the highlights of his negoti-
ation to sell the herd. That is regrettable because the experience changed his life.
From his 1,100 head, only a quarter of which he owned outright, Littlefield realized
enough to satisfy all of his creditors and still enjoy $3,600 in pure profit. The
accomplishment surprised even him. More important than the money, though,
was what he learned of himself. He discovered that he was his own best salesman,
that he truly delighted in the deal making, and that limits he had placed on himself
had held him back and cost him money. These realizations, or maybe admissions
of what he knew deep inside, caused him to refocus his business interest. Littlefield
left home a farmer. Ninety days later he returned a cattleman—a businessman
trading in the commodity of cattle. With that $3,600 and his new knowledge of
himself, at twenty-nine years of age, George Washington Littlefield set out, in his
words, "to begin business."

FIG. 1. George Washington Littlefield. Portrait by Solomon Salomon, 1910. Littlefield approved of this likeness so heartily that he commissioned at least two copies for family members. Reminiscent of the piercing fixation he commanded upon those with whom he spoke, his left eye in the painting follows the viewer. *University of Texas. Photograph by Sergio Santos of Holland Photo Imaging.*

FIG. 2. Fleming Littlefield (1814–53) This late nineteenth-century copy photograph is inscribed "To Georgie from Grandpa." Georgia Cole's grandfathers were Fleming Littlefield and Whitfield Harral. Only Harral was alive when the inscription was written. But the image does not resemble the figure in the only known image, a painting, of Harral. From her long study of the lives and natures of the two men, family historian Alice Duggan Gracy concluded that the man pictured is Fleming Littlefield. *Author's collection.*

FIG. 3. Mildred Terrell Satterwhite White Littlefield (1811–80). The painting, thought to have been created during Mildred's life in the 1870s, is the only known likeness of her. J. Evetts Haley's *George W. Littlefield, Texan* presents a sketch of a young Mildred, but no image has been found in the Haley archives or elsewhere to provide a basis for this sketch. *Author's collection.*

FIG. 4. Capt. George Washington Littlefield, CSA, January 1863. "My Idolized young husband," Alice Littlefield wrote on the reverse of this photograph. *Courtesy Dr. William A. Wroe.*

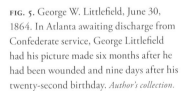

FIG. 5. George W. Littlefield, June 30, 1864. In Atlanta awaiting discharge from Confederate service, George Littlefield had his picture made six months after he had been wounded and nine days after his twenty-second birthday. *Author's collection.*

FIG. 6. Littlefield Cattle Ranches letterhead, 1883.

George W. Littlefield Papers, Dolph Briscoe Center for American History, University of Texas at Austin.

FIG. 7. LIT brand on George Littlefield's pocket watch. This lone contemporary depiction of the brand is incongruous. The LIT Ranch deed of sale and the 1906 *Brand Book of the Territory of New Mexico* both specified that Littlefield's LIT was burned on the right side. The initial brand registration in Gonzales County did not specify a side. The left-side depiction represents either Littlefield's aborted initial intent or an engraver's mistake. Whichever, Littlefield nevertheless used the watch with its Knights Templar fob. *Courtesy John David White.*

84

FIG. 8. The White brothers. *Left to right:* Thomas David "Tom," James Phelps "Phelps," and John Wilburn "Will." *Courtesy Nancy White DeYoung.*

FIG. 9. Shelton Clark Dowell (1853–85), taken in San Antonio, ca. 1882. *MSS 0050, Dowell-Littlefield Collection, Houston Public Library, HMRC.*

FIG. 10. Brothers Tom (*left*) and Phelps White (*right*) at the Bosque Grande Ranch headquarters, 1883. Although J. P. White II and Mrs. Hamlin Hill offered different identifications for the rider on the viewer's left, Phelps White III's research strongly suggests that it is Phelps I's brother Tom. This is both the earliest image of Littlefield ranch leadership and the only known contemporary picture of the Bosque Grande headquarters. *Author's collection.*

FIG. 11. Bosque Grande site. Flowing south, the Pecos River bows to the west (*right*) away from the first rise, back from the river on the east side, to create a gently sloping oval-shaped terrain forming a natural holding pen for cattle. The width of the stream, pictured in normal flow of late summer, compared to the width of the river bed, shows the potential for quicksand so treacherous for cow and cowboy both. *Author's collection.*

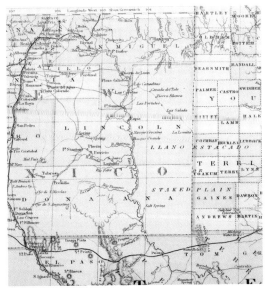

FIG. 12. Mitchell's "County Map of the State of Texas, Showing Also portions of the Adjoining States and Territories," 1884, detail. Bosque Grande is on the east side of the Pecos River south of Fort Sumner. Roswell has yet to appear near the mouth of the Hondo River. The part of eastern New Mexico that would become the Four Lakes Ranch is void of landmarks, including Mescalero Spring.

FIG. 13. George Littlefield. *MSS 0050 Dowell-Littlefield Collection, Houston Public Library, HMRC.*

FIG. 14. Alice P. Tillar Littlefield. These two *cartes de visite* of George and Alice were taken in Kansas City between 1874 and 1881, but most likely in 1881, the year of the LIT sale. *Author's collection.*

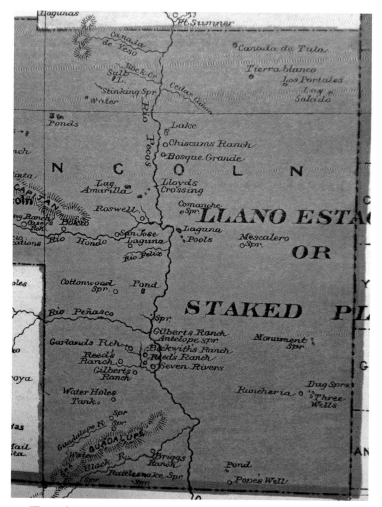

FIG. 15. "Tunison's New Mexico," 1889. Lincoln County detail. Mescalero Spring appears as the only landmark in the seven-thousand-square-mile vastness bounded by Los Portales, Lagunas Pools (Bottomless Lakes), Monument Spring, and the Texas state line. Though sited too far south, Bosque Grande appears here on a commercial New Mexico state map for perhaps the last time. Chisum's Ranch is misplaced north of Bosque Grande.

FIG. 16. Four Lakes Ranch outbuilding. The earliest stones were laid without mortar. *Author's collection.*

FIG. 17. Ranch house at Hidden Spring. William P. Littlefield, wife Euphemia, and family in front of their new Hidden Spring adobe ranch house, 1880s or 1890s. *Courtesy Pat H. Boone IV.*

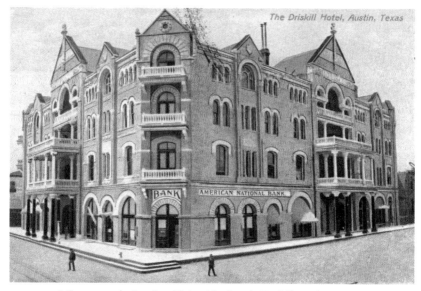

FIG. 18. Entrance to the American National Bank in the Driskill Hotel. *Author's collection.*

FIG. 19. The Littlefield home, ca. 1900. Littlefield kept his yard bushes shaped—
these as cones and cylinders. *Author's collection.*

FIG. 20. GWL crest on the doors of the Littlefield home. The intertwined initials appear also on the newel post and over the entrance to the carriage house. *Author's collection.*

FIG. 21 (a & b). Littlefield home brickwork. Note the careful finish of each brick, the thin and exceptionally precise mortar work, and the unusually bright white resulting from the quartz dust. *Author's collection.*

FIG. 22. Still life by Alice Littlefield. Painting of chrysanthemums.
Author's collection.

FIG. 23. George Littlefield's favorite sculpture. Though the LFD bull is losing the fight, perhaps Littlefield liked the piece because it so effectively displayed his brand as he positioned it on the bull's right side. The sculptor and date are unidentified. *Courtesy John David White.*

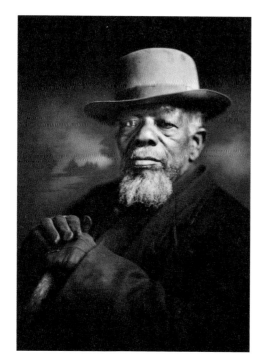

FIG. 24. Nathan Stokes, ca. 1910–16. Portrait of "Uncle Nathan" dressed, as he insisted, in clothes formerly belonging to George Littlefield. *Courtesy Susan Wroe Perry.*

FIG. 25. George Littlefield, miniature, 1890s. *Author's collection.*

FIG. 26. Terry's Texas Rangers Monument, by Pompeo Coppini, Texas State capitol grounds.
Author's collection.

FIG 27. Bank president George Littlefield posed in the American National Bank, 1912.
Author's collection.

Littlefield Building, Austin, Texas.

FIG. 28. Littlefield Building, 1911. This postcard shows the roof garden and bank entrance facing the Congress Avenue and Sixth Street intersection on the recently completed building, before installation of the bronze doors. *Author's collection*

CONNECTING THE FOUR-DOLLAR COW WITH THE FORTY-DOLLAR MARKET

Having decided to go into the cattle business, George Littlefield needed cattle. There were four ways to get them. He could raise them. But whatever stock remained on the acreage he managed in 1871 could not multiply rapidly enough to form the foundation of a business making the profits he had seen being made in cattle. He could buy them outright and get them on credit against their sale at the end of the trail in Kansas, as he had done for half of the animals in his 1871 drive. But his resources would allow him neither to acquire cattle sufficient to "make a rise in the world," as he would say, nor to utilize all the energy he was mustering for the business. Cattle could be had in trade for store goods. But he no longer had his roadside store. Finally, he could round up "mavericks," a term then coming into popularity for wild, unbranded cattle free for the taking.[1] But that was a haphazard approach for a man who had built a thriving enterprise running multiple plantations and a store brought down only by horrific weather events beyond his control. Before cattle, then, what Littlefield needed in the summer of 1871 was a business structure that would increase the capital at his disposal, systematize the work of gathering stock, and position him to exploit his potent ability to negotiate advantageous deals. Though he probably thought little of laying a foundation for a future beyond the drives of the next year or two, the best organization would be one he could replicate as business opportunities warranted. And for a perceptive man on the make in the cattle trade in the decade and a half after the Civil War, opportunity would crowd upon opportunity.

With the profitable sale of his herd in 1871, George Littlefield's three years of ill fortune began to change. First, the profit lifted him from debt, pointed him to a business that truly attracted him, and gave him working capital. Then, in October in Gonzales, just when he needed it, a business opportunity opened when James Colwell "Dock" Dilworth and his partner dissolved their mercantile business. Littlefield bought out the partner and brought to the new enterprise a substantial stock of goods from the store he had closed.[2]

Partnerships were fine structures for conducting business when they yoked the strengths of capable and compatible men. Dilworth was as good a partner as Littlefield could have hoped to find. He was a live wire and a money-maker, Will White recalled.[3] With only a three-year age difference and having arrived in Gonzales County from Mississippi within months of each other, they had been best of friends as playmates, schoolmates, and finally tentmates and officers in I Company during the war. Moreover, Dock brought to the arrangement both competence in running a store and access to capital. He had served as commissary officer for the regiment. The year after the war he had joined his brother, George Norwood Dilworth, and Hugh Lewis in opening not just a mercantile business dealing in groceries, iron, and plantation goods but also Gonzales's first bank.[4] When Dock formed a partnership with Littlefield that actually competed with Dock's Dilworth and Lewis arrangement, it raised no eyebrows. In fact, the practice seems to have been common in Gonzales and to have knitted the community of businessmen together. Finally, the location of the store in the county seat town of Gonzales promised a stronger trade area than Littlefield had enjoyed in his roadside store. Having contributed the greater part of the capital to the partnership, Dilworth would manage the store while Littlefield tended to the cattle side of the business.[5]

Not just any cattle, with no rail lines yet connecting the Texas cattle kingdom with northern markets, Littlefield needed animals robust enough to take themselves to Kansas. And with high tariffs for shipping cattle from railheads in Kansas to markets in the north and east, he needed ones strong enough to gain weight grazing along the way so as to arrive at trail's end in a condition to command a good price. Texas longhorns fit the bill. Longhorns were long legged, angular, and rough, and their hardy constitution outfitted them to transport long distances such beef as they had on their bones. The best time to find likely animals was early spring, when range cattle were in their poorest condition after foraging for whatever nourishment they could come across during the winter. To judge animals offered to him, cowman Littlefield made their owners run them through a gate one at a time. Those that appeared weak he jumped at. If they fell down when scared, he rejected them.[6]

Paying for his purchases was not the simple transaction it would later become. Into the 1870s, Texans continued to be skittish of paper currency. Sellers wanted something of intrinsic value for their animals. The first year of the Dilworth and Littlefield partnership, Littlefield paid the greater cost of the two herds he bought by giving store credit. Of course, markup in the store goods added to the profit realized in the cattle. Sellers distant from Gonzales preferred specie. For them, cattle buyers carried silver. Arriving at the rendezvous point Littlefield, as was common, simply dumped out the coins on a blanket under a tree. Since cattle in those days were bought and sold by class, that is, by a fixed amount for yearlings, two-year-olds, and so forth, rather than by weight, calculating the amount due each seller was simple. While Littlefield was choosing his purchases, his men sorted the coins into sacks of twenty dollars each. After his animals had been counted out to him, Littlefield and his men handed the sellers the number of sacks due each.[7]

Rather than spend two months plodding up the trail out of touch with his business affairs, Littlefield hired crews of cowboys to move the herds.[8] He took trains to the market towns to arrange sales. In making a business of acquiring, driving, and selling herds, Littlefield seized an opportunity most stock raisers avoided but all needed. Most either could not afford the annual cost of outfitting a drive or simply did not want to undertake the endeavor. With no ranch to confine him, Littlefield joined the small fraternity of entrepreneurs who embraced the opportunity of making an enterprise from taking the supply to the demand, or as one of them phrased it colorfully, of "connecting the four dollar cow with the forty dollar market."[9]

With initial 1872 sales being half of what he hoped for, Littlefield no doubt launched his 1873 drive sharing his fellow Texans' anticipation that the year would reward their enterprise handsomely. It didn't. While the good market of 1872 drew in 1873 the second largest number of cattle ever trailed, the buyers of stocker cattle for northern ranges who had made 1872 such a good year had been satisfied and did not return. A poor corn crop diminished demand for feeders. Cattlemen held their herds hoping for an upturn in prices. To hang on, they borrowed, one estimate being as much as $1.5 million. The upturn never came. Fewer than three-fifths of the trail herds sold. Then in September the Panic of 1873 abruptly called in the loans. Cattlemen sold for whatever they could get, often below the capital they had in their herds. "Cattle men, as well as cattle, are slaughtered every day," wrote a Wichita, Kansas, observer.[10]

Not George Washington Littlefield. "Here is the money—And Here is the Field to opperrate in," he announced exuberantly in July, reveling in the challenge and excitement of the deal making that had attracted him to the cattle business in the first place and confirmed his decision to make handling beeves his life's work.[11] Quantifying his achievement, he noted that he would leave the market with ten thousand dollars in profit. That was a stunning sum. A trail boss drawing $150 per month would have to work more than five years to equal Littlefield's take. A cowhand earning a good wage of a dollar a day could not pocket that much before the trailing era ended a decade and a half later.

If Littlefield ever paused to regret the money he had forfeited by failing to enter the business in 1869 when he had marveled at the profits Gonzales men were making, he needn't have. In fact, he had entered the trailing business in good time. John Thomas Lytle, who in one year drove ninety-one thousand head and whose prominence in the cattle trailing industry catapulted him to leadership of several cattlemen's associations, made his first drive in 1871, the same year as Littlefield. The Blocker brothers of Blanco County, who made trailing pay as well as any of them, began driving only in 1873. And Isaac Thomas "Ike" Pryor, who would net in one later year a fabulous $130,000 profit, inaugurated his trailing one or maybe two years after the Blockers, in 1874 or 1875.

A lifelong friend, the calm-natured Pryor shared with Littlefield a defining characteristic of the entrepreneurs of the cattle-trailing industry.[12] They were young. In 1871 Pryor was twenty. At twenty-nine, Littlefield was two years younger than the average. The industry required young men, its historian, Jimmy M. Skaggs, surmised, because of both the rigors of the trail and the necessity of being adaptable to changing conditions in a business that functioned for only half a year. Though Littlefield invested his time in ways other than making the protracted trail rides with his product, he fit the mold as a man who not just adapted to conditions but turned them to his advantage.[13]

The calamity of 1873 confirmed it. The misfortune of other trailing entrepreneurs opened opportunity to Littlefield. Saying that when others wanted to buy, he sold, and when others wanted to sell, he bought, he made plans to acquire cattle cheap to hold through the winter. He anticipated the normal loss from bad weather on the Kansas plains would be offset by the higher price the cattle would bring in the spring. Wintering in climates materially colder than their home ground relieved the south Texans of Texas Fever. And being free of it raised the animals' value by one-third or so.[14] Since to manage his business interests at home he could not spend the winter just watching cattle in Kansas, Littlefield needed a partner on the ground. Excitement filled the letter he dashed off to twenty-year-old bachelor nephew Shelton Clark Dowell:

> I am satisfied that next month I can buy cattle at Ellsworth at my own figures and Time. Now Shelt I am not asleep. Nor am I in the least deceived When I tell you This is our Place. This is the Place, *and This the winter,* for *You* and *I* to make *a rise in the world.* I say, if I can buy 1000 head of cattle cheap on one years time next month . . . I am going to dispatch for you to come. come, without delay. Don't talk to anyone. Pack up, and leave. Bring all the money you can control of yours as you will find a place for it here.

Here we meet *Live, energetic men.* and I only want you to assist me and in one year from now we will have made at Least $6,000.00. . . . Shelt now is the time for us. . . . Don't show this. But prepare so you may be ready whenever I dispatch for you.[15]

Some said that Greenoville and Sallie Dowell's second child and Littlefield's second oldest nephew was a favorite of Uncle George. If so, it was not because Shelton took to stock raising and farming. Born on January 24, 1853, Shelt at age fifteen first went to work for his uncle helping with the stock and corn crop. But he didn't stick with it long. His father invited him to make a life in the city by becoming a printer's devil so he could take over the Galveston printing office in which his father was producing the first medical journal in Texas. "There is no business more profitable in a large city nor anything more honorable and elegant or causes more respect," Dowell advised.[16] Perhaps father Dowell, who had not seen his son in nearly a decade, took the young man's handwriting that incorporated elegant loops and flourishes to express a love of the written word. Whatever the fancy script expressed, it was not an interest in printing. Shelton didn't go. Instead, he went to clerking in yet another of the Gonzales stores of intertwined partners—the one of Hugh Lewis and Littlefield partner Dock Dilworth.[17] A handsome man, maybe the option of taking his salary in clothes attracted him (fig. 9).

Shelton had been in his new job only months when he was summoned home. On November 20, 1869, he stood with his grandmother, his brother and sister, and Uncle George at his mother's bedside and watched as she asked George to sit beside her. Sallie White Dowell kissed her half brother goodbye and used her last breaths to murmur, "George take care of my children. Educate them *if you can.*" She had grieved that Shelton had not received the schooling his brother John had. But destitute after her divorce and loss of her property in slaves, she couldn't afford to send him. If nothing before had, Shelton's mother's dying request completed for the young man the transformation of his uncle, only ten and a half years older, into a father figure. George Littlefield accepted it. "Then it was, my Heart was fullest," Littlefield relived the emotion decades later. "No one Knows, only He, who has been [in] alike situation, what that feeling is. Whether I have done my duty in trying to bring those two boys up, and raising that Girl as she should be, God in Heaven must be the Judge."[18]

As fate would have it, Littlefield never dispatched for Shelton to come in the fall of 1873. If conditions that turned dry, aggravated by a plague of grasshoppers, had not scuttled his wintering scheme, the terrible financial Panic of 1873 did by paralyzing the fall cattle market. But only for 1873. And Littlefield's infectious, exuberant enthusiasm for the cattle trade animating the letter not only outlasted the conditions but thirty-nine years later blossomed in his commissioning a pair of massive bronze doors that are a unique celebration of the great age of the range-cattle industry created by a cattleman who lived it.[19]

With a dozen or so men to drive some 2,500 longhorn cattle that could run with the speed of deer in wide-open spaces, losses occurred. There were two ways to deal with them. One was to buy herds arriving at trail's end. Littlefield did. "Cherokee and Texas Cattle," read the Dilworth and Littlefield advertising card promoting stock acquired at or near the end of their trek.[20] The other way was to absorb the attrition. Cattlemen considered 3 percent normal. Most losses resulted from stampedes sparked by thunder, sudden unusual noises, and startling movements. Attrition from these trail losses the owner simply had to absorb.

Losses to Indians demanding compensation for herds crossing their reservations were different. Cowboys with a herd that Wash Harris drove for the captain in 1879 thought they might not live to tell the story of their encounter. From Matagorda on the Texas Gulf Coast, the drive proceeded routinely until the mile-or-so-long string of cattle snaked into Indian Territory. Without warning, a band of Kiowas and Comanches wearing war paint and numbering in what the terrified nineteen-year-old tenderfoot Louis Hamilton Hill recalled as thousands (but certainly not more than hundreds) confronted the drive and demanded beef. Outnumbered and outgunned, the drovers handed over about ten animals and watched the Indians slaughter them in what appeared to the cowboys to be a reliving of a buffalo hunt on the plains. Not once, but for seven or eight days straight as the drovers pushed the herd north, the Indians dogged the drive and repeated the demand and the disturbing slaughter. Never once did the small military detachment assigned to escort the Indian group leave its bivouac several miles distant to challenge their charges.

As the herd approached the relative safety of the Kansas state line, the Indians' demand changed ominously. Appearing out of dusk's deepening dark as the cowboys were catching their night mounts, the warriors this time wanted not cattle but horses. Refusing the demand meant at the least dealing with a stampede the Indians could be expected to start at the worst time—at night. Or it meant being killed outright. Appreciating the Indians' love of horseflesh, the quick-thinking drovers postponed their fate by convincing the Indians to wait to take the horses until morning, when they could see to select the best mounts. Then a cowboy stole through the darkness to the soldiers. When morning's light revealed the drovers and the soldiers ready to receive an attack, the Indians withdrew.

Trail boss Harris secured a signed statement from the detachment commander documenting that the braves had commandeered several thousand dollars' worth of beef. With proof of this requisition, Littlefield appealed to Congress for compensation. First Representative Christopher C. Upson in 1880, then Banking and Commerce Committee chair and Littlefield attorney James F. Miller in 1886 introduced bills to reimburse the trailing entrepreneur. Neither measure left committee, and Littlefield never received a penny in reimbursement.[21]

An annoyance, Littlefield termed the Indians, perhaps because he utilized the cattleman's way of obtaining reimbursement. Beginning in 1871, the federal government began purchasing cattle to feed Indians on newly established reservations. Littlefield wanted in on this market that had to grow and by 1879 had grown to absorb some 50,000 to 60,000 head annually, the equivalent of 20 to 24 average sized herds. Under the contracts, cattle were paid for on the basis of weight—the average of the heaviest animal (selected by the trail boss) and the lightest (selected by the Indian agent). For sufficient cash, the agent could be induced to select the Guernsey cow brought along for the purpose. Readily recognizable and weighing about the same as a good-sized longhorn steer, the agent's selection of the Guernsey ensured that the cattleman received a good return for his stock.[22]

The Guernsey strategy also made up for the government's contracting rules. They reserved awards to Northerners alone. Texans were relegated to subcontracting. As a result, contractors commonly profited as much as the subcontractor who bore the expense and work of driving the herd to the reservation. This arrangement, concluded a historian of cattle industry business methods, was one reason that "Yankees continued to be 'damn Yankees' to Texans as long as they did."[23]

When asked in 1884 about trailing, Littlefield counted dealing with the "cursed aborigines," as he called them, using a term rarely heard in America, as one of the two reasons he quit driving. "I am tired of the trail," he told a Dodge City reporter. "In the future I will ship by rail. The annoyance of crossing the Indian's reservation and getting through the settled up portion of the country with our cattle is enough to drive a man crazy." The advantages of transporting cattle expeditiously on the cars followed his accounting of negative reasons.[24]

For thirteen years, from 1872 through 1884, George Littlefield made a business of trailing herds on commission, on his own, and in partnerships with Dilworth in the store and with several cattlemen. Surviving figures for his herds traveling to Kansas, Colorado, Wyoming, and the Dakotas, though incomplete, nevertheless permit a calculation of the level of Littlefield's participation in the trailing industry. Littlefield recalled decades later that he drove between 5,000 and 30,000 head every year. During the nine of the thirteen years for which figures survive in newspaper accounts and in reminiscences of men who participated in the drives, herds Littlefield sent north totaled some 111,000 head. Of the estimated 2,826,124 head that made the trek during those nine years, Littlefield's contribution amounted in round numbers to 4 percent.[25] In the two years for which Littlefield's numbers likely are close to accurate—1877 (23,000 head) and 1879 (30,000 head)—he drove 11.5 percent of the 459,086 total head trailed. Men positioned to support Littlefield's trailing enterprise noticed. Based on his profit from the 1877 trailing season, Dun and Company raised his credit rating in May 1878. That year, when more cattle trudged north than in either 1877 or 1879, Littlefield's reported participation with 14,000 of 265,646 head considerably lagged that of his years before and after, yet still represents 5.3 percent of the two years' drive.

Two facts indicate that 4 percent does not exaggerate Littlefield's participation in trailing. First, contemporary numbers for his herds come from the incomplete runs of two newspapers—the *Fort Griffin Echo* reported herds passing by the Texas frontier town and Dodge City, Kansas, *Ford County Globe,* which chronicled only one of Littlefield's destinations. Second, in two years for which figures for Littlefield clearly are incomplete, the *Ford County Globe* reported that Littlefield's activity ranked with that of the most productive trailing entrepreneurs and cattlemen. In 1878 the twenty cars of cattle Littlefield shipped out by rail in August stood second only to Jesse Lincoln Driskill's twenty-four cars, and these two men together accounted for two-thirds of the total. In 1880, for which extant figures report only 11,000 Littlefield cattle out of 394,784 trailed, or 2.7 percent, the *Ford County Globe* declared that, judging trailing entrepreneurs by the value of the cattle they traded in Dodge City, Littlefield joined Texas Panhandle cattlemen Charles Goodnight of the JA Ranch and David Thomas Beals of the LX in topping all others by marketing half a million dollars' worth each.

Moving 4 percent of the head driven during his years in trailing ranks Littlefield among the eleven most significant figures in the business. Trailing industry historian Jimmy Skaggs calculated that the most active trailing contractor, John Lytle, accounted for about 15 percent of all the cattle driven. The Blocker Brothers drove between 7 and 10 percent, Dillard Fant between 4 and 5 percent, and Eugene Bartlett Millett and Seth Mabry, whose operation "served as the standard of excellence by which all other contracting concerns were judged," just 3 percent. Skaggs drew the line between minor and major names in the trailing business at 3 percent.[26]

Men in the business of trailing cattle were especially awake to opportunity, decisive in accepting the risk in seizing it, and within reach of the financing that afforded them the opportunity to be decisive. Finding unexpected promise in the exhilarating return born of the desperation that launched his first drive, George Littlefield propelled himself into the trailing business. Maybe certain at first of no more than his skill at trading, the entrepreneur in him did not hesitate to embark on the specialized work of acquiring and transporting meat between a place of almost unlimited supply and one of nearly insatiable demand. The nature of the business saddled those successful in it with two significant challenges. Its short annual duration was one. That placed stress on demands for capital to finance product acquisition and for labor to staff the drives. Then, at the sale table, the trader had to be prepared to conduct his negotiations while possessing minimal, if any knowledge of the size and condition in which his product would arrive after two-or-so month's transit. "Do think that you Boys [in Texas] ought to write me often and not wait for me to answer every letter," Littlefield expressed the cattleman's cry for information in a missive admonishing a nephew who had failed to send news.[27]

During his years in trailing, Littlefield laid the foundation for the remainder of his life with cattle. As a trailing entrepreneur, he established himself in the fraternity of leaders in the cattle business. The association afforded timely knowledge of developments that informed business decisions of a man alert to prospect. Only five years into trailing and while it remained a lucrative enterprise, Littlefield capitalized on this familiarity to time his entry into large-scale ranching.

When measured historically by volume of cattle driven, George W. Littlefield stands among the dozen or so figures most prominently associated with trailing. When judged contemporaneously by the use of information Littlefield gleaned from conversations within the trailing fraternity, his timely move into ranching would be celebrated even before the trailing era closed.

7

THE FASTEST MONEY-MAKING BUSINESS

Trading in cattle in the volume that trailing entrepreneur Littlefield did meant spending two to four months at a time away from home. Alice took to traveling with her husband. The trip in 1873 provided one eye-opening or luxurious experience after another. Alice could have iced treats whenever she wanted. "This summer I have often thought of you all at home, how hard living was there and how hot and not a single iced soda or plate of ice cream. Some days we would drink three glasses of soda," she wrote in the only one of her many letters that has survived. The waitstaff "in the best [lodging] which the market affords" affected her stereotype of the work suitable for the races. A bit astonished, she confessed that "I am as much pleased to have white girls and boys to wait on me now as I ever was" to have black waitstaff. But it was railroad travel that gave her to realize how isolated life in Gonzales truly was. "I declare, it is awful that we have been deprived of so many blessings which the cars would bring," she summed up both her amazement at all she had experienced and her eagerness to live in a place linked to the rest of the country by steel rails.[1]

As long as he had cattle to work and trade, George Littlefield felt no deprivation. He enjoyed cowboying in its way as much as trading in its way. In July 1875 he labored zealously in Kansas City to sell his remaining bunches within twenty days so he could leave "to assist in working those cattle down in Texas." Two years later at trail's end, he had only minutes, not days, to join his cowboys. On June 9, 1877, a pelting sleet and rain storm raked a herd his men were holding so close to Dodge City that they could hear the music and merriment in town. Rather than endure the torment, a number of the trail-weary hands abruptly quit their jobs and rode to shelter in Dodge. Without replacement hands to corral them, the restless cattle were likely to mix with herds of other cowmen camped only a mile or so away. Trail boss George Hodges sent Phelps White into town to tell his uncle to send men. Along with his recruits, Littlefield loped out to join in holding the herds apart.[2]

Weathering the late spring storm, as important as it was in the moment, was not the watershed event of the year for George Littlefield. Dock Dilworth's death three weeks earlier on May 17, 1877, was. To pay the Dilworth heirs their share of the Dilworth and Littlefield partnership, Littlefield liquidated the store. The enterprise, he said later, earned the partners "handsome fortunes." It had. Dun and Company correspondents judged that, counting personal and business assets, in the six years between June 1871 and July 1877, Littlefield's worth had swelled more than seventeen times from $5,500 to $95,000.[3]

As profitable as the store had been, closing it was not the consequence of Dock's death that marked the watershed in cattleman Littlefield's life. Rather, the turning point was the termination of the partnership. The arrangement that had so facilitated Littlefield's entrance into the cattle business had developed strains between its two sides—the Gonzales store and the trailing operation. If Littlefield wintered a herd in partnership with Dilworth, "I would have to stay up Here [in Kansas] all the time, away from my business," Littlefield wrote, "while He [in Gonzales] would Have all of His well attended to."[4] Littlefield's situation in the partnership contrasted with his position in the other business relationships he established. To extend his trailing ventures, he had been forming transitory partnerships with cattlemen to invest in individual herds. These were affiliations of equals. The Dilworth and Littlefield partnership was not. Littlefield was the junior in the pact. Dilworth's death ended the one time in Littlefield's life that he was so subordinated.

It seems to be no coincidence, then, that in a way unique and personal to cowmen, Littlefield proclaimed the change. On July 23, 1877, he registered a new brand distinctly his. Though easy enough to read, the Diamond 7 of his youth had offered no logical link to him. Moreover, it was not a brand for the trail herds that were Littlefield's staple. For them he and his partners used simple road brands like F, L, and Bar F (backed up with documents from owners of cattle he was driving). That July day in Gonzales, Littlefield registered the brand no cowman, cowhand, or cattle inspector would mistake as belonging to anyone but George Washington Littlefield: **LIT**. The first three letters of his name emblazoned on the animal proclaimed Littlefield's ownership more boldly and plainly than any artful brand could (fig. 7).[5]

LIT, of course, was no more a trail brand than was the Diamond 7. It was a ranch brand. George Littlefield had decided to expand into another sector of the cattle business. The LIT Ranch he meant to establish would be unlike properties in Gonzales and the settled regions of the state, where a man first had to buy the land on which to hold his animals. Littlefield had his eye on unappropriated land in the Texas Panhandle. The time was right to claim such a domain. Littlefield knew it from conversations among trailing contractors. Maybe anyone could have known, but few had the ready capital, men, and cattle available to take advantage of the moment. Some $12,350, one authority calculated, was the investment required just to open a free-range operation running a thousand head in Texas.[6] Littlefield had them all—just short of $100,000, mostly from liquidation of the Dilworth partnership, established hands driving for him and nephews ready to join his enterprise, and cattle on his Gonzales property.

When on his 1871 drive George Littlefield first entered the cattle country of north Texas, Indian Territory, and southern Kansas, it was common knowledge that there was one place where white men did not go. The Staked Plain, the elevated southern extent of the Great Plains that stretched from Canada well into Texas, was an inhospitable if not hostile territory. In eleven words the Texas plate in *The Peoples' Pictorial Atlas* of 1873 told why. "Elevated Table-lands without wood or water" meant there were no building materials and, as far as white men knew, no way to sustain agriculture. The real reason, though, took only five of those words: "Comanches" on the western side and "Kiowa & Middle & Southern Comanches" to the east. Whites who ventured into the domain of these Indians beyond the 100th meridian, a portion of which separated the Texas Panhandle from Indian Territory, took their lives into their own hands.[7]

Comanches and Kiowas protected the plains expanse south of the Cimarron River fiercely. It was theirs under the 1867 Treaty of Medicine Lodge. Well they knew it was their last refuge from the ever-encroaching whites. It was the last domain where they could live as their ancestors had lived, striking out in raids to steal the horses that formed their wealth. It was the last ancestral land on which they could follow their traditional nomadic life, pursuing the buffalo that provided them with the essentials of food, clothing, and tools. Some four million buffalo roaming these plains in the 1860s could sustain the tribes indefinitely.

White men saw in the shaggy beasts little more than sport and profit in the robes made from their hides. As railroads pushed westward across Kansas, white men in increasing numbers came with their new, powerful, long-range Sharps Big Fifties (.50 caliber rifles) to slaughter America's largest land animal by the thousands, then tens of thousands annually. Between 1871 and 1874, the economy of Kansas rested on what William T. Hornaday in his contemporary government report on *The Extermination of the American Bison* called the buffalo "product." By 1874 the southern herd had nearly vanished from Kansas and was a shadow of itself farther south. "By the close of the hunting season of 1875," Hornaday wrote, "the great southern herd had ceased to exist. As a body, it had been utterly annihilated. The main body of the survivors, numbering about ten thousand head, fled southwest, and dispersed through that great tract of wild, desolate, and inhospitable land stretching southward from the Cimarron country across the 'Public Land Strip' [present-day Oklahoma Panhandle], the Pan-handle of Texas, and the Llano Estacado, or Staked Plain, to the Pecos River."[8]

Buffalo hunters pursued them into the Texas Panhandle and the breaks west of Fort Griffin (located about one hundred miles west of Fort Worth). The first into the Texas Panhandle set up camp in 1873 at Adobe Walls, an abandoned trading post on the Canadian River. They trespassed. The next summer a large force of Comanches, Kiowas, Arapahos, and Cheyennes attacked. Raiding parties pillaged and murdered settlers and travelers east of forts meant to protect the whites from the Indians to the west. In retaliation, with a mission of not just punishing the Indians but wiping them out altogether, five columns of soldiers converged on the Panhandle. The Fourth United States Cavalry dealt the Red River War's decisive blow in the Battle of Palo Duro Canyon on September 28, 1874. Though few were killed on either side, the cavalrymen destroyed both dried meat the Indians had stockpiled to sustain them through the winter and the horses that provided their mobility to hunt buffalo and to evade pursuit. Nine months later, in June 1875, Quanah Parker finally gave up the struggle to maintain the traditional Comanche way of life and led his band into submission on the reservation. With the Indian threat on the southern plains reduced to scattered forays launched from reservations to which the loss of the great buffalo herd further forced the Indians to retreat, the land was opening for whomever had the strength to take and use it.[9]

While these events were unfolding in the early and middle 1870s, a few Texas cattlemen ventured into Indian domain in the rolling plains country east and south of the Staked Plains. The Ikards and the Harrolds claimed territories about one hundred miles northwest of Fort Worth along the Red River border with Indian Territory. Christopher Columbus Slaughter staked out his range some two hundred miles west of Fort Worth. But trailing contractor John Lytle marked the changing landscape the most dramatically when in 1874 he pioneered a trail along the ninety-ninth meridian through Comanche and Kiowa country, some one hundred miles west of the Chisholm Trail, the principal cattle highway of Littlefield's early drives. The Western Trail ran past Fort Griffin, whose newspaper editor likely gave not one thought to how helpful his reporting of the owners and numbers of passing herds would be to historians, and continued north and northwest to Dodge City and beyond. So many drovers followed Lytle's route once the Indian presence on the plains was minimized that the Western became the most heavily traveled of all the cattle trails.[10]

Unlike the Ikards, Harrolds, and Lytle on the east, Charles Goodnight approached the formerly forbidding country from the west. Goodnight had interests in Colorado, having blazed the Goodnight-Loving Trail around the southern end of the plains and north up the Pecos River to Fort Sumner. Aware of the Indians' failure to overrun Adobe Walls the year before, late in 1875 he drifted a herd to winter pasture along the Canadian River in eastern New Mexico. The following summer he pushed into the former Indian country nudging the cattle down the Canadian in the direction of Adobe Walls to graze on the nutritious grama grasses of the Texas Panhandle. Rather than contest the Mexican sheepherders in the valley for territory, in October 1876 he left the river and settled the herd east and south in Palo Duro Canyon, where Col. Ranald S. Mackenzie had routed the Comanche concentration two years earlier.[11]

Few if any cattlemen learned of Goodnight's move before early summer, when they congregated at trail's end to market their herds. "Dodge City boiling over with buyers and drovers," the *Dodge City Times* described the scene in 1877. Trailing entrepreneurs and their men lodged in the same hotels. And they talked. With some, as Seth Mabry, Littlefield developed a close friendship along with the business connection. In this way, if no other, Littlefield learned that several trailing contractors, Mabry among them, had ranches in south and central Texas and that they increased their earnings by raising some of the cattle they marketed. Maybe casual conversation rekindled Littlefield's decade-old interest in going into ranching. However long Littlefield had been thinking about adding ranching to the ways he made money from cattle, it appears that closing the Dilworth and Littlefield store precipitated his move.[12]

Numbered among the partnership's assets were at least four trail herds. For Littlefield, the Dilworth, Littlefield, and Dowell bunch in the Cross L brand stood apart from the others. In the outfit driving the herd and making his first trip up the trail rode twenty-year-old James Phelps White. Born four days before Christmas in 1856, the second son of Littlefield's half brother Thomas White, Phelps and his uncle had been practically inseparable from the moment Littlefield returned from the war. When only seven-going-on-eight years old, Phelps began riding behind his twenty-two-year-old uncle as Littlefield went about his work on the plantations. The two shared a work ethic. "There wasn't a lazy bone in that boy," trail boss and family friend Jim Roberts said of Phelps. He was a good worker, "a goer." Littlefield was the same way. "He worked fast," Edgar Harral said. "He would never get tired. . . . He would work all day and . . . follow those hounds all night hunting civet cats and 'coons." Phelps accompanied Littlefield on the hunting trips too.[13]

The two grew even closer when Littlefield penned a little bunch of Circle 9 cattle at Phelps's father's place to separate the calves from the older and stronger animals Littlefield would take on his 1871 drive. Phelps was fourteen. "You can have all of those calves you can catch," Littlefield told Phelps and his younger brother, Thomas David White. "We caught nine of them," Phelps recounted, "and that was my start in the cattle business." Though in reminiscing to J. Evetts Haley Phelps didn't say what he did with those calves, he must have learned a great deal from them about cattle and their handling. Beginning with those nine, he began learning the business from the ground up. It didn't take long. "In his young days he could punch cattle, could rope, was a good rider, and all that," recalled cowman and friend Charlie Ballard, who knew him well. Littlefield saw it. Before Phelps completed his first drive, his uncle asked him: "It looks like I'm going to make a pretty good profit. I wonder if you'd like to go to ranching with me."

"'Sure,' I said. 'I'll go anywhere with you.'"[14]

And so began the partnership that would become legendary in the history of the range-cattle industry for its longevity and profitability. In the second striking coincidence in six years, just when Littlefield needed a partner, the right man appeared. Just when Littlefield lost in Dock Dilworth the close friend whose partnership allowed him to make a real rise in the cattle trade, Phelps White joined the Littlefield operation and filled the void. Like Dock, Phelps had a good head for business. He was "a good businessman—held his money together; made a little more always. Was a bright fellow. . . . It takes a businessman to hold a big lot of money together," Ballard observed.

What distinguished Phelps from Dock, though, was his insight into and love of handling cattle. Phelps was a cowman the equal of his uncle. As Littlefield described him years later in a wonderful mixing of metaphors, Phelps was "a dyed in the wool cow man." In fact, Phelps was a cowman who thoroughly understood business. Littlefield was a businessman who thoroughly understood cattle. So Phelps did not just fill the void of Dock's death. He brought the talents that formed the foundation on which Littlefield could far extend his enterprise. Finally, he brought judgment. "I rely upon him more than any one to help me," Littlefield would declare more than once.[15] On the LIT the two would seal the business and personal partnership that would sustain them for forty-three years, until closed by Littlefield's death.

After disposing of the herds trailed north in the spring drive, Littlefield sent his top hand, thirty-one-year-old Charles S. "Mac" McCarty, to find a ranch location in the newly opening country. Though ranchers of the Gonzales region gravitated to the Trans-Pecos country, Littlefield directed Mac to the Texas Panhandle. Increasing his incentive to select a range rich in good grass and groundwater, essential in the days before windmills substituted for springs, Littlefield told Mac that he, McCarty, would have management of the ranch.

Of these two basic characteristics of good open-range ranch property, water was the more important. Control of the water meant control of the land ranging back from it. In a day before fences laced the plains, ownership of water rights, whether held by purchase or gentleman's agreement, secured the grass for the rancher who fronted the stream or occupied the land around the spring. McCarty rode to the most important watercourse flowing across the Panhandle. The Canadian River "was a beautiful stream, no sand bars at all," Jose Romero described the generally northeast-flowing watercourse. "It was hardly more than 20 feet wide and had deep clear living water. Its banks were fringed . . . [with] wild berries, grapes, plums," and little cottonwood groves. On his course to that beautiful water, McCarty passed through a land rich with wildlife—antelope, buffalo, coyote, wolves, mustang horses—but vacant enough to accommodate thousands of resilient longhorn cattle.[16]

If Littlefield and Mac thought that Mac would have nothing more to do than take his pick of unclaimed territory, they were mistaken. A handful of Anglo cattlemen had beaten them to the valley. Thomas Sherman Bugbee had located 1,800 Quarter Circle T cattle in Bugbee Canyon, about seventy-five miles downstream from present-day Tascosa (established later but grown from a settlement the LIT range surrounded). West of Bugbee, only weeks before McCarty began his search for a location, David T. Beals and W. H. Bates declared a huge swath of territory to be their LX Ranch. To the south, on Alamocitos Creek, Ellsworth Torrey had located his TS range where he appears initially to have grazed sheep. The river available for McCarty, then, lay to the west and north of these two.[17]

In fact, the Canadian was populated by more than cattle. Scattered plazas of a well-organized society of sheepmen from New Mexico dotted the river's banks. McCarty would have to deal with these men as well. The most prominent of the New Mexicans was no simple herder. Around forty years old and a former comanchero who traded between the Comanche Indians and the whites, Casimero Romero projected a commanding personality. The entourage he organized to take him and his family to the settlement he established where Atascosa Creek empties into the Canadian left no doubt. McCarty arrived with a comrade and a packhorse. Not Romero:

> Romero had come in the grand manner. He was a *"mucho grande"* operator, a cultured and wealthy Castilian. . . . Casimero moved on a scale befitting a grandee of Mexico. The train was composed of fourteen great lumbering schooners, peaked like a boat in front and back, which Romero had purchased from the United States Army. . . . The coach in which the family rode was a magnificent conveyance not unlike the stagecoaches plying the mail routes.[18]

Charles McCarty was not the first or even the second cowman Romero had faced since his arrival less than a year earlier. First, he and Goodnight struck an agreement that Romero would keep his sheep out of Goodnight's Palo Duro and the eastern Panhandle, and Goodnight would keep his cattle out of Romero's Canadian and the western Panhandle. With Bates and Beals, Romero evidently concurred that the remaining Canadian was big enough for them both. Bates and Beals located the west line of the LX on John Ray Creek, only twenty miles down stream from Romero's settlement (a few miles northwest of present-day Amarillo). How much more of the Canadian east of his settlement would Romero give up?

Phelps White said that McCarty, handsome and thickset but not large, was "a gentleman in every respect." "As social and agreeable a man as will be found on the Canadian," the *Ford County Globe* would echo. And so he must have been in their negotiations. Though plenty of land for both made Romero's agreement with Goodnight workable, still Goodnight made plain that his men would deal harshly with transgressors (and so they did with one). Whether Bates and Beals promised to use their cowboys similarly, McCarty had no force behind him to dictate the boundaries he wanted. Still, McCarty had come for land and a lot of it. On average to fatten one longhorn steer for market, open-range cowmen then considered twenty-five acres necessary—62,500 acres, or 97.5 square miles, for the average herd of 2,500 head. Mayordomo Romero recognizing that his three thousand sheep and the flocks of the several New Mexican *pastores* needed far less acreage—10 acres per animal in the worst years—evidently concluded that he could afford or that he had no choice but to relinquish yet more acreage to the advancing land-hungry Anglo cattlemen. He sold McCarty a location at the mouth of Pescado Creek, about three miles east of his settlement at what became Tascosa, a corruption of Atascosa, meaning "boggy," where the mayordomo had built a dugout and pens. This would serve as the headquarters for the LIT Ranch, and probably the boundary between Littlefield's cattle and Romero's flock. By gentleman's agreement with Bates and Beals, the LIT's eastern boundary would be where Bates and Beals had established it with Romero.[19]

Not just any cattle would Littlefield throw onto his new ranch. While McCarty was meeting Romero, in Gonzales Littlefield seared the new LIT brand on some 3,300 south Texas cattle—two-thirds choice females, the balance in steers, and all "as wild as polecats," family friend Jim Roberts said. Then he sent them up the Chisholm Trail the long way to Dodge City to meet McCarty. In September McCarty led the bunch down what became the Tascosa–Dodge City Trail some 225 miles to begin his work managing the expansive LIT Ranch.[20] And with their arrival, cowboy, trailing contractor, and cattleman George Littlefield became a rancher, the role that, more than any other, seared his name into the history of the great age of the range-cattle business.

The work and responsibilities of the rancher were significantly different in four ways from those of either the cowboy or the cattleman. One was ownership of the land over which his animals grazed. Beyond the obvious acquisition and sale, the rancher had to improve and continually maintain the property with buildings from bunkhouses to the blacksmith shop at the headquarters and, after the open range period, with fences, windmills, and surface tanks (depressions) for holding groundwater. Another rancher responsibility was breeding. For some, that was little more than leaving bulls and cows to produce calves as they would. For a few, it included spending substantial sums on prize-winning bulls to put on the herd's cows. Littlefield early on began upgrading his stock, first with shorthorns, then with the Herefords that constituted his staple thenceforward. Unlike orienting the year to the driving season, a rancher had a twelve-month operation to oversee. The most important task of a rancher who did not live on the property, as Littlefield would not, was selecting the right man as manager. This individual had to be effective in assembling and directing the workforce, in managing and accounting for the costs of the operation, and in anticipating needs of all kinds, especially for delivering herds to purchasers. He had to be both knowledgeable and skilled in cowboying and willing to join his hands in the work as need be. Perhaps most important of all, he had to be faithful to the rancher and his business.

George Littlefield saw his LIT Ranch for the first time the following spring of 1878, when he made the first of his annual visits to inspect his ranch properties and select the animals he would send to market. The country and how well his cattle had survived the winter pleased him as much as it had the visitor to the region whose report moved the editor of the *Dodge City Times* to proclaim that it was "the finest stock country in the world." And there was "room for millions of cattle." Not just space, "room" meant grass enough to nourish them. If hundreds of thousands of buffalo had not eaten the land barren, it stood to reason that hundreds of thousands of cattle wouldn't either. Finally, Littlefield, the good cowman who appreciated the importance of knowing the country as well as the cattle, saw the contour that, along with water, made the Canadian River location superb. The bluffs above the river and extending up the creeks emptying into it afforded protection from frigid winter northers.[21]

What no one could see was that in appropriating this land, George Littlefield and his hands and his neighbors were forging the final piece of what western historian Howard R. Lamar called "probably the most classic example of all western nineteenth-century frontiers." In the twenty-year period between 1870 and 1890, the Texas Panhandle saw the concluding campaigns of its Indian wars, the slaughter of the last great buffalo herd, and the conversion of the lush, seemingly unbounded grassy plains into vast cattle ranching domains. "Overnight," Lamar summed it up, "the Texas Panhandle Frontier came to epitomize the popular romantic image of the Wild West at its wildest and most colorful."[22]

Wouldn't a rancher want to own land with the promise Littlefield saw on his LIT? Jot Gunter and William Benjamin Munson saw a market. Shortly after the Panhandle opened, they began surveying so as to offer certificates ranchers could use to secure their range. In the summer of 1878, a representative of their land firm met McCarty on the ranch and offered 16,500 acres in blocks located along the river. For only seventy-five cents an acre, Littlefield could take title to water that occurred the grassland he was grazing for free. Rancher Littlefield thought about it, but instead of paying the $12,000 Gunter and Munson asked, Phelps White gave $150 for a place on Cheyenne Creek some five miles as the crow flies west of Pescado Creek. Not only did the purchase expand the western boundary of the ranch to Cheyenne Creek, but it also gave the men an adobe building for the ranch headquarters to replace the Pescado Creek dugout. Gunter and Munson persisted. And the story is that when Gunter, passing through the Panhandle in 1879, took Littlefield aside in the shade of a wagon and pressed him, the rancher replied firmly, "Jot, you might just as well try to sell me 100,000 acres of that blue sky as this land. I don't want it."[23]

With Phelps's acquisition, the dimensions of Littlefield's open-range LIT grew to encompass a good twenty-five miles of river front along with grazing rights back ten or more miles on both sides of the stream. "The Cattle business here is conducted on a large scale," Shelton Dowell wrote after he first saw the operation there four years later. The five hundred square miles, more or less, of the LIT made it the second largest outfit along the Canadian.[24]

For Littlefield the LIT solved a problem that tormented all who drove cattle from south Texas. Texas Fever. Though still unaware of its cause, cattlemen had learned that south Texas animals that spent a winter in a cold environment no longer infected cattle with which they came into contact (because the toxic tick froze). For this benefit, Panhandle ranch historian Laura Hamner labeled properties like the LIT "halfway ranches" where south Texas cattle could be driven to spend the winter before trailing the final few hundred miles to market. While it cost about fifty cents more to maintain an animal in the Panhandle than in south Texas, the wintered cattle free of the malady could be sold for six times the slightly higher maintenance cost. Moreover, the nutritious Panhandle grasses proved to fatten yearling south Texans some one hundred to two hundred pounds more than grasses of their birth country.[25]

Two years after McCarty drifted the first 3,000-plus herd onto LIT grass, the *Dodge City Times* reported that 120,000 cattle roamed the Panhandle. On the Canadian, Bates and Beals ran 30,000 and Torrey and Littlefield 8,000 each. Cattle were flooding into the region. During these two years, Littlefield more than doubled his number. He would repeat that increase in the next biennium. To this, the LIT's natural increase contributed up to 4,500 calves yearly.[26]

Counting total numbers alone missed a smaller figure more important to the future of the cattle business. It was the number of blooded bulls being brought onto the range to upgrade both the quality and the quantity of beef per animal. Shorthorn breeds—Durham cattle—came first. "A few short-horns, from Kentucky, have, years ago, been taken to Texas with an effort to improve the native Mexican stock," Lewis F. Allen wrote in *American Cattle: Their History, Breeding and Management*, "but we hear of no results worth noting; nor can there be much improvement, so long as they retain their wild and vagrant habits." Results soon came. "It is beginning to dawn upon the understanding of the Lone Star ranchmen that his only hope, as well as imperative duty toward himself, lies in improving the blood of his stock even at the expense of numbers," Joseph McCoy proclaimed in 1874. Three years later, Charles Goodnight trailed one hundred Durhams to the Palo Duro. Another three years and Driskill threw shorthorns into his bunch.[27]

Better than any shorthorn, Allen asserted, was the Hereford. "They feed kindly, are thrifty in growth, mature early—at three and four years old—and prove well on the butchers' block." Five years after Allen wrote, Hereford cattle were introduced into Texas. Two years later, in 1878, William Susan "Sude" Ikard brought the breed to the Panhandle. They thrived. That brought more. In 1880 William McDole Lee and Albert Eugene Reynolds brought seven carloads to their LE Ranch across the Canadian southwest of the LIT. C. C. Slaughter, who would turn heads a decade later with the prices he would pay for champion white-face bulls, placed the first Herefords on his southern plains ranch in 1880. The ranchers found, as Hereford breeder and Chicago businessman T. L. Miller of Illinois proclaimed, that Herefords "are the most hardy; they are the best grazers; they mature earlier; they are nearer the ground; they are more compact; they have more hair; they have thicker and softer hides; although shorter on the leg, they are better travelers, and as grazers they become higher-fleshed and riper steers; they carry their flesh to market with less shrinkage; they are heavier topped steers, and the best animal in the family of Herefords is the steer." Then, after the hard winter of 1880–81 showed "the white-faces as the one breed best capable of facing grief," the *Clarendon News* declared with enthusiasm unrestrained in mid-1881 that Herefords were not just coming but had already reached "the zenith of their popularity."[28]

George Littlefield noticed. Without newspaper fanfare, he set about joining the switch to blooded bulls. Though Herefords would become his mainstay, evidently he began with shorthorn sires that, the *Austin Daily Statesman* trumpeted, had "done more to improve the beef producing ability of the United States than all other breeds."[29] Littlefield worked fast. The year after Lee and Reynolds brought the first one hundred or so Herefords to the Canadian, Littlefield had double that number of blooded bulls in his herd. Not only that, the 254 outnumbered their longhorn counterparts two to one.

In May 1881 Littlefield was working with the roundup to return to their home grounds cattle that had drifted off during storms of the previous winter. It was hard work. He was thirty-nine years old, and apprehensive over his losses. Moreover, he was "having a hard time of it this Spring, living rough," he wrote Alice. Maybe he felt the exertion more strongly as he thought about his future in ranching. Should he sell the LIT? In Kansas City, while Littlefield was on his way to the Panhandle, Augustus H. Johnson, a former livestock agent for the Santa Fe Railroad, approached him with an offer to buy the ranch lock, stock, and barrel. Johnson represented C. C. Quinlan and Alexander Frazier of Kansas City, who in turn represented the vanguard of moneyed men from Great Britain who saw a bonanza for investment in the American cattle business. Indeed, James S. Brisbin's *The Beef Bonanza, or, How to Get Rich on the Plains, Being a Description of Cattle-Growing, Sheep-Farming, Horse-Raising, and Dairying in the West*, published that very year in Philadelphia and London, blared that beckoning word—bonanza. It wasn't the first siren song. Changes in beef consumption in Britain focused interest on America's expanding cattle range. And just at that time developments in the science of refrigeration were providing the means for transporting meat over long distances and long periods without spoilage. Despite the British calling the product "dead meat," importation and sales skyrocketed in two short years from 134,000 pounds in 1875 to 49 million pounds in 1877. To study the phenomenon, *The Scotsman* sent James MacDonald across the Atlantic. His *Food from the Far West, or, American Agriculture with Special Reference to the Beef Production and Importation of Dead Meat from America to Great Britain* resulted in appointment of a Parliamentary Commission to study the matter. When the researchers reported that annual profits of 33 percent could be expected, investors jumped to get in on the opportunity. Between 1880 and 1886 thirteen companies organized in Great Britain to heave money into the American cattle business.[30]

Scots led. The Scottish American Mortgage Company, organized in 1880, created the Prairie Cattle Company with a grand vision of fashioning a range covering millions of acres. Early in 1881 agents of what one historian called "the mother of the British companies" fanned out, contacting the Jones brothers on the Purgatoire River in southeastern Colorado, the Hall brothers on the Dry Cimarron in northeastern New Mexico, and George Littlefield and Tom Bugbee on the Canadian in the Texas Panhandle. What a spread the combined JJ, Cross L, LIT, and Quarter Circle T ranches would make![31]

"I have been offered a very good price for my Beeves," Littlefield wrote, as though it was just another topic, on the second page of a long letter of May 7, 1881, to his wife. "If I was to Sell then I would have nothing to do this Summer after I got through delivering." He was not a man to do nothing, especially when there was money to be made. And the LIT was making money. "I will be able to ship off from sixty to seventy-five thousand dollars worth of Beef this year. And every year after this I will be able to trim off Fifty thousand Dollars worth," he calculated. "So you See only a few years and the Ranch would pay for itself." Clearly the prospect pleased him.[32]

Maybe it was to lessen the chances of a sale if the Scots realized that the ranch could be expected to net a profit of only around 20, not 33 percent per year. Maybe it was to ensure that a sale would enable him to take care of the family and live comfortably for the rest of his life. Maybe the most compelling reason for setting a figure on the LIT was the change Panhandle ranchers could see coming. First, those like Littlefield along the Panhandle's western boundary were about to lose some of the free land on which their cattle grazed. Needing a larger capitol, the land-rich and money-poor State of Texas had provided for trading three million acres of public land in the lightly populated Panhandle and South Plains to fund the construction. The acreage included at a minimum the LIT headquarters and rights north of the river that Phelps had acquired three years earlier. When the Capitol Board approved a design for the building in May 1881 and advertised for a contractor to erect the grand edifice, Littlefield knew that the days were numbered for his use of the western part of his range. Second, then, as cattlemen followed the LE Ranch in acquiring title to land, remaining on the LIT would necessitate diverting thousands of dollars from the profit-making business of trading cattle to investing in pasture for the animals. That would simultaneously increase his operating cost and diminish his return.[33] Whatever drove him to it, Littlefield set a price on the ranch of a handsome $230,000 cash.

On June 21, 1881, Littlefield's thirty-ninth birthday, the buyer accepted the rancher's terms. A month to the day later, for $248,024.50, George Littlefield turned over "all right to what is commonly known as the Littlefield ranch situated in Oldham and Potter counties, together with all privileges, rights of range, wagons, machines, implements, guns, saddles, equipage, outfit, &c." and something more than 17,000 cattle (about 13 percent of the roughly 226,000 head in the Panhandle), including 113 Texas longhorn bulls and 254 graded bulls, 250 horses, and 1,602 head of through cattle on their way to Kansas.[34]

Dodge City's *Ford County Globe* pronounced this "the most prominent sale of the season." The *Fort Griffin Echo* reported, not entirely accurately, that "Ten years ago Capt. Littlefield sold his farm in Gonzales county for $2,000, which constituted the whole amount of his wealth. He is now worth over $300,000." Watching developments from his saddle, Shelton Dowell marveled that "this is the fastest money making business I ever was in."[35]

And Dowell could see only the half of it. For the Scottish investors with their eyes fixed on impossible profits, money was no object.[36] They offered Bugbee $175,000 for his rights and 12,500 cattle. On his wife's advice, Bugbee refused to sell, and the following year accepted double the amount from a competing British firm. For the 300 horses, 55,000 cattle, and water rights owned or claimed by the JJ Ranch, the Prairie Cattle Company paid $625,000. Figured at half the price for which he was then sending a herd to Kansas, Littlefield's cattle alone should have been worth just under $200,000. Though he would learn it only later, for his LIT the Prairie in fact paid the brokers about double the $230,000 Littlefield had asked. Years afterward, the Prairie management discovered the double dealing but never recovered all it lost in the fraud.[37]

What George Littlefield had accomplished in cattle during the decade that culminated with the sale was extraordinary by any standard. Whether he entered the cattle business with $2,000 as the newspaper said, with $5,500 as the Dun and Company correspondents believed, or with the $3,600 he calculated, he had not just pulled himself back from financial collapse but had built a modest sum into a fortune dwarfing those of all but the most successful men in the business (fig. 13).

8

A LITTLE BIT WIDER

As spring warmed toward summer in 1881, George Littlefield felt he needed a change. Open-range ranching, he wrote Alice from the grueling spring roundup on the Canadian River in the Texas Panhandle, "is a very rough life." "They move around a little faster than in our Country," Shelton Dowell described it, "never start any where unless in full speed. It seems mighty rough on horses & men too. But they say that is the only way to work this Country." Whether or not it was the only way, Littlefield knew it was "not suited to any one of my age and one that can be more comfortable." With a quarter million dollars, that summer he could afford to think about comfort. In one lump sum he had not just far more money than he ever expected to have but so much more that he told Alice he could consider "clear[ing] up my business now so as to have time for us to locate at some place and improve us a nice House."

Yet the thought of retiring and settling down troubled him. Thirty-nine years old, he could not picture himself being idle. He could concentrate on developing his central Texas ranching operation, but should he continue in ranching at all? "While I like a Ranch, and there has been good pay in it to me, yet there is some things about the business which I do not like," he wrote, without spelling out any of them. And even if he continued ranching, his central Texas operation could not quickly put the new money to profit. What should he do with the cash? As conflicted and uncertain as he was, George Littlefield was not a man to flounder in indecision. In sorting things out, he came to realize the continuity that had taken him to the LIT sale and would continue to propel his life. It was, he said years later, that "the more money a man makes, the more he has to make, that a man's world opens up a little bit wider with each deal and demands become heavier."[1]

Whatever about the ranching business bothered George Littlefield, it was not investing in ranchland. In October 1878, while declining to pay seventy-five cents per acre for title to about 5 percent of his year-old Panhandle free range, he gave three times more per acre for the 3,745-acre Foster Ranch, plus seven dollars per head for two hundred cows in the JF Under Crescent brand. Lying between the San

Marcos and Guadalupe Rivers in Gonzales County more than three miles north of the Old Littlefield Place, the property would be a breeding ranch. Experience had taught cattlemen that a larger proportion of cows produced calves in the warm Texas climate than did she-stuff on northern ranges. They saw that cows in central and south Texas dropped more calves per female. And they were seeing that larger ranches reduced the operating cost per head. Consequently, Littlefield enlarged the Foster by more than a third to nearly six thousand acres.[2]

To manage the ranch, Littlefield might have called on Shelton Dowell. But after the 1873 cattle proposition evaporated, Shelt had become a storekeeper. Littlefield gave no thought to Theo Harral, who had tried making a go of a mercantile business in town and failed. Littlefield had moved his brother-in-law back to his farm to bail him out a second time. Nor did George consider his brother William, whose dedication to wasting himself tormented the older brother almost beyond his patriarchal tolerance. The two men could not have been more opposite in their approaches to living. William drank to excess. He gambled. To support his habit, he mortgaged his property, burned through money George provided to support his household, sued family members to get more, and owed everyone who would loan him money. And that was not the worst of it. William's dissipation ensnared their mother. Maybe it was Mildred's motherly instinct; maybe it was her pleasure in the company of her attentive daughter-in-law; maybe it was enjoying William's two children, especially his firstborn, who was named for her. Whatever drew her, Mildred took up residence at the rundown old farm with her youngest son and his family. Enduring the deprivation and witnessing the dissipation was not the way George envisioned his sixty-plus-year-old mother enjoying her last years. "John," George unburdened himself in six tortured pages to his half brother in Mississippi, "I never had any thing that give me half the truble as it does."[3]

Instead, Uncle George gave the job and a one-third interest in the profits to Shelt's younger first cousin twenty-three-year-old John Wilburn "Will" White, Phelps's older brother. Born on July 22, 1854, the second child and oldest son of Thomas and Martha White, Will grew up on his father's farm and attended the Presbyterian Tehuacana Academy (later renamed Trinity University) for a year or so before, at seventeen, he began cowboying on Littlefield's 1871 drive. Rather than sticking with cattle, Will then clerked for Dilworth and Littlefield and for Shelt Dowell, taking time off only once to help drive a Littlefield herd to Dodge City. But Will wanted to make more money than clerking and cowboying paid. Gambling failed him. Though squandering time and money in games of chance made his uncle wary of him, Will had a redeeming trait. "I always had a saving screw in my head," he said. With the nest egg he accumulated, Will talked his

Uncle George into buying one of the two livery stables in Gonzales for him to run. "There was big money" in livery stables, Harrison McClure recalled, and the partners made a tidy profit when after one year they sold out for Will to take charge of the Foster Ranch.[4]

The Foster demanded all the cowboying skill Phelps White's older brother and his hands could muster. Enclosed within a rail fence, the ranch was nothing like the open Panhandle range. Rather, it was "the brushiest pasture you ever seen," recalled Theo Harral's son, Edgar, who was a fourteen-year-old runaway from school when Uncle George sent him to the ranch to begin cowboying. Long adapted to such terrain, wild longhorns by nature took shelter in thickets during the day and emerged into open country at night to graze. And they learned from repetition. "We had to catch cattle with hounds," he said. "A cow gets awful smart. They would get in the brush and never move when they had been got up a few times." Littlefield's hunting dogs came to serve a double purpose. "A man wouldn't think it, but them dogs would sure bring them [cattle] to the corral."[5]

As George Littlefield thought things through, the difficulty of working cattle on the Foster Ranch and the hard life for cowboys and horses on the LIT Ranch, along with the other considerations that argued for quitting ranching, did not outweigh two reasons for continuing in the business. The more immediate was the need to invest advantageously his sudden mountain of cash. Sure, he could lend it out. And to cattlemen friends, including James Monroe "Doc" Day, Jesse Driskill, James F. Ellison, John W. Gamel, John Lytle, and Seth Mabry, hunting money for their own investment opportunities, he loaned "considerable." Speculation on trail herds nearing Dodge City brought quick return from a portion but increased the pressure to find good long-term investments for his mounting pile of cash. "It seems when a person has money that Everybody wants to beat him out of it," Littlefield wrote as he struggled to rid himself of the vultures.[6]

The more deep-seated reason to continue ranching was his responsibility for his family. Ranches provided places where the businessman could employ nephews. Employing nephews positioned the patriarch to look after them all. The family knew it. "If he has as much money and property as I hear he has he needs good young men to work for him and he can help them greatly. Try and please him if you can," John Dowell summed it up for his brother, Shelton. Shelton just then needed looking after—needed employment to replace his failed dry goods business. Managing the Foster Ranch would get him back into profitable cattle in a location where he could continue courting the woman he would marry a year later. Will White needed looking after too. A situation on the frontier far from any town would employ Will's cattle strength while curbing his penchant for spending on the good life. Will's brother Phelps, by contrast, needed opportunity. "Phelps is a man. So far comes right up to the mark," Littlefield approved of the twenty-year-old after watching him for two years. "I am going [to] make him well off yet,"[7] he vowed. And he did.

Central Texas was not the place to invest heavily and grow in ranching, though. Its confines lacked the expansion potential of the open range. In his heart, then, George Littlefield knew what he had to do. But he had known it all along. The sentence in his May 7, 1881, letter to Alice first saying he might open a ranch in New Mexico Territory followed the sentence first announcing the offer to buy the LIT. Though for nearly a year he would doubt his decision to sell, hardly a month after he relinquished the Panhandle property he began looking for a location to replace it.[8]

After rejecting a site near Las Vegas, New Mexico, about two hundred miles due west of the LIT, perhaps because the carrying capacity of the country had been reduced by overstocking, Littlefield focused on the watershed of the southward flowing Pecos River. The Pecos "run lots of water in them days, and it was really good water. It was muddy all the time; it wasn't salty like it is now," Edgar Harral looked back to the good times a half century earlier. Paralleling the Rio Grande that bisects New Mexico to its west, the Pecos for much of its journey drains a treeless, rolling prairie approximately ninety miles wide between the Sacramento, Jicarilla, and Gallinas Mountains on the west and the high plains on the east. The monotony of the grassy expanse gives way on the west side of the river to heaving foothills and on the east side to some sand and gypsum hills and a few canyons where arroyos emptying the prairie cut through the bluffs fronting the river valley. Crooked, never exceptionally wide even when its valley stretched three miles across, and often shallow, the river looked placid. Looks were deceiving. Cow-punchers feared two things, cowboy James F. Hinkle declared, emphasizing the two in capital letters: the PECOS RIVER and RATTLESNAKES. Charles Goodnight and Oliver Loving learned that about the river on their first drive in 1866. Quicksand and pools of stagnant alkali water decimated the herd they drove establishing the Goodnight-Loving Trail that in turn initiated the era of the rancher and cowboy in southeastern New Mexico. From that first drive, Goodnight hated the Pecos. It was, he said, "the graveyard of the cowman's hopes."[9]

Be that as it may, Goodnight not only continued driving cattle along the river but established the first ranch beside it. For six years he worked on the Pecos. While most Texas cattlemen after the Civil War pursued markets in the meat-starved northern states, Goodnight and Loving took their beeves west to New Mexico to supply four-year-old Fort Sumner on the Pecos and the eight thousand Indians incarcerated on the adjacent Bosque Redondo Reservation. So successful was their first venture, despite the animals they lost to the river, that they determined to continue serving the market and to look for other outlets farther north. Consequently, the partners sought a place along the river where they could receive and dispatch herds. The site they selected was a stretch of flat land on the east side of the river, where the stream on its west side bowed gently away from a low bluff line on the east, creating an oval of some five hundred acres. It was a fine place for working cattle. Bosque Grande they named the location, for the grove of cottonwood trees, huge falling remnants of which stood through the twentieth century beside stream beds the Pecos had abandoned along the site's southern extent. By the time Goodnight relinquished the place, about fifty miles south of Fort Sumner, he had put it on the map—literally. Not five years after the cattlemen named the Bosque, Samuel Augustus Mitchell sited it on the small map of Arizona and New Mexico he published a half a continent away in Philadelphia (fig. 11).

In 1871 Goodnight abandoned Bosque Grande to Texan John Simpson Chisum, who had become familiar with the place from delivering herds. Chisum developed the Bosque into the headquarters of the first breeding ranch in southern New Mexico. The "cattle king," as territorial newspapers soon styled him, loosed some twenty thousand Jinglebob cattle (so called for the dangling ear mark that was more distinctive than Chisum's Long Rail brand) on a range stretching probably one hundred miles down the Pecos. By 1875, when he left the Bosque for better water south on the river's South Spring tributary near Roswell, Chisum had what he called trouble. "I can not dispose of my stock as fast as it increases," he said. In four years, twenty thousand head enjoying the plenteous grass had multiplied by three times to sixty thousand head.[10]

The increase reflected the expanding cattle industry in New Mexico. After Goodnight and Loving showed profits could be made there, cattle by the tens of thousands pounded the trails into and through the territory. At first they came in consequence of Texas ranchers' desperation to pasture cattle they could not sell following the Panic of 1873. In 1874 alone, around 110,000 beeves plodded by Roswell on their way up the Pecos. Though only a small handful of adobe buildings made up the settlement not yet ten years in existence, Roswell nevertheless was a welcome sight for outfits needing to replenish supplies. Though most of the passing cattle were headed to market, plenty remained to stock pastures. By 1880–81 around three hundred thousand head grazed the thirteen million acres of southeastern New Mexico grass; in 1884 one-third more (four hundred thousand); and by 1889 the region had become the second most densely stocked (indeed, overstocked) American range.[11]

After Chisum the vacant Bosque headquarters passed through hands to Ella Lea Calfee, sister of Roswell founder Joseph C. Lea.[12] If she meant to go into ranching, she had prime property for it. Around the time she acquired the location in the fall of 1881, George Littlefield dispatched Phelps White to the Pecos region to search for a location to replace the LIT. Two considerations likely topped his concerns.

One was rustlers, whom the National Live Stock Association so elegantly styled as "enterprising western men of loose ideas about the rights of property . . . who regarded as a 'dead letter' that part of the tenth commandment that tells us we shall not covet our neighbor's ox." With so many Chisum cattle ranging along the Pecos, stealing them had become, as one historian termed it, "a popular pastime." Rustling was easy. On the open range, thieves had little difficulty appropriating branded cattle that strayed off unfenced pastures and that grazed out of sight of cowboys riding line to keep the beeves on home ground. But when they were caught, justice often came swiftly. "Boy, in later years there was so many durned cow rustlers and hoss thieves hanged from the limbs of them cottonwood trees" at Bosque Grande, reminisced an old-line rider named Shorty, that "the grove came to be plumb ha'nted. Night horses staked out with a rope would get scared, break loose, and run off. . . . I've heard cowpunchers claim they could hear . . . sounds like someone gasping for breath with a rope around his neck."[13]

Among the outlaws, Billy the Kid raised appropriating horses and cattle to a way of life in New Mexico and the Texas Panhandle in the very years in which Littlefield was growing his LIT. For the National Live Stock Association, a quarter century after his death, Billy was counted as one of the two most notorious of his kind in all the Great Plains. Phelps White knew the Kid. Though their one recorded meeting was amiable, Billy did not let sociability interfere with business. He helped himself to steers of the LIT and its LX neighbors. The ranches lay close to the New Mexico line, across which the young rustler had buyers who asked no questions about his title to the cattle he brought for sale. In the fall of 1880, the Texas ranchers had had enough. The Panhandle Stock Association dispatched a party, made up largely of LIT and LX cowboys, to recover the lost stock. In the posse rode twenty-two-year-old Littlefield half-nephew John Henry White III—"Little Johnny White," his Mississippi neighbors called him informally. Whether or not he sought adventure when he left Mississippi to punch cattle on the LIT, he found it in the hunt for Billy the Kid. Some 250 miles southwest in White Oaks, New Mexico, on the west side of Capitan Mountain, the posse discovered hides of stolen LIT cattle. But learning that Billy, who had been in town only three days earlier, threatened to wipe them out if he came upon them with his force larger than theirs, the group returned without encountering their quarry. Even so, White never tired of recounting the story of his ride to the men who gathered for conversation in the Longtown, Mississippi, corner store. The experience became so much a part of "Little Johnny" White that his obituaries sixty-three years later highlighted it. If continuing trouble with the young outlaw figured in Littlefield's initial thinking about a location for his new ranch, fate intervened three weeks after the LIT sale was completed and before Littlefield dispatched Phelps to New Mexico. In a split second of hesitation on a dark night in Pete Maxwell's home in Fort Sumner, Billy died as he lived—by the gun. Though never eradicated, cattle theft no longer afflicted Pecos ranchers as it had.[14]

The most important consideration, of course, was the country. Plentiful rain in a period of unusual bounty had thickened the carpet of nutritious grasses and raised the tallest to brush riders' stirrups. "It was the finest country I ever rode over," Edgar Harral recalled his first sight of the immense green expanse stretching to the mountains, which become increasingly distinct as the sun sets behind them. "Upon the second bottom [back from the river] and over the foot-hills the pasturage . . . was very good and water was plentiful in springs which sank before they reached the river," Clarence W. Gordon confirmed Edgar's memory. But "the immediate river valley of the Pecos, from latitude 34-20 down to 33-30 [roughly Fort Sumner to Roswell], was nearly bare of vegetation," Gordon wrote in the cattle section of the 1880 U.S. Census. In six years, Goodnight's and Chisum's cattle had "wholly eaten off" every blade of grass at Bosque Grande.[15]

From his travels throughout this cattleman's paradise, cleared of Indians and buffalo and vacant for appropriation, Phelps saw one other singular advantage making the Bosque Grande the best location on which to center Littlefield's new ranch despite the bare river bottom. It had a good four-room house, stables, corrals, and store building left from Chisum's days.

Having settled on a site encompassing a range unclaimed by any cattleman, stretching maybe fifty miles on both sides of the river, beginning at Chisum's north line about fifteen miles below the Bosque (approximately where the railroad crosses the river), Phelps traveled the six hundred miles to Gonzales to present his findings to Uncle George. Beside him rode Thomas David White, the third of the three White brothers. Though two and a half years Phelps's junior—born on June 20, 1859—Tom had gotten his start in the cattle business with Phelps in capturing the Circle 9 calves in 1871. About ten years later, he joined Phelps and cousin Little Johnny White cowboying for Uncle George on the LIT. From his arrival on the ranch, Tom fit into the outfit. He was outgoing. More important, he showed the cattle, ranching, and business savvy that distinguished all three of Thomas

Jefferson White's sons. Those brothers, said Roswell newspaperman Cecil Bonney, "literally 'thought cattle'" (fig. 8).[16]

After hearing Phelps's and Tom's report, George Littlefield naturally formed a business relationship with his nephews to operate the New Mexico property. But departing from his practice of constituting partnerships, he thought to join the contemporary convention and incorporate a company—until he ran into New Mexico government red tape. On March 3, 1882, he and the brothers signed articles of agreement written in Uncle's bold hand creating the Littlefield Cattle Company. Having sold the LIT brand with the Panhandle ranch, the company's brand would be **LFD**, burned into the right hip, ribs, and shoulder.[17] Littlefield would put up $100,000 to stock and fund operation of the ranch for a year, for which he would hold a 75 percent interest. For their 25 percent interest, the brothers would put up $25,000, and Phelps would manage the ranch. But that day, together, the brothers had only $10,000. True to his word that in making business deals Uncle accorded nephews no preferential treatment, Littlefield had them execute promissory notes for the balance at 9 percent annual interest. Then, so that all three could know the condition and profitability of the ranch, the agreement required the keeping of multiple sets of books. This would be no hip pocket operation as was common in trailing days. Books on the ranch would account for "all cattle and Horses put upon the Ranch, As well as all calves Branded thereon, Also . . . all cattle Killed on the Ranch, or sold, or Driven to market from it, Also . . . a regular Set of Books that the Expense of and Standing of the Ranch may at any time be determined." Littlefield's set in Gonzales would account for cattle sales, the final decisions on which he reserved to himself.[18]

Continuing the work begun on the LIT of putting more meat on Littlefield cattle, the agreement called for purchase of two hundred "good grade yearling Shorthorns or Hereford Bulls." More than just personal interest in upgrading the quality of his beef drove Littlefield's attention to developing heavier animals. Not three weeks earlier he had been appointed to a committee on the improvement of stock. This was no routine assignment. Rather, the cattlemen of Texas, meeting in Austin in mid-February 1882, placed in the hands of the committee's five members nothing less than the future of the cattle business. Rangy Texas longhorns were losing value. Year by year their ability to get themselves to market mattered less, and the amount and quality of meat each one carried mattered more. No issue on the minds of Texas cattlemen ranked higher than ensuring the marketability of their product.

Change was coming—had to come—in the commerce of cattle. Individual initiative had created the business. The Charles Goodnights and John Lytles established cattle trails to markets where none existed before. The Ike Pryors and

Seth Mabrys fashioned businesses from trailing cattle between ranch and market. The Jesse Driskills and C. C. Slaughters converted open grassland into ranches of nearly unimaginable breadth stocked with nearly innumerable cattle. The Doc Days made money just trading beeves. Like them all, George Littlefield built his operation trusting his own knowledge and instinct telling him when to move, in which direction and how far, and when not to move at all. But the time had come when acting individually and in partnerships no longer sufficed for meeting the challenges of the industry they had created.

If cattlemen from north, central, and south, from the trans Pecos, Permian Basin, south plains, and Panhandle regions of Texas, and in all phases of the business could anticipate only dimly the extent of the change coming, they knew full well that they needed to direct it as much as they could. Forty of them, including Slaughter of the Long S, John Simpson of the Hashknifes, and Samuel Burk Burnett of the Four Sixes, had pointed the way five years before, in 1877, when they joined together to form the first cattlemen's association in Texas. Combating theft, facilitating cooperation in open-range roundups, and inspecting trail herds to return to home ranches cattle that had strayed into them—these three most immediate rancher concerns had driven creation of the Northwest Texas Cattle Raisers Association. The same motives led to organization three years later of the Panhandle Stock Association that, in an initial action, had sent the posse with Johnny White after rustler Billy the Kid. "District" associations as these "have accomplished a noble work," the *Austin Statesman* complimented them, but their activities naturally were limited to the boundaries of each district. Some matters required confederation on a larger scale. Disease, leasing of public lands, trail restrictions, transportation (railroad freight rates and the conditions of animals riding the rails), fencing, and perhaps most important of all, improving the animals' quality headed the list. In the state that produced not only more cattle than any other but also more horses and sheep and ranked second only in burros, these were interests not just of cattlemen but in fact of stockmen broadly. Not just of stockmen broadly but in fact of Texans all, the *Austin Statesman* reported. "To no influence does Texas owe more, in its present day of great prosperity, than to the stockmen of the Lone Star State," proclaimed the paper in preparing its readers to receive the stockmen converging on the capital city in mid-February 1882 to form the first statewide organization in their industry—the Texas Live Stock Association (TLSA).[19]

In creating the TLSA, to whatever extent they sensed it then, the delegates were making history. Looking at the eighty-year era of cattle raising, 1847–1927, seasoned livestock reporter and historian Frank Reeves Sr. discerned four periods. The exponential increase in the number of free-ranging cattle in the state easily characterized the first. The second, 1867–87, distinguished by the rise and decline of trailing, focused on marketing that volume of cattle. The third two-decade period, the one in which the founders of the TLSA were organizing themselves, was, in Reeves's words, "the most volatile" of the four. The passing of the open range into fenced ranches that facilitated upgrading herds and issues related to transportation—from railroads to refrigeration—distinguished it. The 275 delegates representing 116 counties who assembled in Millett's Opera House on February 14, 1882, meant to take the next step in advancing the course and conduct of their business. And in four days they would set in motion the transition between the third marketing-trailing period and the fourth beef improvement–transportation period.[20]

Until the longhorn and shorthorn, horse, and sheep raisers of Texas came together to create a statewide organization, George Littlefield, though certainly a man on the make, nevertheless was simply one among many trailing contractors, ranchers, cattle and horse traders, even personal bankers. But as the Texas cattlemen had been building toward this broader level of activity, so his prominence among them had been rising with it. In the deliberations of the TLSA, he stood out.

The *Austin Statesman*'s lengthy convention coverage named far fewer than half of those attending beyond their listing as delegates. Of those mentioned for appointment to a committee, fewer than half appeared again. George Littlefield, by contrast, in his first experience participating in the work of an industry organization, made news in each of the four days and in both aspects of the meeting. Of the committees constituted to tackle the ten broad issues of the industry, President James Miller, the Gonzales attorney who had represented Littlefield after the Watson shooting, appointed him one of five with John Lytle under the gavel of ex–lieutenant governor (and Terry Ranger) Joseph Sayers to make recommendations on stock improvement. More important in this first meeting even than beginning work on the ten most vital issues was providing a robust structure to support that work. Littlefield received appointment to not one, not two, but three structure committees. If the basis of representation group credentialing all the stockmen was the easiest of the three assignments, appointment to chair the select group to choose an executive committee of twenty-five to guide the organization spoke volumes regarding George Littlefield's standing among his colleagues. Finally, whether or not he expected it, on the final day, the committee for which Littlefield had moved two days earlier charged him and President Miller in a group of six to draft a constitution and bylaws to firm up the organization.[21]

As pleased as they were with the work they had done in forming the Texas Live Stock Association, the stockmen had to feel even better about the money being made in cattle. While prices had been rising during the second half of the 1870s, a combination of factors sent money cascading into the business in 1880, 1881, and 1882. The British headlong rush to own ranching empires made many like Littlefield wealthy. But a rancher did not have to sell his range rights to do well. After cattlemen's initial rush in 1880 to cash in on sale of the 394,000 head trailed to market, prices remained good because the supply diminished. Only 250,000 beeves trailed north in 1881 and 1882, nearly two-fifths fewer each year than the 1880 high. Cattlemen had oversold their herds. Then, in 1882 a short corn crop in the Midwest that increased demand, combined with a mild winter from which cattle emerged heavy and desirable, sent prices climbing. "Those who had raised fat cattle on buffalo grass found themselves in clover," wrote James Cox who saw it all. For cattle that had brought only two dollars per hundredweight a decade earlier, nine cents a pound became the new benchmark. By the head, Texas beeves that had sold for seven dollars in 1880 commanded three and a half times that in 1883. "Everything was rosy and delightful," Cox added, "and many a handsome fortune was made by men who, less than ten years before, had been almost in the depths of despair, with ruin staring them blankly in the face."[22] George Littlefield had been one of them.

Cattlemen became heady. "We find ourselves at the threshold of a new era in the cattle business, not only of Texas, but of the entire Western section of the United States," William Kuykendall told readers of the *Texas Stockman and Farmer*. James S. Brisbin confirmed it. "For the next ten years, I believe cattle-raising will be one of the most lucrative callings in the United States, and those who have the good fortune to be able to engage in it will rapidly grow rich," the *Statesman* in July 1882 quoted Brisbin's 1881 book *The Beef Bonanza, or, How to Get Rich on the Plains*. Texas cattlemen could believe it. "Without some unforeseen disaster," the *Statesman* quoted the *Texas Live Stock Journal*, two months after the stockmen adopted it as their official organ, "West Texas will reap a larger money harvest from the sale of beef cattle this year than ever before."[23]

Seizing the prospect, Littlefield sent at least 10,000 head north in 1882. James F. Ellison trailed double that, probably more. No stranger to the business, in the early 1850s the Central Texan had begun driving herds to the best market of the antebellum years—New Orleans. In the decade after the Civil War, he rose to the heights of the trailing business. A partnership with Seth Mabry and two others dominated cattle trailing in 1875 when the group accounted for two-thirds of the 100,000 to 150,000 head driven north that year. Three years later, a careful observer thought him to be worth more than $100,000 and to have cattle to three times that value on the trail.[24]

To make his killing in the good markets of the early 1880s, Ellison took the risk George Littlefield had taken a decade earlier to reap the greatest profit from his first drive. He borrowed—and heavily. Littlefield joined others in backing him. As the trailing season was ending in August 1882, while Littlefield was in Lockhart for a meeting, he "got to thinking about the money Mr. Ellison owed me—$20,000," and rode the sixteen miles to San Marcos to check on it. Maybe Littlefield was uneasy, since, contrary to what twenty years later he said he never did, he also had guaranteed and thus was liable for an Ellison note. Littlefield's sixth sense served him well. "I was Just in time," he wrote Alice, "as He was preparing to leave Home, I think to try and beat us all out of what He owed." Despite the *Kansas City Price Current* trumpeting the "healthfulness in the trade and confidence in the future most gratifying to western cattle owners," Ellison evidently had badly overextended himself and could not hope to satisfy all of his creditors. Whether or not he accurately assessed Ellison's intentions, Littlefield flew into action.[25]

A cattleman might think about "us all," but each took care of himself first. When he differentiated between "damn rascals" and the legitimate transactions "Big Men" made among themselves, Abel Head "Shanghai" Pierce (his nickname coming from his long neck that reminded friends of a Shanghai rooster) must have spoken for his friend Littlefield too. Styling his a legitimate big man's transaction, Shanghai described a move he made when, like Littlefield, he became privy to information:

> Dillard Fant once inspected a herd belonging to "Old Man" Fleming. I heard that Dillard was going to offer the "Old Man" twelve thousand dollars for all the cows he had in a certain brand. I slipped down there before Dillard could make the offer, and hurried up and bought every critter in that brand, except one poor one. Then Fleming, who buys his own drinks when he should have been buying me one, too, wrote a bill of sale specifying "every cow I own," and he took Fant's money. . . . Yes sir: that was a square deal . . . and besides that, Fleming "set-em-up" so often to keep me from telling it, that I almost drank myself to death.[26]

Littlefield remained with Ellison until he believed he had worked out a deal "by which I will save myself." Some would style it a careful businessman's transaction; those less attentive to their investments probably reckoned it a damn rascal's work. For canceling all of Ellison's indebtedness to him and covering what he owed in the cattleman's behalf, Littlefield bought two properties for $55,000. One was Ellison's Dinner Bell Ranch of about 13,000 acres stretched along and east of upper Plum

Creek, about fifteen miles south of Austin and only eight miles east of the shipping station of Kyle. The other was a 13,000-acre Pedernales River pasture. Adding in cattle from the places bought on equally favorable terms, Littlefield's payout apparently totaled somewhere around $90,000. Ellison wanted more. Littlefield cursed him. At the same time, though, before other creditors, evidently including even friends Jesse Driskill and Doc Day, might "catch me," Littlefield traveled 130-plus miles without sleep to file in three counties the deeds giving him title to those of Ellison's assets he had marked for himself and others he bought outright, including the Ellisons' Presidio County ranch.[27]

Ellison never recovered fully from his losses. Littlefield, on the other hand, used the Plum Creek property to get Shelton Dowell back into ranching. Uncle installed Shelt on the Foster and moved Will White to the Dinner Bell. How do you like it? How many cattle do you intend to pasture? Phelps White asked his cousin. The questions went to the heart of Shelt's job as manager, his first. Grass was short. The Foster had been overstocked during the summer. With only five acres for each of the two thousand head on the place that fall, it was overstocked still. "Shelt that is what always plays the wild with Pastures," Phelps cautioned. "One will get too many cattle in before he can think about it."[28] Whatever Shelt answered has not survived. But one thing was certain: winter would come—both literally and figuratively. It always does. And it tests resolve and stamina.

In the meantime, cattlemen enjoyed the rosy years. For Littlefield, cattle prices were climbing at the same time that the number of animals carrying LFD, LF Running W, and Bar F brands was continuing to grow (fig. 6). As 1882 reached its close, book count on Littlefield's Central Texas and New Mexico lands tallied some eighteen thousand head. George exulted, writing that he didn't care if prices "go as high as the moon." No wonder. Central Texas land values were rocketing upward right along with cattle prices. Not three months after he bought the Dinner Bell for $3.30 an acre, Littlefield refused to sell it for nearly double that. "Our Country is very prosperous this fall," more so than for several years past, he observed. "Every one feels more confidence all around."[29]

The confidence that enveloped Littlefield marked a dramatic change from his questioning at the time of the LIT sale whether he should continue ranching at all. A year later, he reversed himself and questioned his judgment in selling the LIT. Speculating in cattle and loaning his quarter million in cash had made money alright. But fretting over the difficulty of finding long-term investment opportunities had caused him to scorn the sale as "a great mistake." Ranching, more than just managing money, was his life. He had become "anxious to get Settled down once more in a Ranch business."[30]

In fact, by the time he expressed his anxiety in April 1882, he was closer to "being settled," as he called it, than he knew. He would see it first when he rode into the Bosque Grande headquarters and learned Phelps's plans for developing the operation. He would see it second when, only days later, he topped the caprock at Mescalero Spring. Spread before him farther than the eye could see lay a carpet of lush plains grass that had sustained buffalo in greater numbers than he would ever have in cattle. And the expanse lay vacant, inviting a rancher confident of himself, of his men, and of his operation to establish range rights over it.

PHELPS HAS DONE WELL

Optimism stirred the five hundred cattlemen who converged on Austin in early February 1883 for the second annual meeting of the Texas Live Stock Association. Demand for beef was growing worldwide. Producing meatier animals that matured faster, George Littlefield's Improvement of Stock Committee reported on February 8, was the Texas cattleman's ticket to remaining competitive in satisfying the hunger for beef and consequently to building their prosperity. Breed out the characteristics of longhorns and breed in the qualities of Herefords, Durhams, Shorthorns, Polled Angus—any meatier strain. Rather than rehash arguments in the livestock press over the strengths and weaknesses of different breeds, Littlefield's committee fixed on the *benefit* of upgrading their product.

Whether or not Littlefield, or any of his colleagues, thought particularly about it just then, the extent to which any one of them would profit from the benefit of improved characteristics depended on the number of better animals the cattleman could raise. In a day when most cattle on the Texas and New Mexico range were fattened on native grass, increasing the number of animals required expanding times over the number of acres available to nourish them. With his newly acquired claim to about as many hundreds of square miles of Pecos River basin pasture as he had of Canadian River range, George Littlefield appeared to be well positioned to implement his committee's recommendation. How well would hinge on how closely New Mexico's cattle country compared to the committee's description of Texas's cattle range.

To Texas cattlemen the report gave every reason to understand that they were superbly located to take advantage of their opportunity. A battery of questions, to which the answers were obvious and positive, gave TLSA members reason after reason after reason to embrace the recommendation. "Is there anything in our climate or soil, or grasses that will prevent the stock breeders of Texas at once advancing to the front and building up for themselves and their posterity a trade in which they will scarcely have a rival?" one question asked. "Our winters as compared with those of Europe and of many portions of the United States are not only short but mild," the answer followed. Maybe in a normal year, but not this one. After the stockmen dutifully approved the document, they fled the frigid hall, summarily abandoning the first day's agenda.[1]

Instead of short and mild, the arctic cold of early 1883 intensified in what was seeming to be a new normal. In 1879 intense cold killed three-fourths of the sheep in Gonzales County. In 1880 frost destroyed the potato crop. But the ferocity of the blast in mid-February 1883 surpassed them both. It froze cattle. Bob Houston, with whom Littlefield had partnered in trailing, lost three thousand head. Littlefield lost a similar number—nearly one-fifth of his Texas and New Mexico herds combined. Will White on the Dinner Bell despaired and wanted out of cattle ranching altogether. Uncle refused to allow it. Staking him with four thousand beeves, Littlefield told his nephew to join his brothers in New Mexico.[2] Then, not yet having seen for himself his Littlefield Cattle Company ranch on the Pecos, George Littlefield headed for the Bosque Grande too.

After Uncle George created the Littlefield Cattle Company with Phelps and Tom White the previous March, Phelps returned straightaway to New Mexico to secure possession of the headquarters ground. Littlefield was anxious for it. "No way to handle a large amount of money to a profit outside of cattle," he declared, by which he meant a ranch operation on the scale of the LIT. Consequently, for the land claim filed on the 160-acre heart of the property, a day's ride from any settlement, the road to which was nothing but a well-beaten cattle trail, the Littlefield Cattle Company paid, by Phelps's memory, an astounding ten dollars an acre in January 1883. The headquarters and range rights at last theirs, shaping and running the Bosque Grande operation inaugurated with nine thousand head, some that Will White trailed from Gonzales, would shortly become Phelps White's first full test as a ranch manager.[3]

George Littlefield rode into the Bosque Grande Ranch headquarters for the first time on May 14, 1883, a year and a half after Phelps opened its Littlefield era. The country "does not look well," he recorded his first impression. It was dry, very dry. Incessant sun had withered the luxurious grass that had attracted Phelps. Nevertheless, Littlefield saw in the location the potential his nephew had seen. "I think it will be a fine paying Ranch," he added in the next sentence, "if I can get my land all located so as to controle the water." Phelps was certain of it. "If we can only get water where I want it," he had declared expansively in December, "then there is Room here for all of the cattle in Tex." Even so, he had not begun the work. Knowing, as Littlefield's managers did, that effecting goals greater than maintaining routine cattle operations required Uncle's approval first, Phelps had awaited confirmation from the more experienced cowman. Once he received the sanction, Phelps bought out prior claimants and used several of the men to file claims. By summer's end, LFD cattle had range rights to graze some thirty-five miles along and as far back (Phelps estimated fifteen miles) from the river as search for good grass would take them (fig. 12).[4]

The condition of cattle and horses came next. The dogies (pronounced with a long O, cowmen's word for calves) he had bought in Louisiana, shipped by rail to Kyle near the Plum Creek Ranch, as Littlefield called the former Dinner Bell, and had Will White drive to the Bosque to begin stocking the property matured nicely. Phelps credited the country. "Shelt there is no use talking about the differance in this country and that [of central Texas]. . . . I can show you yearling here [born of those Louisiana cows] that are as large as your four year old steers."[5]

To the Louisiana bunch, Phelps had added several herds. In one instance, he had contracted for a bunch, counting on Uncle George to pay for them. When nephew Shelton Dowell wanted to buy cattle, he had to describe the animals to Uncle to obtain his authorization to make the purchase. But Phelps had not asked permission. And every day that passed before Littlefield accepted the commitment, the new manager, remote from the man to whom he must account, became increasingly nervous. The deal turned out to typify the manner in which he and his brothers bought cattle for the Littlefield ranches.

> I had bought them conditionally [for] . . . fourteen thousand dollars. . . .
> I had very little prospect of paying for them, but paid . . . [owner Roger Sikes] a thousand dollars, and then he and I went down the Pecos to Pecos City, and from there over the railroad to [Sikes's home at] Colorado City, where we were to wait until I could catch Major Littlefield, notify him that I had bought the cattle, and he would pay for them. We stayed there about a week trying to catch the Major, who was out receiving more cattle. I was getting uneasy about the matter, as I was still just a boy. But finally one of my messages got to him, and he caught a train and came right up and paid Sikes the thirteen thousand dollars for the cattle and thirty-five head of saddle horses that went in on the deal.[6]

Equally characteristic of Littlefield's way, he gave cash, not promissory notes. Cowman Rufe O'Keefe appreciated what many did not. When inevitable changes in market conditions occurred, cattlemen caught owing more than they could satisfy in cash had to pay with fat cattle. Steers first. If the debt forced selling cows and heifers too, the rancher then shipped off that much of his foundation for rebuilding his herd. Littlefield knew it. In a bad market, he said summarily, "steers would break you."[7]

The number of cattle was one measure of the operation. Quality was another. Fulfilling the Littlefield Cattle Company agreement and, not coincidentally, implementing the Improvement of Stock Committee recommendation, Phelps began buying bulls to improve the herd. He didn't have to go far. "I wish you could see old man [John] Chisoms Ranch and cattle," Phelps described the operation across his southern boundary. The cattle are "the best in the Territory." Chisum prized blooded bulls. He brought in the first registered Herefords in 1878. Herefords quickly came to dominate his herd. One group he brought to his ranch, the contemporary press reported, was "as fine a bunch of animals as ever held down hoofs." For thirty dollars per head, Phelps bought fifty "very nice young Bulls" to upgrade his longhorns. George Littlefield approved.[8]

Before the sun set on his first day at Bosque Grande, Littlefield concluded that "Phelps has done well, and I think He will make money" from the ranch (fig. 10). So pleased was the ranch owner with what he saw that then and there he made two changes in his organization. First, he confirmed Phelps as the manager. Second, he amended the Littlefield Cattle Company charter to reflect the changes in responsibility. Calling the White brothers and Charles McCarty together, as Littlefield told it, he said:

> "Now we will all get well off on this ranch and investment if we will all act right, use good judgement and energy." [Littlefield] said he thought he would Incorporate the New Mexico ranch and wanted them to take an interest. So he called McCarty "how much money have you Mack." "None," he said. Well he had a few cattle, he said. "Well put those in." Littlefield said to him, that he would put him in for $10,000.00 and if he was not satisfied next spring he would give him that and 10% on it and he could get out. "Tom, how much have you got?" He said only $250.00. "Well, you can come in for $18,000.00 stock. And Phelps you have the $10,000 I gave you when I sold the Potter county ranch in 1881. I will put you in for $60,000.00. Now that will be the interest you each will have and I hold the balance."

Totaling the interests, Littlefield assessed his New Mexico place to be worth every bit of the $350,000 valuation he had put on it the previous November.[9]

At last to his satisfaction fully reestablished in the cattle business, George Littlefield was ready, as he had written Alice two years earlier, "to locate at some place and improve us a nice House" (figs. 13 and 14).[10]

Gonzales was out. Though convenient for being close to family and the several cattlemen friends who continued to live in the spacious and comfortable community at the confluence of the San Marcos and Guadalupe Rivers, the town had stagnated. Only 1,581 souls called it home for the census taker in 1880. Though percentage-wise a considerable increase from the population thirty years earlier when the Littlefields arrived, in absolute numbers the growth was modest. The railroad line built from Houston to San Antonio missed the town. Not until 1882 did a twelve-mile tap line reach Gonzales, and it lost $1,200 in its first year of operation. The decline of the Chisholm and rise of the Western cattle trails was preventing Gonzales from reaching its potential as a financial center of the trade. While Gonzales County's population nearly doubled in those thirty years, the county's economy decayed. Land prices collapsed. "The cotton farms are still worked on a large scale as the Lands are River bottom land and to divide them into small farms would leave some of them away from wood and water. The lands in the River Valleys . . . [in the years after the Civil War] were valued at $30 per acre. Now," Littlefield summed up the change, "they are valued at $15 for the reason that it is impossible to cut them up into small farms." He had abandoned cotton altogether, instead raising corn, oats, and millet to mix with cotton seed for a nutritious feed on his Plum Creek Ranch.[11]

Seth and Elizabeth Mabry begged George and Alice to join them in Kansas City. Mabry struck a figure so notable among Texas cattlemen that, despite having moved out of state, he had been proposed to head the Texas Live Stock Association at its inaugural meeting. He declined to stand precisely because of his out-of-state residence. So likable was Mabry that "everybody in anywise connected with the livestock trade . . . feels the right to call him their friend; for he knows every one, and has a pleasant word for each," Joseph G. McCoy characterized him in the first substantial contemporary description of the cattle trade. For its part, Kansas City was a transportation hub with two railroads positioning it between markets in Kansas, Colorado, and Nebraska to the west and Chicago to the east. And meat-packing houses made it a cattle destination of its own. So important had Mabry considered his move there that he and Elizabeth had left the magnificent Italianate home Austin master builder Abner Cook had completed for them only four years earlier in 1876.[12] As enticing as his close friend's entreaties were, for George Littlefield in 1883 Kansas City lay too far from his family and properties in Texas and from his large new ranch in New Mexico.

The capital city of Texas, by contrast, lay between the two. Twenty years after he dreamed of establishing himself at Austin, George Littlefield paid ten thousand dollars cash for liquor dealer Martin McCarty's "elegant place" on the half block at 300 West Orange (later renamed Twenty-Fourth) Street on July 3, 1883. For bustle, Kansas City had nothing on Austin. Austin's businessmen made manifest the bright future they anticipated when, in the single year of 1882, they spent a quarter million dollars erecting splendid homes. Fifty more new houses were going up in 1883. Continuing arrivals so swelled the population, which already had trebled in the decade of the 1870s, that vacant rooms could be found only in hotels. Rentals were not to be had. With railroad lines connecting Austin east to Houston, north to Saint Louis, Missouri, south via Kyle and San Marcos to San Antonio, and building northwest toward intersection with the Texas and Pacific at Abilene, Texas, Austin boasted its own transportation advantages.[13]

Better yet, Austin was a cattleman's town. A feeder of the Chisholm Trail led herds across the Colorado River ford at Shoal Creek and up Congress Avenue through the heart of the business district. Passing herds made news. Only two months before Littlefield bought, a trail boss confronting the swollen river decided to push his six hundred longhorns across on the wooden toll bridge at the foot of Congress Avenue. A wagon hauling bricks caused the animals to begin milling. Shortly, a 120-foot span gave way, sending cattle plunging to their deaths. After the remainder of the animals were quieted, the trail boss found that his impatience had cost him about one-eighth of his herd.[14]

More than the seasonal passage of trail herds, it was the year-round business of cattle that made Austin a cattleman's town. During the early 1880s, in a population of eleven thousand that made Austin the fourth largest city in Texas, cattle dealers outnumbered barbers 16 to 15 and Texas Live Stock Association cattlemen members outnumbered doctors 26 to 22. For a city without the cattle pens and shipping facilities that transformed towns into cattle meccas, the magnetism for cattlemen of Texas's westernmost metropolis was astonishing. But so many came that their presence and prominence struck even newcomers. "In those days, cattlemen were the anointed," recalled the writer O. Henry, who arrived only months after Littlefield bought his place. "They were the grandees of the grass, kings of the kine, lords of the lea, barons of beef and bone."[15]

Grandees, kings, lords, and barons brought wealth, and a lot of it. The Austin paper in 1886 listed fifteen cattlemen worth between $100,000 and $1.8 million. Three accounted for nearly two-thirds of the fifteen's $5.835 million total. Of the three's $3.6 million, Littlefield and Doc Day each accounted for $900,000— together making one-half. "Caught in a stampede of dollars," as O. Henry put it, they spent their good fortune lavishly. They "are constantly adding to the beauties of Austin by handsome and costly residences and all the adornments which the taste and ingenuity of modern civilization can supply," touted a city directory. Jesse Driskill topped them all. In building and furnishing his palace a little more than a block from Littlefield's property, Driskill spent a reputed staggering $120,000.[16]

The dynamic cattle business, vibrant local economy, and state government marked Austin with a character and vigor, but still did not fully embrace the city's vitality. The *Statesman* newspaper called for the town to become "the great health resort of the southwest, and the chief educational and manufacturing center." With little infrastructure for manufacturing and less for health, the single certainty was education. On College Hill in north Austin, the first building was rising on the forty-acre tract designated in 1881 for the campus of the University of Texas. Even before it was ready for them, twelve faculty opened the university on September 15, 1883, welcoming 221 students in temporary quarters. Then, within two months of each other, the school and the Littlefields moved into their new homes. Maybe chance pointed the Gonzales couple to the half block across Orange from the campus; maybe in Austin's tight housing market the McCarty place was the only property that suited them. Whatever drew the Littlefields to the modest estate, the man who quit university because he found nothing practical in the subjects offered would contribute time, treasure, and a sense of duty that not just built the institution during his lifetime but will continue to mark it for as long as there is a University of Texas.[17]

But that was decades on. In the fall of 1883, with Alice in Gonzales, the work of supervising repairs and an addition to their new house as well as selecting furniture and fixtures fell to George. In Kansas City he bought a boxcar load of carpets and curtains, lamps and mirrors, dressers and such. Alice's letters helped, but still "as for little ornaments you don't Know how lost I am in such selections." Costs mounted. Frustration built. Littlefield even second-guessed their decision, writing that "when we come to consider expense, it would have been better to of built than to repair the old House." Adding to his frustration, Austin was not the place for him to be that fall. "No cattlemen here," he wrote in October. "I leave on tomorrow morning train" for Kansas City.[18]

Cattlemen in Kansas City continued to be hungry to milk the boom of the last couple of years for all it was worth. Littlefield found the Saint James Hotel "crowd[ed] with Texas men. Nearly every one wanting to borrow money." Not him. "Do not lets get impatient," was his motto of long-standing: "Economy, Industry, guided by good judgement, will bring all things right for any one."[19]

All things were coming right in New Mexico. Rain was falling on the Bosque Grande range in the Pecos valley. In fact, reported Phelps, "more rain than ever was Known before." Better even than rain, which they could not control, was land—vacant land or, rather, in the mindset of the times put into words by the Kansas *Parsons' Memorial and Historical Library Magazine*, "waste lands of the boundless West" waiting for entrepreneurial men to make it productive.[20] Phelps and Mac McCarty had found such land.

Two or three days' ride southeast of the Bosque in the fall of 1882, they, in a company of LFD and Chisum men, arrived at the caprock, where a steep trail led to the top of the rocky escarpment, three hundred to six hundred feet up.[21] There were easier places to climb up, but the beautiful stream that flowed from a considerable spring one-third of the way up the bluff had attracted Native Americans and all variety of animals to this place long before the cattlemen arrived. In fact, the rivulet of Mescalero Spring ran so ample that it could water a herd, Phelps noted. On the plains about eighteen miles east-northeast, they came upon more water. Spread over a couple of square miles lay four lakes. Three were wet weather basins, but beside the fourth, South Lake, flowed a spring of cool, sweet water. And in every direction stretching past the nearly level horizon was grass—beautiful tall, luxuriant grass. The "waste land" of grass and water became more important to Phelps than the small herd of buffalo they had come hunting (fig. 15).

To take control of this cattleman's paradise, Phelps needed to file claims on the water. That meant a trip to the government land office in Las Cruces, more than two hundred miles away over the Sierra Blanca mountains, around the southern end of the white sands spreading miles across the dry, sun baked Tularosa Basin, and finally over the lower but rocky Organ Mountains. Until he could get to Las Cruces, Phelps sent Harry Robinson, "a man not afraid of anything," as Edgar Harral remembered him, to squat on Mescalero Spring.[22]

Losing no time, the day after he arrived at the Bosque, about six months after the hunting trip, George Littlefield set out on an eight-day ride to see the springs and plains for himself. Throwing his bedding in a buckboard driven by "an Old English man [who] done our cooking, The best and most attentive man I ever Saw," he, McCarty, and Will White saddled up and headed for the plains. Littlefield liked what he saw. By putting in windmills to provide water at sites beyond the springs and to ensure the availability of water during dry periods, the plains could "be made very valuable," he said, confirming Phelps's assessment.[23]

Phelps had waited on his uncle's inspection trip before starting the process of registering formal claim to the lush plains, but Littlefield let not another moment pass. Only three months after he saw the potential of the seemingly unending carpet of grass, two trusted men of his outfit had completed the process of filing on the Middle and North Lakes.[24] Not just any men, one was the fearless, attentive cook Harry Robinson. Born in England, "Old Man Harry" abandoned his early life when he jumped ship on the Gulf Coast and made his way to the cattle country of the plains. Fellow waddy (cowboy) Vivian H. Whitlock said Robinson joined the Littlefield outfit on the LIT, then moved with it to New Mexico where he was important to establishing its hold on the plains.[25] The other was the extraordinary black cowboy Addison Jones. If horses and cattle had not been his life during twenty years of slavery, mounts became his calling after emancipation. He could break any horse to the saddle. Some said it was because he could look a horse in the eye and tell what it was thinking. Others thought it was the way he caught a horse by the ear with one hand and the nose with the other. Those who knew him were sure of his prowess after they saw him master Whistlin' Bullet, the worst outlaw horse in the LFD remuda. Add was a top hand in every way but name, the prejudice of the period refusing the designation to blacks. McCarty, who apparently saw the lakes first, took South Lake.[26]

Back at the Bosque, "sun burned more than I ever was in my life," George Littlefield was pleased with himself for bringing in antelope meat for the men. Having shot three of the five antelope the party killed, Littlefield bragged to Alice that "I came out first best on the hunt." Tell Mr. Lewis, he added, that "his fishing don't compare with Killing Antelope on the Plains."[27]

With twelve live water filings completed, improving the land came next. Littlefield didn't have to tell Phelps about windmills. Phelps learned from former buffalo hunter Thomas L. "George" Causey. Moving south in pursuit of the ever-decreasing number of shaggies, as many called the buffalo, Causey landed in 1877 at the Yellow House site on the Texas south plains, some 115 miles below the Canadian River where Littlefield was opening his LIT Ranch that year. Named for a row of shallow caves just below the top of a bluff that, seen from across normally dry Yellow Lake in the soft maize hue of early morning, looked for all the world like Indian dwellings, the place offered shelter and a spring of life-giving water. Causey settled in, building a sod or adobe house and damming the spring to enlarge the water supply. However comfortable he was with his headquarters, after five years he had to move. No buffalo remained. He killed the last substantial herd on the south plains in 1882. More to the point, though, the land set aside to pay for construction of the state capitol—which had precipitated Littlefield's own move from the Canadian River area—included the Yellow House country (fig. 46).

Causey settled about seventy-five miles southwest of the Yellow House at water he had found while exploring Indian trails in New Mexico. Enclosing the spring at Ranger Lake, he increased the water supply for his stock, including mustangs, cattle, buffalo grown from calves, and work teams. As numbers grew, the natural flow could not support them all. Digging down, he told his nephew Vivian Whitlock, Causey discovered that the water table lay only feet below the surface. To tap it more efficiently than he had at Sulphur Draw with rawhide buckets, he erected a windmill—the first on the Llano Estacado—and found to his delight that he had acquired all the water he could want.[28]

During the trip exploring the plains, Phelps apparently rode up on Ranger Lake, about ten or so miles east of the Four Lakes. He and Causey recognized each other, having met in Dodge City, probably in 1877 at the end of Phelps's first drive. If not at Ranger Lake then and there in the fall of 1882, then shortly after Uncle George assessed the plains, Phelps bought Causey's place with its water and windmill. And he contracted with Causey to buy a rig with which to sink shallow wells about ten miles apart at the corners of squares so that no cow would have to walk farther than five miles to water.[29]

In June 1883 the LFD outfit, commonly known in the cattle country as "the LFDs," as all ranches were referred to by their brands, began taking control of the land to establish the operation they would call the Four Lakes Ranch. George Littlefield sent cattle from the Bosque to fatten. Causey began hauling drilling equipment and supplies to put in the windmills. Likely he opened the trail to what became the ranch's supply point, some 120 miles away at Midland Station (named for being halfway between Dallas and El Paso) on the Texas and Pacific Railroad. Causey put teams to work creating tanks to catch rainwater. And he sent men to help build a blacksmith shop and bunkhouse (both still standing) on the claim McCarty filed beside South Lake. "Mac's Ranch," Littlefield called the place until he bought it a year or two later to serve as the ranch headquarters. At Mescalero Spring Phelps established a horse camp for resting their mounts. He piped some of the flow from Mescalero Spring to water troughs and built a one-room adobe house for the wranglers (figs. 16 and 42).[30]

Will White's departure for New Mexico after the die-up of February 1883 left only Shelton Dowell to run the central Texas ranches. Uncle sent him to the Plum Creek operation and sold the Foster, which his cattle enterprise had outgrown.[31] What on the surface seemed to be an easy transition in fact required close attention.

Ever protecting his managers, Uncle had absorbed the die-up loss himself— but not silently. Help one, and inevitably another felt slighted because he did not receive the same amount of money or enough money to set something just so or the infusion just when he thought he had to have it. To control inevitable jealousies, Uncle freely told managers, even family members, what he was doing for each of them. "As far as the loss in Foster Ranch is concerned I don't care for it if our business is run all right," he wrote Shelton Dowell in a typical letter:

> But you must see my situation and how I am working to help you all in every way I can to make money. You Know I pay out to Miller & Sayers [bank] the Balance P.C.R. [Plum Creek Ranch] account and then place 3000$ to its credit with State Nat. Bank [in Austin] so as to get the Pasture

in a good paying shape. . . . I really needed that money, As I feel it my duty
to arrange something to get Edgar started out, and to give [brother] Bill a
chance to do something. But now you see, this P.C.R. gets out of me over
$6000.00 cash, and then McCarty finds a cheap bunch of Cattle and it
takes $8,000.00 to get them, and His Ranch is like the P.C. Pasture[,]
needs them in order to make business pay. I buy them for Him. This will
fix Mack all O.K. and your place will be very well fixed. Next comes Edgar
& Bill if I find they will bear fixing.[32]

As trying as George Littlefield's personal challenge in overseeing his ranches
might be, it paled against what he sensed looming in the future—the near
future—for cattlemen. A slight decline in prices caused him to feel as 1883 closed
that "there is a hard time comeing for cattle men who are in debt." If he were
right, Littlefield needed to be especially careful of his expenses. And following
his contrarian philosophy, in that strife he could look for opportunities. In fact,
Littlefield was right. The boom was reaching its climax, and men with his vision
who "allowed enthusiastic would-be buyers full leeway . . . realized on their investments," wrote James Cox, looking back on it.[33]

Whether or not George Littlefield just then had money to lend, he had become
associated with the State National Bank of Austin, which did. After Littlefield confirmed his move to Austin, bank president Eugene Bremond, eight or nine years
Littlefield's senior, "insisted" (Littlefield's word decades later) that the increasingly
wealthy and prominent cattleman join the board.[34]

The Bremonds were an old Austin family. Irishman John Bremond had settled
in the community the year before it traded its status from the capital of a country to
that of a state. In fact, the family had made Austin home almost four-fifths as long as
a settlement had existed on the north bank of the limestone ford over the Colorado
River. Two years after he arrived, in 1847, Bremond opened a store for which five
years later he erected a larger building to accommodate his expanding trade. John's
sons, John Jr. and Eugene, continued the business after their father's death in 1866.
If advertising in the *Texas Almanac* is any guide, the brothers doubled the number of
banks in Austin when they added banking to the Bremond and Company enterprise
in 1869. In fact, by safeguarding money and issuing notes of exchange, as many
businesses did, they had been offering a form of banking service even before formally
opening their private bank. In 1870 Eugene relinquished his interest—whether in
Bremond and Company entirely or just in the merchandising side is unclear. But
banking had gotten into his blood. In 1873 he bought stock in and accepted a seat
on the initial board of the aptly named First National Bank of Austin. After the bank

opened for business in April 1874, appropriate to the community and region it meant to serve, Austin's First National catered to the needs of cattlemen.

In this approach the bank was following the lead of the fourth national bank to be organized in Texas—the San Antonio National. No wonder. San Antonio National founder and president, George Washington Brackenridge, stood behind Austin's First National. Attuned to business opportunities in western Texas, Brackenridge had made most of his money from the cattle trade. Though he worked with ranchers from one end of the state to the other—from Shanghai Pierce in south Texas to Charles Goodnight in the Panhandle—Brackenridge found the most lucrative facet of the cattle business for him was underwriting trailing contractors who needed large sums for the short, quick-return trailing season.

Unlike the San Antonio National, the Austin bank would employ George Brackenridge's brothers: John Thomas ("Tom"), James Madison, and Robert John. George didn't need them to help him manage in San Antonio. Patriarch of his family that he was, the second oldest Brackenridge brother found the Austin bank useful for providing employment for his three male siblings and at first, for investment for his mother and sister.[35] If he thought about it, one patriarch to another, George Littlefield would have appreciated George Brackenridge's attention to his family that mirrored his own. But there it ended. George Brackenridge's brothers as bankers were not of the caliber of George Littlefield's White nephews as cattlemen. The difference would hurt Brackenridge's bottom line and enhance Littlefield's. But for the first few years, the bank prospered from its investments in the thriving livestock trade.

Sometime in 1881, if not earlier, Eugene Bremond left the First National to organize the State National Bank of Austin. With a hundred thousand dollars capital, the institution opened its doors on February 1, 1882. If the prosperous livestock business had drawn Bremond to make the move, his timing could not have been better. Less than two weeks after the State National opened its doors, the stockmen of Texas assembled in Austin to form the Texas Live Stock Association. The gathering provided an optimal opportunity for Bremond to introduce Austin's second national bank to this important group of the state's businessmen, and Bremond positioned himself with his banking rival, the gregarious Tom Brackenridge, on Austin's reception committee. Bremond accomplished his purpose and recruited the customer base he desired. In the bank's second quarter, deposits jumped by one-third from $333,000 to $436,000.[36]

When Littlefield accepted Bremond's invitation to join the State National board, the cattleman was not the novice in banking that a casual observer might have thought him to be. For a town its size, Gonzales was well endowed with private banks. In 1870 it had as many as Austin. Hugh Lewis and the Dilworth brothers, George and Littlefield's future partner, Dock, opened the first in 1866. It began when, to save carrying $5,000 in gold to New York, a traveling grocer asked whether the firm could give him a bill of exchange against money the firm had on deposit there. Receiving $1 per $100 for the service, the Dilworths added banking to their services. Two years later Littlefield attorney James F. Miller and friend from Terry Ranger days William B. Sayers opened the second. Littlefield knew banking from the customer's side, having borrowed from Gonzales banks to survive the three years of crop failures and then get into the cattle business. In fact, what he had learned by 1883 was enough for a man to be able to get into the banking business. Indeed, by the rules for operating private banks, from his lending activity, he *was* a bank. "The environment under which private banks operated was one of complete freedom," historians of Texas's state-chartered banks state, "as they were responsible to no supervisory authority and were free to follow whatever policies they desired. There were no restrictions on entry; any individual or firm could operate a 'banking' business regardless of the amount of net worth, or capital, in hand to support it. They could make loans for any purpose whatsoever, in any amount, for any duration, and for whatever rate of interest the market would bear, as long as the usury laws were not violated."[37]

In joining the board of a national bank, Littlefield did have something to learn, though. Banking within the twenty-year-old national bank system was different— regulated. Created by the National Banking Acts of 1863 and 1864, the system had the goals of regularizing the currency by issuing banknotes uniform and accepted throughout the country, of stimulating the market for U.S. bonds, initially to finance the war, and of creating a banking system without a central bank. Required of each national bank was raising and maintaining a minimum capital, initially fifty thousand dollars, of which a high percentage had to be invested in U.S. bonds. Deposited in the federal treasury, these bonds then underwrote the paper currency. The greenbacks were put in circulation by the banks, each institution receiving bills in an amount corresponding to a percentage of its bond deposit. Banking inspectors visited the banks to ensure adherence to the rules.[38] Whatever timely knowledge of trends in the financial world Littlefield expected to gain from his position on the State National board, certainly intimate knowledge of the operation of the national bank system would stand him in good stead if and when, as Brackenridge and Bremond had done before him, he determined to organize and head a national bank.

In 1884 Littlefield also felt foreboding related to new difficulties with transporting cattle to market. Mention trailing, and temperatures rose. Settlers and cattlemen from Kansas northward demanded that trailing end in their neighborhoods. Trailed beeves trampled their fields and brought Texas Fever that decimated their stock. To mitigate this confrontation, every year or two, trunk trails had developed new branches to the west. Every few years a trunk trail was abandoned in favor of one farther to the west. From the Shawnee Trail to Missouri, drovers took the Chisholm Trail to central Kansas, then drove the Western Trail to western Kansas. But by the mid-1880s, drovers had run out of vacant country farther west into which to shift the trunk trail. Fellow cattlemen in the Texas Panhandle north of the Texas Fever line (above which the winter freeze killed the Texas Fever ticks) even threw up an armed Winchester Quarantine to keep south Texas herds from using the Potter-Bacon Cutoff from the Western Trail to angle west across their pastures before turning north. But trailing afforded the most economical means for south Texas cattlemen to deliver their product to market. They demanded that trailing not be interdicted.[39] Could establishment of a designated national trail be the compromise to end the confrontation and save trailing?

In a grand effort to find consensus, cattlemen from one end of the plains to the other, from as far east as Pennsylvania and New York, from Mexico and Canada—some 1,365 delegates in all—gathered in Saint Louis, Missouri, in the third week of November 1884 to hold the first National Cattle Growers' Convention. The assemblage attracted attention. "There is an unmistakable class look about them.... In matters of dress and bearing the cattlemen are peculiar; they wear wide white hats, long, black coats, and as a rule, long silky beards," wrote one observer. "No one could fail to notice the stalwart, robust physical manhood of the delegates, and no one standing up before the convention, and looking in the faces of the vast body of sun-tanned men, could fail to note the evidence of superior intellectuality, the bold self-reliance, the keen, penetrating, character-reading eye, . . . [and] the marked individuality of the members," observed another.

Establishing a national trail would be the work of Congress. Presence was important for gaining a hearing, money for influence. Reporters calculated. "The men represent many millions of capital, and the most tremendous new industry of America." In short, *Parsons' Memorial and Historical Library Magazine* continued, the cattle industry "represents more capital than would be required to pay off the national debt." The magazine then listed men of wealth. Second on the non-alphabetical list of "solid millionaire ranchmen from Texas" was George Littlefield.

That, however, was the only Littlefield notice. Others spoke for the Lincoln County Live Stock Association, from which he was credentialed, supporting the New Mexico position that as long as it avoided that state, the national trail afforded a lever for checking railroad freight rates. Credentialed also from the Texas Live Stock Association, which included south Texans ardently in favor of a national trail, Littlefield was on record with the stock improvement committee telling Texas ranchers that cattle cars, not cattle trails, were the means for transporting the high-er-quality beeves the committee advocated. Though two bills would be introduced calling for a national trail, one sponsored by Congressman James Miller of Gonzales, neither passed. Whether or not at the end of 1884 he really had realized his first million dollars, Littlefield was prepared for the outcome. Four months before the cattlemen convened, he had announced publicly that he was quitting trailing.[40]

If on New Year's Day 1885 George Littlefield reflected on events of the last four years, he should have remembered feeling exhilaration in 1881 from receiving that quarter million dollars for the LIT, then emptiness in 1882 from frustration in struggling to invest it, then great pleasure with Phelps's work in finding and making plans to develop the Bosque Grande range. The view from decades later confirmed it. The Bosque "became equal to a gold mine," Littlefield reminisced proudly near the end of his life. "From those 9000 cows and heifers put there in 1882 sprang the greatest growths we ever had in cattle."[41] In fact, he knew it long before he penned that autobiography. When he sold the LIT after four years, Littlefield turned over seventeen thousand head of cattle. After only two and a half years on the Pecos, he was running twenty-five thousand head. In one-third less time, he was running half again more cattle. And that was just on the Bosque. The salvation of the Four Lakes Ranch awaited the inevitable next drought.

Where some counted prosperity in terms of numbers of cattle and acres, others described it in dollars. After the LIT sale, the *Fort Griffin Echo* thought Littlefield to be worth $350,000. Three and a half years later, *Parsons' Memorial and Historical Library Magazine* pegged his standing at triple that—a solid $1 million. A rise on that scale and in such a short time created opportunity. His peers called him to leadership positions beginning with the founding of the Texas Live Stock Association. Eugene Bremond invited him into banking, which in time widened his world in ways that neither of them could have imagined in 1883.

Certainly, no one could know how events would have transpired if Littlefield had not sold his LIT Ranch. But on that New Year's Day of 1885, George Littlefield surely could begin to see the LIT sale in yet a third light. The combination of the White brothers team under Phelps running the Bosque Grande ranch and opening the Four Lakes range of virtually unlimited free land onto which Littlefield's New Mexico cattle operation was spreading, of the favorable years in the cattle business, and of his own skill in trading turned what at first had seemed to be a triumph, then to be a mistake, into a widening of his world that his move to Austin would both accelerate and channel far beyond cattle and the half block where his home would stand for the rest of his life and beyond.

THE WAY TO MAKE MONEY

When George W. Littlefield opened his morning paper on January 2, 1885, he saw himself in the news. It wasn't just that his name appeared in the newspaper. In that period when gazettes published lists of hotel arrivals and addressees with letters to be picked up in the post office, almost anyone's name could show up in the notices. Rather, it was that his name appeared in a way it never had before. In the chair of the committee planning "proper entertainments" for those attending the upcoming Texas Live Stock Association annual meeting sat *Major* George W. Littlefield.[1] He had been promoted. Whether the advancement in social title from captain to major originated with someone who heard Littlefield himself describe the battlefield recognition he so valued or with someone who heard the story secondhand, the preferment signaled simultaneously recognition of accomplishment and anticipation of grander achievement. Sometimes, the grandest feat is emerging from a long and difficult period in a position stronger than when the trouble began.

George Littlefield's prominence among Texas stockmen had risen in concert with the ascension of the Texas Live Stock Association itself. In its three years, the statewide organization had grown to be among the largest and richest, if not *the* largest and richest of its kind in the country. Members owned some one million cattle (about 15 percent of the total of beeves in the state), one million sheep, and 350,000 horses, the value of which Secretary Will Lambert estimated to be around $45 million. Within two years, the number of cattle of the six-hundred-some members would increase six times and be worth more than $71 million, a capital exceeded only by the assessed value of land in the state.[2]

To deal with the matters for which the stockmen had built their association, 150 members converged on Austin in mid-January 1885 for their third annual meeting. In contrast to the unpleasant cold, muddy slush in the streets outside, proceedings in the Travis County district courtroom moved in warm harmony. Perhaps the diminishing importance of formerly prominent issues played a role. Stock improvement was one, they learned, when Littlefield's committee recommended its own dissolution, not because upgrading of stock had become inconsequential, though.

Just the opposite. The recommendation documented the progress that had been made in undertaking the work. As the report so artfully worded it, the committee "beg leave to report that the importance of the use of improved blood in the herds throughout the country is now so universally believed that we consider it useless to discuss the question in the presence of a meeting composed of so much intelligence and business capacity." Maybe the accord resulted, too, from delegating the TLSA work to a small core of members. Eighteen of the more than 150 delegates filled a seat on at least two of the thirteen committees. Only one committee failed to have at least two of the eighteen. Seven of the eighteen were appointed to three committees. Appointed to three, Littlefield accepted election to his fourth, the executive committee, whose members then elevated him to the chair.[3]

Surely, he recognized the choice before him—the choice that confronts every leader—to lead by asserting a vision for making the organization more than it was when he came to the chairmanship or to simply advocate the prevailing sentiment in the conduct of the association's routine business. Surely, he recognized, too, that his was not a choice for the faint of heart. Despite the cordiality of the meeting, conflict over Texas Fever was pulling the TLSA apart. The south Texas majority demanded to be allowed to continue driving cattle straight through to market. They had succeeded in securing from the Saint Louis convention in November 1884 endorsement of their call for congressional establishment of a defined national trail through the lands of hostile cattlemen and settlers to railroad loading pens. Texas cattlemen members north of the thirty-second parallel (a line that runs through Midland, Texas, and forms the boundary between southern New Mexico and Texas) not only offered no support for the national trail but instead pushed for drawing the "dead [quarantine] line" yet farther south.[4] Following, then, meant advocating the south Texans' position in favor of a national trail. Leading meant convincing Texas cattlemen that more important to them than any single issue was a strong state body. With the organization's officers, he accepted responsibility to do both—to do the impossible.

The front page of the Austin paper on October 10, 1885, reported Executive Committee Chair Littlefield's twofold solution to the deadlock. First, avoiding siding with scientists who suggested that Texas Fever originated with grass contaminated in some way or with executive committee colleague Shanghai Pierce, who claimed it resulted from bad handling of stock late in the season, Littlefield steered a middle course. "The best thing, I think, is for the [Texas] legislature to offer an appropriation and employ expert veterinary surgeons to investigate this Fever, and get at the root of it; then a quarantine ground should be established and the infected cattle be compelled to stay on the quarantine grounds for a specified time." All the state's stockmen could support this call for legislative contribution to ensuring the well-being of the second most important pillar of the state's economy. Why, seven months earlier the Cattle Raisers Association of Northwest Texas had petitioned for establishment of a state sanitary commission. The legislature had even seemed friendly to cattle interests, having petitioned Congress to legislate a national trail. Evidently meant to quiet the conflict, Littlefield's recommendation showed no urgency. Short of a called session, the legislature would not meet again for fifteen months.[5]

Second, echoing the recommendation of his stock improvement committee and despite the urging of the majority bloc to pursue establishment of a national trail, Littlefield advocated abandoning the trail altogether in favor of rail transportation. Likely he saw the handwriting on the wall. Ten months earlier, in January 1885, Kansas had adopted a quarantine measure that prohibited Texas longhorns from entering or passing through the state without spending a substantial period in quarantine. And this measure followed and broadened narrower quarantines, one of which two years earlier, in 1883, had closed Dodge City, the Queen of Cow Towns itself, to trail herds. Moreover, Kansas joined states from Arizona to New Mexico and north to Canada in restricting the movement of cattle carrying Texas Fever. Though an estimated total of 220,000 head made their way north in 1885, this smallest number in nearly a decade foretold the complete collapse of trailing. The experience of the most successful of the trailing contractors and TLSA executive committee member John Lytle showed it. In the three years between 1884 and 1887 when he closed his business, the number of head his firm handled plummeted by half each year from ninety-one thousand to just twelve thousand. The coup de grace from the quarantines came in 1886, when buyers shunned south Texas longhorns so completely that their value fell by 70 percent.[6]

If cattlemen listened to voices as Littlefield's, they did not hear. They did not respond to association president John N. Simpson's appeal to renew memberships in arrears. They ignored the executive committee's call to attend the 1886 annual meeting to settle the location of the dead line. Of the three hundred to four hundred expected to overflow the seats in the House chamber in the temporary capitol, on January 12, 1886, only fifty-four members showed up, barely one-third of the previous year's number. Worse yet, almost all were south Texas cattlemen. Northern Texas cattlemen returned the favor of the south Texans, who had boycotted a called meeting the year before. Seeing little else he could do to bridge the sectional division, President Simpson lamented to the nearly empty chamber that "The one thing which, I believe, is the primary cause of the greater part of all our troubles is the want of friendly and united feelings amongst stockmen of our own

State."[7] Having interests on both sides of the dead line, Simpson was genuine in his entreaty to come together for the good of all.

Littlefield followed with the executive committee report so lengthy and detailed that it alone consumed almost one-sixth of the printed proceedings of the four-day meeting. Opening with the committee's investigation of a false report of Texas Fever, Littlefield derided the quarantines as "an injustice to the cattle world." Northern ranchers, he asserted, needed south Texas cattle to fatten. Then he reported action on a range of matters important to all cattlemen from leasing public lands to feeding. He recounted expenditures, including out-of-pocket payments TLSA leaders made while lobbying for the national trail. Members commended their executive committee chair, "who had been so indefatigable in the discharge of his duty, and who wrote the very able and lengthy report," then punctuated their approval by electing him to another term. But no one moved to reimburse the not-inconsiderable personal expenditures.[8]

The last hope for breaking through the quarantines died in April 1886. The U.S. Senate had approved the national trail bill. But for lack of a quorum, induced by cattlemen opposed to the measure, in his U.S. House commerce committee, Texan John H. Reagan could not send Gonzales congressman James Miller's bill to the full house. That brought cattlemen face to face with the issue behind transportation. However the cattle reached them, "the great dressed beef ring," as Littlefield scorned the big four meat packers in Chicago, set the market price of cattle to suit themselves, not the producers. To Littlefield's executive committee, the solution was not only simple but totally Texan. Open a packing and refrigeration plant in Texas. Locate it in the rail hub of Houston to reduce shipping costs by shortening hauls. And supply the plant with Texas cattle fattened on the product of Texas farms. Farmers would benefit from the ready market. Cattlemen would benefit from gaining farmers as allies. Texas would benefit by keeping Texas money at home. So evident were the plan's advantages that Houston businessmen encouraged it. Texas bankers endorsed it. Texas cattlemen adopted it, despite Charles Goodnight's assertion that Panhandle ranchers would benefit only from the value bestowed on otherwise nearly worthless south Texas stock.

Its response to the packers adopted, the executive committee focused on the association's finances. If the treasury could be returned to solvency, which included discharging the State National Bank loan made to keep the organization afloat, the TLSA leaders would complete the other half of their agenda for the 1887 meeting. The total of dues outstanding had risen to $8,000, against which members had paid in during the year a paltry $72. Sensing the need for drastic action then and there, Littlefield moved to lock the doors and allow none to leave without satisfying his debt to the association. A majority of the 250 in attendance adopted the motion. But whether the desperate deed met its goal no record survives to say.[9]

In his two years heading the executive committee, Littlefield had tried to lead the Texas Live Stock Association away from the breakup toward which it was headed when he took the chair. He had offered ways forward that had favored neither one side nor the other, but instead aimed to advantage all of his colleagues. Nevertheless, he did not return for a third term at the center of TLSA affairs. And within two years the organization in which he had invested so much energy from its founding died. Maybe failures in pursuing the Houston refrigerator project doomed it. More likely the division over Texas Fever had so poisoned the fiber of the organization that not even identification in 1890 of the tick *Boophilus bovis* as the cause of Texas Fever resuscitated it. Perhaps cattlemen so valued regional associations' roles in combating theft and recovering cattle that they could not see the worth in supporting the policy-oriented state organization along with the regional associations that directly supported their daily activity. Though a Texas Live Stock Association would function for more than a decade longer, it was a new body created in 1890 simply using the old name. George Littlefield took no part in it. He had done his duty serving his fellow stockmen.[10]

While Littlefield labored on the executive committee, conditions on the Plum Creek Ranch began to change. By late summer 1883, Plum Creek had dried up, forcing him to transfer three thousand head to New Mexico. What rain fell during the winter stopped altogether in the following spring. As the grass wilted and stock tanks dried up, a buyer offered $100,512 for the place, a profit of about 50 percent on Littlefield's two-year investment in the Dinner Bell outfit. Ever ready to accommodate a serious buyer, the Major simultaneously accepted the proposition and by fortuitous circumstance avoided having to see cattle through a three-year dry spell so desperate that the locals compared it to the benchmark central Texas drought of 1857.[11]

Within a year, though, "desperate" was beginning to describe conditions in the Pecos River basin below Fort Sumner. On average, the country received nine to twelve inches of rain a year. The thick, beautiful, and nourishing black grama and other grasses that attracted the White brothers and so impressed Edgar Harral grew, spread, and replenished only as fast as showers favored them. Rains had been good. So had markets. The two brought stockmen to claim shares as large as each could get of what Littlefield effusively called "the best Cattle breeding Country in the United States." Littlefield's LFD in 1882 was the first large cattle outfit to come into the valley after Chisum's Long Rail. The next year, a Missouri group organized the Cass Land and Cattle Company and carved out what became the Bar V domain between the LFD and Chisum's Jinglebobs. Roswell resident Joseph Callaway Lea fashioned the Lea Cattle Company in 1885, occupying land west and south of the LFD. Small ranchers came too. "Complaints come from different parts of the county," editorialized Lincoln County's *Golden Era* late in 1884 "of parties who secure a small seepage of water, either by purchase or location, only calculated to accommodate a few head of cattle under the most favorable circumstances, and turn loose thereon from one to three hundred head of cattle, and this to[o] within the lines [of] or contiguous to other ranges already overstocked, allowing them to roam at will . . . thereby consuming the grass and water of their neighbors." The total of cattle they all pushed onto the Pecos grass and water each year numbered in the tens of thousands. Representative, the LFDs disregarded Phelps's 1882 warning to Shelt Dowell about overcrowding and in less than three years had exploded the number of head almost three times to twenty-five thousand. Lincoln County Live Stock Association member Littlefield had to have known and disregarded the reality reported in the *Golden Era's* October 23, 1884, editorial that "overstocked ranges . . . is a problem whose solution is now disturbing stockmen in this country more than the spread of the cattle plague."[12] Grazing twenty-five thousand head on seven hundred square miles, the LFD outfit at the end of 1884 had on its domain one cow for every eighteen acres, about the same density as on the LIT when Littlefield sold it three years earlier. If purchase and calving enlarged the herd in 1885 by just the ranch's average annual increase of 6,400 head, then at the beginning of 1886 the ranchers expected each animal to subsist on only fourteen acres.

The few years' experience that ranchers of the postwar cattle kingdom had with both rainfall and running cattle on huge swaths of land in the plains environment told them that between ten and twenty-five acres would be sufficient to fatten one cow. New Mexico Governor Edmund Gilbert Ross pegged the number at twenty acres in 1885.[13] If that were true for a year or two, or maybe a couple more, of normal rainfall, then when precipitation fell below average, crowded cattle suffered. Meatier blooded stock suffered more. Rangy longhorns grown up for generations in semi-arid south Texas tolerated drought conditions better. "No animal of the cow kind will shift and take care of itself under all conditions as will the longhorns," said Charles Goodnight. "They can go farther without water and endure more suffering than others." In fact, he added, "they have at least double the endurance."[14] But experience would teach that neither ten nor even twenty-five acres of arid-country grass under normal rainfall could sustain even one longhorn year in and year out. Unfortunately, experience offered no counsel on the number of acres it took when rain stopped.

In the first years of the 1880s, stockmen saw abundant grass and had no rain-fall averages by which to judge how normal or unusual the plenty was. Clashes over land resulted. "You know this is all U S land here and every body think they have a perfec right to use it," Phelps wrote Cousin Shelton late in 1882.[15]

For Pecos valley cattlemen, "every body" described two groups—cattlemen and sheepmen. Each needed large territories for grazing. Both saw two reasons they had a perfect right to appropriate the public land. First, the government gave them no legal means to secure use of the inviting unappropriated land. The land system encouraged settlement and commercial exploitation of timber and coal parcels. "The classification of surveyable lands made by Congress," New Mexico surveyor general Henry M. Atkinson stated six months after he took office in 1876, "precludes the survey of portions of this Territory that are valuable for grazing pur-poses and which could be rapidly sold by the Government were they surveyed and subject to sale." Second, making no effort to exclude the graziers, the government left them to settle their contests for the land. That did not bode well. Cattlemen despised sheepmen. "There is more real mean men in the sheep business than any one thing on earth," Phelps minced no words.[16]

Just how mean the LFD ranch manager was about to find out in dealing with the sheepman who claimed domain below the Bosque south line. The cattle and sheep grazed some of the same ground. John Chisum had allowed it after he and Jim Miller settled on a way to share the range. After Chisum died late in 1884, Phelps concluded he needed to make an arrangement with his neighbor and sent Charles Walker to see him. Normally, the woolies hurt cattle range by clipping the grass too close to the ground for cattle to graze easily after them. Somehow, though, Miller's sheep shunned the native course grass cattle liked, while LFD cattle bypassed the lower-lying grass and weeds sheep enjoyed. That made it easy for the two men to work to mutual benefit. They agreed that Phelps would keep cattlemen off their shared domain and Jim would reciprocate with sheepmen. "I believe that I, and the L.F.D. Company and the three Walker brothers must have broken all records for sheep and cattle harmony," Miller recalled years later. "I do not believe another instance can be found in the west to match it. Our stock ran together, and we borrowed coffee and flour of each other in perfect harmony."[17]

Competition among cattlemen for grass and water was not as easily resolved. Miller had acquired his sheep in 1881 from Joseph Callaway Lea, who by then was well into building his reputation as Roswell's founder, not because he arrived first but because he so fully invested himself in making the fledgling community into a fine little town. Captain Lea, as everyone addressed him, had arrived about three years earlier as a sheepman. But dissatisfied with his experiment of sheep and cattle sharing the range, he decided to concentrate on cattle. Disposing of some of his flock to Miller, he secured substantial backing from men distant from New Mexico but eager to get into the cattle business (principal among whom was Horace K. Thurber, whose interests included manufacture of the cowboy favorite, Arbuckle Coffee).[18] Lea aggressively expanded his LEA land and herds west of the Pecos until they overlapped other outfits. Retaliating, the LFDs, Jinglebobs, and Diamond As excluded the LEAs from participating in roundups, which threw the LEAs behind the others in gathering and branding, and then in preparing bunches for market. After a time, Captain Lea had had enough. He called a meeting in the county seat of Lincoln to confront his adversaries. Lea's range foreman, Charlie Ballard, watched as his boss "told them they had hammered him around and that he wasn't going to stand it any more, and was afraid his boys were going to take it up, and that if there was any fighting to be done, it would be done right there, and that he was ready." No one doubted that this one of William Clarke Quantrill's Civil War irregulars meant business. Ballard knew Phelps White as "a bull-headed kind of fellow" but also "a smart man—a good businessman." Whether Phelps suggested it, after the men on his side heard Lea out, they said they wanted to make friends. They did, and that ended it. As Jim Miller, who had no stake in the outcome, saw it: "In the division of the large Chisum domain among Chisum himself, Captain Lea, the L.F.D. people, the Cass Land and Cattle Company, Milne and Bush, and the Diamond A, there was no killings because these men were all big men with large brains and cool heads."[19]

Finding an accord among outfits was one thing, accommodating changes in the weather was quite another. In the summer of 1885, a "swollen sun that burned with a quiet fury" began "The Big Dry," a two-year spell that withered cattle forage, cracked the barren bottoms of stock tanks, and shriveled the river. As ranchers searched vainly for greener pastures, President Grover Cleveland compounded the drought's effects when he ordered stockmen off leased lands in Indian Territory. Owners threw thousands of beeves onto any acreage they could find to accommodate them. Eaten-down ranges in nearby states shortly swarmed with cattle that cropped and trampled the parched grass more completely yet. To mitigate the damage, ranchers began thinning their herds. The dull market Littlefield experienced that August collapsed. By year's end, cows bought for thirty-five dollars the year before fetched as little as five dollars.[20]

Then conditions turned bad. Phelps White saw the thin Pecos River freeze over in January 1886. Rufe O'Keefe said that the winter of 1885–86 on the high plains east of the LFDs when he was a young cowboy was one of the two coldest of his decades in the cattle business. Spring saw the Pecos lined with cattle dead of cold, thirst, hunger, and bogging in the river's treacherous quicksand. The second summer's drought exceeded the first. Cattle suffered more than ever. Men suffered not just from the desperate drought but also from the stench of carcasses rotting along the river. What scorching summer heat did on the Pecos, the following bitterest of winters did up and down the Great Plains. When in the spring of 1887 cattlemen of the Pecos and southeastern New Mexico counted the survivors, they found only half the number of head they had on their books two years earlier. And these cattlemen were fortunate. The farther north, the greater the loss, on some ranges reaching 90 percent. The Great Die-Up, Pecos cattlemen called the summer drought and plains cattlemen called the winter wet and cold. It "will live in the history of the range-cattle industry as the most destructive season that western stockmen ever knew," an observer wrote of the winter, without realizing he was summing up the summer on the Pecos too.[21]

In the wake of the disaster, investors whose interest in cattle ran no deeper than the pages of Brisbin's get-rich-quick sure thing unloaded. They had more to lose than Brisbin had suggested. As investors had invaded the business, the cost of ranching had gone up, sharply reducing profit margins. With so many like the Prairie Cattle Company rushing to get into ranching on a grand scale, free grass disappeared. To ensure use of land, investors had to acquire not range rights but legal title by purchase or lease. Then, to reserve their territory for their cattle alone, they had to buy barbed wire by the miles to fence it in. Confining cattle within pastures on the plains where springs, lakes, and water courses were mighty few and far between required investors to drill wells and erect windmills. Not just here and there, wells were placed to ensure both that concentrations of animals had adequate water and that cattle would not walk off their flesh traveling more than five miles from good grass to water. Distances between good grass and wells, steadily increased as cattle crowded onto the range to maximize short-term return, forced cattle to eat and trample the nourishment in their pastures. In a very few years, overstocking on average reduced the carrying capacity of the land by one-half.[22]

The Big Dry and Great Die-Up spelled the end of the cattle boom on the Pecos thirteen years after John Chisum and only four after the LFD began spreading their herds through the valley. Losses broke small cowmen. Some lost too many animals to continue as independent ranchers. Others could not afford the cost of providing water to sustain their operation. Even the valley's large Hashknife outfit sold out. From the Texas plains to the east, the Francklyn, Kentucky, and Espuela cattle companies disappeared. The flight from cattle flooded the market. Prices fell further.[23]

Against the odds, the LFD outfit survived the calamity in remarkably strong condition. In the spring of 1887, Phelps White reported the birth of so many calves that he was taking the uncommon step of spaying two thousand heifers to mature for beef. Major Littlefield anticipated selling $150,000 worth of cattle. Cowhand Frank Lloyd credited native longhorns for the LFD's good fortune. The work of a couple hundred blooded bulls introducing their characteristics into the herd of maybe twenty-five thousand females had progressed only so far. "White had these Texas cattle, and he never lost one-third as many as Chisum did," Lloyd said. "Chisum had his bred up to Durhams, and . . . they just died like sheep."[24]

But longhorns were not the only reason, nor even the main reason. Phelps White's foresight four years earlier to secure Mescalero Spring, the Four Lakes, and Ranger Lake provided the Littlefield outfit with its ace in the hole. Unlike other cattle companies along the Pecos, the LFDs had a large reserve of grass and sufficient water on it from three years' work putting in windmills. However dry the plains grass was, having been grazed only by antelopes and mustangs since extermination of the buffalo, the carpet was thick and ready. Before conditions could deteriorate further, in 1886 Phelps drove between fifteen thousand and twenty thousand head off the river and onto the plains.[25]

Confirmed in his belief that the future of the LFD operation lay on the high plains, Littlefield moved to enlarge and consolidate his hold on the vastness. To Addison Jones's claim at the Four Lakes, for which Littlefield had paid Jones a month after the filing, the rancher added McCarty's South Lake claim and improvements to solidify the headquarters. Establishing what became the LFD south line, stretching from the Texas state line to the caprock and running just north of present Lovington, New Mexico, Littlefield bought Jim Campbell's small OJIM outfit with its 336 mother cows and the watering places Campbell had developed. Uncle sent Edgar Harral to run the place in August 1886, promising that if he remained there only a year, Uncle would give him the little ranch.[26] The Four Lakes Ranch's north line lay in a stretch of sand hills about five miles north of the headquarters.

With Littlefield still backing him, in 1886 McCarty picked a site for his new, small T71 ranch on a spring at the base of the San Juan Mesa extension of the west slope of the Llano Estacado (one mile due north of present-day Kenna). The location was opportune. It would provide a link between George Littlefield's Four Lakes Ranch to the south and the Bosque Grande Ranch to the west. The ranch George would help his brother open along the Mesa's base north of the T71 would significantly enlarge the link.[27]

William Littlefield had come to New Mexico in 1883 with the herd Will White drove from the Plum Creek Ranch.[28] The next year he brought his wife and five children, the youngest not a year old, to make their home at the Bosque headquarters. The story told both inside and outside the family is that one day maybe four years later, while riding miles into the great open country east of the Bosque headquarters, he happened upon one or a band of men herding horses around another spring at the base of San Juan Mesa. The colorful version says that the life-giving water had been discovered in 1881, when a rider heard a curious hollow sound as his horse walked over a little patch of dry ground. Investigating, he found a structure of lodge poles covered with Indian blankets, dirt, and rocks that Native Americans had constructed to hide the year-round spring underneath. The more likely version says that a margin of unusually green grass betrayed the water under the covering. However the Hidden Spring had been found, it was precious. Its three-gallon-per-minute flow was enough to water men and animals too. William bargained with the horse herders until he acquired the place to establish a ranch of his own.[29]

For the younger Littlefield, finding the good water with a breadth of land unsurveyed and unclaimed at least ten miles in most directions could not have been more timely. From the east, ranchers had been advancing onto the New Mexico plains, centering their outfits on spring-fed pools. The Carters at Lake Tierra Blanca about 1879, Doak Good at Portales Spring with the 9-R in 1880, and Jim Newman, who, after the Capitol Syndicate forced him off its southern division headquartered at the Yellow House bluff and spring, bought out an outfit at Big Lake to establish his enormous DZ in 1884—all were pasturing herds to the north and east by the time William acquired the Hidden Spring. Brother George confirmed William's hold on the place by funding construction of a nice adobe dogtrot home. In 1888 William and his family moved into the ample house with walls eighteen inches thick supporting roof timbers freighted in some 170 miles from Las Vegas (fig. 17).[30]

For Phelps the move could not have come too soon. The loose, easygoing William, then in his late thirties, was not the cowhand others were, and children running loose at the Bosque headquarters distracted if not disrupted the cow work. Nevertheless, Uncle had insisted that Phelps accept William and his family until Uncle could provide a ranch for them. The Hidden Spring site satisfied both of George's criteria. It made a good headquarters for a ranch, and it was well situated for growing the Littlefield domain in southeastern New Mexico.[31]

William's ranch, for which he adopted the LIV brand, with McCarty's T71 some five miles to the southeast, occupied the center of the Littlefield range that stretched more than one hundred miles from the Four Lakes Ranch southeast corner on the Texas line to the Bosque Grande Ranch northwest corner on the Pecos River. Though the territory was roughly barbell in shape, the Bosque headquarters lay about thirty-five miles west of the center, the Four Lakes head-quarters about forty miles south. Of this expanse of approximately 1.75 million acres, the Littlefield outfit held title to only a few thousand covering river banks and water holes.[32]

Leaving nothing to chance in securing the vastness, the Major bought the T71 in 1892, shortly after McCarty received his patent to the ground around the spring.[33] If the purchase cleared another of McCarty's money shortages, ensuring control of water likely motivated Littlefield to send his faithful war servant Nathan Stokes to occupy a little seepage that lay about a half mile southwest of the T71 headquarters. After seeing his master home from the war, Nathan dropped from records until Christmas Day 1867, when the thirty-four-year-old married Mary Grants, mother of three, with whom he fathered three of his own.[34] By 1880 he had moved his family from the Littlefield area of Gonzales County into adjacent Caldwell County, likely to work on the Foster and Plum Creek ranches. Though neither a bronc buster nor even a horseman like what he called "the crack riders," Nathan nevertheless had a way with horses and mules. He made a good hand. He could rope, handle a branding iron, and cook. In fact, he did whatever the whites told him to do. However much George Littlefield appreciated him and however widely the ranch owner's feelings were known, in the cow camp Nathan was just another hand on the black side of the color line. And he was careful to stay on his side. "I don't think I ever gave them any trouble much," he said decades later. "I never did cross them."[35]

Establishing William in his ranch released George not one iota from his patri-archal duty. To the contrary, he seems to have felt the obligation even more deeply since their mother's death on June 8, 1880. "I have to get a teacher for Williams Children in New Mexico as the one I have there wants to quit in May," George documented just how closely he oversaw the well-being of his brother and family. "I want to get a Settled woman. No young woman would Suit the place. And an old one would not probably get along with the children. The Lady that's there has taught for two years and gets along very well. The oldest children are very well advanced, and a teacher has to have some experience to teach them."[36]

As remote as their home was—and geographically it was very remote, with Roswell being about fifty miles away by horseback—William and Euphemia ensured that their children did not lack for good reading. Their library boasted Dickens, Longfellow, Tennyson, Bryant, and Washington Irving, as well as works of English history. A talented musician, Euphemia brought in a piano too. Daugh-ter Christine, five years old when the house was completed, played it avidly, no doubt learning from her mother, who had mastered the instrument in her youth.[37]

Patriarchal motives had to account substantially for George Littlefield's investment in McCarty's T71 and William's LIV because the national cattle market offered no encouragement. While the Major was expanding through creation of these two ranches, the prices paid for cattle remained depressed. So hard on the American economy was the continuing slump that the United States Senate formed a select committee to investigate in 1888. As cattlemen and meat packers argued over whether overproduction or low prices lay at the root of the misery, Texas Cattle Raisers Association President A. P. Bush Jr. blamed overextended credit. He was right. Since the mid-1880s, picturing themselves as millionaires, cattlemen had borrowed to expand their holdings of both cattle and land to accommodate them.[38]

Not George Littlefield. Having since 1883 anticipated the downturn, he waited for the falling market to present investment opportunities for a disciplined contrarian investor. "You Keep a watch out for any thing cheap in cattle," he counseled Edgar Harral. "There is always some one wanting to raise a little money and have to sell cheap, and thats the way to make money."[39]

Littlefield was right too. In 1890 John A. Hullum of Midland sold the Major his cattle and claim twelve miles south of the Four Lakes headquarters for twenty-three thousand dollars, a price "considered very cheap for the outfit as they were a good lot of cattle and well bred up," reported the *Fort Worth Gazette*. Settling a debt of thirty-nine thousand dollars that year possessed Littlefield with James Ellison's sons' Presidio County ranch in far west Texas. But of such transactions, one was different. More than just a way to make money, it laid the foundation for a ranching operation that became legendary and continues in 2018 as one of only two in Littlefield's portfolio still in family hands.[40]

For at least a decade and a half since ranching's introduction on the western side of central Texas's Hill Country, John W. Gamel had been growing his Mason County range. Apparently, in the market slump of the late 1880s, his debt grew well beyond what his sales could support. Maybe Littlefield heard about Gamel's trouble from their mutual friend Ike Pryor, who had neighbored and trailed cattle for Gamel. However he learned of it, on August 11, 1888, Littlefield salvaged Gamel by buying his 33,033-acre fenced and well-watered Mill Creek Ranch straddling the Llano River. "Mr. Gamel was once offered $150,000," the Austin paper told, "but that was several years since, when times were much better."[41]

To manage the new range one hundred miles northwest of Austin, Littlefield approached Will White. Uncle apparently knew his nephew better than the nephew knew himself. White had yet to find his footing. He had not continued in the livery stable business in Gonzales, yet declined to leave central Texas to work on the LIT in the Panhandle. He had become dissatisfied with the Dinner Bell

Ranch but found no pleasure in working in the Bosque Grande country. Through these years, though, Uncle had seen him mature as a cowman. Will accepted both the job and a one-fourth interest in the operation. The partners sealed the deal by registering the Square Top 3 for their brand.[42]

Where the Major and his nephew managers had used the lowland Foster and Dinner Bell as breeding ranches, Uncle and Will designed the Mill Creek, at its 1,200-foot-higher elevation, for maturing. Stream beds channeling through the mostly grassy rolling hills, affording protection from winter's winds, suited the arrangement. Their routine became as steady as the market allowed. They bought yearlings and two-year-olds in the spring and sold threes and fours in the summer. Will said they bought quantity over quality. Said he of his uncle, "A cow was a cow to him. He bought lots of them, just so they were cheap"—in cost, not quality, which Littlefield had been building since bringing blooded bulls onto the LIT.[43]

Though they disagreed as partners do from time to time, neither let it strain their relationship. Three things likely accounted for it. First, Littlefield held controlling interest in this, as in every operation, and he knew each intimately. Second, White admitted, "I always jumped to his beckoning. . . . I was always afraid of him. . . . I just didn't want to have a fight with him." Will was not alone. "The rest," he said, "were so afraid of him, they wouldn't talk back to him." Third, Uncle gave his trusted nephew managers considerable latitude in running their outfits. With few exceptions, "he never paid any attention to what I bought," White said. He "just furnished the money and we furnished the work . . . and when I made one dollar for myself, I made three for him." All things considered as he looked back over their thirty-one-year partnership, Will White concluded that "we never had a cross word in our settlement. He was fair in all his dealings." On the Mill Creek Ranch, Will White at last had found his place.[44]

The Mill Creek property likely would have been the extent of Will's operation but for another rancher in distress. The effects of the dry years of the early 1890s in the Hill Country, compounded no doubt by the economic downturn from the Panic of 1893, broke Seth Mabry. Though Littlefield was spending heavily in 1894 on construction of his grand home, he nevertheless bought Mabry's thirty-six-thousand-acre Saline Ranch on the Llano River adjacent to and west of the Mill Creek.[45] The money slaked but did not resolve Mabry's troubles. A few years later, Littlefield bailed out his friend again by buying his thirty-thousand-acre Menard Ranch, adjoining the Saline to the north.

By simply following the plain charge he had given Edgar Harral, Littlefield had acquired in the three ranches a block of around one hundred thousand acres of pasture. Surely equally important to the Major, he had helped a dear friend. As Haley got Mabry's story from those who knew, the former trailing contractor "was virtually pensioned by old cowmen friends."[46] For Uncle, the Mill Creek Ranch in particular served as more than a business proposition and contributed more than family security. Once or twice a year "He come out there and run them hounds until their feet would get so sore they couldn't go," Will said.[47]

On the Four Lakes, his men remembered not his hunting but Littlefield's camaraderie. "He wasn't highhanded a bit," Jim Roberts said. "He made his boys like him instead of using them like they were servants." Wearing "duckin's just like us cowboys," why, "in his younger days, Major would come out to the wagon, wrestle with all the doggone boys there. He used to box. . . . He'd just go and catch all the dirtiest and toughest old boys and wallow out there like a kid."[48]

To a cowman outside the LFD outfit like Charlie Ballard, George Littlefield appeared to be not a warmhearted sort at all but rather "a cold and hard-headed businessman." LFD men knew that side of him too. "He was business, though, by George," Charlie Walker confirmed. "He wanted you to keep tab on everything." But, added Walker, as though being business-like in running an operation was unfriendly, "he was fine in every other way." Indeed, continued Walker, "If you wanted to do anything [in cattle], he was just as willing for you to go on and help you do it." He favored regular hands like Gonzales natives Bud Ratliff and range boss William John "Bud" Wilkinson by letting them run their own brands on the Four Lakes. The practice even attracted such hands as J. D. Hart from the Bar V and Ben Baker from the Jinglebob. All that the ranch owner asked in return was that when a herd grew to three hundred to four hundred head, the rancher-hand provide a windmill watering place.[49] How a man perceived the Major depended on the capacity in which he knew him.

As Charlie Walker documented, George Littlefield kept his finger on the pulse of his ranches. Not just through communications, he monitored them also by having the managers come to Austin for an annual face-to-face settlement of accounts and by visiting the properties for an extended period at least annually in the spring to see how the cattle had wintered. On the Four Lakes, after he could travel to Roswell by rail, he visited again for roundup and branding, then a third time in the fall, when cattle were being delivered to buyers. No detail escaped him in the cow work and in preparing cattle for market, however far in the future delivery would come. "Did you brand those cattle through a chute?" Uncle once asked Edgar Harral pointedly. Uniformly branded steers signaled a careful rancher and sold better. "If you put them in a chute and don't have a squeezer you will brand all over them," he continued, before instructing that "You should handle them so you will have the best branded bunch." Like any good manager wanting to know his operation and product thoroughly, Littlefield participated in the work. He particularly enjoyed "cutting" the cattle. On a horse especially adept, on the one hand, at making quick moves corresponding to those of a cow trying to avoid being singled out and, on the other hand, at understanding the job so that the rider need do little more than identify the animal to be cut, the rider would work individual animals out of the herd, normally calves for branding and animals from other ranches that had wandered onto the Four Lakes ground.[50]

The weather, of course, defied control. Drought returned to the Pecos in 1889 so severely that the outfit had to ship thirteen thousand steers and cows to Indian Territory for grass and water. Following a wet spring in 1891, then a deadly blizzard, drought resumed. And by "'94 it was sure enough dry," recalled Edgar Harral. "Nothing but whirlwinds, that was all you could see." That year—eighteen after Charles Goodnight's cattle began the eating of virtually every blade of grass in their section of the Pecos basin—Phelps finished moving all but cattle remnants off the river. "That was one of the finest business moves there was," Charlie Walker lauded the multiyear transfer, "because along from '94 on that river was just et out, perfectly bare—nothing could stay there. . . . [The desperately dry spell] didn't affect them because they had most all their stuff out on them Plains, and they had fine grass out there."[51]

Actually, fine grass was only the half of it. The Major's profit was more than good because of the foresight to tap the underground water. In the estimation of General Land Office Commissioner William A. J. Sparks nine years earlier, "the choicest cattle raising portions" of the territory had been taken. By "choice," he meant parcels along streams or beside lakes. George Littlefield and Phelps White knew better. Windmills provided an abundant flow of water unaffected by any drought. No cow on the Four Lakes had to walk more than five miles to reach the Double Star, West Jim, East Jim, Hightower, 7HR, Shiloh, Eight Mile, or another of the dozens of windmills spotted over the ranch, most of which Phelps had contracted Causey to put in. The benefit of the move was immediate. "I made a good Sale yesterday. Cattle are going up. And," the Major congratulated himself early in 1895, "we who have stayed in the business and attended to them properly will make good mony."[52]

Maybe Sparks's belief accounted for the high plains being the last substantial chunk of ground within the territory to have the surveyor's chain laid on it. More likely it was that the land office saw other priorities after Congress failed to provide a mechanism for collecting the twenty-five-dollar yearly rent per section for which it called in 1885. Washington's negligence allowed the LFD to utilize the some nine hundred thousand acres rent-free. Eight years of the twentieth century would pass before surveyors climbed the caprock to delineate townships and the Major had to add the expense of leasing more than a minimum of his partially surveyed north boundary to the cost of running the Four Lakes Ranch.[53]

In the cattle community, George Littlefield had earned his promotion. The Major had devoted six years to helping found the Texas Live Stock Association, then working with the small, compatible group of elected leaders guiding its fortunes. They built the association to the pinnacle in size and importance among the nation's livestock organizations, then did their best to hold the TLSA together as its members confronted the single but singularly divisive issue of Texas Fever. Though unsuccessful in saving the first statewide livestock organization, George Littlefield earned the respect of his colleagues. "Indefatigable in the discharge of his duty," they praised his leadership.

As a cattleman, the Major had seen his Littlefield Cattle Company through times that broke unnumbered others. His accomplishment rested on two foundations. First was assembling a team of exceptionally talented and dedicated ranch managers. Fifteen years it took him trying a cowman, then one nephew, then another in his search for the right men—the three White brothers—who brought to their work an implicit understanding of cattle management, a thorough knowledge of the cattle business, and a personal commitment to him and to the work that would sustain their shared interests and relationships for as long as they lived.

Under George Littlefield's direction and the skillful management of Phelps and Tom White, the Littlefield outfit in New Mexico had survived the bad times. Not just survived, Phelps and Tom had managed so deftly that each year even through the bad times they had increased the value of their interest in the company until they had worked themselves out of debt to Uncle. Appreciating their unswerving dedication, when they visited in Austin, Uncle devoted himself to seeing that they had "a good time while here as they have such a poor opportunity to enjoy themselves in New Mexico." Alice Littlefield confirmed to Will White that Uncle felt the same about him and his management of the Mill Creek Ranch. "My Aunt used to tell me," Will recalled years later, "Now, when you buy these cattle and put them on the ranch, George is coming home every night, and saying 'Those boys are going to break me yet.' But when they commenced to sell the cattle and send the money into Austin, why, it was a different tune."[54]

The second foundation on which his achievement rested was his innate business sense and talent. A handful of men handled more cattle than he, but, testified drover and founder of a successful livestock commission company George W.

Saunders, "none of them showed his ability as a financier."[55] On the one hand, he had the strength of character to maintain a contrarian investment philosophy. On the other, his remarkable deal-making talent at which Will White so marveled amassed the financial reserves that supported his way. Undergirding both was supreme confidence. He could not have put it more succinctly than when he told Edgar Harral that he ran his business; it didn't run him.

A man able to do that could not help but attract notice at home.

11

MY OWN MAN

On June 28, 1884, six months after George and Alice Littlefield moved into their Austin home, George and fellow cattleman Jesse Lincoln Driskill were driving down Congress Avenue when something spooked the horse pulling their buggy. Instantly things became "quite lively." As sixty-year-old Driskill vaulted free of the vehicle, forty-two-year-old Littlefield sprang forward "cow-boy like," reported the newspaper. Experience propelled him toward the horse's neck. Once having hold, he bulldogged the animal to the ground, where he held it until it was quieted. From their ringside seat at the Raymond House Hotel, onlookers "were loud in praise of Mr. Littlefield's coolness and dexterity," the news story concluded.[1] If any in Austin wondered whether Littlefield, and Alice with him, would make their presence felt in the city, they might have taken Littlefield's decisive resolution of the sudden calamity as a sign.

Atop the hill up Congress Avenue from the Raymond House, the State of Texas had begun erecting its new capitol. Superlatives described the building. More than a replacement for the plain 1853 pile preceding it on the site, the majestic new structure would be without rival in size and appointment among the capitols of all the other thirty-seven states. The 326 feet to the tip of the lone star held high by the Goddess of Liberty surmounting the dome would soar taller even than the national capitol. Why, proclaimed the state officials overseeing construction, the architect's conception was larger and finer even than the buildings of the German Reichstag and English Parliament. Most singular of all, construction was paid for not with tax money but with three million acres of West Texas land (which few beyond ranchers wanted).

For an edifice of this magnitude, grandeur, and statewide importance, the cornerstone laying could not help but be the biggest event in Austin since the government of the Republic of Texas inaugurated Austin's tenure as the capital four and a half decades earlier. To make the date even more meaningful, the event was scheduled for March 2, 1885, the forty-ninth anniversary of the signing of the Texas Declaration of Independence. Austin leaders knew that, paraphrasing capitol

167

historian Fred Rathjen, everyone of any distinction would be present, and just about everyone of no particular distinction would be there too. George Littlefield would join prominent local cattlemen representing the Texas Live Stock Association, the *Statesman* reported four months out. But on New Year's Day 1885 came the real news, when the paper reported that the chair of Austin's central committee for the celebration—civic leader and banker Alexander Penn Wooldridge—had selected Littlefield to serve on the celebration committee's finance subcommittee. The newspaper mention was small—in a list and on an inside page—but the meaning of the appointment was profound. Littlefield's designation elevated the increasingly wealthy resident of a year and a half into the ranks of the city's movers and shakers.[2]

If any doubt about the meaning lingered, invitation to membership in the Washington Steam Fire Company No. 1 three months later confirmed George Littlefield's integration into Austin's inner circle of catalytic achievers. The city's second-oldest fire company, organized in 1868 by Eugene Bremond's father, lately enjoyed the prestige earned by having been first to put water on the 1881 fire that destroyed the 1853 capitol. But as renowned as the volunteers were for firefighting, the singular distinction of the Washington Fire Company lay in the persons of its members. The "kid-glove company," locals called the group, because so many moneyed men and leading citizens filled its ranks.[3]

In a day when social activities bonded the volunteers who staffed fire companies, George and Alice fit right in. "Major and Mrs. Littlefield know how to entertain to perfection," the *Statesman* declared. Just three months after Littlefield's induction into the fire company, the paper treated readers to a lengthy description of "the usual hospitality received at their hands," this time in a large party for the two nieces living with them. Among the tables of fruits, ices, and beverages scattered around the Littlefield's half block, the party featured a delectably light-hearted but devilish twist. In a pond containing German carp, "patient anglers fished with varied success, though each secured at least one member of the finny tribe. None were pulled out of their boots in their endeavors to land their prizes, but some of the hauls created considerable excitement, as when an eel was fished out to the dismay and fright of some of the ladies." And "one fish . . . turned out to be a large onion, much to the chagrin of the fair capturer."[4]

Thoroughly integrated into Austin's power and social circles, the Littlefields' involvement in local affairs blossomed. George served in 1886 on the committee planning the January cattleman's ball, judged the March races at the fairgrounds, chaired the committee planning the January 1887 gubernatorial inaugural ball (the first to be held in the sumptuous new Driskill Hotel), and served on the 1888 capitol dedication General Reception Committee. Alice joined the women's social scene. Along with taking turns hosting elegant lunches, the ladies banded together to raise funds for settlers in West Texas suffering from the same drought afflicting the LFD in New Mexico.[5]

Sympathy for the victims surely motivated Alice and her friends. By contrast, a "sentiment of fraternity born of the hardships and dangers shared in the march, the bivouac and the battle field" summoned Civil War veterans. George Littlefield felt it. He had felt it in his days at the front. But after the war, it appears cattle and family occupied him until 1884. In November, just months after settling into his Orange Street home, he joined with sixty-three comrades in the capital city in forming the John Bell Hood Camp, the first Texas organization embracing Confederate veterans no matter their unit.[6]

The Hood Camp was the second such organization in the entire South, following the formation of the Robert E. Lee Camp in the former Confederate capital of Richmond, Virginia, by just a year. Fellowship drew the Austin veterans together, certainly. But two larger goals drove them. One was guarding portrayal of the history of the Lost Cause, an anxiety that would simmer in George Littlefield for three decades until he created the country's first endowment in support of a full and impartial history of the South.

The other was following the Lee Camp's lead in filling an increasingly visible void of providing relief for comrades disabled from their wounds. In the years after the Confederate surrender, those who attended memory of the lost country memorialized the dead locally. The death of Robert E. Lee in 1870 changed the approach. Groups sprang up to venerate the fallen leader, tend memory of their shared cause, and rekindle former camaraderie. In Houston a group of Eighth Texas Cavalrymen met in May 1871 to form the Association of Survivors of Terry's Texas Rangers. On his cattle drive to Kansas, Littlefield missed the founding of this social organization of which he would become a stalwart. For all the communal spirit represented by such groups as the Terry Ranger association, members by and large were those prosperous enough to be able to afford to participate. Left aside were those just able to take care of themselves. Though the national and northern state governments established homes for incapacitated Union soldiers, no southern state or local government offered assistance or succor to its veterans. Then a generation removed from the war, southern thinking came to focus on the reconciliation for which Lee himself had called and thus on remembering the war through the battlefield experience common to both sides. This sentiment in the 1880s not only emphasized the common soldier but simultaneously illuminated the plight of those whose war injuries, aggravated by advancing age, were diminishing their abilities to support themselves. Confederate veterans on the streets begging for their living offended the sensibilities of their comrades. The "living monuments to the South's most sacred virtues of honor and chivalry," as some called them, deserved better. If relief were to reach the sinking, the veterans who had fought beside them would have to provide it. The Hood Camp set about establishing a home in Austin for these unfortunates.[7]

Maybe Maj. George Littlefield felt the drive because he himself had come so near to being one of the incapacitated. His social promotion to the rank associated with his wound came concurrently with his commitment to the Hood Camp. Those who knew him had every reason to anticipate he would involve himself vigorously in camp affairs. But camp records seem to tell a different story. For nearly six years after the home, the third in the South behind Virginia's and Louisiana's, opened its doors in 1884, his name appears nowhere in camp minutes.[8]

Far from holding Confederate veteran activities at arm's length, though, the Major reveled in them. When the Terry Rangers held their 1887 annual meeting at the Driskill Hotel, he was there. And what an occasion it was. In reporting the speeches and exuberance of the evening's social, the reporter summoned the most expressive words and phrases at his command. The "dithyramb of exultation" that began at ten o'clock in the evening produced "an inspiration animate with the grand spirit of the occasion." The succession of talks, one running for two hours, built to a "diapason of expression." So long into the night did the partying continue that, to have any description in the next day's paper, the reporter had to leave early. He apologized, and readers are left to wonder what climax had topped the dithyramb and diapason that preceded it.

For Littlefield, the meeting's high point likely occurred in the afternoon, when his colleagues selected him to serve on the committee to review the regimental history then being compiled, appointed him to chair the committee arranging the next year's reunion also in Austin, and elected him the association's second vice president. In every aspect of the Rangers association life, Littlefield had become a fixture.[9]

As with the Rangers, once George Littlefield took a role in Hood Camp affairs, the veterans vaulted him to leadership. In January 1890, one month after his first recorded committee assignment, he accepted election to the board of directors.[10] Since the Hood Camp was a business operating the Confederate Home, members surely picked their leaders for strengths essential to managing the project. The Major's entrepreneurial acumen was well known, of course. But a further forte may have attracted the membership. George Littlefield was blossoming into a force in state politics.

Having the State of Texas assume responsibility for the Confederate Home had been a goal of the camp from the beginning. After a legislature dominated by former Confederates failed to find in the eleven-year-old state constitution any authorization for providing support, in 1889 the Austin veterans met their champion when Attorney General James Stephen Hogg identified an appropriate provision. As happy as the resulting income was, it fell far short of expenses. Consequently, Confederates throughout the state made public funding a campaign issue in the 1890 gubernatorial election. Democratic candidate Hogg, the son of a Confederate brigadier but himself without Confederate credentials, having been too young to join the fight, campaigned on it, won, and within two months of taking office signed into law a bill under which the state took charge of the facility.[11]

Littlefield made friends with Hogg. "The people's governor," the Major would call him. Though Littlefield's correspondence documenting his lifetime of political activity has not survived, some of the basis of Littlefield's embrace of Hogg seems evident. Both men opposed prohibition, though neither drank to any extent. For Littlefield, it was an issue of personal freedom. Further, Hogg fought abusive corporations and business combinations. Long outraged over railroad practices detrimental to cattlemen, Littlefield had to have been pleased with Hogg's successful pursuit of railroad regulation through creating the Texas Railroad Commission. Underlying everything, of course, Hogg was a Democrat. "Could not support any Republican for any thing." "Carpetbaggers," he often called them.[12] Along with most of the electorate, he held that position from Reconstruction, if not the 1860 presidential election, until his death.

For a politician, Littlefield's friendship had concrete benefits. If George Littlefield was your friend, later governor James E. Ferguson recounted his experience, "he put his money on you. He'd go to the limit. . . . He would bet all that anyone and everyone could put up against a cause he was interested in and then get out and spend that much to get his party elected." Having come of age politically in the unsettled Reconstruction years, the Major "believed it was perfectly all right to buy an election with silver dollars if that was the way to get it," commented another. A generation would have to pass, Littlefield had prophesied in 1868, to get beyond "the death and destruction that's abroad upon the land."[13] Whether he remembered his prediction, he was one of the new generation rising in the late 1880s. And by that time, he had the means to commit to winning elections.

In Jim Hogg's 1892 reelection campaign, Littlefield for the first time through the *Statesman* challenged anyone willing to put his money on the governor's opponent. Two men arrived in Austin to accept the wager, reported the paper, but in the time it took other Hogg supporters to sweeten the pot, the men departed for

Houston, never to be heard from again. Hogg won, but by a plurality—the first time a gubernatorial candidate in Texas failed to receive a majority.[14]

If George Littlefield's money helped to secure the narrow victory, as likely it did, then equally probable is that his strong and newsworthy fidelity accounts for his appointment to a vacancy on the Blind Asylum's Board of Trustees. No association with the blind community or with state government suggests a basis other than political reward. Hardly a plum, though, the commission placed Littlefield on the board of an institution that was not only regularly scrutinized by the legislature because it cost more than most state agencies to operate but also just then was begging for a greater appropriation to repair decaying facilities. One term was enough. The only connection Littlefield developed from the appointment was a lifelong friendship with superintendent Frank Rainey, fellow Hood Camp member.[15]

The year Hogg moved into the governor's mansion, Hood Camp members elevated George Littlefield to their treasurer. On this officer's shoulders in 1891 rested the weight of the camp's principal work of ensuring funding to operate the Confederate Home. Surely Littlefield accepted the job knowing of the camp's troubled finances. Shortly after he took office, the board required him to move against the property of his predecessor delinquent in rent payments for use of camp properties. Camp members knew they had the right man for the job. Littlefield's integrity was newsworthy. In the only feature of its kind in years, if ever, the Austin paper reported the incident when, after finding fifty dollars on the sidewalk, Littlefield returned the large sum to the dry goods merchant who proved his loss. For a sound money manager, camp members could hardly have selected better than the president of Austin's newest bank.[16]

Some heard that a disagreement with State National Bank directors impelled George Littlefield to want to open a bank to run as he judged best. Maybe, instead, the fine potential for profit in the cattle industry that had come to rely on borrowed money enticed him. And there was just then Austin's soaring economic prospects. Whatever his motivation, on March 27, 1890, he joined about two dozen business friends in organizing the American National Bank.[17]

So buoyant in anticipation of their future were Austinites in 1890, they were ready to mortgage the city to secure it. A generation earlier, in the 1870s, the coming of railroads invigorated the place by turning it into the trade center of its neighborhood. In the 1880s construction of the capitol and the opening of the university animated spirits. Cattle substantially undergirded the economy. The stately Driskill Hotel, opened in 1886, displayed it: over each entrance presided the bust of a Driskill rancher supported by a steer's head. But in neither decade had the good times lasted into the following decade. To invigorate Austin's economy in the 1890s and beyond, City National Bank president A. P. Wooldridge told his fellow residents that as it approached the new decade, Austin needed to harness its one great untapped asset—the Colorado River. Supporters erupted in rhyme. Bubbled one:

> A dam! A dam! . . .
> Here's the place for speculation,
> With no fear of defalcation,
> And no dread of retrogression,
> For we're working on a dam.
> Come for health and come for pleasure,
> Come for work or come for leisure,
> Come whate'er it is you treasure

Contributed another, envisioning the economic impact:

> The most important mission of all when done,
> Manufacturers by score to Austin will come,
> Setting the wheels of industry in motion,
> Advertising Austin from ocean to ocean.

Water and electric power exceeding that produced anywhere else in the South would propel the future, Austinites were told. And they believed. So did George Littlefield and his friends. Hardly had the consultant finished describing the magnitude and benefit of the dam project than they met, subscribed double the fifty-thousand-dollar minimum capital requirement, formed the board of directors, and elected officers from their number to launch the American National Bank. For president they elected George Washington Littlefield. He was the wealthiest among them, his $1 million representing one-third of their estimated combined worth. Liquor dealer John Henry Houghton received the vote for vice president. If particular business savvy characterized these two, then far-reaching connections distinguished William Robert Hamby, the board's choice for cashier. On top of managing the local newspaper, Hamby was holding a seat in the Texas House of Representatives. The board had good reason to anticipate that the three would work well together. Littlefield and Hamby shared commitment to the Hood Camp and officed adjacent to each other. Littlefield and Houghton belonged to the exclusive Washington Fire Company and, with their families, spent time in the summer rejuvenating in the waters of Waukesha, Wisconsin.[18]

In May 1890 Austin residents justified the expectation of the American National's financiers when they voted in a 27-to-1 tsunami to issue construction bonds valued at $1.4 million—a stunning amount, eleven times larger than all other bonded indebtedness combined and fourteen times annual revenues. Entrepreneurs interested in banking in Texas pointed to less dramatic but equally solid figures. Ratios of both dividends and earnings to capital bettered the national average. For financiers, "National bank stock is the very best kind of investment in the country," Hamby's paper editorialized in March. Though unregulated private banks had dominated banking in Texas since Reconstruction, by the last decade of the nineteenth century the accumulation of wealth in Texas cities, combined with the greater safety of the national banking system, turned capitalists to national banks. With the investors, public opinion swung from hostility toward banks to approval. It was a sea change, one excited banker told his colleagues convened in the 1889 Texas Bankers Association annual meeting. The number of new national banks organized in Texas in 1889 proved it. Thirty-six placed the Lone Star State ahead of all states. And that number paled before the sixty-three in 1890. Combine the optimism in Austin with the enthusiasm for organizing national banks, and Littlefield's board could not have been surprised when shortly after they selected their officers, a group organized the Austin National Bank.[19]

For President Littlefield, the new bank was something more than simply the fifth national bank in the capital city. From the Austin National's opening two weeks ahead of the American National's on July 1, 1890, he saw the Austin National as his bank's chief rival. For those who read between the lines, editor Hamby told the paper's readers why. Like Eugene Bremond's State National, Tom Brackenridge's First National, and Alexander Wooldridge's City National, the American National Bank was "a home institution composed of home men." The Austin National was not. Pennsylvania financiers established it. C. W. Gilfillan and his son-in-law Edward P. Wilmot searched the Southwest for someplace to open a bank until they found Austin. Southerner Littlefield bristled. While the competitive Major worked incessantly to best every competitor bank, throughout his twenty-nine years heading the American National he went to extra lengths to upstage the "northern" Austin National.[20]

It began with location and appointment. In a two-story business building of no distinguishing character, the Austin National outfitted its space with "richly and chastely carved" antique oak furniture pieces "that for finish and style there has never been anything in Austin to equal them." The banking rooms presented "perhaps as handsome an appearance as any bank in this section." The steel-lined safe protected by time locks was "the first of the kind ever brought to Austin," if not to Texas, the paper added.

By contrast, the furniture of the American National was utilitarian. And its new safe would not arrive until after opening day. But if location was key to success, the American National bested its rival hands down. The American National occupied space on the main floor of *the* place to be in Austin, *the* place to which Austinites came to negotiate business deals and socialize. The three-year-old Driskill Hotel offered every convenience and luxury. To dine in the most elegant eating place in town, come to the sky-lit main dining room. For the finest glass of soda, visit the fountain in the hotel's drug store. The telegraph office attracted businessmen requiring the speediest communication to distant parts. The ladies' entrance on the east protected the sensibilities of the fair sex from assault by the rough talk of gentlemen coming and going through the south and west entrances. Littlefield's bank was strategically positioned between the men's and women's entrances (fig. 18).[21]

Whether or not location trumped appointment, Littlefield saw his bank embraced by the community. Only eight business days after opening, he told Shelton Dowell's widow, Shelt having died at home in Lockhart, Texas, on December 2, 1885, that response had been so strong that "if I have any opportunity in future to buy any [American National Bank stock for you at a reasonable price] . . . I will let you Know and it may be best to do so as it would be a *permanent* investment." He was right. The bank's first year mirrored its first days. Not only did the American National pay what the newspaper styled as "a handsome dividend," but at its first anniversary it increased its paid-up capital to two hundred thousand dollars, doubling the capital of the State and City Nationals and leapfrogging the Austin National by fifty thousand dollars.[22]

Capital offered one measure of a bank's strength. Cash on hand provided another. And that was the one a president could affect on short notice. To make "our Deposits on the day of opening heavier," Littlefield took advantage of what later would be called a float. He had Alice, visiting in Houston, withdraw the money she needed from a bank slow to present drafts out of town.[23]

While every penny counted, the truly important days for having the largest sum in the safe were those on which the bank examiner appeared. But bankers in institutions such as Austin's American National and First National that catered to the cattle trade often knew their customers personally and sometimes made short-term loans on the insubstantial collateral of a cattle herd that dropped the bank's cash on hand below the required minimum. When bank presidents such as Littlefield learned that an examiner was coming when their vault was too bare, the exertions they made to pull money from friendly banks to cover the shortage became legendary.

Short story writer O. Henry turned the legend into a gripping story. The scrambling he evidently witnessed from his First National teller's window gave him the plot of "Friends in San Rosario." San Rosario is an ill-disguised Austin. The main character, according to banker George Brackenridge biographer Marilyn McAdams Sibley, is a composite of bank presidents George Littlefield and Tom Brackenridge, "with Brackenridge contributing most to the name and Littlefield most to the characteristics of the fictional man." In the story, a fastidious bank examiner shows up unannounced at Major Tom's bank. Knowing that after inspecting the First National the examiner will visit the Stockman's National, the First National's messenger reports the man's presence to the Stockman's National. Hastily the Stockman's National president scribbles a note for Major Tom. The rest of the tale recounts what Major Tom does to stall the examiner until the train arrives carrying the Stockman's salvation.[24]

Competition continued on balance sheets and statements of condition for five years until 1895, when President Edward Wilmot took it to a different plane. He announced plans to move. The Austin National's space no longer accommodated the bank's volume of business. Rather than securing more square feet in its two-story location on Sixth Street, though, Wilmot was taking the bank to a three-story building on Congress Avenue.

George Littlefield had to respond. Rather than leave the Driskill, he determined to cement the hotel yet more solidly as Austin's centerpiece. Before Wilmot could move, the American National's president counted out $106,000 in cash to buy the Driskill lock, stock, and barrel on May 24, 1895. However hasty his decision to buy was, Littlefield acquired the property for between one-quarter and one-third of its initial cost. Jesse Driskill had lost his hotel after the Big Die-Up of 1887–88 and a severe spring cold snap that destroyed his herds and left him without means to pay on his loans. Then with each subsequent sale, the hotel's value dropped, and the property's future darkened. Littlefield's purchase changed that. More than just stabilizing ownership of his bank's home, the Major announced his intention to add two floors to accommodate demand. And he was exploring building an 1,800-plus-seat opera house next door. Ambitious plans these, but as they were coming from Major Littlefield, citizens could have confidence in them, the paper said. If any doubted, a glance at the *New York Tribune*'s June 1892 supplement "American Millionaires" should have reassured them that the Major could finance his intentions. Littlefield's name appeared on this first list of the 4,047 wealthiest Americans. And buoying their confidence, locals would have noticed that Austin's other millionaire, sugar plantation owner Leigh A. Ellis, sat on Littlefield's American National Bank board.[25]

Austinites could be confident of Littlefield's financial strength, too, when they passed by the home George and Alice completed in 1894. San Antonio architect James Wahrenberger, a native of Austin renowned for placing second in the design competition for the Texas capitol and for admired residences in San Antonio, was told to outdo himself. "Yes, when our house is complete," George observed during construction, "it will be the best in this City. I hated to put so much money into a home, but there are no children and Alice and I should just as well enjoy it."[26] The Littlefield home would eclipse all others in Austin, Littlefield could say, because he had turned down buying what up to then was Austin's most modern and elegant mansion.

Built by millionaire Jesse Driskill in 1881, Driskill Hall, only three blocks up Whitis from the Littlefields, was a palace. In design, construction, and furnishing of his residence, Driskill spent a reputed staggering $120,000. Walls were twenty inches thick. Each brick cost ten cents, not counting shipping from Saint Louis. It was the first house in Austin to have indoor plumbing with pipes for both hot and cold water and a shower bath, whose water temperature could be regulated to suit the bather. For beauty, cut-glass door panels complemented cut-glass transoms and chandeliers, and even the maid's room contained one of the eleven marble mantles.

What good years in the cattle trade brought him, losses from the winter die-up and killing cold the following spring took away. Debts mounted until Jesse Driskill had to sell his house too. Sometime before his death in 1890, Driskill approached George Littlefield about buying the mansion. With his own finances crimped by the bad times in the cattle trade, George declined, adding that when he could afford the house he and Alice wanted, he would build it.[27]

In the fall of 1892, work began on the Littlefield home. Like Driskill Hall, the mantels and fireplace surrounds are works of art, the walls are twenty inches thick, and the bricks came from Saint Louis, still at ten cents each. But how the craftsmen assembled the building blocks set the Littlefield residence apart. It began with remarkably precise laying of each course. Then a mortar compound containing quartz dust was worked into a convex curvature to give the exterior a subtle but unique sparkle. Exquisite woodwork using several woods matched Driskill's cut-glass appointments. Marshall Field and Company of Chicago furnished the 8,140 square feet of living space on two floors. Initials worked into the fabric of the house both outside and inside telegraphed unmistakably that this was George Littlefield's home. An architectural historian saw the owner's hand displayed more deeply in the home's "extreme ornateness" that exhibited "an exacting intent which directly reflects the man's character." Completed and furnished, the Texas Victorian mansion cost the Major two and half times Jesse Driskill's outlay for Driskill Hall (figs. 19, 20, 21).[28]

If to decorate the interior walls Marshall Field provided the period generic art, Alice Littlefield personalized the spaces with works she painted (fig. 22). One depicted a tranquil sylvan scene featuring a lake with three black and white cows standing in the water in the foreground. When he saw the canvas, her Hereford rancher husband balked: "Oh, Alice, they're just milk cows." George contributed to the interior decoration by displaying his favorite cattle sculpture in the turret off the library on the main floor. Like any rancher who ensured that all his cattle were branded, George had LFD etched into and highlighted in black on the bull whose full right side is visible, even though that animal is losing the fight. When she saw the addition, Alice returned his compliment, chiding him that it ruined the aesthetic of the piece (figs. 14 and 23).[29]

Having built the mansion immediately behind the house in which they were living, the old building had to be removed. Uncle's habit being to provide family brides with a house, he meant to move this one to a nearby Whitis Avenue lot for Alice Daniel. But trees he had planted some years earlier blocked the most direct route southeast to Whitis. Other foliage obstructed the route south to Orange Street. To save the landscaping, he approached his neighbor on the west. Professor George Bruce Halsted was a man of extremes. He was a theoretical mathematician whose brilliance brought distinction to the university. But said one who knew him, he was inordinately impractical, "a victim of higher education." His house exemplified it. He perched the eyesore atop poles to save it from a flood that could never reach his property even if the Austin dam did break to bring his nightmare to pass. Would he sell? Incensed at the proposal, the intensely hotheaded Halsted shot back that if Littlefield thought that just because he was rich, he could acquire anything he wanted, he was wrong. Halsted's half block was not Littlefield's to have or even use. So Littlefield accomplished the move by uprooting the trees. Not content with telling Littlefield off, the young professor encouraged his sons to pester their wealthy neighbor by heaving dead chickens and cats and rotten vegetables over Littlefield's west wall. The unpleasantness ended a few years later, when Halsted was summarily dismissed from the faculty for being too free in his criticisms of university administration.[30]

Little time elapsed after removing the old house before the Littlefields threw their showplace open for parties. As if the magnificent home was not spectacle enough, the first, on December 18, 1894, featured "the handsomest and largest order" ever served in Austin of "brick mould (Harlequin) ice cream." So large was the stream of guests to the second party, on New Year's Day 1895, that Alice Littlefield engaged thirty-three women to assist in serving the crowd.[31]

For the Littlefields' horses and conveyances, the architect designed a carriage house matching the home. To tend the animals and drive him to his destinations,

primarily the bank, Littlefield summoned Nathan Stokes (fig. 24). When not dot-
ing over the horses, the sixty-plus-year-old man busied himself tending the yard's
flowers, running errands, and milking the cow, as long as the Littlefields kept one.
While a passerby could not surmise by watching Nathan's activity, the former slave
occupied a singular status within the Littlefield community. No work was required
of him. For all that Nathan had done for the Major, especially tending him during
his recovery thirty-plus years earlier, George Littlefield provided for his every need.
The Major furnished quarters on the commodious second floor of the carriage
house. Continuing the habit begun during the war, Littlefield gave him two dollars
spending money every Saturday. "War money," they called it. So hallowed was the
ritual that in his will the Major provided for its continuance as long as Nathan
lived. Far from a provision buried deep in the lengthy document, it was the fourth
item, preceding mention even of Alice herself. "They just took care of him, I tell
you right now," milkman Henry A. Dunn summed up what all who knew the
Littlefields knew.[32]

"Uncle Nathan" was the way whites young and old, family members and the
Major's friends and associates spoke of him out of respect for his absolute devotion
to the Major and for the pleasure they had in listening to his stories of the war, the
cattle range, and life as he experienced it. Many teased him playfully just to hear
him respond. If the whites' reminiscences are representative, Nathan sometimes
taught them something and other times had as much fun with them as they had
with him.

Henry Dunn recalled a tease, the reply to which took him aback:

"I'd always heard about people rustling cattle, and I always thought it was
a joke, you know. I didn't mean it to [upset him], but he couldn't stand you
talk about stealing anything."

"How many cattle do you suppose that you swiped for Major Littlefield?" [Dunn asked playfully once].

"Oh! but," he said, "we didn't never use words like that. That's a strong
word. We used mild words."

"Well," I said, "didn't some . . . cattle [of other ranchers] take up with
some of your bunch?"

"Yes, sir, yes, sir, they took up with us, but they wanted to be sociable,
and we didn't run them off like a dog. When you tell a dog to go, you just
say, 'Git.' We didn't do calves like that. You just kind of let them alone, and
we didn't shoo them away. We let them stay."

"Well," I said, "What did you do at round up time?"

"Well," he said, "if they wanted to be sociable and be with us, well we just let them alone."

"Well, did you brand everything?"

"Yes, sir, we had to brand. That's the only way we could keep up with our cattle, you know. We had to brand everything."

"Well, did other people get some of your cattle?"

"Oh! yes, sir, I suppose they did, but we didn't run after anybody. The Major, he wanted everybody to get along with everybody. That's the way he wanted to run his business."

"If I'd say a curse word," Dunn continued, "he'd say, 'Un, oh. Don't use those words. They don't sound right. You're not going to go to heaven if you don't use better language than that.'"[33]

Accountant Mood Cicero Landrum's daughter said her father enjoyed asking Uncle Nathan how he was doing, how the Littlefields were treating him. Terribly, Uncle Nathan would reply. "My father came home just dying because he thought it was the funniest thing he'd ever heard of, terribly treated, so hard on him."[34]

Not just Nathan Stokes, George Littlefield looked after former slaves from his growing-up years like he did members of his biological family, said niece Alice Daniel. One was the slave woman who, typical of plantation life, looked after him as though he were one of her own children. When the Major learned of the destitution into which Mama Lucy in Gonzales had fallen, he came to her relief. Her fifty-nine-year tie to the Littlefields had been broken, first, by George's mother's death, then by George's move to Austin. Childless and twice widowed, seventy-one-year-old Lucy Littlefield had been left with neither family nor home until, with the Major's support, the Methodist preacher who reconnected them took her into his Austin home to finish her years. When Mama Lucy, as they called her, died, George and Alice gave her a burial in Austin's city cemetery and funded a funeral of unusual personal attention and lavishness. Flowers imported from Houston and arranged by Alice Littlefield herself covered the grave. Finally, George marked the spot more prominently than most whites evidenced their own final resting places in the nearly sixty-year-old Oakwood burial ground.[35]

Appreciative of all they knew of Major Littlefield—not least his purchase of and plans for the Driskill Hotel—a group of prominent Austinites began circulating petitions promoting the handsome businessman and civic figure for mayor in the December 1895 election (fig. 25). The energetic campaign made news even two hundred miles away. "Everybody they encountered was anxious to sign," the *Dallas Morning News* reported. Everybody but George Littlefield. When he heard of the drive, the Major announced bluntly "that he would not accept the mayoralty or any other office if petitioned to do so by every man, woman, and child in Texas, as his private affairs demand all his attention." Writing about the political aspirations of a great nephew, the man who had said that the more money a man makes, the more he has to make, summed up in one sentence the path he had followed and thought a responsible male member of his family should follow too. "I had rather have a Peanut Stand on the Street corner than any office at $100.00 per month, for I would then be my own man and have a chance to build and get up in the world."[36] In opening and running a bank, by buying Austin's finest hotel to upstage a rival bank, with building the best house in town rather than settling for what used to be the best, even in inserting an occasional playful twist into lavish entertainments, George Washington Littlefield left no doubt that he *was* his own man.

$\longleftrightarrow\!\!\longrightarrow$ **12** $\longleftrightarrow\!\!\longrightarrow$

PEOPLE MAKE
THEIR OWN LIVES

"Speaking about management, major, will you run the hotel yourself or lease it to somebody?" a *Statesman* reporter asked the day-old owner of Austin's premier hostelry, the Driskill. "I will run it myself," George Littlefield answered. "That is, I will look after the details and see that it is run as a first-class house should be. I will employ a first-class manager who will supply the experience I lack."[1] He did. But after the third in three years left, the businessman would quit his declaration and revert to the policy that was serving him in his cattle operation. He would look for a manager among the men of his extended family.

Though childless himself, George Littlefield was a family man to an unusual degree. He needed to be. From his mother he inherited not one but two families—the Whites from her first marriage and the Littlefields from her second. Overseeing the relatives, increasing throughout his lifetime to total in the sixties, was as central to his being as was trading in cattle and running a bank. With the affectionate but firm patriarchal manner of his mother, he combined the determined but caring head of household tone of his father. However strained his relationship might become with any one of them, Uncle maintained his attachment even into his will.

As Littlefield appreciated family tradition, all had paths to follow dictated by gender and age—men worked, women kept house, children learned lessons. The majority of his seventeen Littlefield and fourteen White nieces and nephews accepted his vision, probably for the reason Will White said. They were afraid to talk back to him. One resisted outwardly. A small number, maybe more, dissented under their breath. Uncle knew little of it. What he did come to know was that, despite his best efforts, not all family men had the drive, acumen, or will to succeed that he hoped if not expected to realize in them.

Major Littlefield's proprietorship of the Driskill Hotel began well. So pleased was the paper with the prospects he laid out that the *Statesman* editorialized against burdening with a yet higher tax rate the property that already paid the largest tax bill in town. Then the money George Littlefield began pumping into his new property made real news. That fall, workers installed circuits to light the hotel as no other west or south of Saint Louis. What luxury! A button just inside the door in each room awaited the press of the entering guest. Push it, and the room lit up "brilliantly." Unfortunately, instantaneous light alone failed to boost profits. "It would have been better if I had not of bought it, for the money could be used to a better advantage in other things," Littlefield moaned a year after acquiring the hotel.[2]

Maybe what the place really needed was a new manager. If he thought back, Littlefield could have seen a parallel with his ranches. A year afterward, he had lamented selling the LIT. But under Phelps and Tom White's skillful management, the successor LFD operation quickly surpassed its predecessor in profitability. So, sometime in 1896, the Major hired Charles P. Shadbolt to take charge of the hostelry. Shadbolt a year later announced that the proprietor would pour twenty-five thousand dollars (almost doubling as the work progressed) into improvements "from top to bottom, inside and out." Without raising the roof as initially contemplated, Littlefield added forty sleeping rooms, almost all with desirable outside views, and, noted the paper, a bathroom with each. Every room and hallway was graced with frescoes "about as near perfection as anyone would care to see." Costing a thousand dollars by itself, the largest of them, picturing an "immense lake with water lilies growing and swans swimming around," soothed patrons in the grand dining room. "Too much praise can not be accorded the proprietor, Col. Littlefield, and the manager . . . Shadbolt for displaying so much taste regardless of expense," applauded the paper.[3]

Just as things appeared to be going well, late in 1898 or early in 1899, "the most efficient and obliging manager" Shadbolt departed. Instead of replacing him with one experienced in running a hotel, Littlefield looked to a farmer turned businessman married into the family—niece Alice Mildred Dowell's husband, Irwin Daniel. When the couple wed in 1890, George was relieved. Uncle and niece had failed to bond. "It seems as if she will never get off our hands," he vented about the thirty-four-year-old the year before she married.[4] Uncle named names and minced no words in criticizing and praising family members one to another. It apparently served him well in stemming confrontations and blunting schemes relatives sought to play one against another.

Fourteen when her mother died in 1869, Alice Daniel had spent more than half of her life with Grandmother Mildred and then with Uncle George and Aunt Alice. If Uncle pushed her toward the union with Daniel, surely he wanted it to succeed. Readily he helped the husband establish himself in business. Some two thousand dollars got him into retailing cigars. The business didn't last. "He never paid me back five Cents of it," Littlefield grumbled. "I told Him it was the first business in all my life that Seemed to Eat itself up." A similar advance staked the nephew-in-law in his own insurance agency. This venture went little better. Irwin Daniel will "never make any thing more than a living," Uncle concluded three years later. "He is what I term a good easy good for nothing Kind of a fellow. Stands well but makes nothing."[5] But he was family.

What commended Daniel for managing a business more complex than those for which he had shown no special aptitude, Uncle never said. But to prepare the novice, Uncle brought him in to learn the work from the professional and then gave the forty-year-old charge a year or so later when Shadbolt departed. A finer opportunity to grow and build up, as Uncle was fond of saying, could hardly have been handed the Daniels. Irwin and Alice both received salaries, he for managing, she for overseeing housekeeping. With room and board included, the couple not only had no monthly expenses but could rent their house for additional income. And following his habit of sharing, Uncle gave the nephew a one-third interest in the profits.[6]

There were no profits. Irwin Daniel gambled. When Uncle confirmed it, he dumped the hotel—on June 19, 1903, not a month after he learned the truth. Some eighty-one thousand dollars he calculated he lost over his eight-year proprietorship. Though he was fond of saying that the place to find lost money was where it had been lost, this time he abandoned the business without regret. "Those that do right and use energy and industry should be helped and those who show that they Have no tact to get along, and never save a dollar you Cant Keep up," he put it in business terms. And, seeming to wash his hands of the Daniels, he added profoundly that "people make their own lives."[7]

Despite everything, though, Uncle ultimately could not bring himself to wash his hands of the niece and her husband. Uncle paid their debts and gave Daniel a thousand dollars to reopen his insurance business. Supplemented by pawning diamonds Uncle had given the niece, Irwin instead began building a house so as to rent theirs for income. Seeing them with no place to live while work proceeded on both places, Uncle George and Aunt Alice boarded the Daniels. "I am done furnishing him for it does no good," Uncle vowed this time. But when Daniel was later committed to an asylum, Uncle paid the expenses. Three years later, on the day his nephew-in-law died, Uncle dropped his work and went to San Antonio to escort the body to his house, from which the next morning it was taken for burial.[8]

Nephew Edgar Harral should have learned from Irwin Daniel's fall. He should have known from his time working on the LFD; in the articles establishing the Littlefield Cattle Company, Phelps could have shown him the injunction against gambling written in Uncle's own hand. But Edgar appears to have had his hands full just trying to find his place in life. He lasted only six months of the year Uncle set for him to stay to earn the OJIM Ranch. When Phelps passed by in March 1887 on his way to the cattlemen's convention in Fort Worth, Edgar joined him. "What did you come for?" Uncle asked. To give you back that ranch, Edgar replied. "Just what I thought," Littlefield answered. But he gave Harral more cattle and sent him back under Phelps's management. If loneliness was Edgar's problem on the plains, having neighbors was worse. On the Menard Ranch in west central Texas where Uncle next placed Edgar, Uncle caught him gambling. Littlefield stripped his nephew of his partnership interest, and when the gambling continued, he removed him from the ranch entirely. "I sure felt sorry to have to turn off a cripple and He with a wife and five children," Littlefield said. "But necessity Knows no law."[9]

Making minimal effort or quitting altogether registered virtually as bad in Uncle's mind as gambling. After Edgar's brother, Victor, walked away from ranching with Uncle, Littlefield determined to "let Him go alone," declaring that he would "not run after any of them after they show they will not try to build up." Said as a businessman, he did not mean it as the family head. Uncle placed Victor with his wife and three children on a Gonzales farm. As with his brother, if Victor managed it well, Uncle would give him the place. Victor was not the manager that Uncle so hoped. Agonized Littlefield in 1909: "I am an old man. It's not money I want, but honest treatment [illeg., and] Evidence [as by tolerable management] that what I do for my people is [illeg.] affectionately appreciated."[10]

Try as he did in merchandising on his own and ranching with uncle, Shelton Dowell had built up little. When he died in 1885, leaving a widow and five children, the youngest barely two months old, Uncle amplified his attention to the family's financial security. Though Shelt had accumulated a small nest egg, he owed Uncle for the advance to get back into ranching on the Plum Creek domain. Never mind. Uncle forgave all the debt and took charge of investing what widow Lizzie Dowell had. That meant finding investments both safe and yielding steady, high returns. The only places that fit the criteria were his ranches under White management. "Your business has done very well by me Keeping your money loaned to the White boys," he told her. "They have prospered and I have made them pay 10% interest on your money." Indeed, "So long as I live and these Boys are under my controle I can Keep your money safe for you." The White nephews understood. Phelps could have paid the notes long before, but understanding the purpose to which Uncle put his interest payments, he agreed to continue the arrangement. "Phelps is a good man," added a grateful Uncle.[11]

All that businessman Uncle asked of Lizzie, as of any manager, was attention to statements of account. "You have never noticed the receipt of the Statement I Sent you of your business Ending January 14th last. Its right," he chided her, "that you examine each Statement I Send you and say if Correct, if not Correct Say where in it is not and if Correct say so." But he recognized that her silence likely spoke volumes. Patting himself on the back, he concluded that "it must be satisfactory for it has shown an annual increase all the time [nine years that spanned the economic collapse of the Panic of 1893] since I took it in hand."[12]

From family with whom he had a pecuniary relationship, Uncle expected attention to money matters. From men brought into his business orbit, Uncle expected management earning a return. Men who failed he dismissed. However summarily he acted, however grievous the transgression that prompted him to dismiss, one thing remained. They were members of the family for which he considered himself responsible. Yes, people make their own lives. But whatever errant way individuals might go, Uncle still held their well-being to be his responsibility. Family ties trumped business relations.

For Littlefield, men worked; girls married. "It will not do for girls to undertake to live Single," Uncle wrote of one. "Cant to save my life see why she does not get married," he anticipated the consequences for another. "It will not be many years before she is an old woman and then when Aunt Alice and I die she will be left alone."[13]

George Littlefield's firm concept of women's role in life was rooted in the code of the Old South that exalted the woman as the ornament of the home, above and separate from the business world. Though his bank would open a women's department to facilitate ladies' conducting their banking business, he perceived little place for females outside of managing hearth and home. William Littlefield's daughter Christine—Euphemia Christine—vividly remembered her experience of it. When her piano teacher recommended she entertain a career on the concert stage, Uncle put his foot down. "Women had no business running round the country like that," he told her flatly. Whether she admitted it to him, Christine did not regret abandoning the musician's career before it began. Just then she "was having plenty of beaus and enjoying University life."[14]

Contrasting starkly with his firm idea of women's role was Littlefield's total acknowledgment of his mother's business acumen that had not just preserved but in fact advanced the family's wealth in the wake of her second husband's death. He never seemed to accept that her sagacious, tenacious, perspicacious faculty could flower in another woman. Rather, it was their mother-son relationship that he held up especially to boys for emulation. "Give me the boy that loves his mother, one who fills with tears when he bids her good bye, Even for only a short time," he wrote to a nephew. "Something lays deep in that heart, and will come to be seen Some day." Indelibly impressed on him were "the tears that my mother used to shed upon me. And how good I would feel after my tears were dried away. Though gone from her I thought of those tears, and how my heart would soften when I would think of [them. Such sentiments] follow all along through life and when given deep hold in childhood, the impress is felt in manhood."[15]

Littlefield took over his mother's leadership role at least as early as 1871. Even with his mind on preparing the risky venture he hoped would rescue him from financial ruin, Uncle "is an indispensable part of home affairs," John Dowell testified.[16] Later that decade, likely beginning with Alice Daniel, Uncle George and Aunt Alice began their nearly forty years of taking first-, second-, and third-generation nieces and nephews into their home, some for years to provide an environment conducive to well-rounded upbringing, many to attend the university, not a few to convalesce, and, on holidays especially, to enjoy their company.

Sister Martha's daughter, Sarah "Sallie" Elisibeth Harral, was one who lived in the Littlefield home for years for the home environment. Her father had been none too prosperous since George had rescued him from bankruptcy and then a failed mercantile business. When Theo died in 1880, he left Martha pregnant, with at least seven of their ten living children, ranging in age from one to fourteen years, still at home and with a broken-down farm for her support. George took the family under his wing. He built his sister a fine house, provided the family's living, and educated the children. He asked in return only rent-free use of that farm, which he fixed up, and frugality.[17]

Economy was his dictum. He taught it to the young. But he recognized that frugality had its limits too. Consequently he felt the need to explain his considerable outlay for quality materials and sound construction of the truly grand house he built for his and Alice's residence.[18] Unlike the robber barons, though, scorned for overbuilding to impress with their conspicuous consumption, Littlefield planned his house to meet daily family needs and no more. For two decades it did, until he had to add rooms to accommodate help for Alice.

Sallie Harral had arrived initially just for a visit. But, said Uncle, "she can never do any good by returning home." Her mother had remarried. It proved disastrous. Her new husband took advantage of George's largess and was a poor father figure. After four years, in 1895 George paid the man $350 to accept divorce and leave.[19]

The niece's stay did not go well at first. Uncle's word was law. "Having never been controlled she does many things to annoy us," Uncle said, "but we will bring her straight after awhile." Uncle took particular pride in that part of parenting. "If

Maurice Should at any time go wrong I will correct him," Uncle wrote Maurice's mother, Lizzie Dowell, assuring her, though, that her boy "seems to want to Keep good company, and I don't anticipate his going wrong."[20]

Uncle's concept of right and good was firm. Resident girls going on a date had to tell him with whom and where they were going and when they would return. Showing just how much he meant it, he waited up to see that they came in punctually. Sallie Harral so chafed under the requirement that years later she displayed her frustration by often failing to favor her husband with day-trip return plans.[21]

Appreciating that finishing schools provided the final polish on the ornament, Uncle sent Sallie to the Baptist-sponsored Mary Nash College in Sherman, Texas, where all students participated in required Bible study and took courses in language, music, and polite behavior. Whether or not the school taught it, Uncle expected Sallie, as he expected all, to be frugal in managing personal expenses. This was nothing new: John Dowell's improvidence had caused Uncle thirty-some years earlier to recall this first family member whose education he had underwritten. But to ensure economy in the fourteen girls whose education he had supported as of 1904, he allowed a paltry ten dollars of spending money per week. Even that, he said, "is to much for any girl to have . . . for if they have that in hand most of them will Spend it carelessly."[22]

Uncle's vision for boys was as definite as that for girls. "Let him go to business as Soon as possible. He will make a better man." Not just any business, though; Uncle meant retailing: "He will learn a great deal in the Bank but He can not learn the mercantile business there," Uncle commented on one nephew's employment. Once the nephew understood trade, Uncle would help him establish a store of his own.[23]

Ranching, rather than merchandising, attracted brother Bill's twenty-four-year-old son George. Having learned cowboying on the LIV, worked on the LFD, and attended the Agricultural and Mechanical College of Texas for a year, George went to see Uncle. Almost every time a family member came, Littlefield expected the individual to want something, usually money. George did. And as the story passed down through the family, he was blunt about it. Uncle had helped his father create a ranch. Now it was his turn. He was ready for Uncle to put him into the ranching business. "No," Littlefield answered gruffly; he would not buy the impertinent nephew a ranch. Instead, "Go into the army. . . . I want it to make a man of you," Uncle commanded. George went. Returning to New Mexico, he enlisted in a cavalry regiment for the Philippine-American War, ignited by United States' acquisition of the island territory in the treaty ending the Spanish-American War. When Uncle learned that his nephew had been sent into conflict, "he grieved and said: 'Oh, if the boy's killed, it's all my fault. I should have helped him.'" In that frame of mind, when George returned safe and sound, Uncle assembled the land he needed, "and that's how the second ranch was formed there right next to the old home [LIV] ranch."[24]

Whatever enterprise the young man pursued, honesty and saving must govern his actions, Uncle told one in his plainspoken way:

> Now what Ever you do, let it be done well and Satisfactory—It makes but little diference what a man starts in so he saves up what he makes. Unless He does that, . . . He will do no good- So it is in life. The best men of our land Started on nothing, but they saved and built up. When you show you can be successful then the world endorses you, but if you show you are a failure then the world is afraid of you- Truth and honesty must prevail. Your words must be good in all things, or Confidence will not exist, and without Confidence no business is Safe.[25]

Extending his paternal disposition to young men outside the family in whom he saw promise, George Littlefield sometimes gave his advice in a lesson, not simply words. Cub reporter Edmunds Travis remembered it vividly. When he brought in the final payment on a note, the Major said:

> "Travis I've been worried about this thing a lot."
>
> I said: "Why are you worried Major? I was always pretty prompt, wasn't I?"
>
> "Well, that's not it," he responded quietly. "I want to help you. You're a young man just starting out. And I've thought many times that I would just charge this note off. Just give it to you. It wouldn't mean anything much to me, and it might mean a whole lot to you. But just because you are just starting out, it's well for you to learn that as you go through life, men expect you to live up to your obligations. And it might just spoil you if I gave you this note, and that's why I didn't do it."
>
> Says "I want you to understand that. Do you understand it?"
>
> And I said, "Yes, sir, I think I do."

At that, Littlefield accepted the principal but canceled the remaining interest. "He was exactly right about the whole thing," Travis concurred a half century later.[26]

By the count of one of them, nearly forty young people spent some of their formative years growing up under Littlefield's tutelage. Likely the total Littlefield counseled is greater because he did not restrict his attention only to those he could meet face to face. "Tell Shelton He must not forget to answer my letter," Uncle wrote the great-nephew's mother. "He will find that writing letters will improve Him more than anything else. I write letters to several of the Nephews and Nieces, and I like to see them improving."[27]

Family obligation grounded on loyalty, responsible money management, and sound business practices permeated George Littlefield's life to a singular degree. His feeling for blood relations ensured that advice and wherewithal flowed from the patriarch. It led him to install family men in his businesses even when he doubted their ability to handle the job. True, he did not shy from summarily dismissing family men when they violated his prescriptions for good business practices. But in the final analysis, business was business and family was family. What was remarkable for capitalist Littlefield was that family trumped making money.

$\sim\!\!=\!\!\circ\!\!\circ$ **13** $\circ\!\!\circ\!\!=\!\!\sim$

THE BEST AND SAFEST BUSINESS

When they made news at all, real estate purchases commonly were buried in a column deep inside a newspaper and attracted no notice beyond the local community. Not so the report that George Washington Littlefield committed $50,000 in October 1898 for a five-hundred-acre tract about five miles southeast of Roswell, New Mexico. Giving $100 per acre in the Pecos River basin in which few people could pay $4.50 for raw land drew notice of the *San Antonio Express* five hundred miles away.[1] If the Texas paper sensed that the substantial expenditure must presage something more than operation of a run-of-the-mill agricultural improvement, it was right. In fact, Littlefield's initiative characterized a period of entrepreneurial expansion begun with acquisition of the Driskill Hotel that, first in the cattle arena, would see him through the transition from open to enclosed ranching and then would take him well beyond the cattle and banking businesses in which he had grown and built up.

What Littlefield bought in the five-hundred-acre Poe Farm was proof of concept. In the seven years from 1887 to 1894, John William Poe had fashioned what the historian of southeastern New Mexico called probably the first stock farm in the Pecos valley, if not in all of New Mexico Territory. Possessed of an "almost uncanny instinct for moving into areas of economic activity just as they were taking on importance or entering the early growth stages," Poe began by demonstrating that, with water from tributaries near Roswell, the Pecos valley could produce abundantly. Tapping the Woodlawn Ditch, which from the South Spring River carried a stream substantial enough to fill its sixteen-by-two-and-a half-foot trench, he reaped four large cuttings a year of a high protein grade of alfalfa.

Selling at ten dollars a ton, Poe's four hundred acres of feed yielded a profit that confirmed James John Hagerman's image of the valley becoming one of the territory's, if not one of the country's, great agricultural oases. "With an abundance of good water at command, a soil that might be used elsewhere with profit as a fertilizer, and a climate of matchless geniality and salubrity," Hagerman's Pecos

Irrigation and Improvement Company had proclaimed since 1891, "the Pecos Valley is destined to become one of the most remunerative farming and fruit-growing regions within the limits of the United States." So many farmers followed Poe's lead that alfalfa constituted one of the valley's two most profitable crops twenty years later.

But growing feed was only half of Poe's plan. In a cattle country in which animals still ranged free and drift fences alone thwarted a cow's wandering, especially in biting winter storms, Poe enclosed his property, introduced purebred bulls and quality brood mares, and began a controlled breeding operation. So productive was the combination of raising feed and upgrading stock that entrepreneur Hagerman in 1892–93 bought the farm and an interest in the Woodlawn Ditch.[2]

Since he had first visited the Pecos valley in 1889 in the company of visionary and promoter extraordinaire Charles B. Eddy, Hagerman had been imbued with the dream of towns, farms, and modest ranches blossoming on irrigated land south of Roswell. Fabulously lucrative investments in railroads and mining—first iron ore in Michigan, then silver and gold in Colorado—endowed the fifty-one-year-old with the millions required to convert vision into reality. In addition to the hundreds of thousands of dollars Hagerman poured into the irrigation projects and related improvements, he laid 160-some miles of track connecting the basin to the nation's rail network. But the combination of floods that destroyed the irrigation infrastructure and the Panic of 1893 that severely constricted Hagerman's access to financing brought him to bankruptcy in July 1898. To salvage for himself both certain acreage southeast of Roswell and his large northern canal, Hagerman needed fifty thousand dollars. Three months later, Littlefield gave him that amount in exchange for the Poe Farm. If, as circumstances suggest, Hagerman's need for cash caused him to price his property to sell, then the deal again validated Littlefield's investment strategy of watching for someone wanting to raise a little money and having to sell cheap.[3]

The impression from the newspaper story that Littlefield's purchase was apropos of nothing did not tell the whole story. By the end of the century, Roswell was a town growing into a new bearing. Since its earliest days in the late 1860s serving as a supply stop for trail herds, it had gained a post office in 1873, been platted in 1885, named seat of the new Chaves County in 1889, and become the railhead of Hagerman's Pecos Valley Railroad in 1894. As the population quintupled in the 1890s from 343 to 2,049, any who looked could see transformation, as frame, brick, and stone buildings began joining their adobe predecessors. But the singular event that distinguished Roswell and sparked the community above all others occurred in 1890, when Nathan Jaffa drilled in his back lot for water. Suffering ill effects from drinking the brackish liquid pumped from shallow wells, he determined to dig deeper. At 250 feet the drill hit a layer of porous limestone from which, wrote one who saw it, "water, as pure as ever gladdened the throat of man, bubbled up over the casing and ran away laughing in a flashing stream." At the very time men were looking greedily at surface water they could divert to irrigation, they discovered that Roswell sat atop an artesian reservoir of untold dimension.[4]

Phelps White didn't have to wait for the dramatic artesian discovery to see Roswell rising. By 1887 he had transferred the Bosque Grande Ranch address from Fort Sumner to Roswell. The next year he took a personal hand in maturing the community when he joined in organizing its Masonic lodge. Phelps knew Roswell. And in fourteen years with Uncle, including a decade setting up and managing the LFD operation, the thirty-five-year-old had proven his judgment in trading cattle and handling business broadly. Maybe, then, Phelps pointed Littlefield to the investment opportunity beyond cattle in New Mexico. Whatever impelled him, in November 1891 Littlefield bought an interest in the growing network of irrigation ditches and land they watered in the Roswell area. Seven years and multiple acquisitions later, purchase of the Poe Farm represented not a unique act but a crescendo.[5]

Building on John Poe's stock farm concept, Littlefield and his nephew partner developed the LFD Farm into a utilitarian showplace. They more than doubled the original five hundred acres into a domain stretching over two square miles. While a fortuitous investment in the Woodlawn Ditch six years before he bought the Poe place may have afforded Littlefield more right to the ditch's water for his new acquisition than otherwise would have been the case, the artesian aquifer liberated the partners to locate water sources where they needed them.[6]

For the Four Lakes ranching operation, the partners increased the alfalfa acreage. Cuttings fed cattle, particularly the three-hundred-some purebred Hereford and Durham bulls brought in to increase beef production on the plains. A spring stand fed horses when hands drove in the remuda from winter camp at Mescalero Spring. "By the time the spring roundup started," recalled waddy Vivian Whitlock approvingly, "the horses had shed their winter coats of hair and were fat and frisky."[7]

While the LFD Farm clearly buttressed the cattle operation, its dollars-and-cents contribution to the ranch's bottom line could be difficult to calculate. Not so the value of the other marketable products raised on its 1,250 acres. During the next twenty-plus years, the partners profited from sales of mules, sheep, hogs, feed corn and oats, corn fodder, hay, apples, wood, honey, watermelons, vinegar, poultry, eggs, butter, and pasturage. Before solid numbers in income tax schedules document return in the thousands of dollars in the 1910s, the farm's profitability has to be surmised from news reports. They show hogs setting Pecos valley records for weight gain. They document the partners seeing profit in once-despised sheep. In 1903 Littlefield bought four thousand head and was looking to double the number, reported the *Roswell Record*, "as he does not believe in doing things by halves." Likely the farm's most lucrative crop grown for sale, though, was apples. After 1892 apple production and profit around Roswell rose to rival those of alfalfa. With plenteous artesian water and no insects or worms to damage the fruit, trees planted during Roswell's peak twenty years, 1892–1914, groaned under the weight of the fruit. Sixty LFD Farm acres yielded thirty-two rail cars full in 1902. An "El Dorado spot in the wilderness," the Austin paper marveled. So good was the income stream that the partners quintupled the size of their orchard to nearly three hundred acres. Investors noticed. Just five years after Littlefield bought the place, he received an offer of 20 percent per acre profit. After the sale fell through, later he refused double that figure.[8]

Maybe good management under men such as nephew-in-law Marion W. Hodges developed the LFD Farm into the property of which Littlefield in 1914 said he was the proudest. Perhaps the business model accounted for it. Where the LFD Farm made money from marketing its wide variety of crops and animals, cattleman C. C. Slaughter's nearby two-thousand-acre version of the stock farm arrangement failed to pay. For focusing almost exclusively on supporting the cattle operation in Texas, the "Slaughter Hereford Home" neglected opportunities the LFD Farm exploited. Expanding his investment strategy beyond cattle had begun to pay Littlefield handsomely.[9]

Apple growers had welcomed Hagerman's Pecos Valley Railroad's arrival in Roswell in 1894. It saved them from freighting supplies by wagon seventy-five miles up from Eddy and provided more satisfactory transportation to market for their crop, which was rising to join alfalfa as the valley's most profitable. For cattlemen, though, the line delivered only expense and delay. It ran in the wrong direction—down into Texas, south of the Texas Fever dead line. Crossing the line meant a ninety-day detention to ensure that the uninfected animals had not picked up the deadly ticks. Having abandoned driving Four Lakes cattle to Midland to board Texas and Pacific trains to market, Littlefield and White were not going to freight them to the Pecos Valley's T&P connection in Pecos, Texas.[10]

To stay north of the Texas Fever line, New Mexico cattlemen had to point their beeves to shipping points east. But the XIT's fence, stretching two hundred miles as the crow flies south from the Oklahoma state line, blocked their way. This left the New Mexicans to drive costly miles around the barrier. Or simply barge across. A fence-cutting war a decade earlier had produced a Texas law requiring a gate every three miles. While the availability of these openings reduced damage from unauthorized herds pushing across a pasture, they did nothing to pacify the rancher whose grass the bunches of 2,000 to maybe 3,000 transients at a time ate and trampled and whose scarce water they drank. Conflict between New Mexico ranchers and the XIT was inevitable. An LEA herd cutting through in 1889 had its ramrod (trail foreman) and four drovers jailed for trespassing. When jailing failed to stay the flow, XIT management turned to the courts. So many LFD herds invaded the XIT in 1893 and 1894 that the ranch sued to stop the incursions.[11]

While a compromise by which the XIT created a mile-wide corridor across its property ended the conflict, the real solution had to be a rail line northward from Roswell. Hagerman knew it. Two years of low-volume shipments of cattle, wool, and fruit south had not just failed to make the PV profitable but had driven it into receivership. Finally, in 1898–99 Hagerman had the capital he needed to build the reorganized Pecos Valley and Northeastern from Roswell to a junction with the Santa Fe in Amarillo, Texas. The rails traversed 112 miles of open country between Roswell and the Texas state line with only the one-store tent city of Portales 22 rail miles from the state line to interrupt the monotony. Hauling a heavy train up the 90-mile incline from Roswell to the spring at Portales without replenishing the steam engine's water supply tempted fate. Railroad builders had to find a place between Roswell and Portales to put in a water stop. Locating good springs about halfway between the two, the railroad erected water facilities, built a station, and named the place Urton, later renamed Kenna for a Santa Fe company official. A bonus of the spot proved to be an adjacent bowl-shaped formation suited for holding cattle awaiting shipment. Consequently, pens were erected, and Kenna rose to be the prime shipping point for eastern New Mexico cattle. The number passing through its chutes swelled until Kenna claimed to load not only the most cattle of any place in its region but the second most of any station in the entire country. For the Littlefield ranches, the siting of Kenna could not have been more favorable. The station and loading pens lay a bare handful of miles from the LIV headquarters and a straight drive on Littlefield land from the Four Lakes Ranch.[12]

Installation of the convenient shipping facility ended the decade that began with the arrival on the Four Lakes of the longest train of freight wagons waddy Eugene Price said he ever saw. The wagons creaked under the weight of wire, staples, posts, and supplies for erecting a drift fence nearly forty miles long from the Texas line to the caprock to stall cattle from wandering southward from the large DZ ranch to the north. Littlefield spent $10,000 if not half again more, for the barrier, a number doubled by erection of the LFD south drift fence fifty miles to the south.[13] Free-range ranching was hardly cost free. The 40-plus windmills cost no less than $15,000 for the wells, towers, and mechanisms. At its height during the decade, many associated with the Four Lakes operation thought that 40,000 to 50,000 animals grazed the land, producing 12,000 to 14,000 calves a year. With one cowboy required under normal circumstances for every 300 to 400 animals on the free range, the Four Lakes can be expected to have employed at least 100 cowboys watching and working the cattle every day. At around $25 per month each, the payroll, exclusive of cooks, wranglers, the range boss, windmillers, and other hands, began at $25,000 per year. If the Four Lakes cost the Major at least $50,000 annually to operate, one good year could make up for periods with few or no sales. At decade's end in 1900, Littlefield expected to realize $270,000 for 10,000 New Mexico steers. "Cattle business seems to be doing very well," he pronounced happily.[14]

The cattle business *was* doing well for George Littlefield, but for reasons more fundamental than favorable markets. He had successfully ridden the wave of the revolution that transformed the cattle business at the end of the nineteenth century. "In none of the large industries or occupations of men has there ever been so great a change, so swift and complete a revolution in methods and in results within so brief a period, as that which has come to pass in the live stock industry in the West since 1885," declared the author of *Prose and Poetry of the Cattle Industry*, the National Live Stock Association's solid and insightful history and analysis published in 1904. "The principal factors in working these radical changes were improved stock, provident management, and individual control more or less of the land upon which each stockman operated, accompanied by the use of fences."[15]

While the importance of each and the combination of all were indisputable, the millions of dollars cattlemen invested in quality bulls led the *Prose and Poetry* author to conclude that stock improvement transcended them all. Not George Littlefield. He lived by his mother's teaching that any and every business began with provident management. His words conveyed it. "Business people," executive committee chair Littlefield referred to cattlemen of the Texas Live Stock Association in 1886 near the beginning of the revolution. His actions confirmed it. In organizing the Littlefield Cattle Company a full four years earlier, he had required two sets of books that would empower him to fully and accurately assess the dollars-and-cents performance of his free-range cattle operation.[16]

Of the three principal factors, only legally sanctioned possession of the land and the value of fencing off pastures had yet to press Littlefield and the ranchers of southeastern New Mexico. Lacking a mechanism for having these cattlemen pay to use the public domain, the commissioner of the General Land Office left them undisturbed until, around the turn of the century, he ordered the drift fences removed. "This left things just right for a real catastrophe," recalled Eugene Price. Ranching just south of the Four Lakes range, he knew that to keep his little herd he would have to fight both the weather and LFD cattle sweeping his animals into the massive drift pushed before the storm. In February 1903 the epic blizzard hit. To protect himself from the bitter, bitter cold as he rode after his cattle, Price "put on about all the clothes I had, then put a slicker on over them, using a grass hobble to strap and tie the slicker more tightly around my body, and wrapped my feet with grain sacks over my overshoes." What he accomplished in restraining his animals the big ranches could not achieve. Desperate cattle traveled so far that the LFD and its neighbors spent two months in "one of the most notoriously big works in the history of the Southeastern New Mexico cattle range" recovering them.[17]

Some way had to be found to keep the cattle on their ranges. Tom White hit on it. Having been elected a Chaves County commissioner in 1900, the personable but sage LFD Tom, as the cow people distinguished him from Tom White of the T Bar T Ranch, realized that a county road could be fenced. So pleased with the stratagem were ranchers both north and south of the proposed right-of-way paralleling the LFD south drift fence that they funded construction all the way into Roswell.[18]

As bad as the blizzard had been and as clever as LFD Tom's ploy was, neither faced the current that almost alone within a decade would end the open range on lands from the Four Lakes north. In two waves the tide came. William Littlefield on the LIV felt it first. The railroad that carried cattle out brought homesteaders in. By 1907 it was said that a dugout or house sheltered a cotton farmer on almost every quarter section in Roosevelt County. The surge pushed the LIV into the San Juan Mesa brakes until the rancher began buying out as many settlers with patents as he could. Though the inevitable succession of dry years that came at the end of the decade drove many off their little places, the second wave—ranchers with small herds—forced more outlays to maintain the Littlefield range until the drought of 1917–18 broke this group.[19]

Small ranchers invaded the Four Lakes and ranges south first. Between 1900 and 1906 men like Eugene Price claimed unsurveyed grass for themselves. However much the big ranches objected to the intrusions, the newcomers with cattle experience did assist in cow works. Some were even recruited. Harve Harris and his brother learned later that they were persuaded to settle on Four Lakes land to combat "one extra bad cattle rustler that kept His cattle under herd and was stealing to many unbranded calves and eating to mutch of other mens beaf and was hard to catch." No similar value accompanied the trickle turning into a wave of homesteaders. Before decade's end, at least eleven settlements dotted the Four

Lakes range, surrounded by dugouts and houses peppering the land around them almost as thick as on the LIV. Government surveyors came to mark sections and townships empowering the settlers to solidify their land claims. With its range severely reduced and fragmented, the LFD operation almost overnight lost room for the forty-thousand-some head that grazed unchallenged in 1900. At decade's end the ranch could accommodate barely one-third as many. But marking the land provided salvation too. Phelps White at the first opportunity in mid-1908 leased fifty-two thousand contiguous acres along the ranch's north line to begin protecting LFD territory for the remaining fifteen thousand head.[20]

The decade of momentous change opening the twentieth century had barely begun before George Littlefield recognized what was coming. "We will have to get some place else as this will soon play out," he told Alice at the end of April 1901, two years after the railroad crossed his brother's range and two years before the great blizzard scattered his cattle far and wide.[21] For such a contrarian investor as Littlefield, opportunity lurked somewhere in the change sweeping across the ranch country breaking up the sprawling domains.

On the Texas plains to the east, the Capitol Freehold Land and Investment Company was hearing the ever louder howls of frustrated investors. In sixteen years its XIT Ranch had failed to make a profit. British bond holders had begun demanding a return on their investments. Since selling cattle from the property too big for lean ranching had failed to meet the company's obligations, the Capitol syndicate was reduced to marketing its very foundation—the three million acres it received for building the state capitol. Ranch managing director John Villiers Farwell did propose withholding some 368,000 acres that stood in the long run to bring the highest return. No. Distant investors wanted out of ranching. And they were in no mood to delay until farmers clamored for tracts of the invitingly level and treeless virgin soil. So in a flyer Farwell announced:

LAND   LAND   LAND

For sale, in tracts to suit, the land comprising what is popularly known as the XIT Ranch. . . . The land is capable of producing forage crops in great abundance. An inexhaustible supply and excellent quality of water is procurable. The greatest opportunity of the time for those desiring to engage in the stock-farming business or for investors who may wish to hold for appreciating values.[22]

If the handbill failed to catch George Littlefield's attention, the letter he received from XIT agent John Henry Stephens in early April 1901 did. It marked the second time in two years that Stephens had approached his friend from trailing days. George Findlay admitted his skepticism that this second contact would bear any more fruit than the first. "I think his idea of values is so much lower than ours that it may be doubtful if anything can be done with him," the ranch's business manager recalled the earlier conversations.[23] But nothing ventured, nothing gained, and men familiar with the cattle business knew that Littlefield was one of the few who, upon making a deal, had the wherewithal to pay cash and pay it promptly. If Stephens's approach in 1899 had yielded nothing because it coincided with installation of the cattle-loading facilities at Kenna that resolved the LFD's shipping difficulties, the playing-out Littlefield saw looming on the Four Lakes Ranch's horizon two years later changed his perspective on his future in open-range ranching. By 1901 he recognized that he needed to look seriously at owning the land his cattle roamed above the caprock.

Whatever the Major knew or did not know of the Capitol syndicate's financial straits, Stephens's second contact may have signaled that Littlefield had found the buyer's market he perpetually sought. At almost every turn, syndicate negotiators bent over backward to accommodate their prospect. First, not just any tract, Littlefield wanted the best—the Yellow House division. Next, he insisted on purchasing by units of land rather than by current survey. Everyone in the plains country knew that the surveyors who marked out the capitol lands had been generously inaccurate in their work and included in each league more acres than the 4,428 normal for this largest capitol lands survey unit. "Of course we would prefer to have the land surveyed, as we believe there is probably two per cent or so surplus," Findlay told General Manager Boyce, "but a man like Littlefield is after those little surpluses himself." And the company was not going to lose the sale by contending the unit of measure. The syndicate even accepted Littlefield's refusal to give a deed of trust securing the company in its land until payments were completed. The Major had never given one in his life, he said, and was not about to start with this sale. Finally, two dollars per acre for some 250,000 acres is "a fearful price to pay for land that is suitable only for grazing," the prospective buyer protested. But the syndicate dug in its heels. Year in and year out, the Yellow House "gives probably more satisfaction [in] the way of the calf increase, the condition of the cattle, smallness of loss, and the good condition of the grass and water," the ranch business manager countered. And on top of that, "for a speculative venture in view of the possible development into an agricultural tract . . . we have nothing . . . more valuable than this." Two dollars the price remained. At that, the Capitol syndicate on its books doubled its money, having received the land at one dollar per acre. And Littlefield had his way, too, as history would show that two dollars fell fifty cents per acre below the average paid by the subsequent early large-acreage buyers (fig. 46).[24]

Arrangements completed, a telegraph key in Chicago tapped out the news on May 9, 1901, that Littlefield would close the sale. Paying $65,000 down, he took possession of some 64 leagues at $2 an acre, plus 5,000 cows and calves and 357 bulls, for which he would pay an additional $222,500. Discharging the total $800,000 obligation in six years instead of the allotted seven, he and three sevenths partner Phelps White were able to save multiple tens of thousands of dollars in interest payments. In acres, the leagues should have given Littlefield 286,000. When in 1912 he had the state surveyor determine the actual acreage, the Major learned that his Yellow House Ranch in fact encompassed 312,175 acres, a surplus exceeding five and a half normal leagues (fig. 47).[25]

"Major George W. Littlefield is the largest cattle owner in the world since his last purchase," the *Austin Statesman* headlined its account of the Yellow House deal. Sixty-five thousand animals the story reported him having on a domain that, were it a half-mile-wide strip, would stretch eight hundred miles from Austin to Saint Louis, Missouri. More vast than the King Ranch, the reporter gushed inaccurately. Nevertheless, George Littlefield continued to be haunted by the playing-out of the great cattle country of eastern New Mexico he believed he was witnessing. In his distress, he concluded to abandon New Mexico altogether, including even the LFD Farm that news reports regularly credited as being the favorite of all his properties.[26]

Only one region in North America remained so uninhabited at the turn of the century that a cattleman could carve out a realm of contiguous unfenced acres sufficient to accommodate a herd of the size of Littlefield's in New Mexico. Only one region remained in which a single expanse could replicate the Four Lakes and Bosque Grande ranges on which LFD cattle had roamed free only a decade earlier. To gain such a territory for his reported fifty thousand New Mexico cattle with their fifteen thousand calves, in August 1902 the Major leased for two cents each some one million acres in western Canada's British Columbia province.[27] Though likely no LFD animal ever grazed the virgin Canadian grass, Littlefield's interest in the huge expanse did not go unnoticed.

Cattleman Charles Goodnight thought he saw an opportunity in Littlefield's initiative, and set out to sell the Major three hundred thousand acres of the Four Lakes range. Goodnight claimed to possess title to the land under a Mexican grant from the 1830s to one John Charles Beales. Littlefield of course declined to buy the grant story without a merchantable title to go with it. Nor was he the first. John Farwell had rebuffed a similar approach fifteen years earlier.[28]

More serious, the highly respected Four Lakes range manager, fifty-year-old Bud Wilkinson, quit. Grown from a boy in Gonzales, Bud had worked himself up in the Littlefield organization from drover to straw boss to trail boss to range manager. Taking advantage of the Major's policy of allowing hands to run their own little herds among the LFD cattle, Bud had built a good bunch in the HUT brand. Seeing the Major leasing Canadian land, maybe it was no coincidence that only months later Bud took his animals north of the border to open a ranch with his brother-in-law. The brutal winter of 1906–7 decimated their stock, causing Bud to return nearly broke to run the remaining HUT cattle and work for the Littlefields.[29]

Maybe events in New Mexico not a year after he executed the British Columbia lease caused Littlefield to reconsider his resolve to leave. First, in the late spring of 1903, the LFD Farm sale for three times Littlefield's purchase price fell through. Then nephew James Phelps White settled in Roswell to start a family. The manager of Uncle's Yellow House and New Mexico ranches and partner on whom Uncle depended completely, Phelps solidified his Pecos valley roots on July 23, 1903, when he wed Lou Lee Tomlinson, daughter of local contractor David Y. Tomlinson.

Marriage changed Phelps's life. Establishing a residence with his wife gave Phelps a quality of life he had rarely experienced in more than a quarter century. For the first time since he left his parents' home twenty-six years earlier, he could expect to spend each night in a home rather than on the range. Uncle understood. "As I tell all our family in offering up their prayers," he wrote Lizzie Dowell, "remember those boys that braved the Storm Sleeping under the wet blankets and Enabled me to assist all who I have aided in life."[30]

As 1903 approached its end, not British Columbia expanse nor short grass in New Mexico nor even the large Yellow House debt directed Littlefield's outlook. Rather, how he stood to weather the poor market on top of those concerns buoyed him. For one, he was upgrading his herd significantly. So proud was he of the work that in 1904 he took the unusual step of taking "some fine stock" to exhibit at the Texas Cattle Raisers Association meeting. For another, he told Lizzie Dowell, "Men who owe large Sums of money and who have to Ship Cattle to pay it are suffering." Unlike them, and even though "our Sales have been less this year than for five years . . . we will have a large number of Steers to sell next year. Cattlemen who are able to hold on to their Stuff are all right. The World needs the Beef, and men who own large tracts of land stocked with Cattle will be independent." Littlefield was right. A population increase of eleven million Americans during the 1890s had been matched by a cattle population shrinking by five million.[31] But large tracts of plains land stocked with cattle could bring hurt in a category all their own—prairie fire.

On March 25, 1904, Phelps White at the Yellow House headquarters noticed smoke on the southwestern horizon. Grass was burning. Nothing commanded attention on a ranch more than smoke moving against the sky. At sight, all dropped whatever they were doing and rode to fight the blaze. Phelps hitched a pair of mules to the buckboard and headed for it. Driven by the constant plains wind, prairie fires spread fast, advanced rapidly, and were dangerously unpredictable. The wind could abruptly shift direction and with it the fire's path. As Phelps approached the all-consuming blaze, it happened the wind changed. Suddenly blowing from the north, it turned the fire to race toward the ranch manager from two directions at once. With the fire moving too fast to outrun and its line extending farther than he could flank, Phelps was trapped. Quickly he unhitched the mules to run for their lives. Then, pulling his hat over his face to protect his eyes, he threw himself face down on the ground. When some cowboys spotted the mules badly singed, they searched frantically until they found Phelps still lying where the fire had passed over him, burning his clothes in some places completely away. They gathered him up, took him back to headquarters, and one rode like the wind the forty-plus miles to Lubbock to bring the town's doctor. For a week Dr. M. C. Overton stayed at Phelps's side, swabbing him in ointment until his condition began to improve. When Phelps could travel, they rigged a hammock in a wagon to minimize the painful jolting of the fifty-plus-mile ride to Portales to catch a train to Roswell, where he convalesced until going to Saint Louis, Missouri, for further treatment. Miraculously, Phelps White recovered, though the fire's scars marked him for the rest of his life.[32]

Accounted as one of the largest wildfires in memory on the south plains, the blaze started in a Slaughter pasture adjoining the Yellow House southwest of the headquarters. Wrote George Slaughter, it burned about eight sections of Lazy S land, then went northeast, blackening about one-third of the Yellow House Ranch on its way into the Spade pasture, where the wind changed. The fire then raced down the east side of Littlefield's ranch for more than half of its twenty-five-mile length before the wind shifted yet again. Blowing from the east, wind chased the fire across the twelve-mile width of the Yellow House and into the Oxsheer Ranch, south of the Lazy S starting point.[33] How many LFD cattle perished in the incineration of approximately two-thirds of the Yellow House range no record survives to tell.

The year 1904 proved to be the first of three back-to-back years of significant losses reminiscent of 1868–70, only fires and cold replaced drought and floods. A savage blizzard in 1905 left nine hundred LFD cattle frozen to death, among the heaviest losses in the region, said Slaughter. In 1906 fire returned. "The loss of Grass was very Heavy about 220,000 Acres burned, and about 300 cattle died,"

Littlefield documented the conflagration, which burned at least as many acres as the 1904 fire. He added, "No telling what loss will be until we get spring." But different from nearly forty years earlier, the three successive misfortunes did not push him to the edge of ruin. As a multimillionaire, he had reserves. More importantly, his array of properties and investments relieved him of being dependent on a single income stream. And development of a pesticide in which cattle could be immersed to kill the Texas Fever tick eliminated that scourge. Consequently, after the 1906 fire, George Littlefield waxed philosophical: "At any rate, I am not bothering over it. We must take all such over which we have no Controle without worry."[34]

On his sixty-fourth birthday three months later, cattleman and rancher George Washington Littlefield was content. As he reviewed his condition in the cattle trade on June 21, 1906, not the changes on the New Mexico range nor the effects of the long-running weak market nor three years of severe losses nor even the remaining debt on the Yellow House Ranch dominated his perspective. Cattle sales that spring had been good. Far more important, Phelps White had fully recovered from his near-fatal burns. And George Findlay's promise on the future value of the Yellow House property was already proving up. "Our lands have all doubled and over in value," Littlefield noted that spring. Whatever ups and downs the cattle market would take, he echoed Worsham and the *Texas Almanac* that the land on which the cattle grazed was "the best thing one can Keep money in in Texas." It was. Settlers wanting small plots to farm would pay to get them. So, with hundreds of square miles of land and tens of thousands of cattle on it, Littlefield declared in the summer of 1906 that the cattle trade "is the best and safest business in Tex. In fact nothing else compares with it."[35]

$\leftarrow\!\!\!\rightarrow$ **14** $\leftarrow\!\!\!\rightarrow$

I'LL DO THE REST

Back in May 1894, when so much was going well—Phelps White was completing his move of the LFD herd and headquarters from the Pecos River with its treacherous quicksand and unrelenting drought onto the lush grass of the high plains, the four-year-old American National Bank was prospering, and Littlefield's grand new house was nearing completion—George Littlefield received the worst news. It came from across the street and from a quarter never before requiring his attention. "I See that Dr. Dabney is to leave the university. After loosing Gov. Roberts, now we loose Dr. Dabney," he emphasized his anxiety to Gonzales County friend, fellow Confederate major, and University of Texas regent Thomas Moore Harwood.[1]

Mental and moral philosophy professor Robert Lewis Dabney and law professor Oran Milo Roberts anchored more than fields of study for Littlefield. They represented a worldview. Roberts was steeped in the rationale for forming the Confederacy to protect the Southern way of life. He had helped call and then led Texas's secession convention. He raised the Eleventh Texas Infantry before becoming chief justice of Texas's Confederate-era supreme court. Dabney, whose star rested most brightly on his service as chief of staff for Confederate hero Stonewall Jackson, went farther. An ordained minister, he preached that his Southern Presbyterian Bible provided a moral justification for slavery. Not only that, it led him to the conclusion that the society of the Old South, fashioned on slavery, represented the zenith of Christian civilization.[2]

"From what I can see and learn, the institution [University of Texas] is becoming entirely to northern," Littlefield expressed his alarm. Why, some teachers were drawing pensions from the federal government for their service against the South. The northern slant "is to be regretted, for we all are desirous of seeing the university prosper," he declared. If others as strong in their Southern perspectives as Dabney and Roberts departed, the conclusion for Littlefield was patent: "the true Southern Sentiment in our university will be a thing of the past." What Littlefield wanted was Texas "to have a Southern University that was as good as any of them" and postwar generations to appreciate their Southern heritage.[3] Though Southern arms had been vanquished on the field, a battle for the hearts and minds of succeeding generations had commenced. And the departures from campus of the war's elder generation signaled that the time was at hand for the Major and his peers to take charge of the struggle.

Confederate veterans cherished "the true Southern Sentiment." They had offered their lives for it. The very phrase "true Southern" had flowed from young George Littlefield's pen as he committed himself to the Confederate fight. Not surprisingly, then, the true Southern sentiment rested on two principal tenets from the war. First, the cause. Although protection of the familiar Southern society based on slavery had motivated them to take up arms thirty years earlier, by the 1890s Confederate warriors maintained that they had joined up to sustain a state's constitutional right to secede, or as Littlefield stated it: "for the cause of liberty and self government."[4] Second, the defeat. It resulted from the weight of overwhelming numbers and was not a verdict on the righteousness of "the Lost Cause." "Uncle George, he told me he wanted the younger generation to understand why the South was in the right," Edgar Harral testified. "He said they *was* in the right."[5]

To these two shared tenets, every "true Southerner" no doubt added personal ones. Littlefield did. His had three threads. First, the difference between Southern and Yankee. If he got it nowhere else, Baylor University had instilled in him that Yankee attitudes were alien. Second, an ideal of the chivalrous South. In the opening hours of the Battle of Shiloh, for example, he had been appalled at the sight of Southern soldiers putting self above country by dropping out of the fight to plunder Union camps. And finally, the relationship between slave owner and slave. "The confidence existing between the slave owner and the slave" he remembered feeling as a teenager when he brought a large group of slaves from Mississippi to Texas was part of it.[6] But Nathan Stokes's lifetime commitment grown from Littlefield's mother's charge to take care of George during the war sealed Littlefield's thinking on the relationship.

For igniting and nourishing the true Southern sentiment flame, veterans such as Littlefield saw three principal agencies. Monuments and statues would remind viewers of what the war generation had fought for and sacrificed on behalf of the cause. Textbooks that conveyed the "truth" would save young minds from being misled into thinking that their fathers and uncles were traitors for having taken up arms against the United States. In 1892 groups within the United Confederate Veterans organization began reviewing every new American history textbook and calling on school authorities to reject those that presented contrary interpretations. Finally, the classroom teacher ranked as important as the textbook. Best were men from the South for whom the true Southern sentiment was instinctive because they grew up with it.[7]

Better than just imbibing it, Robert Dabney worked to shape Southernness. With a venomous hatred of Yankees buttressed by an increasingly calcified Calvinist fervor, Dabney in print and in the classroom devoted himself "to teaching Southern youth not to despise the cause for which their fathers died, not to forget the proud traditions of the past, not to repudiate the blood of patriots shed, and to study the constitutional question settled in this world by the late war; but, in his opinion, never to be ultimately decided on a basis of right and wrong until the great hereafter." So said Thomas Watt Gregory—former student and ever-ardent university supporter, future regent, and later President Woodrow Wilson's attorney general—at the high point in Dabney's career at the University of Texas when faculty and former student friends presented the school in 1891 with a portrait they had commissioned of the great man.[8]

However much Littlefield concurred in Dabney's views from having served with him on the Hood Camp board, he was unwilling to come out on Dabney's behalf and instead wrote Harwood, "trusting you may find a remedy." No remedy was to be had, and certainly not from Harwood. Littlefield had heard it wrong. Far from losing Dabney, after eleven years, the board of regents was inviting his resignation. "His orthodox and conservative views were not altogether in accord" with those of the board, reported the Louisville *Courier-Journal* diplomatically. And though Littlefield could not know it, Dabney received the board's decision from regent executive committee member Harwood himself.[9]

The Louisville paper had it right that in Dabney's mind, his efforts "to maintain a Christian influence" caused his downfall. Not the first time. His extreme orthodoxy had brought about his ouster from the Union Theological Seminary in Virginia. The publicly funded University of Texas was drifting "into a mere nest of infidelity and Atheism," Dabney declared after learning of his dismissal, adding that "in comparison with cotton, money, and spoils politics," the "Texas people" cared little about "the pride and trust of a Christian people."[10] If the loss of Dabney's voice caused Littlefield to give more attention to ways he could contribute to imparting the true Southern sentiment to the second generation born since the war, the time was right for stirring patriotic memory by raising monuments recalling military service defending that sentiment.

Nearly twenty years had elapsed since the proposition to raise a memorial to the Eighth Texas Cavalry Regiment's dead had been advanced at a Terry Ranger reunion, fifteen since the Texas legislature authorized erecting it on state property.[11] Obtaining legislative permission, and thus sanction, as difficult as that was, turned out to be the easy part. Raising the necessary funds proved more difficult. During the latter 1880s, preparation of a unit history that never came to fruition held the veterans' attention and thus diverted energy away from the monument project.

Maybe similar to the Hood Camp's giving Littlefield charge of its treasury only months after the comrade became a bank president, the Terry Ranger veterans during the October 1890 Bastrop reunion sought to tap his financing skills too. If appointing him to a newly constituted monument committee was intended to open doors to dollars, the stratagem bore no immediate fruit. In frustration at the Austin reunion the next year, monument committee chair George B. Zimpelman spoke frankly. The time had come, he said, to set aside the floundering written history project and devote themselves to erecting the monument. If they could not raise enough to fund the monument they wanted, then they should accommodate their want to the amount in hand. Challenged, the assembled veterans pledged $4,665 to the work, Littlefield and another each pledging nearly a quarter. The Austin paper took notice and editorialized its support, even supposing the state must contribute to "this noble work." Having for a decade devoted their monument building to the Texas Revolution, capped that year of 1891 with completion of the Heroes of the Alamo monument on the capitol grounds, lawmakers had satisfied their appetite for state monument building. If the Confederate veterans wanted monuments, they would have to raise them themselves.[12]

Despite the pledges and the editorial, still the Terry Rangers' monument project languished. Insufficient money played a role. Perhaps, though, the idea of siting the monument in a cemetery, which was what the legislature had authorized, cooled their ardor. Survivors of one of the two most famous Texas Civil War units wanted to be memorialized among the living. Happily, the purpose of monuments and their role in Confederate memory-making had begun changing about the time the legislature acted in 1879. From burial grounds, desirable placement had moved to bustling public spaces where the community would see and thus profit from what the memorial recalled. The survivors set their sights on the grounds of the Texas capitol. Major Littlefield and monument committee colleague E. M. Phelps made the case and in 1897 secured legislative authorization. Then, during the association reunion in June 1898, the attendees accompanied President Littlefield to the capitol where, with the governor, they selected the site for the monument—across the front walk from the prominent Alamo memorial.[13] Surely, soon the Terry Rangers would be able to celebrate their monument.

From the capitol grounds, President Littlefield led his happy band of sixty-five Terry Ranger survivors to Camp Mabry, northwest of Austin, to watch battalion drills of regiments forming for service in the Spanish-American War. When they reached the encampment, the Confederate "boys" made a beeline for the cavalry regiment where the recruits were selecting their mounts from the seven train-car loads of horses that had arrived earlier in the day. After a while "Colonel" Littlefield formed the "gallant heroes" in line and marched them across the parade ground. Catching the spirit, the Third Regiment band struck up "Dixie." The Confederates answered with a lusty Rebel Yell. Battalions cheered. Superlatives flowed. "The Terry Rangers can fight yet if necessary," observers pronounced, perhaps aware that "Fightin' Joe" Wheeler, who had dispatched the captain on his night ride over the Chickamauga Battlefield, had been given command of a cavalry division already engaged in Cuba.[14]

George and Alice Littlefield crowned the exhilarating day at their home by treating the reunion attendees to a reception like none before. First, arriving at the front gate, visitors saw "an elaborate design made of electric lights [that] shone out brilliantly. It was a star, with 'Texas' spelled out, one letter between each of the star's points, and in the center was an 'R,' for Rangers, the design worn by members of the regiment on their caps and hats during the war." The electric light display could hardly have been more arresting. Lighting with electricity was still so new that gas flame illuminated the four-year-old home's light fixtures, and it was less than three years earlier that Littlefield had turned the Driskill into the most modern of hostelries by outfitting it with electric lighting.[15] Then, in the long receiving line, no less a personage greeted the veterans than the last living member of the Confederate cabinet, Texan John H. Reagan.[16]

The unique, lighted Ranger R that captivated the reporter and the veterans closed a day of high points, the most sentimental of which had been the surprise that animated the morning. During the business meeting, Henry W. Graber read a communication from Major John J. Weiler, Seventeenth Indiana Mounted Infantry, concerning a Ranger flag the Hoosiers held as a war trophy. Subsequent exchanges between Graber's Terry Ranger committee and the Indiana legislature and governor succeeded in arranging the treasure's repatriation. Twenty-four Eighth Texas veterans assembled in Dallas on October 5, 1899, to cheer the Indiana governor as he handed the colors to the Texas governor, brother to a Terry Ranger, who then returned it to Ranger custody, handing the banner to Ranger and former congressman James Miller. "Terry Rangers flag returned, event of national importance," the Austin paper headlined its account of the ceremony. What should have been a red-letter day in the Terry Ranger survivors' history wasn't. George Littlefield and a majority of association members boycotted the return that Littlefield himself had helped to arrange. "Petty jealousies," Graber called it later. And so it was. Though he had no firsthand knowledge of the incident, having left the service months prior, Littlefield bitterly resented the Indianans' claim that the flag had been captured—that the Yankees had overrun the Texans. Major Weiler himself said he found the flag lying sheathed on the ground, having been dropped. The real reason for the snub, though, said Graber, was that he, Graber, ignored the Austinite's recommendation to hold the ceremony in the Texas capital.[17]

But on June 1, 1898, the inhospitality in Dallas lay in the future. In Austin the exuberance of the Terry Ranger parade continued to stir men forming at Camp Mabry in answer to President William McKinley's call for volunteers to avenge the sinking of the battleship *Maine* in Havana Harbor and help the Cuban people wrest independence from Spain. Following tradition, company units took names to hearten and inspire the ranks. For the company he was raising, Captain Robert L. Ralston had chosen the name Dewey Rifles in honor of Admiral George Dewey, who had defeated the Spanish fleet in Manila Harbor. But in July, recognizing their local luminary's "distinguished and daring service in the Texas Rangers, in behalf of the 'lost cause,'" Ralston's Austin area "country boys in the pink of condition" discarded the Dewey name to march as Littlefield Rifles.[18]

No sooner had Ralston's company adopted its new title than American arms triumphed in Cuba and the Philippines. The victories ended the foreign war and with it the need for volunteer companies like the Littlefield Rifles. While the disbanding of the Littlefield Rifles and evaporation of the war spirit would not take interest in the Civil War with them, still the Confederate veterans could not afford to relax their campaign extolling their Southern sentiment. Members of the John Bell Hood Camp knew it. For six years they had been working to raise a monument to Confederate dead on the capitol grounds. Obtaining legislative authority consumed two years, and another four went to settling on the design and exact location. With a treasury comfortable from sale of the Confederate Home, the fund-raising committee including Littlefield accomplished its work in the remarkably short span of six years. By contrast, production of the actual monument threatened to take longer than anticipated. In 1901, two years after contracting for the monument with granite man Frank Teich of San Antonio, the veterans flatly rejected the first of the five figures planned to stand atop it. Agreeing to switch to bronze, Teich fished around until Pompeo Luigi Coppini walked into his shop unannounced.[19]

Thirty-one years old, only five years in the United States from his native Italy, and not yet an American citizen, Coppini had never set foot in the South until he stepped off the train in San Antonio. But his acceptance of the commission changed both his life and the course of Confederate monument-making in Texas. Whatever cultural differences separated the Confederates and the Italian, the

A Man Absolutely Sure of Himself

purposes of the art that the old warriors wanted and that the sculptor saw as his product harmonized completely. "It has . . . always been my strong belief that art, without an uplifting mission, is not really a fine art, but a simple commercial decoration . . . missing thus its high philosophic and moral ideal of educating mankind and failing to become the perpetual teacher of virtues and truth," Coppini wrote in his autobiography. "An art that has no effect on the betterment of the soul, and on the building of better character, by a strong message that portrays the better events of the past as a philosophical teaching, or that brings emphasis to the greatest deeds of our contemporary people, is to my way of thinking as degenerating as are those who like it that way."[20] Teaching virtue and truth from the better events of the past could not have expressed more succinctly the Confederates' resolve in erecting their monuments.

If the artist had latitude in molding the faces of the figures representing the four branches of military service that would occupy the corners of the monument, the real test of his skill would come in how he captured the facial expression, in heroic size, of the most important figure in the group. The likeness of the president of the Confederacy, Jefferson Davis, would surmount the large monument. Upon entering Coppini's work place with his fellow committee members to see the Italian's creation, Texas Civil War governor and subsequent Davis aide-de-camp Francis Lubbock took a position in a corner silently studying every feature. Then Coppini saw the old man's "eyes moistened by deep emotion" as he avowed that the face "looks as if he could speak to me."[21]

That was all camp executive committee member George Littlefield needed to hear to cast his vote accepting the monument. On April 16, 1903, two years after Coppini gave new life to the monument, a large crowd gathered to watch the Hood Camp dedicate the most lasting work it would send into the battle for hearts and minds of postwar generations.[22] And if he did not suspect it just then, in time the Major would appreciate that he had met the sculptor for the Terry's Texas Rangers monument.

But that, too, lay in the future. After having its site designated, the Terry Ranger monument stalled. Monument chair Littlefield had his hands full working on multiple Confederate matters at once. Along with his role in completing the Hood Camp's monument, he took charge of raising funds to realize a Terry Ranger window, one of three representing Texas, for the White House of the Confederacy Museum in Richmond. And he was responsible for donating two portraits to the museum. In Dallas he joined in chartering the Texas Reunion Association, whose board raised funds to host the 1902 United Confederate Veterans Reunion and erect a grand statue to Gen. Robert E. Lee.[23]

In pursuing Confederate memory-making so heartily, George Littlefield had turned a corner and risen to a new level of participation in perpetuating the Southern sentiment. No longer would he find and meet his obligations only by carrying out commitments to the Terry Ranger and Hood Camp associations. No longer would he shy from acting alone as he had done in trying to reverse the Dabney departure. For the remainder of his years, the Major would invest not just his time but also his wealth in what he saw as duty. "It's a duty of such Confederates as yourself and myself," he would lay it on the line to a comrade, endowing the word "duty" with the deepest level of commitment, "to do all they can to have the true history of our Country given to the Young men and women."[24]

If a single act could mark the turn, surely it occurred in 1898 when George Littlefield commissioned Lawrence Ludlow Cohen, Confederate veteran and German-trained portrait painter then in Houston, to produce paintings for Littlefield's home. This was no insignificant move. Art had been no part of the Major's life before he married Alice, who was accomplished in needlework and painting. Since no portraits of hers have ever been spoken of, much less survived, it is unlikely that her brush produced the earliest portrait of a Littlefield family member; son George must have commissioned the unsigned portrait of his mother (fig. 3). If made during her life, as it appears, the work dates before Mildred Littlefield's June 1880 death. If so, then twenty years, give or take, passed before Littlefield engaged Cohen and adopted art as a stimulus to Confederate memory. Cohen's work featured four Confederates: three nearly life-sized paintings of Robert E. Lee, Jefferson Davis, and John H. Reagan and a mounted Stonewall Jackson. Along with the Confederates, the Major had Cohen paint the first life-sized canvas of himself. Rather than take time to pose, Littlefield provided the painter with a photograph to duplicate, a habit the Major followed thereafter. From another artist, he commissioned a portrait of Thomas Harrison who had promoted him to major for gallantry in action.[25]

The seeds of Littlefield's turn may have germinated in the very Spanish-American War fervor that raised the battalions cheering the Terry Rangers as they marched smartly across the Camp Mabry parade ground. Though the 1898 conflict, and the Littlefield Rifles with it, came and went in only months, excitement over the war distracted attention from the Civil War and the Southern sentiment the Major's war symbolized. Beginning with commissioning the Confederate paintings for his home, George Littlefield so broadened his activity in behalf of appreciation of southernness that in chairing fundraising for both the Ranger Monument in Austin and the Ranger window in Richmond, he would compete with himself in tapping similar pools of money.[26]

As his devotion to the Confederates' duty increased, so the Major encouraged it in others. Work on the Terry Ranger monument for the capitol grounds was dragging on, he concluded, because the very men most interested in and who would be honored by having the work created were lagging the step. They lacked the motivation of a deadline. During the December 1903 reunion, Littlefield proposed and the attendees dutifully adopted the goals not just of raising the wherewithal to complete their monument but also of erecting and dedicating it, all in a year's time. If he truly thought that a tight deadline would speed the work, he was mistaken. A year later, with the project little advanced, he tried having his bank loan a tidy sum to the Rangers. While leaving a modest amount more for the men to raise, this put the survivors in the position of owing on the loan taken out in their name. From the money, he and a few others even borrowed amounts just to pay the interest into the monument fund. When the treasury still remained short, only one ploy remained for his committee to try to bring the project to completion—force the issue by contracting with a sculptor.[27]

A dozen or so sculptors from around the country submitted designs. "An Equestrian statue, after all, is the great achievement dreamed of by sculptors," wrote Coppini, who in 1904 still only dreamed. Paying for a mounted Terry Ranger would be a great achievement of its own. For their single-figure monument, the survivors would have to pay about as much as the Hood Camp spent for its monument with five statues.[28]

Texas's most widely known and praised sculptor of course wanted the job. German born and trained, Elisabet Ney had arrived in the United States in 1871, well after the war. Like George's mother, Ney was her own woman. For two decades in East Texas, she managed the family plantation. Defying convention, she went by her maiden name professionally. Her classic, delicate artistry spoke for itself in the commissions awarded her. Prominent Confederate Francis Lubbock had sat for her. Oran Roberts not only had sat but also housed Ney for a time. The legislature had commissioned her to sculpt Stephen F. Austin and Sam Houston for display in the Texas building at the 1893 World's Fair. (These figures are Texas's favorite sons in the National Statuary Hall in the national capitol in Washington, D.C. Copies may be seen in the Texas state capitol.) More important for the Confederate association, the legislature also commissioned the recumbent Gen. Albert Sidney Johnston that marks the Texas State Cemetery grave of the most famous and mourned Texas Confederate. The Major must have noticed when his Democratic presidential candidate, William Jennings Bryan, came to Austin to sit for a bust.[29] Ney had every artistic qualification.

Since the monument committee chair had not contacted her, Ney approached him. Nephew Maurice Dowell recalled the occasion:

One evening, we, Uncle George, Aunt Alice and I, were talking in their
room, when Selma, the faithful housekeeper, entered and said, "Mr. Littlefield, Miss Ney wishes to see you."

It upset Uncle George, and he bounded up out of his rocking chair and
said, "Tell her I am not at home!"

Aunt Alice quickly said, "George, you are at home. You must go down
and see her."

He said, "I will not go and see her. She calls herself a *Miss*, and lives
with a man and I don't know if she is married or not. She wants to see me
about the Terry Ranger Monument."

Aunt Alice said, with righteous resignation, "George, I am going down
to talk to Miss Ney."

"Well," he said, "I won't see her, and I am going to give the job to a *man*."

So dear Aunt Alice went downstairs and was most gracious to Madame
Ney.[30]

The Major was not alone in being appalled at Ney's ways. And this was not the
first time it had come up. Littlefield had been fending off Ney for a decade since
the Hood Camp and Terry Ranger groups had begun talking seriously about erecting monuments. Maybe John Reagan's vitriolic campaign only a few years earlier
against Ney's statue of Sam Houston in "Indian apparel" weighed in Littlefield's
mind too.[31] Whatever his combination of reasons, for Littlefield, born of the Old
South, only a proper man was the right choice to sculpt a Terry Ranger on his
warhorse heading into the fight.

The Major could dictate because he held the overriding vote on the monument committee. At the 1904 reunion, his comrades entrusted the project to him
when, in addition to having him chair the committee, they elected him association
vice president and treasurer as well. After six months of winnowing the field, in
May 1905 the monument committee awarded the work to Pompeo Coppini. What
a statue he would produce. The figure would be nothing like the "conventional
good looking and well fed lazy boy in dress parade attire and at rest," Coppini
wrote, disparaging his own work that had satisfied the Hood Camp veterans.
Reported the Austin paper, the Italian's bronze would portray a Terry Ranger

> leaning forward on the neck of his fiery charger, holding in one hand his
> closest companion, the rifle, while in the other he unconsciously guides
> the steed into the thickest of the battle. A look of daring fearlessness,
> unconcern of the dangers surrounding, eagerness for the fray, with that
> keen, piercing gaze, that dare-devil appearance which strikes terror to the

soul of the enemy, is portrayed in the face of the man. The most striking and commendable characteristic of the figure is the animated life which is portrayed in every feature of the statue.

George Littlefield and his comrades could not have described better how they remembered their unit and wanted others to picture it (fig. 26).[32]

"Unveiling of Terry statue, program of ceremonies has been completed": the June 21, 1907, *Austin Statesman* headline surely animated George Washington Littlefield's sixty-fifth birthday. Behind him lay two years' work overseeing erection of the monument, beginning with securing the site. Behind him lay the delay caused by having to engage a New York foundry after the Chicago facility, where the five tons of molded clay was sent first for casting, could not accommodate the largest of the statue's twelve units. Behind him lay overcoming the Austin City Council's initial refusal to allow the monument's Texas gray granite die stone to travel up Congress Avenue, the only street whose slope was gentle enough for hauling the seventy-thousand-pound behemoth measuring ten feet long by five and a half feet wide by six feet tall from the railroad to the capitol grounds. More importantly that Friday, ahead of him in five days, as president of the Terry's Texas Rangers Survivors Association, lay overseeing the grand dedication culminating thirty-one years of dreams and persistence.[33]

With thousands expected to crowd the capitol grounds, "This is going to be a great event . . . in the history of Austin," the *Statesman* told its readers as it asked them to deck downtown streets with bunting, flowers, and tributes. "Pull for Austin," read one editorial. "Here is to greater Austin," another expanded on the theme.[34]

George Washington Littlefield understood. Littlefield had been pulling for Austin almost since he had moved there. As a member of committees of local leaders convened to show Austin hospitality to visiting groups, he had been boosting his home at least since the Texas Live Stock Association planned its Austin meeting in 1885. For eight years, as proprietor of the center of Austin's civic, and much of its business life, Driskill Hotel owner Littlefield held arguably the highest stake in Austin's future.

But as singular and important as the hotel was to Austin, it was not the capitol city's signature institution. For city booster Littlefield, the state university was.[35] Yet in 1897, fourteen years after the University of Texas opened, the school's main building still stood unfinished. The wooden fence surrounding the campus to keep stray cows out instead demonstrated the animals' intelligence in learning to operate the turnstiles so as to pass to the forbidden grass on the forty acres. Though the city had begun paving streets two years earlier, in 1897 the ways beside the campus remained simply dirt tracks. If the school were to look more like a flagship university, then citizens and faculty interested in the institution had to contribute.[36]

So on Tuesday evening, December 7, 1897, George Littlefield invited eleven faculty, business, and civic leaders to discuss the matter. They arrived at the Littlefield home anticipating nothing out of the ordinary for a business meeting, and for two hours, late into the night, they talked until they determined to request the board of regents' authorization to construct a walk and bicycle way around the campus. Constituting themselves as the Campus Improvement Society executive committee, each pledged a contribution, Littlefield doubling the next largest amount. Business accomplished after selecting the American National Bank to hold the account, near midnight the group and the *Statesman* reporter discovered that "never did a committee meet under more favorable auspices." The hospitable major directed all to the dining room for what the *Ranger* student reporter called "a splendid 'bumper.'" Upon the host's invitation, "the chairman stampeded, with the entire committee close at his heels" where, among refreshments of the season that glistened in cut-glass serving dishes, they partook of eggnog "that was never surpassed since Columbus discovered America."[37]

The regents accepted the donation, stipulating that the committee relinquish all ownership of the finished product. In the face of design changes, work proceeded slowly. When after a year the "broad golden band" of the peripatos, as the way was called, extended only along the south and west sides of campus, Littlefield moved to encourage work on the north side in front of his residence by offering to plant and water a row of hackberry trees beautifying that stretch.[38]

Upgrading byways for the comfort and pleasure of visitors, locals, and the university family, students especially, was one thing; ensuring Austin's livability and growth was another. Attention to the city's quality of life and expansion required nearly annual dedication. In 1897, the same year that he led the drive securing the capitol grounds site for the Terry Ranger monument, Littlefield became involved with selecting members of Austin's Water and Light Commission. In the face of the dam's failure to produce the volumes of promised water and power, the two-year-old body would set rates affecting the entire community, since the shortfall would saddle taxpayers with considerable of the burden of retiring the $200,000 bond obligation contracted for building infrastructure to extend service beyond the 750 water and 766 electricity customers. In 1898 he accepted appointment to a committee to draft amendments to the city charter and presided over the Travis County Fair. "Put me down in favor of the bonds first, last, and all the time," he told a *Statesman* reporter canvassing prominent figures in 1899 about moving the high school from rented space into a purpose-built facility. To secure the Missouri, Kansas and Texas Railway as Austin's third major transportation link to the rest of the country, in 1902 Littlefield joined fifteen other guarantors of right-of-way and depot facilities. He and Joseph Nalle pledged the largest amount. "No set of men . . . worked harder for an enterprise than did these," the paper lauded conclusion of the eighteen-year campaign. For assistance to the city's needy, beginning in 1903 the Major occupied a seat on the board guiding the new United Charity Association. If there were one other way in which Littlefield personally could serve the city directly, the *Statesman* headlined it on July 29, 1905, "Major Littlefield is surety for the city" in its case against the Austin Water, Light, and Power Commission.[39]

Behind the scenes, city affairs could be influenced indirectly but powerfully through the ballot box. Challenging opponents to wager on an election, as he had begun doing in Hogg's reelection campaign, might influence voters by signaling Littlefield's candidate, but it could not deliver votes. For that, silver dollars talked. One who knew John Dodd McCall quoted the late 1890s two-term Austin mayor as saying that Littlefield "was as smart as he could be" about securing votes. He would delay until near poll-closing time, then go into a black precinct where men stood around to see what their vote was worth. When the election judge signaled that a man had voted Littlefield's way, the Major handed the voter a silver dollar.[40]

However common this practice was, not everyone approved. Nephew George T. Littlefield related the story Nathan Stokes told him of the occasion when a poll watcher notified Littlefield that his candidate was losing. Quickly, the Major gathered his silver dollars, hustled into his buggy, and with Nathan driving, tore out to the polling place. While the Major was passing out the coins,

> A policeman came up and said, "Why, Major Littlefield, you ought not to be doing this. We might have to arrest you."
>
> "I don't have time to see you now," he replied, "Come around tomorrow and we'll talk it over."
>
> The Major's candidate won, but said Stokes, "I shore thought we was going to de calaboose."[41]

By a two-to-one margin, Texans in November 1902 approved a constitutional amendment instituting a poll tax prerequisite for voting. Intended as an assault on voter fraud by requiring registration, the levy instead disenfranchised the poor and minorities who could ill afford the $1.75 outlay. Where proponents saw beneficial restriction of the voter pool, those able to spend to sway elections saw opportunity and began buying poll tax receipts in bulk. Appalled, the Good Government League went to the city council. The police chief and members of the force were acting illegally as middlemen in the distribution of the certificates, the league protested, so as to swing the referendum in favor of the chief's reelection. Everyone knew that the charges simply established a basis for the league to argue against bulk sale of poll taxes. Expecting a "hot time" when the city council convened on the evening of March 24, 1903, for the first of three days hearing the league's case, observers packed city hall and were not disappointed.

In the two months after poll tax receipts went on sale, testimony revealed that more than half of them had been bought by other than individual voters. The American National and Austin National Banks were singled out because each supported one of its officers as a candidate for city treasurer. Hardly altruism, the successful candidate would move the city's money into an account at his bank. So when George Littlefield was called to the stand, the first question asked him was, in effect, whether he underwrote the purchase of poll tax receipts. If the Good Government League thought the hearing would intimidate him, it was mistaken. "Yes, sir, I paid them," Littlefield answered tartly. "Littlefield's money paid them—nobody else's money paid them." In fact, he bought eight hundred in one $1,400 transaction shortly after poll tax receipts went on sale. "Major Littlefield stated he exercised his right to buy poll tax receipts," the paper headlined his testimony. Why did he do it? He "wanted to be in position to have everybody to vote," he said, to which he added honestly that then he "would have as good a chance at the voters as anybody else." No "club or organization ought to run the city," he continued. "It ought to be run by the people." Regarding police involvement, Littlefield said he simply told officers that if they encountered individuals "who wanted their poll tax paid to bring them to him and he would pay them." But police were only one source. Littlefield acquired lists of potential voters from what he called "a good many people." Some he asked to gather lists. Others, as Alex Gamble, went to him themselves. The black man told the council he wanted the Major "to pay my taxes because he is my friend." When Littlefield had had enough of the questioning, he looked directly at the league's lead interrogator and asked if he was finished with him. "Yes, major," came the reply. "Thanks," Littlefield answered "amid a roar of laughter."[42]

From its three days of testimony, the Good Government League failed to accomplish its stated purpose of dismissal or at least disciplinary action against the chief and his officers. And the chief was reelected. But it accomplished its real goal when the city council instructed election judges to see that none of the illegal poll tax receipts was voted. If the league had hoped with its success to change the nature of the competition for the city treasurer post, it failed when the city council took the selection back from the voters. Unbowed in the city in which money still often moved decisions in city hall, Littlefield then out-lobbied his rival bank and secured the treasurer job for American National vice president Hiram Augustus Wroe.[43]

So prominent had George Littlefield become in Austin's civic and political life that even his health made news. "Major Littlefield may have blood poison: Boil pricked by small pocket knife resulted in very serious and painful complications" a December 30, 1905, *Statesman* headline announced. The news "created a great deal of talk on the streets," the New Year's Eve edition followed up, "as he is so well known and liked." If the decision taken by the black Shriners were representative, then the white reporter would have heard similar talk on the black streets. Just the previous month, the organizers of Austin's Mystic Shrine, Colored, had named it the George W. Littlefield Temple.[44]

Whatever else naming the temple for Littlefield might have recognized, it had to have spoken to his fraternal work as a Mason in Gonzales and as a Shriner, an organization of master masons, in Austin. The Masonic society had become a part of Littlefield's life more than forty years earlier when he affiliated with the Terry Ranger Military Masonic Lodge. In Gonzales Lodge No. 30, shortly after the war, he earned his Master Mason degree and served as an officer. A member of York Rite bodies in Texas, he became a member of Gonzales Royal Arch Chapter No. 51, Gonzales Council No. 8, and Gonzales Commandery No. 11. Maintaining his Commandery membership in Gonzales lifelong, he invested his Austin activity in the Shriners.[45]

When June 26, 1907, finally arrived, it was clear the *Statesman* had been right. Dedication of the Terry's Texas Rangers monument *was* going to be a big day in Austin's history. Streets decked, plans ready for execution, onlookers gathering, and "the old soldiers in splendid fettle," only a blistering sun could interrupt the proceedings. After an hour's postponement, at three o'clock the parade stepped off from the Driskill Hotel and traveled up Congress Avenue to the capitol grounds. There, "amid the booming of cannon, the strains of 'Dixie,' and the cheering of 5000 people," the monument to the Terry Rangers was unveiled. Leaving the speech making to the governor and others, Terry Ranger Association President Littlefield played so minimal a part in the formal proceedings that the paper took no notice of him.

Comrades knew, though, that but for George Littlefield, where the monument stood would have remained just a grassy patch on the capitol lawn. In his hands elevation of the Southern sentiment was secure. Speaking for the Rangers, Capt. Rufus Y. King of A Company likened the I Company captain's unwavering support to the power and pull of magnetic force. "At times the task seemed great and not possible," King said, "but when it seemed as if we must stop for want of means, when all discouraged and almost hopeless, a crisis close at hand, then Mr. President, you and comrades like you came to the rescue and the work moved on to this perfect consummation. You, sir, have been as faithful, as devoted to this interest as is 'the needle to the pole.'"[46]

Captain King said it well, but didn't say it all. A correspondent of the *Statesman* four days later, quoting ten words of Littlefield himself, completed the story. Though "One of J. E. B. Stuart's Men," as the author signed himself, repeated the Major's words to characterize his accomplishment with the Terry Ranger monument, in fact, the sentiment telegraphed just as firmly the nature of Littlefield's posture toward his commitments all, not the least of which were the university community, Austin, and Confederate memory. "His comrades say and they will rejoice to know," the correspondent wrote, "that his neighbors of all classes and arms give credit to the gallant Littlefield for the expression 'Boys, do the best you can. I'll do the rest.' And it is done."[47]

$$\text{---}\!\!\infty\!\!\text{---} \quad 15 \quad \text{---}\!\!\infty\!\!\text{---}$$

SYNONYMOUS WITH AUSTIN'S ASPIRATIONS AND AMBITIONS

Though the little story was buried next to the "Social Mention, Fashion Notes, and Clubdom Gossip" in the back half of the *Austin Statesman*, observant Austinites two days after Christmas of 1906 must have noticed the report that some forty-six feet of expensive Congress Avenue frontage had changed hands in a pair of transactions. The American National Bank had acquired the Goldstein tobacco store on the corner of Congress and Sixth Street. And George Washington Littlefield had bought the nearby, notorious Iron Front Saloon. Through most of its forty-one years, the Iron Front stood out among the town's many drinking and gambling dens. A cockpit in the rear enlivened the alley between the Iron Front and the Driskill Hotel. For a period, the second floor hosted the gambling business of legendary sure-shot and sometime city marshal Ben Thompson. "Stories are still told," the paper chronicled later

> of the high stakes played for and of money thrown about in drunken revels. In one instance a player became enraged with the dealer, and, picking up a stack of $20 gold pieces, threw them at the dealer's head. The rash individual paid for his outburst with his life and a scramble ensued for the money, but much of it was never recovered. It is thought that some of it rolled through holes in the floor and may still be lodged in the rafters or stowed away in crevices in the wall.

Neither recovering the elusive coins nor operating the place during the remaining four years of its lease beckoned the Major who not only refused to loan money to a gambler, but even dismissed family member partners for gaming. George Littlefield wanted the location. And paying a combined forty-five thousand dollars for the two properties, a sum the average American workingman with a family of five would need 763 years to save, was not too much for Littlefield. Better than any other city-center location, the Sixth Street intersection where all five trolley lines converged marked the heart of Austin's business district. Littlefield meant to move

his bank there and to house it in a structure that would top all others and herald
the city as the vital business and financial center he envisioned.[1]

After sixteen years in its original space in the Driskill Hotel, the American
National Bank was cramped. Its rival Austin National Bank, whose $2.5 million
resources at the June 1906 accounting exceeded the American National's by
$400,000 (19 percent), had enlarged its accommodations twice since the two
banks' 1890 founding, the last time four years earlier, in 1902. Pressure on the
American National's space after sixteen years arose from the bank's own growth, of
course, but also likely from President Littlefield's significantly expanding business
and personal interests both within and outside Austin's banking community.[2]

Trailing the Austin National had to needle George Littlefield every day that
he saw the competitor's advertisement in the morning paper. "We wish to call your
attention to the fact that our CAPITAL AND SURPLUS IS LARGER THAN ANY BANK
in Austin," the piece's uppercase letters rubbed in the further fact that during the
year the American National's assets had fallen $150,000 farther behind its rival's.
Nevertheless, Littlefield's second largest of Austin's four national banks was doing
well. Acquisition of the Travis County account added five hundred thousand dollars to the institution's deposits in 1905, and with Vice President Wroe continuing
as treasurer, the Austin city account remained secure. Of all the statistics, though,
one stood out by which Littlefield's bank soundly beat Wilmot's. As the American
National's ad boasted, the wealth of its bank's officers totaled $3 million, besting
its Austin National counterparts by a half million.[3]

In fact, banks as a whole in Austin were doing well. A year and a quarter
after the frustrating bank-to-bank comparison, the *Statesman* announced that
on a city-by-city basis, Austin's financial institutions, with total capital of eight
hundred thousand dollars, average dividend rate of 6.25 percent, and annual dividend disbursement of sixty thousand dollars, had advanced their city into fifth
place among Texas cities. And Austin mirrored the favorable banking environment
across Texas that on a state-by-state basis exceeded the national average. During the
period 1894–1905, the ratio of net earnings to capital for national banks in Texas
averaged 11.1 percent compared to 7.55 nationally. Of that profit, Texas's national
banks' 9.0 percent return on capital bettered the national average by more than
a full percentage point. Concluded the historian of banking in Texas, the state's
national banks for more than a decade spanning the turn of the century were
highly prosperous institutions.[4]

If continuity of leadership contributed to its success, the American National's
board and officers brought strength. Sixteen years after the bank's founding, nearly
half of the initial twelve officers and directors remained with Littlefield running

the institution.[5] Yet Littlefield's two eventual successors joined the bank only in the twentieth century.

Major Roger Courtland Roberdeau, the thirty-six-year-old son of a Hood's Brigade company commander, left the state treasury in November 1905 to take the assistant cashier position. When the Spanish-American War had loomed, he had led his national drill competition champion Governor's Guard into service as L Company, First Texas Volunteer Infantry, one of the units that cheered the animated Terry Rangers' march across the Camp Mabry parade ground. Discharged with the rank of major, he returned to the state treasury where he rose from assistant bookkeeper to chief clerk. In joining the bank, Major Roberdeau (his name and title always were spoken together to distinguish him from *the* Major) apologized publicly to supporters for abruptly abandoning his ambition to run for election as state treasurer.[6]

Where Roberdeau joined the bank in a line position, Hiram Augustus "Gus" Wroe entered in January 1903 as both a bank director and vice president. It was not because he had banking experience. Since 1895 he had been managing his father's Austin saddlery business. Rather, in 1898 he had married Littlefield's niece Pearl White. Maybe Littlefield knew young Wroe through his growing-up years when Wroe's father, a trooper in Littlefield's I Company, attended Ranger reunions and after he moved his business from Gonzales to Austin. Certainly, Uncle had abundant opportunity to assess the new family member after Gus and Pearl moved into a house across the street from the Littlefields and then on August 24, 1899, named their firstborn Ed Rhodes Littlefield Wroe for Uncle and Aunt's lost son. In place of the partnership formed with ranch managers, Uncle gave his nephew-in-law bank stock worth ten thousand dollars to cement his interest in the institution.[7] Wroe integrated quickly, particularly by being the bank's successful candidate for city treasurer.

To Roberdeau and Wroe fell the job of staffing the bank. The recollection of one hire gives a glimpse into President Littlefield's routine. Alfred Ellison said that in filing checks near the president, he and Littlefield developed a camaraderie.

> He'd come in there and say, "Well, good morning, Alfred." He'd make different remarks to me, and then some fellow would come in there and ask him for a donation to help building his church. Oh! They were in there every day. Lots of them every day. Some of them he would turn down, and he'd turn to me and say, "Did you ever hear of such a yarn in all your life?" And then another one he'd give him $200.00. . . . He was as generous as he could be.[8]

Many say that Littlefield could not refuse a loan to an old cowboy or rancher or to a Confederate veteran or a preacher. One who knew him said that often the Major made small loans from his own money, rather than the bank's, and without taking a note. Doing little favors leavened by nostalgia was one thing. Handling the bank's money was another and outweighed personal relationships. In 1905, after founding bank director Leigh Ellis's heirs fell delinquent on a seventeen-thousand-dollar note, Littlefield at first upbraided the borrowers, writing that "It seems to me you should feel obligated to me for endorsing the note, for the Bank could not make the loan direct to you on its own stock" that they had offered as collateral. Matters then went from bad to worse. If the heirs thought that threatening to take their business to the Austin National would soften the Major, they thought wrong. Littlefield bought the delinquent note, took his debtors to court, and won judgment.[9]

Heading a bank positioned Littlefield superbly for pursuing his strategy of making money by picking up cattle and land that a debtor pressed for money had to sell cheap. When General Land Office Commissioner William L. McGaughey had trouble meeting his payments, Littlefield steered him to sell stock to Will White. But that failed to end it. Discrepancy in classification of the land collateral and the number of cattle led Littlefield to demand payment, adding "if you insist on further trouble, we will give it to you." In fact, the matter dragged on until the bank sold the land to further satisfy the debt.[10]

Work being George Littlefield's recreation, even when the bank was closed, he went to his office. On Sundays he opened himself to chatting with employees who dropped by. "I'd come down before church knowing that Major was down," recalled teller Ed Cravens. "I kind of looked forward to the situation. He'd be there by himself. He loved to talk about various instances of the Civil War. When he talked to you, he looked you square in the eye, and he did most of the talking in our conversations."[11]

"His desk was piled high with stuff," said another. "Nobody knew what all was there, and he kept pushing the accumulations back from a tiny space before him just enough upon which he could sign his name." George Washington Littlefield knew what was there. "A great hand to keep every[thing] under his immediate direction," wrote nephew-in-law manager Arthur Pope Duggan, "he actually writes all of his o[wn letters,] and it is very seldom that he ever requires the service[s of a] stenographer in the Bank" (fig. 27).[12]

Some piles may have held communications from the range of investments into which he expanded beginning late in the nineteenth century. The 1898 Poe Farm purchase moved him into apples, produce, and stock farming. He even tried gold mining when he accepted the invitation of fellow cattleman and active Hood Camp member Dudley Hiram Snyder to invest in a Sinaloa, Mexico, shaft Snyder was working. "You will remember you told me when you agreed to put up the $5,000 that you would depend upon my judgment," Snyder reminded him in August 1898, "hence, I am doing as I would if the money was all coming out of my own pocket." Good intentions were one thing, profit another. As the mine failed and "all I have left is my home, one buggy horse, three jersey cows, and my courage, honor and determination," Snyder appealed for help. How Littlefield answered is lost to history.[13]

In 1902, while paying $121,400 on the Yellow House Ranch purchase, Littlefield further expanded his investments when he joined a group of prominent city and state business and political leaders in forming what became the Austin Fire Insurance Company. The firm achieved good profitability when, in its fourth year, it paid claims totaling just 32 percent of premiums.[14] In 1904 Littlefield added sugar. While still paying $49,000 annually on the Yellow House, he bought the 12,500-acre Stratton Plantation near the Texas coast. A mere $19,000 acquired the sugarcane plantation his bank carried on its books for $40,000. To manage the Stratton, a half interest secured niece Georgia Harral's husband, Seth Emmett Cole. Four years after he bought it, Littlefield sold the Stratton for triple what he had paid.[15]

One accumulation of papers on the desk doubtless dealt with missing cattle cars in 1907 and the resulting Littlefield Cattle Company suit that worked its way to the United States Supreme Court. The day after George Littlefield's sixty-fifth birthday, three days after the American National won its 1907 bid to handle Austin's money, and only five days before dedication of the Terry Ranger monument, the Major's blood must have boiled. The paper reported that railroads were failing to deliver cars to move cattle to market. While 3,900 Yellow House Ranch cattle waited at Kenna, the Santa Fe sent cattle cars Littlefield had contracted for them in pursuit of more lucrative business elsewhere in the Southwest and in Mexico. For weeks cowboys held the large herd until it became clear that the two hundred cars would never come for the Herefords. Returning the cattle to the ranch completed a fruitless, nearly two-hundred-mile roundtrip. Thirty-five thousand dollars the trip and lost sales cost the ranch. Littlefield sued. The jury awarded damages. The Santa Fe appealed. Eight years passed before the Supreme Court in 1915 ruled in Littlefield's favor.[16]

Another stack documented Littlefield's takeover of Austin's Capital Bank and Trust Company in 1908. Organized not three years earlier, the institution barely weathered the Panic of 1907, which so pressed Austin's five banks that, led by Littlefield and Wilmot, they formed a clearinghouse to protect themselves by limiting the amount a depositor could withdraw on a single day. But the Capital Bank could not survive the death of its president. Maybe Littlefield was motivated to acquire the little institution so as to even the score with Wilmot, who three years earlier had bested the American National by absorbing Wooldridge's City National Bank. Perhaps simply gaining its assets spirited him, or he saw it as a way to have a Littlefield bank on Congress Avenue with the Austin National before the Iron Front lease expired and he could build and move the American National. Whatever his reason, he invested himself so fully in the bank's operation that the Texas banking commissioner commended him for "remarkable progress" in upgrading the bank's condition.[17]

About the time the Major was taking control of his second bank, he received the deed to the Yellow House Ranch and a visit from land colonizer William Pulver Soash. If the LFDs thought the ranch, located more than ninety miles east of the Kenna shipping pens and nearly sixty miles south of the Bovina, Texas, facility, was remote from the changing world, it wasn't. To land promoters, the South Plains on which it sprawled was inviting ground. Whether or not the value of the 312,000 Yellow House acres had doubled in five years, as George Littlefield wrote Lizzie Dowell, without question it was increasing as colonizers began bringing land seekers to and promoters began projecting rail lines across Texas's Panhandle Plains. So many farm families seeking new land in the first years of the twentieth century began staking their dreams on tracts of the level, treeless acreage, virgin to the plow, that the region was blossoming as the fastest growing section of Texas. In six plains counties in the seven years between 1906 and 1912, land sales enterprises spawned no fewer than seventeen towns. In Lamb County north of the Yellow House in 1906, a Kansas City land promoter opened Springlake on the Halsell Ranch, and Iowan W. P. Soash two years later platted Olton on C. C. Slaughter's Running Water Ranch. Soash ferried his prospects (as they were called) from the Santa Fe Railroad at Plainview, closer to the Yellow House than either Kenna or Bovina. By year's end, Soash had sold more than half of his nearly ninety-thousand-acre tract, organized the county with Olton as its seat, and begun paying Slaughter the handsome eleven-dollars-per-acre purchase price.[18]

If settlers carving out locations at their pleasure on the public domain of the Four Lakes range drove Littlefield to seek a location that would not play out, even before he had paid off the Yellow House purchase, he faced the cattleman's dilemma that Slaughter articulated at the 1907 Texas Cattle Raisers Association meeting. While cattle prices in the twentieth century were depressed by 10 to 60 percent, increasing land values were driving up ranching's cost. Consequently, in the face of the demand for farm plots for which settlers would pay times more than the land had cost the rancher, cattlemen had to decide whether to sell at the first good opportunity, knowing that they well might "sit down in days to come and tell sons they sold too cheap."[19]

Maybe Slaughter assumed Littlefield's interest in colonization from reading press stories about his entertaining propositions to route rail lines across the Yellow House; perhaps Phelps's and Uncle's conversations about the proposition reached beyond family ears.[20] Whatever his basis, in 1908 the Running Water owner suggested that Soash visit Austin. Littlefield listened but rejected the colonizer's $3 million offer. "The real reason that the deal did not go over," Soash said later, "was that colonization methods were too new, too little understood, for Mr. Littlefield to make a deal that would leave me free to colonize the lands."[21] Soash's revolution was simple enough for anyone to understand. With "Soash Specials"—chartered trains made wholesome by the absence of liquor, the presence of wives, and the comfort of Pullman sleeper cars that allowed him to concentrate, herd, control, and whip up excitement in his prospects—the land colonizer generated sales volumes theretofore unknown.

> Oh Texas land, great Texas land
> We look across the waving grain,
> And in our hearts we do proclaim,
> On a better land the sun ne'er shown,
> We'll set our stakes and build our home,

went the chorus of one song composed for passengers to sing over and over and over as they traveled to his property. But the ranch owner perceived the consequence all too well. Soash's terms meant a return to the Four Lakes experience. The Iowan insisted that upon completion of a purchase, Littlefield deed over the little farm island wherever it might be on the vast cattle ranch. George Littlefield was not about to compromise his realization of the best and safest business in Texas by checkerboarding his ranch. When it heard that the Austinite rejected the multi-million dollar offer, the *San Antonio Express* gushed "that Mr. Littlefield is probably one of the richest men in Texas."[22]

As the years passed, Littlefield channeled increasing amounts to Confederate memory and well-being. Among the multiple piles of papers concerning Confederate veteran activity, surely the one rising to rival the Terry Ranger monument stack concerned the Major's devotion to the third and last Confederate monument to be erected on the capitol grounds. "Hoods Brigade stands first with me," Littlefield responded with a pledge of one thousand dollars to Hood's Texas Brigade

Monument committee chair, Frank Bowden Chilton, on September 20, 1907. "In my opinion to them belongs more credit than can be claimed by any command that served during the war, and to their memory should be erected a grand monument. We who are left from that army owe it to Hoods Brigade, and I as a citizen and confederate soldier, feel its my duty to do what I can that Hoods Brigade may have a monument in memory of their gallantry and suffering endured for the cause we all loved so well."[23]

Littlefield meant it. "It is part of his religion to love the cause of the South and to honor the memory of our gallant dead," William Hamby testified to Chilton at the beginning of their campaign to erect the monument. "I was intimately associated with him for nearly twenty years [as founder and cashier of the American National Bank until he left in 1905 to organize his own state bank], and during all that time, he was working with untiring zeal and energy to erect the monument to Terry's Texas Rangers, and but for his labors and his own large subscription, I do not believe that monument would ever have been built." Just how intimately Littlefield was involved in all arrangements culminating in the Hood's Texas Brigade Monument Hamby characterized probably better than he knew when he wrote Chilton on one occasion that he would confer with the Major and then "write you what *our* [italics mine] ideas are."[24]

With his Terry Ranger comrades, George Littlefield's association with the Hood's Brigade men stretched back twenty-five years to the reunion to which the Hood's Brigade Association invited the Terry Rangers group. That 1882 gathering may have been seminal in intertwining each group's interest in erecting a monument to both celebrate and avoid losing its history. During the meeting, the Hood men called for a marble shaft to be put up at the capitol. Three years earlier the Rangers had charted a path when they obtained legislative approval to erect a commemoration on state property. Like that of the Rangers, though, the Hood association's effort languished until, for the Hood group, the unveiling of the Rangers' imposing equestrian statue reinvigorated it.[25]

Though the Hood and Terry men remained so close that in time the Hood group adopted the cavalrymen as honorary members, Littlefield's relationship with Hamby mattered more. Circumstances drove Hamby to Littlefield. Not only did Littlefield have the experience on which Hamby needed to draw, but also the monument project treasurer had no Hood's Brigade comrade in Austin with whom to consult. After taking Littlefield onto the monument committee in 1908, the questions followed. What were his recommendations as to the best way to proceed with fundraising? with site selection? on the unveiling ceremony? And could he secure project oversight by the architect he had engaged to design his building?[26]

With the 1909 date for the unveiling nearing, the statue to top the shaft arrived. Hamby recoiled. One leg gave the appearance of the soldier having a broken knee; the rifle was positioned at an angle no soldier would hold it, and overall to him the figure looked like a recruit standing for a portrait rather than a veteran on the line. With Littlefield and the governor concurring, Hamby rejected the work, which canceled the unveiling.[27]

Knowing that difficult moments lay ahead, Hamby went to Littlefield to discuss hiring the Major's favorite sculptor. Chilton preferred anyone but Coppini, with whom he had had an unpleasant exchange after the volatile Italian vilified the monument committee's method and then initial selection of a sculptor more prominent than he. For his part, Coppini felt doubly spurned. Littlefield, he claimed, had promised him the job. If the Major did so, surely he hadn't done it, as Coppini asserted, two years before the monument project took flight and three before Littlefield had a hand in it. Wherever Hamby stood between the two sides, he lobbied Chilton for Coppini. As he wrote the association president: "to please Major Littlefield personally in addition to [satisfying] his professional pride as a sculptor, he [Coppini] will do everything within his power" to fashion an acceptable statue as quickly as possible.[28]

The monument men concurring, Littlefield summoned Coppini to Austin. Coppini refused to come. So monument committee members Hamby, Littlefield, and top donor John Henry Kirby the next day journeyed to San Antonio to wait on the artist in his studio. Would Coppini accept the commission? No, he had other pressing work. The delegation pleaded. Whether it was to please Littlefield or, as he wrote later, because he "felt sorry for their plight [and was] proud to believe that people were beginning to see straight," Coppini "reluctantly gave in." Finally, a year and a half late, the Hood's Brigade survivors and their admirers gathered on October 27, 1910, to dedicate the monument in a grand celebration that, in the length and community participation in its parade, surpassed that for the Terry Ranger monument three years earlier.[29]

Paralleling work toward the monument, the Hood's Brigade Association gave member Joseph B. Polley the job of writing the unit's official history. Would Littlefield provide a photographic portrait of himself? Embarrassed by the request since he was not a brigade veteran, Littlefield agreed to comply "if you tell me that all of the Committee on monument for Hoods Brigade have agreed to furnish their photos for the History. . . . While I appreciate the honor shown me, yet you know we must not overlook our modesty." Chilton insisted, and Littlefield's picture appears in the book, but identified only as a Terry Ranger. And as to modesty, the monument's second largest donor rode to the unveiling in the second automobile in the parade, sitting governor Thomas M. Campbell two automobiles back and monument committee members still farther behind.[30]

Among the last acts of their emotional reunion, the veterans called on the state to take responsibility for the Texas Confederate Woman's Home, as it had for the Texas Confederate Men's Home, then journeyed to north Austin to pay their respects to the indigent wives and widows.[31]

George Littlefield knew the facility well. Wife Alice belonged to the United Daughters of the Confederacy, whose Texas Division conceived, supported, and had managed the home since its 1903 opening. For years Littlefield had given both time and wherewithal to ensure that the home fulfilled its mission. From 1905 to 1908 he served on a three-man building advisory committee. Then he chaired the executive and arrangements committees of the June 3, 1908, official home dedication, scheduled on the South-wide observance of the centenary of Confederate President Jefferson Davis's birth, the Austin celebration of which Littlefield also chaired. Even before the dedication, he had accepted appointment to the new management advisory board.[32]

Like the Hood men, Littlefield advocated ensuring stable support by lodging the home's administration with the state instead of continuing to rely on the Confederate daughters' private fundraising. But that was only the half of it. Behind his advocacy lay his desire that control be wrested from the fair sex. "Ladies," he pontificated to thirty-four "grizzly" Terry Rangers assembled in their mid-December 1910 reunion, "while very excellent and loveable characters, are not inclined to get along together in the conduct of business as harmoniously as men manage to do." The women's lackadaisical handling of his payments for the United Daughters of the Confederacy scholarship he funded in 1909 frustrated him. State administration would open the door to positive change. Men could be installed on the home's previously all-female board of directors "for the avoidance of possible dissention" and "an excellent balance." Contradicting not only the governor, who had commended the UDC for "courage and patriotism to do what men failed to do," and next UDC Texas Division president Mrs. A. R. Howard who, at the formal dedication, pointedly called on men to "cast off your indifference," George Littlefield persisted that "inasmuch as the Confederate veterans had aided in the support and conduct of the present home it was not presumption in them to suggest the placing of Confederates at the head of the state institution." Unpersuaded, state authorities appointed Hood's Brigade daughter and three-time UDC Texas Division president Katie Litty Daffan as administrator, making her the first woman to head a unit in state government.[33]

Maybe some undocumented conflict bubbling up in the organization of the Texas Library and Historical Commission to which Governor Campbell had appointed the Major in March 1909 hardened Littlefield's thinking on the place of women in society. Members of the decade-old Texas Federation of Women's Clubs had been principal, steadfast, and aggressive through four legislatures to achieve passage of the library and historical commission bill. And they expected to be well represented on the commission. But the governor shared Littlefield's antipathy toward women's participation in business and public affairs. With two men ex officio—the superintendent of public instruction and University of Texas history department head George Pierce Garrison—but accepting that he had to appoint a woman, Governor Campbell needed two more men to fill out the five-person commission. To minimize confrontation over the appointments, surely he needed men he could get both over the weekend after Friday's bill signing and without lengthy arm-twisting to accept the not-inconsequential job of overseeing the shaping and running of a new state department. By Monday, the chief executive had his two.

Banker Littlefield's interest in adding the commission's work to his load would seem to have harmonized with the governor's on the history side of the agency. He had only a small library at home and did most of his reading in periodicals at the bank. But his concern for Confederate history was patent. Whatever his motivation, he dove into the work. For the commission's first item of business, and the only motion whose mover is identified, he accomplished the successful election of Garrison to the chair. Mary Terrell accepted election as vice chair. No lightweight, for her unflagging and dogged pursuit of the bill's passage, library supporters bestowed on her the sobriquet "Mother of Texas Libraries." Elected himself to the executive committee composed of the Austin members, which excluded Mary Terrell, Littlefield missed only one of the nine committee and commission meetings called during his twenty-two-month tenure. But on the contribution of individual members, the minutes are silent.[34]

More likely, the seed of George Littlefield's disdain of women in business and administration sprouted within the family and matured in the 1880s, when his sister and her large family became substantially dependent on him, especially after her husband's death. Buttressing the contempt surely must have been his growing revulsion at the financial ineptitude of Littlefield nieces, Alice Daniel especially. Whatever the timeline, by 1910 he could not see the contradiction of his disparagement of women in business with his unwavering esteem of his mother's acumen manifested in her deft management of Littlefield properties before the war. Nor did he perceive the contrast with the business wisdom he had seen in his bride's 1864 recommendations on the disposition of slave property. Nor further still could he admit that but for the assertive women who found business footing and mission in the UDC, the Texas Confederate Woman's Home never would have come to be.[35]

Creating and running the home gave one perspective on women's judgment, selection of a scholarship recipient gave quite another. Sometime between his appointment to the home's building and dedication committees, Texas UDC president Ella Peyton Dibrell proposed to Alice Littlefield and her husband that the UDC offer a scholarship to a University of Texas student in exchange for the student writing a history of the Confederate war from the southern point of view. And would Alice Littlefield head the fund-raising committee? If Dibrell singled out the Littlefields because she knew that the Major was willing to put money into Confederate projects, the proud Terry Ranger monument being the most recent, she didn't know him well enough. "Anxious to see the scheme carried out," the Major pledged $1,200, ending the fundraising campaign before it began.[36]

After such a propitious start, the initiative soured. Apparently no scholarship committeewoman, Alice Littlefield included, told the freshman recipient the commitment he was making in accepting the subsidy. Well, have the young man sign a pledge, Littlefield suggested, admitting that it "would be only a moral obligation . . . but a moral obligation is better than nothing."[37] A year passed. Not the first page of a manuscript nor even an outline for the work appeared. Littlefield's anticipation withered. "We all know that but few are ever history writers and . . . taking the chance of the young student they might educate proving faithful to his promise was taking a risk. Historians are born and not educated to it. By nature they must be adapted to such work. All of this we learn by experience."[38] Whether or not Littlefield's assessment of historians was accurate, his estimation of the student was. Though the UDC had promised that the selection committee "will take into consideration . . . any special indications of interest in or fitness for historical work," and though the recipient earned baccalaureate and master's degrees in history, including Phi Beta Kappa honors, Eugene Osborne Tanner centered his career on teaching Latin and government, not history.[39]

With as many irons as George Littlefield had in the fire, disappointment in one quarter often would be offset by good news in another. And so it happened that a month after the Major saw his student-written history from the Southern point of view wither, the Austin paper headlined his "phenomenal deals in land and cattle." Some 43,000 of his 100,000 Menard County acres brought him nearly $163,000 dollars, and sale of 4,000 three-year-old steers doubled that amount. Those two sales equaled more than three-quarters of his 1909 total. Whether he would have sold the land otherwise, 1910 was a contrarian's year to sell. "I never saw such a demand for money as there has been this spring," he wrote brother Bill's son George in July 1910. "Every boddy seems to want to speculate."[40]

Remarkably, neither of the sales was said to make a noticeable dent in Littlefield's operation that reportedly added 7,000 to 10,000 calves a year to the some 50,000 head roaming his Texas and New Mexico lands, which had grown to include 73,000 leased Z Bar L acres for wintering New Mexico steers in Texas's Crosby and Garza counties. Consequently, the *Statesman* reporter felt safe in asserting that Littlefield probably owned more land and cattle than any other Texan. And with that much property, he must be worth somewhere between $5 million and $8 million. The paper exaggerated. By his calculation in July 1910, the Major's assets totaled $4,586,000. As had been the case since he committed to the cattle business in 1871, his wealth rested on land and cattle, to the tune of $2,585,000 (56 percent) in 1910. Though banking had been a large part of his life for twenty years, stock in three banks accounted for a paltry $216,500 (about 5 percent). He was holding about as much in cash to cover upcoming Littlefield Building construction costs.[41]

In the years after his poll tax purchases ran afoul of the emerging Progressive Democrats' good government push, the Major's politics made news only in regard to that issue which, since the mid-1880s, not only tested the Democrats' unity but also subjected friendships and family ties "to the keenest trial"—prohibition. Littlefield opposed it. Where progressives saw moral uplift in banishing alcohol, conservative Democrats including Littlefield saw restriction of personal liberty. The clash came to a head in a local option election on June 1, 1907.

For four years in anticipation of the showdown the pros recruited their strength. From its inception, Littlefield joined the contest, as usual for him, by handling campaign money "in the interest of the cause," which was all that anti leaders wanted said of how the funds were employed. When the Travis County antis only a month before the election fully awoke to their adversaries' muscle, they called the Major to chair their finance committee. If the locals waited to elevate him thinking to take advantage of his vote-mobilization strategy of distributing paid poll taxes and silver dollars, they failed to appreciate their peril. "Owing to our divided [white] vote it's going to be a hard fight and very expensive to the town," Littlefield warned just three and a half weeks before the polls opened. And expense might not be the worst of it. "Should we lose this county," he added, "the prohibitionists will be very much emboldened and no telling what their next demand may be." The antiprohibition leadership's complacent neglect of black voters was playing with fire.[42]

Positioning Littlefield seems to have marked a turning point. The Texas Brewers Association that was coordinating activity statewide responded to him by dispatching John Baptis Rayner to Austin. An effective black pro preacher in earlier years,

Rayner had switched sides with the dedication of a convert. It was not on account of having been driven to drink. Rather, the invigorated hateful racist theme of the pro-oriented Progressive Democrats drove him away. Moreover, to raise the funds essential to building Conroe Normal and Industrial College into Texas's equivalent of Alabama's Tuskegee Institute, he needed white philanthropy. The anti group had money. Maybe the activist knew of Littlefield's generosity from news reports of the rancher-banker's strong support of the State Colored Orphans' Home at Gilmer. Perhaps the grapevine told Rayner of the Major's simple benevolences with black preachers. However it was, Rayner came to know Littlefield particularly from the Austinite opening his wallet to the Conroe school. Consequently, it is little surprise that when Rayner arrived in Austin in May 1907, he judged Littlefield to be "our only hope." Littlefield would act. As soon as Rayner opened the headquarters for his evangelism, the banker furnished him with "a full supply of refreshments" to begin wooing preachers and their flocks away from the pro ticket.[43]

Rayner and refreshments turned the tide. Not just turned it, they hushed it. While the turnout exceeded that of any previous election and the antis won in a landslide, the contest "passed off as quietly as any election ever held in this city," marveled the *Statesman*. Though he had not headed the wet forces, George Little-field sensed that as a prominent Austinite, he needed to address his fellow citizens. Maybe seeing the victory coming, he wanted to assuage the local pros and focus the citizenry on their Austin bond. "Go like men of nerve," he urged in his open letter, published on Election Day, "and stand by your convictions, sustain your city as in your mind you believe to be the best." But afterward, "put energy in our efforts to build up Austin." As it should be, commented the *Statesman*: "Major Littlefield's Card . . . was what might have been expected from so public spirited a citizen as Major Littlefield is known to be. Indeed, it was a straightforward talk from one whose conspicuous fidelity to this city in the upbuilding of which he has been so influential a factor that its very terms evidence the good intentions of the man." Take the sentiment to heart, the *Statesman* concluded. "With the Littlefield spirit that we are all still Americans and to Austin's prosperity wedded, let's do it."[44]

Do what? Austin had lost its optimism and direction of the previous decade. Destruction of the dam in 1900 had snuffed out the city's dream of becoming a manufacturing center. Four railroads serving Austin had not salvaged its primacy as a commercial center so pronounced after the first tracks reached town. The four institutions of higher education—two for whites, two for blacks—were too small to make Austin an education mecca. As important as it was, state government and its asylums at the mercy of a stingy legislature both lacked much potential for growth and were beyond the city's control anyway. Though Austin's population doubled between 1880 and 1900, the 22,258 residents at the turn of the century were too few to keep the city's rank among Texas's largest metropolitan centers from dropping two notches in those two decades to sixth place. All that Austin's leaders could see as Austin's attraction was well-being. A "delightful place to live" and "a beautiful healthy city," the press styled the community. Below the surface, though, heavy municipal indebtedness that building the dam had saddled on the population and persistent neglect of city services resulting from both the debt service and public reluctance to approve new bond issues compromised the surface serenity.[45]

What George Littlefield envisioned for Austin and what he meant by "building up" was raising the city's future on a vigorous business base centered on the city's strong financial institutions. Emerson Monroe Scarbrough imagined something similar and lost no time in making his move. In the last days of 1905, as the year's bountiful cotton harvest was replacing citizens' economic listlessness with a boom mentality, the department store owner shelled out a staggering $145,000 to acquire the half block on the southwest corner of Sixth Street and Congress Avenue. If from news of the purchase Austinites sensed that Scarbrough thought on a grand scale, in June 1906 they learned just how grand it was. Along with remodeling his shop, he would build an eight-story skyscraper to dominate Austin's business hub. Towering more than twice the height of the next tallest business house between the river and the capitol on the city's most important street, Scarbrough's office building would outshine all competitors, equipped as it would be with the finest amenities, including hot and cold air, local-made lights, and motive power for elevators and fans generated in a "mammoth" basement steam and electric plant.[46]

However pleased George Littlefield should have been with his friend's plans, two sentences in the news report could not help but prick the Major's competitive instinct. When finished, the block of buildings "will be among the handsomest in the south," read one. If superlative in the South did not provoke the Major, then the next sentence surely must have: "There may be imitators to follow, but Mr. Scarbrough leads in the matter of substantial testimonials of his faith in Greater Austin."[47] Accepting no backseat to anyone in demonstrating commitment to his city, and no imitator he, George Washington Littlefield accepted the challenge.

Barely a month after news spread of Scarbrough's purchase, a rumor began circulating that "a certain corner in the center of the city will be bought and that a five or six story building will be there erected." A year it took, but in December 1906 Littlefield and his bank acquired that corner diagonally across the intersection from Scarbrough. Architects went to work. Three years later, Scarbrough had plans for a "Giant Sky Scraper" containing "one of the most up-to-date office buildings architects can design." A month afterward Littlefield matched his rival floor for floor with an office building "as complete and perfect as it was possible to build."

But Littlefield charged young Austin architect Charles Henry Page, whose particular triumph was the Texas Building at the 1904 Saint Louis World's Fair celebrating the Louisiana Purchase's centennial, to deliver more than just up-to-date, complete, and perfect: Create a monument. Spare no expense to fashion a testimonial to George Littlefield, the businessman, banker, and civic force. Realize a structure that will be "one of the best . . . in the south," "that will ever be in the eyes of the commercial world," and "that would be equal to any that would or could be erected in Austin for at least twenty years" (fig. 28).

For Austin, "establish a new skyline . . . that must be quickly built to." For Austinites, design a roof garden "modeled on the latest and most successful in the northern cities." That amenity, topped by a prominent structure supporting a grape arbor would, not incidentally, thrust his building above Scarbrough's. Beginning in May 1911, for one dime Austinites would be able to retreat for an evening's entertainment in the cool breeze 136 feet above the street. And if cool air, music, a meal, movies, and overlooking the Scarbrough Building weren't attraction enough, "the biggest searchlight that was ever brought to Texas," whose beam could reach five miles, could be flashed "on your favorite spot in the city" or on unsuspecting couples below.

As 1910 opened, the rivalry seemed to turn into a race when clearing of the diagonally opposed properties began simultaneously on January 3. A year later, Scarbrough won. His three-hundred-thousand-dollar building was ready for move-in. Littlefield's structure, with its $480,000 completion cost, the furnishings and fixtures for which brought the total to almost three-quarters of a million dollars, was still under construction.[48]

For all the rivalry over their respective office buildings, Scarbrough and Littlefield of course launched their construction projects to improve the facilities for their department store and bank businesses, respectively. As much as the American National needed the new and expanded space, its Driskill location did not prevent it from earning inclusion on the 1910 national bank roll of honor. Reported the *Texas Bankers Journal*, only 15 percent of the country's 7,821 national banks achieved a ratio of surplus and profits to capital high enough to earn the distinction, and an even lower percentage of Texas's 520 national banks. Probably most satisfying to President Littlefield, though, was that the American National stood first in Austin with the best ratio.[49]

When in June 1911 George Littlefield began taking possession of his Littlefield Building, the banking room remained unfinished. It couldn't have been for the fixtures. Wroe and Page had bought them a year earlier. It wasn't because of installation of the largest and likely most difficult unit to mount. The one-ton hinge and its eight-ton "most modern and most nearly perfect vault door anywhere in the South" had been fixed in place two months earlier. Evidently, the delay arose in completion of the artwork that would turn the American National Bank of Austin, Texas, from just one more fine facility for conducting routine financial transactions into a unique and exuberant celebration of the open-range and early enclosed ranching periods of the American cattle industry. With his décor George Littlefield would do what no other cowman, cattleman, or rancher who had prospered through those times had done. And he would do it in a personal way, by depicting in murals and on a pair of bronze doors the cattle and men and the ranching and ranch land that had laid the foundation for his success and were his greatest pride and joy.[50]

He began with the paintings. Typical of him, for his artist Littlefield hired a young and budding but proven painter. Ernest Martin Hennings was a 1904 graduate of the Art Institute of Chicago and later highly acclaimed Taos artist who was establishing his credentials and developing his style by painting murals on order. Littlefield's was no small order. Canvases were to be ten to twelve feet long by almost three feet high. To ensure that each presented the subject and perspective that he wanted, the Major presented Hennings with photographs to copy. Made in 1908, documenting that the ranching art was no spur-of-the-moment impulse, the images included the most handsome and heaviest bull, a cowboy selecting his mount from a group of horses within a rope corral, and also a large herd of cattle passing before the viewer on a drive. Along with those scenes from the Yellow House Ranch, Hennings rendered from the LFD Farm in New Mexico a group of sleek horses grazing, cattle lazing in a field oblivious to a spectacularly exaggerated artesian water spout erupting nearby, and apple trees weighed down by their fruit.

At the bank's opening in 1911, these six distinct scenes decorated the walls. Four years later, for the bank's silver anniversary, a seventh had joined them. The addition of horses and a mule at a hay crib ensured that an expansive LFD scene caught the eye from every angle of the banking room. The ubiquity of the cattle scenes overpowered at least one colleague with no western roots. Seeking the Major's full attention to his letter, the writer begged Littlefield to take it home to read. "Don't try to read it at the bank with the cattle looking on," he pled.[51]

Seven paintings, in fact, were not all. Hennings produced nine murals for the Major. Two were near duplicates of two of the initial six. Though he did not mount them, Littlefield clearly liked them. He had photographs of them included in the booklet published to celebrate the bank's opening.

If surviving correspondence is a reliable indication, the rancher-banker turned his attention to the bank's entrance well after he determined to cover the walls with murals. Writing in March 1910, in the earliest mention of doors, Littlefield told Pompeo Coppini that he wanted "a design showing horses and cattle above and cotton bales on one panel[,] and oats and wheat in shocks on the other." The bank's entrance would herald the agricultural economy on which the institution rested. The Major emphasized it in greeting customers. "You will note that if a farmer and a cer tain dude who has a wholesale house come to see me," young employee Carl Widen remembered him saying, "I greet the farmer first." But what Littlefield envisioned for the doors and what his favorite sculptor delivered failed to correspond. The allegori- cally minded Italian offered panels exhibiting "economy," "providence," and a ranch scene centered on a bust of the Major attended by two cupids representing the sowing and gathering of crops. Unimpressed, literalist Littlefield abandoned the classicist.[52]

The Major discarded the agricultural theme too. Ranching views would better engage passersby and beckon customers to the colorful murals inside. At the sug- gestion of Tiffany and Company of New York, which would cast the plaster models in bronze, Littlefield selected Harry Daniel Webster for the work. Only slightly older than Hennings and having produced a figure for statuary hall in the national capitol, the sculptor, like the muralist, fit the bill of a talent clearly accomplished but still very attentive to building his reputation. Littlefield of course provided the tenderfoot with photographs to orient him to the scenes the cattleman wanted. But appreciating that the easterner lacked familiarity with cattle and ranching, in late spring 1911, the banker sent the artist to New Mexico to see and feel the land, the cattle, and the cowmen going about their work.[53] In those three essential compo- nents of his or anyone's ranch, Littlefield ensured that, as with the murals, the five scenes on the doors, ten-plus feet tall and nearly seven feet wide when closed, were at once unique to his ranch and universal to ranching. (For more on the murals and bronze doors, see appendix C.)

With the murals and doors distinguishing the American National Bank, and the bank the centerpiece of his magnificent Littlefield Building, George Littlefield had his monument. On August 15, 1911, he threw the bank's doors open for the public to see. Throngs came and approved. When the first number of the Texas Bankers Association's *Texas Bankers Record* proclaimed the "palatial apartments" to be "the finest banking room in Texas and the finest of its size in the entire South," the Major had full affirmation that the seventy-five thousand dollars he invested in furnishings, fixtures, and décor had been money well spent.[54]

In creating his monument, George Washington Littlefield did more than he could have known when he began. What started in 1906 as the solution to the bank's constricted space and at the same time cleansed Austin's main street of some of the town's infamous past simultaneously took on the aspect of a competition between Austin's two most prominent businessmen in encouraging Austin's growth as a commercial hub. In time, Littlefield added to it a personal recognition of accomplishment displayed in heroic-sized artwork, unique as documentation of the cattle industry commissioned by one who experienced its every phase.[55] As the *Austin Statesman* contemplated the totality of the Littlefield Building, it saw not just Austin's tallest office home and entertainment venue but a true turning point in the community's history. The showplace banking room paid tribute to the past while meeting the needs of the day. The office building accommodated the demands of Austin's business present while anticipating those of its coming commercial generation. Declared the *Statesman*, Littlefield's building signified "the closing of the provincial or town era . . . and the beginning of the metropolitan or city era." In marking the transition, the Littlefield Building in fact embodied the spirit of Austin a decade into the twentieth century. Pronounced the booklet published for the bank's silver anniversary, George Washington Littlefield gave his hometown a structure "synonymous with the aspirations and ambitions of 'Austin of Today.'"[56]

THE TRUE HISTORY

Elected Governor of Texas on November 8, 1910, Oscar Branch Colquitt turned at once to finding state offices for his supporters. Seats on the governing board of the University of Texas ranked among the most important. And with a single holdover in its eight members, this board would bear the new chief executive's stamp to an unusual degree. Announced only days after the victory, three early choices attested his design to give the board a business frame of mind.

The board needed the business orientation because its school was outgrowing the arrangement that, from its opening, saddled the day-to-day business affairs on the academician head. It needed the orientation, too, because in addition to sharing some of the administrative load, the regents administered the university's endowment of millions of West Texas acres and the property's revenue. The need must have seemed all the greater because, in numbers of students, the state university and its sister public institutions of higher learning drew into their classrooms barely half as many pupils as registered in denominational colleges.[1]

Houston lumber magnate John Henry Kirby led the list of businessmen appointees. Neither former student nor benefactor, Kirby's selection paid a personal debt. Rumor had it that, to facilitate repair of Colquitt's finances, strained during his years on the Texas Railroad Commission, Kirby had offered Colquitt a position in his company.[2]

San Antonio banker and public utility president George Washington Brackenridge stood in stark contrast. The longest-serving board member at twenty-four years, he was deeply invested in the school. His innumerable gifts included even the fledgling institution's first dormitory. Spartan enough to keep rent low for young men struggling to afford higher education, B Hall, as the 1890 structure became known, nevertheless was billed in the university catalog as being "as attractive as a first-class modern residence."[3] And in one respect, it absolutely was. Nine years after Jesse Driskill introduced the luxury to Austin and four years before George Littlefield would enjoy it, B Hall provided hot and cold running water.

Austin rancher and banker George Washington Littlefield's relationships with

Colquitt and the university lay somewhere between those of Kirby and Bracken-ridge. As Kirby had, Littlefield had offered Colquitt financial help. If Colquitt could arrange sale of the entire Yellow House Ranch for $3 million, the Major would pay him a commission 2 percent above what he allowed commercial agents. Like Brackenridge, though to a lesser extent, Littlefield had contributed to the school in multiple ways. In addition to serving as surety for the university auditor and contributing meaningfully to the Young Men's Christian Association residence hall, he had given both money and time to beautify the campus across the street from his home.[4]

The governor's unsolicited offer of a seat on the board of regents presented Littlefield a dilemma. "I don't believe in the finished Educations. More men ruined by them than made," he had declared a decade earlier. If he continued to believe that business courses provided the best foundation for young men's futures, the university was irrelevant. It had none, though it was searching for a professor to establish this curriculum.[5] However entrenched these views remained, he never-theless invited all family young wishing to attend the university to make Aunt and Uncle's home theirs.

Weighted against his disdain for finished educations was the Major's sincere regard for duty. Here was an unusually special opportunity "to do my duty in honor to yourself [the governor] and our great state." But with the outgoing board chair saying that the new board had a clean slate, that no substantive old business required the new board's attention, and lacking any bearing from the governor, what might the sixty-eight-year-old businessman have considered his duty to be?[6]

Six words in the Constitution of 1876 charged the school to be "a university of the first class." Drawing from the 1858 first bill to implement the concept inherent in that charge, the future university president whose leadership the Major particu-larly admired, Robert Ernest Vinson, characterized in two sentences the duty those words invested in the institution. "The University of Texas was from its beginning meant to be 'a means whereby the attachments of the young men of the state to the interests, the institutions, and the rights of the state and the liberties of the people might be encouraged and increased.' The worthiest possible compliment to be given the institution," Vinson concluded, "is that its students (and through them other Texans) should feel an increased responsibility and love for the interests, institutions and rights of the state." George Littlefield embraced that obligation to the school even before Vinson so succinctly expressed it. Just how deeply anyone could hear when he pronounced "the University of Texas": he emphasized "Texas."[7]

Apart from state loyalty, the Major needed no reminder of his duty to the South. The triumphal dedication of the Hood's Texas Brigade monument had occurred not three weeks earlier. And just then in early November, Hood Camp veterans watching for histories expounding the Yankee view of the plantation South and the war were up in arms over a high school reader containing such offensive poems as "We Will Hang Jeff Davis on a Sour Apple Tree." The book disappeared from school shelves, and the incident should have reinforced the Major in the commitment of United Confederate Veterans members to, in his words, "have the *true* history of our Country given to the Young men and women."[8]

Few appointments could match a seat on a university governing board for positioning a man to affect the content of United States history classes. Consequently, the Major's initial answer upon learning that the governor-elect had appointed him to the university's board of regents is puzzling. Littlefield declined. Not because he did not want to serve, Colquitt recalled. Rather, he demurred on account of having to associate with George Washington Brackenridge.

From a distance, in dress and cut the two could be mistaken one for the other. Not only that, both were bankers. And both early made their fortunes in the cattle business—Brackenridge loaning money for trail drives, Littlefield in trading and ranching. But there the correspondence ended. "Mr. Littlefield and I have never been intimately associated either socially or in a business way," Brackenridge allowed, "but I have no prejudice against him—on the other hand, admire him for his ability which is illustrated by his great financial success." Maybe so, but privately Brackenridge only "somewhat" regretted the news story reporting his "disinclination to associate with Mr. Littlefield and that our relations were not entirely harmonious."[9]

"Disinclined" put it mildly for Littlefield. He despised Brackenridge. The turncoat "took the oath of allegiance to the Confederacy, then ran off and came back with northern troops after the War" to trade in cotton confiscated from Texas Confederates, the young Maurice Dowell heard Uncle say about a decade before the Major's feelings became consequential in November 1910.[10]

Colquitt tried to change Littlefield's mind by saying he needed him on the board to increase revenue from the university's West Texas lands. First, that was true only if Brackenridge had failed in his duty as chair of the board's land committee. He hadn't. And what might have been within the governor-elect's knowledge, most recently Brackenridge had instituted a study of underground water, the presence of which would provide the basis for further increasing the lease income. Second, positioning Littlefield for the duty could happen only if the governor-elect declined to reappoint Brackenridge. He hadn't. Consequently, the land committee chair was not open for Littlefield to fill. Exercising all of its influence, the "university bunch," as Colquitt called the lobby, had prevailed on him to reappoint the regent popular for his benevolence and leadership.[11]

What should have charged Littlefield to jump at the opportunity to join the board of regents was a vote Brackenridge had taken the previous year. On a motion to accept the Austin United Daughters of the Confederacy chapter's offer of an annual prize of twenty-five dollars for the best paper "on a subject selected from the field of Southern History," Brackenridge startled his colleagues by voting "No." With the proposal coming from the UDC, he must have concluded that the field would center on the war. Of course, when the Confederate Daughters listened to Major Littlefield and veterans talk of the War between the States, they heard warm stories of camaraderie fused in campaigning. When Brackenridge thought of the Civil War, he remembered a cold noose around his neck. One night, as the fortunes of war were turning dark for the Confederacy, a group of vigilantes caught up to him. Fuming over his Unionist sentiment or his profiting from trading cotton across the Mexican border rather than fighting with his brothers for the Stars and Bars, they meant to hang him. At the last minute, one of them reflected that, though a Unionist, Brackenridge was not an abolitionist. Brackenridge was saved. "Be gone by sunup," they ordered. And away he rode for the Rio Grande and subsequent service as a U.S. treasury agent on the river. This was all that Brackenridge ever revealed about his life during the war. Not only did he not talk about those years, but in opposing the prize offer he signaled his desire that the university follow his lead—that it "not encourage Keeping alive and discussion of Civil War subjects."[12]

Though he meant every word of it, Brackenridge knew full well that his lone opposition was symbolic and affected neither acceptance of the prize nor the state of the university. Upon his departure from the board eight months later, he must have known, too, that no other member would pick up this mantle. But if he thought the matter would end there, he underestimated George Littlefield. Contrary to Brackenridge's symbolic action, the Major's response was concrete and affected the university profoundly. Disclosed in November 1920 in Littlefield's will, it may even have contributed to Brackenridge's demise a month later, Brackenridge's biographer believed.[13] But those events lay a decade off.

Whether the governor's persuasion or Brackenridge's vote or both changed his mind, Littlefield accepted the position. The Austin paper in November 1910 declared that the governor-elect had brought together "the best selections that could have been made." Six of the eight were businessmen, five of them millionaires. The student newspaper reported predictions of "the best business administration at their hands the university has ever had." All that the *Statesman* said of the hometown choice was that he would be "a valuable addition."[14] What did that say? Before the board ever met, couldn't each of them be presumed to be a valuable addition? Whether the paper was prophetic about its local regent remained to be seen.

What was certain on Friday, January 27, 1911, when the new Austin regent walked into his first meeting of the board was that he would be called on to take charge of matters best handled by the local member. Littlefield's previous two years on the Texas Library and Historical Commission told him so. But little else from his commission years prepared him for his regental duties. The library and historical commission administered a library and archives run by a small staff in the capitol. The regents had responsibility for a large community of a couple of thousand persons, within which were distinct groups, most obviously faculty and students. The regents owned buildings and land, including the main and medical school campuses in Austin and Galveston, respectively, and the West Texas acreage, whose revenue contributed also to supporting the Agricultural and Mechanical College of Texas in College Station. More than a job of simply overseeing it all, vested in the board alone were significant responsibilities including leasing that West Texas domain.

Sure enough, the first agenda item on January 27 was disposition of some Austin property. The previous October, the board had accepted George Brackenridge's donation of 458 undeveloped acres stretching along the Colorado River from above the dam toward town.[15] More than just an act of disinterested generosity, the San Antonio regent meant for his benevolence to become the university's new main campus. Unlike on the crowded original forty acres, there the school would have space to accommodate its growth into a future beyond imagination. It was no secret that Brackenridge intended that his gift of land once belonging to Governor E. M. Pease honor the former chief executive. In his antebellum terms, Pease had hoped to sign the 1858 bill, Vinson had quoted, to establish the university. Be that as it may, glaring to Littlefield was that Pease, like Brackenridge, had failed to follow his state into the Confederacy.

As fate would have it, the board chairman assigned administration of this land to Littlefield, the man most ardently opposed to honoring a Republican and to moving the campus away from its setting across the street from his home. Whether or not anticipation of this appointment weighed in his decision, Brackenridge concluded that a quarter century on the board was long enough. He resigned, postponing what would be a titanic clash over the land and move.[16]

Since a move on the scale that Brackenridge proposed would not happen overnight, the board asked Littlefield to lease the property for income in the meantime. Littlefield sensed opportunity. Of course he would accept a university group's bid and lease portions as dearly as possible for timber harvesting and dairying. But in the arrangement with the city, he thought to accomplish three ends more valuable to each than just funneling cold cash into university coffers. First, "in line with public policy" he favored leasing a portion to accommodate the city's interest in developing a public park. Second, believing that the university was the city's most significant asset, he negotiated for payment in kind. The city, which had few paved streets, agreed to pave streets on two sides of the Forty Acres to enhance the asset. Third, in exchange for adjusting priorities in its paving program, the city gained a new park at a popular location.[17]

Though the board chair normally assigned leadership for only one committee, newspaper editor and chairman Clarence N. Ousley asked the Austin member to head two. Construction of the school's sorely needed first library building had fallen behind schedule. Thinking to push the project, the previous board had entrusted New York architect Cass Gilbert with subcontracting the many facets of the job. The arrangement apparently intended the building committee chair's role to be giving nominal oversight and writing checks. Taking the oversight duty seriously, on an early inspection, Littlefield spotted discolored limestone high in the walls. Chemicals could whiten it, said Gilbert's construction superintendent. Not in his experience, Littlefield replied, his familiarity likely grounded in the Littlefield Building, then about two-thirds complete. Speed or specifications: choosing expedience to relieve the overcrowding as quickly as possible or fulfillment of the contract to the letter—that was the question. Not one who lived by expedience, Littlefield nevertheless lacked knowledge sufficient to make the decision in every case. "It is out of the question that your Chairman could be there all the while or that he could be a competent judge of the work," Littlefield protested to Ousley. No response. "I do not think its to the interest of the State that I should go ahead and approve . . . contracts when I do not know whether I am agreeing to a swindle or something right. No one but a builder can tell," the Major wrote again. No response. So Littlefield himself hired a professional to represent the university. The man noted twelve times more inferior stones than the rancher-banker had seen and reported that the walls were out of plumb. Littlefield stopped approving payments. Construction slowed. Upset followed, especially among members of the predecessor building committee that had made the arrangement with Gilbert. For his part, appreciating the university's strained financial condition, the governor endorsed Littlefield by hiring his man as state superintendent of masonry to continue supervising. Ousley's contribution to ensuring that the new university library met its specifications was to extricate himself from the uncomfortable choice between speed and specifications Littlefield's earnest fulfillment of his chairmanship had placed him in by removing Littlefield as building committee chair. Pleased to be relieved of the duty while appreciating the importance of completing the project as early as possible, Littlefield provided the board an interest-free line of credit from his American National Bank.[18]

The demands of the building and land committee chairmanships saddled on Littlefield an extremely heavy workload for a volunteer. Littlefield saw it clearly. While on November 11, 1912, the board loaded on him the work, regarding just the Brackenridge property, of commissioning a survey, hiring counsel to resolve boundary issues, paying back taxes, and negotiating with the attorney general in hopes of channeling the lease income to the university instead of to the state treasury, it accepted his resolution to create the position of business manager. Accomplished finally in April 1913, this was no functionary position. The board set the salary only slightly below the president's.[19]

Different from the library and historical commission, too, seats on the board of regents attracted favor seekers. Upon learning of Colquitt's election and Littlefield's appointment, sculptor Coppini rushed to Austin to propose that Littlefield sponsor a bust of the governor, and not incidentally one of the Major himself (fig. 55). What the artist particularly wanted, though, was the opportunity of the sittings. During Littlefield's, he designed to convince his subject to endow the university with an art school that he would head. Donating land and a building and underwriting initial operation would accomplish it. With the university then in the legislature pursuing taxing authority for the school's support, Littlefield answered that the time was not ripe. Though the artist failed during this very time to satisfy the Major with his conception for the bronze doors, Littlefield nevertheless gave hope to the man he called "the greatest sculptor this Country has" by finding a personal reason for considering the art school project. Perhaps it could assist in accomplishing his emerging dream of raising on campus a grand memorial to the Confederacy.[20]

While Coppini was making his proposition, Frank Rainey wrote the regent about prewar plantation masters' sexual misconduct with slave girls. Were American history students being taught from Yankee historian and Lutheran minister Henry William Elson's *A History of the United States*, which pictured an unwarranted depravity in the South? asked Littlefield's friend since at least the early days of the Hood Camp and the Major's term on Rainey's blind asylum board. If that was the case, Littlefield replied, "I promise you that the Regents will have it stopped." No, the book was not used as *the* text in history classes, History Department Chair Eugene Campbell Barker reported to Littlefield and university president Sidney E. Mezes. Acknowledging the book's failings, he added as the academic he was that including it among the eight to ten books used in American history gave students the opportunity to evaluate for themselves its worth relative to others.[21]

Having taken Barker's measure during the months in 1910 when the two served together on the Texas Library and Historical Commission, in replying to Rainey, Littlefield added reassuringly that Barker "would not countenance the use of any history that he thought would influence or be [the] cause of any student to form a wrong impression of the South." He was a southern man, a native Texan whose grandfathers and uncles had fought for the Confederacy. A generation apart, Littlefield and Barker shared Southern sympathies, an appreciation of the importance and power of history, and a deep commitment to the University of Texas.[22]

Still, appreciating his duty to Confederate history, he would get and read the book. Whether or not the Major ever turned a page, Barker withdrew the work from the department's reading list. And at its June 1911 meeting, the board closed the matter by adopting a committee recommendation both praising the department for its action and directing that Elson's book be excluded until "those passages not sustained by the facts of history and the true theory of our national life and institutions are omitted."[23]

Serving historical fact was one thing; obliging requests for positions was another. Littlefield would have none of that. "I know of no vacancy at present, and there will be none for [State] Senator [Robert E.] Cofer so far as I am concerned," Littlefield responded bluntly and publicly to the approach of U.S. Senator Joe Bailey, whom Littlefield continued to befriend with time and treasure. Despite the Major's and the governor's opposition, the lawyers on the board persuaded their colleagues to make the hire anyway. To a proposal that he displace an employee to open a spot for a friend of the governor, Littlefield answered, "When I am expected to look at the interest of the University, I would be obliged to admit it would be a loss to give him the place at this time. If it was politics alone, then I would not hesitate. . . . I don't think any man can be more loyal to his party or friends than I am, but when other things have to be considered, I reserve the right to do what I think best."[24]

Whether a majority in the Texas Senate thought it right or, as the paper said, they were simply "unwilling to allow one session of the Texas legislature to pass without an investigation," on March, 3, 1911, they seized on a student shooting the evening before to order an investigation. Texas Independence Day, March 2, had been a day joyously and raucously celebrated on campus since 1896 with, among other events, the firing of a cannon in front of the main building. This year, the sophomore men determined to force the freshmen men to return the field piece to the location from which they had appropriated it. Do it, or else! "Or else" meant "rushing," that is, being set upon with paddles. One freshman refused, and that evening a group of sophomores went to the off-campus house in which he boarded, intent on rushing him. "You had better go away, we have a gun in here," those outside heard a warning from behind the freshman's locked door. Disregarding the threat, with a skeleton key, three sophomores forced entry. The gun fired. The principal rusher fell, mortally wounded.[25]

The faculty and administration cannot control the institution, charged some senators. Students are running the place, echoed others. "We call upon the Board of Regents and the faculty of said University of Texas . . . to put an end to all 'hazing and brutal practices,'" declared the senate resolution empowering the investigation. Chairman Ousley dutifully proposed calling a meeting. Littlefield counseled not. Let the university president and faculty "master the situation and quiet all parties who have shown excitement over difficulty." Supported as the faculty and administration were by the student body at large, Littlefield believed that hazing would end and that the investigation had been brought on by senators with "little good feeling for the University" who seized "that unfortunate occurance . . . to blow off and say some hard things." Only four days after the event, he assessed that "its all over with now and everything will move along nicely." He was right. And the board closed the incident in its regular meeting on April 6, 1911, by commending student efforts to quiet the campus and abolish rushing.[26]

Littlefield's response signaled no apathy toward students. Three years before his appointment to the board, the Major had made the initial contribution toward construction of a large Young Men's Christian Association hall to serve as a center for that side of student life unmet in classroom, dormitory, and administration buildings. Some in the YMCA's building committee had been ambivalent about asking him for the kickoff gift. He could afford it, of course, but he was not a churchgoer, maybe not even a Christian, they seemed to think. So, before approaching him, the committee held "a long season of prayer asking God to move on the Major's heart to receive us cordially and to give generously." Four thousand dollars he pledged. When the committee then said it would like to receive the money in a lump sum up front, the benefactor replied with a smile that "I don't want to give you my money to place in some one else's bank to draw interest. I can make more interest on my money than you can. I will pay as you build, but not . . . for what you have not built."[27]

Rarely darkening a church door was one thing; following Christian tenets was quite another. True, the committee could not know, as documented in more than two decades of Uncle's letters to Shelton Dowell's widow, Lizzie, that George Littlefield had never lost the faith ignited by Reverend Bunting in Rome, Georgia, during the war. Outsiders who challenged his commitment quickly learned the tenacity with which he held it. In July 1911 he shot back at a correspondent questioning how he could oppose prohibition and consider himself a Christian: "The idea that no man can be a Christian unless he is a prohibitionist is outrageous and unbecoming of the ministry of our State. I believe there are good men that are prohibitionist and I grant them the right of their belief." The committee in fact should have recognized that faith influenced the Major's civic life at least because of his work only the year before, in 1906, with the Austin Business League heartily urging fellow citizens to invest in their city and its religious life by contributing to settlement of the Austin Presbyterian Theological Seminary in a location where seminarians could easily attend university classes. Despite what they could or should have known going in, before the building committee left his office, the members must have learned the reason Littlefield supported the YMCA so heartily. The nondenominational organization, he said, "provides probably the strongest element the university has to offer in character building."[28]

For George Littlefield, good character as much as duty, marked a man of affairs and certainly a university graduate. No doubt with the shooting incident in mind, President Sidney Mezes had told the regents in June 1911 what the Major had been grumbling about concerning his White and Littlefield nieces and nephews for years: "The country over, children are not held to obedience to their parents, and are . . . allowed to dispose of their own time and to determine their own conduct with little advice or control." The family youth who lived with Uncle would have seen the Major in Mezes's next words that "when young people who have not been controlled in their earlier years come to enter college, men and women who should be more reasonable at once demand that they [the students] shall be subjected to strict discipline." Continued the president, "Colleges will continue to give their best efforts . . . but until our homes and lower schools deal with them [students] more effectively there is not very much hope that colleges can be wholly successful."[29]

Doubtless having gotten the Major's attention on the topic of students, Mezes turned to control, specifically the "acute need" for dormitories. For its 1,676 students, the main campus had two. B Hall, enlarged in 1899, accommodated 124 men; the Woman's Building, erected in 1903, housed 86—together 210, or 12.5 percent of the student body. And of course, matriculations were increasing each year, jumping by 112, more than 7 percent, between the 1910 and 1911 school years alone. Mezes could have added that numbers was only the half of it. As the school newspaper reported, refuting the charge that the University of Texas was a rich man's school, nearly one-third of the students were farmers' children; two-fifths supported themselves wholly or in part. In other words, a healthy segment of the student body had little means. "It is bad education to submit a body of students of whom much is expected as future citizens of the State to living conditions that are neither sanitary, orderly, nor conducive to rudimentary good manners or the elementary conditions of self-restraint," Mezes told the board. "The carelessness of the University as compared with some private colleges in allowing its students to room and board anywhere and everywhere, with practically no supervision, is very widely criticized, and the criticism is in large measure just."[30]

Mezes's words sounded a clarion call to Littlefield. Four months later he presented the board with a fully developed proposal. Enlarge each dormitory to accommodate 250 students, and require freshmen to spend their first year in the residence hall unless they had a relative in town with whom to live. Such an arrangement, he said, "will be the biggest move that can be made for the University" because "it will establish confidence over the State that the young boys and girls will be cared for their first year." Construction could be funded by selling West Texas land. As he was developing his plan, the board was approached about selling 311,000 acres in Andrews County. At his recommendation, the regents sent him at the head of an inspection party to assess the territory. They found little of value. Much was sandy and poorly watered, suitable only for cattle raising, and inferior even for that, as twenty to twenty-five acres were required to support one animal on the sedge and shin oak. The possibility of oil beneath the surface was of little consideration. Finding none yet in the well he was drilling on the Yellow House land discouraged anticipation of hitting any of significance under the property. (The first successful Permian Basin well would not be brought in for a decade. The university's Santa Rita No. 1 gushed in in 1923.[31]) And as land committee chair, Littlefield had negotiated not only a healthy price but also five years' interest payment up front. Interest alone, not principal, could be used for construction.[32]

President Mezes liked the plan. Woman's Building matron Asenath Wallace Carothers thought it was "the best thing we could do." But the board rejected it. Maybe it was something about the buildings; more likely it was objection to selling the land. The minutes are silent. So be it, but a seed had been planted with George and Alice Littlefield.[33]

In the meantime, the YMCA's fundraising campaign dragged on for two years after New York oil magnate John D. Rockefeller's $10,500 pledge stimulated it. Then on Monday, July 1, 1912, with the oil man's noon match deadline unfulfilled and the entire $94,500 project in jeopardy, an anxious group including Presbyterian seminary president Robert Vinson filed into the Major's office, hats in hand. To their relief and delight, the banker responded with the $3,500 needed to secure the New Yorker's pledge and conclude the public campaign.[34]

The next request for money was very different—only thirty dollars and benefiting George Littlefield as much as the fifteen-year-old Texas State Historical Association from which it came. Eugene Barker invited him to buy a lifetime membership. Whether Barker judged the time to be right because Confederate veterans were excited again over textbooks or perceived that Littlefield was feeling the history in his seventy years, the professor's letter arrived at an opportune moment. The day he received it, Littlefield replied, not only buying the membership but also taking the occasion to lay bare his feelings to the historian. "A great many persons do not sympathize with movements of the University, as a great many of the Professors and teachers employed there seem to prefer giving their support to Northern institutions of this City. Not one, but dozens of times I have heard some of the best citizens say that the University needs a cleaning out, that it is politically rotten, and I hate to see such a feeling," both for the educational institution and for Austin's biggest asset. Littlefield had Austin high on his mind, having just opened the tallest building between New Orleans and San Francisco. "We are a Democratic [Party] State and a Democratic people," Littlefield concluded, "and it seems to me those employed about the University should be in sympathy with the State and citizens, and I believe such men as yourself would like to see it that way."[35]

After replying that he thought the faculty *was* in sympathy and sending a copy of his new *School History of Texas* for Littlefield's inspection, Barker began thinking. What might he suggest to the regent that, in one fell swoop, would emphasize the South, promote history, and distinguish the university, thereby bringing reflective prominence to the city?

Trained in the scientific school that focused historians on writing their narratives from original sources, Barker valued archives and historical documentation. So should the historically minded, he told a UDC audience in a talk titled "The Value of Letters to History." When in 1910 direction of both the history department and the Texas State Historical Association passed to him, responsibilities with the archival and library operations of the university came too. The state historical association collected historical material and placed it in the university library. For its archival holdings, the University of Texas was spending virtually nothing; for books on the South, little more. Compared with institutions across the South, UT's expenditures fell probably in the lower half of the range from a high of four hundred dollars in Mississippi to less than fifteen dollars in Florida. The University of Wisconsin, by comparison, allocated eight thousand dollars annually for the purchase of American historical materials. Then, as an ex officio member of the Texas Library and Historical Commission by virtue of chairing the history department, Barker had an oversight role for Texas's state archives. Formalized under its commission in 1909, the state library and archives of Texas came late to the movement. Alabama established its department of archives and history in 1901. In the eight years before Texas acted, eight other Southern states formalized their state archives and thus led Texas in gathering the documents and relics of Confederate veterans.[36] By any measure, Texas was behind.

Not quite three months later, Barker had formulated his answer. On December 5, 1912, with the approval of Dean Harry Yandell Benedict, he accepted Littlefield's courtesy invitation to contact him and volunteered the fruit of his thinking. The letter was structured masterfully. First the North: "The accumulation of historical material in northern libraries has attracted to the universities of the North the greatest historical scholars and teachers of America." Then the historians: "Historians of the younger generation are honest. Many of them are absolutely without conscious sectional bias." Then the foundation of historical writing: "The historian must draw his conclusions from the material that he has at hand. . . . As a result he goes to the libraries [located in the North] which have the largest collections." Barker's answer—create a repository of historical sources unrivaled on the South, in the South: "The remedy for the situation is perfectly simple. In the last analysis it is merely a matter of money to collect the historical materials of the South, and time to use them." Veteran objections: "Until this collection is made the resolutions and protests of patriotic societies against the misrepresentation of the South are 'as sounding brass and tinkling cymbals.'" The incentive: "Texas would then begin to remove from the South the reproach of neglecting its own history."[37]

When Littlefield responded asking for figures, Barker rejoiced. "I have taken . . . the occasion to stir up some of the University Regents and well to do Confederates on the subject of adequate library provision for the history of the South," he told Reuben Gold Thwaites of the State Historical Society of Wisconsin whom he asked for advice. For the amount needed for, in Barker's words, "curing the histories unfair to the South," Thwaites advised that $200,000 was not too little. Barker must have gasped. Just $250 immediately and $100 annually would acquire all pertinent historical documentation in Louisiana, William Beer had advised him. Thwaites's figure was more than forty times what R. D. W. Connor thought would scoop up all appropriate material in North Carolina. It was more than twenty times larger than the precious few endowments so far given to the university and more than one-quarter of the university's annual budget. So, continued Thwaites, $25,000 would do but was the smallest amount that would produce meaningful results. Barker steeled himself and proposed $50,000 to Major Littlefield in March 1913.[38]

The historian's jubilation was short lived. A month after he sent the figure to Littlefield, encouraging him "that we have at the University of Texas the opportunity to do for the South and for the nation an invaluable service by gathering the materials for fair and complete study of the history of the South"—using "fair and complete" instead of the veterans' preferred word "true"—the veterans rose again. At the end of April 1913, the Hood Camp scorched the *Austin Statesman* pages with its rebuke of the newest text, Edward Channing's *Student's History of the United States*. How could "any regent or professor of the University who has a drop of Southern blood in his veins . . . recommend Channing's book . . . or teach it to our Southern sons and daughters?" they asked, putting Littlefield on the spot with Barker. "As a rule the Veterans are not informed as to the method of instruction followed in the history courses," Barker repeated to Littlefield the message he had sent the year before. "The book . . . is only one of a number . . . to which the students are referred," the intent being "to lead students to do their own thinking." Furthermore, "all the courses in United States history are taught by Southern men," he assured the regent. Nevertheless, the history department chair removed Channing from the reading list, this time without regents' commendation.[39]

Silence followed. A year passed without protest, but also without communication from Littlefield. It wasn't because his focus turned from the university.

Beginning with and extending beyond his exchange with Barker, celebration of the school's thirtieth year commanded his attention. Grown from a faculty of 8 to near 200; from a student body of 221 to 1,993; from temporary quarters on Congress Avenue to a forty-acre campus crowded with some nine brick-and-mortar structures and a pack of wooden classroom and gym buildings, spiced in the spring with a blanket of bluebonnets illuminating the ever shrinking grassy stretches, university faithful meant to mark the 1913 milestone of preparing the coming generation of state leaders. "Varsity Celebration to be Greatest Ever," the paper anticipated the festivity organized by a who's who of city, state, and university figures under the Major's chairmanship. More than ten thousand invitations brought uncounted thousands to Austin on June 9–10 to rekindle friendships and thrill to a parade, declared by the paper in its usual superlative to be the "most brilliant" the city had ever seen. Leading the nearly two-mile-long caravan in a convoy of fifty-eight automobiles rode Regent Littlefield in "his profusely decorated" car.[40]

Outwardly just a happy occasion, the occasion could not have been timed better for the future of the institution. Or so it seemed. To relieve the crowded forty acres, in July voters would be asked to pass a constitutional amendment authorizing issuance of bonds to fund land acquisition and construction of fireproof brick-and-mortar structures to replace five frame classroom shacks on the Austin campus. With the bonds to be retired without taxpayer dollars but rather from income realized from leasing the West Texas land, passage would seem to be easy.

The House of Representatives so indicated when it authorized the referendum by a 113-to-2 vote.

Even with the governor's active support, the board of regents must have sensed otherwise. For the first time ever, it appealed directly to Texas voters. Who better to lead the Austin campaign than celebration chair George Littlefield? Whether or not loss of the amendment really would carry with it loss of the university to a larger, financially stronger city, Littlefield painted it so. "Every Austin Man Expected to Do Duty," he christened the campaign, soliciting $15,000 to $20,000 on top of the $5,000 he had just raised for the celebration. The work proved to be difficult. Weekly reports on progress and appeals for contributions, including the news that he personally wrote letters to absentee voters, filled the paper. Littlefield contributed liberally. The *Statesman* printed cheery accounts of rising support around the state. But it wasn't enough. Though carried in Travis County, the amendment failed statewide by a six-to-one margin.[41]

Next, it was nothing less than the governor's veto of the institution's funding for the second year of the following biennium. Though no record survives of Littlefield's work to reinstate the money the governor meant to save so as to avoid a fifteen-cent property tax increase, as a continuing member of the board's legislative committee and as a friend of the governor so close that Colquitt would write at the end of his term thanking the Major for his steadfast support, Littlefield undoubtedly played a central role in achieving continuing state funding of the school.[42]

While the financing issue was running its course, Barker wrote the Major in March 1914 in hopes of rekindling the Southern history collection flame he thought he had lit. But he took a different tack—vanity:

> It has always seemed to me that a man could build no more conspicuous and useful memorial to himself on a university campus than by endowing a branch of the library. . . . Frankly, I want the library to grow strong in southern history because . . . I should like to see Texas take the lead in studying and writing southern history. I know your interest in the subject, and I hope that as one of the leading and most conspicuous representatives of the South in Texas the memorial idea may appeal to you.[43]

It did. They talked. Littlefield drafted a letter. Barker edited. A month later, George Washington Littlefield addressed Chairman Ousley:

> It has been my desire to see a history written of the United States with the plain facts concerning the South and her acts since the foundation of the Government, especially since 1860, fairly stated, that the children of

the South may be truthfully taught and persons matured since 1860 may
be given opportunity to inform themselves correctly, and to secure such a
history I feel that some one must make the sacrifice to get it. I will give to
the University of Texas the sum of $25,000.00, which shall be known as
the Littlefield Fund for Southern History.[44]

Interest from the principal was to be used to "purchase of books, pamphlets,
newspaper files, maps, manuscripts, etc.," so as "to lay . . . the foundation of a
collection that shall be of fundamental value for the full and impartial study of
the South and of its part in American History." Littlefield's and Barker's wording
of the gift's purpose united the goals of the old warrior and the scholar. On his
side, Littlefield coupled the proudest day of his life and all that it represented to
him with his hopes for the future when he wrote: "I feel it is but just to the cause
I gave the best four years of my life to defend, and I feel that I owe such to those
patriots who gave their lives to sustain it and for the benefit of the young people of
this time, as well as the generations to come." For scholarship, Barker masterfully
laid a scope broad enough that the proceeds could be used for almost the breadth
of American history. And deftly, he skirted the interpretation-tinged phrase "true
history" for the historian's more objective "full and impartial study."[45]

While it had appeared to Barker that appeal to self-interest might be the key to
achieving the Confederate veterans' goal of righting the wrongs of written history
and his goal of creating an endowment that would raise the University of Texas
to undisputed leadership in the study of the South, appearance was deceiving.
Though Barker could not know it, in suggesting a memorial, he revived the idea
of the fund at a propitious moment. In March 1914 George Littlefield despaired of
life. As the nearness of death had gripped the captain in the bitter December winds
of 1863, so an uncharacteristic desolation possessed the aging husband in 1914. To
James H. Parramore, "the one man [of his childhood and war experience] I love
and esteem more than all my friends," whose name Littlefield mentioned in the
gift letter, the Major revealed his anguish. "Time has taken your wife from you,"
he wrote, "and mine is suffering afflicted. . . . Jim to tell you my heart is sad and
heavy does not feebly express it. No one knows the trouble but they who bear it."[46]

In January 1912 Alice Littlefield began suffering from what her husband diag-
nosed as a "severe nervousness." Their Austin doctor thought it would pass. It did
not. A month later, Dr. Joe Sil Wooten recommended that George take Alice to
Battle Creek Sanitarium in Michigan, a facility popular with those who could
afford its treatments, advocating a healthy lifestyle grounded in diet, fresh water,
and exercise. Among other treatments, Alice's Battle Creek physician prescribed

walking outside for four hours a day, even in the snow. That did not help either. Not quite two months later, George took her to the renowned nervous conditions specialist Dr. Hugh T. Patrick in Chicago. He saw, as George described it, that "she has a delusion, fears that we will all be murdered, and she to witness it, and then she kidnapped and driven over the Country like a beast. She begs to die, and for something to take her life. Anything she sees that could be used to take her life excites her and throws her into nervous spell." But Dr. Patrick saw as well that "her mind was not gone." Recovery was possible, he thought, though only a one-in-eight chance. The long road ahead required that her husband either commit her to a sanitarium or modify his home to care for her. "I told him I would not think of leaving her with strangers, but I would carry her home, so I could look after her and care for her in comfort. He told me he thought I was right and that I would do as well by her as any Sanitarium."[47]

Though likely it never entered the Major's mind that the work of the Littlefield Fund would provide him genuine respite in the midst of his agony over Alice, in fact the acquisitions quickly came to do just that. Shortly, all saw how little the interest on twenty-five thousand dollars contributed to accomplishing the fund's purpose. In October 1914, only six months into the fund's first year, its projected available money already had been spent on runs of two newspapers. The Major loaned the fund seven hundred dollars. Expenses mounted. The fund fell deeper and deeper into his debt. Then, in 1916, runs of Charleston, South Carolina, newspapers became available. Wanting top dollar for them, the Charleston Chamber of Commerce solicited sealed bids rather than offering them for sale at auction. The Littlefield Fund needed the runs that covered more than a century and the significance of Charleston in the history of the South. Several northern libraries wanted the papers too. Barker went to Littlefield. "Is it good stuff?" the Major asked. "Yes, sir," Barker answered. "Then go get it!" the Major replied. University librarian Ernest William Winkler (whom Littlefield respected highly from his days as state librarian under the Texas Library and Historical Commission) carried the bid in person: $4,200. When the offer of Chicago's well-endowed Newberry Library was opened, it was higher. Having expected or feared as much, the university tender read in its entirety: "We bid $4,200 and ten per cent above the highest bidder." Texas won.[48]

Initially Littlefield treated overruns of the endowment's income stream as loans. But the ever-increasing debt came to so burden the purpose of the fund that the Major canceled the loan arrangement and in December 1916 commanded Barker thereafter to "secure the data and I will pay the cash for same. . . . I trust you may be watchful and secure all data that may be useful for the history." Barker was, and

Barker did. Between May 1916 and October 1920, at Barker's summons the aging Confederate contributed an additional $30,566.65 for purchases. "Without any doubt," the fund's principal historian summarized, "these were the most exciting years of the Fund's history. Almost every year, and sometimes more often, there was some large acquisition, some big find." Littlefield had to have been gratified to learn early in 1920 that students of multiple disciplines interested in Southern history already were being attracted to the fund's collection.[49]

With the gift of the Littlefield Fund, the Major stimulated a research focus central to the fuller understanding of not just Southern but the whole of American history. In fact, that was only the half of it. In the gift, the Major moved down the road from pressuring removal of offensive books to accepting the worth of what academic historians meant by full and impartial history. In two years, by coming to embrace, above dogma, the fundamental value of history's documentary foundation, he moved a significant way toward appreciating the academics' understanding of the distance between "true" and "full and impartial." In the coming two years, Governor Colquitt's successor would test the regent-benefactor's judgment of the political distance between the two. Nothing less than the integrity of the University of Texas would hang on his conviction.

FIG. 29. "Cattle on the Move," E. Martin Hennings mural, the all-Herefords version that was mounted over the bank vault door. *Albritton Collection.*

FIG. 30. "Cattle on the Move," four with mottled hides. The four with hides similar to those of longhorns and substituted for Herefords are located left, center, and right.
From American National Bank Opening Day Booklet.

FIG. 31. "Cattle on the Move," Hennings's mural above the bank vault door. Parts of "The Round-Up" and "Cattle on the LFD Farm" are visible to the left and right.

From American National Bank Opening Day Booklet.

FIG. 32. Yellow House Ranch cattle drive. This photograph taken by Mrs. Hamlin Hill shows the cattle moving in a thinner line than Hennings pictured.

Hamlin Hill Family Photographs, courtesy Patsy Hill Rahn.

FIG. 33. "The Pride of the Herd." *From American National Bank Opening Day Booklet*

FIG. 34. Cutting the bull for his portrait, 1908. Yellow House Ranch manager
Hamlin Hill driving the bull for a picture Littlefield could give to the mural painter.
Hamlin Hill Family Photographs, courtesy Patsy Hill Rahn.

FIG. 35. "The Round-Up." The white-shirted figure left of center is Hamlin Hill. *Albritton Collection,*

FIG. 36. Setting up "The Round-Up" shoot, 1908. Mrs. Hamlin Hill's photograph
of her husband working with the horses inside the rope coral. Phelps White stands to the left.
Hamlin Hill Family Photographs, courtesy Patsy Hill Rahn.

FIG. 37. "Thorough-Breds." Hennings's mural of sleek horses on the LFD Farm near Roswell,
New Mexico, enjoying leisure before returning to the Four Lakes Ranch for work. *Albritton Collection.*

FIG. 38. Cattle on the LFD Farm. Hennings's mural showing an exaggerated artesian water spout. *JPMorgan Chase Art Collection*

FIG. 39. Mural showing horses and mule at hay crib. *From American National Bank Silver Anniversary Booklet* Austin Yesterday and Today *by Pearl Jackson.*

FIG. 40. Littlefield bronze doors. Curved for mounting in the original Congress Avenue and Sixth Street entrance to the American National Bank, they measure 10.3 feet tall by 6.75 feet wide, closed, and weigh 2.5 tons. They are on display in the University of Texas System building in Austin. The door's riders are Tom White and Phelps White at Bosque Grande (*top left*), Ham Hill, Bud Wilkinson, and Will McCombs (*top right*), and Bud Wilkinson and Ham Hill (*middle panels, left and right, respectively*). *University of Texas System.*

FIG. 41. Mescalero Spring, 2001. Pictured from about twenty yards below the position from which sculptor H. Daniel Webster presented the view on the Littlefield bronze doors. *Author's collection.*

FIG. 42. Cowboys' cabin at Mescalero Spring, looking west. Little more than vigas remain of the adobe structure the LFDs built to house hands who managed the remuda at Mescalero Spring.
Author's collection.

FIG. 43. Littlefield bronze doors, steer-head handles. *Author's collection.*

FIG. 44. The LFD brand in bronze. Littlefield hired an engraver to sink the brand into every animal whose right side was exposed on the bronze doors. *University of Texas System.*

FIG. 45. Phelps White (*left*) and George Littlefield (*right*) on the Yellow House Ranch, 1908.
Hamlin Hill Family Photographs, courtesy Patsy Hill Rahn.

FIG. 46. Yellow House Ranch headquarters, 1907. Seen in early morning light, caves below the escarpment rim gave the place its Yellow House name. A 118-foot-tall windmill projects above the horizon to catch the constant plains wind. *Hamlin Hill Family Photographs, courtesy Patsy Hill Rahn.*

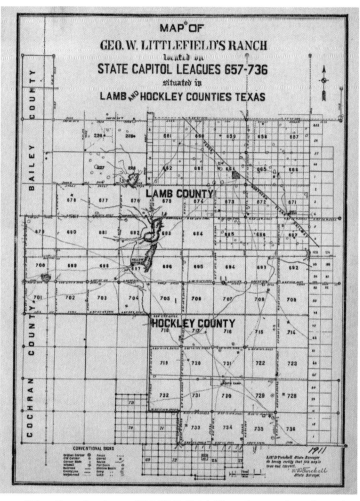

FIG. 47. Yellow House Ranch map, 1912. W. D. Twichell's ranch survey shows the northeast corner Littlefield designated for colonization. *Author's collection.*

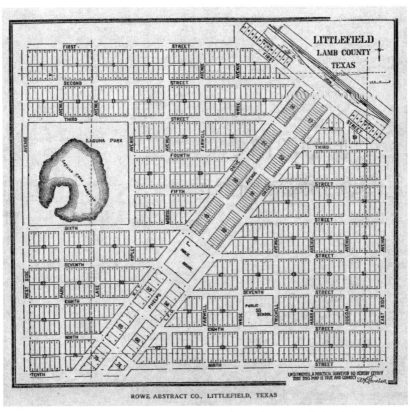

FIG. 48. Littlefield Townsite plat, 1912. Accommodating the Santa Fe Railroad, Duggan and Twichell laid out the main street to terminate at the depot. For good measure to ensure having the Littlefield name, the Littlefield interests named streets for Santa Fe president Edward P. Ripley and chief engineer Charles A. Morse. *Author's collection.*

267

FIG. 49. Jefferson Davis birthplace medal, 1917. Obverse of medal struck to reward Jefferson Davis Birthplace Obelisk donors. Young is pictured top left, Littlefield top right. *Author's collection.*

FIG. 50. Jefferson Davis Birthplace Medal, 1917. Reverse of medal struck to reward Jefferson Davis Birthplace Obelisk donors. *Author's collection.*

FIG. 51. Obelisk at the Jefferson Davis State Historic Site, Fairview, Kentucky. *Author's collection.*

FIG. 52. Main approach to the University of Texas, 1915. Littlefield wanted his arch to span the walkways from the head of University Avenue to the main building. *From American National Bank Silver Anniversary Booklet* Austin Yesterday and Today *by Pearl Jackson.*

FIG. 53. Littlefield Memorial Fountain, University of Texas. Postcard view in front of Old Main, likely in 1933, the year the fountain began operating. In Coppini's words, the centerpiece is Columbia on the prow of the ship of state "bringing, for the first time, her Army and Navy [a figure representing each flanking Columbia] across the water in defense of World Democracy; and driven by three sea-horses, symbolizing the sea power of the United States; the center sea-horse, the wild force of mob hysteria, kept in check by strong disciplined manpower of the Navy as well as of the Army." (*From Dawn to Sunset,* 344, illustration following page 288). *Author's collection.*

FIG. 54. Littlefield plot, Oakwood Cemetery, Austin, Texas. *Author's collection.*

FIG. 55. George W. Littlefield
bust, 1910, by Pompeo Coppini.
*Harry Ransom Center, University
of Texas at Austin.*

FIG. 56. George Washington Littlefield's bold signature. *Author's collection.*

17

WATCHMAN ON THE TOWER

Concluding its meeting on October 27, 1914, the University of Texas Board of Regents elected George Washington Littlefield its chairman by unanimous vote. But the Major "felt compelled" to decline the position. Ill health, he said. It had been building. Bilious attacks beset him. He ate steak every day. Either his doctors were unaware of the connection or he was too set in his ways to cut back on red meat. Bouts of influenza—La Grippe, they called it—confined him to bed for days at a time. Thankfully, at least from these he could recover. From Alice's affliction he had no respite. "It is so very trying on me as she clings to me all the time I am with her and appeals to me so pitifully it Keeps my nerves Excited," he confided to Lizzie Dowell. Travel in search of relief for her wore him down. Constant worry about her wore him down further. All told, "I have Weakened more in the last six months than last ten years," he assessed himself late in 1912. Adding to the stress, his ill sister moved in with them in 1913. The character of life had changed for George Littlefield.[1] How profoundly so he would admit to himself when he recognized that the time was at hand to pass forward the sacred trust of overseeing the family that his beloved mother had passed to him so many decades earlier.

As much as they affected the Major, the trials of advancing age were not the stuff of news. His health did not make the paper in these years as had the scare from the boil he pricked nearly a decade earlier. So to those who saw him only through news reports, he appeared to have lost none of the energy of his business enterprise. "Littlefield's large deal" headlined the July 12, 1912, story of three thousand LFD yearling heifers and two-year-old steers sold for one hundred thousand dollars. The largest sum reported in years for similar cattle, the transaction nearly equaled his previous year's income. And the six-figure sale was no fluke. Two years later the *Statesman* reported that five thousand Yellow House calves, about three-fifths of the combined annual crop of the Yellow House, Four Lakes, and Mill Creek ranches, brought half again more. Marveled the 1912 piece, Littlefield stood as "one of the few men in Texas who has made a fortune in the cattle business."[2]

True, he was one of the few, but when the Austin paper focused on eye-pop-
ping deals, it missed the inauguration of a new business that was as responsible as
the Major's health and home life for his refusal to head the board of regents. On
American Independence Day 1913, the Littlefield Lands Company threw open for
settlement a one-hundred-square-mile tract in the northeast corner of the Yellow
House Ranch. The colonization venture saddled the Major with a workload heavier
than that loaded on him by any of his other businesses. Streams of paperwork
demanded his attention guiding property development and tracking sales. In
October 1914 the detail-oriented rancher-banker recognized that the volume so
crowded his twenty-four-hour day that he simply had no more time to devote to
university affairs.[3]

Actually, he would not have opened a portion of his ranch for sale in small
units to settlers if he could have sold the ranch outright. He was an old man, he
said. And, admitting it, he began to think about how to distribute his assets in his
will. So hardly had he completed paying for the sprawling Yellow House than he
began entertaining offers to sell it.[4] Will Soash offered. His $3 million proposal in
1908 would have yielded a 200 percent profit in seven years if paid simply in cash
and notes. But as it was a colonization proposal that paid him as settlers bought
and then saddled the ranch with homesteads scattered here and there, Littlefield
rejected it.

No sooner had Soash fixed his sights on Slaughter land far south of the Yellow House than the Atchison, Topeka, and Santa Fe Railroad sent men in 1909
to scout a route between Lubbock, Texas, and Texico, New Mexico. Of course,
railroad lines had been plotted across the south plains before, even across Littlefield's ranch, and evaporated. Most recently, the Panhandle Shortline, proposed
to connect Soash's town of Olton to the national network, progressed no farther
than the paper it was written on. But the Santa Fe was different. The AT&SF was
an established company operating thousands of miles of track. The ninety miles
it meant to lay across the South Plains would complete the company's most direct
route between Galveston on Texas's Gulf coast and Los Angeles on the Pacific
Ocean. Confirming the priority it placed on ending four years of rumors, the
company had its colonization department assign a local land agent to the work of
platting towns as nuclei for newly opening acreage.[5]

George Littlefield saw his opportunity. In exchange for agreeing to deed right-
of-way and pay a fifty-thousand-dollar bonus, subsequently doubled to a hundred
thousand, payable after the first passenger train steamed across his acreage, in
1909 the Major secured the railroad's promise to lay what became about ten miles
of track across the ranch, accept a townsite, and provide a rail siding for cattle

shipping pens serving the Yellow House and adjacent Spade ranches. But there the Yellow House colonization matter lay for nearly two years.[6]

Even before the lull, the Major had hit on a way to help land agents trying to sell the entire ranch, including gubernatorial aspirant Colquitt, to push their prospects to close. Bring in a gusher. In July 1909 Littlefield sent oil wildcatter J H. Mook to the vicinity of South Camp to begin boring the first exploration well on the south plains. "No time to fool around," Littlefield wrote one land agent. "Let them [prospective buyers] prepare themselves and come prepared to close for if I were to strike oil all would be off." When five years later he reached the contracted depth, Mook had brought up only gas. Hoping to convince the Major to let him bore deeper, the driller primed the hole with oil. Littlefield remained firm. Two thousand feet and no farther. The endeavor produced no buyer for the entire property then or during the Major's lifetime. But the black gold was there, just thousands of feet farther down.[7]

In mid-1912 the time had come for the Major to launch his colonization venture. The Santa Fe was ready to receive his deed for right-of-way over the Yellow House. As he gave it, Littlefield marked some seventy-nine thousand acres in league units on either side of the track to be subdivided into labor units for sale. For the convenience of the Littlefield Lands community, he sited his town near the halfway point of the ranch's ten miles of railroad. With a view to wresting the county seat from Olton, he located it as close to county center as he could. Finally, to run the operation with the title of sales manager, he engaged Sallie Harral's lawyer husband, Arthur Pope Duggan, then head of a North Texas real estate firm's farmland department.[8]

What to name the new town? "Littlefield" seemed obvious. But not to the railroad. Of the initial eleven stops between Lubbock and Texico, the Santa Fe named at least three—Lariat, Roundup, and Bainer (known as East Camp then Yellow House Switch to the Littlefields)—and possibly as many as six. Appreciating that the railroad preferred to name stops, promoters of one townsite thought to curry favor by naming the place for the railroad's president, E. P. Ripley. But the railroad already had a Ripley beside its tracks in Oklahoma. So Afton, evidently recognizing another Santa Fe figure, designated that stop in the railroad's earliest public passenger timetables that included the Texico-Lubbock Cutoff. Frustrated and uncharacteristically submissive considering the large bonus he guaranteed, on October 7, 1912, the Major wrote the railroad's Chicago head office that "If you don't want to call the town Littlefield, call it White. If you cannot do that, then do what you please."[9]

For once the owner's people would not follow his lead. "With your permission," his new sales manager wrote on October 30, in the earliest letter in the Littlefield

Lands Company records, "I will advise Mr. Weidel that you will deed the Santa Fe Railway company the strips . . . , the consideration being that the name of Littlefield be preserved." Phelps White wrote Uncle on November 3 that he would accept the railroad's reneging on its promise of a siding for shipping pens if that would secure the Littlefield name.[10] Neither concession was enough

The Santa Fe held out for one more. It wanted the depot accentuated by having the town's main street terminate at it on a plan like that of the railroad town of Sla ton fifteen miles southeast of Lubbock. This was no small request. The lands given for building the capitol had been surveyed on a north-south, east-west grid. But the rail line ran on a southeast-northwest diagonal. Consequently, State Surveyor Willis Day Twichell, who had recently surveyed the ranch, and Sales Manager Duggan together began by laying out the townsite "square with the world," as Duggan said. Then they drew the main street and the ones on either side to suit the railroad. This threw the east and west sides of town out of parallel, resulted in the ends of four of the eleven north-south streets not meeting in the middle, and created along the diagonal streets thirty-eight lots of varying size and shape amid otherwise uniformly rectangular units (fig. 48). With this last consideration granted, the Santa Fe accepted the name. Never mind that, unlike with Ripley, this would be the first and only Littlefield along Santa Fe tracks in the twelve states the railroad served. For whatever reason, no other townsite along the Texico-Lubbock stretch accommodated itself to the diagonal by orienting its main street to its depot.[11]

As negotiations over the town's name were concluding, the Littlefield interests faced a chicken-and-egg question. Should they concentrate on populating the land with farmers to create demand to attract merchants or work to establish the town with an array of services to beckon land buyers? The Major argued it both ways. After only two farm sales had been made and before the buyers occupied their land, he wrote Duggan that "If we can get Farmers to buy and settle on the land[,] that will bring people to build the town." But in the very next sentence, written before even one town lot had been sold, he proposed advertising a sale of town lots for a day certain in order to bring "a good crowd who would buy lots." Plans for the day certain developed into the grand opening scheduled for July 4, 1913, that the Austin paper failed to notice. A roundup of some 2,700 yearling heifers, highlighted with a branding exhibition and barbecue lunch, serenaded by Lubbock's fifteen-piece band, was sure to attract a throng. Would the Major attend to receive proceeds from the many sales Duggan expected? No. By then second-guessing the idea, he would be in Waukesha, Wisconsin, where he hoped the waters would give Alice relief. About 1,400 people came from far and wide for the opening day festivities, some on special trains over tracks that had barely reached Littlefield.

The hoopla overshadowed actual business. Only a single sale materialized. "Yes, I expected a light trade on the 4th," the Major wrote Phelps. "It was really a foolish thing to have had the Barbecue but a man lives to learn in this world although the Experience sometimes comes high."[12]

Experience told Sales Manager Duggan, who had arrived the previous fall of 1912 to launch the Littlefield Lands Company, that having a bank builds confidence in a new town. Early on he began "working on" the owners of the only financial institution in the county to move it from Olton to Littlefield. In mid-January 1913 he reported to the Major that in exchange for two business lots, two residential lots, and two thousand dollars to buy the holdings of Olton stockholders who might want to sell, they would make the move. One success presaged another. Being able to conduct banking and county business in the same town meant that for getting the one, Littlefield stood to get the other too. Phelps agreed that it would be "the most important step we could take toward moving the County Seat" to Littlefield. Lost on none of them was that having a bank in Littlefield, rather than routing financial transactions through institutions in Plainview that had their own correspondent banks, would ensure that company business flowed directly to the American National in Austin.

The practical Major did not share his men's enthusiasm. Sparsely settled ranching country lacked activity enough to support a bank. A drugstore would mean more to the fledgling community, he countered. Nevertheless, to facilitate the move, the American National would advance five thousand dollars to cover anticipated loss of deposits. And Duggan, Phelps, and Bill Littlefield's son George bought stock from Olton residents unhappy with the bank's decision to move. But as months passed, it became clear that the Major had been right. Olton's First State Bank failed before it could move. "I don't care to go into another bank until there is some thing like Enough people settled out there to give it business that it can live off of," the Major concluded. Though a bank that opened in Littlefield two years later would survive, neither the Major, Duggan, nor White lived to celebrate the referendum that in 1946 moved the county seat to Littlefield.[13]

Maybe trying to boost himself against Littlefield's initial failure to capture either the bank or the county seat, newspaperman C. Grover Pipkin arrived in the spring of 1914 and put out two issues of the *Littlefielder*. A town with "the possible future of Littlefield" could not afford "to go without a paper," he wrote the Major, seeking support. To go without "would mean that the dozen or more towns around her would eclipse her for so long a time that her future would certainly be in doubt." Confident he had made his case, Pipkin awaited the Major's reply before publishing his next issue. While Pipkin was surely correct about a newspaper's role in promoting a fledgling town, his strategy with the Major could not have been worse. He criticized Phelps White. The town needed his paper to counterbalance what Pipkin asserted was a sour relationship between Phelps and buyers. The Major rejected both the accusation against Phelps and the assertion that the town's existence hung on the publisher's rag. "I am aware of the trouble of every newspaper making its start in the West, but not knowing you and for what you stand and your ability to maintain a respectable paper," the Major replied bluntly, "I am not prepared to say what I consider right and proper to extend to you toward a support." To Duggan, Littlefield grumbled that a good crop is better than any newspaper. Then Duggan's report of Pipkin's unwarranted assertion of being a company agent made the Major's decision easy and ended the *Littlefielder*'s short life.[14]

Pipkin's insinuation notwithstanding, the Major needed no newspaper to know conditions on the ground. Though a four-day drive or a two-day train ride away, he not only kept himself fully informed of developments with his colonization enterprise; he directed them. Unlike with his ranching businesses, Littlefield hired Duggan outright without giving him a partnership interest. Maybe the Major preferred the arrangement because Phelps White, on whom he increasingly relied, could oversee the colonization operation as general manager. Whatever the reason, Duggan felt constrained in decision making. To a land agent friend, he griped that the arrangement "is certainly not a sinecure to attempt to please two men with diametrically opposed notions as to the way this thing ought to be done; both separated and neither ever having had any experience in this particular line of work."[15]

Duggan overstated the case. George Littlefield was the man to please. He made the big decisions. Chief among them was how he wanted his Littlefield Lands presented. "We have had nothing in the way of a boom," Duggan described the Major's approach, "have not wanted it; have made no particular effort to build up the town but have directed our attention to the selling of the land, knowing that if we can settle up the country with good, prosperous, progressive farmers, that the town will take care of itself."[16]

The Major's way could not have been more different from that of seasoned colonizer Will Soash. After failing to make a deal with Littlefield in 1909, the Iowan staked his financial future on colonizing that Slaughter land 125 miles south of the Yellow House. Soash promptly sank tens of thousands of dollars into developing his town of Soash. He built a large, expensive reinforced concrete building to house the company office, installed an electric light plant and a telephone exchange, financed a bank, and moved some of his Iowa employees to the town. He hired an experienced railroad surveyor to find a route and begin grading roadbed for the Gulf, Soash, and Pacific Railroad that he hoped the Santa Fe would absorb into the final leg of its yet-unbuilt Galveston-Texico route. But three years of searing drought snuffed out Soash's $1 million company and left the concrete building to deteriorate to lonely, bare walls in an open field.[17]

As of mid-July 1913, Littlefield had spent only some thirty thousand dollars on his town, none of it on concrete or electricity or telephones or a bank. The Major based his approach on history. He had been observing the progress of town building for a decade and a half before Will Soash even entered the business. "Towns that are Boomed are generally bad places to invest money," he had concluded as early as 1891 from observing the growth of Velasco, Dallas, and Fort Worth. What he thought he saw is unclear. Dallas and Fort Worth were established metropolises. Already Texas's most populous city in 1890, Dallas continued to grow, its economy resting smartly on banking and insurance along with cotton. Fort Worth's ascendency as a rail hub permitted the city's rise as the dressed beef center of Texas. Velasco, by contrast, was entering its second life, sixteen years after having been devastated by a hurricane. It had hardly had time to begin its redevelopment. Nevertheless, the lesson the Major took from what he saw remained to guide development at Littlefield.[18]

And guide he did in letter after letter. Products of the land—from money crops to show crops to livestock—engaged him as fully as the money side, dealing with land agents and buyers. Don't forget to plant a few acres of early cotton near the railroad, he counseled in one letter. Plant it thick in rows two and a half feet apart, followed in another. "I am writing this [instruction] for I am afraid your farmer does not know much about cotton cultivation," came a third. "If You can show that you can raise one-third of a bale of cotton per Acre, Then that land will Sell fast," he summed up the thread. Try wheat. If it does well, Kansas farmers will "come to it fast." But for looks, raise pumpkins. "They certainly do show up a crop biger than any thing, and lay so thick on the ground that it attracts Every ones attention." Don't raise so much feed because it is hard to sell every year. And watch hogs, or they will eat more than they are worth.[19]

Outlays for hog feed they could control themselves. Not tax increases. In late spring 1914, rumor reached the Major that Lamb County commissioners intended to raise levies on the southern portion of the county on the grounds that train service had increased the land's value. Littlefield objected. Raising the cost of owning land would hurt both sales and new owners already bearing the expenses of moving and putting up house, barn, windmill, and related structures, he argued. Moreover, bonds could finance the county's needs as the tax base grew. "Commissioners should study the welfare of their people on all sides and in a newly settling country it is necessary to care for them," he told Duggan.[20]

The Major's protest to his sales manager created nothing like the "storm of discussion" his letter to the Austin City Council had kicked up five months earlier in December 1913. Then, as never before for him in Austin, taxes pitted personal interest against public spirit. The city assessed land at fair market value, improvements at a lesser figure. With the Littlefield Building returning only 3 percent after two years, the Major objected to the policy. Totaling the two figures for the Littlefield Building, he said, produced a tax bill out of proportion to his income from the property. He was not alone in objecting to the dual valuations. The Major's letter brought out what the paper called a "general disaffection with existing methods of tax assessments." Littlefield called for valuation based on profitability. Mayor Wooldridge countered that the city could not afford to lose revenue by removing vacant property from the tax rolls. There the matter lay until the Major received the next year's valuation for his Congress Avenue holdings—the Littlefield Building and a movie theater. It had skyrocketed by a staggering $39,200. To the paper, he said: "My present feeling is that about thirty of us should get together and say, 'Here, collect your taxes,' the major declared yesterday, 'and fight 'em as long as there is a court to fight in.' 'I want to bear my fair share of the public burden,' Major Littlefield continued, 'but I don't want to be singled out, year after year, and made to dig up, just because the city administration doesn't like me.'"[21] In fact, he didn't blame the impersonal administration for the increase but rather the mayor, who "has it in" for him. Then, in an unusually personal attack, Littlefield added that the mayor "is going to ruin this town if we don't put him out." And if city voters continued to elect "that sort of man," Littlefield blustered that he would let the town suffer the consequences.[22]

To abandon Austinites to their suffering, George Littlefield would have to turn his back on encouraging the city's growth. He didn't. He couldn't do it when there was money to be made and work to do promoting the city's prosperity. Austin was growing alright, but at a pace slower than competitor municipalities. The addition of seven thousand souls between 1900 and 1910 had not saved the capital from slipping from sixth to seventh place among Texas's largest municipalities. Cotton alone simply was a weak foundation for the city's economy. Contemporaries saw it clearly when the 1920 census showed that the city had fallen to tenth place behind such metropolises as Wichita Falls, Beaumont, and Waco.[23]

So, to lift Austin's economy, on January 22, 1914, at the midpoint of his seventy-second year and only three months after he registered his tax protest, George Littlefield announced big plans. He would spend nearly one hundred thousand dollars to enlarge the Littlefield Building by enclosing its roof garden and adding a nine-story annex. When he constructed the tallest building between New Orleans and San Francisco, "it was not generally supposed that the growth of the city would so soon call for a big addition to the giant office building," the *Statesman* reported. But anticipating the time would come, the Major had had the steel skeleton designed to support up to four additional floors.[24]

If the building's lackluster returns hardly cried out for his plans, the American National Bank's stunning performance delivered support for them. "Largest dividend ever paid in Austin" the *Statesman* headlined its July 1, 1913, story on the two-percentage-point increase in the bank's dividend, which brought the annual rate to an astounding 16 percent.

The remarkable dividend reflected the prosperity of national banks in Texas, especially the country nationals like Littlefield's American outside the state's six largest cities. During the thirteen years from 1906 through 1918, Texas's country national banks outshone the nationals across the nation in three principal categories. Comptroller of the Currency reports revealed that their 12.69 percent average ratio of dividends to capital beat the U.S. number by nearly a full percentage point. The ratio of dividends to capital and surplus showed up even better. The Texas country institutions' 8.49 percent ratio bettered the U.S. figure by one and a half percentage points. Best of all, at an average of 12.12 percent of net earnings to capital and surplus, they surpassed the U.S. average by nearly two and a half percentage points.[25]

Clearly, the times accounted in some measure for the American National Bank's prosperity. But George Littlefield's management accounted for more. In 1913 and 1914 his bank topped its Austin competitors on the national bank roll of honor. In 1915 it achieved a double distinction. With $4,027,000, it was the only Austin and the only country national bank listed among the top ten nationals in Texas, measured by the total of deposits. He had been building the bank to such hegemony. Twenty years and counting after the American National's organization, he remained not just the only founder still with it but also the only president the institution had ever known.[26]

Like any good bank president, he followed system rules conscientiously. Like any good leader, he projected a vision. His vision was that the American National was a home institution built on personal relationships with stockholders, customers, and employees. So it had been from its founding. So it remained. "It is purely a simple business proposition to try and get the stock of this Bank in the hands of persons who do their business with the bank," the Major wrote to one inheritor of stock. "We know you are our friend, but situated as you and your son are [in New York City], you can't be worth anything to the Bank. [Others similarly distant are] sitting in wait for dividend day . . . but they are slow about moving to the relief of the bank."[27]

Personal relationships similarly marked dealings with correspondent banks. When the Lampasas First National pulled an account away from the American National, Littlefield wrote Harry Newton Key, the First National's cashier, that "we, of course, regret [it], as you would the loss of any of your good friends." But with the Major and his extended family, kinship and Southern loyalty often entwined with friendship. So it did here. Littlefield continued, "And when you took it from us to a blue breasted Yankee concern, who would take pleasure in saying that account is from the Key boys in Lampasas, life long friends of Littlefields and one of them a nephew by marriage, People will wonder what could have caused that. . . . Most men of the south do not turn down Southern Institutions to go to Northern." Key understood. In a letter lost to history, he explained the move in a way that gave Littlefield to respond that "when I am right and my heart feels right, it does me good to know my friends realize and appreciate it."[28]

Littlefield's sense of right and that Southern orientation could not help but have a political cast. And to Governor Colquitt on May 27, 1911, he laid it on the line:

> Now my friend, I can't see the justness of a Republican Bank getting the business of a Democratic Administration. While its true that we have some good accounts of the Administration offices, its also true we are more entitled to them than any bank in the town. First is we are the only out and out Democratic Bank in the City and next is we stood by you through every race and never refused at any time to carry your account. I really think we are entitled to that deposit and we have always expected it and do trust you may look at it as we do and give it to us.

The governor satisfied the Major.[29]

Right, too, meant that friendship had its limits. "One thing to a certainty, I always look to the upbuilding and sustaining of the bank first and ahead of any individual interest," Littlefield explained to a Terry Ranger friend, "and I can't help it if any one becomes dissatisfied." The president might occasionally bend the rules, for example by allowing extra time for a borrower to repay a loan, but "I never borrow of the bank and I never allow any stockholder to ride it."[30]

As strong as the fundamentals of the bank were in their way, so too were those of the colonization company in theirs. Yet where bank stockholders far from Austin held their stock tenaciously for the dividend, Phelps and Tom White, a year after the grand opening, wanted out of their combined half interest in the colonization acres. Uncle had let them have the interest at the ranch's two dollar purchase price when he took them in as partners on the Yellow House. So would Uncle let them out by paying them half the amount he was netting from buyers? No. "I have all my life tried to treat Each of my nephews Justly," he explained. "Therefore I can say right now I will not allow Phelps and Tom to Sell me their interest in that 79,000 acres for $7.50 per Acre. While that makes them a good profit Yet the property is worth more."[31]

Then would Uncle allow the transaction at all? As never before, dollars and cents were the least of the considerations. Explained the Major: "I don't care to go Into It for it increases business to fall on me, and I am in no shape to take on more." The loss of Phelps's participation in running Littlefield Lands he would feel first. But worrying the Major more was the shift their departure would create in the dynamic that for so many decades had contributed meaningfully to Uncle's prosperity. The nephews were debtors. Despite all the money they had made through the years, they continued paying Uncle interest on land and cattle loans. As the years passed, the loans grew larger than they needed to be and ran longer than they needed to run. Nevertheless, Uncle asked the nephews to continue carrying the debt so as to provide him with reliable funding to support family members' needs. Uncle readily acknowledged to family members the White brothers' unselfish devotion to them all. To Arthur Duggan he wrote that "Phelps Tom and Will White I am indebted to for my Prosperity. They did the rough work and it was their work that has brought the prosperity we enjoy." Altogether just then, Phelps and Tom owed Uncle a staggering $340,000-something, on which they paid 6 percent interest. "Now that makes it [the 79,000 acres] live property for $20,000.00," Uncle calculated. In short, then, the heaviest burden their departure would saddle on Uncle would be replacing the safe and lucrative income stream.[32]

But one concern loomed larger yet: Littlefield's health. "If I do trade with Phelps and Tom," Littlefield wrote on September 24, 1914, "it will be to Ease them of their fear and dread of consequences to come after my death." Separating their land and cattle interests would not be simple. Hardly a new concern, Littlefield and Phelps had been corresponding about the matter since before Alice's affliction so changed Uncle's condition. Likely, then, fear and dread of the inevitable sealed the decision. In mid-October, three weeks after he wrote, Uncle agreed to the deal, apparently at nine dollars per acre. "I am sorry I had to buy it for I am sure the boys would have made more money to of remained in on it," Uncle wrote. The transaction came none too soon. Two weeks later, on October 29, 1914, fifty-five-year-old Thomas David White died of a kidney infection he had disregarded.[33]

Loss of the good-natured cowman hit them all hard. Tom's father and Littlefield's oldest half brother, Thomas Jefferson White, took it the hardest. Though a widower for fourteen years, in just fifteen days he cried himself to death. Six days on he would have reached his eighty-sixth birthday. Seeing Tom's demise coming, seventy-two-year-old George Littlefield confided to Phelps that "I am an old man. I have grown weak, and I must watch myself[,] be careful for fear of any exposure for that is what takes old men off. Neglect." Tom's loss meant much more, though. Uncle saw that the time was upon him to choose a successor to receive the mantle his mother had bestowed on him as head of her extended Littlefield-White family. So, to James Phelps White, the nephew closest to him for the half century since he had returned from the war, he wrote: "I have lived to help to build you up and you have built me up. As it is and when my life goes out, I shal leave my life earnings to you to see after and care for all. I have been a Watchman on the tower careing for all our family."[34] So he had been. So he would continue to be for as long as he lived. But in his remaining time on earth, he would be content that he had ordained the next patriarch of the lineage.

In late October of 1914, George Washington Littlefield had every reason to feel old and weak. Alice's condition weighed on him; his own health was declining noticeably; and Tom White's death not only saddened him but also took away one of the three brothers whose work sustained him in the charge consecrated by his mother of serving the Littlefield-White clan. When he went to the office, the workload of the Littlefield Lands operation taxed him, and how he would replace the income stream lost from the White brothers' sale of their Littlefield Lands interest worried him. Oppressing him further, the dramatic jump in the tax bill on his Congress Avenue properties drove him, beyond his usual restraint, to publicly blame Mayor Wooldridge, and on the ranch the exploration oil well begun so expectantly was proving to be a costly dry hole.[35] The weight of it all became stark when he refused election to head the university's board of regents.

As dark as the days were for the Major, though, one date on the calendar was sure to buoy him—election day. The fall of every even-numbered year brought a Texas gubernatorial election. For the Major, the Democratic candidate that year, assured of election after having won the primary, generated unusual excitement. James Edward Ferguson was a new face. Though barren of experience in government, he excelled in appealing to the electorate. He epitomized the "successful man of farm origin that every small town in Texas knows well," wrote the earliest student of his gubernatorial administrations. "He wore a black felt hat of semi-western effect, and the black string tie of the politician. . . . He was a man inclined to express his own opinions in his own terms, regardless of the effect they may have on the other fellow." Wrote another, he combined "his power of persuasion and likability with an innate ability to size up his listeners and play to their vulnerabilities." Ferguson was a born campaigner and stump speaker. "His good ol' boy delivery and down-home style were messages in themselves," giving his rural poor tenant-farmer audience to feel that he was one of them.[36] Moved by Ferguson, too, Littlefield joined his bandwagon early. Not just joined cash in hand, he paraded to it—literally, if Ferguson can be believed.

On "Farmer Jim's" first campaign stop in Austin in the spring of 1914, a crowd of thousands, tenant farmers mostly, gathered in a tabernacle rented for his preaching. Littlefield came too and took a place in the rear of the sweaty assembly, watching for his moment. The Major was a real politician, Ferguson reminisced admiringly years later. And he showed it then and there. Just before the speaking began, Littlefield strode forward. "Dressed in a pearl hickory shirt with a red handkerchief around his neck [and] a pair of big suspenders and a pair of old blue jeans on," he carried an oak bucket filled with water and a gourd dipper. "I caught the cue," Ferguson recalled, "jumped up and drank while he, the richest man in Austin, but dressed worse than the poorest one there, held the bucket."[37]

A relationship so propitiously begun would climax in three years, with Littlefield having "his fangs back at Ferguson as big as a wolf" and his break with the governor propelling the Major to his finest moment as a regent.[38]

18

IN A MAN'S SIZED WORLD

"Major, what was it that made you rich?" asked a friend who came by the bank on June 21, 1915, to congratulate George Littlefield on his seventy-third birthday. "Well," he responded, stroking his iron-gray beard, "I cannot say, except that I got into a good business and stayed with it." Had the well-wisher asked what was a good business, the Major surely would have demurred. "It makes no diference what Kind of a business a young man may start in," he had counseled Maurice Dowell. "He must Expect very slow growth." Compared to the quick glamour of election to political office that Maurice later pursued, there was no debate. Give the Major a lowly peanut stand on the street corner, he had said. With a peanut stand, a fellow was his own man. In the business world, George Littlefield was his own man. Temple, Texas, banker, retail merchant, farmer, and rancher James Edward Ferguson was his own man too. Being your own man in business was one thing. Being your own man in politics and government was quite another. In the fall of 1914, Ferguson had been elected to his first political office. As governor, Ferguson exposed a stubborn arrogance and demanded an absolute loyalty beyond what a businessman, the Major for one, required of his managers and employees. A showdown between the resolute governor and the independent board of regents over university employees politically offensive to the governor was bound to come. When it did, Major Littlefield would have to decide whose man he was on the board. Were he to downplay the importance of his decision, the student-produced *University of Texas Magazine* reminded all of its magnitude. In June 1917, as the confrontation moved toward its climax, the magazine editorialized that "'The Eyes of Texas' are to-day centered upon the Board of Regents. The man [among them] who is ultimately expected to clear up the whole unpleasant affair is none other than Major Littlefield."[1] Would he side with the authority of the governor of Texas, whom he had helped to elect and ardently supported, or would he stand with the integrity of the University of Texas, in which he had taken keen interest since he had moved to Austin more than thirty years earlier and on whose governing board he served?

When the board of regents met not two months before the Major's birthday in 1915, it entertained an unusual offer. Former regent George W. Brackenridge proposed giving the school his seagoing houseboat. The thirty-thousand-dollar *Navidad* meant a lot to George for the family outings he had held on it for more than a quarter century. Among other excursions, he and brother Tom had used it to enjoy each other's proximity. Fishing brought them together. Though George held Tom to be his favorite brother, the two could not tolerate each other for long. George had been a Unionist, Tom a Confederate; George a Republican, Tom a Democrat. Their conversations commonly ended in acrimony, ever more so as the years passed. Whether the increasing unpleasantness moved George to make the donation, he thought the university could make good use of the craft to study Texas's coastal marine fauna. The board agreed and accepted his offer.[2]

Perhaps it was only a coincidence, but within days of the Brackenridge offer, the Austin paper reported that George Littlefield bought a similar boat for himself. The Major's motivation is a mystery. He had never spent time around watercraft, nor had he written of them since his 1863 offer to serve on a gunboat in exchange for passage across the Mississippi River. Nevertheless, the Major purchased a sixty-eight-foot pleasure cruiser and had it freighted from Houston to Lake Austin, just formed behind the city's recently completed second dam on the Colorado River. Some sixteen thousand dollars the *Statesman* reported Littlefield paid for the vessel. The paper never told what he spent to transport the exquisite craft, whose mahogany woodwork beautified the six sleeping compartments, one with "a brass bedstead of artistic design," and a dining room that could be transformed into a dance floor for one hundred revelers. Hauling the massive vessel by rail required not only three flat cars under it but also a route with bridges wide enough to accommodate its thirteen-foot beam. Then, getting the boat into the lake necessitated laying track into the water. Between four hundred and five hundred onlookers flocked to the shore to watch twelve men labor for more than an hour to ease the boat into the lake.[3]

The next day, April 16, 1915, a crew of sailors, a chef, waiters, and maintenance men the Major brought with the boat from Houston nosed the launch into the current to take him and eight guests for the *Terry Ranger*'s maiden voyage. "For fourteen miles along the river the sound of the discharging engines echoed and re-echoed between the hills . . . and the entire trip of twenty-eight miles was finished in a little over two hours, doing even better than the highest expectations of the most optimistic seaman aboard," the *Statesman* reporter described the experience.[4]

Austinites were ready to regain the pleasures of the lake lost after the first dam broke. Fondly they remembered gliding over the normally serene water of that first lake on the side-wheel paddle boat *Ben Hur*. The *Terry Ranger* picked up where the *Ben Hur*, grounded after the first dam broke, left off. Littlefield's craft took group after group on cruises to leave "behind in the heat-smitten city their weighty cares and problems."[5] Joining the *Terry Ranger*, cotton broker E. H. Perry's *Nanette* hosted its share of the pleasure seekers too.

Gliding down the lake ten miles above the dam in the deep dusk of August 2, 1915, *Terry Ranger* master Nelson Sweet noticed a light he thought to be on the west bank. Suddenly it turned and headed across the river on what appeared to be a collision course with the *Terry Ranger*. Sweet slowed. The light disappeared. Sweet reversed his engines and spun his wheel. To no avail. The *Terry Ranger* crashed into the *Ermine*, throwing four of the stricken craft's nine passengers into the river. Two died. The right leg of C. Ramsey, father of the *Ermine*'s pilot, was mangled by the *Terry Ranger*'s propellers. The Ramseys sued for damages. Testimony showed that young Ramsey had steered deliberately into Littlefield's boat's path in hopes of extracting from the Major a sum equivalent to the *Terry Ranger*'s purchase price. Instead of enriching themselves, the Ramseys suffered a settlement in Littlefield's favor that left them owing court costs and the elder man crippled.[6]

If the Major thought that a collision and suit were the worst that could happen from owning the craft, barely four months after the *Terry Ranger* had been launched, he found otherwise. At 9:20 p.m. on Thursday, September 16, 1915, the river began to rise. It was runoff from exceptionally heavy rain over the Pedernales River watershed that emptied into the Colorado River above Austin. In fewer than six hours, the level at the dam had gained twenty-two feet. Five and a half hours later, with the angry water a foot higher yet, the *Terry Ranger* could resist the current no longer. Or maybe it was the *Nanette* tethered to it. Whichever it was, eleven hours after the flood began, the two boats joined the flotsam racing downstream. The *Nanette* crashed against the dam first but when found a few days later was thought to be salvageable. What was left of the *Terry Ranger* "is swinging now from the cable which anchored it to a 500 pound concrete block, the concrete anchorage still being above the dam, the bow of the *Terry Ranger* at the other end of the cable below the dam."[7]

A month later, the university's nautical venture ended, too, when the regents returned Brackenridge's handsome benevolence. The school lacked the means to maintain and operate the vessel.[8]

Money was becoming tight everywhere. George Littlefield had seen it coming even before he shelled out multiple thousands for the *Terry Ranger*. It began with a gunshot. On June 28, 1914, half a world away in Sarajevo, Bosnia-Herzegovina, the assassination of Archduke Franz Ferdinand propelled Germany to declare war on Russia and France, then Britain to reciprocate against Germany. Though

President Woodrow Wilson reflected American sentiment by promptly issuing a declaration of neutrality, Littlefield surmised that the war would affect business on the high plains by staunching European immigration.

How unfortunate. Sales Manager Arthur Duggan just then was courting two German Mennonite groups. Their numbers had enlarged until sons in the second generation needed land of their own. It was not to be had on the northern plains, where their immigrant parents had settled. For Littlefield Lands, their coming stood to be propitious. "I do not know of anything that could happen to Littlefield that would be as much advantage as having this class of people move here and make their home," Duggan exulted. "As you know they are very religious; also very hard workers, and very successful farmers."[9] For Europeans unfamiliar with American soils, indeed, for tillers all, their move to Littlefield Lands would signal the property's quality better than any advertising.

The Mennonites came. As happy as that was, though, until the Great War ended, "it seems to me that it will be an impossibility to sell lands," the Major advised Duggan. "Only where you find a man with the ready money could we reasonably expect sales to be made. . . . Every man that has any management about him now is studying how to Keep from spending any money." While he would continue to sell on credit, the Major dreaded the consequences: "The trouble with all those who have attempted to colonise or to settle up landed estates, is there expense list, and the holding down losses by Extending credit to liberally to those who they have sold land to. Let the owner of lands do what he may, He will be called and looked upon as a hard man." Would the Major trade for something of value—a car? No. "An Auto is an Expensive Luxury at best," he rejected the prospect's proposal, "and I do not want any man to think I am silly enough to trade land for one." So in mid-October 1914, "I cant see how we are going to . . . [meet expenses] without a continual going down in our pockets after fresh money."[10]

In that gloomy picture, Uncle offered Duggan a proposition. Would the nephew by marriage be interested in opening a ranching partnership on two unsold leagues? Stocked with five hundred head of cattle and managed by a good hand, the entrepreneur in service to his kin thought the New Ranch in a couple of years should make up for commissions Duggan would lose from the slow sales. With Uncle's ranching experience to guide him, Duggan accepted.[11]

If land sales did shrink to a trickle, the Major still had his ranch for making money. Banks unable to collect on loans lacked such security. And those dependent on cotton were suffering. Facing depressed prices, farmers were holding their crops in hopes of better returns. Two more such years, the American National's president prophesied, and half of the banks and two-thirds of the merchants would be forced out of business. In fact, "Texas will soon confront a condition of general bankruptcy," he joined the other three Austin bank presidents in writing to his former American National Bank board member and current advisor to President Wilson, Edward M. House. Action by the federal government, the bankers argued, was needed to prevent the cotton depression from dragging down the national economy. "I want to stay open," Littlefield declared. And doing so would not be easy, because the only way, he saw to survive was "to see that our customers do not involve us."[12]

How easy it was to become "involved," even for one who warned to beware of it. After news of the Major's gift of the Littlefield Fund for Southern History resonated across the South, United Confederate Veterans commander Bennett Henderson Young expressed the veterans' appreciation by commissioning Littlefield a brigadier general on his staff. A year later, General Littlefield sent an innocent one hundred dollars for staff expenses. Not needing it for that purpose, Young asked whether Littlefield would allow him to apply it toward memorializing Confederate President Jefferson Davis at his birthplace in Todd County, Kentucky. Young did not have to ask twice.[13]

The Jefferson Davis Home Association had been formed in 1907, a year or two after the Lincoln Farm Association organized to mark the sixteenth president's Kentucky birthplace about one hundred miles distant. Display of Lincoln's reputed birth cabin in a national park motivated that group. Not to be outdone but lacking the Davis cabin, the Davis Home Association bought nineteen acres at the Davis birth site on which to erect the best monument that five thousand dollars appropriated by the Kentucky legislature would buy. Association president Young still needed to raise enough to build roads on the property. And he knew where he might get some of it. To Littlefield he bragged that he had raised one thousand dollars, which "I consider . . . quite good, because I may say to you what I would not say outside—that Mr. Davis was never popular in the South and it was difficult to excite and evoke enthusiasm in regard to things which affect him." Then the master salesman made his pitch. First, the softening up: "You were so good to me that I hate to make any suggestions to you at all." Then the flattery: "You are evidently a man of large means, certainly a man of large heart." Then the ask: "I would like to see your name connected in some way with Jefferson Davis Park. I would like to see an Avenue named after you, and if you have more money than you know what to do with you might take up the question of helping to build one of these avenues, call it the 'General George W. Littlefield Avenue.'"[14]

The proposition must have struck a chord. In September 1916 Littlefield made a weeklong excursion to see this place into whose development Young was drawing him ever deeper. What began as a simple business trip turned into a "triumphal march through Kentucky," as the *Statesman* headlined its coverage. After reporting the disappointing Lincoln site visit in three lines, the Austin paper took two paragraphs to describe the Major's emotional trip to the Confederate Men's Home that Young not only had been instrumental in building but also presided over as board president. After brief remarks by the two men, a choir sang "God Be with You till We Meet Again." At the conclusion, as Littlefield shook the hand of every soldier, many were moved to tears "as they realized that of those who sang the song and shook the hand of General Littlefield many would never see him again." Two days later, during Littlefield's visit to the Davis homesite, word came that the students of nearby Elkton High School wanted to see the celebrity. After Littlefield addressed them, Young asked: "What is the matter with Gen. George W. Littlefield?" In "a great cheer," the two hundred young people responded, "Gen. George W. Littlefield is all right."[15]

"My trip was very pleasant," the Major wrote Phelps. "I put new life in the movement, which had become very quiet." An infusion of $2,000 and promise of another $8,000 after Young and the board raised $5,000 could hardly do other than excite. "The Great trouble," Littlefield recognized, though, "is the old Confederates are getting few, and men born or grown up since the War don't feel like them."[16] Major Littlefield was accepting that the weight of memorializing the true Southern sentiment for which he and the veterans whose hands he shook had fought was falling ever more heavily on him.

Littlefield was right that he with money had kindled new interest. In the absence of Davis's birth cabin, owners of the house in which the president had married offered it to the home association for five thousand dollars. Probably as a way of assuring his donor and newly elected board vice president that the association would be judicious in proposing expenditures, Young wrote Littlefield that "of course you know that being a Presbyterian I cannot cuss, but I found a wicked friend who greatly relieved me by telling him to 'go to hell.'"[17]

For Young, both the marriage home proposition and a five-thousand-dollar monument had come to represent small thinking. With Littlefield behind him, Young could envision a mighty work. Less a memorial to a man, he projected a monument to the cause so grand that it would be "the greatest monument to the Confederacy." His mind's eye pictured a towering obelisk as "an outward, visible exponent of a great idea [that would be] a national shrine which will draw to it people of all parties, colors and conditions" in recognition "of a fundamental principle of the political creed of the Old South—that of Constitutional States Rights, and of the heroic effort to sustain it." At 351 feet, the column would top all others but the magnificent Washington Monument itself. To ensure that Littlefield shared his vision, Young reminded him that "*We* cannot afford, after the talks we have made, to let this be ordinary. We must let it be extraordinary." And so "I told the architect what *we* wanted was immensity, not artistic lines alone."[18]

Should they be unable to raise the money necessary to reach 351 feet, then Young identified acceptable lesser heights, each taller than a prominent national monument. "You never saw a lawyer who could not make a good excuse for any thing that would happen," he told the Major, "and if we have to shorten the shaft, why we can give a most excellent reason for it." That said, "I hope you will concur . . . that it is a heap easier to do a big thing than a little thing, and that our only chance of a great success is to go after the big thing." Major Littlefield signaled his concurrence by accepting elevation to chairmanship of the board three months after joining the group. Surely he appreciated what that meant. For the man who felt overworked already, the chairmanship brought with it the weight of passing on every new or large expenditure. No wonder, since most of the money underwriting the project would be his.[19]

In a year and a half, a simple one hundred dollars had grown into a stagger-ing fifty-thousand-dollar commitment to raising what would become the world's tallest poured concrete obelisk. Not lost on Young, it paired two of the most prominent Confederates—the richest and the most eloquent. At the Daughters of the Confederacy November 1916 Dallas convention, Young sought to show off his "Big Money Man" in making his pitch to the women for support of the Davis monument. Littlefield declined to go. The women were worn out with giving, he said. They had given so generously already that they ought not be asked. Young went alone and reaped a healthy eleven-thousand-dollar contribution. "You are a much better judge of cows and calves than I am," he wired Littlefield triumphantly, "but I can beat you all holler when it comes to judging women."[20]

The monument project reached a high point in late January 1917, when Young sent Littlefield the design of a medal he proposed giving women who donated substantial sums to the obelisk and painted his vision of a vast throng gathered for the unveiling (figs. 49 and 50). Then, German torpedoing of American ships and a German diplomatic initiative to bring Mexico into the war against the United States pushed America to declare war on Germany in April. Suddenly, Littlefield found himself caught between a coming wartime economy unfavorable to the project and his want to realize the object to which he had committed so much time and money. Time becoming ever more imperative for the aging Major, work began. Within months, rising costs of supplies and labor beset the undertaking. A year later, an exhausted Young reluctantly raised consideration of suspending work until the war ended. "It has been my earnest desire to get this monument [completed] before you and I should die," he wrote Littlefield on March 2, 1918, with the obelisk ninety feet above ground. "If we stop now the chances are we will never see it finished." He was right. Bennett Young died eleven months later with the monument stalled only halfway up. By the time the final pour dried in 1924, George Littlefield had gone to his grave too (fig. 51).[21]

The sixth sense friends said Major Littlefield had for spotting snares failed him twice in mid-decade, first with Bennett Young. That said, Littlefield never regretted his involvement in the Jefferson Davis obelisk project, though its increasing demands did frustrate him. Regret and frustration would be the least of his grief from misjudging Jim Ferguson.

Forty-three-year-old Farmer Jim, as his admirers called him, had secured the governor's office by mobilizing the voting power of poor tenant farmers. At the same time, he gave men of means like Major Littlefield plenty of reasons to warm to him. And Littlefield did. Both had farmed, ranched, and run a bank. Both were Masons and took Scottish Rite degrees together only a month after the new governor's inauguration. Moreover, Ferguson commended wealthy men to his adherents. Texans "ought to welcome all the rich men who are willing to invest in Texas," he said, "and join in the development of this state." Not only welcome them, Texans should "guarantee them absolute protection for their capital." And for cattlemen, he called for a massive appropriation aimed at eradicating the Texas Fever tick. Perhaps paramount, Ferguson favored education, and Littlefield was entering his fifth year on the state university's governing board.[22]

By almost every measure—length of the school year, percentage of children attending school, teacher salaries, and amount spent per pupil—Texas's primary and secondary schools fell below the national average. The $2,284,632 Texas spent on public education in 1908–9 ranked it thirty-seventh among the forty-nine enumerated states, territories, and the District of Columbia. In fact, Texas fell five hundred thousand dollars short of the expenditure in adjacent Oklahoma. Nevertheless, Texas's average outlay of fourteen dollars per student in 1914 evidently sounded princely to state leaders. For 1915–16 they decreased the amount by more than half to a pitiful six dollars. Proclaimed candidate Ferguson, "If we get our money's worth, let us buy all the education we can pay for" to uplift every level, from the rural schoolhouse to the state university. That sounded good, but what did he mean by "if we get our money's worth"?[23]

The discrepancy in expenditure between rural (by which he meant primary and secondary school levels) and university students was stark. On his second day in office, January 20, 1915, Ferguson highlighted it. "When we consider the seventy thousand children in Texas who never get a chance to go to school," he told the legislature, "and against this put the fact that the Texas Legislature is today being asked to appropriate over $325.00 per student for the benefit of those fortunate enough and able to go to the Agricultural and Mechanical College and the University [of Texas], you can begin to see that there is a real danger of somebody going hog wild about higher education." That somebody would not be him. To Jim Ferguson, the state was not getting its money's worth from higher education by comparison with schooling at the lower levels.[24]

Dollars and cents in fact were only part of it. Whether he had grounds for it, Ferguson believed that Austin's university community—he called them "the university crowd"—looked down on him and his wife. Of the two, only Miriam had attended college. Daughter Ouida decades later described the Fergusons' feeling that "The University group . . . bask in their intellectual superiority, but . . . for the sake of University appropriations, tolerate, and at times are very sweet to, the political group on Capitol Hill."[25]

Ferguson in fact broadened his definition of "university group" to degree holders as a class. Friends of state librarian Ernest William Winkler knew it. Even before inauguration day, rumor spread that Ferguson was looking for positions from which to remove incumbents so as to provide openings for rewarding supporters. To preempt a move against Winkler, Texas Library and Historical Commission chairman and university faculty member Eugene Barker wrote Ferguson's brother at Texas A&M, asking him to intervene on Winkler's behalf. He pointed out to Alexander Ferguson that Major Littlefield had once remarked that Winkler was the most efficient man for the position. No matter. Soon afterward, Governor Ferguson confronted Winkler, saying: "You are the son of a farmer; you know what it costs to obtain an education; it was through the sacrifices of your father that you obtained an education. Now that you have an education and have occupied an important position, you have turned away from the teaching of your father and . . . proclaimed that a man without a college education is not fit to hold office." Winkler was speechless. The governor's conclusion was as baseless as his description of Winkler's background was accurate. And Ferguson would not be dissuaded by the testimony of a supporter as generous as George Littlefield.[26]

Beyond dollars and cents, and the feeling of being snubbed by the university community, the governor's rising abhorrence of the university crowd had a political tone to it too. True, politically active individual faculty and staff members headed a progressive wing of the Democratic Party opposed to him. But the governor thought he saw wholesale political insurgence where it did not exist. In addition to writing brother Ferguson, Barker obtained the governor's permission to describe the job to the governor's intended Winkler replacement. Barker's note concluded by observing that the law required the state library head to be a qualified librarian, which Reverend Cunningham was not. And Barker stated plainly that he was writing in hopes of dissuading the reverend from accepting the governor's offer. Upon reading the letter, Ferguson lashed out at the statement of facts as being just "a long discussion of politics."[27]

In this frame of mind about the university, the governor called acting university president William James Battle to his office in July, 1915, to discuss the university budget. A professor of classics and the son of a former president of the University of North Carolina, the forty-four-year-old Battle was deeply invested in the university. After fifteen years in the classroom, he had been elevated to dean of the College of Arts, three years later to dean of the faculty, and three years after that, in 1914, to acting president. Battle knew his mind and was not reticent in speaking it.[28] The firm temperaments of the two men did not bode well for harmony, even in a routine meeting to clarify budget lines.

The university financial plan had been crafted by President Mezes, who had subsequently resigned, leaving his successor to defend it. As the document awaited his signature, Ferguson summoned Battle for explanations. What was the name of the professor who would fill the sociology teaching position? the governor asked. Replied Battle, the position was unfilled, and the administration planned to use the money for other purposes. Ferguson was incredulous. "Dr. Battle, let me understand you," Ferguson began; "do you mean to tell me that you have come down to this Legislature and told the Appropriation Committee that you wanted to pay him $3250 a year knowing that you did not have such a man, that you never did have such a man and that you intended to divert the money to some other use which you did not disclose to the Appropriation Committee of the Legislature?"[29] Whatever Battle's explanation, Ferguson understood him to have admitted the validity of the assessment, damning in the governor's mind.

Though he later declared that Battle had fooled him, Ferguson nevertheless signed the bill without requiring a change. Battle was astonished. Never before within his twenty-one years at the university had a governor accepted the appropriation as passed. If, after reporting his observation to the regents, they and he thought that Ferguson's signature signaled his acceptance of university expenditures, they soon learned otherwise. Support education as he did, Governor Ferguson could not ignore what he had learned of the way the university handled its appropriation. He would address it by having his state comptroller appointee set up accounts for university spending. True, Governor Colquitt had vetoed a portion of the 1913 university appropriation for not being itemized, which had led to President Mezes's resignation. But neither Colquitt nor any predecessor had taken so singular a step of trying to impose the specific budget lines. Battle's executive experience told him that an administration the size of the university needed flexibility to move money between lines as changing situations required. Consequently, he asked an attorney general's ruling on whether the governor's mandated budget lines would bind the school. After the answer endorsed the regents' authority over its appropriation, the governor declared that the issue was drawn "whether the University, through its President, shall be permitted to thwart the will of the people or whether that will must be respected and carried out."[30]

Checked in his effort to have his way with the university by controlling its funding, the governor shifted his focus to personnel. Seven faculty and staff drew his wrath. But not stopping with individuals, Governor Ferguson imagined a conspiracy against him. A clique "absolutely ran the university," he told regents David Harrell and chairman Fred W. Cook, adding ominously that he would "get them out before I get through."[31]

What the governor needed was a university president who would do his bidding. Expecting dutiful compliance, to the regents he named his choice. They disregarded it. Instead, the board surprised the university community by selecting Austin Presbyterian Theological Seminary president Robert Vinson. This affront proved to be a turning point in the governor's relation with the university. Said Littlefield looking back, it turned Ferguson bitter. Suggestions became demands.[32]

As customary before taking office, Vinson called on the governor. Major Littlefield accompanied Vinson for the visit on June 20, 1916. The meeting did not go well. Hammering his desk, Ferguson demanded dismissals. Vinson resisted, saying he had "never been accustomed to acting upon another man's dictation and wasn't going to commence then." Replied Ferguson, manifesting what one biographer described as "a propensity for unprovoked acrimony," then Vinson should expect "the biggest bear fight that had ever taken place in the history of the State of Texas." Unintimidated, Vinson replied simply: "I would not go into a fight voluntarily, but . . . I wouldn't run from one if it was forced upon me." No record documents what part Littlefield took in the meeting, but he had to have left it conflicted. As a strong political friend of the governor, he had proposed that the board recover authority to make appointments, promotions, and dismissals at its will, rather than continuing to act only on the president's recommendations. But he had defied the governor in joining the unanimous vote electing Vinson, whom he had liked since meeting him fourteen years earlier when the cleric joined the seminary faculty. Seeing the mettle of the governor and the university president, surely the Major had to sense that one day he would have to choose between them.[33]

At President Vinson's request, in October 1916 the board met in special session to hear and act on the governor's charges against the seven men. Ferguson demanded summary dismissals. The regents balked. Led by vice chairman William Clifford Hogg of Houston, the liberal-minded, independent son of Littlefield's favorite governor, the regents insisted upon hearing charges. Staunch in his stance that, as he told Hogg, "I don't have to give any reasons, I am Governor of the State of Texas," Ferguson blustered that he would replace every regent who opposed him. Nevertheless he offered his charges—some financial, some political. As they voted on each of the accused, a majority of regents stood firm against dismissal and for what the *Statesman* called "a continuance of university authority rather than state domination." Not Littlefield. He held with the three "standing staunchly together like Dumas's musketeers—one for all and all for one" behind the governor. "I believe it's the duty of the University Regents to back up the Governor in his contentions," Littlefield had declared philosophically three years earlier. Whether or not the often gruff, brusque Hogg had expected it of Littlefield, he was appalled at the older man's position. And the vice chairman, whose friends were given to saying that the C in his name stood for Combustible, told him so. "Major," he began, "I'm going to talk to you like no man ever talked to you before. You've been the bull-tongued banker in a one-horse town, sitting up in your saffron-colored cage so long that you've lost the power to tell right from wrong." Then, "the fearless Major listened to a lurid description of his ancestry—and he didn't shoot," Hogg's friend, John A. Lomax, concluded his account of the unbridled rebuke.[34]

Whether or not Hogg's chastening moved him, at the next opportunity to support the governor unequivocally, Littlefield didn't. Failing to secure dismissal of journalism professor and former lieutenant governor William Harding Mayes for having "skinned me from hell to breakfast" in his *Brownwood Bulletin*, Ferguson turned to elimination of the university's school of journalism. Mayes had been hired to establish it two years earlier. Littlefield took a middle course. He voted against the proposal, then moved a palliative prohibiting employment of anyone owning an interest in a newspaper within the state.[35]

Next, Littlefield focused the board's attention on good news from his land committee. First, he reported income from the West Texas lands had reached a record $182,000 per year, adding nearly one-quarter to the legislative appropriation. Second, proceeds from the Brackenridge tract totaled their own six-thousand-dollar record. Rather than dump that sum into the general fund, the Major led his colleagues in devoting it to curbing and paving campus driveways to improve the university's central Austin prominence he considered so valuable to the city.[36]

When the regents next met five months later, at the end of April 1917, Major Littlefield found himself with an immediate decision to make. Passing over the man who had chaired the board for more than two years, Ferguson appointees placed in nomination for chair the names of George Littlefield and Dr. Ashley Wilson Fly, the board's senior member by two years, but Littlefield's junior by thirteen. The Major asked not to be elected. "Although he looked to be a well man, he was not," he said. Heavy obligations weighed on him, too, he added, no doubt high in his mind being the Davis monument pour just beginning. For a Ferguson board, Fly then would seem to have been a shoo-in. He was the only regent who, on every ballot, had voted for dismissal. Nevertheless, through four votes Littlefield tied with Fly. Finally, to break the stalemate, the two candidates talked, then recommended thirty-eight-year-old Austin lawyer, cattleman, and American National Bank board member Wilbur Price Allen, who accepted election.[37]

Littlefield got what he wanted. And so too, thought Governor Ferguson, would he. In the six months after the contentious October meeting, he had made four appointments. Counting Chairman Allen and the two confirmed by the previous legislature, Ferguson had appointed six of the nine members. "The Governor once told me that if this board did not do what he wanted it to do, he would get one that would," Littlefield recalled him saying. What the governor expected of his nominees, the university's rejuvenated Ex-Students Association feared of them. Led by then former regent Will Hogg and John A. Lomax, secretary to several university departments, the Ex-Students requested a legislative inquiry into the four new appointees' independence.[38] So confident was Governor Ferguson of his appointee's fealty that he asked the state senate to just leave the board free to carry out its work. After the Senate finally confirmed the last appointees on March 19, its last day in session, only one matter remained for completion.[39]

On May 17, 1917, a special session took care of it by adopting a biennial budget for the university and then adjourned. In the quiet that followed, observers hoped the conflict had ended. It hadn't. Ten days later a front-page headline reported that the governor had summoned the regents to meet in his office the next day to consider a matter "of utmost and grave importance." Chairman Allen disclosed to President Vinson, whom the governor pointedly excluded from the meeting but who reported the chairman's words to the *Statesman*, that Ferguson was going to demand both his ouster and elimination of fraternities. Fraternities were an easy target. Rich playboys, as the governor characterized fraters, could afford these exclusive groups, not the poor, rural, salt-of-the-earth young men whose parents formed the core of his supporters. To ensure the governor got his way, Allen continued ominously, he hinted that he was "inclined" to withhold approval of the university appropriation until after the board had acted on the matters he would raise at the meeting.[40]

Though his appointees and supporters constituted a supermajority of eight, Governor Ferguson still had reason to be apprehensive about the board's vassalage. George Littlefield's response to Ferguson's demands told him so. Contrary to the governor's assertions, Vinson had not mismanaged seminary affairs, Littlefield reported to the chief executive after conducting his own investigation. Not only was Vinson the best man for the job, but the fact that he was a cleric who had preached a couple of sermons since becoming university president did not violate the constitutional provision separating church and state, the Major added. Finally, Ferguson should not disapprove of Vinson because he wouldn't stand hitched" to the governor, as Littlefield worded Ferguson's objection. Vinson appropriately considered it his duty to answer to none but the board of regents that had appointed him.[41]

If, as later events strongly suggest, Littlefield had been behind Ferguson's appointment of his bank director Allen, and Allen had accepted both appointment and the chairmanship at Littlefield's urging, in no time he confronted his own conflict between the governor's demands and his personal interests. Allen was not just a fraternity man. He was the Grand Counsel of all of Sigma Chi Fraternity and, reported the *Statesman*, "one of the leading fraternity men of the United States." But far from being the elitist for which Ferguson denounced fraternity men, Allen had created two funds to pay the way for four young men and women to attend the school. The new chairman would have to declare his allegiance soon enough. And he had to decide whether as chairman he would try to lead the board in choosing its way or just facilitate its proceedings.[42]

In the four days between the governor's office meeting, which ended unfinished in the cacophony of a student protest march, and the June 1 adjournment of the board's next regular meeting, the board found itself in turmoil. Two regents resigned. Ferguson removed a third and appointed three—one-third of the total board. This left George Littlefield unsettled. If events continued moving as they were, the Major would have to choose between personal allegiance to the governor and institutional loyalty to the university. While he lacked sympathy for the academic freedom the professorate cited against moves to dismiss instructors unsympathetic with the state's political leadership, the governor's dictatorial shuffling of board membership so as to have his way in university administration "sat uneasily on his own strong stomach."

Hardly had the board convened on May 31 in Galveston than it formed a committee to satisfy itself on the governor's power of removal without trial. Chair Judge

John M. Mathis, seated only that morning, read the law in the governor's favor. Committee member Littlefield objected. The law could be read differently, and he called for a more thorough investigation. "We all make mistakes," Littlefield continued. "The governor has made one in this case [dismissing an unsubmissive regent] I hope that he recognizes it." But even were the governor's dismissal power deemed to be legal, new appointee James P. Tucker's commission was not, the Major declared. It lacked the state seal. Motion then followed motion. Littlefield moved to reject the commission and not seat Tucker. Fly moved to table. Fly lost, with Allen breaking the tie. Two-month regent Charles E. Kelly moved that a lawyer be engaged to advise the board in the morning. With Littlefield's second, Cook moved to substitute June 11 for the next day. Allen scuttled that by siding with the majority against Littlefield. On the morrow, Friday, June 1, rather than the legal advice it sought, the board found itself served with two injunctions. One restrained Tucker from taking his seat. The other, initiated in Ex-Students Secretary Lomax's name, prevented three Ferguson regents from voting to remove faculty members. With the orders effectively preventing the board from acting on any matter, it adjourned to Monday, June 11, the day set for the Lomax injunction trial.[43]

The governor could not wait that long. If he did not redline the appropriation by June 7, it would take effect without his signature. The only way to preserve the veto threat was to use it before June 7. A proclamation drafted before the deadline would serve because it could be withdrawn.

"GOVERNOR CUTS OFF UNIVERSITY FUNDS," proclaimed the banner headline stretched across the *Statesman*'s Sunday, June 3, front page in letters larger than those of the masthead. "*Opinion Is Expressed That State's Greatest Institution of Learning Must Be Closed for Two Years*," the *Dallas Morning News* eye-catching italicized subhead summed up the general feeling.[44]

Still, hope for preventing the veto flickered. A committee of the Major and two regent colleagues met a counterpart group from the Ex-Students Association on Monday, June 4, seeking a resolution to the impasse. They failed. Maybe a smaller group could find a way. Chairman Allen and the Major met two Ex-Students leaders on Tuesday, June 5. They failed. Chairman Allen took the news to the governor. What could save the appropriation? he asked. Vinson's and Lomax's resignations and withdrawal of Lomax's injunction suit, Ferguson said. Allen and Littlefield took that proposition to Vinson, Lomax, and one or two others from the Ex-Students Association meeting in the president's office about five o'clock. To Vinson the chairman presented the desperate alternative—resign or see the biennial appropriation of his school eliminated. Robert Vinson two decades later told what happened next:

As I now recall that meeting, Major Littlefield proceeded to emphasize the obvious results that would ensue upon the veto of the measure, but expressed no opinion as to the kind of action on my part that he would recommend. My first reaction to the proposal was that a pretty high value was being placed upon my decision and that I must have been far more of a thorn in the flesh of certain people than it had been possible for me to imagine, accompanied by quite a strong feeling of indignation at both the proposal itself and the fact that it had been timed in such a manner as to leave no opportunity for reflection or mature consideration. Just at that moment the ringing of the telephone interrupted the proceedings and the voice of [Episcopal] Bishop [George Herbert] Kinsolving came to my ears. "No matter how I know it, but I know what is going on," he said, "but don't you resign." That message had much to do with the decision then made. After some rather heated exchanges, I turned to Major Littlefield and asked him to put himself in my place and tell me frankly what sort of an answer he would make if he were faced with the same alternative. His reply was immediate, direct, and I have always considered quite adequate and suitable. "I would tell him to go to hell," he said. That remark concluded the meeting, for while I told him that his language was somewhat out of line with my own customary forms of expression, I would authorize him to convey the substance of his statement to the Governor as my reply, leaving the exact verbiage to his own discretion. Within an hour word came that the appropriation had been vetoed and the bill filed with the Secretary of State, which, of course, made the action final.[45]

Littlefield had made his choice between personal and institutional loyalty. "Disagreeable," he politely described the experience of the meeting. In fact, if a moment of satisfaction had occurred, it came in making his immediate and direct answer to Vinson's question. Littlefield was addressing the governor. Ferguson "has fallen out with me for I would not be driven by him and that against this community [the regents?] and the university," Littlefield wrote privately on June 4. "I do not intend to give one inch. He will know me when ever he meets me in future as a stand patter." Not one to shrink from his convictions, Littlefield declared it publicly in the injunction trial. "Fangs back," as Ex-Students Central Committee representative Dudley K. Woodward recalled, Littlefield said that "he would not accept having matters 'ramrodded' down his throat," that the governor had no right "to step in and say [to the regents], 'you shall do these things.'"[46]

The disagreeableness went even deeper than that, as the Major scrawled in his heavy hand in a letter to Ferguson on June 22, 1917:

Now Governor, no man in this great State stood closer to you and your principals than I did in both your campaigns, but it seems to me you forgot all that and undertook to throw the pressure on to me.

You were down to see me at bank on May 29th. I had gone home between eleven and twelve o'clock and you said you were coming to see me that evening. I waited up to 5:20 o'clock. You did not come. I went with my wife riding, as I do every day. Went up by the capitol, told my family I would stop at Capitol to see you. Just as I had gotten up there I saw you had some gentleman with you in office and I went on my ride. I have not seen or sought to see you since. The next day at noon I went to the Galveston Regents meeting. The first day I was there I saw an infernal dispatch you had sent Wilbur Allen saying to watch me, that I was not his friend and wanted to keep him off the board. I considered it an insult. Wilbur has been my friend for years. I gave you no just cause to treat me in that way.

Your Secretary of State jumped in on the 29th of May and withdrew $250,000.00 from this bank in favor of your Temple State Bank. I thought it looked as if you wanted to press me. It did not and never will. I will say I am your friend in all that's just and right but I will not be coerced or forced to do anything against my judgment. No man regrets the situation more than myself but its your making not mine. . . . If you wish to come down and talk over affairs all right.[47]

The day after the veto's filing was one of stock taking. Hopeful for the future, George Littlefield in reserved tones answered reporters' questions about the regents' options. President Vinson spent the day "searching of heart and an almost frantic effort to find some way out." Two courses occurred to him. First, he should study the veto message. He noted to his surprise that after marking out virtually all of the specifics of the appropriation, the governor had failed to redline the total. Vinson immediately notified the attorney general asking his concurrence in the interpretation, opposite to the governor's intent, that the full appropriation could be used entirely at the regents' discretion. Then, he got in his car and drove to San Antonio.[48]

Talking with George Brackenridge cheered Vinson further. The former regent's support of the university continued stout. John Lomax had told the president that after a conversation he had had with Brackenridge, the *San Antonio Express* owner had directed his editor to "hop onto the governor. He's wrong, and we'll fight him to the end." Emboldened, Vinson then made an extraordinary request. Would

Brackenridge underwrite the university's biennium? Yes, even if the $1.6 million amount took every cent he had (which it very nearly would have done).

Perhaps appreciating his precarious finances, Brackenridge suggested Vinson take up the matter with Littlefield too. Tell him that Brackenridge offered to fund the entire figure. Then add that the San Antonio philanthropist suggested that Littlefield "perhaps . . . might like to join in this engagement for a part, even as much as one-half the amount." If Vinson had approached Brackenridge in the prospect that whatever Brackenridge might do would persuade Littlefield to open his pocketbook similarly, Brackenridge anticipated him. As Vinson said later, all three knew that between Littlefield and Brackenridge, "any yielding of one to the other would have been regarded by both as a surrender of . . . principles." For Vinson, then, Brackenridge had suggested a perfect strategy. And the Major rose to the occasion. Not just accepting the challenge to fund half, he declared that he would underwrite the full biennium himself.[49]

Before week's end, news broke that the attorney general concurred with Vinson. The regents had the full appropriation at their disposal. Neither philanthropist had to cover the biennium.[50]

Its 1917–19 years secured, the board returned in July to consideration of faculty dismissals. It voted to relieve the school of six, only to reinstate them all in September. Some of the dismissals Littlefield, as the governor's friend, initiated, but contrary to Lomax's later, widely circulated assertion, not all. In the recanting, Littlefield joined his colleagues only twice. But watching him reverse himself on even those two gave returning board member George Brackenridge "grim pleasure." Whether on account of the satisfaction he must have known Brackenridge was finding in those two actions or for his own conscience, the Major took the privilege of the floor to justify his position with regard to each faculty member. Regrettably, his words never left the board room, for the secretary failed to record or even to summarize them.[51]

Maybe Littlefield in September had asked to speak in confidence. He hadn't done so in July, when the secretary recorded him saying that the Home Economics Department's female instructors' salaries "were too high for women," after which he joined the majority in passing Wilbur Allen's motion reducing faculty women's pay 20 percent below faculty men's. Suffragists erupted. Clubwoman Helen Knox wrote former Texas and General Federation of Women's Clubs president Anna Pennybacker to denounce this "challenge to womanhood." Knox had heard that in the meeting the Major had "exclaimed" that "No woman in the world is worth $3,000" (the female department chair's proposed salary) and "declared" "the Department of Home Economics a farce, . . . that his $40.00 cook could do better." If he had indeed disparaged the department, the Major did not act on his opinion. In fact, Littlefield specifically opposed scuttling the unit. If she knew it, it made no difference to Austin Equal Suffrage Association President Jane Y. McCallum. "It may be wicked," she confided to her diary, "but how delighted, and supremely happy we'd all be if Ferguson, [Regents] Littlefield, Allen, Fly and McReynolds were to be killed."[52]

Littlefield took Alice and fled the state. For more than a month in August and September, 1917, they traveled in the North for her health and visited his New Mexico ranches. He was running alright, but not from threats on his life. Rather, the Major absented himself to avoid a subpoena. In the House proceedings to determine what, if any, articles of impeachment to prepare against Governor Ferguson, Littlefield had testified concerning faculty dismissals. Had he allowed himself to be put on the stand in the actual impeachment trial, "other things would have been brought out that would of injured" Ferguson, Littlefield from Chicago wrote his private secretary. "I prefer that no one Knows just how I feel." However he did feel, Ferguson changed it. The governor attempted "to ruin me with Wilber Allen by misstating the facts," testifying that the Major had opposed Allen's appointment. "Since he has said what he has about me and what I did, I do not expect any favors at his hands, though he is under obligations," Littlefield fumed, then concluded "that its dangerous to allow politicians to get to friendly. They all will use you if they can."[53]

Exhaustion from their travels drove George and Alice home. Though the senate trial was concluding, Littlefield was not called to bare his fangs again. But that did not spare him from becoming the target of a final shot growing out of trial testimony. State senator Isaac E. Clark introduced a resolution calling for Littlefield's removal as a regent because his American National Bank paid the state no interest on the university's daily balance of some seventy thousand dollars. The *Statesman* sprang to the Major's defense. "There are some things in this world a whole lot bigger than politics," the editor wrote, "one of them being the clean record and splendid reputation which a man attains by years of integrity in business and devotion to his country and his people. This is beyond price and any effort to destroy such must meet with the contempt of all good citizens." The senate expunged Clark's resolution from the journal.[54]

The Ferguson trial took its tolls. In September 1917 Jim Ferguson resigned. But it failed to save him from conviction, removal from office, and being barred from ever holding public office again. Likely wearied by all he had been through as regent chairman at the center of the Ferguson unpleasantness, Wilbur Allen resigned before the October meeting. And as the Major left in August to avoid involvement in the senate trial, he took an uncharacteristically submissive tone. "If not Impeached we have him [Ferguson] for Eighteen months, and it may be 3 1/2 years," he wrote. "Then why should citizens take so much stock" and press the issue?[55]

In fact, the stocktaking of affairs that citizens did in light of Littlefield's offer to fund the university, thus nullifying the effect of Ferguson's veto, President Vinson declared to be the Major's greatest contribution to the university and the state. In the fullness of reflection two decades after the Major had passed from the scene, Vinson told an audience of historians that

> In the course of my experience as a university executive I have had many occasions to be grateful for whole-hearted generosity, in some instances for sums larger in fact than the amount involved in this transaction, but among them all this one stands out as the superlative example of its kind. It was particularly valuable because it really defeated itself. It aroused public opinion. It renewed hopes that had almost disappeared. It had tremendous weight in bringing about the final result of the struggle that left the University both whole and free. . . . Other men were the founders of the University. These men [Littlefield and Brackenridge] were, in their hearts, its saviors.[56]

The *University of Texas Magazine* had expected as much from Major Littlefield. The *Statesman* had anticipated the eventuality Vinson described. Contemporaneously with the student publication, the newspaper editor explained why. George Washington Littlefield, it said, stood stout on his better judgment. In some seven and a half column inches in the issue that followed the hectic four days leading up to the veto proclamation, the paper editorialized under the title "Littlefield":

> There are so many distasteful features to the University controversy that it is a pleasure to turn to something different, to discuss something in connection with it which must be grateful to every patriotic citizen of Austin. This something is the conduct of Major George W. Littlefield. . . . The Major is a man of strong opinions. If he doesn't approve of a man or a measure he is quite likely to say so without reservation. . . . He acts upon his judgment of right and wrong, and it is yet to be shown that he can be intimidated. . . . Those who know him can hardly doubt that he would have preferred standing with the Governor in advocacy of a reasonable measure, to opposing him. It was the innate manhood of the Major which would not allow him to follow the Governor in the University matter. . . .

The Statesman said something a week ago about being 'a man in a man's sized world.' That is what the Major has been so long that he couldn't change now, if he wanted to change.[57]

Fifty-nine years, in fact, was how long ago the Major's mother had validated teenage George's innate manhood by dispatching him to Mississippi to close his older half brother's estate. But as the 1910s passed, George Littlefield became increasingly conscious of a struggle in which manliness provided little guidance. The concerns of aging gripped him ever tighter. But things remained to be done. Watching it all from her room in the Littlefield home, a niece marveled: "I never saw any body fight off infirmity and death with the courage he does."[58]

19

TO ACCOMPLISH WHAT OUGHT
TO BE ACCOMPLISHED

In 1914, about the time George Littlefield's gift of the Littlefield Fund for Southern History brought the Major's appointment to Bennett Young's United Confederate Veterans staff, Phelps White began to worry. Responding to a now-lost letter from Uncle, he concurred that: "Yes of all the fools it is the man that gives away his Stuff before the End comes. So dont do it is all I have to say."[1] In twenty-eight words, Phelps expressed Uncle's last great work—securing the future for family members and institutions meaningful to him. Arraying his substantial estate of cattle, real property, and securities and cash to protect memory, advance education, and provide family support was no fool's errand. For this businessman, it was a responsibility. The time had come to determine what he wanted yet to accomplish and how much of his wealth he would allot to achieving each ambition.

If Phelps had in mind Uncle's continuing donations forwarding the Littlefield Fund's work, then his admonition fell on deaf ears. Uncle enjoyed ensuring the fund's acquisitions. More likely on Phelps's mind was Uncle's talk of disposing of the Yellow House Ranch and retiring from ranching altogether. No doubt he remembered, too, that eleven years earlier Uncle had sold the Driskill Hotel precipitously at a heavy loss just to get the property off his hands. But as much as he lost in absolute dollars, the sale diminished the Major's total worth by only a small degree. In comparison, the Saline, Four Lakes, Mill Creek, and Yellow House Ranch lands and stock constituted just short of two-thirds of the $4.59 million the Major had calculated as his worth in 1910.[2]

Actually, Littlefield had begun reducing his ranching realm in 1909 when he concluded the first of two transactions disposing of the 33,000-acre Menard Ranch in the Texas Hill Country for $277,700. Tom White's death pushed the process along with 1915 sales of the Four Lakes, by then reduced to just 6 townships (138,000 acres), and the T71. The 40,000-acre Saline Ranch with its cattle and horses followed in February 1916 for $600,000. Littlefield got out none too soon,

307

recalled Will's son Walker. The drought of 1917–18 broke the buyer. Observed Walker, "He couldn't skin the cattle as fast as they died."[3]

The last of Littlefield's Central Texas holdings, being his three-fourths interest in the thirty-thousand-acre Mill Creek Ranch, Littlefield turned over in June 1916 to Will White, who had been operating the place since Uncle had acquired it. Not only did Will want to continue the cattle operation, but the Mill Creek land was productive in other ways. Uncle and nephew had been training race and harness horses on a track they had built on the property. And only the fall before, Littlefield called the *Statesman's* attention to production of its ten-year-old irrigated farm. "Some of the finest apples ever displayed in Austin," the *Statesman* gushed. Not missing the opportunity to boost central Texas, the paper even crowed that though Mason County lay far south of apple-growing country, the fruit demonstrated that irrigating its soils could overcome latitude. Concluded the paper, Littlefield "is a 'foxie' farmer, ranchman and producer when it comes to getting results."[4]

One ranch remained. But a bond at the Yellow House made closing out there more difficult and agonizing than had been arranging disposal of his interests in all the other cattle lands. It could have been how much he enjoyed the place. George Littlefield readily admitted he felt physically better on the ranch than in Austin. In part it was the crisp high plains air. Alice did well in it too. In part it was that in the expanse he could vicariously relive horseback days. On one occasion, while he was being driven around inspecting the cattle, a coyote sprang up, startled by the car. Chase him! Littlefield ordered his driver. Away they sped hither and yon, to his pleasure but his National automobile's ruin. Above all, the bond was the connection between him and Phelps (fig. 45).[5]

Uncle, aging and aching, wanted to cash out. Phelps, hardworking and happy, didn't. Their fourteen-year age difference had caught up with them. Parting their interests in the some 250,000 acres of remaining ranch land would test the attachment between them as nothing else had in more than fifty years. Uncle held doggedly to his hope of selling the entire Yellow House Ranch in one fell swoop. Recognizing how elusive the prospect was after several years of trying, still he wrote Phelps in mid-1916 to "write me if I should strike a Sucker, and He would tie up to take all our Yellow House land to net us $12.00 [per acre] and wanted the cattle and Horses what should I do. . . . I now have a Party who has been very successful that want to invest about three or four million dollars in good lands and they say that they might take our land and cattle." Just think of a cash deal: "Phelps if we could clean up at such figures, we could afford to buy 2% U.S. Bonds and quit, look after your children and dabble in only such as showed a profit." Increasingly enfeebled by the advancing pains of rheumatism, aggravated by the lingering effects of a fall on the land office steps in 1915 that occasionally left him so debilitated he could not push himself to write the several letters that characterized his normal business day, Uncle was ready to retire to the life he pictured before Phelps.[6]

For all of his adult years and more, Phelps had followed Uncle's lead. "You Know I made all the plans that have made us what we are," Uncle reminded him. Phelps knew it: "I had nothing to start life on[,] only You to help me on. . . . I have gotten all I wanted at any and all times." That said, Phelps felt himself still in his prime and not at all ready to retreat to a rocking chair on the porch of the grand house he had built in Roswell.[7] For four years they corresponded, sometimes bluntly, without coming to agreement. Will White watched. "I do not know what to think of him," Will told his brother after visiting Uncle late in the back-and-forth. "He got out the map and tried to show me how he waunted to devide the land. I could see that he had all kinds of arguments that he was doing fair. I told him that I knew that you was getting all the bad land. Of course he did not think so." Seeing Uncle's obstinacy, Will advised Phelps to "just do as he says for he will not do any thing else. Then you will have your deed." Commiserating, Will added that Uncle "has always helped me but not for nothing. I have paid dear for all that I ever got and still will have to do so." Whether Phelps felt similarly, he could follow Uncle's lead only so far this time, and he told Littlefield so.

All I ask is that don't sell my land but go on and Sell all of yours at any time you wish. I think I know what is best for me. I care nothing for any money and all I want is to fix up [division of] our land. . . . I was surprised at what you said the Ranch was worth to you as it Stood today. You get the Same as I and I know that [working] my Cattle pays me more than the money I would get out of them would. But that too is all rite. You have your way of seeing things and I have my way.[8]

Just how much working his cattle meant to Phelps could be measured in dollars and cents. He valued it more than his half of the $197,994.30 in 1915 ranch sales. So, after speaking his peace, Phelps agreed to Uncle's division. From it, Phelps got what he so wanted—his own ranch, free and clear. Uncle realized his want only partially. He did eliminate a large undivided interest from his estate. But he was left with more than twenty leagues of ranch land for the sale of which he had little prospect. Paramount to them both, however, the bond that through forty-one years had made them highly effective partners in cattle and trusted confidants in other matters had held firm, and Phelps continued to manage the Yellow House Ranch for them as he always had.[9]

No sooner had Littlefield positioned himself to sell his Yellow House interest at his discretion than he retreated from it. The likelihood of American intervention in the European war loomed. In wartimes, he said, land unencumbered made a better investment than promises to pay.[10] And devaluing any sale would be the bite of the new tax on individual income.

In 1913 the Sixteenth Amendment to the United States Constitution validated the levy of a personal income tax. For a man with holdings as extensive as Little field's, the new tax brought considerable strain. Internal Revenue Service agents audited each of his first three returns. Some questions involved substantial sums, as his declaration of a one-dollar-per-acre profit on the seventy-thousand-some acre Mill Creek and Saline ranch sales. He died before the government finally accepted his claim. Other questions from the IRS collided with decades of custom. The government disallowed his deduction of $3,200 spent to win a $5,000 bet on an election outcome.[11]

After the United States entered the war, on top of the income tax came an excess profits tax. Judging in December 1917 that the two federal levies were exacting about half of the profit from his land sales, the Major took almost all Littlefield Lands off the market, leaving just enough for Duggan to realize some sales income. Though J. C. Whicker's land agent business suffered from the decision, he opined that the Major took the right course. "I do not know how I would feel if I had more money than I knew what to do with," Whicker confided to friend Duggan, "but I expect I would be a little like Mr. Littlefield, I would feel perfectly safe if I had it tied up in such land as he has." Only four months later, after the sales manager left the company to enlist in the Texas National Guard, the Major closed the operation. In just short of six and a half years, the colonization business earned George Littlefield $243,473 after all expenses, including those for securing the railroad. On his books, sales of Littlefield Lands' 20 percent of the ranch acreage returned the Major 30 percent of the purchase price of the entire Yellow House property. Even so, he had to have been satisfied to conclude the land sales business. Equal to the tax consideration for abandoning sales, the profit no longer outweighed the physical burden on him of overseeing the operation's details. Along with the real struggle of managing the office work, visiting the property became an ordeal. "I am afraid of the trip for I am very weak, and don't feel well," he wrote Phelps in November 1917, "but I want to come, and will try to take care of myself."[12]

While Littlefield's outlay to satisfy the federal tax didn't make news, his local taxes did. The September 16, 1915, *Statesman* reported the Major to be the largest individual taxpayer in Travis County, paying $3,809.95 (a scant 1 percent) on an assessed valuation of $388,770. Like its president, the American National Bank received the largest tax bill of Austin's banks for 1916. If the Major gritted his teeth over it, he had to have been pleased too. The American had surpassed its Austin National rival in assessed value. Marking the triumph, he led the board in raising the bank's surplus from $600,000 to $700,000. Only two other Texas banks could stand beside the American in boasting a surplus of 2.3 times capital. No small matter, "the big Surplus shows to the business man that Energy, good Judgement and efficiency is used" in running the American National, he would declare. The board then rewarded stockholders with a remarkable 18 percent dividend, three percentage points above the previous year's high.[13]

For the bank president and building owner, 1916 truly had been a banner year. Workers completed the hundred-thousand-dollar Littlefield Building expansion. Beyond office space, the "commodious annex" and the enclosed roof garden offered features unusual for an office building. A "luxurious Turkish bath" and compressed air connections for physicians distinguished the facility. But George Littlefield was not done. Though he sold the Littlefield Building to the bank on the last day of 1917 for seven hundred thousand dollars, later that year the American National spent seventy thousand dollars to enlarge its space. The new configuration moved the entrance and bronze doors from their commanding position facing the Sixth and Congress intersection to a location fronting Congress alone. His work at the bank at last done and advancing rheumatism affecting his movement so noticeably that his appearance in town made news, Major Littlefield relinquished his active leadership of the institution he had helped found twenty-eight years earlier. At three o'clock on November 12, 1918, he resigned as president. The board immediately elevated him to its chairmanship. Judged by the three center-column spread below the banner head on the *Statesman*'s November 13, 1918, front page, the American National Bank leadership change rivaled in magnitude the previous day's news of the signing of the armistice ending World War I.[14]

As his dividend and ranch and building sales money came in, the Major acquired bonds to underwrite his and Alice's remaining years. America's entry into the European war gave those purchases an additional, important meaning. More than just a personal investment, buying these securities became a patriotic duty. Barely a month after passage of the First Liberty Bond Act at the end of April 1917 to raise money to prosecute the war, President Wilson made national news when he invested $10,000. Only local press reported that George Littlefield contemporaneously dwarfed that by pouring $300,000 into the Liberty Loan. His singular commitment was remarkable against the backdrop of the issue's tepid national reception. His purchase accounted for nearly half of the $685,000 that Austinites invested and vaulted the capital city to first place by dollars' worth sold among

Texas municipalities of similar size. Answering the October 1917 Second Liberty Loan call with another $300,000 singled him out for holding the most Liberty bonds of any Texan.[15]

Patriotic to the core, the Major did not leave his participation in the war effort to financing alone. Nor did he await eventual direct American involvement to take part in elevating the country's military posture. He funded training in a United States Naval Reserve school and contributed to the work of the Navy League and the American Red Cross. In November 1915 he accepted election to the board of the new American Defense Society created to promote a citizen soldiery ready to defend the country. Whatever the old warrior could do, he would do. "Major Littlefield is an ardent believer in preparedness and is working to that end," reported the *Statesman*.[16]

Theodore Roosevelt advocated readiness too. But his was readiness for offensive operations. Americans, the former president of the United States said, should enter the fight in Europe against what he cast as barbaric Germans. But who was American? Not "hyphenated" Americans. German Americans, particularly, were a national weakness, Roosevelt preached. They did not see themselves as totally American, totally loyal, for the simple reason that, by definition, they regarded themselves as having sentiment for if not outright loyalty to two countries. For a bully pulpit for his crusade to push America into the war, Roosevelt seized on the American Defense Society, which had made him its honorary president. And the dynamic hero of the charge up San Juan Hill in the Spanish-American War galvanized the militarist and wealthy conservative membership, Littlefield among them, in rejecting dual loyalties. Where German Americans had been valued in 1914, when Duggan courted the Mennonites, by 1917, no longer.[17]

When the University of Texas Board of Regents met on April 24, 1917, loyalty was the byword. Governor Ferguson spoke of it in personal terms. Most associated it with a country at war. Two and a half weeks before the regents convened, the United States had declared war on Germany. By the time the board gathered, President Vinson had led the school in significant planning for full mobilization of the university's capabilities. Faculty had modified courses. Instruction in military science and tactics was being introduced. Action he proposed for the board to take included offering the school's laboratories in the national service, applying for a Reserve Officers' Training Corps camp, and accepting the faculty recommendation to award full credit to students who had enlisted before completing final course requirements. The board adopted the recommendations and added an action of its own. It terminated all non-Americans, targeting the one German American faculty member who had failed to complete his citizenship application and declared he would not do so while the war raged. Its war work done, members broke for lunch.[18]

Following the board's authorization, President Vinson arranged with the War Department to open a school to teach the rudiments of the newest form of military service—military aeronautics. Texas was one of six universities selected to offer the instruction. One course, uniform across the six schools and lasting eight weeks, would incorporate drill, instruction in officers' duties, map drawing, wireless telegraphy (radio communication), and understanding of airplane engines. Acting with exceptional expedition, Texas began its instruction on May 21, 1917, not a month after the board meeting and less than a week after the consortium of schools agreed on the course's contents.[19]

Sometime between the regents' October 1917 and April 1918 meetings, the War Department approached the university about opening a School for Automobile Mechanics to prepare men for service in another field new to military operations. With the movement of men and supplies in the war zone changing by the substitution of internal combustion vehicles for horses, specialists trained to keep the vehicles running became a need so urgent that the War Department wanted ninety thousand ready within six months. Of the university it asked training for at least 2,500. The regents wanted to accommodate the extreme urgency but recognized themselves with what the *Statesman* politely called a "financial problem." They lacked the $465,000 Vinson estimated they would need. Though the aeronautics school did repay the university some of its costs and the auto mechanics school could be expected to do the same, the federal government offered no subsidy with which to launch the installation. Finding a way to pay for the auto mechanics school the board in April 1918 assigned to the finance committee, chaired since his return to the board the previous September by George Brackenridge.

If the long-generous Brackenridge had been given committee leadership because of his seemingly bottomless reserve of wherewithal to answer university needs, then one other action taken in the April 1918 meeting had greater significance than a simple reading of the minutes tells. Though appearing in a single inconspicuous line, it nevertheless confirmed a major shift in the principal source of external funding for the university's large special needs. The board chairman reversed his September 1917 assignments and in the last substantive action of the day returned George Littlefield to the committee.[20]

Inspiration for the reversal likely had its root in English professor Reginald Harvey Griffith's startling discovery during the 1917 Christmas break. Using the period to search for elusive, rare publications he needed to study to complete a comprehensive bibliography of eighteenth-century English poet Alexander Pope,

Griffith—the same whom Littlefield the previous July had voted to reprimand for leading a student protest against Governor Ferguson—chanced to learn of and gain access to the English literature collection of the late capitalist John Henry Wrenn of Chicago. To his delight, Griffith found items he was looking for. To his amazement, he discovered more riches than he ever expected to find in a single library in America. The assemblage of some 5,300 specially and beautifully bound, mostly first editions from the late sixteenth through the nineteenth centuries, Griffith recognized to be unrivaled in America and hardly matched even in Britain. "With his artistic soul set afire," the professor straightaway described the beauty of his find to President Vinson. Vinson was "greatly moved." Continued Griffith, the university should try to acquire the library. How much would it cost? Circumstances suggested that a half million dollars could secure it. Nearly two-thirds the outlay for running the university for a year, the figure "quickly brought me back to earth," Vinson recalled. Nevertheless, if there were one man of means who would need no convincing of how significantly having this library would advance the university as an institution of higher learning, it was George Brackenridge, the same man who had pledged his all to support the university following the governor's June veto. As Vinson described him, Brackenridge was

> by instinct a scholar. His mental companions were Charles Darwin, Alfred Russell Wallace, Thomas Henry Huxley, Herbert Spencer, John Tyndall, and curiously enough, Isaiah and Paul. He kept their writings by his bed and on his table. He read them and as he used to say "quarreled with them" every day. Any extended conversations with him would always arrive, sooner or later at cosmogony, the origin and evolution of life and its destiny. This was the circle of his thoughts.[21]

On the board, Vinson had the one philanthropist for whom securing this library was a tailor-made task. But the president turned not to him. Instead, he approached George Littlefield, for whom "Mr. Brackenridge's familiars were but names . . . if that." True, the Major did have an interest in libraries, as his continuing donations to the Littlefield Fund showed. And he had amply demonstrated the seriousness with which he took his regental obligation. So, feeling that "nothing attempted, nothing done," the president traveled the seventeen blocks from his office on campus to Littlefield's in the American National Bank.[22]

After laying the proposition before the Major, the president's spirit rose when Littlefield said that were the library all that Vinson described, then yes, the university should acquire it. Did the university have the funds necessary? No, replied Vinson. How the conversation then proceeded, Vinson recounted:

He then asked where I expected to find the money. That question was so direct and pertinent that it sent shivers down my spine, but having gone so far I was determined to see it through, so I took my courage in hand and told him that I had come to see him in the hope that he might find it possible to provide the necessary funds. His answer was, "But that's a lot of money, Doctor." I agreed to this but reminded him that he had always been urging me to make the University first class and that if this library were so beautiful and complete as Dr. Griffith had described it, its acquisition by the University would enable the institution to take a long step in the desired direction. It would give the University possession of a treasure so unique and valuable that scholars from all over the world would, sooner or later, be compelled to find their way to the University of Texas, and our own faculty and students would find in it materials for research of incomparable value. He was thoughtful for a moment and the room was filled with a sound of stillness, and then all tension was removed and all hopes revived when he said, "I don't know whether I have that much cash on hand or not." Picking up his telephone he called his bookkeeper in the bank and asked him to bring him at once a statement of his balance. In a few minutes a slip of paper was laid before him and he immediately wrote a check to my order for $500,000 [actually $225,000] and handed it to me. Having done this, his enthusiasm began to mount until it was soon equal to my own, which was considerable, and he requested me to leave the next morning for Chicago and get the Wrenn Library and if the amount provided should prove to be insufficient for that purpose to let him know and the balance would be forthcoming.[23]

"Probably the largest single check for a similar purpose ever written in this country," submitted one paper. "Princely gift," the *Statesman* characterized the donation on first blush. And so it was when measured in dollars and cents. The purchase price equaled roughly one-third the cost of annual university operations. Moreover, the collection was worth more than the price paid. Some three hundred thousand dollars Wrenn's estate estimated the books would bring if sold singly at auction. But to ensure that the collection would remain forever as the "the Wrenn Library," the estate parted with the volumes for three-fourths of their full value.[24]

"Marks epoch in history of University of Texas," the *Statesman*'s headline in half-inch-tall letters assessed the donation five days later after reporters had reflected on the gift's meaning. "No event connected with the history of the University of Texas is perhaps of more far reaching importance" because "the adding of this collection of books to the University of Texas places it among the world's great libraries." For such a jewel, housing had to be equal to the gem. To have Wrenn's personal architect outfit the rooms designated for the library, Littlefield donated half of the $10,000 the regents appropriated. In a spirit of goodwill, the Major accepted Brackenridge's $8,000 contribution toward the $20,000 cost of an exquisite five-volume limited edition catalog.[25]

Likely the two men most pleased with the Wrenn purchase were Professor Griffith and President Vinson. Griffith was awarded charge of the treasure as the Wrenn's first curator. Vinson had found his new most reliable source of funding for large special needs. Showering his wealth on a library he esteemed only because academics he trusted avowed its value confirmed that George Washington Littlefield had supplanted his rival Brackenridge as the principal to whom the university should turn first in decisive moments.[26]

Decisive moments followed quickly. Not four months after documenting praise for donation of the Wrenn Library, board minutes for June 1918 record that Littlefield was loaning the university some three hundred thousand dollars to permit erecting buildings to accommodate the School for Auto Mechanics.[27] And events precipitating the next decisive moment already were in train. No modest moment this one, the amount would equal the total of the gift and the loan combined.

In January 1918, during a meeting of university presidents in Washington, D.C., at which Vinson secured approval for the Reserve Officers' Training Corps camp the regents had authorized the previous April, the attendees fell to discussing training for radio operators. The value of wireless communication having been recognized by militaries before outbreak of the war, combatants exploited the technology from the conflict's beginning. British front-line positions employed it to warn rear elements of spreading poison gas. German spotters used it to direct Zeppelin bombing. French counterintelligence transmitted erroneous signals to confuse the bombers. Appreciating radio communication's established and growing consequence to warfare, Vinson offered his university to meet the want of operators. The offer should have been especially attractive to the War Department. Unlike with flying and auto mechanics, the university had a history with radio. One of the first two wireless facilities in the state had been constructed on campus seven years earlier (the other was at Texas A&M College). More notable yet, the school already was teaching a course in wireless. Distinct from the brief instruction included in the air school training introduced in the summer, classes in a course designed for men intending to enter military service groomed in radio skills had begun meeting a month earlier, on December 10, 1917.[28]

The university's School for Radio Operators began to take shape with the arrival on March 20, 1918, of its commanding officer. Ten days later enlisted men from San Antonio's Ellington Field arrived to be billeted in B Hall, displacing civilian university students. About two months after instruction began on April 1, the nature of the radio school changed dramatically. The War Department transferred it from the signal corps back to the army's air service. "Now instead of the instruction being along two or three lines as it has been, it will be along the line only of radio operating," the *Statesman* advised readers. Lieutenants replaced civilian instructors. Significant from a funding perspective were the physical facilities required. New buildings for housing and instruction had constituted the bulk of the expense to accommodate the previous two military training operations. But with instruction and drill for the radio school concentrating on communication between ground and air, the installation required also a flying field. Sometime in mid- to late summer 1918, President Vinson went to see Littlefield. One-half million dollars the university needed to purchase some 320 acres south of town and to erect on it Penn Field, a complete facility for training radio operators and all other jobs related to military aviation. "Without the Government's guarantee of replacement or compensation," Littlefield met the request.[29]

Students applauded. Regent Littlefield "made it possible for the University to take the lead of all other educational institutions of the country in the matter of training young men for the Army," the 1919 *Cactus* yearbook declared. The *Statesman* marveled. "Financial assistance" of more than $1 million George Littlefield had provided to the University of Texas within the previous twelve months.[30] Something approaching one-quarter of his wealth the three sums totaled. If Phelps's admonition about giving it all away prematurely weighed on Uncle's mind, Uncle disregarded it concerning the eight hundred thousand dollars for wartime construction. These were loans—investments. If he pondered Phelps's words in that quiet time before writing the check for the Wrenn Library, Littlefield must have concluded that enough would be left, even counting the six thousand dollars he was sending each month to the Davis obelisk project, to answer all the needs he had for distributions in the will he was working to finalize three months later, in July.

George Littlefield continued on the board for another year and a half to the end of 1919. Eight times the board met. The Major was able to attend only three of those meetings. The special meeting of July 21, 1919, had been called to investigate the Texas Senate's grave concern that "we have reached a crisis in the world's history that demands the earnest attention of every citizen who has at heart the welfare of the people and the creation and perpetuation of Democratic Government." Bluntly stated, against the backdrop of the Russian Revolution, "there is now propaganda going on throughout the world which has for its purpose . . . the enthronement of Socialism which is the forerunner of Bolshevism, the arch-enemy of all free government[s], and . . . it is commonly reported that these Socialistic doctrines are being taught in our great Texas State University." After calling on the board to investigate, the senate resolved that any faculty found so doing should be dismissed "to the end that our great University may stand as the exponent of the great principles for which our soldiers fought and died, and which true Americans cherish above all else." The board's investigation showed the allegations to be false. Nevertheless, the regents directed faculty to teach their courses in such a manner that it would be "practically impossible for students of reasonable ability and for the citizens of Texas to misunderstand the attitude of this institution."[31]

Its principal work done, the board opened its agenda to "miscellaneous" items. After consideration of three, the Major asked the privilege of the floor. Would the gentlemen of the board allow him, at his expense, to erect a grand gateway gracing the main entrance—the south entrance to which the main building faced? Before them he pictured a large bronze arch, passage through which would lead to the main building atop College Hill. More than just a simple arch, though, he visualized the span "adorned" with statues of five eminent men—Jefferson Davis, Robert E. Lee, John H. Reagan, James S. Hogg, and Woodrow Wilson. If the Major's proposal erupted in the fervor of the meeting's main business, buried in it no doubt was his intent to thwart any campus move to Brackenridge's riverside tract. Whatever his fellow regents cared of his motives, they joined him in the spirit of the moment. Seizing the opportunity to both distinguish the entrance to the school and set before the university community examples of illustrious Americans, the board "not only granted the permission requested, but voted its very cordial approval of the plan and its sincere gratitude to Major Littlefield for his thoughtful generosity." The day's final substantive business concluded, the board adjourned. And George Littlefield left the board room for the last time.[32]

However spontaneously Littlefield chose the occasion for proposing his gateway, if Pompeo Coppini was right, the Major had begun developing his arch concept sometime after the Hood's Brigade Monument dedication and about the time he was appointed to the board of regents. Nothing came of it in 1911. Five years later, Littlefield had called Coppini to design and erect the gateway for fifty thousand dollars. So insignificant was that amount for the immensity and complexity of the structure Littlefield described that Coppini left the Major before they lost patience with each other arguing about it. Still, Littlefield must have heard the artist's argument. In the will he signed on July 1, 1918, the Major quadrupled the amount for the arch to two hundred thousand dollars. Item 6 in the will both included a sixth figure—Gen. Albert Sidney Johnston, killed at Shiloh where Lieutenant Littlefield received his baptism of fire—and recommended placement of the statues to emphasize the Confederates. Providing that work not begin until three years after conclusion of the Great War, when the cost of materials should have fallen to "a fair level," he apparently had been awaiting the most propitious moment to offer the work to the university and found it in the special meeting of July 21 emphasizing American values.[33]

With the board's approval, Littlefield summoned Coppini. "You know me and I you and I think we could get up something grand for old Texas as well as ourselves," the Major encouraged the artist in offering him the work. Coppini exulted. "The lucky strike," he wrote on the envelope, underlining it. For three if not seven years the sculptor had been waiting for this commission. But by 1919 it meant even more to Coppini than just a commission. "This work of yours should be the means to vindicate myself and prove that I know better," Coppini responded. Vindication from what? Better than what? He didn't say. A strong motive, he admitted to Vinson, was the chance to sow "a healthy seed" he hoped would blossom into that school of fine arts at the university that Littlefield had dismissed years before, saying only the time was not right.[34]

As certainly as Littlefield's goal in the monument seemed to be established by specifications in the will, in fact it remained in flux. In the letter to Coppini, the Major pictured not Jefferson Davis but World War I victor President Woodrow Wilson in the place of honor atop the arch. Neither what the gateway most fundamentally would memorialize nor the amount he would donate to accomplish the work had the Major resolved totally in his mind. The will had quadrupled Littlefield's 1916 figure to two hundred thousand dollars.[35] On the heels of such a large increase, could it not be augmented again? The scene was set for hard feelings to follow.

When he saw Littlefield in his office to talk about the project, Coppini was shocked. The Major "had aged very badly and was using crutches. His leg, that had been shot during the Civil War and that had always been bothering him, was giving away." No matter. They drove to the site for the gateway where University Avenue dead-ended into the campus (fig. 52). Observing the distance to be spanned, Coppini shrank from the job. The structure he envisioned for it would be larger and more costly than the Major acknowledged. Coppini tried to bow out, saying the arch was a job for an architect. No. The statues he wanted in the structure made it the job of a sculptor, Littlefield countered, flattering Coppini by praising his talent. The remainder of their conversation Coppini recalled in his autobiography:

> "But Major," I remonstrated, "look at this ground, at the immensity of space. It has to be something of a large proportion, not to look like a dwarf among all these big trees, and to do that the cost will be far above half a million dollars."
>
> "Now, Coppini, I do not want to hear anymore about that. Two hundred and fifty thousand; that is all I have left to you for this, and I cannot and will not add another cent. I know your ability, your talent; go back to Chicago and study the plan, get estimates, and you will see that we can do just what I have in mind to do."
>
> What else could I say? I left him that very morning. I did not even accept his invitation for lunch, for fear that I might say too much and make him mad again.[36]

Coppini went to work. But two hundred thousand dollars remained restrictive. Would President Vinson help with the Major? "What the Major can afford to do and what he may make up his mind to do" were two different things, Vinson replied matter-of-factly.[37]

In that sentence, Vinson captured Littlefield's struggle over the grand memorial. On one hand, he considered its cost weighed against the other ends set down in his will. On the other, recalled the president, "Of all his gifts to the University that which lay closest to his own heart was the gate to the University campus. He talked about it more, and more feelingly, than about anything else. He gave much thought to the significance and symbolism of this monumental structure. It represented, in a sense, a life-long dream or hope or ambition and he went through much struggle to make it really represent his mind."[38]

Struggle led to frustration. Trying to harmonize outlay and idealism, Littlefield could hardly escape it, as proposals put before him failed to meet his spending cap or his concept or both. Finally, from convalescence in Hot Springs, Arkansas, he exploded: "I don't want Coppini and Vinson to go wild about that work. We can get another Artist besides Coppini rather than have him Skin us on the Job, or we could put it off for a few years, as after my death its left to you [Wroe,] Vinson and Will Hogg to look after." Precisely on this account, Littlefield had put Wroe on the committee to oversee the gateway. "Those university men and Hogg don't care how fine its made, or may cost," the Major asserted.[39] Coppini cared. But his approach only made matters worse. "He wants to go into a contract and We not Know what it might cost to complete the memorial," Littlefield complained in December 1919.

For a man who, as Vinson said, "is able to count dollars just about as accurately as any man of my acquaintance," that would not do, even if it meant the Major would not live to see completion.[40]

Frustration rose in Coppini too. While needing to secure his none-too-flush finances with a contract, he spent money creating plans and models to go with them. Then, out of the blue, apropos only of the artist's relationship with Littlefield, Wroe solicited ten thousand dollars from him. The banker headed the Wroe-Hogg Syndicate project to build Austin's next modern hotel. Located in the block fronting the capitol, with the *Statesman*'s blessing, it was to be named The Littlefield Hotel. Coppini could not refuse but needed the contract to afford the contribution. Quickening his anxiety, through the fall and winter, he lost almost complete contact with his patron.[41]

No wonder. Since late summer, Littlefield's deteriorating health and its treatment left him unable to tend to business for extended periods. "When a man cant walk or get up when down he is in a bad fix," he described his condition in October 1919. Advanced Bright's disease Vinson had assessed as its cause a month earlier. Rheumatism that had bothered him for more than twenty years took its own toll. So much so that he tried any remedy. At the end of November, he had all his teeth pulled in hopes that would help. Adding to his discomfort, he was away from home. "I cant say when we can return to our home," he wrote in January 1920, having missed Christmas in Austin. "There is no place like home, and the better the man the more he loves his home. I have not improved as I expected. Yet, I am going to try it longer, for I do hate to think that I would have to be a cripple and suffer from Rheumatism for balance of my time to live."[42]

Sometime probably around mid-March 1920, Coppini learned that Littlefield had returned to Austin. Desperate to talk with his patron, he wrote saying his newest plans were ready, though assuring Littlefield that if he only reconsidered the earlier, grander (more expensive) plan, "you would not want me to change it for any thing else, as it would be one of the most unique Memorials in the World and would make a great name for you and myself." No answer. Twice more he wrote before hearing that the Major would welcome him. About two weeks later, when he arrived at the front door, a nurse refused him admission on doctor's orders. The next day the rebuff was repeated. And the next. The heirs, Wroe in particular, were against him, he concluded. "Almost delirious, I started pacing the grounds around the house, and in the back of the entrance, when all of a sudden, looking up to the second-floor porch, I saw the Major sitting in a large rocker, braced up by pillows." "Hello, Major," Coppini hollered up, after which the sculptor gained entry.[43]

Coppini laid out figures showing the arch would cost at least $494,000. Too much, Littlefield repeated. Coppini boiled over. But remaining as calm as he could, he addressed the feeble patron frankly. Or so he claimed:

> "Look here," I said. "I have worked hard and spent quite a bit of money in trying to convince you that you could not build a half decent arch memorial for less than a half million dollars. . . . You have forced me into this. . . . I want you now to be reasonable and listen to me, a person who is more anxious than you seem to be, to leave an imperishable good name in connection with this memorial, with which I would not like to have anything to do unless I, too, can make a bigger reputation."[44]

Coppini then told the Major that the symbolism in antiquity of arches as structures through which the defeated were made to pass was un-American and "stupid." In the same blunt tone he continued: "Let me tell you what my honest opinion is as to where you are wrong." As time passed, the Civil War would be seen "as a blot on the pages of American history, and the Littlefield Memorial will be resented as keeping up the hatred between the Northern and Southern states." Many faculty already opposed a Confederate memorial on campus. But Coppini had the solution. World War I reflected a nation united. "Why not dedicate your memorial to the boys of the University of Texas who died so that American democracy might spread all over the world, while also honoring the leaders you most admire as America's great men? Let me build a fountain, a fountain symbolic of the perpetual flowing of American patriotism and American enlight[en]ment?"[45]

After the sculptor finished, "My dear Major remained silent, as if in very deep thought, while I was pacing the floor . . . very much concerned for the outcome." Finally emerging from his silence, George Littlefield spoke "with real emotion":

> Well—you may be right. I always have trusted you, and a few times I have discovered that I have done wrong by not listening to your advice in matters in which you are more competent than I. I do believe that you are my friend and that you are also deeply interested in making a bigger name for yourself, in which case I am also sure to gain, so I will let you have it your way this time. Go back and make the plan you have in mind; but be sure to limit it to the $250,000, as I cannot invest one cent more. Then let us drop the arch idea once and for all.[46]

Maybe it happened as the sculptor claimed to recall with such precision. Maybe it didn't. Coppini's published autobiography reversed the discussions of this March meeting with those of the April meeting during which the contents of the contract were settled.[47] The word "arch" remained in the codicil Littlefield signed the day before he died. Nephew Maurice Dowell disputed that the sculptor first proposed the fountain. Before a Texas State Historical Association audience, Dowell credited Alice Littlefield with it. Returning from a trip to Europe, Dowell offered his step-aunt any of the pictures he had taken. She chose only one—"a remarkably fine one of the Trevi, or Wishing Fountain, in Rome, which she saw and admired when she went to Europe." Putting two and two together, Dowell "always thought our Aunt Alice Littlefield was the inspiration of the fountain project."[48]

However many different influences combined in the concept of the gateway on which Littlefield settled, President Vinson's account of the evolution of the Major's thinking stands to be the most accurate, as he was in touch with Littlefield more frequently than either Coppini or Dowell. While by Coppini's account Vinson played a significant role in turning the Major's thinking to the dual memorial, for his part Vinson clearly was moved by the maturing he observed in that thinking.

> At first it was his purpose to make it a monument solely to the Confederacy, for to a degree unsurpassed by any man I have known, Major Littlefield lived and died in the firm conviction of the righteousness of that cause. It is therefore no small tribute to the qualities of his mind and heart that this life-long conviction came to be included in, if not supplanted by, another which grew out of his observation that the American nation had finally emerged out of the World War as one whole, fused, as it were, in those new fires. He wanted to give physical expression to this thought.

Placement of the memorial gateway held as much significance for George Littlefield as did the symbolism represented in it. Continued Vinson:

> He considered that a university campus was the best place in the world to hold such a memorial to one, united, free nation. I can see him now as he talked about the symbolism of the gate, sitting squarely in his chair, his feet firmly planted upon the floor, gesturing with a pencil in his hand. He talked not only about a memorial to one free nation, but about keeping the nation for the future, both one and free. "Education," he would say, "is the only way to do it. It will be a long and a hard fight but it is sure, and I want to build something on the campus of our University to be a permanent reminder to our boys and girls of Lamar's words that 'Cultivated mind is the guardian genius of democracy.'" That was characteristic of him, even though that quotation is the only one I ever heard him make, for he always was opposed to short-cuts to either wealth or Utopia. He believed in the long way, the hard way. He always considered that the future is long

enough to accomplish what ought to be accomplished and if brought about by the slow processes of education, it would be sound and sure.[49]

On April 20, 1920, Littlefield's committee of the university president (Vinson), an alumnus (Will Hogg), and an executor (Wroe) reached agreement with Coppini on the "Littlefield Entrance Gate." Littlefield inked his signature a month and a half later, on June 9, providing for a memorial to both the Confederacy and winning the World War that materialized not as a gate but as a fountain.[50]

By the time Littlefield signed the contract approving his memorial gateway design, he had left the board of regents in January 1920. But his influence remained undiminished. At the Major's request, Ferguson's successor as governor, William P. Hobby, appointed in his place Littlefield's representative in business matters and successor in the bank, Hiram Augustus Wroe.[51]

Returning to Austin in mid-February after months in Hot Springs, Arkansas, Littlefield had business to attend to. Permitting his health to dictate no short-term outlook, the *Statesman* reported in March and April that Littlefield spent forty thousand dollars for the Congress Avenue property adjacent to the Queen Theater with the intent of spending two hundred thousand dollars to expand the venue into a 1,200-seat auditorium. And he acquired another property on which to build a hotel. Neither required his presence in consummating the purchases. Scheduled to speak at the dedication of the Wrenn Library on March 26, however, he had to call on Wroe to represent him.[52]

As the Major's pleasure in cultivating business opportunities back in Austin rose above his frailty, so did the vigor and compassion that characterized the uncle-patriarch in bringing up nephews in the ranching business. Great-nephew Patrick Henry Boone II had arrived on the Yellow House Ranch in 1918 with saddle and bridle, two good cow ponies, a change of work clothes, and a Sunday suit to accept a ranching partnership with Uncle George. To the arrangement, Boone brought a high school diploma with a medal in track and a year's experience doing hired hand work on his grandfather Bill Littlefield's ranch.[53] Uncle's direction for their partnership was simple: follow Uncle's advice and consult with Phelps. In a cattle sale several months into their relationship, Boone didn't. He took a check. Uncle demanded cash. As he had done through the decades with Will White, Edgar Harral, and others, Uncle minced no words in rebuking his partner: "If you have mind to not follow his [Phelps's] advice when you know I requested it of you, Then you and I had better separate." Lest Boone misunderstand, Uncle added later: "I was anxious to Start you on in safe way, and you must understand if we do business togather and I furnishing the money it must be done in my way."

One other thing, "Don't think you have got to get married then take on yourself additional burthen. You have a mother and two sisters to look after [his father having died four years earlier]. Much better to protect your own than some one else Sister." Boone obeyed. After two years' tutelage, Uncle praised him for having "done exceedingly well with what you have handled." Whether or not on Uncle's admonition, Boone married only after Uncle's death.[54]

Only one pleasure matched that of mentoring nephews, and it was the annual Terry Ranger reunion. On October 12–13, 1920, fourteen of the fewer than fifty remaining veterans met in the Driskill for the association's forty-ninth anniversary. Too feeble to attend, President Littlefield had them to his home. He enjoyed their afternoon together to the fullest. "Those old men, I can hear them laughing now," recalled niece Ruth Key, who as the house manager had prepared their reception. During the business meeting, the veterans elected Littlefield president for the fourth year in a row. And in a sign of great respect, they voted Nathan Stokes a Terry Texas Ranger.[55]

Maybe it was about that time that a neighbor brought his eight-year-old granddaughter to entertain the Major. "Uncle sat there in that big old Morris chair, they called it, and had his cane on there by him," Key recalled. The second of two melodies the granddaughter presented was the ballad "The Blue and the Gray," telling of a mother's grief over the loss of her three sons, two in the Civil War and one in the Spanish-American conflict. Sung three times, the chorus told that:

> One lies down near Appomattox, many miles away,
> Another sleeps at Chickamauga, and they both wore suits of gray,
> 'Mid the strains of "Down to Dixie," the third was laid away
> In a trench at Santiago, the Blue and the Gray.[56]

As the little girl sang, "the tears just rolled down his cheeks. And when she finished, he took that little girl in his arms, and he sobbed like a baby." Overcome with emotion herself, Key left the room. "I'll never forget that," she said softly fifty years later.[57]

On Tuesday, November 9, Major Littlefield had one more business matter to conclude. To account for circumstances and wishes changed since he had executed the first codicil of his will, he signed a second. Then, with his affairs arranged as exactly as he could make them, he lay back.

As night darkened on November 10, lying in his bedroom on the second floor, Littlefield called for nephews and executors H. A. Wroe and Whitfield Harral. Upon his arrival, Wroe asked the attending physician of his uncle's condition. "His pulse is better than it has been for several days now," the doctor said.

"It would seem as though he will make it safely through the night. But he has stated he will not live—that he feels he will not—and sometimes those who are as rational as Major Littlefield is now, can tell of the end's approach better than the physician."[58]

Before retiring to his room on the second floor of the carriage house, faithful Nathan, white-headed and stooped with the weight of his eighty-eight years, went up to see Littlefield. Later "in the night as the last hours came, the Major, a little boy again, called for his old nurse. Nathan because of his deafness failed to hear the summons from the foot of his stairs. In the morning when he awoke his master was dead." Recalling the moment he learned the sad news, Nathan's "shoulders droop and a tear steals down the furrowed brown cheek as he murmurs: 'I ain't never lef' him, but he lef' me.'"[59]

AS EVER YOURS

Final expressions of respect for all that George Washington Littlefield had meant to Austin and the University of Texas dominated Friday, November 12, 1920. The city council adjourned, the university dismissed classes, and merchants closed during the funeral hour. At 10 A.M., the body was taken to the university library to lie in repose for two hours, the first time this ultimate honor had been accorded. At three o'clock, under the gray and threatening sky that marked the day, members of the Austin Commandery, Knights Templar conducted the burial ceremony in Oakwood Cemetery, after which Rev. William Ramseur Minter, pastor of the Southern Presbyterian Church, chaplain of the Terry Ranger organization, and close friend, pronounced the benediction.[1]

When the sun rose the next morning, attention turned to the estate. How big was it? No one knew. "He was a man with such quiet and unoffending dignity that not even his closest friends or relatives had discussed such matters with him," reported the *Statesman*. What distribution had he made of it? The answer made front-page reading a week later. "Maj. Littlefield's estate left to widow," the banner headline, stretching from side to side on the page, told readers. "Bequests to many relatives totaling $1,500,000 cancelled; Great property to be kept intact while Mrs. Littlefield lives; provision made for university war memorial, girls dormitory, and school of American history; some minor legacies made," the subhead elaborated.[2] As accurate as those characterizations of the will were, the paper overlooked the most important passages the effect of which on the university and Austin would be incalculable. Missing them was easy in scanning the will's twenty-three typed pages, plus two codicils of seventeen pages more. The provisions were brief. But George Littlefield inserted them because he knew what would follow if he omitted them and died before George Brackenridge.

President Vinson knew what would follow too. For three years he had been waiting for it, not without sorrow at the prospect of losing Littlefield but with anticipation over opportunity. As Littlefield had talked to him with great feeling about his memorial gateway, so George Brackenridge had talked to him with similar emotion about moving the university to the Brackenridge tract along the river. And not just the ample tract he already had donated: Brackenridge spoke of committing his wealth and energy to tripling the property's acreage and erecting the necessary buildings.[3]

No one disputed that the historic campus had become too small for the demands being made on it. The 1,993 students in 1914 crowded the campus at 50 per acre. Faculty and support staff drove the density higher. Then matriculations exploded, the number of faculty and staff increasing proportionally. The enrollment that had taken thirty years to build to near 2,000 doubled in the following six years.[4]

In fact, university presidents had been talking forcefully about the increasingly cramped space for almost as long as Littlefield had been a member of the board of regents. In 1913, two years after Littlefield joined the board, President Mezes told the regents that "there are now so many [temporary wooden buildings] on the campus that three more [he called on the regents to fund] will not appreciably add to its unsightly appearance. On the other hand, it is impossible, without them, to conduct the work of the divisions concerned with even approximate efficiency."[5]

Mezes's successor, William Battle, spoke more bluntly in 1915: "Serious and pressing as our needs for buildings are, it would be well, in my judgment, for the board to consider first whether we have sufficient land for present use and for a reasonable development. Our present historic campus, noble in its situation and hallowed by the memories of the years, is yet too small for the University of today, and yearly its inadequacy becomes more apparent. . . . It simply is not big enough." Admitting that "the arguments for keeping the University where it is are many and cogent," Battle nevertheless articulated the obvious solution. Move to the Brackenridge donation. "The possibility of a new university there, on a scale truly commensurate with the greatness of Texas, appeals wonderfully to the imagination," he dreamed.[6]

Not in Littlefield's mind. For him, the campus belonged where it had begun, on the ground across the street from the property he had bought specifically to front the university, and nowhere else. The memorial entrance gate blazoned his determination to anchor it there. That said, he understood fully the need and difficulty of expanding the historic campus to accommodate growth. He had been in the thick of board efforts to acquire properties south, east, and north of campus. As of his departure from the board, expansion into those residential areas had eluded the university.[7] The stage was set for a showdown one day.

Maybe not if Brackenridge outlived him. Though ten years Littlefield's senior and suffering health issues of his own, as fate would have it, Brackenridge did outlive Littlefield. And he lost no time in moving to achieve his last, greatest dream. The

Monday after Littlefield's service on Friday, Governor Hobby appointed the San Antonio philanthropist to yet another term on the board of regents (his previous term having ended the year before), and plans were quickly laid for a special board meeting to be convened on January 5, 1921, at his San Antonio home to discuss relocation. For a week Brackenridge and Vinson enjoyed delicious anticipation. Then, to borrow Vinson's phrase from the Wrenn Library purchase, a close reading of the will brought them back to earth.[8]

It began with item 7 of the July 1918 base will that bequeathed the land a short distance north of campus and $250,000, increased in the second codicil to $300,000, for construction of a dormitory to accommodate 150 young women, primarily freshmen, "as they need assistance and protection more than girls who have been in University before them." This bequest carried the specific stipulation, overlooked in the paper's report, "that the property shall revert to my estate if the Main University shall within 21 years after my death be changed from its present location near my home in Austin, Texas." George provided further that this home away from home for young women be named the Alice Littlefield Dormitory as a memorial to his wife. To great nephew Maurice Dowell, that was not just good but right. Alice herself, he believed, had "inspired the idea . . . as I heard her make the statement years ago that a girl during her first year from home needed special care and protection."[9]

Then, item 32 provided that $1 million, subsequently reduced to $500,000, be donated to the university for construction of a main building "on the campus now used and occupied by the said University and nowhere else. . . . This gift is made on condition that the Board of Regents shall pass a resolution that the location of the University shall not be removed from its present position." Item 6 provided $200,000, increased the day before he died to $250,000, to erect "at the south entrance to the campus" the memorial entrance gate. Finally, item 10 of the second codicil bequeathed his $91,500 house to the university, with the stipulation that Alice could live out her life in it.

These bequests, dependent on the university remaining on its historic campus, totaled $1,141,500. As if dedicating more than one-quarter of his $4,159,330 worth to the university was not remarkable enough, one more bequest remained.[10] And the Major considered the accomplishment of that bequest at least as important as the school's location on College Hill. Item 5 of the base will added $100,000 to the Littlefield Fund to continue collecting documentation and books of Southern history and to publish the history of the United States for which he had called in creating the fund. The proceeds from the publication he directed to establishing a chair of American history to perpetuate instruction in this subject so vital to him.

Library acquisitions have built at Texas the largest collection *at a single institution* in the South of documentation on the South, by which to encourage study *of the South* and its part in American history.[11] That said, in contrast to the stipulations the Major placed on other dispositions, the requirement he did *not* place on Littlefield Fund purchases has added value to them. The Major did not require that fund items be maintained as a separate Littlefield collection as were the works in the Wrenn. Available on the library's open shelves, Littlefield Fund acquisitions have enriched beyond measure the library's support of teaching and research.[12]

When Littlefield executor Wroe heard of the proposition to move the campus, he announced that were it to move, the university would lose the entire bequest—$1.25 million. The prospect staggered George Brackenridge, as Littlefield intended, and also possibly shortening Brackenridge's life, opined the San Antonian's biographer. Brackenridge's wealth had shrunk such that if he forced the issue of moving, he could do no more than match Littlefield's largess. But doing even that would mean neglecting his kin. He spoke to President Vinson of writing a new will. But he never did. Then, three days after Christmas 1920, George Brackenridge died. "Whether by intent, default, or carelessness," the biographer concluded, the San Antonio philanthropist himself "spelled the doom of his dream."[13]

President Vinson decided to pursue the move without his money man. Proponents, who assumed that Brackenridge was worth much more than he was, argued for it at the expense of Littlefield's bequests. Opponents called on the legislature, then in session, to secure the Littlefield gifts and solve the space problem by appropriating funds to expand the historic campus. A third set of voices suggested that if moving were such a good idea, bidding for the institution should be opened to communities throughout the state. That proposal immediately united Austinites against the move. In the end, the legislature and governor obliged the opponents. The state provided $250,000 to acquire land for expansion adjacent to College Hill. For better or worse, Littlefield's vision of the University of TEXAS, as he enunciated it, as integral to its community and the people who support it, not as an institution set apart on the periphery, prevailed. And acquisition of expansion property, which had eluded him in life, Littlefield accomplished by his generosity to the university after his death.[14]

In arranging for matters after his death, businessman Littlefield would be expected to plan for a final resting place. He did. But rather than following common practice, Littlefield's design reflected a principal sentiment of his life. After Austin's original burying ground was enlarged, the Major in his prime of life in 1899 took the occasion to acquire half of the summit of Oakwood Cemetery's highest hill. As his time on earth grew short, he earmarked an astounding forty thousand dollars and had sketches drawn for the monument to distinguish the plot and the markers for the graves in it. So great was George Littlefield's grandest monument in the eighty-two-year-old cemetery that delivering the thirty-thousand-pound outsized base slab from the railroad brought out a reporter and photographer. Transporting the massive stone required a special four-axle wagon pulled by four teams. The heaviest drayage movement undertaken in Austin, trumpeted the reporter, unaware of the job of moving the seventy-thousand-pound base slab of the capitol's Terry Ranger memorial. Rather than use Texas pink, the Major obtained (Confederate) gray granite from Vermont. And most significant of all, he specified that, different from almost all the others in the memorial park sited in the traditional east-west orientation, the graves on his plot were laid out north-south, feet to the north (fig. 54).[15]

Alice was the next after George buried on the plot. For slightly more than fourteen years she lived a widow. They were better years than anyone could have expected. George's death had affected Alice in a way totally unanticipated. Though he left his wife with multiple millions for her care, large expenditures did not bring respite from her nervous condition. Ironically, her revival emerged simply from his passing. No longer tormented by uncontrollable worry over his safety, Alice ascended from her anxiety. Her nervous condition ameliorated until negligible, if it lingered at all.

Restored, Alice resumed annual pleasure trips. Accompanied by great-niece Ruth Key, who had moved into the home early in 1919 to manage the household and remain to the end of Alice's days, Alice traveled within the United States and overseas.[16] She returned to her gardening by having a greenhouse constructed on the second-floor balcony, and Key in 1924 planted the deodar cedar that grew to dominate the front yard. Moreover, reminiscent of the way things had been before her condition arose, Alice opened the house to family members. Young children came to spend a week or two at a time; older nieces and nephews dropped by. The Littlefield home returned to being a lively place energized by the family's second and third generations.[17]

To children, septuagenarian Aunt Alice presented a calm but friendly, expressive, and patient presence. She entertained them by telling stories. Well read, Aunt Alice encouraged them to read. Patiently she had each child tell her about the book he or she had most recently completed so as to help the child remember it. At mealtime, she admonished them to put no more food on their plates than they could eat. Punctuating the caution, she added that she knew a community in which diners who failed to eat all of their food had to pay a fine for anything left on their plates. What her price was, young minds wondered. But bravery eluded them. None left a morsel to find out. "Everyone in the family worshipped Aunt Alice," said Alice Dowell Daniel. "I couldn't have loved her more if she'd been my mother."[18]

As Alice Littlefield Dormitory neared completion in 1927, the university asked its namesake for a portrait to grace the lobby. Alice complied, but in a way unexpected. She delivered a portrait not of herself but instead of her mother-in-law, Mildred Terrell Satterwhite White Littlefield. The dormitory should have been named for her, Alice explained, because George's mother had been such a profound influence on him. Though they did not receive the picture they wanted, the university leaders received a gift that said far more of Alice in 1927 than paint on canvas ever could have. That she declined to have her portrait made for the lobby silhouetted how much Alice eschewed ostentation and notoriety in the fifteen years since she had developed her nervous disorder. University president Harry Yandell Benedict even noted in mourning her death seven years after the dormitory opened that "she did not seek, but on the contrary steadily sought to avoid all praise for these benefactions, never, I think, giving even the girls who have lived in the Alice Littlefield Dormitory a chance to thank her in any even semi-public way." At the same time, focusing attention on her mother-in-law confirmed how unreservedly Alice esteemed the family in which she had found stability in life.[19]

Withdrawing from the outside world personally was one thing. Defending her husband's wishes was quite another. In mid-1924 the architect hired to plan the dormitory concluded that the lots provided by the Major across Whitis from the Littlefield Home could not accommodate a building of the size specified in his will. The architect settled on a site that incorporated the former grand Driskill Home, then renamed Driskill Hall and serving as the university's faculty women's club. Regents favored razing the structure to provide for the dormitory. When she heard that, Alice Littlefield put her foot down. The Littlefields and Driskills had been friends, she said, and she would not approve tearing down the historic home. Period. The regents "will have to comply with Mrs. Littlefield's desires in the matter or it [the dormitory] will not be built at all," Wroe told his board colleagues. Unwilling to defy the widow, the architect and regents selected the present site backing on Twenty-Sixth Street between Whitis and University Avenues.[20]

Five years later the memorial gate location came into question. On November 7, 1929, the board voted to site the gateway on the east side of campus. If the Houston highway could be routed by the east side, the Littlefield gateway and the football stadium would make an impressive presence to motorists. Maybe so, but the regents forgot to reckon with Alice Littlefield. Build it where her husband stipulated it be, she insisted, or it would not be built at the university at all. Period. Students petitioned their concurrence. And again the regents reversed themselves.[21]

Three months short of her eighty-ninth birthday, Alice P. Tillar Littlefield died at home on January 9, 1935.

Before the sun set that day, attention turned to her home. The paper's notice of her passing reported that her husband had willed the Texas Victorian masterpiece to the university for a president's home. The matter seemed to have arisen from President Vinson's wishing in 1918–19 that an official residence be provided for him. Who better to fund the purchase on short notice than George Littlefield? No sooner had the board relieved the Major of that call and bought a property than Vinson himself, appreciating the greater need for university housing for women, recommended the new housing be converted for dormitory use. Events suggest that wishing to satisfy Vinson after his selfless act and to provide for future presidents motivated Littlefield to change his will the day before he died, replacing a great nephew with the university as the house's inheritor.[22]

Fourteen years after the Major's death, the university sought possession of its house as soon as the family could clean it out. But not for a president. With the 1936 Texas Centennial looming, the school first utilized the Littlefield home to house the headquarters of its year-long celebration. Kappa Alpha Theta Sorority occupied the building for two years until the music school moved in in 1938. Upon completion of the music building on the South Mall early in World War II, the Naval ROTC arrived, installing a massive steel backstop (still in place) for a rifle range in the attic and protecting the property with antiaircraft and deck guns on the front lawn. The music school returned in 1957, partitioning the once commodious spaces into fifteen practice rooms, fourteen faculty offices, and two classrooms. A decade later, after a complete renovation returned the first floor to a semblance of its as-built appearance, the oldest building on campus was added to the National Register of Historic Buildings on August 25, 1970. In 1998 the university's development office occupied the second floor, leaving the first for university events.

Behind the home, the architecturally matching carriage house was given initially to university broadcasting. Remodeled in 1939 to accommodate Radio House, in 1955 a two-camera chain for rehearsing shows developed in the university's three-year-old television workshop squeezed into Nathan's longtime home. After University News and Information Service's use, a development office unit occupies the building in 2018.[23]

The last interment on the Littlefield plot in Oakwood Cemetery was Nathan Stokes, who outlived his contemporaries all. George provided for every need of "my old war servant," even down to the clothes in which the man who began life as a slave would be buried on the most prominent plot in Austin's oldest cemetery. As Nathan wore outfits that had belonged to the Major, Ruth Key went to the cedar chest for Littlefield's Prince Albert suit. "Uncle had them show it to me—his suit, white shirt, tie, socks, and underwear to always keep, and if I was living when Nath died to be sure and put on him. So I did."[24]

In addition to all of Stokes's living and medical expenses, Littlefield directed that every Saturday he receive his two dollars "war money," a practice Littlefield had begun during the Civil War. Some scoffed at this bequest as being a pittance typical of white men intent on keeping black men in their place. Not John Lomax, who sincerely disliked Littlefield but appreciated the full breadth of his provision for Stokes in life and death. "Hats off to the man who does not forget the lowly," he wrote in his review of J. Evetts Haley's Littlefield biography.[25]

In the background all his life, Nathan Stokes made news in death. No less a paper than the *New York Times* recorded his passing on February 1, 1936, at 105 years of age.[26] (The *Times* neglected George Littlefield's death despite his wealth and spending in support of the country's recent war.) No less an entourage than one of American National Bank officers served as pallbearers with the Reverend Minter officiating. Finally, recognizing the strength and length of the bond between Nathan and George, some whites suggested using Stokes's likeness as the model for a monument to faithful former slaves.[27] Despite the notoriety, George Littlefield's executors failed to execute the Major's wish in marking Stokes's grave. Over it they installed a small, simple block glaringly out of character and harmony with the markers over the other three burials.

Remembering all the members of the extended Littlefield-White family presented a problem thornier to Uncle than caring for his immediate household. "My feeling with them all is of the best but I might have a wrong way of showing it," he wrote late in life, without spelling out what he meant by "wrong way." Though lavishing his generosity on them, he knew what could result from including thirty-nine named individuals. Contention. The prospect troubled him. Since 1911 he had been trying to work it out in two different wills. Five years later he still was toiling "to Straighten out my business, so when I die the Trustees who will Close up my Estate will not be bothered with Contentious persons whom I might name in my will." His generosity with family members, in fact, staunched dispute, even from the niece for whom he included a special provision. Embarrassed by her lifestyle, he directed that she receive her inheritance as a stipend paid on condition that she continue to reside in California (thereby staying out of Texas) for at least nine months of every year.[28]

Sale of the Yellow House Ranch, which had eluded Littlefield in the tight economy of the 1910s, his executors accomplished in the rising good times of the 1920s. "Famous Yellow House Ranch passes out of existence," *Austin American-Statesman* readers learned on January 10, 1924. Some 230,000 of the original 312,000 acres passed into the hands of the Yellow House Land Company, formed to market the grazing land for cotton cultivation. The $3.5 million reportedly paid for this three-fourths of the entire property returned in twenty-three years more than three times the purchase price of the entire ranch and easily funded Littlefield's bequests.[29]

After the American National Bank moved out of the Littlefield Building in 1954 and into Austin's first facility designed to accommodate drive-through banking, the bronze doors and murals became forever separated. The building entered a fifteen-year period alternating between proposed grand renovations and sale. Likely important in ensuring the Littlefield Building's survival was its owner's 1970 decision to bring it into the automobile age by providing a parking garage. Eight years later the Austin City Council recognized the historical significance of its community's finest office building for a generation by zoning it as historic. The bank stored the bronze doors until finally donating them to the university in 1960. In 2018 they can be viewed in the University of Texas System Building in downtown Austin. Apart from three that were sold, the Littlefield murals passed through the hands of successor banks; in 2018 they reside in the JPMorgan Chase Art Collection in Chicago.[30]

The University of Texas shied from significant recognition of Littlefield's beneficence, which had showered on it the largest documented contribution in its first half century, before oil-enriched fortunes and inflation supported larger gifts. A press report in 1924 on the university's endowments did not occasion it. Of the total $176,500 in eleven endowments, the Littlefield Fund, valued at $125,000, stood eleven times larger than the next largest, worth $11,000. The Littlefield Fund's $6,668 annual income accounted for 63 percent of endowment income. *Dallas Morning News* and *Austin American-Statesman* features on Littlefield's unsurpassed total of giving did not occasion recognition. Noting the passing of the Littlefield era with Alice Littlefield's death, Ruth Key's ex-student father wrote members of the board of regents proposing the university name something physical for the Major, say the grand new main building under construction. Maybe Key's proposal caused a totaling for the regents of Littlefield's gifts since 1914. If so, the $1,515,500 figure did not occasion recognition. True, by the time Key wrote, Littlefield's name already identified a prominent campus structure. Littlefield Fountain, his memorial distinguishing the south entrance, had begun flowing in 1933 (fig. 53).[31]

Finally, in 1991, "when The University of Texas at Austin decided . . . to recognize its most generous benefactors through an honorary society, the question arose as to what to call the new organization. One name stood out as an exemplar of the many distinguished individuals who have sustained and advanced the University throughout its history," the development office's website stated. George Washington Littlefield. "Through his gifts and active engagement, he personifies the philanthropic spirit at UT Austin." And so the university named its most prominent donor group the Littlefield Society. Mature reflection on the magnitude of individual giving and the significance of the pledges and gifts to the school through 110 years finally occasioned the university making a significant recognition of Littlefield's beneficence.

A quarter century later, public reference to the Littlefield Society disappeared as the university rethought ways to engage and honor society members. Whether by coincidence or not, it happened in an environment on campus and in Austin that discredited historical figures who had Confederate association or slave ownership in their past. Further in that spirit, in 2017 the university removed from their positions along the South Mall behind the Littlefield Fountain the six statues (two in Confederate uniform, two civilians identified by their Confederate affiliation, two with no Confederate affiliation or slave ownership in their past) that formed the Littlefield Fountain's theme of North and South uniting in the World War I crusade to save democracy. To turn the removal into an educational benefit, the university installed the Jefferson Davis bronze, that had been at the center of calls for removal, in the Briscoe Center for American History. An interpretive exhibit gives a context and meaning to the piece that it lacked on the plinth from which it was removed.[32]

"My Every act was as I saw it for the best," Littlefield summed up his years as regent. The words in fact portrayed the Major's approach to every endeavor in which he engaged—managing plantations before and after the Civil War; leading his men during the war; running cattle ranches from central Texas to the Texas Panhandle and South Plains and eastern New Mexico that branded the distinctive LIT, LFD, and Square Top 3 on thousands of calves per year; directing Austin's American National Bank; overseeing the Littlefield Lands Company; raising memorials to the Confederate cause, which veterans justified later as defense of state's rights, for which he nearly gave his life; and attending to the men and women of the extended Littlefield-White family. To achieve his best, he adhered to the principles he repeated over and over to nephews, great nephews, and any young man who listened.[33]

Do not lets get impatient[,] Economy-Industry, guided by good judgment, will bring all things right for any one. Be honest, and upright. Keep out of bad habbits. And your friends will love you.

Now What Ever you do, let it be done well and Satisfactory. . . . Truth and honesty must prevail, Your word must be good in all things, or Confidence will not exist, and without Confidence no business is Safe.

Now couple those traits [honesty, industry, and promptness in fulfilling promises] with an affectionate heart and Christian disposition and your success is assured . . . And to love and obey your mother gives you a good standing with the best people of the country.[34]

Adhering to these values in his own works, George Washington Littlefield lived as a man absolutely sure of himself.

APPENDIX A
Littlefield, Nance, Satterwhite, and White Genealogies

Lineages display individuals mentioned in the book. Consequently, not all siblings are included. Spouses are included only where the couple had one or more children mentioned in the book.

The meaning of the numbers:
- The number before the decimal is the generation.
- The generation number corresponds across all four genealogies to facilitate seeing relationships. For example, Philip Bryant Littlefield, Shelton White, Margaret "Peggy" Nance, and James Satterwhite II are of the same generation.
- The number after the decimal is the birth order.

LITTLEFIELD GENEALOGY

Generations 1–3

1.1 William Littlefield II
    b. 1756, d. 1836
    m. Rebecca Bryant

    2.1 Philip Bryant Littlefield
        b. 1778, d. 1864
        m. Martha "Patsy" Nance 1805
        b. 1787, d. 1859

        3.1 William Martin Littlefield
            b. 1809, d. 1880
            m. Jane McGarity 1826 (?)
            b. 1803, d. 1890

        3.2 Zachariah Nance Littlefield
            b. 1809, d. 1865
            m. Mary Ann McGarity 1836
            b. 1812, d. 1864

3.5 Fleming "Flem" Littlefield
    b. 1814, d. 1853
    m. Mildred "Milly" Terrell Satterwhite White 1841
    b. 1811, d. 1880

3.6 Oliver Hazard Perry Littlefield
    b. 1816, d. 1893

Generations 3–6

3.5 Fleming Littlefield
    b. 1814, d. 1853
    m. Mildred Terrell Satterwhite White 1841
    b. 1811, d. 1880

    4.1 George Washington Littlefield
        b. 1842, d. 1920
        m. Alice P. Tillar 1863
        b. 1846, d. 1935

        5.1 Edward Rhodes Littlefield
            b. 1866, d. 1867

        5.2 Infant daughter
            b. 1869, d. 1869

    4.2 Martha Mildred Littlefield
        b. 1844, d. 1919
        m. Theophilus "Theo" Eugene Harral 1858
        b. 1837, d. 1880

        5.3 Edgar Fleming Harral
            b. 1864, d. 1956

        5.4 Lula Alice Harral
            b. 1866, d. 1904
            m. James Richard Key 1886
            b. 1864, d. 1936

            6.2 Ruth Key
                b. 1890, d. 1970

        5.6 Whitfield W. Harral
            b. 1871, d. 1938

5.7 Georgia Harral
 b. 1872, d. 1930
 m. Seth Emmett Cole 1899
 b. 1864, d. 1944

5.9 Sarah "Sallie" Elisibeth Harral
 b. 1877, d. 1964
 m. Arthur Pope Duggan 1902
 b. 1876, d. 1935

  6.1 Alice Tillar Duggan
   b. 1903, d. 1995

5.10 Victor Phelps Harral
 b. 1879, d. 1954

4.3 Fleming Littlefield
 b. 1846, d. 1846

4. 4 William Philip Littlefield
 b. 1849, d. 1927
 m. Euphemia K. Mathieu 1871
 b. 1849, d. 1942

 5.1 Mildred F. Littlefield
  b. 1872, d. 1921
  m. Patrick Henry Boone 1890
  b. 1852, d. 1910

 5.2 George Theodore Littlefield
  b. 1874, d. 1942

 5.3 Alice T. Littlefield
  b. 1877, d. 1958
  m. Bernard Wright 1906

 5.5 Euphemia Christina "Christine" Littlefield
  b. 1883, d. 1974
  m. Robert A. Buford 1912
  b. 1881, d. 1942

 5.6 Edna Earle Littlefield
  b. 1886, d. 1969
  m. Rosser L. Malone 1909
  b. 1879, d. 1948

NANCE GENEALOGY

1.1 Zachariah Nance
    b. ? d. 1829

      2.6 Martha "Patsy" Nance
          b. 1787, d. 1859
          m. Philip Bryant Littlefield 1805
          b. 1778, d. 1864

      2.7 John Nance
          b. ca. 1800, d. 1838

      2.8 Fleming B. Nance

      2.9 Mary Nance
          m.——McGarity

      2.10 Margaret "Peggy" Nance
          b. 1793, d. 1835
          m. Flemming Hall
          b. 1793, d. 1832

      2.11 Martha Elizabeth "Patsy" Nance
          b. 1788, d. 1859
          m.——Hall

SATTERWHITE GENEALOGY

1.1 James Satterwhite I
    b. 1758, d. 1810

      2.? Charles Satterwhite
          b. 1783, d. 1869

      2.? James Satterwhite II
          b. 1788, d. 1846
          m. Mildred Wyche
          b. ?, d. 1838

          3.1 Mildred "Milly" Terrell Satterwhite
              b. 1811, d. 1880
              m. John Henry White 1826
              b. 1806, d. 1838

      3.2 James Sanders Satterwhite
         b. 1822, d. 1849

2.? Reuben Satterwhite

2.? Elizabeth Satterwhite
     b. ?, d. bef. 1864?
     m. Frank S. McGuire
     b. 1801, d. ?

WHITE GENEALOGY

Generations 1–3

1.1 Thomas White
    b. ca. 1745, d. aft. 1802

      2.1 Shelton White
         b. 1771, d. 1853
         m. Mildred Clark 1794
         b. 1779, d. bef. 1850

           3.3 John Henry White
              b. 1806, d. 1838
              m. Mildred "Milly" Terrell Satterwhite 1826
              b. 1811, d. 1880

           3.7 David Shelton White
              b. 1814, d. 1859

Generations 3–7

           3.3 John Henry White
              b. 1806, d. 1838
              m. Mildred "Milly" Terrell Satterwhite 1826
              b. 1811, d. 1880

               4.1 Thomas Jefferson "T.J." White
                  b. 1828, d. 1914
                  m Martha Elizabeth Phelps 1851
                  b. 1830, d. 1900

5.2 John Wilburn "Will" White
  b. 1854, d. 1939
  m. Cora Jane Bridges 1891
  b. 1867, d. 1951

  6.5 Walton Walker White
    b. 1905, d. 2002
    m. Virginia McGaha 1929
    b. 1907, d. 2000

5.3 James Phelps White
  b. 1856, d. 1934
  m. Lou Lee Tomlinson 1903
  b. 1879, d. 1972

  6.1 James Phelps White Jr.
    b. 1904, d. 1987
    m. Mary Beers 1927
    b. 1905, d. 1970

    7.1 James Phelps White III
      b. 1932

  6.3 George Littlefield White
    b. 1908, d. 1978

5.4 Thomas David White
  b. 1859, d. 1914

5.5 Ida White
  b. 1862, d. 1954
  m. Robert Hamilton Walker
  b. 1858, d. 1930

  6.1 Jennie Knox Walker
    b. 1888, d. 1983
    m. Benjamin F. Harless 1914
    b. 1876, d. ?

5.6 Sarah Z. White
  b. 1865, d. 1944
  m. James M. Murphy Jr.
  b. 1858, d. 1926

5.7 Pearl White
    b. 1868, d. 1918
    m. Hiram Augustus "Gus" Wroe 1898
    b. 1867, d. 1943

      6.1 Ed Rhodes Littlefield Wroe
         b. 1899, d. 1961

5.9 Edna Hildegarde White
    b. 1874, d. 1937
    m. Marion W. Hodges 1896
    b. 1867, d. 1936

4.3 Sarah "Sallie" Zalinda White
    b. 1832, d. 1869
    m. Greensville Dowell 1849
    b. 1822, d. 1881

    5.1 John Henry White Dowell
       b. 1850, d. 1917

    5.2 Shelton "Shelt" Clark Dowell
       b. 1853, d. 1885
       m. Elizabeth Harriette "Lizzie" Gillespie 1879
       b. 1855, d. 1934

      6.4 Maurice Hood Dowell
         b. 1884, d. 1944

      6.5 Dora Alice Dowell
         b. 1885, d. 1947

    5.3 Alice Mildred Dowell
       b. 1855, d. 1941
       m Irwin Daniel 1890
       b. 1858, d. 1909

4.4 David Shelton White
    b. 1834, d. 1863

4.5 John Henry White Jr. (called himself "Senior")
    b. 1836, d. 1929

    5.1 Rosalie H. White
        b. 1857, d. 1943

    5.2 John Henry "Little Johnny" White III
        b. 1858, d. 1942

    5.3 Sarah Gertrude White
        b. 1876, d. 1907

4.6 Charles E. White
    b. 1838, d. 1866

APPENDIX B
Capt. George W. Littlefield's Route over the Chickamauga Battlefield, September 20, 1863

Three accounts tell the story of Littlefield's ride.[1] The earlier two, published by Lewis E. Daniell in 1890 and 1918, twenty-nine and fifty-five years after the event, and approved by Littlefield, give similar details from which Littlefield's route can be deduced. The third, published in 1924, four years after Littlefield's death, reports the emotion that one person heard him express about the ride.

Six clues from Littlefield's accounts in the Daniell works identify his likely route:

(1) *Who gave him the order.* The accounts record that at division headquarters Littlefield received the order "to move back over the battlefield" to secure a ford. Both accounts mention corps commander Gen. Joe Wheeler by name, not division commander John Wharton. Had Wharton delivered the order, surely Littlefield would have indicated it. Littlefield and Wharton had been well acquainted at least since Littlefield's promotion incidents of May 1862. Most likely, then, Wheeler personally gave him the order.

(2–3) *The time and location that he received the order.* Littlefield reported receiving the order at night. As night fell, Wheeler and the main body of his corps, including Wharton's Division with the Eighth Texas, had entered the Chattanooga Creek Valley in pursuit of Union wagons and supporting troops that had abandoned the large Federal hospital complex at Crawfish Spring (present-day Chickamauga, Georgia). Heading for Chattanooga, the Federals had taken the road west over Missionary Ridge and north down the valley. On this route, they kept Missionary Ridge between themselves and the battlefield's congested roads. By his account, about two hours after dark Wheeler broke off his pursuit and sent the bulk of Wharton's division back to its camp of the previous night at Rock Spring. To have received his order from Wheeler, Littlefield had to have begun his ride somewhere in the Chattanooga Creek Valley about the time that Wheeler concluded his pursuit and dispatched Wharton to return to his camp far south of West Chickamauga Creek. Had the order come from Wharton at the Rock Spring camp, Littlefield could have reached his assignment without having to cross West Chickamauga Creek at all, and certainly without having to travel a portion of the Chickamauga Battlefield.

(4) *Where he crossed West Chickamauga Creek.* The accounts indicate that Littlefield's order instructed him to cross from north to south at a ford guarded by the Fourth Georgia Cavalry. The Fourth Georgia was stationed at the Glass Mill Ford, a location the Rangers knew well from fighting the previous day.

(5) *The distance he traveled.* In the third account, Mrs. Samuel Posey recollected Little-field having reckoned his ride to have covered twelve miles.

(6) *The engagement at the ford the following morning.* After the wagon train and its sup-port whose passage Littlefield was to stop arrived the following morning, Littlefield engaged its advance elements until General Wharton overwhelmed the defenders. Wheeler's after-action report documents the location as being Owen's Ford.

In summary, Littlefield must have received the order about two hours after dark in the Chat-tanooga Creek valley, when Wheeler abandoned his pursuit of the fleeing Federals. The most direct route from Wheeler's location to Littlefield's assignment would have been returning to Crawfish Spring by the way he had come and from there taking the road to Glass Mill Ford. The morning fighting along this route occurred not in the Chattanooga Creek valley but between Crawfish Spring and Glass Mill Ford. This engagement threw five thousand Confed-erate cavalry, including the Eighth Texas, against four Federal regiments (about nine hundred men) and a two-gun battery. The battery retired without loss of horses or guns. The afternoon fight was a much lesser engagement and occurred north of Glass Mill Ford, away from the Crawfish Spring–Glass Mill Ford road. Even taken together, these encounters could not be considered what Littlefield described as "one of the hardest fought fields of the war." Nor did they result in death and wounding sufficient to produce the sounds that Littlefield described as "the screams of the mangled artillery horses made the night hideous with their heart-rending appeals for relief. Everywhere lay the wounded and dying and the slain of both armies."

Consequently, to have seen and heard on his way to the Glass Mill Ford what he said he saw and heard, Littlefield had to travel some part of the Dry Valley Road east of Missionary Ridge, on the west side of the battlefield. To reach the Dry Valley Road through unfamiliar terrain in the dark, he had to have followed a distinguishable path over Missionary Ridge. The most northerly track intersected the Dry Valley Road just below McFarland Gap and would have taken him by the Vittetoe place, in the vicinity of which he would have encoun-tered the aftermath of the afternoon's terribly desperate and bloody fight for possession of the western end of Horseshoe Ridge. The middle trail hit the Dry Valley Road in the mile or so stretch between the Vittetoe place and the burned-out Widow Glenn cabin. On this portion of the Dry Valley Road, he would have traveled ground over which Confederate forces had driven Federal troops after the breakthrough earlier in the day.

The southern trace reached the Dry Valley Road at the Widow Glenn's where that afternoon John T. Wilder's Union Brigade's repeating rifles turned the exuberant charge of the Twenty-Fourth and Twenty-Eighth Alabama regiments into bloody and disorganized flight. By whichever route he reached the Dry Valley Road, Littlefield's travel would have taken him by Bloody Pond, the only water of consequence north of Crawfish Spring. For nearly twelve hours, wounded who could manage it had been taking themselves to the fetid cattle pool to drink, many to die. At Crawfish Spring, he passed again the extensive remains of the large Union hospital complex where more than one thousand wounded littered the ground. Instead of continuing down the road from Crawfish Spring directly to Owen's Ford, Littlefield had to turn east to reach Glass Mill Ford to cross to the south side of West Chickamauga Creek. This would take him by the scene of the morning's fight, in which he had participated, where the dead and wounded continued to lie where they had fallen.[2]

APPENDIX C
George W. Littlefield's American National Bank Ranching Art

HISTORY

To decorate his American National Bank in the new Littlefield Building, George Washington Littlefield commissioned art depicting his LFD cattle, the land they roamed on the Texas and New Mexico high plains and in New Mexico's Pecos River valley, and the LFD cowboys and cowmen working their charges. In those three essential components of land, animals, and men, Littlefield ensured that he would have art that was at once unique to his ranch and universal to ranching. The art is unique, too, in that Littlefield's is the only such visual celebration and historical record commissioned by one who participated in, indeed led events of, the open-range and early fenced ranching periods.

Though Littlefield likely gave no thought to the place of murals in American art, his commissioning of expansive paintings to illuminate the bank's walls mirrored the mainstream. Proclaimed contemporary muralists, mural painting at the turn of the century represented a new American aesthetic. John LaFarge's murals for Trinity Church, Boston (1878), launched the new creative form, and the paintings gracing buildings of the World's Columbian Exposition in Chicago (1893) that Littlefield attended advanced it. Stated contemporary muralist and teacher Kenyon Cox, "in no field have American artists more decisively taken their own way than in this of mural painting, in none have they produced an art more their own." Beyond simply reflecting the mainstream, commissioning murals fit the spirit of the times perfectly. Mural themes constituted "statements of America's unlimited and virtuous powers of industry" and in so doing took their place in "educating the Public in national history, values, and morals in order to spur on national intellectual development," added prominent contemporary muralist Edwin Blashfield. In animating the bank's grand lobby in the tallest building between New Orleans and San Francisco, the Littlefield murals were at home in every way.[1]

Six paintings enlivened the walls on August 15, 1911, when the bank hosted a reception to show off its new quarters. With the single exception of a view of an apple orchard at harvest time on the LFD Farm near Roswell, they pictured blooded cattle and horses in their native pastures. In a 1915 booklet marking the bank's silver anniversary—Pearl C. Jackson's *Austin Yesterday and Today*—a seventh mural of horses and a mule at a hay crib is pictured on a wall. Since two versions exist of two of the initial six murals, artist E. Martin Hennings actually produced nine separate paintings.[2]

Contrary to the 1911 booklet published on the occasion of the bank's opening, not all of the murals were painted from photographs. Octavia F. Rogan's June 4, 1916, *San Antonio Express* feature story, written from a lengthy interview with Littlefield, reported that only four of the six were so copied. The two LFD Farm scenes of the apple orchard and the cattle in the field with the artesian fountain, then, were done from life.

Though the photographs from which Hennings worked have not been located, snapshots taken by Jesse (Mrs. Hamlin) Hill, the Yellow House Ranch Foreman's wife, of preparations for scenes depicted in the murals date Littlefield's interest in commissioning artwork for the bank to 1908.[3] One photograph that she taped over the opening day booklet picture of the "Pride of the Herd" captures Hamlin Hill cutting the big bull for his portrait. Two others show cowboys managing horses in a rope corral and on a drive.

When the American National Bank left the Littlefield Building in 1954, the murals were removed from the walls, rolled up, and stored. In the late 1980s, after the bank passed from family hands, becoming successively part of M Bank, Bank One, and JPMorgan Chase, three of the murals were sold, three continued in bank hands, and three disappeared.

THE PAINTINGS

Titles are known for only four of the murals (marked by asterisks), all of which are pictured in the opening day booklet.

Cattle on the Move*

Hennings painted two versions of this scene, the difference between them being the hides of four animals. Figure 29 presents all Herefords (Albritton Collection), while figure 30 shows a cow near the left side, the two nearest the viewer, and the one coming into the scene from the right with mottled hides reminiscent of the longhorns with which Littlefield entered the cattle business. The all-Hereford mural on the wall at the bank's opening was positioned over the massive vault door (fig. 31), behind which three sets of time locks guarded the books vault and two sets secured the cash vault, on the inside of which another time lock protected the money chest, further marking it as one of Littlefield's favorites. In both views, showing the animals' left side saved the artist from having to brand any of them. Mrs. Hill's photograph of a similar scene (fig. 32) shows the cattle moving in a thinner line than Hennings pictured.

Pride of the Herd*

Hennings painted two versions of the herd's largest bull, one with the animal standing alone (JPMorgan Chase Art Collection), the other with a cowboy holding its halter (fig. 33). Mrs. Hamlin Hill's photograph of her husband cutting the bull for his portrait dates the scene's composition to 1908 (fig. 34). Since Mrs. Hill's photograph shows the bull to have been on the Yellow House Ranch, it is clear that Hennings took artistic license to make the setting visually more appealing.

The Round-Up*

In *The Round-Up* (fig. 35; Albritton Collection), the white-shirted figure having just thrown his loop is ranch foreman Hamlin Hill. Mrs. Hill captured a photograph of this scene too (fig. 36).

Thorough-Breds*

Thorough-Breds (fig. 37; Albritton Collection) pictures well-tended horses on the LFD Farm.

Cattle on the LFD Farm

This mural (fig. 38; JPMorgan Chase Art Collection) depicts cattle lazing in the tall grass of the LFD Farm, oblivious to an exaggerated artesian water spout.

Horses and Mule at Hay Crib

This seventh mural (fig. 39; JPMorgan Chase Art Collection) is documented on the wall only in the bank's silver anniversary booklet.

Apple Orchard at Harvest Time on the New Mexico Ranch near Roswell

Neither this mural nor a picture of it in its entirety has been located.

BRONZE DOORS

After considering an agricultural motif illuminating the foundation on which the bank rested, Littlefield switched to a ranching theme to harmonize with the murals enlivening the banking room's walls. Scenes of men, cattle, and the place that was at once the most important single location and the most dramatic landscape of Littlefield's ranches constitute the imagery on the massive doors, which stand 10 feet, 4 inches tall, span 6 feet, 9 inches when closed, weigh 2.5 tons, and cost $4,000 in 1911 (fig. 40).

In the top panels, Littlefield displayed his ranch leadership. Reproducing, the earliest image of any Littlefield operation, taken in 1883 (fig. 10), the left panel pictures managers Phelps and Tom White at the Bosque Grande headquarters. To the right, posed in 1910 and to an extent representing overlapping generations, are Yellow House Ranch foreman Hamlin Hill and New Mexico top hands Bud Wilkinson and Will McCombs.

Cattle well-proportioned and content fill the two bottom panels. These are not just the first animals the photographer or the sculptor happened upon. Littlefield was too particular about his cattle for that. While he approved of the specimens captured in the photographs provided to Harry Daniel Webster, he nevertheless instructed his sculptor to study the animals grazing on the Four Lakes Ranch and substitute any that exhibited better lines.[4] No doubt the bottom right scene pleased Littlefield, especially because some of its cattle are standing in a wet-weather lake filled knee deep by good rains.

The drama of men managing cattle at Mescalero Spring animates the middle panels (fig. 42). In picturing the panorama, Webster had to divide the scene with the vertical stile members. So skillfully did he meet the challenge that only someone familiar with the scene will notice that Mescalero Spring itself is not pictured. It lies behind the decorative rivets and the astragal. No matter. The stream watering robust, thirsty cattle watched by Bud Wilkinson on the left and being driven in by Ham Hill on the right unites the companion panels. Finally, emphasizing the trail Littlefield traveled twenty-eight years earlier to have his first look at the expansive eastern New Mexico plains, Webster included a detail still common to large ranches in the early twentieth century—the hoodlum wagon carrying bedrolls and supplies.

No longer flowing and far off the beaten path in 2018, Mescalero Spring lies beneath the grove at center (fig. 41). The trail descends the caprock from the dip in the rim above the grove and bends around the spring. As on the doors, the streambed runs off the picture to the right. The photographer's position is perhaps twenty yards below sculptor Webster's.

For all his powers of observation, Daniel Webster missed one essential matter. And when the bronze doors arrived in Austin, George Littlefield noticed. Not one animal was branded. For a rancher who enjoyed seeing his LFD brand so much that he had it engraved on the bull being gored in the delicate fighting bulls statuette, Littlefield straightaway hired engraver Minnie Allen to sink "LFD" into every animal whose right side was exposed. Allen didn't stop there. She branded the horses—both hips—though the LFDs put the Bar F only on the left. She even marked the hoodlum wagon (fig. 44).[5]

The piece de resistance of the doors is their handles (fig. 43). Two steers' heads, suitably haltered with a bronze rope, bid welcome and guard the bank entrance.

The American National Bank donated the doors to the University of Texas in 1960, and they are displayed for the public in the University of Texas System Building.

NOTES

INTRODUCTION

1. Robert E. Vinson, "The University Crosses the Bar," *Southwestern Historical Quarterly* 43 (January 1940): 284.

2. See Matthew Josephson, *The Robber Barons: The Great American Capitalists, 1861–1901* (1934; repr., New Brunswick, N.J.: Transaction Publishers, 2011), 75–120, 363; Richard White, *The Republic for Which It Stands: The United States during Reconstruction and the Gilded Age,*

1865–1896 (New York: Oxford University Press, 2017), 2–7, 655–75; Larry Tye, *Rising from the Rails: Pullman Porters and the Making of the Black Middle Class* (2004; repr., New York: Henry Holt, 2005), 1–29, 70–71, 98–99.

3. Littlefield to Maurice Dowell, September 11, 1894, Littlefield Letters, Dolph Briscoe Center for American History, University of Texas at Austin, and Texas State Archives (hereafter LL).

4. Walter L. Buenger, "Texas Identity: Alternatives to the Terrible Triplets," in *This Corner of Canaan: Essays on Texas in Honor of Randolph B. Campbell*, ed. Richard B. McCaslin, Donald E. Chipman, and Andrew J. Torget (Denton: University of North Texas Press, 2013), 21.

5. Ibid., 22.

6. J. Evetts Haley, *George W. Littlefield, Texan* (Norman: University of Oklahoma Press, 1943), viii (quotation); Eugene C. Barker to JEH, February 7, 1938, Alice Duggan Gracy to JEH, November 14, 1943, Papers and Correspondence Re: Book, J. Evetts Haley Collection, Nita Stewart Haley Library, Midland, Tex. (hereafter JEHC).

7. J. Frank Dobie, "Having His Own Way," in *Cow People* (New York: Little, Brown, 1964), 271.

8. T. U. Taylor, "Major George W. Littlefield," *Frontier Times* 13 (September 1936): 575; Octavia F. Rogan, "Converts Cattle into Gold to Give Nation True History of War," *San Antonio Express*, June 4, 1916. See also David B. Gracy II, "Cows Have Calves: The Hesitant Beginning and Remarkable Career of Cowboy, Cattleman, Rancher George Washington Littlefield," *West Texas Historical Review* 89 (2013): 8–26.

9. In his *Life and Literature of the Southwest* bibliography (available at Project Gutenberg, www.gutenberg.org/files/314/314-h/314-h.htm#link2H_4_0022), Dobie included several rancher biographies and even Haley's *The XIT Ranch of Texas and the Early Days of the Llano Estacado* (Chicago: Lakeside Press, 1929); Haley, *George W. Littlefield*, 3 (quotation).

10. Fred A. Bailey asserted in "The Best History Money Can Buy: Eugene Campbell Barker, George Washington Littlefield, and the Quest for a Suitable Past," *Gulf South Historical Review* 20 (2004): 29; Fred Arthur Bailey, "The Textbooks of the 'Lost Cause': Censorship and the Creation of Southern State Historics," *Georgia Historical Quarterly* 35 (Fall 1991): 507–33, and "Free Speech and the 'Lost Cause' in Texas: A Study of Censorship and Social Control in the New South," *Southwestern Historical Quarterly* 47 (January 1994): 453–79.

11. Bailey, "Best History Money Can Buy," 29; Eugene C. Barker to Editor of the Nation, May 1, 1914, Eugene C. Barker Papers, Dolph Briscoe Center for American History (hereafter BCAH), University of Texas at Austin; Ernest William Winkler to Littlefield, May 7, 1914, Littlefield Fund, George Washington Littlefield, Papers (hereafter GWL), BCAH. See, for example, Librarian's Report on Expenditures for the Littlefield Collection for Southern History [1918] in GWL.

12. Marilyn McAdams Sibley, *George W. Brackenridge: Maverick Philanthropist* (Austin: University of Texas Press, 1973), 245.

13. Ed Cravens to the author (hereafter DBG), interview, January 29, 1970; Alice Duggan Gracy to Sharon Wallace, interview, June 17, 1982, Winedale Historical Center Collection, Alexander Architectural Archives, University of Texas at Austin; Lewis E. Daniell, *Types of Successful Men of Texas* (Austin: E. Von Boeckmann, 1890), 352. The eye follows viewers as they move before the painting.

14. Harrison McClure to J. Evetts Haley (hereafter JEH), interview, September 22, 1935 (first quotation), Dudley K. Woodward to JEH, interview, January 14, 1939 (second quotation); Tom H. Wells to DBG, June 11, 1964, Littlefield File, author's collection (hereafter cited as DBGC).

15. Alice Gracy to Wallace, interview, June 17, 1982 (first quotation); Jeff Connolly, "Hit the Trail in High Places," in J. Marvin Hunter, comp. and ed., *The Trail Drivers of Texas* (1924; Austin: University of Texas Press, 1992), 188–89 (second quotation).

16. *Austin Statesman*, April 29, 1919; *Houston Chronicle*, May 12, 1919; Hunter, *Trail Drivers*, 5–7.

17. W. F. Cody to Joe Booth, November 11, 1908, Niles-Graham-Pease Collection, Austin History Center; *Austin Statesman*, April 29, 1909.

18. Littlefield to Oscar Porter Littlefield, December 3, 1918, Leona Littlefield, Roots Webpage, March 20, 1998 (removed after her death in 2015); Ruth Key to DBG, interview, January 26, 1970; Alice Daniel to JEH, interview, July 18, 1939.

19. John Wilburn "Will" White to JEH, interview, October 18, 1935 (first and third quotations); S. E. Cole to JEH, interview, January 23, 1939 (second quotation), Alice Daniel to JEH, interview, July 18, 1939 (fourth quotation); Jennie Walker Harless to DBG, September 13, 1970, Littlefield File, DBGC. A nephew said it was the same with dominoes (Edgar Harral to JEH, interview, June 13, 1939).

20. Key to DBG, interview, January 26, 1970; Jennie Harless to DBG, October 6, 1970, and Ruth Pennybacker to DBG, April 27, 1970, in Littlefield File, DBGC; McClure to JEH, interview, September 22, 1935.

21. Jennie Harless to DBG, October 20 (quotation), November 12, 1970, Woodul to DBG, April 5, 1971, both in Littlefield File, DBGC; Key to DBG, interview, January 26, 1970; Alice Gracy to DBG, interview, more times than I can remember; Edgar Harral to JEH, interview, June 13, 1939; Alice Daniel to JEH, interview, July 18, 1939; Edward Crane to JEH, November 15, 1943, Book Wallet 1, JEHC; Maurice Hood Dowell, ["George Littlefield Reminiscence"], Dowell-Littlefield Collection, Houston Metropolitan Research Center, Houston.

22. *Austin Statesman*, May 19, 1901 (first quotation), November 10, 1920 (fourth quotation); *Austin American*, October 16, 1916 (second quotation); Rogan, "Converts Cattle" (third quotation).

23. Maurice Dowell to JEH, January 18, 1937, in Maurice Dowell Letters, JEHC; Walter E. Long to DBG, interview, May 18, 1968; Key to DBG, interview, January 26, 1970.

24. Alice Gracy to DBG, interview, July 4, 1973 (first quotation), Edmunds Travis to DBG, interview, June 9, 1971; Harral to JEH, interview, June 13, 1939 (second quotation), McClure to JEH, interview, September 22, 1935; John A. Lomax, "Review of *George W. Littlefield, Texan* by J. Evetts Haley," in *Southwest Review* 29 (Spring 1944): 440 (third quotation); Rogan, "Converts Cattle."

CHAPTER I. TROUBLES ENOUGH

1. George W. Littlefield to John W. Dowell, September 1, 1868 (first quotation), August 10, 1869 (fourth quotation); Alice M. Dowell to John Dowell, July 18, 1869 (second quotation); Shelton Dowell to John Dowell, July 31, 1869 (third quotation); George W. Littlefield to John H. White [Jr.], September 26, 1868, LL. Hereafter, "Littlefield" will identify George W. Littlefield. All other Littlefields will be cited with first names.

The 1869 flood stood as the worst in Gonzales's recorded history until the 1913 flood eclipsed it by six inches (Gonzales County Historical Commission, *The History of Gonzales County, Texas* [Dallas, Tex.: Curtis Media, 1986], 94).

2. Littlefield to John White, September 26, 1868, LL; Littlefield to John White, September 12, 1869, John H. White Jr. Family Papers, Betsy Anne Springfield Lindstrom Papers hereafter (BL); George Washington Littlefield, "Autobiography," 1919, transcription DBGC; McClure to JEH, interviews, September 22, 1935, January 14, 1938; Thomas J. White to Littlefield, July 7, 1868; T. E. Harral to Littlefield, October 6, 1868, Deed Book Q, 367 and 504, Gonzales County Clerk; Daniell, *Types of Successful Men*, 351.

3. Littlefield to John White, September 26, 1868, LL (quotation); Randolph B. Campbell, *Gone to Texas: A History of the Lone Star State* (New York: Oxford University Press, 2003), 274–83; Robert A. Calvert, Gregg Cantrell, and Arnoldo De León, *The History of Texas*, 3rd ed. (Wheeling, Ill.: Harlan Davidson, 2002), 155–65; Roger A. Griffin, "Pease, Elisha Marshall," *Handbook of Texas Online*.

4. Rogan, "Converts Cattle into Gold."

5. Littlefield to John White, September 12, 1869, BL (first and second quotations); Littlefield to John Dowell, September 1, 1868, LL; Littlefield, "Autobiography," 1919; Taylor, "Littlefield," 575 (third quotation).

6. McClure to JEH, interview, September 22, 1935. I have not repeated McClure's use of the then-common derogatory word for black people.

7. This account relies on the recollections of McClure and Will White (to JEH, interview, October 18, 1935; to Brockman Horne, interview, September 9, 1936, Nita Stewart Haley Memorial Library, Midland, Tex. [hereafter HL]). See also Charlie Walker to JEH, interview, August 7, 1937. White said that Littlefield's first shot hit Watson in the arm, spinning him away from the tree. A second shot killed him as he tried to regain the safety of the tree (Will White to Horne, interview, September 9, 1936). John H. Watson's headstone establishes the encounter's date as March 13, 1871 (Charles Kimes, Coe Valley Cemetery, Gonzales County, Tex., U.S. Genweb, http://files.usgwarchives.net/tx/gonzales/cemetery/coe.txt).

8. Littlefield's memory may have inflated the figure. Dun and Company's correspondent reported on June 7, 1871, that Littlefield had less than half that—only $1,500 (George W. Littlefield, Farmer and Trader, R. G. Dun and Co. Credit Report Volumes, Vol. 11, Gonzales, 175, Baker Library, Harvard Business School). For prices the sellers hoped for and Littlefield evidently realized, see James Cox, *Historical and Biographical Record of the Cattle Industry and the Cattlemen of Texas and Adjacent Territory* (Saint Louis: Woodward and Tiernan Printing, 1894), 90.

9. McClure to JEH, interview, September 22, 1935 (first quotation); Littlefield, "Autobiography," 1915 (second quotation); Littlefield, "Autobiography," 1919 (third quotation); William Littlefield to George Littlefield, Property and Cattle, Deed Book R, 434–35, Gonzales County Clerk; Donald Emmet Worcester, *The Chisholm Trail: High Road of the Cattle Kingdom* (Lincoln: University of Nebraska Press, 1980), 15–16; William Curry Holden, *Alkali Trails: or, Social and Economic Movements of the Texas Frontier, 1846–1900* (Dallas: Southwest Press, 1930), 29; Edward Everett Dale, *The Range Cattle Industry: Ranching on the Great Plains from 1865 to 1925* (Norman: University of Oklahoma Press, 1960), 42–43; Mary G. Ramos, "Cattle Drives Started in Earnest After the Civil War," *Texas Almanac*, http://www.texasalmanac.com/topics /agriculture/cattle-drives-started-earnest-after-civil-war.

10. John Dowell to Littlefield, May 9, 1917, James Phelps White Papers (hereafter JPW); McClure to JEH, interview, March 25, 1937, cited in Haley, *Littlefield*, 54–55; Gonzales County, District Court, Journal Book D, 398, 474, 513 (Gonzales County's only record of the trial).

11. Charles Lynch, twice governor of Mississippi, reformed the penal code to reduce the number of death penalty offenses (David G. Sansing, "Charles Lynch, Eighth and Eleventh Governor of Mississippi: June to November 1833; 1836–1838," Mississippi History Now, http://mshistory .k12.ms.us/index.php?s=extra&id=114). No court records preserved in the Mississippi Department of Archives and History (hereafter MDAH) document this case, and ordering a killing seems out of character for him.

12. Greensville Dowell, "Autobiography," Texas State Archives, 41–42, 105–6 (both quotations); George W. Littlefield to ADG, August 26, 1961, February 11, June 12, 1963, Oklahoma Littlefields, Alice Duggan Gracy Papers (hereafter ADG). It is curious that Dowell, who knew Fleming well and professed to record in his autobiography only plain facts, chose to describe Littlefield through the eyes of a third party and to repeat rumor that depicted Fleming in the worst light. Perhaps Carroll's acrimony reflected a loan agreement gone bad. Carroll advanced Littlefield $1,700 in exchange for a deed of trust to a half section of land (Fleming Littlefield to William H. Carroll, Mortgage, November 24, 1846, Panola County, Chancery Clerk, Sardis, Deed Book F, 86; William H. Carroll and Eliza Jane Carroll to Fleming Littlefield, Deed [of Trust], November 20, 1846, Deed Book F, 100). No resolution is recorded. The 1845 Personal Property tax roll for Panola County shows Carroll and Littlefield possessing comparable wealth (Panola County, Tax Roll, Personal assessment, 1845, MDAH).

13. Philip Bryant Littlefield Genealogy in Maxwell Littlefield Genealogy Documentation, DBGC; Alice Duggan Gracy, "Fleming Littlefield," ADG. Fleming himself—born May 16, 1814, and the first in the Littlefield line to have this name—could have been given it in honor of either or both Fleming B. Nance, his mother's brother, or Flemming Hall, his mother's brother-in-law (husband of her sister Margaret) and apparently the uncle of Robert Hall to whose place in Texas Littlefield traveled after departing Mississippi. See Zachariah Nance, Will, August 1, 1828, Will Book B, Probate Court, Union County, South Carolina, 135–37; Ann Littlefield Coleman to DBG, November 21, 2012.

14. In 1836 Mary McGarity married Philip's second son, Zachariah Nance Littlefield. Her sister, Jane, had married Philip's oldest son, William Martin Littlefield, in 1826 (Maxwell, Littlefield Genealogy Documentation, DBG).

15. Perhaps Nance family patriarch and planter Zachariah Nance's death further loosened remaining bonds (Zachariah Nance, Will, August 1, 1828, Will Book B, Probate Court, Union County, South Carolina, 135–37; Coleman to DBG, September 10, 2012).

16. Philip Littlefield v. John Nance, Union District Court; State of South Carolina v. Philip Littlefield, Union District, Peareson, October 1826; John Nance, Arson, Criminal Case file 992, 1828, all in Union County, General Sessions Court Records, South Carolina Department of Archives and History, compiled in Coleman to DBG, September 26, 2012; Carroll County Commissioners Court, Minutes, March 12, 1827, Minute Book 2, 1826–1833, Carroll County, Tenn., Courthouse; Philip Littlefield enumeration in United States Census, Population, 1830, Gibson County, Tenn.; Coleman to DBG, September 10, 2012, May 21, 2013; [John Monroe Littlefield], "Supplement to 'The Life of Major George W. Littlefield,'" [1944], in Oklahoma Littlefields, "Tradition Says," in Littlefield, Geo W., Parentage, ADG; David B. Gracy II, "George Washington Littlefield: A Biography in Business" (PhD diss., Texas Tech University, 1971), 12–15.

17. *The Lynx*, January 18, 1845, quoted in Lula Mae Fowler, "A History of Panola County, 1836–1860" (master's thesis, University of Mississippi, 1960), 15 (quotation); Dowell, "Autobiography," 106; Mississippi State Census, 1841, Panola County; Combined Tax Rolls, Panola County, MDAH; Maxwell, Littlefield Genealogy Documentation; Zachariah Littlefield, Gibson County, Carroll County, Tennessee, Early Tax List Records (available on Ancestry.com). If C. C. Littlefield's obituary is correct that Zachariah moved to Panola County in 1838, barely two months after C. C.'s birth, Zachariah avoided paying county taxes in 1839 (Captain C.C. Littlefield, Obituary, Gonzales File, ADG).

18. Her second child, James L., had died in 1838, not yet eight years old (John Henry White genealogical chart, Littlefields—Mississippi, ADG).

19. Dowell, "Autobiography," 106 (quotation); Probate Court Minutes, Chancery Clerk's Office, Sardis, 79; Bertram Wyatt-Brown, *Southern Honor: Ethics and Behavior in the Old South* (Oxford: Oxford University Press, 2007), 226–53; Anne Firor Scott, *The Southern Lady: From Pedestal to Politics, 1830–1930* (Chicago: University of Chicago Press, 1970), 4–79; Patricia Garrett Iverson, comp., "White and Allied Families of Virginia, Elbert County, GA, North Mississippi, and Beyond" (Roundup, Mont.: Patricia Garrett Iverson, 2007), 39; United States Census, 1840, Population, Carroll County, Tenn., Philip Littlefield; Oliver Hazard Perry Littlefield in Maxwell, Littlefield Genealogy Documentation, DBGC; Kenneth M. Stampp, *The Peculiar Institution: Slavery in the Ante-Bellum South* (New York: Vintage, 1956), 37–42. O.H.P.'s father, Philip, owned two slave women in 1840.

20. Dowell, "Autobiography," 106. In his reminiscent work, *The Pavilion: Of People and Times Remembered, Of Stories and Places* (New York: Charles Scribner's Sons, 1951), 22–25, Panola County native Stark Young tells a story of Uncle David White's confrontation with the overseer who secretly married his daughter and its aftermath. The tale is said to have been inspired by the rancor boiling from Mildred's and Fleming's marriage.

21. [George Rockingham Gilmer], *Sketches of Some of the First Settlers of Upper Georgia, of the Cherokees, and of the Author* (1855), 6 (quotation) (available on Ancestry.com); Ellis Merton

Coulter, *Old Petersburg and the Broad River Valley of Georgia: The Rise and Decline* (Athens: University of Georgia Press, 1965), 8–30; Genealogical notes in Wyche Family folder, ADG; Wyatt-Brown, *Southern Honor*, 117–25.

22. Satterwhite family Bible, BL. See also: D. M. Satterwhite, "Satterwhite Family History with Ancestors Names," DBGC. For biographical sketches, see David B. Gracy II, "Mildred Satterwhite Littlefield (1811–1880)" in *Women in Early Texas*, ed. Evelyn M. Carrington (Austin: Jenkins Publishing, 1975), 163–67, and Alice Duggan Gracy, "Fleming Littlefield," in *History of Gonzales County*, 395–96.

23. John Henry White was his wife's mother's first cousin. Though only five years older than his wife, he was a generation ahead of her genealogically. He traced his paternal ancestry to his great-grandfather John White (1695–1788), who arrived in Virginia from England in 1717. Whites fought in both the Revolutionary War and War of 1812. John Henry's grandfather Thomas became wealthy and left tidy sums to his children (Iverson, "White and Allied Families," 2, 20–22, 29–31; Patricia Garrett Iverson to DBG, April 7, 2012).

24. Five children followed in biennial succession: James L., 1830–38; Sarah Zalinda, 1832–69; David Shelton, 1834–64; John Henry Jr., 1836–1929; and Charles E., 1838–66 (Iverson, "White and Allied Families," 40; Charles E. White, Pennsylvania, Philadelphia City Death Certificate, available on FamilySearch.org; and Philadelphia, Pennsylvania, Death Certificates Index, available on Ancestry.com).

25. John H. White and Milly Satterwhite, Marriage License, December 19, 1826, Satterwhite Family Bible, BL; Elbert County, Georgia, Will Book, 1825–29, 409; Wyatt-Brown, *Southern Honor*, 203–4, 251–52; Monroe Lee Billington, *The American South: A Brief History* (New York: Charles Scribner's Sons, 1971), 75. Of John Henry White's siblings whose marriage dates are known, two sisters and his brother, David Shelton White, wed when fifteen years old (Iverson, "White and Allied Families," 36–41).

26. Charles Satterwhite to James Satterwhite, October 26, 1834, C. B. Spencer Collection, BCAH; Satterwhite, "Satterwhite Family History"; Coulter, *Old Petersburg*, 120, 167–70; Ray Allen Billington, *Westward Expansion: A History of the American Frontier* 2nd ed. (New York: Macmillan, 1960), 320–24. U.S. Census, 1820, Population, Elbert County, Ga., 161, shows the James Satterwhite and Shelton White families as neighbors. U.S. Census, Population, 1830, Wilcox County, Ala., lists only Reuben Satterwhite.

27. Sections 33 and 34, Township 6 South, Range 8 West, about five miles west of present-day Como, Miss.

28. Iverson, "White and Allied Families," 36, 39–40, 130–31; Mississippi State Census, 1837, Pontotoc County, MDAH; U.S. Census, 1840, Population, Pontotoc County and Panola County, Miss.; John S. McGehee and Malinda McGehee to John H. White and James Satterwhite, Deed, April 7, 1837, Deed Book B, 252, Chancery Clerk, Panola County, Sardis; Fowler, "History of Panola County," 1–26. In the 1830 census, John Henry White possessed eight slaves (U.S. Census, 1830, Slave Schedule, Elbert County, Ga.).

29. Iverson, "White and Allied Families," 39.

30. Littlefield, George W., Parentage file; John M. Littlefield to ADG, interview, May, 1954, Oklahoma Littlefields, ADG.

31. Billington, *American South*, 101; William Kauffman Scarborough, *The Overseer: Plantation Management in the Old South* (Baton Rouge: Louisiana State University Press, 1966), 196–98.

32. Panola County Probate Court, Sardis, Minutes, October 18, 1841, Book A, 73–74, 79–80, 82, 87–88, 115, 247; Book B, 330; Panola County Tax Rolls, 1842–44; Wyatt-Brown, *Southern Honor*, 255. Fleming may have acted first. On the 1842 county tax roll, he alone of the three declared a weapon—a Bowie knife, one of only seven in the county.

33. Panola County, Circuit Court, Sardis, Minute Books: November 1843–April 1847, 27, 57, 62, 68, 96, 103; April–October 1846, 15–16; April 1847–May 1848, 257–61, 271–73, 383, 622–25; October 1847–May 1849, 77–79, 345.

34. Gracy, "Fleming Littlefield"; Photograph of Fleming Junior's grave in Heaton Research, Littlefields—Mississippi, ADG.

35. The spelling and source of her maiden name are unclear. Her mother did not include it on Sarah's funeral notice. "Zalinda" was the spelling given her granddaughter. "Zelinda" appears on a copy of an 1854 appointment of attorney she and her husband executed. Though "Zelinda" was the only known contemporary spelling, it is unclear whether this was her spelling. (Sarah Zelinda Dowell and Greenville Dowell, Appointment of Attorney, January 16, 1854, Deed Book I, 574, Gonzales County Clerk; Zalinda Gertrude Dowell, Funeral notice, 1884, in Dowell family Bible; Dowell, "Littlefield Reminiscence").

36. Dowell, "Autobiography," 41.

37. Ibid., 106–10; W. H. Alexander, "History of Panola County," *Southern Reporter*, November 7, 1963; Greensville Dowell, Petition for Divorce, March 21, 1859, Case 2349, District Court, Brazoria County, Tex.; Dowell Family Bible, cited in Haley, *George W. Littlefield*, 10n6; Inci A. Bowman, "Dowell, Greensville E.," *Handbook of Texas Online*. The Dowell family Bible quoted in Haley was subsequently lost.

38. James S. Satterwhite, Will, December 18, 1849, Panola County, Sardis, Will Book A, 76–77; Dowell, "Autobiography," 112.

39. Victor Harral to ADG, interview, January 19, 1944, DBGC; Maurice H. Dowell to JEH, interview, March 24, 1937, December 6, 1941; Rosalie White West to Louise Heaton, interview, January, 1941, in Heaton Research, Littlefields—Mississippi, ADG. Harrison McClure said he heard Mildred Littlefield say that a political disagreement brought matters to a head (McClure to JEH, interview, January 14, 1938).

40. For some, the rancor long outlived the parties to it. Mississippi native and professional researcher Louise Heaton wrote nearly a century after the Littlefields departed: "Now, I am going to tell you frankly, why you are having such a time with the Littlefield [research]. My father came from that county, and I have often heard of this." After recounting the White-Satterwhite objection to Mildred's marriage to Fleming and the assassination attempt, she added that "due to a division of land, there is a feeling that exists among relatives now, and so one gets data [only] here and there, in bits" (Louise Moseley Heaton to ADG, January 24, 1941, Heaton Research, Littlefields—Mississippi, ADG). See also Taylor Pointer to ADG, interview, September 19, 1970, Littlefields—Mississippi, ADG. Stark Young published *The Pavilion* about the time that Heaton wrote.

CHAPTER 2. LIKE A MAN

1. Brazos, *The Life of Robert Hall* (1898; repr., Austin: State House Press, 1992), xi–xiv, 3–36; A. Ray Stephens, *Texas: A Historical Atlas* (Norman: University of Oklahoma Press, 2010), 135–37; "Oak Forest," in *History of Gonzales County*, 165; Harral to Alice Gracy, interview, January 19, 1944. If Hall received Littlefield at Oak Forest, as Harral said, it must have been at a King home. In mid-November 1850 the census reported Robert Hall to be living on Sandies Creek more than ten miles south (U.S. Census, 1850, Population, Gonzales County, Tex.).

2. Frederick Kemp Dixon, "A History of Gonzales County in the Nineteenth Century" (master's thesis: University of Texas, 1964), 5–7, 14, 22–23; Dorcas Huff Baumgartner and Genevieve B. Vollentine, "Gonzales County"; Stephen L. Hardin, "Gonzales"; Craig H. Roell, "DeWitt's Colony"; and Craig H. Roell, "Linnville Raid of 1840," *Handbook of Texas Online*; Campbell, *Gone to Texas*, 187, 207; James L. Rock and W. I. Smith, *Southern and Western Texas Guide for 1878* (Saint Louis: A. H. Granger, 1878), 73–75; Brazos, *Life of Robert Hall*, 60; *Gonzales Inquirer*, June 4, 1853. Subsequent boundary changes placed the Plum Creek Battle site in present-day Caldwell County.

3. Baumgartner and Vollentine, "Gonzales County," *Handbook of Texas Online*; Fowler, "History of Panola County," 22, 25–26, 29, 40.

4. Frederick Law Olmsted, *A Journey Through Texas; or a Saddle-Trip on the Southwestern Frontier* (New York: Dix, Edwards, 1857), 234; Dixon, "History of Gonzales County," 7, 46–49.

5. George W. Littlefield was well known for giving nicknames to members of his family (see introduction). With no basis in genealogy but showing respect for an elder, Phelps White called John Chisum "uncle" (J. Phelps White to JEH, interview, March 2, 1933).

6. That Victor Harral meant *the* Bob Hall is clear from Harral's reference to Cousin Bob's distinctive fur hat. Described in *Life of Robert Hall*, the hat was "composed of very many pieces of pretty fur, and ornamented with a pair of antelope horns."

7. Thought when the sale was closed to total 1,760 acres, after the property was surveyed, it turned out to be only 1,470 acres (John Oliver Jr. to Fleming Littlefield, Deeds, June 11, 1851, Book H, 56; December 9, 1852, Book J, 145, John and Nancy Cooksey to Littlefield, Deed, June 18, 1851, Book H, 54, all in Deeds, Gonzales County Clerk).

8. Tax rolls, 1851, 1852; Index to Marks and Brands, Inventory of Fleming Littlefield Estate, January 31, 1853; Fleming Littlefield, Will, January 3, 1853; and Codicil, January 4, 1853, Cause 293, Probate Records, all in Gonzales County Clerk; F. Littlefield in R. G. Dun and Co. Credit Report Volumes, Volume 11, Gonzales County, 164; McClure to JEH, interview, September 22, 1935, January 14, 1938.

9. When he registered to vote in 1867, George Littlefield declared he had lived in Texas for sixteen years (1867 Voter Registration Lists, Texas State Archives, available on Ancestry.com).

10. Walter W. Walker to JEH, interview, August 7, 1937; McClure to JEH, interview, September 22, 1935; Property statement in Noah Webster, *An American Dictionary of the English Language* (Springfield, Mass.: George and Charles Merriam, 1855), C. B. Spencer Collection, BCAH; Captain Charles W. Allen, Interrogation, n.d., Case 2349, Brazoria County District Court; Charles W. Allen, U.S. Census, 1860, Population, Belmont, Gonzales County, 96; David S. White, Promissory Note, October 28, 1853, Cause No. 267, Probate Records, Gonzales County Clerk.

11. Mrs. R. H. [Ida White] Walker to JEH, interview, March 29, 1937 (first quotation); Walter Walker to JEH, interview, August 7, 1937 (subsequent quotations); McClure quoted in Haley, *Littlefield*, 13–14. Walter Walker was the son of the Littlefield's family doctor (Charles and Walter Walker to JEH, interview, August 5, 1937).

12. Fleming Littlefield, Will and Inventory of Estate, Cause 293, Probate Records, Gonzales County Clerk.

13. McClure to JEH, interview, September 22, 1935; Elizabeth York Enstam, "Women and the Law," *Handbook of Texas Online*.

14. Caroline Merrick quoted in Wyatt-Brown, *Southern Honor*, 230, 226–71; Scott, *Southern Lady*, 3–44.

15. U.S. Census, 1850, Slave Schedule, Panola County; Panola County Tax Rolls, 1840, 1841; Inventory of Estate, Fleming Littlefield, Gonzales County Clerk, Probate Records; Wyatt-Brown, *Southern Honor*, 255. Their combined wealth in real estate, slaves, and agricultural production as they left Mississippi placed them in the upper 20 percent of Southerners economically (Mrs. R. H. [Ida White] Walker to JEH, interview, March 29, 1937; Walter Walker to JEH, interview, August 7, 1937; U.S. Census, 1860, Population, Gonzales County, Tex., Mildred T. Littlefield; Gracy, "George Washington Littlefield," 25–26).

16. Charlie Walker to JEH, interview, March 5, 1937. An example of her management of family affairs is in Mildred T. Littlefield to John White, March 8, 1860, BL.

17. Mrs. R. H. [Ida White] Walker to JEH, interview, March 29, 1937. Judging by the date of a power of attorney, Mildred left Panola County in mid-November 1850, shortly after the census taker's visit (Mildred T Littlefield to Green Bowldin, Power of Attorney, November 16, 1850, Deed Book H, 109, Chancery Clerk, Panola County, Sardis). Littlefield family memory is that Philip Littlefield added his family to Mildred's entourage (John M. Littlefield, "A Supplement to the 'Life of Major George W. Littlefield,'" ADG).

18. Mrs. R. H. [Ida White] Walker to JEH, interview, March 29, 1937; Rosalie White West note, 1933, C. B. Spencer Collection, BCAH; Betsy Anne Springfield Lindstrom Genealogy,

ms., BL; Greensville Dowell, Petition for Divorce, March 21, 1859, Case 2349, Brazoria County District Court; Littlefield, "Autobiography," 1919; Wyatt-Brown, *Southern Honor*, 241.

19. Mildred Terrell Littlefield to Mr. and Mrs. Darst, June 4, 1854, quoted in Annie Reese, "Famed Letter," *Gonzales Inquirer*, June 4, 1953; Walter Walker to JEH, interview, August 5, 1937.

20. Charles R. Matthews, *Higher Education in Texas: Its Beginnings to 1970* (Denton: University of North Texas Press, 2018), 166–67 (quotation); "Gonzales College," *Handbook of Texas Online*.

21. *Sixth Catalogue of the Trustees, Faculty and Students of Baylor University, Independence, December, 1857* (Independence: Baylor University, 1857), 23 (first quotation), 24 (second quotation), 11, 29–30; *Catalogue of the Trustees, Faculty and Students of Baylor University, Female Department, Independence, Texas, for the Year 1857* (Independence, Tex.: Baylor University, 1857), 8, 10, 14, 18; Lillie M. Russell and Lois Smith Murray, "Baylor University," *Handbook of Texas Online*; Guy Bryan Harrison to Alice Duggan Gracy, February 1, 6, 1962; John M. Littlefield to Alice Gracy, interview, May, 1954, ADG, Littlefield, "Autobiography," 1919; Gracy, "George Washington Littlefield," 10–11; Daniell, *Types of Successful Men*, 345; Matthews, *Higher Education in Texas*, 163–69. Philip Littlefield joined Belmont's Mount Hope Baptist Church (*History of Gonzales County*, 73).

22. Littlefield, "Autobiography," 1919; Charles E. White to John H. White, Deed, March 1, 1859, Deed Book M, 456, Chancery Clerk, Panola County, Sardis; Mildred T. Littlefield to John White, March 8, 1860, BL; Iverson, "White and Allied Families," 41.

23. Littlefield, "Autobiography," 1919; U.S. Census, 1860, Slave Schedule, Gonzales County, Mildred Littlefield.

24. Mildred T. Littlefield holdings recorded in U.S. Census, 1860, Population and Slave Schedules, Gonzales County. See also John H. White to George Littlefield, Deed, July 30, 1868, Deed Book Q, 397, Gonzales County Clerk. Having married in 1858, daughter Martha Mildred Littlefield and her husband had charge of her property.

25. Littlefield, "Autobiography," 1919 (first quotation); Littlefield to John Dowell, June 25, 1869, LL (second quotation); Key to DBG, interview, January 26, 1970; *History of Gonzales County*, 121–23; "Gonzales College," *Yesterdays* 16 (September 1981), 15–16 (March 1982), 84–87; V. R. Cardozier, "Higher Education," *Handbook of Texas Online*. George Littlefield read neither avidly nor widely beyond business publications and books about successful men.

26. One who knew recalled that Alice so disliked her middle name, Payne, that she refused to use it (Dot B. Fraser to Alice Gracy, February 22, 1944, ADG). For an extended biography of Alice Tillar Littlefield, see David B. Gracy II, "Alice P. Tillar Littlefield: Her Life," DBGC.

27. McClure to JEH, interview, September 22, 1935; Harrell [Harral] and Son, R. G. Dun and Co. Credit Report Volumes, Vol. 11, Gonzales County, 162; Alice Gracy, "Whitfield Harral Jr.," ADG; Theophilus Eugene Harral and Martha Mildred Littlefield, Marriage License, July 9, 1858, Gonzales County Clerk; Gracy, "Alice Littlefield"; "City Population History from 1850–2000," Texas Almanac, texasalmanac.com/sites/default/files/images/CityPopHist%20web.pdf.

28. Gracy, "Alice Littlefield"; List of United States Citizens arriving Honolulu, Hawaii, on the ship *Malolo* on May 19, 1928, on Ancestry.com. As with her middle name, Alice evidently wished to conceal the community of her birth. Where all other passengers declared the town and state of their nativity, she gave only the state. The town of Emporia clearly was divulged later, as it is typed on the form in a different font.

29. Dowell, "Autobiography"; Mississippi Masonic Lodges, http://www.icrr.net/lodgelist1.htm; Jeanne Hand Henry, comp., *1819–1849 Abstradex of Annual Returns: Mississippi Free and Accepted Masons* (New Market, Ala.: Southern Genealogical Services, 1969); Morris Terry to DBG, interview, n.d. Panola County has two courthouses, one north, the other south of the Tallahatchie River.

30. George Littlefield to Alice Tillar, January 24, March 2, 1861, Alice Littlefield Papers, Gracy-Littlefield Collection (hereafter ALP). See Gracy, "Alice Littlefield." (Hereafter, "Alice" will identify Alice P. Tillar Littlefield. Other Alices will be identified by their full names.)

31. Greensville Dowell, Petition for Divorce, March 21, 1859 (first quotation), January 26, 1860; Sarah Dowell, petition, April 4, 1860, in Greensville Dowell vs. Sarah Dowell, Case 2349; Dowell, Petition, February 16, 1861; Sarah Dowell, Answer to petition, April 14, 1861, in Greensville Dowell vs. Sarah Dowell, Case 2473, Brazoria County District Court; Sarah Zelinda Dowell and Greensville Dowell, Appointment of Attorney in Fact, January 16, 1854, Deed Book I, 574, Gonzales County Clerk; James B. Sharp and Co. (Greenville Dowell, Wm. B. Morris), Dry Goods, Monthalia, Dun and Co. Credit Volumes, Vol. 18, Panola County, 64; Littlefield to Lizzie H. Dowell, January 9, 1890 (second and fourth quotations); Mildred T. Littlefield to Children, September 15, 1860 (third quotation), LL; Mildred T. Littlefield to John White, March 8, September 1, 1860; Littlefield to John White, April 14, 1861, BL. Greensville and Sarah Dowell offered substantially different dates for his trip to Gonzales. Greensville said 1857, only a few months after his wife left. Sarah recalled 1859. Four months after losing his case in October, 1860, Dowell filed again. This second divorce petition was granted. Eight or nine years passed before the property claims were finally settled.

CHAPTER 3. THE "SISING" OF MINIÉ BALLS

1. Mildred Littlefield to John White, September 1, 1860, BL; Donald E. Reynolds, *Texas Terror: The Slave Insurrection Panic of 1860 and the Secession of the Lower South* (Baton Rouge: Louisiana State University Press, 2007), 1–50; Robert Pattison Felgar, "Texas in the War for Southern Independence, 1861–1865" (PhD diss., University of Texas, 1935), 13–14, 22–23; Campbell, *Gone to Texas*, 240.

2. Alf Satterwhite to JEH, interview, January 14, 1938 (quotation); Mildred Littlefield to John White, September 1, 1860, August 19, 1861, BL; Baumgartner and Vollentine, "Gonzales County," *Handbook of Texas Online*.

3. Sallie Dowell to John White, November 19, 1860 (quotations); T.J. White to John White, December 1, 1860, BL; Campbell, *Gone to Texas*, 241–44; Stephens, *Texas: A Historical Atlas*, 168–70; *History of Gonzales County*, 36.

4. Littlefield to John White, April 14, 1861, BL. If George's uncle Zachariah Littlefield, who had followed his brother Fleming to Texas, typified the family, he opposed secession, then pledged his loyalty to Texas after secession (Frank W. Johnson [Eugene C. Barker, ed.], *A History of Texas and Texans* 4 vols. [Chicago: American Historical Society, 1916], vol. 4, 1670–1671). Charles David Grear, *Why Texans Fought in the Civil War* (College Station: Texas A&M University Press, 2010), 13–28, describes Littlefield's motives exactly in relation to slavery. Defense of his former home was not the motivation Grear contends in discussing Terry's Rangers (81–85).

5. Littlefield to John White, May 20, 1861, also April 27, 1861, BL; Felgar, "Texas in the War for Southern Independence," 64–65.

6. Littlefield to John White, May 20, 1861; David S. White to John H. White, April 15, 18, May 16, 1861, BL.

7. "Uncle Nathan Talks of Major Littlefield," *Austin American-Statesman Magazine*, October 14, 1928 (first quotation); Dowell, "Autobiography," 12. This is the only instance reproducing Nathan's manner of speaking. Nathan and his mother were common property until Fleming willed them to Mildred, who gave Nathan to George. Nathan said he had been born in Mississippi, and his Stokes surname indicates not in a Littlefield community. Though Nathan was unclear as to the year of his birth, his statements to census takers basically corroborated the Whites' conclusion that he was ten years older than George (Fleming Littlefield, Will and Inventory of Estate, Cause 293, Probate Records, Gonzales County Clerk; *New York Times*, February 3, 1936; Clement A. Evans, *The Confederate Military History*. [Atlanta, GA: Confederate Publishing Company, 1899] quoted in Carl J. Eckhardt, *The Promise of Greatness: Early Experiences at The University of Texas* [n.p.: n.p., 1978], 88-89 [second quotation]).

8. Confederate Muster Roll 1411, Texas State Archives, Texas State Library and Archives Commission (first quotation); Littlefield to John White, August 17, 1861, BL (second quotation);

Muster Roll, Eighth Texas Cavalry, September 11, 1861, Compiled Military Service Records, Confederate, National Archives and Records Administration (hereafter NARA).

9. L. B. Giles, "Terry's Texas Rangers," in Thomas W. Cutrer, *Terry Texas Ranger Trilogy* (Austin: State House Press, 1996), 9–10; Thomas W. Cutrer, ed., *Our Trust Is in the God of Battles: The Civil War Letters of Robert Franklin Bunting, Chaplain, Terry's Texas Rangers, C.S.A.* (Knoxville: University of Tennessee Press, 2006), xxii–xxiv (quotation); McClure to JEH, interview, September 22, 1935, Will White to Horne, interview, September 9, 1936. To preserve the horn, which had been cracked by the blow, he encircled it with four silver bands.

10. Cutrer, *God of Battles*, xxii–xxiii (quotations); C. C. Jeffries, "The Character of Terry's Texas Rangers," *Southwestern Historical Quarterly* 64 (April 1961), 454–62; Kenneth W. Hobbs, "Terry, Benjamin Franklin," *Handbook of Texas Online*; Cutrer, *Terry Texas Ranger Trilogy*, x; Thomas J. Goree to My Dear Mother, July 6, 1861, in *Longstreet's Aide: The Civil War Letters of Major Thomas J. Goree*, ed. Thomas W. Cutrer (Charlottesville: University Press of Virginia, 1995), 20; B. F. Terry to Dear John or Clint, August 27, 1861, B. F. Weems Papers (copies in possession of Paul Robert Scott); Jeanette H. Flachmeier, "Johnston, Albert Sidney," *Handbook of Texas Online*.

11. Littlefield to John White, May 20, 1861, BL (first quotation); Cutrer, *God of Battles*, xxiii (second quotation); Muster Roll, September 11, 1861, Eighth Texas Cavalry, NARA.

12. Littlefield to John White, December 1, 31, 1861, February 4, 27, 1862, BL; Littlefield to Alice, January 26, 1862, William A. Wroe, Littlefield Collection, in possession of William A. Wroe; Stanley F. Horn, *The Army of Tennessee* (1941; repr., Norman: University of Oklahoma Press, 1955), 67–107.

13. Littlefield recounted the story in his "Autobiography," 1919; Muster Roll, Eighth Texas Cavalry, NARA; Bunting, February 26, 1862, in Cutrer, *God of Battles*, 31–33.

14. Littlefield to John White, February 27, 1862, BL (first quotation); Bunting, February 26, 1862, in Cutrer, *God of Battles*, 31 (second quotation).

15. Bunting to Cushing, April 19, 1862, in Cutrer, *God of Battles*, 33 (first quotation); Littlefield to Alice, April 29, 1862, Littlefield Civil War Letters home, typescripts, DBGC (hereafter LCWL) (second quotation); William Preston Johnton, *The Life of General Albert Sidney Johnston, Embracing His Services in the Armies of the United States, the Republic of Texas, and the Confederate States* (New York: D. Appleton, 1878), 557; Timothy B. Smith, *Shiloh: Conquer or Perish* (Lawrence: University Press of Kansas, 2014), 224–25; Atwell Thompson and David W. Reed, *Map of the Shiloh Battlefield Positions on First Day, April 6, 1862* (1904).

16. Littlefield to Alice, April 29, 1862, LCWL. Terry Ranger hats, with their bright single star front and center, identified the unit to both sides.

17. Littlefield to Mother, April 27, 1862 (quotations); Littlefield to Alice, April 29, 1862, LCWL.

18. Littlefield to Alice, June 13, 1862 (quotations), LCWL; Littlefield, Autobiography, [1919]; Muster Rolls, Eighth Texas Cavalry, May 7, 1864, June 1, 1862, NARA; David B. Gracy II, "With Danger and Honor: George W. Littlefield," *Texana* 1 (Winter 1963), 11.

19. Robert Selph Henry, *"First with the Most" Forrest* (Indianapolis: Bobbs-Merrill, 1944), 85 (quotation); Gracy, "With Danger and Honor," 13.

20. Littlefield to Alice, August 11, 1862 (first and third quotations), June 13, 1862 (second quotation), LCWL; Henry, *Forrest*, 85–90; Jeffrey D. Murrah, *None But Texians: A History of Terry's Texas Rangers* (Austin: Eakin Press, 2001), 49–53.

21. Littlefield to Alice, August 11 (first quotation), 13 (second quotation), 1862, LCWL; Bunting, July 26, 1862, in Cutrer, *God of Battles*, 70–71.

22. Littlefield to Alice, August 11 (first quotation), 13 (second quotation), 1862, LCWL.

23. Littlefield to Alice, August 13, 1862, LCWL.

24. Daniell, *Types of Successful Men*, 347; Cutrer, *God of Battles*, 87; Mrs. Samuel Posey, "A Story of Terry's Texas Rangers," *Confederate Veteran* 32 (April 1924), 137–38. H. W. Graber, *A*

Terry Texas Ranger: The Life Record of H. W. Graber (Austin: State House Press, 1987), 163–64, describes a similar encounter involving Littlefield on the way to Perryville.

25. Daniell, *Types of Successful Men*, 347; Gracy, "With Danger and Honor," 17; Cutrer, *God of Battles*, 99.

26. Daniell, *Types of Successful Men*, 347; Paul Robert Scott, "Eighth Texas Cavalry Regiment, CSA" (master's thesis, University of Texas at Arlington, 1977), chapter 4, "Return to Kentucky," http://web.archive.org/web/20101130130136/http://terrytexasrangers.org/histories/scott_thesis .html.

CHAPTER 4. THE PROUDEST DAY

1. *History of Gonzales County*, 36–39.

2. *Richmond Dispatch* quoted in E. Merton Coulter, *The Confederate States of America* (Baton Rouge: Louisiana State University Press, 1950), 316 (first quotation), 311–21; Littlefield to Alice, April 27 (second quotation), August 13, 1862, LCWL; Bunting, November 3, 1862 (third quotation), March 12, 1863, in Cutrer, *God of Battles*, 83, 136; Daniell, *Types of Successful Men*, 347; Calvert, Cantrell, and De León, *History of Texas*, 143. If Littlefield gathered any men, Bunting missed it.

3. Littlefield to Alice, December 10 (quotation), 14, 28, and n.d. (2), 1862, LCWL; Littlefield to John White, March 2, 1862, BL; Marriage License, Harris County, Tex., Records, Vol. D, 313; Daniell, *Successful Men*, 348.

4. Littlefield to Wife, February 13, 20, 26, March 9, 1863, LCWL; Littlefield to John White, March 2, 1863, BL; Robert Franklin Bunting, Diary, March 6, 1863, Robert Franklin Bunting Papers, BCAH; J. C. Dilworth to Mrs. George N. [Marsha Ellen] Dilworth, March 9, 1863, "Civil War Letter," *Quarterly of the South Texas Genealogical Society* 1 (June 1967), 60; "Battle of Memphis," Wikipedia; J. G. Randall and David Donald, *The Civil War and Reconstruction* 2nd ed. (Boston: D. C. Heath, 1961), 409–10. Circumstances forced Littlefield to travel a circuitous route from Houston to Marshall, Tex., Shreveport and Alexandria, La., Jackson, Miss., Mobile, Ala., and Chattanooga, Tenn., to rejoin the Rangers at Wartrace in Middle Tennessee.

5. Littlefield to Wife, February 26, March 9, 1863, LCWL; Horn, *Army of Tennessee*, 240.

6. Littlefield to Wife, March 9, 1863, LCWL; Randall and Donald, *Civil War and Reconstruction*, 409.

7. Littlefield to Wife, March 9, 1863, LCWL; Littlefield to John White, March 2, 1863, BL.

8. Littlefield to Wife, April 3, 1863, LCWL.

9. Henry A. Dunn to DBG, interview, December 31, 1963.

10. Ibid. (quotation); Littlefield to Wife, July 7, 1863, LCWL.

11. Littlefield to Wife, August 26, 1863 (first and second quotations), LCWL; Dunn to DBG, interview, December 31, 1963 (third quotation).

12. Horn, *Army of Tennessee*, 229–40; Murrah, *None but Texians*, 70–72; Scott, "Eighth Texas Cavalry," 68–132; Littlefield to Wife, July 7, 1863, LCWL.

13. Littlefield to Wife, August 6, 1863 (quotations), LCWL; Bunting, August 11, 23, 1863, in Cutrer, *God of Battles*, 182–89, 195.

14. Littlefield to Wife, April 20, May 1, 12, June 12, 17, July 7, 1, August 2, 6, 22, 26, 1863, LCWL; Horn, *Army of Tennessee*, 230–37; Bruce Mercer to DBG, email, September 6, 2018; Paula Mitchell Marks, "Bunting, Robert Franklin," *Handbook of Texas Online*; Lewis E. Daniell, *Texas: The Country and Its Men: Historical, Biographical, Descriptive* (Austin: n.p., ca. 1918), 142; Cutrer, ed., *God of Battles*, 149; Littlefield to Mary M. Birge, October 16, 1917, Box 3L457, United Daughters of the Confederacy Papers, BCAH. See image of Bunting misidentified as Littlefield in Gracy, "With Danger and Honor," opposite p. 17 and correctly identified in Cutrer, *God of Battles*, 28.

15. "Uncle Nathan Talks of Major Littlefield," *Austin American-Statesman Magazine*, October 14, 1928.

16. Peter Cozzens, *This Terrible Sound: The Battle of Chickamauga* (1994; repr., Urbana: University of Illinois Press, 1996), 534; Horn, *Army of Tennessee*, 239–73; Bunting, Letter, September 29, 1863, in Cutrer, *God of Battles*, 196–98; Scott, "Eighth Texas Cavalry," 150–54.

17. Cozzens, *This Terrible Sound*, 283 (McGee, Griest, and Collins quotations), 285 (McGee second quotation), 356–404, 462–66, 517; Giles, "Terry's Texas Rangers" in Cutrer, *Terry Texas Ranger Trilogy*, 47 (last quotation), 49; David A. Powell, *The Maps of Chickamauga: An Atlas of the Chickamauga Campaign, Including the Tullahoma Operations, June 22–September 23, 1863* (El Dorado Hills, Calif.: Savas Beatie, 2009), 185, 189; Kate Scurry Terrell, "Terry's Texas Rangers," in Dudley G. Wooten, *A Comprehensive History of Texas, 1685–1897* (2 vols.; Dallas: W. G. Scariff, 1898), vol. 2, 690; Littlefield to George Boothe, June 9, 1919, enclosure in R. W. Harless to DBG, February 9, 1998. Apparently Ranger presence in the detail was minimal. Neither Bunting nor any Ranger letters mention it.

18. The quotation is a mingling of the descriptions in Posey, "A Story of Terry's Texas Rangers," 130, Daniell, *Types of Successful Men*, 348; and Daniell, *Texas*, 138. See also Littlefield to Whitfield Harral, October 26, 1863, LCWL. Ranger Giles described how easy it was to get lost even in moonlight, how difficult it was to ignore appeals for aid of wounded of both armies, and how mentally trying was being on the battlefield that night (Giles, "Terry's Texas Rangers" in Cutrer, *Terry Texas Ranger Trilogy*, 47–49). For Littlefield's route, see appendix B.

19. Daniell, *Types of Successful Men*, 348 (first quotation); Littlefield to Wife, November 2 (second quotation), [December?] 23 (third quotation), 1863; Littlefield to Whitfield Harral, October 26, 1863 (fourth quotation), LCWL.

20. Littlefield to Wife, October 26, 1863, LCWL; Scott, "Eighth Texas Cavalry," 154–61; Horn, *Army of Tennessee*, 281–82; Bunting, October 20, 1863, in Cutrer, *God of Battles*, 211–12.

21. Scott, "Eighth Texas Cavalry," 161–62; Horn, *Army of Tennessee*, 278–95.

22. Bunting, January 11, 1864, in Cutrer, *God of Battles*, 222–23.

23. Ibid., 222–34.

24. Ibid., 235. Longstreet had full command after Wheeler returned to Bragg's army in Georgia.

25. Littlefield to Wife, [December?] 23, 1863, LCWL.

26. Bunting, January 11, 1864, in Cutrer, *God of Battles*, 235.

27. J. W. Gulick to Bunting, January 10, 1864, quoted in Bunting, January 24, 1864, in Cutrer, *God of Battles*, 237. The full Bunting letter giving more detail of the day is available in "Typescript of Letters," Vol. 2, Robert Franklin Bunting Papers, BCAH. See also Andrew Jones, "Thomas Walker Jones and the Skirmish at Mossy Creek, TN," unpublished ms., DBGC.

28. Littlefield to Boothe, June 9, 1919, in Harless to DBG; Giles, *Terry's Texas Rangers*, 57; Gulick to Bunting, January 10, 1864, in Bunting, January 24, 1864, in Typescript of Letters, Vol. 2, Robert Franklin Bunting Papers, BCAH. Perhaps the Rangers were exposed in order to focus the Federals away from a Confederate movement flanking the Union position (see Gen. S. D. Sturges, December 26, 1863, 11 A.M., in *The War of the Rebellion: A Compilation of the Official Records of the Union and Confederate Armies* [128 vols.; Washington, D.C.: Government Printing Office, 1880–1901], series 1, vol. 31, pt. 3, 505).

29. Daniell, *Texas*, 139. This is Littlefield's account of his wounding and recovery.

30. Daniell, *Types of Successful Men*, 349–50; T. H. Bowman to JEH, interview, January 8, 1938; Littlefield, "Autobiography," 1919; Ed T. Rhodes to Littlefield, March 17, 1867, transcript in possession of the author.

31. Dr. William A. Wroe to DBG, interview, June 17, 2013; Howard Baade to DBG, interview, June 15, 2013; John W. Hill to Mary S. Hill, January 10, 1864, John W. Hill Papers, BCAH; Terry L. Jones, "Under the Knife," Opinionator, *New York Times*, November 17, 2012, http://opinionator.blogs.nytimes.com/2012/11/17/under-the-knife/.

32. J. W. Gulick to Bunting, January 10, 1864, in Bunting, January 24, 1864, in Bunting, Typescript of Letters, Vol. 2; Hill to Hill, January 10, 1864, John W. Hill Papers, BCAH. In

Littlefield to Boothe, June 9, 1919, in Harless to DBG, Littlefield described the time that Ranger Boothe became so emotional when visiting him that Boothe's tears fell on Littlefield's face.

33. E. T. Rhodes to Mrs. [Alice] Littlefield, January 8, 1864, LCWL; Muster Roll, February 29, 1864, Eighth Texas Cavalry, NARA; Cutrer, *God of Battles*, 322.

34. "Uncle Nathan Talks of Major Littlefield," *Austin American-Statesman Magazine*, October 14, 1928. Perhaps where Nathan found George was in the Confederate hospital in Marietta, Ga., that admitted Littlefield on April 16, 1864. (See Marietta, Georgia, Academy Hospital, 1863–1864, Samuel H. Stout Collection, BCAH; Frank Batchelor to Wife, April 24, 1864, in *Batchelor Turner Letters, 1861–1864*, comp. Helen J. H. Rugeley [Austin: Privately printed: 1961], 79–81). The Rangers returned to the Western Theater when they reached Marietta three days after Littlefield's admission (Paul Robert Scott to DBG, July 26, 2016).

35. Ruth Key to DBG, interview, January 26, 1970.

36. Elizabeth Satterwhite, wife of Francis "Frank" S. McGuire, was George Littlefield's maternal grandfather's sister. George and his mother had visited the McGuires late in 1860 for settlement of the estate of Charles Satterwhite—Mildred's uncle and Elizabeth McGuire's brother (T.J. White to John White, December 1, 1860, BL).

37. Littlefield to Wife, April 22, May 26, June 21, July 29, 1864, Littlefield to Mother, June 21, 1864, LCWL; Littlefield to Wife, May 2, 28, 1864, William A. Wroe Collection; Frank Batchelor to Wife, June 30, 1864, William T. and Sallie Turner to Brother and Sister, July 23, 1864, in Rugeley, *Batchelor-Turner Letters*, 81, 84; Hill to Hill, June 26, 1864, John W. Hill Papers, BCAH.

38. Daniell, *Types of Successful Men*, 351. Daniell's 1918 *Texas*, 140, says November 4.

CHAPTER 5. TO BEGIN BUSINESS

1. Littlefield, "Autobiography," 1919 (quotation). The Littlefield Place, bought in 1851 and lying about five miles west of the town of Gonzales, south of the Guadalupe River and along the San Antonio Road, contained about six hundred acres. It caused Fleming's initial acquisition to become known as "the Old Littlefield Place." George and William gained controlling interest in the Old Littlefield Place after their mother, as their guardian, bought for them the interest of their sister Martha and her husband. In August 1856, for eighteen-year-old son Charles White, Mildred bought 940 acres in the forks of the San Marcos and Guadalupe Rivers (Deed Book H, 20 Deed Book K, 789–90; Deed Book M; 563; Deed Book Q, 383; Deed Book 83, 7, Gonzales County Clerk).

2. John Henry White Dowell, "Land Titles of Texas," *Gonzales Inquirer*, January 24, March 3, 5, 21 (quotation), 1914; Littlefield to John White, March 2, 3, 1863, BL; U.S. Census, 1860, Slave Schedule, Gonzales County. See Stampp, *Peculiar Institution*, 36–58.

3. Mildred Littlefield Obituary, *Gonzales Inquirer*, June 12, 1880 (first quotation); Dowell, "Land Titles," December 30, 1913, January 24, 1914 (second and third quotations).

4. Littlefield to Alice, October 26 (first quotation), November 2 (second quotation), 1863; Littlefield to Whitfield Harral, October 26, 1863, LCWL; McClure to JEH, interview, September 22, 1935; Wyatt-Brown, *Southern Honor*, 254–71; Enstam, "Women and the Law." Perhaps because of this early experience, when George traveled alone during the 1870s and 1880s buying and selling cattle, he wrote long and newsy letters keeping Alice abreast of his activities.

5. Walter Walker to JEH, interview, August 5, 1937; Littlefield to Wife, June 21, 1864, LCWL.

6. Randall and Donald, *Civil War and Reconstruction*, 424–34, 523–29.

7. Dowell, "Land Titles," January 27, 1914; McClure to JEH, interview, January 14, 1938. Dowell's portrait of his grandmother's state of mind is poignant. Though in freeing his two young servants, fourteen-year-old Dowell lost nothing comparable to his grandmother's loss in plantation the labor, unlike her he regretted slavery's end to his dying day.

8. McClure to JEH, interview, September 22, 1935 (first and second quotations); G. W. Littlefield, "Remarks on Cattle and Agriculture," Bancroft Library, University of California,

Berkeley; Harral to JEH, interview, June 13, 1939. Mack Benson [Henson], "Finally at Rest," *Austin Statesman*, March 18, 1893 (third quotation) echoed McClure in this touching tribute to Lucy Littlefield.

9. Littlefield, "Autobiography," 1919; Harrell [Harral] and Son, R. G. Dun and Co. Credit Report Volumes, Vol. 11, Gonzales County, 162 (quotation); McClure to JEH, interviews, September 22, 1935, January 14, 1938; Walter Walker to JEH, interview, August 7, 1937; U.S. Census, 1850, Population, Whitfield Harral, DeSoto County, Miss., U.S. Census, 1860, Population, Whitfield Harral, Gonzales County, Tex.; Daniell, *Texas*, 140.

10. Littlefield to J. W. White, July 2, 1874, LL (first quotation); Will White to JEH, interview, October 18, 1935 (second quotation); Daniell, *Types of Successful Men*, 352 (third quotation).

11. Will White to JEH, interview, October 18, 1935.

12. Ibid. (first quotation); Charlie Walker to JEH, interview, August 5, 1937 (second quotation); Arthur P. Duggan to Robert C. Rawlings, June 27, 1913 (third quotation), Littlefield Lands Company Records, Southwest Collection, Texas Tech University; Will White to Horne, interview, September 9 (fourth quotation), 13, 1936 (sixth quotation); McClure to JEH, interview, September 22, 1935 (fifth quotation).

13. Alice Dowell to John Dowell, July 18, 1869 (quotation), LL; Littlefield to John White, March 2, 1867; T.J. White to John White, October 21, 1867, BL; Littlefield, "Autobiography," 1919; Walter Walker to JEH, interview, August 5, 1937; Will White to Horne, interview, September 9, 1936; Daniell, *Types of Successful Men*, 351; "Washington and Lee University," Wikipedia.

14. Ruth Key to DBG, interview, November 13, 1964; Ed T. Rhodes to Littlefield, March 17, 1867, Gracy-Littlefield Collection, BCAH (hereafter GLC); Daniell, *Types of Successful Men*, 352; Edward Rhodes Littlefield tombstone, Littlefield Plot, Masonic Cemetery, Gonzales, Tex..

15. Walter Walker to JEH, interview, August 7, 1937; Littlefield, "Autobiography," 1919; Littlefield to Boothe, June 9, 1919, in Harless to DBG.

16. *History of Gonzales*, 3 (first quotation); Dixon, "History of Gonzales County," 26–27; Littlefield to John White, September 26, 1868 (second quotation), Littlefield to John Dowell, June 25, August 10, 1869, LL; Thomas J. White Bankruptcy Sale, July 7, 1868, Deed Book Q, 367; Thomas White to Littlefield, Purchase of Interest in Charles White Estate, July 16, 1868, Deed Book Q, 368; T. E. Harral to Littlefield, Deed, October 6, 1868, Deed Book Q, 504; T. E. and Martha Harral to Littlefield, Deed, November 26, 1868, Deed Book Q, 519, Gonzales County Clerk; Rogan, "Converts Cattle." Shortly before the war began, Charles E. White was admitted to the Pennsylvania Hospital for the Insane for treatment of his deteriorating mental state. Though he may have returned home briefly after the conflict, he died in the hospital on March 3, 1866, apparently because of the effects of scarlet fever (Mildred Littlefield to John White, September 1, 1860, Littlefield to John White, March 2, 1863, BL; Charles E. White, Death Certificate; Jennie Walker Harless and Pearl Walker Dobbins to DBG, interview, August 14, 1970).

17. Littlefield, "Autobiography," 1919; Daniell, *Types of Successful Men*, 140; J. Frank Dobie, *The Longhorns* (New York: Little, Brown, 1941), 51 (quotation); Walter Walker to JEH, interviews, August 5, 7, 1937. As late as September 1869, debts due Charles Satterwhite's estate were being paid in Confederate currency (Littlefield to John Dowell, September 12, 1869, BL).

18. Haley, "Survey of Texas Cattle Drives," 62–63; McArthur, "Cattle Industry of Texas," 62–65; Brand Book A–R, brands 6, 10, 12, 16; Division of Estate, August 28, 1854, Fleming Littlefield, Cause 293, Probate Records, Gonzales County Clerk.

19. Littlefield to Alice, November 2, 1863, LCWL; Brand Book A, 161, Inventory of Estate, January 31, 1853; Fleming Littlefield, Cause 293, Probate Records, Gonzales County Clerk; McClure to JEH, interviews, September 22, 1935, March 25, 1937.

20. Littlefield to Whitfield Harral, October 26, 1863 (quotation), LCWL; P. B. Littlefield, PL Brand, Marks and Brands Record 1, 70, August 5, 1863, Travis County Clerk; Index to Marks and Brands, Book A, brand 13, Gonzales County Clerk; McClure to JEH, interview, September 22, 1935; P. B. Littlefield in W. H. Jackson and S. A. Long, *Texas Stock Directory, or Book of Marks*

and Brands (San Antonio: Herald Office, 1865), 366; Dixon, "History of Gonzales County," 39; McArthur, "Cattle Industry of Texas," 64, 70; Wayne Ludwig, *The Old Chisholm Trail: From Cow Path to Tourist Stop* (College Station: Texas A&M University Press, 2018), 58–59.

21. Jackson and Long, *Texas Stock Directory*, 365; *Gonzales Inquirer*, December 9, 1864; Daniell, *Types of Successful Men of Texas*, 351; Littlefield, "Autobiography," 1919.

22. Charlie Walker told Haley on August 5, 1937, that he recalled Littlefield taking a herd to Shreveport in 1866 or 1867 for shipment to New Orleans; B. B. Hoskins and Jack Blackwell, "Gonzales: One Hundred and Ten Years a Cow-Country," *The Cattleman* 26, no. 5 (October 1939), 23–24, stated that, with J. C. Dilworth and Doc Burnett, Littlefield drove a herd to Salt Lake City in 1866. Neither happened. Gonzales County's record of herds driven that could have enumerated Littlefield's drives after 1871 burned in an 1890 courthouse fire.

23. Jimmy M. Skaggs, *The Cattle-Trailing Industry Between Supply and Demand, 1866–1890* (Lawrence: University Press of Kansas, 1973), 5; Edward Everett Dale, *The Range Cattle Industry: Ranching on the Great Plains from 1865 to 1925* (Norman: University of Oklahoma Press, 1960), 33–43; Haley, "Survey of Texas Cattle Drives," 179–203; Worcester, *Chisholm Trail*, 9–16; Jimmy M. Skaggs, *Prime Cut: Livestock Raising and Meatpacking in the United States, 1607–1983* (College Station: Texas A&M University Press, 1986), 44–47.

24. Littlefield to John White, September 12, 1869, BL.

25. Ibid.; Haley, "Survey of Texas Cattle Drives," 163–64, 184–87.

26. Walter Walker to JEH, interview, August 7, 1937; McClure to JEH, interview, September 22, 1935; Littlefield to John White, August 7, 1866, September 12, 1869, BL.

27. Littlefield to John Dowell, August 10, 1869, LL; Daniell, *Types of Successful Men*, 351.

28. Littlefield to John White, September 26, 1868, LL; Littlefield to John White, September 12, 1869, BL; Littlefield, "Autobiography," 1919.

29. Littlefield to John White, September 12, 1869, BL.

30. Daniell, *Texas*, 141; *History of the Cattlemen of Texas: A Brief Resume of the Live Stock Industry of the Southwest and a Biographical Sketch of Many of the Important Characters Whose Lives are Interwoven Therein* (1914; repr., Austin: Texas State Historical Association, 1991), 27. For a description of this activity, see Joseph G. McCoy, *Historic Sketches of the Cattle Trade of the West and Southwest* (1874; facsimile reprint, Columbus, Ohio: Long's College, 1951), 78–86; J. Marvin Hunter and George W. Saunders, *The Trail Drivers of Texas* (1924; repr., Austin: University of Texas Press, 1992), 21; Haley, "Survey of Texas Cattle Drives," 203–5.

31. Great-nephew Maurice Dowell said that Littlefield put a doubled-up coat under Watson's head and sent a hand to bring a doctor (Dowell, ["Littlefield Reminiscence"]).

32. "Cowboying" knowledge included techniques of *herding* (reading the mood of and moving a bunch of cattle in part by listening to the sound of the horns hitting each other as the cattle grazed and milled about), *cutting* (separating individual animals from a herd), *castrating* (for improving the quality of a herd by eliminating weaker bulls from breading, increasing meat production in the sterilized males, and rendering males less rowdy and dangerous—a vital skill once ranchers began upgrading their stock), *sorting* (segregating cattle into classes, for example, by age and gender, and males by bulls and steers), and *marking and branding* (using a red-hot branding iron and cropping the ears to show ownership) (J. Phelps White III to DBG, September 10, October 1, 2012).

CHAPTER 6. CONNECTING THE FOUR-DOLLAR COW WITH THE FORTY-DOLLAR MARKET

1. The term "maverick" arose from the refusal of Sam Maverick of San Antonio to brand his cattle. Having minimal interest in the animals, he did not carefully confine them to his Conquista Ranch. By 1867 when the term first appeared in print, cowmen had extended the recognition of Maverick's unmarked cattle to any cow unbranded and running wild (Paula Mitchell Marks, "Maverick, Samuel Augustus," *Handbook of Texas Online*).

2. Littlefield, "Autobiography," 1919; Littlefield to H. A. Wroe, November 5, 1919, H. A. Wroe Papers, GLC. The Dun and Company documentation shows the partner to be Hugh Lewis, yet two reminiscences identified the partner as a man named Anderson (R. G. Dun and Co. Credit Report Volumes, Vol. 11, Gonzales County, 166C; Will White to Horne, September 9, 1936; Mrs. J. C. [Sarah Ellen] Dilworth Jr., "George Norwood Dilworth," in *History of Gonzales County*, 287). On December 26, 1871, and January 4, 1872, the Dilworths and Littlefield exchanged deeds and notes sealing the deal (George N. and James C. Dilworth to Littlefield, Deed of Sale, December 26, 1871, Book T, 60–61; Littlefield to J. C. Dilworth, Deed of Sale, January 4, 1872, Book T, 251, Gonzales County Clerk); Joe E. Ericson, *Banks and Bankers in Early Texas, 1835–1875* (New Orleans: Polyanthos, 1976), 58.

3. Will White to Horne, interview, September 9, 1936.

4. "The best house in the county," a Dun and Company correspondent wrote in 1876 after the firm survived the failure of a correspondent bank [Lewis and Dilworth Banking, R. G. Dun and Co. Credit Report Volumes, Vol. 11, Gonzales County, 200, 166C].

5. Daniell, *Texas*, 141; Gracy, "With Danger and Honor," 127; Cutrer, *God of Battles*, 320–21; Littlefield, "Autobiography," 1919; *History of Gonzales County*, 103, 105, 287; Kent Gardien, "A Sketch of J. C. Dilworth," *Quarterly of the South Texas Genealogical and Historical Society* 2 (June 1968): 150, 155; R. G. Dun and Co. Credit Report Volumes, Vol. 11, Gonzales County, 166C, 166K, 174, 188; *Southwestern Index* (Gonzales), January 10, 1873; Phelps White to JEH, interview, March 2, 1933; Will White to Horne, interview, September 9, 1936; Will White to JEH, interview, October 18, 1935. George Dilworth's capital came largely from trading cotton across the Rio Grande during the Civil War, an enterprise that decades later would fuel Littlefield's loathing of George Brackenridge. Unlike Brackenridge's enterprise, Dilworth's benefited the Confederacy.

6. Edgar Harral to Haley, interview, June 13, 1939; Frank Reeves Sr., "Sketch of Texas Cattle Industry," in *A Century of Texas Cattle Brands* (Fort Worth, Tex.: Fair Publishing Company, 1936), 12.

7. Will White to Horne, interview, September 9, 1936; Jim W. Roberts to JEH, interview, June 24, 1937; Worcester, *Chisholm Trail*, 15; Hunter, *Trail Drivers of Texas*, 438–39, 923–24; David J. Murrah, *C. C. Slaughter: Rancher, Banker, Baptist* (Austin: University of Texas Press, 1981), 24.

8. Driving cattle was a science of its own. Littlefield picked men who understood it. "Use the tenderfoot best in day service and his best place was on the side or swing of the herd, never on the points nor in the rear," Littlefield advised. "The rear cattle had to have careful handling and certain men were adapted to that place. If crowded the cattle would often injure each other by treading on the heels of those ahead of them" (Littlefield quoted in *Austin American*, January 6, 1918).

9. Robert H. Thonhoff, "Butler, William G.," *Handbook of Texas Online*; Harral to JEH, interview, June 13, 1939; Will White to Horne, September 9, 1936; Shelton Dowell to Lizzie Dowell, June 7, 1882, LL; Littlefield, "Autobiography," 1919; Hunter, *Trail Drivers of Texas*, 476–78; Lester Fields Sheffy, *The Francklyn Land and Cattle Company: A Panhandle Enterprise, 1882–1957* (Austin: University of Texas Press, 1963), 160–67; Skaggs, *Cattle-Trailing Industry*, 1–11.

10. Quoted in Robert R. Dykstra, *The Cattle Towns* (New York: Alfred A. Knopf, 1971), 77, 74–78; Littlefield to John White, July 5, 1872, BL; Joseph McCoy quoted in James Cox, *Historical and Biographical Record*, 93.

11. Littlefield to Shelton Dowell, July 30, 1873, LL; Ike T. Pryor, "The Old Trail Drivers" in *The New Encyclopedia of Texas*, ed. and comp. Ellis A. Davis and Edwin H. Grobe (4 vols.; Dallas: Texas Development Bureau, 1929), vol. 1, 64; Haley, "Survey of Texas Cattle Drives," 232; Holden, *Alkali Trails*, 29–30.

12. Pryor and Littlefield became close friends even though Pryor had been on the other side in the Civil War. A boy of nine when the war erupted, Pryor participated only as the mascot of the Third Ohio Cavalry. As fate would have it, the Third Ohio clashed with the Eighth Texas on Chickamauga's Glass Field. Pryor came to Texas in 1870 and first hired out to work cattle the

year Littlefield bossed his herd up the trail (Jimmy M. Skaggs, "Pryor, Isaac Thomas," *Handbook of Texas Online*; J. Frank Dobie, *Cow People* [Boston: Little, Brown, 1964], 3–24; Chris Emmett, *Shanghai Pierce: A Fair Likeness* [Norman: University of Oklahoma Press, 1953], 10).

13. Skaggs, *Cattle-Trailing Industry*, 14–15, 45, 53–57, 71–72; Dale, *Range Cattle Industry*, 41–42; Haley, "Survey of Texas Cattle Drives," 232–33; Jimmy M. Skaggs, "John Thomas Lytle: Cattle Baron," *Southwestern Historical Quarterly* 71 (July 1967): 48–50.

14. Phelps White to JEH, interview, March 2, 1933. In the late 1880s and early 1890s, scientific experiments proved that Texas Fever was a condition spread by ticks. It was eradicated by "dipping" cattle, that is, running them through a vat with a chemistry toxic to the tick (Mary Whatley Clarke, *A Century of Cow Business: A History of Texas and Southwestern Cattle Raisers Association* [Fort Worth: Texas and Southwestern Cattle Raisers Association, 1976], 63–64).

15. Littlefield to Shelton Dowell, July 30, 1873, LL.

16. Greensville Dowell to Shelton Dowell, June 22, 1869, LL.

17. "Lewis and Dilworth (J.C.)," 166C; "Lewis (Hugh) and Dilworth (J.C. and G. N.)," 166K, R. G. Dun and Co. Credit Report Volumes, Vol. 11, Gonzales County.

18. Littlefield to Lizzie Dowell, January 9, 1890, Sallie Dowell to John Dowell, January 3, 1869, LL; Sallie Dowell to John Dowell, April 6, November 22, [1868]; Shelton Dowell to John Dowell, January 31, 1869, Dowell-Littlefield Collection; Dowell, [George Littlefield Reminiscence]; Sallie Dowell to John Dowell, March 14, 1869, JEHC.

19. Littlefield to Shelton Dowell, September 5, 1873, July 6, 1875, LL; Littlefield to Shelton Dowell, July 27, 1875, JEHC; Phelps White to JEH, interview, March 2, 1933; Cox, *Historical and Biographical Record*, 93.

20. Dilworth and Littlefield advertising card, n.d., DBG; Littlefield to Alice, August 3, 1881, ALP.

21. *Congressional Record*, 46th Congress, 2nd Session (Washington, D.C.: Government Printing Office, 1880), X, 3977, 3988; *Congressional Record*, 49th Congress, 1st Session (Washington, D.C.: Government Printing Office, 1886), XVII, 486; [Dodge City] *Ford County Globe*, July 1, 1884; *History of the Cattlemen of Texas*, 29; McArthur, "Cattle Industry of Texas," 194–95; Jo Toland Ackman and Glen Sachtleben, *Gonzales Drovers, Brands, Cattle and More* (1996), 30. Louis Hamilton Hill, who told the story of the 1879 Indian encounter in "Louis Hamilton Hill," in *History of the Cattlemen of Texas*, 123–24, seems to have embellished it. Reporting a bill filed in Congress to reimburse Littlefield, the *Dallas News* (January 7, 24, 1886) documented that on June 16, 1879, a Littlefield herd supplied $282 worth of beef to the army for starving Indians. Hill reported, likely accurately, that "I think most of us aged about ten years as a result of that experience."

22. H. Bailey Carroll to DBG, interview, February 2, 1965; and William Curry Holden to DBG, interview, January 27, 1967, reported their conversation with Phelps White; Phelps White to JEH, March 2, 1933; *Ford County Globe*, July 1, 1884; McArthur, "Cattle Industry of Texas," 309–10; Dale, *Range Cattle Industry*, 62–65. Dale too referred to Indian demands as an annoyance (40–41).

23. T. J. Cauley, "Early Business Methods in the Texas Cattle Industry," *Journal of Economic and Business History* 4 (May 1932): 461–86.

24. *Ford County Globe*, July 1, 1884. Looking back on it, Littlefield admitted that "losses by Indians were little" (Littlefield, "Autobiography," 1919).

25. Joseph Nimmo Jr., *Report in Regard to the Range and Ranch Cattle Business of the United States* (1885; rep., New York: Arno Press, 1972) is the foundation source for annual totals. Though he repeated Nimmo's numbers, Dale (*Range Cattle Industry*, 43–44) reckoned them to be low. Ike Pryor ("The Old Trail Drivers" in Davis and Grobe, *New Encyclopedia of Texas*, 1:64) estimated that some ten million cattle traveled the trail between 1870 and 1890. If his half-million-head annual average is accurate, the number trailed in the 1871–84 heyday must have greatly exceeded the average because the annual number dropped dramatically after 1884. Skaggs (*Cattle-Trailing Industry*, 18–23) found no documentation allowing him to offer more accurate numbers.

26. Skaggs, *Cattle-Trailing Industry*, 10, 40 (quotation), 50, 64, 71, 123; Littlefield, GW, and White, JW, Gonzales, Livery Stable, 204; Dilworth and Littlefield General Store, 192, R. G. Dun and Co. Credit Report Volumes, Vol. 11, Gonzales County; *Ford County Globe*, September 3, 1878, March 18, May 6, 1879, March 23, April 20, June 29, November 2, 1880, May 24, June 14, 1881, February 14, April 18, 1882, July 1, 1884; *Dodge City Times*, May 26, 1877; *Fort Griffin Echo*, May 31, June 7, 1879, May 22, 1880, April 30, 1881; Littlefield, "Remarks on Cattle and Agriculture"; Littlefield to Abel Head Pierce, January 4, 1879, Correspondence, 1879, Abel Head "Shanghai" Pierce Papers, BCAH; Rogan, "Converts Cattle"; Phelps White to JEH, interview, March 2, 1933; Hoskins and Blackwell, "Gonzales: One Hundred and Ten Years," 24; A. E. Scheske, "Sold Cattle in Natchez for $4.50 a Head," in Hunter, *Trail Drivers of Texas*, 569–70; James W. Mullins quoted in George W. Saunders, "More Lore of Cattle Trails," *Frontier Times* 4 (October, 1926), 42–43; Charles A. Siringo, *A Texas Cowboy* (1886; repr., New York: Signat, 1951), 35; Worcester, *Chisholm Trail*, 137–42. Skaggs gives two figures for the number of major contractors—twenty-two on page 71, eleven on page 123.

27. Littlefield to Shelton Dowell, July 6, 1875, LL; Gracy, "Cowman's Eye View, 176–79."

CHAPTER 7. THE FASTEST MONEY-MAKING BUSINESS

1. Alice Littlefield to Shelton Dowell, September 28, 1873, LL. Historian Daniel McArthur ("Cattle Industry of Texas," 197) may have been too modest in asserting only that the cattle trails were "in a measure educative."

2. Littlefield to Shelton Dowell, July 27, 1875, JEHC; Phelps White to JEH, interview, March 2, 1933; Harral to JEH, interview, June 13, 1939. Littlefield had arrived in Dodge City no more than a day or two earlier (*Dodge City Times*, June 9, 1877).

3. Daniell, *Types of Successful Men*, 341 (quotation); Daniell, *Texas*, 141; Littlefield, "Autobiography," 1919; Dilworth and Littlefield General Store, 186; George W. Littlefield Gonzales Farmer and Trader, 175, 192; S. C. Dowell and Co., Gonzales, Rancho, 183, R. G. Dun and Co. Credit Report Volumes, Vol. 11, Gonzales County.

4. Littlefield to Shelton Dowell, July 6, 1875, LL.

5. George W. Littlefield, Entry L159—LIT, July 23, 1877, Entry L168—L (road brand), April 16, 1878; Dilworth and Littlefield, Entry 79—F and 80—Bar F (road brands), November 8, 1875, Brand Book A–R, Gonzales County Clerk. The registrations failed to specify on which side of the animal the brand appeared.

6. Clarence W. Gordon, "Report on Cattle, Sheep, and Swine, Supplementary to Enumeration of Live Stock on Farms in 1880," part 3, *Tenth Census, 1880: Report on the Production of Agriculture* (Washington, D.C., 1883), 17–18.

7. Charles H. Jones, Theodore F. Hamilton, and J. David Williams, comps. and eds., *The Peoples' Pictorial Atlas: Being a Complete and Popular Account of All the Countries of the World, in Their Geographical, Statistical, Topographical and Commercial Aspects, with 52 Maps* (New York: J. David Williams, 1873), 15.

8. William T. Hornaday, *Extermination of the American Bison* (Washington, D.C.: Government Printing Office, 1889), 501.

9. Ibid., 492–504; Holden, *Alkali Trails*, 12–14; S. C. Gwynne, *Empire of the Summer Moon: Quanah Parker and the Rise and Fall of the Comanches, the Most Powerful Indian Tribe in American History* (New York: Scribner, 2010), 258–87; Rupert Norval Richardson, *The Comanche Barrier to South Plains Settlement: A Century and a Half of Savage Resistance to the Advancing White Frontier* (Glendale, Calif.: Arthur H. Clark, 1933), 291–397; James L. Haley, "Red River War," *Handbook of Texas Online*.

10. Joseph Andrew Blackman, "Ikard, William Susan," *Handbook of Texas Online*; Dale, *Range Cattle Industry*, 104–5; Murrah, *Slaughter*, 35–37; Jimmy M. Skaggs, "Northward across the Plains: The Western Cattle Trail," *Great Plains Journal* 12 (Fall 1972): 52–68; Skaggs, *Cattle-Trailing Industry*, 17–18, 90–91. The locations were in the vicinity of Wichita Falls and Harrold, Tex..

11. J. Evetts Haley, *Charles Goodnight: Cowman and Plainsman* (1936; repr., Norman: University of Oklahoma Press, 1949), 276–82; Pauline Durrett Robertson and R. L. Robertson, *Cowman's Country: Fifty Frontier Ranches in the Texas Panhandle, 1876–1887* (Amarillo, Tex.: Paramount Publishing, 1981), 128–29.

12. *Dodge City Times*, June 2, 9, 16 (quotation), 1877, June 1, 8, 1878; *Ford County Globe*, May 11, June 22, 1880; Littlefield to Alice, May 7, October 29, 1881, ALP; Roberts to JEH, interview, June 24, 1937; Haley, *Charles Goodnight*, 284–87. Almost like a herd themselves and like clockwork, the trailing entrepreneurs arrived and took rooms in the principal hotel at trail's end. In 1877 and 1878, for example, James F. Ellison, Jesse Driskill, William H. Day, Seth Mabry, and John W. Gamel of Austin and central Texas checked into the Dodge House in Dodge City to spend June meeting their herds (Grand Central Hotel, Register, 1873–1904, Kansas Historical Society).

13. Jim Roberts to JEH, interview, June 24, 1937 (first quotation); Harral to Haley, interview, June 13, 1939 (second quotation); Littlefield to Phelps White, September 2, 1916, JPW; Phelps White to JEH, interview, March 2, 1933.

14. Phelps White to JEH, interview, March 2, 1933 (first and third quotation); Charles Littlepage Ballard to Hervey E. Chesley, interview, n.d., in Hervey E. Chesley, *Adventuring with the Old-Timers: Trails Traveled—Tales Told* (Midland, Tex.: Nita Stewart Haley Memorial Library, 1979), 64 (second quotation).

15. Ballard to Chesley, interview, n.d., in Chesley, *Adventuring with the Old-Timers*, 64 (first quotation); Littlefield to Arthur Duggan, December 20, 1915, Littlefield Lands Company Records, Southwest Collection, Texas Tech University (hereafter LLSWC) (second quotation); Littlefield to Lizzie Dowell, May 14, 1894, LL (third quotation); Ruth Key to Alice Gracy, interviews, November 29, December 5, 1943. Cowman, rancher, and author J. Evetts Haley defined "cowman" as "a man who is a careful judge of cattle, who knows the fine points of managing them on the range, who can shape a herd for breeding or selling, and who can look at a range or a herd and prophesy the potentialities of either. Hence, among those who know, the designation of 'cowman' is a rich encomium that indicates much more than the possession of enough money to buy a herd of cows" (*Littlefield*, 111). For the depth of Littlefield's cow knowledge, see Littlefield to Edgar Harral, March 12, 1899, February 7, 1900, January 2, 1901, Littlefield Biographical File, HL.

16. Jose Romero quoted in John L. McCarty, *Maverick Town: The Story of Old Tascosa* (1946; Norman: University of Oklahoma Press, 1988), 39; Littlefield, "Autobiography," 1919; Calvert, Cantrell, and De León, *History of Texas*, 185–86.

17. Robertson and Robertson, *Cowman's Country*, 106–9, 112–15; Anderson, "Torrey, Ellsworth," *Handbook of Texas Online*.

18. McCarty, *Maverick Town*, 38. McCarty apparently got his information from Roy Riddle, "Casimero Romero Reigned as Benevolent Don in Brief Pastoral Era," *Amarillo Sunday Globe-News*, August 14, 1938. See also Frederick Nolan, *Tascosa: Its Life and Gaudy Times* (Lubbock: Texas Tech University Press, 2007), 9–11; Anderson, "Romero, Casimero," "John Ray Creek," and "Pastores," *Handbook of Texas Online*.

19. Phelps White to JEH, interviews, January 15, 1927, March 2, 1933 (first quotation); *Ford County Globe*, February 15, 1881 (second quotation); Harry Ingerton to JEH, interview, June 12, 1937, in Nolan, *Tascosa*, 282 (third quotation), 6, 18; William H. O'Brien to DBG, interview, October 3, 2003; Haley, *Charles Goodnight*, 280; *History of the Cattlemen of Texas*, 43; Anderson, "John Ray Creek"; McCarty, *Maverick Town*, 35–36.

20. Phelps White to JEH, interviews, January 15, 1927, March 2, 1933; Roberts to JEH, interview, June 24, 1937 (quotation). This account of the establishment of the LIT is based on reminiscences, not all of which agree on all details. But on the founding of the ranch they are in accord. It was not, as John McCarty in *Maverick Town*, 43, and writers following him have asserted, a sudden decision motivated by ruinously low prices for cattle Littlefield had driven to Dodge City for sale. Neither Phelps White nor Jim Roberts gave market conditions as the reason. The first herd

intended for the ranch, they maintained, was formed and branded in Gonzales. Moreover, cattle prices in 1877 were up from previous years. See Cox, *Historical and Biographical Record*, 88.

21. *Dodge City Times*, February 28, 1878, quoted in Nolan, *Tascosa*, 62 (quotation); McCarty, *Maverick Town*, 3–18; Frank Collinson to JEH, March 3, 1939, Haley File, Panhandle-Plains Historical Museum; Patrick H. Boone IV to DBG, interview, May 24, 2007; Ramon F. Adams, *The Cowman & His Philosophy* (Austin: Encino Press, 1967), 5; Charles L. Wood and James E. Brink, eds., "Cowboy Life on a Western Ranch: Reminiscences of Alexander Mackay," in *At Home on the Range: Essays on the History of Western Social and Domestic Life*, ed. John R. Wunder (Westport, Conn.: Greenwood Press, 1985), 184.

22. Howard R. Lamar, *Charlie Siringo's West: An Interpretive Biography* (Albuquerque: University of New Mexico Press, 2005), 69.

23. Phelps White to JEH, interview, January 15, 1927; Gunter and Munson to Littlefield and McCarty, November 16, 1878, Letter Press Books no. 10, pt. 2; Gunter and Munson to Littlefield, January 18, 28, 1879, Letter Press Books no. 11, pt. 2, Jot Gunter Papers, BCAH. The *pastores* were not party to the transaction that encompassed land on which their flocks grazed, but they "gave us no trouble, as most of them were good people," Phelps White recalled. Though some of the sheepmen were elected officers upon organization of Oldham County, taxes were laid on the *pastores* so as to push them back to New Mexico.

24. Shelton Dowell to Wife, May 17, 1881, LL (quotation); Phelps White to JEH, interviews, January 15, 1927, March 2, 1933. McCarty, *Maverick Town*, 43, and writers who followed him state erroneously that the headquarters of Littlefield's LIT was first located west of present Tascosa, then moved to the east. The move east to the present location occurred after Littlefield had sold his interest and after establishment of the XIT Ranch required the Prairie Cattle Company to pull in its western boundary.

25. Laura Vernon Hamner, "Panhandle Ranch History at a Glance," *Amarillo Sunday News and Globe*, August 14, 1938; Clara M. Love, "History of the Cattle Industry in the Southwest," *Southwestern Historical Quarterly* 19 (April 1916): 388; *Ford County Globe*, September 3, 1879; J. Evetts Haley, *The XIT Ranch of Texas and the Early Days of the Llano Estacado* (1929; repr., Norman: University of Oklahoma Press, 1954), 70.

26. *Dodge City Times*, September 27, 1879, quoting the *Henrietta Journal*, cited in Robertson and Robertson, *Cowman's Country*, 125; Littlefield to Alice, May 23, 1881, ALP; Phelps White to JEH, interview, March 2, 1935; Love, "History of the Cattle Industry," 388.

27. Lewis F. Allen, *American Cattle: Their History, Breeding and Management* (New York: D. D. T. Moore, 1871), 178 (first quotation); McCoy, *Sketches of the Cattle Trade*, 237 (second quotation), 6; Haley, *Charles Goodnight*, 296, 316–17; "Shorthorn Cattle," *Handbook of Texas Online*.

28. Allen, *American Cattle*, 68 (first quotation); *Clarendon News*, June 15, 1881 (second quotation); Alvin Howard Sanders, *The Story of the Herefords: An Account of the Origin and Development of the Breed in Herefordshire, a Sketch of its Early Introduction into the United States and Canada, and Subsequent Rise to Popularity in the Western Cattle Trade, with Sundry Notes on the Management of Breeding Herds* (Chicago: Breeder's Gazette, 1914), 694, 697; Alvin Howard Sanders, *The Cattle of the World: Their Place in the Human Scheme—Wild Types and Modern Breeds in Many Lands* (Washington, D.C.: National Geographic Society, 1926), 79, 82; "Hereford," Animal Science Department, Oklahoma State University, http://www.ansi.okstate.edu/breeds /breeds/cattle/hereford/index.htm; Haley, *Charles Goodnight*, 318; Murrah, *Slaughter*, 74; Joseph Andrew Blackman, "Ikard, William Susan," *Handbook of Texas Online*; Donald F. Schofield, *Indians, Cattle, Ships, and Oil: The Story of W. M. D. Lee* (Austin: University of Texas Press, 1985), 52. Unlike Lee and Reynolds, Littlefield was not remembered as having been an early adopter.

29. *Austin Daily Statesman*, March 18, 1882.

30. Littlefield to Alice, May 18, 1881 (quotation), ALP; J. Fred Rippy, "British Investments in Texas Lands and Livestock," *Southwestern Historical Quarterly* 58 (January, 1955): 331–32; Nolan, *Tascosa*, 120–21.

31. Worcester, *Chisholm Trail*, 149 (quote); "Prairie Cattle Company," in Oklahoma Historical Society, *Oklahoma Encyclopedia of History and Culture*, http://digital.library.okstate.edu /encyclopedia/entries/p/pr002.html; H. Allen Anderson, "Prairie Cattle Company" and "Quarter Circle T Ranch," *Handbook of Texas Online*; Margaret Lancaster, "James Columbus 'Jim' Jones," FindAGrave; Robertson and Robertson, *Cowman's Country*, 129.

32. Littlefield to Alice, May 7 (first quotation), 18 (second quotation), 1881, ALP.

33. Schofield, *Indians, Cattle, Ships, and Oil*, 51–53; Robertson and Robertson, *Cowman's Country*, 64, 106, 125; William Elton Green, "Capitol," *Handbook of Texas Online*; Shelton Dowell to Lizzie Dowell, June 26, 1881, LL; "Map of the L.I.T. Ranche Situated in the Panhandle of Texas, the Property of the Prairie Cattle Co. L'd, 1898," Archives, Panhandle-Plains Historical Museum.

34. George W. Littlefield with C. C. Quinlan and Alexander Frazier, Agreement, June 21, 1881, Oldham County Deed Book 1, 95–98; George W. Littlefield with C. C. Quinlan and Alexander Frazier, Agreement, November 4, 1881, Oldham County Bill of Sale Book 1, 1–2; Shelton Dowell to Lizzie Dowell, July 21, 1881, LL; Laura Hamner, "The LIT's Were Squatters," unpublished ms. in Earl Vandale Collection, BCAH; Ike Pryor quoted in Louis J. Wortham, *A History of Texas: From Wilderness to Commonwealth*, 5 vols.(Fort Worth: Wortham-Molyneaux, 1924), vol. 5, 169. When the Prairie Cattle Company liquidated in 1913, Amarillo cattleman Lee Bivins bought the LIT. At his death it passed to his sons, in whose hands it remained until the present owners, the William H. O'Brien family of Amarillo, Tex., acquired it in the 1980s (LIT Ranch website, http://www.litranch.com/; Robertson and Robertson, *Cowman's Country*, 109).

35. *Ford County Globe*, July 5, 1881 (first quotation); *Fort Griffin Echo*, July 2, 1881 (second quotation); Shelton Dowell to Lizzie Dowell, June 4, 1881, LL (third quotation).

36. The highest single return the Prairie investors received appears to have been 20.5 percent, not long after the company's founding (Robertson and Robertson, *Cowman's Country*, 108).

37. "Prairie Cattle Company," *Oklahoma Encyclopedia of History and Culture*; Delbert A. Ritchhart, *Breathing Life into Family Ancestors: About the Richard, Dean, Bush, O'Malley, Schmidt, McConnell, and Other Associated Families* (Bloomington, Ind.: Author House, 2011), 78; Anderson, "Quarter Circle T Ranch"; Phelps White to JEH, interview, March 2, 1933. According to Colorado Preservation, the Prairie bought Littlefield's LIT the year before, not after, it acquired the JJ on the Purgatoire River in Colorado ("Open Range Cattle Ranching in the Purgatoire River Region," http://coloradopreservation.org/crsurvey/ranching/sites/rch_contexts_openrange .html); Anderson, "Prairie Cattle Company."

CHAPTER 8. A LITTLE BIT WIDER

1. Littlefield to Alice, May 7, 20 (first and third quotations), 23 (fourth quotation), June 6 (fifth quotation), 1881, ALP; Shelton Dowell to Wife, May 17, 1881, LL (second quotation); Littlefield, "Autobiography," 1919; Rogan, "Converts Cattle" (sixth quotation). Littlefield appears at first to be like the cattlemen in whom the writer O. Henry observed a self-consciousness brought on by feeling they had "more money than was decent" (Trueman O'Quinn, "O. Henry in Austin," *Southwestern Historical Quarterly* 43 [October 1939]: 148).

2. J. M. and E. F. Foster to Littlefield, Deeds, October 30, 31, 1878, Deed Book Y, 108, 110–13, Gonzales County Clerk; Gonzales County Surveys Map, 1880, Texas General Land Office, Austin; Littlefield to Shelton Dowell, May 17, 1880, LL; Nimmo, *Report in Regard to the Range and Ranch Cattle Business*, 3, 21.

3. Littlefield to John White, December 28, 1876, BL; S. C. Dowell and Co., R. G. Dun and Co. Credit Report Volumes, Vol. 11, Gonzales County, 183; *Gonzales Inquirer*, April 25, 1874, July 28, 1877; Dowell family Bible, genealogy pages, DBG; Littlefield to Shelton Dowell, April 5, 1875; S. C. Dowell, G. W. Littlefield and Wm. M. Phillips, Articles of Agreement, February 1, 1876; Littlefield to Shelton Dowell, September 5, 1877, June 29, 1879, LL; Littlefield to Shelton Dowell, July 27, 1875, Littlefield-Dowell Letters, JEHC. Euphemia K. Mathieu married William

Littlefield on September 11, 1871. Proud of their French heritage and a line that extended to President Benjamin Harrison, the Mathieu family disapproved of the union and snubbed Euphemia (Pat H. Boone III, "An Oral History: The Pat H. Boone Family, the William P. Littlefield Family, the Kenna, NM Ranch," December 1986 [original in possession of Pat H. Boone IV]).

4. White to Brockman Horne, interview, September 9, 1936 (first quotation); Littlefield to J. W. White, July 2, 1874, Littlefield to Shelton Dowell, May 17, 1880, LL; McClure to JEH, interview, September 22, 1935 (second quotation); Littlefield, G. W., and White, J. W., Gonzales, Livery Stable, R. G. Dun and Co. Credit Report Volumes, Vol. 11, Gonzales County, 204; *Southwestern Index*, January 10, 1873, *Gonzales Inquirer*, June 1, 1878; Daniell, *Texas*, 696–97; "Passing of a Lifelong Friend [John Wilburn White]," *Frontier Times* 17, no. 5 (February 1940): 230. Will said that the livery stable was part of the Foster purchase price (White to Horne, interview, September 9, 1936). The first year with Dilworth and Littlefield, Will White worked for board and clothes instead of a salary.

5. Harral to JEH, interview, June 11, 1939; Lamar, *Charlie Siringo's West*, 61; James M. Cook, *Fifty Years on the Old Frontier*, quoted in Wortham, *History of Texas*, 5:142–51.

6. Littlefield to Alice, August 3 (first quotation), October 29 (second quotation), 1881, ALP. Mabry, Gamel, and Ellison ended up repaying their loans with much or all of their ranch property (See Harral to JEH, interview, June 13, 1939; Charles Walker to JEH, interview, August 5, 1937). Being a cash business, this short-term speculation could make sleep uneasy. One December night in Kansas City, Littlefield slept fitfully on paper bundles containing forty-two thousand dollars.

7. John Dowell to Shelton Dowell, February 28, 1882 (first quotation); Littlefield to Shelton Dowell, June 29, 1879 (subsequent quotations), LL.

8. Littlefield to Alice, May 18, 20, June 6, August 3, 1881, ALP; Littlefield to John White, April 10, 1882, BL; *Ford County Globe*, January 3, 1882. Locating in New Mexico was no passing fancy, as he wrote about it twice more before completing the LIT sale.

9. Harral to JEH, interview, June 13, 1939 (first quotation); James F. Hinkle, *Early Days of a Cowboy on the Pecos* (1937; repr., Santa Fe: Stagecoach Press, 1965), 44; Haley, *Charlie Goodnight*, 134 (second quotation); William A. Keleher, *The Fabulous Frontier: Twelve New Mexico Items*, rev. ed. (Albuquerque: University of New Mexico Press, 1962), 60; Dale, *Range Cattle Industry*, 120.

10. Albuquerque *Republican Review*, April 10, 1875 (quotation), cited in Gerald Baydo, "Cattle Ranching in the Pecos Valley of New Mexico," *Rocky Mountain Social Science Journal* 8 (1971): 85–92; Haley, *Charlie Goodnight*, 92, 147, 233; Carole Larson, *Forgotten Frontier: The Story of Southeastern New Mexico* (Albuquerque: University of New Mexico Press, 1993), 106–9; Harwood P. Hinton, "Chisum, John Simpson," *Handbook of Texas Online*; R. A. Campbell, S. A. Mitchell, and H. F. Walling, *Mitchell's New General Atlas* (Philadelphia: Samuel Augustus Mitchell Jr., 1870), 53, 56; Keleher, *Fabulous Frontier*, 34, 60. Mitchell's 1870 map showed Bosque Grande on the west side of the river, but his 1874 map sited it correctly on the east bank.

11. Cox, *Historical and Biographical Record*, 18, 98; Keleher, *Fabulous Frontier*, 65; William W. Dunmire, *New Mexico's Spanish Livestock Heritage: Four Centuries of Animals, Land, and People* (Albuquerque: University of New Mexico Press, 2013), 72, 91–97; James D. Shinkle, *Fifty Years of Roswell History, 1867–1917* (Roswell, N.Mex.: Hall-Poorbaugh Press, 1964), 9–13.

12. Larson, *Forgotten Frontier*, 107; Shinkle, *Fifty Years of Roswell History*, 42.

13. National Live Stock Association, *Prose and Poetry of the Live Stock Industry of the United States, with Outlines of the Origin and Ancient History of Our Live Stock Animals* (1904; repr., New York: Antiquarian Press, 1959), 627 (first quotation), 628–39; Keleher, *Fabulous Frontier*, 61 (second quotation); Clarke, *A Century of Cow Business*, 2–3, Vivian H. Whitlock, *Cowboy Life on the Llano Estacado* (Norman: University of Oklahoma Press, 1970), 77–78 (third quotation).

14. McCarty, *Maverick Town*, 81–84; Nolan, *Tascosa*, 41–51, 78–90; Lamar, *Charlie Siringo's West*, 70, 81–85; Robert M. Utley, *Billy the Kid: A Short and Violent Life* (Lincoln: University of Nebraska Press, 1989), 2–8, 16, 145–47; Larson, *Forgotten Frontier*, 111; John H. White obituaries, newspaper clippings, July 31, August 1, 1942, BL; Morris Terry to DBG, interview, October

12, 2011; Littlefield to Alice, May 23, 1881, ALP; Phelps White to JEH, interview, March 2, 1933; Whitlock, *Cowboy Life*, 65–74. Regrettably, no one recorded White's stories.

15. Harral to JEH, interview, June 13, 1939 (first quotation); Keleher, *Fabulous Frontier*, 34, 60; Gordon, "Report on Cattle, Sheep, and Swine," 34 (second quotation).

16. Cecil Bonney, *Looking Over My Shoulder: Seventy-Five Years in the Pecos Valley* (Roswell: Hall-Poorbaugh Press, 1971), 140 (quotation); Littlefield to Alice, May 20, 23, June 6, 1881, ALP; Joseph B. Calhoun to James P. White, Deed, December 3, 1885, JPW; S. C. Dowell and Co., R. G. Dun and Co. Credit Report Volumes, Vol. 11, Gonzales County, 183; Littlefield to Shelton Dowell, fragment n.d., Dowell Littlefield Documents; Littlefield Wallet 4, Littlefield-Dowell Letters 2; George Littlefield, Texan, Literary Productions, JEHC; Littlefield to Shelton Dowell, June 29, 1879, May 17, June 22, July 23, 1880, August 24, 1881; Shelton Dowell to Littlefield, August 27, 1879, Lizzie Dowell to Shelton Dowell, July 8, 1881, LL. Conversation was so much a part of Tom White that those who knew him recalled only one man who was his match. The story is told that one evening when Tom and "Massa" John Beal fell into conversation Tom "couldn't finish a sentence or get a word in edgewise without Beal's drowning him out. They slept in the same room, and the last thing White said before dropping off to sleep, was, 'As I was going to say awhile ago . . . ' Beal cut him off before he could finish. White awakened about daylight the following morning, raised up on his elbow, looked over at Massa John, and said, 'As I was trying to tell you last night . . . ' But Beal again interrupted, and Tom White never did get to finish what he was going to tell" (Whitlock, *Cowboy Life*, 139).

17. LFD stood for "Littlefield," Phelps White stated unequivocally to JEH, interview, March 2, 1933. Through the years, creative imaginations fancied other meanings in the initials. "Littlefield Freight Drivers" was said to refer to the men "driving long mule teams strung in double tandem and responsive to a single jerk-line, . . . a familiar sight on the plains, hauling the mountains of supplies necessary to keep the giant ranches operating" (Gil Lea Hinshaw, *New Mexico's Last Frontier* [Hobbs Daily News-Sun, Hobbs, N.M., 1976], 78, and "History: Ranching," New Mexico Art Museum, http://online.nmartmuseum.org/nmhistory/growing-new-mexico/ranching /history-ranching.html). "Left For Dead" was said to refer to Littlefield hands picking up stray, weak cattle in the arid New Mexico climate, nursing them back to health, and thereby substantially enlarging Littlefield's herd ("Texas Ranchers, George Littlefield and the LFD Brand," Western Trips, http://westerntrips.blogspot.com/2012/04/texas-ranchers-george-littlefield-and- .html). Littlefield hand Charlie Walker claimed (to JEH, interview, March 5, 1937) that L stood for Littlefield, F for Phelps, and D for Tom (Thomas David) White.

18. G. W. Littlefield, J. P. White, Thomas D. White, Agreement, March 3, 1882, Littlefield Cattle Company, GWL and JPW; Hendrix, *If I Can Do It Horseback*, 46; William Martin Pearce, *The Matador Land and Cattle Company* (Norman: University of Oklahoma Press, 1964), 7. Phelps said (to JEH, interview, March 2, 1933) that the brothers owned one-quarter interest each, which was how the relationship matured.

19. *Austin Statesman*, February 12–18, 14 (second quotation), 15 (first quotation), 1882; *Ford County Globe*, February 28, 1882; Murrah, *Slaughter*, 39–40; Nolan, *Tascosa*, 78; Chester V. Kielman, "The Texas and Southwestern Cattle Raisers Association Minute Book," *Southwestern Historical Quarterly* 71 (July 1967): 100. A substantial minority were sheepmen. After the Civil War, Texas experienced a boom in sheep ranching for wool. Expanding rapidly, flocks spread to the far limits of West Texas in the 1870s, but the boom peaked in the 1880s (Paul H. Carlson, "Sheep Ranching," *Handbook of Texas Online*).

20. Reeves, "Sketch of Texas Cattle Industry," 11–13. The fourth period, from 1907 to 1927, focused on methods of further upgrading, that is, fattening, the stock. Reeves admitted, though, that he was too close to the period to tell whether it "will develop some outstanding change in the cattle business." See convention reports in the *Austin Statesman*, February 14, 17, 1882. Curiously, the historian of the Texas and Southwestern Cattle Raisers Association ignored this first statewide organization primarily of cattlemen, except in regard to a position it took on fencing (Clarke, *A*

Century of Cow Business, 39).

21. *Austin Statesman*, February 14–17, 1882; *Ford County Globe*, February 28, 1882.

22. Cox, *Historical and Biographical Record*, 98–99 (first quotation), 87–99; Dale, *Range Cattle Industry*, 111.

23. *Austin Statesman*, April 12 (second quotation), July 27, 1882 (first quotation). For market fluctuations during the 1870s and 1880s, see "From Panic to Boom, with Extremes of Prices in Both Directions," chapter 6 in Cox, *Historical and Biographical Record*, 87–102.

24. James F. Ellison, R. G. Dun and Co. Credit Report Volumes, Vol. 5, Caldwell County, 131; McArthur, "Cattle Industry of Texas," 67; Skaggs, *Cattle-Trailing Industry*, 10, 59–61; Dale, *Range Cattle Industry*, 43; *Austin Statesman*, March 12, 1882.

25. Littlefield to Alice, August 21 (first and second quotations), 1882, ALP; *Austin Statesman*, July 9, 1882 (third quotation).

26. Emmett, *Shanghai Pierce*, 144–45.

27. Littlefield to Alice, August 21 (first quotation), 22 (second quotation), 1882, ALP; James F. Ellison and wife E. J. Ellison to Littlefield, August 21, 1882, Deed Book 10, 255–56, Caldwell County Clerk; Jacob J. Ellison and wife Belle Ellison to Littlefield, August 21, 1882, Deed Book P, 456; James F. Ellison Sr. and Mrs. E. J. Ellison to Littlefield, Deed, August 21, 1882, Book P, 458, Hays County Clerk; J. J. Ellison and Wife to Littlefield, Deed, August 21, 1882, Travis County Deed Book 53, 179; *Austin Statesman*, September 3, 1882, March 24, 1889; Littlefield vs. Ellison, Case Papers No. 9293, Travis County District Court. Littlefield sent Charlie Walker to manage the Presidio County property (Charles Walker to JEH, interview, August 5, 1937).

28. J. F. Ellison Jr., "Sketch of Col. J. F. Ellison," in J. Marvin Hunter, comp. and ed., *The Trail Drivers of Texas* (1924; Austin: University of Texas Press, 1992), 478; J. P. White to Shelton Dowell, December 2, September 29, 1882, LL; Littlefield to John White, November 4, 1882, BL. Ellison Jr. misremembered his father's downfall as occurring two years before it actually did.

29. Littlefield to John White, November 4, 1882, BL.

30. Both quotations in Littlefield to John White, April 10, 1882, BL.

CHAPTER 9. PHELPS HAS DONE WELL

1. Texas Live Stock Association, *Proceedings of the Second Annual Session of the Texas Live Stock Association* (Texas Live Stock Association, 1883), 22 (quotation), 23; *Texas Live Stock Journal*, quoted in *Austin Statesman*, October 28, 1882; *Austin Statesman*, January 30, February 7, 9, 1883; Phelps White to JEH, interview, March 2, 1933; T. R. Havins, "The Passing of the Longhorn," *Southwestern Historical Quarterly* 56 (July 1952): 54–55.

2. Dixon, "History of Gonzales County," 33–34, 46; Ackman and Sachtleben, *Gonzales Drovers, Brands, Cattle*, 123; Littlefield to John White, November 4, 1882, BL; Littlefield, "Autobiography," [1919].

3. Littlefield to John White, April 10, 1882 (quotation), BL; Shelton Dowell to Lizzie Dowell, March 6, 1882, LL; *Ford County Globe*, April 18, 1882; Charles Walker to JEH, interview, March 5, 1937; Harral to JEH, interview, June 13, 1939. Phelps recalled giving Mrs. Ella Lea Calfee $1,600. The deed record shows the company paid $1,300 to the Rogerses. If Phelps's memory is accurate, then Calfee made $300 on her investment (Phelps White to JEH, interview, March 2, 1933; A. C. and Amelia D. Rogers to Littlefield Cattle Company, Deeds, January 1, 15, 1883, Deed Book, A, 42–43, Chaves County Clerk, and in Real Estate, GWL).

4. Littlefield to Alice, May 14, 1883 (first quotation), ALP; Phelps White to Shelton Dowell, September 29 (second quotation), December 2, 1882, LL. For examples of filings and purchases, see Frank Jennings, Homestead Claim 536, August 20, 1883; Thomas D. White, Homestead Claim 538, August 30, 1883, LFD Ranches,; and Jackson to Littlefield Cattle Company, Deed, November 2, 1885, Littlefield Misc., JPW; Harral to JEH, interview, June 13, 1939.

5. Phelps White to Shelton Dowell, September 29, 1882, LL; Phelps White to JEH, interview, March 2, 1933. Though the Louisiana cattle were bought for $1.50 a head, Phelps said they sold

a year or two later for $20 per head, a profit of no less than four times even after subtracting the costs of trailing and maintenance on the ranch.

6. Phelps White to JEH, interview, March 2, 1933; Littlefield to Shelton Dowell, June 19, 1882, LL; Littlefield to Alice, May 14, 1883, ALP. For Littlefield's social promotion from captain to major, see chapter 10.

7. "Rancher [Will H. Johnson] Remembers Early Centexas Days," *Austin American-Statesman*, June 5, 1966; Rufus W. O'Keefe, *Cowboy Life: Reminiscences of an Early Life, Early Boyhood and Experiences as a Cowboy on the Range, on the Trail, as Manager of a Ranch and Then Owner and Operator in Cattle* (San Antonio: Naylor, 1936), 104.

8. Phelps White to Shelton Dowell, September 29, 1882 (first and third quotations), LL; Keleher, *Fabulous Frontier* (second quotation), 64, 63; Dunmire, *New Mexico's Spanish Livestock Heritage*, 98.

9. Littlefield to Alice, May 14, 1884 (first quotation), ALP; Littlefield, "Autobiography," 1919 (second quotation); Littlefield to John White, November 4, 1882, BL. In his autobiography, Littlefield may have been melding two different events. First, his and Phelps White's recollections of the contributions of the White brothers to the Littlefield Cattle Company and the interests held by the parties to the agreement vary in some significant details. Second, it is unusual that the detail-oriented Littlefield would, without written record, so significantly amend the formal, lengthy agreement he himself had written out in 1882. On the other hand, both McCarty and Shelton Dowell witnessed but were not party to the 1882 agreement. If McCarty became a shareholder, the New Mexico meeting must have occurred as Littlefield described it. In time, Littlefield included Will White as a partner (White to Horne, interview, September 9, 1936).

10. On June 29, 1885, Littlefield made a final adjustment in the legal basis of his operation when he filed incorporation papers in Texas. In addition to nephews Phelps and Will White and John Dowell, Littlefield brought two prominent Austinites into the directorate. Twenty-five-year-old Austin city attorney Dudley Goodall Wooten was said to be "probably the most scholarly and extensively read and informed man of his age in the state" (Daniell, *Types of Successful Men*, 478). John Orville Johnson, one year Littlefield's senior, was leaving the state comptroller's office for postmastership of Austin, after which he served as city clerk (John O. Johnson File, Austin History Center). Though initially set up for a ten-year life, the company continued into Littlefield's estate (see Articles of Incorporation, Littlefield Cattle Company, June 26, 1885, GWL).

11. Littlefield, "Remarks on Cattle and Agriculture"; John M. Hendrix, "Perpetuating the Epoch of Cattle," *Cattleman* 23 (June 1936): 27; Dixon, "History of Gonzales County," 127–28; *History of Gonzales County*, 140–41; *Austin Statesman*, January 13, 1885. For county population statistics by decennial census, see *Texas Almanac*, https://texasalmanac.com/sites/default/files/images/topics/ctypophistweb2010.pdf.

12. McCoy, *Historic Sketches of the Cattle Trade*, 111–12 (quotation); *History of the Cattlemen of Texas*, 28; "Seth Mabry," in Hunter, *Trail Drivers of Texas*, 718; S. S. Mabry, U.S. Census, 1880, Population, Ancestry.com; Kenneth Hafertepe, "Cook, Abner Hugh," *Handbook of Texas Online*.

13. *Austin Statesman*, July 4, August 21, 1883; "The Story of Austin's Railroads" in *Along the Granite and Iron Route: A Guide to the Hill Country's Historic Excursion Railroad* (Cedar Park, Tex.: Austin Steam Train Association, 2011), n.p.; S. G. Reed, *A History of the Texas Railroads and of Transportation Conditions under Spain and Mexico and the Republic and the State* (Houston: Saint Clair Publishing, 1941), 211, 213–15, 315, 320. A resident of Austin at least since 1878, John Dowell, handled the purchase.

14. *Austin Statesman*, May 24, 1883.

15. O'Quinn, "O. Henry in Austin," 148; *Edwards and Church's General Directory of the City of Austin for 1883–4* (Austin: Edwards and Church or E.W. Swindells, [1883?]), 2; *Morrison and Fourmy's General Directory of the City of Austin, 1885–86* (Austin: Morrison and Fourmy, 1885), 230; Austin, Tex., listings in U.S. Census, Population, 1880, Ancestry.com; Texas Live Stock Association, *Proceedings of the Fourth Annual Session* (Austin: Warner and Draughon, 1886), 6–7, 48–49, 53–54; Joe B. Frantz, *The Driskill Hotel* (Austin: Encino Press, 1973), 6.

16. O'Quinn, "O. Henry in Austin," 148 (first quotation); *Edwards and Church's Directory, 1883–1884*, 2 (second quotation); *Austin Statesman*, July 13, 1886; unidentified ms. in Jesse Lincoln Driskill File, Austin History Center; Texas Live Stock Association, *Proceedings of the Fourth Annual Session*; Love, writing thirty years later, while many were still alive, charged inaccurately that the wealthiest spent "their time in luxury and travel, while their wealth increased faster than they could spend it" ("History of the Cattle Industry," *Southwestern Historical Quarterly* 20 [July 1916]: 16). While many such as Driskill and Littlefield built luxurious but not excessively large homes, these two, typical of the fraternity, traveled only on business, and cow business kept them away from home for extended periods.

17. *Austin Statesman*, May 1 (quotation), 17, 24, July 1, 4, September 7, November 15, 1883; Littlefield to Alice, October 29, 1881, August 28, 1883, ALP; Martin McCarty and Wife to Littlefield, Deed, July 3, 1883, Deed Book 56, 441, Travis County Clerk; John Dowell to Shelton Dowell, March 9, 1878, LL; Mary Starr Barkley, *History of Travis County and Austin, 1839–1899* (1963; 2nd ed., Austin: Steck Company, 1967), 261.

18. Littlefield to Alice, October 15 (second quotation), 21, 24 (first quotation), November 10, 1883, M. M. Harral to Alice Littlefield, October 12, 1883, ALP.

19. Littlefield to Alice, October 24, 1883, ALP; Littlefield to Shelton Dowell, April 5, 1875, LL.

20. Littlefield to Alice, October 24, 1883, ALP; Mrs. Augustus Wilson, ed. and comp., *The Opening Session of the First National Cattle Growers' Convention Held at St. Louis, Missouri, 1885 [1884] Extracted from Parsons' Memorial and Historical Library Magazine* (Bryan, Tex.: Fred White Jr., Bookseller, 1970), n.p. (second quotation).

21. On an average day, traveling at a comfortable pace, a rider could cover twenty to thirty miles. The caprock's height was judged from where the observer thought its base met the valley floor.

22. Harral to JEH, interview, June 13, 1939 (quotation); Whitlock, *Cowboy Life*, 10–11, 136; Eugene H. Price, *Open Range Ranching on the South Plains in the 1890s* (Clarendon, Tex.: Clarendon Press, 1967), 47–48; United States Geological Survey, Mescalero Point Quadrangle, New Mexico, Map, 2013.

23. Littlefield to Alice, May 23, 1883, ALP.

24. Harry Robinson, Desert Land Filing 167, June 8, 1883; and Addison Jones, Desert Land Filing 168, June 8, 1883, in JPW.

25. Though Robinson's life is shrouded in sketchy and contradictory details, eventually, after acquiring some dozens of head, he left the LFDs and built a one-room place a few miles south of Mescalero Spring as the headquarters of his small ranch. Everyone who visited remembered him playing music on the only phonograph for tens of miles around (Whitlock, *Cowboy Life*, 136, 183; Hinshaw, *New Mexico's Last Frontier*, 102–3; Lynn C. Mauldin, *Lea County, New Mexico: A Pictorial History* [Virginia Beach: Donning, 1997], 34–35).

26. See Michael N. Searles, "Addison Jones: The Most Noted Negro Cowboy That Ever 'Topped Off' a Horse," in Sara R. Massey, ed., *Black Cowboys of Texas* (College Station: Texas A&M University Press, 2000), 193–205; Boone, "An Oral History"; Frank Collinson to JEH, March 3, 1939, Haley File, Panhandle-Plains Historical Museum.

27. Littlefield to Alice, May 23, 1883, ALP.

28. Whitlock, *Cowboy Life*, 19; James I. Fenton, "Causey, Thomas L. [George]," *Handbook of Texas Online*; Haley, *XIT Ranch*, 45–46. For the full Causey story, see Whitlock, *Cowboy Life*, 3–20.

29. Whitlock, *Cowboy Life*, 3–4, 19, 134; Phelps White to JEH, interview, March 2, 1933.

30. Whitlock, *Cowboy Life*, 14, 134–35; Littlefield to Alice, May 14, 28, September 7, 1883, ALP; Harral to JEH, interview, August 7, 1937; Charles Walker to JEH, interview, March 5, 1937. To provide shade at his headquarters, Littlefield stuck a cottonwood buggy switch cut at the Bosque in the ground beside the bunkhouse. It grew into a tree massive in size as late as 1968 (J. R. Tipps to DBG, interview, October 31, 1968). Not the only such instance, a planted row of cottonwoods guided travelers along the northern trail into Roswell (Lucius Dills, "Retrospects on Early Roswell," in Shinkle, *Reminiscences of Roswell Pioneers*, 112).

31. *Ford County Globe*, January 3, 1882; Littlefield to Lizzie Dowell, May 3, November 3, 1886, LL.

32. Littlefield to Shelton Dowell, March 24, 1884, LL.

33. Littlefield to Alice, October 24, 1883, ALP; Cox, *Historical and Biographical Record*, 99.

34. Rogan, "Converts Cattle"; David C. Humphrey, *Austin: An Illustrated History* (Northridge, Calif.: Windsor, 1985), 54.

35. *Austin Statesman*, March 21, May 31, 1882; Marilyn McAdams Sibley, *George W. Brackenridge: Maverick Philanthropist* (Austin: University of Texas Press, 1973), 89–115; Joe E. Ericson, *Banks and Bankers in Early Texas, 1835–1875* (New Orleans: Polyanthos, 1976), 13, 55, 74, 89; Joseph M. Grant and Lawrence L. Crum, *The Development of State-Chartered Banking in Texas: From Predecessor Systems Until 1970* (Austin: University of Texas Bureau of Business Research, 1978), 25; Ann Johnston Dolce, *John H. Robinson: A Pioneer Austin Family, 1815–2010* (2010), 31–33; Barkley, *History of Travis County and Austin*, 68; *The Texas Almanac for 1868* (Galveston, 1868), 263; *The Texas Almanac for 1869, and Emigrant's Guide to Texas* (Galveston, 1869), 184; U.S. Census, 1860, 1870, 1880, Population, Austin, Travis County, Tex.

36. *Austin Statesman*, February 12, 23, March 21, May 31, 1882. As the bank prospered, so did Eugene Bremond. Two years later, in 1884, his wealth caused him to pay the largest tax bill of any Austin resident (*Austin American*, January 3, 1885).

37. Grant and Crum, *Development of State-Chartered Banking*, 23–24; Dixon, "History of Gonzales County," 55; *History of Gonzales County*, 287; White to Brockman Horne, interview, September 9, 1936.

38. "National Banking Acts of 1863 and 1864," *American History: From Revolution to Reconstruction and Beyond*, http://www.let.rug.nl/usa/essays/general/a-brief-history-of-central-banking /national-banking-acts-of-1863-and-1864.php.

39. Skaggs, *Cattle-Trailing Industry*, 106–7; Jimmy M. Skaggs, "The Great Western Cattle Trail to Dodge City, Kansas" (master's thesis, Texas Technological College, 1965), 1–2, 12–21.

40. Wilson, *Opening Session of the First National Cattle Growers' Convention*, 1 (first and third quotations), 8 (second quotation), 12 (fourth quotation). For a full account of the convention, see Cox, *Historical and Biographical Record*, 103–18; Skaggs, "The National Trail Issue and the Decline of Trailing," in his *Cattle-Trailing Industry*, 103–21.

41. Littlefield, "Autobiography," 1919.

CHAPTER 10. THE WAY TO MAKE MONEY

1. *Austin Statesman*, January 1, 2, 1885; Grand Central Hotel (Ellsworth Hotel Register, 1873–1904, Kansas State Historical Society). Many men were called by a military rank, whether or not earned. Never in uniform, Ike Pryor came to be addressed as "Colonel." A legitimate captain from his Confederate service, Littlefield was commonly so addressed until he received a social promotion to major, the rank of his battlefield promotion.

2. *Austin Statesman*, November 18, 1884, January 12, 1886. Estimates of the total of cattle varied widely. The percentages are computed from the contemporary estimates that some 19.2 million beef cattle roamed the states west of the Mississippi, of which 6.75 million—35 percent—grazed in Texas (Cox, *Historical and Biographical Record*, 119, 125–26; Nimmo, *Range and Ranch Cattle Business*, 54–55).

3. *Austin Statesman*, January 10, 1884, January 14, 15 (quotation), 16, 1885. Though the need for improvement had been accepted, members continued to discuss preferred breeds (see *Austin Statesman*, January 19, 1898, January 12, 1899). Finance, Protection from Disease, and the Improvement of Stock were Littlefield's three committees.

4. Skaggs, *Cattle-Trailing Industry*, 118–19.

5. *Austin Statesman*, October 10, 1885 (quotation); Cox, *Historical and Biographical Record*, 71–82; Texas Live Stock Association, *Proceedings of the Fourth Annual Session*, 32.

6. Cox, *Historical and Biographical Record*, 74–76; Skaggs, *Cattle-Trailing Industry*, 66, 96,

103–21; Dale, *Range Cattle Industry*, 43; *Austin Statesman*, October 10, 1885; *Las Vegas* (N.Mex.) *Stock Grower*, September 18, 1886.

7. Texas Live Stock Association, *Proceedings of the Fourth Annual Session*, 5; *Austin Statesman*, November 6, December 16, January 10, 13, February 6, 1885.

8. Texas Live Stock Association, *Proceedings of the Fourth Annual Session*, 8–9, 52.

9. *Dallas Morning News*, December 29, 1886, January 12, 14, 15, May 3, 1887; *Austin Statesman*, January 19, August 7, 12, 13, 1886, January 27, 1888, January 8, 1890, December 28, 1893, January 27, 1895; Skaggs, *Cattle-Trailing Industry*, 115–18; Skaggs, *Prime Cut*, 90–98. Holden, *Alkali Trails*, 50–51. Voiced for at least three years, the plan had failed to be adopted earlier, partly on account of what the Austin paper called "the Evil of Live Stock Transportation" by rail (*Austin Statesman*, February 13, July 24, 1883). Elegant in concept, the scheme lacked only the essential component that doomed the earlier and less ambitious plan of the Northern Pacific Refrigerator Company. It neglected provision for marketing the dressed beef, except for calling on the state to build a deep-water port to facilitate export.

10. Cox, *Historical and Biographical Record*, 223, 238; *Austin Statesman*, March 17, 1887, January 19, 1898, January 12, 1899; Skaggs, *Cattle-Trailing Industry*, 120–21; Skaggs, "John Thomas Lytle," 14; Clarke, *A Century of Cow Business*, 92–93; Bank Book, 1894–1896, GWL. In 1893 south Texas cattlemen and counterparts from the Northwest Texas Cattle Raisers Association formed the Cattle Raisers Association of Texas. Maintaining the Northwest Association's emphasis on combating theft, it in time supplanted the second TLSA. Littlefield did not join the Cattle Raisers Association of Texas until 1902 because of a dispute over rendering twenty-five thousand head of cattle for dues (Executive Committee Minutes, April 22, 1895, August 30, 1897, March 13, 1902; *Souvenir Programs*, 1899, 1904, Texas and Southwestern Cattle Raisers Association Records, BCAH; Larry Marshall, T. C. Richardson, and Dick Wilson, "Texas and Southwestern Cattle Raisers Association," *Handbook of Texas Online*). The historian of the Texas and Southwestern Cattle Raisers Association, which claimed the Northwest association as its beginnings, made no mention of the Texas Live Stock Association (Clarke, *A Century of Cow Business*).

11. George and Alice Littlefield to M.A. and C. M. Rogers, Vendor's Lien, July 8, 1884, Deed Book S, 507–15, Hays County Clerk; Martha A. and C. M. Rogers to George and Alice Littlefield, Promissory Notes, July 8, 1884, Book 1, 187, Caldwell County Clerk; Littlefield to Shelton Dowell, July 7, September 3, 1884, March 6, 1885, LL; *Austin Statesman*, September 15, 1883, July 9, 1884; Dixon, "History of Gonzales County," 29–30.

12. G. W. Littlefield, "Remarks on Cattle and Agriculture"; *Golden Era*, quoted in Keleher, *Fabulous Frontier*, 113–14. To his dying day, Littlefield held his high opinion of the Pecos as cattle country (Littlefield, "Autobiography," 1919). Crowding onto the Pecos range increased until by 1889, only Texas's open range region was more densely stocked (Cox, *Historical and Biographical Record*, 18).

13. *Prose and Poetry*, 682; *History of the Cattlemen of Texas*, 43; Keleher, *Fabulous Frontier*, 112. Unlike buffalo, which roamed widely, cattle were confined, so grass constantly trampled and grazed had little opportunity to recover.

14. Haley, *Charles Goodnight*, 256 (quotation); Patrick Dearen, *A Cowboy of the Pecos* (Plano: Republic of Texas Press, 1997), 119, 126.

15. Phelps White to Shelton Dowell, December 2, 1882, LL.

16. Victor Westphall, *The Public Domain in New Mexico, 1854–1891* (Albuquerque: University of New Mexico Press, 1965), 24–25 (first quotation), 27–28; Phelps White to Shelton Dowell, December 2, 1882, LL (second quotation); Cox, *Historical and Biographical Record*, 98.

17. James M. Miller, "Sheep Ranching on the Chisum Cattle Range," in James D. Shinkle, *Reminiscences of Roswell Pioneers* (Roswell: Hall-Poorbaugh Press, 1966), 62, 25–63; Charles W. Walker to JEH, interview, March 5, 1937.

18. B. Byron Price, *The Chuck Wagon Cookbook: Recipes from the Ranch and Range for Today's Kitchen*, rev. ed. (Norman: University of Oklahoma Press, 2004), 119–21.

19. Ballard to Chesley, interview, in Chesley, *Adventuring with the Old-Timers*, 63 (first quotation); Miller, "Sheep Ranching," in Shinkle, *Reminiscences of Roswell Pioneers*, 55 (second quotation); Shinkle, *Fifty Years of Roswell History*, 41; Littlefield to Lizzie Dowell, June 24, 1886, LL; *Austin Statesman*, February 10, 1886; Elvis E. Fleming, *Captain Joseph C. Lea: From Confederate Guerrilla to New Mexico Patriarch* (Las Cruces, N.Mex.: Yucca Free Press, 2002), 52–53, 67–75, 123–24, 220; Daniell, *Types of Successful Men*, 351. So close did Phelps White and Joseph Lea become that White served as a pallbearer in Lea's funeral.

20. Dearen, *Cowboy of the Pecos*, 185 (quotation), 186; *Austin Statesman*, August 5, 7, 1885; *Prose and Poetry*, 689; Dixon, "History of Gonzales County," 29–30.

21. *Prose and Poetry*, 707 (quotation), 707–9; *Austin Statesman*, January 30, 1886; O'Keefe, *Cowboy Life*, 234; Dearen, *Cowboy of the Pecos*, 185–99; Murrah, *Slaughter*, 57–58; Miller, "Sheep Ranching," 44–56; Shinkle, *Fifty Years*, 51–56, 61–63; *Las Vegas Stock Grower*, February 26, July 9, 1887; Fleming, *Lea*, 123–31; Larson, *Forgotten Frontier*, 242; J. Phelps White III to DBG, December 19, 2015. For a moving description of the die ups on the northern plains, see Mari Sandoz, *The Cattlemen: From the Rio Grande across the Far Marias*, 2nd ed. (Lincoln: University of Nebraska Press, 2010), 249–71. So widespread was it that the drought was "a landmark" in West Texas history too (Holden, *Alkali Trails*, 129).

22. Texas Live Stock Association, *Proceedings of the Fourth Annual Session*, 30–33; Cox, *Historical and Biographical Record*, 136–42; *Prose and Poetry*, 682, 702; *History of the Cattlemen of Texas*, 43.

23. Shinkle, *Fifty Years*, 55–57; Keleher, *Fabulous Frontier*, 58; Dearen, *Cowboy of the Pecos*, 192–93; *Prose and Poetry*, 691; Holden, *Alkali Trails*, 45; Cox, *Historical and Biographical Record*, 145–58; Murrah, *Slaughter*, 60; H. Allen Anderson, "Hashknife Ranch," *Handbook of Texas Online*; "Legends of Arizona: The Aztec Cattle Company and the Hashknife Outfit," http: //www.legendsofamerica.com/az-hashknife.html.

24. Frank Lloyd to JEH, interview, June 12, 1939 (quotation), quoted in Dearen, *Cowboy of the Pecos*, 190; *Ford County Globe*, May 13, 1884; Littlefield to Lizzie Dowell, June 24, 1886, LL; *Las Vegas Stock Grower*, February 26, April 30, July 9, 1887; Charles Walker to JEH, interview, March 5, 1937; Harral to JEH, interview, June 13, 1939.

25. Charles Walker to JEH, interview, March 5, 1937; Whitlock, *Cowboy Life*, 134–35.

26. Addison Jones to Littlefield, Deed, July 16, 1883, Real Estate, GWL; Phelps White to JEH, interview, March 2, 1933; Harral to JEH, interview, June 13, 1939; Charles Walker to JEH, interview, March 5, 1937. Likely the offer had a dual purpose, as Phelps found Harral's service at Bosque Grande unsatisfactory (Shelton Dowell to Lizzie Dowell, May 4, 1885, S. C. Dowell Items, GWL).

27. Lowell O'Hare, "Social and Economic History of Roosevelt County to 1925" (master's thesis, Texas Technological College, 1949), 18–19; Mary Lee Robinson, "History of Roosevelt County, New Mexico" (master's thesis, University of Texas, 1947), 68; Charles Walker to JEH, interview, March 5, 1937; Harral to JEH, interview, June 13, 1939. Though memories disagree on the year McCarty made his move, he had established the T71 in time for the *Las Vegas Stock Grower* to report on January 15, 1887, that he took his bride to his ranch.

28. Most called him Bill or Uncle Billy, but not older brother George.

29. Boone III, "Oral History," December, 1986; George T. Littlefield to JEH, interview, March 4, 1937; Harral to JEH, interview, June 13, 1939; Edgar Harral, manuscript fragment, n.d., Edgar Harral File, HL; Shelton Dowell to Lizzie, May 4, 1885, S. C. Dowell Items, GWL; Littlefield to Lizzie Dowell, February 23, 1889, LL; Grace Margaret Evans to DBG, interview, July 25, 1970; Murphey, "Kenna"; O'Hare, "Roosevelt County to 1925," 18–19; Charles F. Coan, *A History of New Mexico* 3 vols. (Chicago: American Historical Society, 1925), vol. 3, 396; Minnie Timms Harper and George Dewey Harper, *Old Ranches* (Dallas: Dealey and Lowe, 1936), 67, 70; George A. Wallis, "Major George W. Littlefield and the Yellow House: A Texas Ranger Who Made $6,000,000 in Ranching," *True West*, 11, No. 4 (March–April, 1964), 9–10. The spring has

alternatively been called Hernandez Spring for the men who found it and from whom William bought it and Barnum Spring. The spring at the T71 headquarters also has been called Hernandez Spring. See Boone, "An Oral History"; John W. Murphey, "Kenna," New Mexico History, http: //www.newmexicohistory.org/places/kenna; Robinson, "History of Roosevelt County," 68; and O'Hare, "Roosevelt County to 1925," 18–19.

30. Price, *Open Range Ranching*, Map; *Rand, McNally and Co's. Indexed County and Township Pocket Map and Shippers' Guide of New Mexico* (Chicago: Rand, McNally, 1891); O'Hare, "Roosevelt County to 1925," 15; Robinson, "History of Roosevelt County," 64–69; George T. Littlefield, "History of the Littlefield Ranch Began in 1884," *Portales Tribune*, April 1, 1938. William's son, George, remembered an H Bar outfit but did not mention its owner.

31. Shelton Dowell to Lizzie Dowell, May 4, 1885, S. C. Dowell Items, GWL; Littlefield to Shelton Dowell, March 24, 1884, LL; Bonney, *Looking Over My Shoulder*, 142.

32. Whitlock, *Cowboy Life*, 135–36; J. P. White to James Sutherland, November 22, 1891, GWL Letters, JPW; Map in Harral to JEH, interview, June 13, 1939. As George drew his LFD brand from his last name, perhaps brother William adopted LIV for his position as the fourth-born of his Littlefield generation.

33. McCarty sold the final portions in 1896. Apparently he abandoned ranching altogether, as he moved into Roswell, where he served as Chaves County's first tax assessor (Abstract of Title in McCarty File, JPW; Shinkle, *Fifty Years*, 110).

34. Polly or Mollie, James, and Jordan (U.S. Census, 1880, Population, Caldwell County, Tex.).

35. Dunn to DBG, interview, December 31, 1963; Stoke[s], Nathan and Mary Grants, Marriage Record, December 25, 1867, Gonzales County Clerk; U.S. Census, 1870, Population, Belmont, Gonzales County, Tex.; U.S. Census, 1880, Population, Caldwell County, Tex.; Nathan Stokes to Littlefield, Deed, June 6, 1892, Book E, 175, Chaves County Clerk; Charles Walker to JEH, interview, March 5, 1937. Nathan's marriage having ended, he bunked at the T71 headquarters.

36. Littlefield to Lizzie Dowell, February 23, 1889, LL.

37. Christine Littlefield Buford, "My Life," ms. in possession of Nancy Buford.

38. Cox, *Historical and Biographical Record*, 117–18, 141–58; *Prose and Poetry*, 683; Murrah, *Slaughter*, 58–64; Dale, *Range Cattle Industry*, 94–98.

39. Littlefield to Edgar Harral, March 12, 1889, Littlefield Biographical File, HL.

40. The other is a portion of William Littlefield's LIV that includes the original headquarters site. Though long out of the family, two ranches still operate under the name Littlefield gave them: the LIT and the Four Lakes.

41. *Fort Worth Gazette*, June 24, 1890 (first quotation); *Austin Statesman*, August 16, 1888 (second quotation); J. W., J. A., and J. C. Gamel to Littlefield, Deed, August 11, 1888, Deed Book N, 369–74; J. W., J. A., and J. C. Gamel to Irving Eggleston, Deed of Trust, August 11, 1888, Deed of Trust Book B, 372–74, Mason County Clerk; George W. Littlefield v. James F. Ellison Jr., et al., Statement, January 9, 1890, Case 9293, Civil Minutes Book T, 398, Travis County District Clerk; Charles Walker to JEH, interview, August 5, 1937; B. B. Paddock, ed., *History of Central and Western Texas* (Chicago: Lewis Publishing, 1911), vol. 1, 449–50; Price, *Open Range Ranching*, 47. For the property, Littlefield paid Gamel $11,573 in cash and assumed $40,000 in land and tax payments. A very brief history of the Mill Creek Ranch is found in Margaret Bierschwale, *History of Mason County, Texas, through 1964*, 2 vols. (Mason, Tex.; Mason County Historical Commission, 1998), vol. 1, 203–4.

42. White to Horne, interview, September 9, 1936; Littlefield to Lizzie Dowell, October 14, 1888, January 11, 1889, LL; Brand 3902, Marks and Brands Book C, 189, Mason County Clerk.

43. J. W. White to JEH, interview, October 18, 1935; Bierschwale, *History of Mason County*, 1:193.

44. White to Horne, interview, September 13, 1936 (quotations), Will White to JEH, interview, October 18, 1935. After marrying Cora Bridges in 1891, Will White settled into the Mason

community. In 1899, as some of his seven children matriculated in the schools, he served on the school board. In 1904 he participated in organizing the German American (later Mason) National Bank, which he served as president for many years, see Kathryn Burford Eilers, "A History of Mason County, Texas" [master's thesis, University of Texas, 1939], 173, 186, 193; Daniell, *Texas*, 696–97.

45. The house's story is in chapter 11.

46. White to Horne, interview, September 9, 1936; Seth Mabry to Littlefield, Deeds, March 31, 1894, Book S, 253–79, Mason County Clerk; Littlefield, "Autobiography," 1919; *Mason County News*, April 6, 1894, cited in Bierschwale, *History of Mason County*, 1:209; Haley, *Littlefield*, 68–71, 70 (quotation).

47. White to Horne, interview, September 13, 1936. More than simply for recreation, Littlefield wrote that hounds should be used to protect cattle from wolves (Littlefield to Edgar Harral, March 12, 1899, Littlefield Biographical File, HL; Littlefield and J. W. White, Statement, March 31, 1894, in Seth Mabry and D. H. Snyder, GWL).

48. Jim W. Roberts to JEH, interview, June 24, 1937 (first and third quotations); "Rancher Remembers Early Centexas Days" (second quotation); Bierschwale, *History of Mason County*, 1:196n.

49. Ballard to Chesley, interview, quoted in Chesley, *Adventuring with the Old-Timers*, 64 (first quotation); Charles Walker to JEH, interview, August 5, 1937 (second quotation); Price, *Open Range Ranching*, 48–50.

50. Edgar Harral to JEH, interview, June 13, 1939 (quotation); Charlie Walker to JEH, interview, August 5, 1937; Ballard to Chesley, interview, in Chesley, *Adventuring with the Old-Timers*, 63–64. See Littlefield to Lizzie Dowell, February 5, 1891, February 26, 1892, LL, regarding annual settlements. For a description of cutting, see Whitlock, *Cowboy Life*, 156.

51. Harral to JEH, interview, June 13, 1939 (first quotation); Charlie Walker to JEH, interview, August 5, 1937 (second quotation); Littlefield to Lizzie Dowell, April 9, 1889, November 7, 1891, June 21, 1893, LL; *Las Vegas Stock Grower*, February 16, March 2, 1889; Ike Pryor quoted in Holden, *Alkali Trails*, 45–46; Hinshaw, *New Mexico's Last Frontier*, 105–6; Murrah, *Slaughter*, 69–70.

52. Westphall, *Public Domain in New Mexico*, 27 (Sparks quotation), 28, 98–99, 119–21, 164–65; Littlefield to Lizzie Dowell, April 9, 1895, LL; Price, *Open Range Ranching*, Map.

53. Hannah and Miller to James P. White, October 14, 1899; Commissioner of Public Lands of New Mexico to James P. White, Lease, July 23, 1908, JPW; Price, *Open Range Ranching*, Map; *Territory of New Mexico* (Map) (Washington, D.C.: General Land Office, 1907). For a broad discussion of cattlemen and land law on the Great Plains, see Everett Dick, *The Lure of the Land: A Social History of the Public Lands from the Articles of Confederation to the New Deal* (Lincoln: University of Nebraska Press, 1970), 220–41; Valerie Weeks Scott, "The Range Cattle Industry: Its Effect on Western Land Law," *Montana Law Review* 28 (Spring 1967): 168 (155–83); *Prose and Poetry*, 743. Even had the land office surveyed the Four Lakes land, Congress had provided no machinery for collecting the rent (Love, "History of the Cattle Industry," 5, 9–11). Had the congressional act been enforced, Littlefield would have had to pay approximately $36,000 annually for use of the some 1,440 sections in 40 townships the ranch was growing rapidly to occupy.

54. Littlefield to Lizzie Dowell, January 11, 1893 (first quotation), Dowell-Littlefield Documents, JEHC; Littlefield to Lizzie Dowell, November 7, 1891, LL; Will White to JEH, interview, September 9, 1936 (second quotation).

55. Saunders, "More Lore of Cattle Trails," 43.

CHAPTER 11. MY OWN MAN

1. *Austin Statesman*, June 29, 1884.

2. Ibid., December 10, 1894, January 1, 1885; Texas Legislative Council, *The Texas Capitol: Symbol of Accomplishment* (Austin: Texas Legislative Council, 1982), 71; Frederick W. Rathjen, "The Texas State House," in *The Texas State Capitol*, ed. Robert C. Cotner (Austin: Pemberton Press, 1968), 11.

3. Barkley, *History of Travis County and Austin*, 233–34; "Washington Fire Company No. 1, 1868–1916," Austin Fire Museum, http://www.austinfiremuseum.org/blog/the-volunteer-fire-companies/washington-fire-company-no-1/.

4. *Austin Statesman*, December 27, 1889, July 10, 1886.

5. Ibid., March 18, December 11, 12, 15, 1886, January 6, 20, 27, March 11, April 10, 1887; *Austin Record*, December 18, 1886; Capitol Dedication Program, ADG. Some of Alice's recipes for these lunches may be among her contributions to *Our Home Cook Book* (1891), Austin's first cookbook presenting recipes of local women. Alice's thirteen offerings, including delicacies as mock turtle or calf's head soup, Christmas plum pudding, and Charlotte Russe, totaled the second most of any contributor. See Michael C. Miller, *Austin's First Cookbook: Our Home Recipes, Remedies and Rules of Thumb* (Austin: American Palate, 2015), 11, 12,18, 23–24, 37, 39, 47–48, 54, 55, 66.

6. *Austin Statesman*, November 6, 1884 (quotation); John Bell Hood Camp, Minutes, September 4, 1894, Minute Book, 1889–1895, 134, John Bell Hood Camp, United Confederate Veterans, 103, Texas Confederate Museum Collection, HL. See also Rusty Williams, *My Old Confederate Home: A Respectable Place for Civil War Veterans* (Lexington: University of Kentucky Press, 2010), 4.

7. R. B. Rosenburg, *Living Monuments: Confederate Soldiers' Homes in the New South* (Chapel Hill: University of North Carolina Press, 1993), xii, 3 (quotation); *Austin Statesman*, November 1, 6, December 11, 1884; *Confederate Gray Book: John B. Hood Camp, United Confederate Veterans, 103, Austin, Texas* (ca. 1913); Terry's Texas Rangers Association, Minutes, May 25, June 14, 1871, Weems Papers; Alice Daniel to JEH, interview, July 18, 1939; Williams, *My Old Confederate Home*, 10; Gaines M. Foster, *Ghosts of the Confederacy: Defeat, the Lost Cause, and the Emergence of the New South* (1985; repr., Oxford: Oxford University Press, 1987), 6–7. Though the name in the November 6 paper is A., not G., W. Littlefield, Austin city directories list no A. W. Littlefield. Since, in the standard type tray, upper case A and G are housed at opposite ends of a row of letters, the compositor must have become momentarily confused as to which end of the row was which (see A. A. Stewart, comp., *Type Cases and Composing-Room Furniture: A Primer of Information about Type Cases, Work Stands, Cabinets, Case Racks, Galley Racks, Standing Galleys, &c.* [1918], https://www.gutenberg.org/files/31704/31704-h/31704-h.htm#structure_of_type_cases).

8. Hood Camp, Minutes, December 10, 1889; clipping, December 7, 1889, Minute Book, 1889–1895, 53–54. The camp's minutes are both incomplete and document little of camp affairs beyond the work of officers and board in financing the Confederate Men's Home.

9. *Austin Statesman*, January 21 (three stories), 22, December 14, 1887, January 11, 26, December 20, 1888; clipping, January 20, 1887, Weems Papers. Terry Ranger association documentation of the period is nonexistent.

10. Hood Camp, Minutes, December 10, 1889, Minute Book, 1889–1895, 53–54.

11. Rosenburg, *Living Monuments*, 32–34.

12. Littlefield to Lizzie Dowell, November 16, 1896 (quotation), LL; Cotner, *Hogg*, 131; Ed Cravens to DBG, interview, January 29, 1970; Key to DBG, interview, January 26, 1970.

13. James E. Ferguson to JEH, interview, January 6, 1938 (first quotation); D. K. Woodward to JEH, interview, January 14, 1939 (second quotation). For the 1868 quotation, see chapter 1.

14. *Austin Statesman*, October 29, 1892.

15. *Austin Statesman*, February 5, 1885; George W. Littlefield, Appointment, January 3, 1893; George W. Littlefield, Oath of Office, January 4, 1893, Texas Bonds and Oaths of Office, 1846–1920, Texas State Archives; *Austin Statesman*, October 22, 1891; James W. Markham and Paulette Delahoussaye, "Texas School for the Blind and Visually Impaired," *Handbook of Texas Online*; Lelia Bailey, "Economic History of Texas' Institution for the Blind" (master's thesis, University of Texas, 1922), 18–25. So completely did Littlefield share his friend's "progressive conservative bent," as Hogg's biographer phrased it, that nearly thirty years later the Major would provide in his will for erection of a heroic-size statue of the popular state leader, to this day the only likeness

in bronze (George Washington Littlefield, Will, July 1, 1918, GWL; Robert C. Cotner, *James Stephen Hogg: A Biography* [Austin: University of Texas Press, 1990], 313). Perhaps Rainey, head of the blind institution for nearly half of its forty-six-year existence and Hood Camp president in the mid-1880s, suggested appointment of Littlefield, whom he knew through the Hood Camp (*Dallas News*, May 23, 1909; Jeanette H. Flachmeier, "Rainey, Frank," *Handbook of Texas Online*).

16. Minutes, 1888–1891, 138; July 13, 1891, 140; September 4, 1891, 146; John Bell Hood Camp, Minutes, 1889–1895, January 14, 1890, 66; January 13, 1891, 91; February 10, 1891, 93; *Austin Statesman*, September 25, 1885, January 15, 1890; E. Zimmermann, U.S. Census, Population, 1880. Securing the owed funds would take more than three years (Hood Camp Minutes, June 5, 1894, 132).

17. Littlefield, "Autobiography," 1919; *Austin Statesman*, March 28, 1890; Mary Toomey Tompkins, "Littlefield Name Texas Institution," *Dallas News*, April 11, 1942; Gene M. Gressley, *Bankers and Cattlemen* (New York: Alfred A. Knopf, 1966), 145; Ruth Ann Overbeck, *Alexander Penn Wooldridge* (Austin: Von Boeckmann-Jones, 1963), 24–26.

18. *Austin Statesman*, January 1, 1885, March 18, April 9, 1886, July 7, 1889, April 11, May 11, May 14 (first quotation), 1890; Humphrey, *Austin*, 128 (second quotation); Monte Akers, *A History of the Driskill Hotel: The Grande Dame of Austin* (Austin: Austin History Center Association, 2017), 21–36; Thomas W. Cutrer, "Hamby, William Robert," *Handbook of Texas Online*; Barkley, *History of Travis County and Austin*, 146; "John Henry Houghton," in Daniell, *Texas*, 246–48.

19. *Austin Statesman*, March 13 (quotation), 28, 1890; Humphrey, *Austin*, 127–43; T. Harry Gatton, *The Texas Bankers Association: The First Century, 1885–1985* (Austin: Texas Bankers Association, 1964), 60, 62.

20. Samuel E. Gideon, *Austin and the Austin National Bank, 1890–1940* (Austin: Austin National Bank, 1984), 4; Avery Luvere Carlson, *A Monetary and Banking History of Texas from the Mexican Regime to the Present Day, 1821–1929* (Fort Worth: Fort Worth National Bank, 1930), 21–46. Despite the well-publicized rivalry, through the years Littlefield and Wilmot continually worked together on committees promoting the civic and financial improvement of the city.

21. *Austin Statesman*, December 17, 1886, April 16, June 22 (quotations), 1890; Gideon, *Austin National Bank*, 4–5; Joe B. Frantz, *The Driskill Hotel* (Austin: Encino Press, 1973), 9–15; Photographs, Banks and Savings, American Bank, Austin History Center; Littlefield to Alice, June 28, 1890, ALP.

22. Littlefield to Lizzie Dowell, July 10, 1890, LL (first quotation; italics mine, emphasizing Littlefield's confidence in his leadership of his new bank); *Austin Statesman*, July 26, 1891 (second quotation).

23. Littlefield to Alice, June 28, 1890, ALP.

24. Sibley, *Brackenridge*, 96–100, 117 (second quotation), 108, 116–19; Bowman to JEH, interview, January 8, 1938; Littlefield to H. G. Seeligson, November 30, 1912, Littlefield Letterpress Book, GWL (hereafter LLPB); O'Quinn, "O. Henry in Austin," 148; O. Henry, "Friends in San Rosario," *Roads of Destiny* (1902; Garden City: Doubleday, Page, 1920), 155–70. For practices in financing the cattle business, see Dale, *Range Cattle Industry*, 161–64. Carlson's description of the small town state banker's relationship with his customers applied as well to bankers specializing in cattle (*Monetary and Banking History of Texas*, 37–38).

25. *Austin Statesman*, April 3, May 31, 1895; "American Millionaires: The Tribune's List of Persons Reputed to Be Worth a Million or More" (June 1892), reprinted in *New Light on the History of Great American Fortunes: American Millionaires of 1892 and 1902*, ed. Sidney Ratner (New York: Augustus M. Kelley, 1953), 53. The list's compilers made no effort to determine approximate worth.

26. Littlefield to Lizzie Dowell, March 7, 1893, LL.

27. Ruth Key to DBG, interview, May 6, 1965; "Jesse Lincoln Driskill," manuscript in Jesse Lincoln Driskill, 96, AF—Biography File, Austin History Center; Christopher Long, "Wahrenberger, James," *Handbook of Texas Online*.

28. Wayne Smith, "Littlefield Home," (ms., 1965, in possession of the author) (quotations); Roxanne Kuter Williamson, *Austin, Texas: An American Architectural History* (San Antonio: Trinity University Press, 1973), 105; White to Horne, interview, September 9, 1936. Niece Sarah Duggan, who lived in both Littlefield homes, recalled the three-hundred-thousand-dollar cost figure (Sarah Harral Duggan to Alice Gracy, interview, September 19–20, 1962). Usable space in the basement and attic bring the total square footage to 13,947.

29. Lou White to DBG, interview, November 5, 1966; Alice Duggan Gracy to Wayne Bell, interview, n.d.; David White to DBG, interview, November 1, 2011.

30. Carl Widen to DBG, interview, June 8, 1971 (quotation); Lomax, "Review of *George W. Littlefield, Texan*," 443–44; John W. Calhoun Narrative, "Trees on the Campus of the University of Texas," John William Calhoun Papers, BCAH; Thomas Ulvan Taylor, *Fifty Years on the Forty Acres* (Austin: Alec, 1938), 87; William J. Battle, "Littlefield Memorial Dormitory," *Alcalde* (January 1928): 136. Lomax, who got the story from his father, supposed that the unpleasant shower precipitated Littlefield's building the west wall. In fact, the wall was built simultaneously with the mansion (photograph in Daniell, *Texas*, 137). In "He Left His Brand," *Houston Chronicle Magazine*, May 25, 1958, 4, Dick King claims erroneously that the incident activated Littlefield's interest in education. Accounts disagree as to whether the cedar elms or hackberries died or were stunted from their disruption. Moved to a location west of the site of Littlefield Dormitory, the house was demolished to make way for the residence hall.

31. *Austin Statesman*, December 19, 1894 (quotation), January 2, 6, 1895.

32. Henry A. Dunn to DBG, interview, December 11, 1963 (quotation); Max Bickler to DBG, interview, May 16, 1968; Maurice Dowell to JEH, interview, January 12, 1939; Alice Daniel to JEH, interview, July 18, 1939; Ruth Key to DBG, interviews, February 4, 1963, November 1, 1964, and January 26, 1970; Campbell Jackson Duggan to DBG, interview, July 17, 1964; Littlefield, Will, July 1, 1918; Austin City Directories, 1897–1901. Nathan was not the only former slave who served Confederate forces to whom Littlefield gave a job and a stipend. When John Price, porter and cook for B Company, Fourth Texas Regiment, Hood's Brigade, could no longer perform his porter work in the Austin post office, Littlefield hired him as porter in the bank simply to provide him an income. Beyond the salary, Littlefield also gave "Uncle John" $2.50 war money every Saturday (Val C. Giles, "A Brave Old Black Confederate," *Austin Statesman*, December 31, 1901).

33. Dunn to DBG, interview, December 31, 1963.

34. Mrs. Berkeley Holman to DBG, interview, January 30, 1970. "Terrible" had a double meaning. To former slave and Littlefield hand Harrison McClure, as clearly to Uncle Nathan, it meant "very good."

35. Alice Daniel to JEH, interview, July 18, 1939; Benson, "Finally at Rest"; *Austin City Directory, 1891–1892*, 146.

36. *Dallas News*, September 11, 1895 (first two quotations); Littlefield to Lizzie Dowell, December 7, 1912 (third quotation), LL. Littlefield was referring to elected office, not board appointments.

CHAPTER 12. PEOPLE MAKE THEIR OWN LIVES

1. *Austin Statesman*, May 25, 1895.

2. Ibid., July 17, 1895; Littlefield to Lizzie Dowell, May 12, 1896, LL.

3. *Austin Statesman*, May 19 (first quotation), September 10 (second quotation), October 1, 1897, February 23 (third quotation), March 30, 1898.

4. Littlefield to Lizzie Dowell, June 24, 1889, LL.

5. Littlefield to Lizzie Dowell, July 10, 1890, March 25, July 10, August 2 (second quotation), September 6 (first quotation), 1904, LL; Irwin Daniel, U.S. Census, Population, 1870 and 1900; Alice Daniel, U.S. Census, Population, 1870 and 1880; Texas Death Certificates for Irwin Daniel, January 6, 1909, Alice Daniel, June 16, 1941, available on Ancestry.com.

6. *Austin Statesman*, July 1, 1898; Littlefield to Lizzie Dowell, September 6, 1904, LL.

7. Littlefield to Lizzie Dowell, March 25, September 6, 1904 (first quotation), January 7, 1905 (second quotation), LL; Ruth Key to DBG, interview, ca. June 1964.

8. Littlefield to Lizzie Dowell, August 22, 1904 (quotation), September 29, 1905, September 6, 30, November 3, 1906, January 9, 1909, LL.

9. Harral to JEH, interview, June 13, 1939; Littlefield to Lizzie Dowell, March 25, May 16, 1904, LL.

10. Littlefield to Lizzie Dowell, July 23, 1898, LL; Littlefield to Victor Harral, November 3, 1909, LLPB.

11. Littlefield to Lizzie Dowell, November 27, 1891 (second quotation), May 14, 1894 (third quotation), February 5, 1895, May 12, 1896 (first quotation), LL.

12. Littlefield to Lizzie Dowell, May 6, 1896, LL.

13. Littlefield to Lizzie Dowell, July 10, 1890 (second quotation), January 12, 1910 (first quotation), LL.

14. Buford, "My Life." Two who knew said that rejection of Uncle's discipline caused Christine to never play a note after she married and left Uncle's home (Harless and Dobbins to DBG, interview, August 14, 1970).

15. Littlefield to Lizzie Dowell, September 23, 1893, LL. See Ed Cravens to DBG, interview, January 29, 1970.

16. John Dowell to Shelton Dowell, January 31, 1871 (quotation), LL.

17. Martha M. Harral to Littlefield, Receipt, April 21, 1891, Accounts, 1891–1919, Family Financial Records, Anglo-American Land, Mortgage, and Agency Co., Ltd. To Littlefield, Assignment of Mortgage, March 15, 1897, Miscellaneous Business; Littlefield, Appointment of T. F. Harwood as Substitute Trustee, June 10, 1897; T. F. Harwood, Statement, August 3, 1897, Land Documents, GWL; Littlefield to Lizzie Dowell, January 18, 1900, LL; U.S. Census, Population, 1880, Gonzales, Theo Harrell [Harral]. Though George built this Gonzales house for his sister and never lived in it himself, the structure is known as the George W. Littlefield House (Paul Frenzel, *Historic Homes of Gonzales* [Gonzales, Tex.: Reese's Printing, 1999], 26–27).

18. Known for the quality materials and construction he required are the Littlefield Building and the Littlefield Dormitory.

19. Littlefield to Lizzie Dowell, November 7, 1891 (quotation), December 10, 1895, LL.

20. Littlefield to Lizzie Dowell, November 7, 1891, June 13, 1893, November 27, 1900, LL.

21. Alice Gracy to DBG, interview, July 4, 1993. Sarah Duggan is the author's grandmother. Her daughter, my mother, Alice Duggan Gracy, on many occasions related this story of her mother's lifelong reaction to Littlefield's supervision. Along with the reaction, my grandmother ever spoke of her love for and appreciation of her uncle.

22. Littlefield to Lizzie Dowell, July 20, 1896, March 25, 1904 (quotation), LL; Lisa C. Maxwell, "Mary Nash College," *Handbook of Texas Online*; Ina May Ogletree McAdams, *Texas Women of Distinction: A Biographical History* (Austin: McAdams, 1962), 87. Sallie Harral graduated valedictorian and received the class medal for excellence in instrumental music (*Austin Statesman*, June 5, 1897).

23. Littlefield to Lizzie Dowell, October 28, 1897, September 17, 1898, LL.

24. Ruth Key to DBG, interview, January 26, 1970 (first quotation); Ruth Key to Alice Gracy, interview, December 5, 1943; Pat Boone III, "An Oral History," 17, 18 (second quotation), 19; George T. Littlefield, "History of the Littlefield Ranch Began in 1884," *Portales Tribune*, April 1, 1938; U.S. Census, 1900, Military and Naval Population, Philippine Islands.

25. Littlefield to Maurice Dowell, December 29, 1904, LL.

26. Edmunds Travis to DBG, interview, June 9, 1971. See also Alfred Ellison's comments in Carl Widen and Alfred Ellison to DBG, interview, June 8, 1971.

27. Littlefield to Lizzie Dowell, February 23, 1889 (quotation), April 9, 1895, LL; Maurice Dowell to JEH, interview, March 24, 1937. The number included Mississippi half brother John White's daughter Gertrude.

CHAPTER 13. THE BEST AND SAFEST BUSINESS

1. *San Antonio Express*, October 18, 1898, Shinkle, *Fifty Years*, 128; Westphall, *Public Domain in New Mexico*, 71.

2. Larson, *Forgotten Frontier*, 218–29, 227 (first quotation), 262 gives the date as 1891; John J. Lipsey, *The Lives of James John Hagerman: Builder of the Colorado Midland Railway* (Denver: Golden Bell Press, 1968), 243 (second quotation), 244; Sophie A. Poe, *Buckboard Days* (Caldwell, Idaho: Caxton Printers, 1936), 260–62; Fleming, *Lea*, 75–78, 137–44; *Roswell Record*, September 5, 1905; Morgan Nelson, "When the South Springs Stopped Flowing," *Roswell Record*, March 20, 2016; Shinkle, *Fifty Years*, 97, 129–30; Phelps White III to DBG, July 20, 2012.

3. Larson, *Forgotten Frontier*, 258–70; Fleming, *Lea*, 75–79, 148–49; Keleher, *Fabulous Frontier*, 200–201.

4. Lucius Dills quoted in Shinkle, *Fifty Years*, 125; Larson, *Forgotten Frontier*, 82, 199; Fleming, *Lea*, 118–20.

5. Case 1790, Solon M. Owens, Ewing Graham, George W. Littlefield and J. Phelps White, a Co-partnership, and R. E. Hornor v. Southspring Ranch and Cattle Company, Complaint, April 29, 1910, Chaves County District Court; Jonathan W. Buck to Littlefield, Deed, November 4, 1891, Book E, 107; Ada B. Davis to Littlefield, Deed, May 9, 1892, Book B, 187; G. A. Richardson to Littlefield, Deed, March 8, 1892, Book E, 133; William H. H. Miller, et ux., to Littlefield, Deed, March 27, 1893, Book B, 353; and M. R. Lewis, et ux., to Littlefield, Deed, November 21, 1893, Book B, 353, Chaves County Deeds; Shinkle, *Fifty Years*, 107–11, 128–35; Larson, *Forgotten Frontier*, 243.

6. Ada B. Davis to Littlefield, Deed, May 9, 1892, Book B, 187, Chaves County Deeds; *Austin Statesman*, April 26, 1903; unidentified clipping, 1914, Littlefield Scrapbook, GWL; Shinkle, *Fifty Years*, 119.

7. Whitlock, *Cowboy Life*, 138; *Austin Statesman*, April 26, 1903.

8. *Roswell Record*, October 15, 1903 (first quotation), February 6, September 8, 1904; *Austin Statesman*, April 26, 1903 (second quotation), March 3, 1918; George M. Slaughter to C. C. Slaughter, April 26, 1903, George M. Slaughter Papers, Southwest Collection, Texas Tech University; unidentified clipping, 1914, Littlefield Scrapbook; Schedule of Farm Income and Expenses, 1918, Littlefield and White Income Tax Return, 1919, GWL; Daniell, *Texas*, 141; Shinkle, *Fifty Years*, 118–23; Dermot H. Hardy and Ingham S. Roberts, *Historical Review of South-East Texas and the Founders, Leaders and Representative Men of Its Commerce, Industry and Civic Affairs*, 2 vols. (Chicago: Lewis Publishing, 1910), vol. 2, 892. The property's fine house played its own role. Phelps's father lived his last years in it with his daughter and son-in-law. And the house hosted great-nieces' joyous parties (*Roswell Record*, January 6, 1904, August 21, 1905, September 19, 1907).

9. Unidentified clipping, 1914, Littlefield Scrapbook; Hardy and Roberts, *Historical Review of South-East Texas*, 2:891; Murrah, *Slaughter*, 80–81.

10. Charles Walker, Answers, May 19, 1894, in Capitol Freehold Land and Investment Company vs. Littlefield Cattle Co., et al., Case 11,569, Travis County District Court; Elvis E. Fleming and Minor S. Huffman, eds., *Roundup on the Pecos* (Roswell, N.Mex.: Chaves County Historical Society, 1978), 19; Shinkle, *Fifty Years*, 118–21.

11. Fleming, *Lea*, 133, 136–37; Larson, *Forgotten Frontier*, 82; Capitol Freehold Land and Investment Company vs. Littlefield Cattle Company, et al., Case 11,569, Travis County District Court; *Las Vegas Stock Grower*, May 14, 1887; Skaggs, *Cattle-Trailing Industry*, 113–17; Wayne Gard, "Fence Cutting," *Handbook of Texas Online*. Haley (*XIT Ranch*, 86–88, 105–16) describes troubles with rustlers but not with New Mexico herds.

12. Capitol Freehold Land and Investment Company vs. Littlefield Cattle Company, et al., Case 11,569, Travis County District Court; Bob Burton, "The Early Days of The Southern Kansas Railway of Texas," *Panhandle-Plains Historical Review* 64 (1991), unpaged version at "A Branchline Comes of Age," Santa Fe Railway Historical and Modeling Society, http://www.atsfrr

.com/resources/burton/branch-1.htm; Larson, *Forgotten Frontier*, 267–69; Murphey, "Kenna"; George T. Littlefield, "History of the Littlefield Ranch," *Portales Tribune*, April 1, 1938; Pat Boone IV to DBG, June 9, 2016; Ann Musser to DBG, June 9, 2016; Bryan Moseley to DBG, June 16, 2016; Robinson, "History of Roosevelt County," 74–75, 214–15; O'Hare, "Roosevelt County," 19, 92–94.

13. The 1880 U.S. census estimated the cost of stringing a barbed wire fence at $110 per mile. Five years later, cattleman Slaughter spent $250. In some places the cost reached $400. And prices rose such that in 1890, fence posts cost Littlefield two and a half times their price half a decade earlier (Love, "History of the Cattle Industry," 9; Henry D. and Frances T. McCallum, *The Wire that Fenced the West* [Norman: University of Oklahoma Press, 1965], 130; Charlie Walker to JEH, interview, March 5, 1937; Haley, *XIT Ranch*, 87; Murrah, *Slaughter*, 46–47).

14. Littlefield to Lizzie Dowell, February 5, 1900 (quotation), April 17, 1896, December 23, 1897, December 1, 1899, LL; Charlie Walker to JEH, interview, August 5, 1937; *Prose and Poetry*, 740–42; McArthur, "Cattle Industry of Texas," 287; *Henrietta Journal* quoted in John Stricklin Spratt, *The Road to Spindletop: Economic Change in Texas, 1875–1901* (1955; repr., Austin: University of Texas, Press, 1970), 90; Tatum, N.Mex., *Golden Jubilee Souvenir*, 1959 (Tatum, N.Mex.,1959), n.p. One author claimed the Four Lakes total to have reached eighty thousand head. This would have packed the animals at one for every ten Four Lakes acres or one for every twenty-one acres over the entire 1.75-million-acre domain Littlefield controlled (Charlie Walker to JEH, interview, August 5, 1937; George A. Lipp, "Passing of the Western Cattle Ranchers," *Overland Monthly* 68 [February 1914]: 138; Clyde Allen True, "Development of the Cattle Industry in the Southwest" [master's thesis, Texas Christian University, 1928], 101).

15. *Prose and Poetry*, 739; Spratt, *Road to Spindletop*, 97–104; Walter Prescott Webb, *The Great Plains* (Boston: Houghton Mifflin, 1936), 237–40.

16. *Prose and Poetry*, 739–40; Littlefield, Executive Committee Report, in *Fourth Annual Proceedings of the Texas Live Stock Association*, 14 (quotation). Neighbor John Chisum's business model, by contrast, appears never to have varied from its focus on upgrading the stock (see Harwood P. Hinton, "John Simpson Chisum," *New Mexico Historical Review* 32 [January 1957]: 61). Littlefield's early twentieth-century feedlot operations with Henry C. Storey depended on solid management more than on cattle breeding (see H. C. Storey File, Littlefield Bankbooks, 1898–1916; Henry C. Storey to H. A. Wroe, May 17, 1917, GWL).

17. Price, *Open Range Ranching*, 40–44 (first quotation), 45 (second quotation); *Prose and Poetry*, 743; *Lubbock Avalanche*, April 1, 1903, cited in John Allison Rickard, "The Cattle Ranch Industry of the Texas South Plains" (master's thesis, University of Texas, 1927), 81. Charlie Walker told Haley (interview, March 5, 1937) how he convinced a land office agent of the drift fences' importance by taking him out in a norther to see one doing its job.

18. Price, *Open Range Ranching*, 45–46; Whitlock, *Cowboy Life*, 138; *Roswell Record*, September 14, 1904, March 20, 1906.

19. Robinson, "History of Roosevelt County," 69–70, 73–79; O'Hare, "Roosevelt County," 22–23; George T. Littlefield to Littlefield, March 9, 1915, George T. Littlefield File, William P. Littlefield to Littlefield, July 23, 1918, W. P. Littlefield File, GWL; Thomas Merlan, *Historic Homesteads and Ranches in New Mexico: A Historic Context* (Santa Fe: New Mexico Office of Cultural Affairs, Historic Preservation Division, 2010), 12; Larson, *Forgotten Frontier*, 268.

20. Harve H. Harris, "Sixty Years in West Texas and New Mexico," Harve H. Harris Papers, Southwest Collection, Texas Tech University; Jefferson Davis Hunter, "Memoirs of a West Texas Cowboy," August 4, 1936, interviewed by and filed under Cornelia Hunter, Manuscript-Interview Collection, Panhandle-Plains Historical Museum, Canyon, Tex.; Mauldin, *Lea County, New Mexico*, 4, 37–29, 91–121; Tatum, "Golden Jubilee," n.p.; Commissioner of Public Lands, New Mexico Territory, to James P. White, Lease, July 23, 1908, May 24, 1912, In re—Townships 34 and 35—11S, 12S, 92,160 acres, n.d.; Mateo Lujan to White, December 26, 1913, JPW. For examples of entries on the Four Lakes, see Kellahin and McDonald to James P. White,

Guarantee of Assigned Soldier's Additional Homestead Right, May 5, 1899; Receivers' Duplicate Receipt, Homestead application No. 1656, January 10, 1901, JPW. O'Hare ("Roosevelt County," 23) reported that Bill Littlefield bought quarter sections to freeze out settlers wishing to claim full sections. In her earlier, longer, and more substantial "History of Roosevelt County," 78–79, 208–15, Robinson noted no such activity. If Bill did do this, it was out of character with brother George, who did not impede settlement on the Four Lakes Ranch (see also Mauldin, *Lea County, New Mexico*, 4, 37–29, 91–121).

21. Littlefield to Alice, April 23, 1901, photocopy in possession of the author.

22. Lewis Nordyke, *Cattle Empire: The Fabulous Story of the 3,000,000 Acre XIT* (New York: William Morrow, 1949), 244–46; H. Allen Anderson, "Boyce, Albert Gallatin"; David B. Gracy II, "Farwell, John Villiers," *Handbook of Texas Online*.

23. George Findlay to A. G. Boyce, April 23, 1901, Boyce-Findlay Letters, XIT Ranch Papers; Haley, *XIT Ranch*, 75.

24. George Findlay to A. G. Boyce, April 15, 23, May 3, 16, May 17 (first quotation), 1901, Boyce-Findlay Letters; Findlay to Frank Crisp, July 12, 1901; Findlay to H. Milner Willis, September 11, 1901, Letterpress book; Findlay to Stephens, April 15, 1901 (second quotation), XIT Ranch Papers; Littlefield to Arthur Duggan, April 9, 1913, LLSWC; Haley, *XIT Ranch*, 218; Nordyke, *Cattle Empire*, 246–47. By 1904 cattlemen generally saw what Littlefield and the XIT leadership perceived three years earlier. Dick Worsham in the *Fort Worth Record*, January 26, 1904 (cited in Rickard, "Cattle Ranch Industry of the Texas South Plains," 136) concurred with A. G. Dawson ("Texas' Great Cattle Industry," *Texas Almanac and State Industrial Guide for 1904* [Galveston: A. H. Belo, 1904], 123) that large ranch owners realized that their land was rapidly becoming "too valuable for grazing purposes."

25. Findlay to William Boyce, June 13, 1901, Boyce-Findlay Letterbook; Findlay to A. G. Boyce, May 9, 16, 1901, Letterbook; Findlay to Frank Crisp, July 13, 1901; Findlay to Boyce Letters, Accounts, Ledger, General, 1893–1902, 372; Accounts, Journal, General, 1893–1906, 175, 218, 223, 264, 275, 307, 343, 399; Accounts, Journal, General, 1906–1907, 43, XIT Ranch Papers; Littlefield to Lizzie Dowell, May 12, 1906, LL; A. G. Boyce to Littlefield, Receipt, n.d.; Quintin Hogg and William Quartus Ewart to Littlefield, Statement, November 22, 1901, Capitol Syndicate File, GWL; Arthur Duggan to Littlefield, April 16, 1913; Littlefield to Duggan, April 19, 1913, LLSWC; *Austin Statesman*, July 21, 1901. In a fat elbow shape, the ranch's longest dimensions stretched almost twenty-two miles east–west by twenty-six miles north–south.

26. *Austin Statesman*, May 19, 1901; Littlefield to Lizzie Dowell, May 31, 1903, LL.

27. *Austin Statesman*, May 19, 1901, August 25, 1902.

28. National Cattle Co., Interstate Land Co., and Charles Goodnight, with George W. Littlefield, Agreement, March 13, 1902, in Miscellaneous Book A, 412, Chaves County Clerk; Carl Coke Rister, "Beales's Rio Grande Colony"; Raymond Estep, "Beales, John Charles," *Handbook of Texas Online*; *Austin Statesman*, March 10, 1887.

29. Collinson to JEH, March 3, 1939; Jayne Taylor, "'Bud' Wilkinson" (ms., Archives, Historical Society for Southeastern New Mexico, Roswell); Margaret V. Watt, "McCord's Ranch: A Chronicle of Sounding Lake," *Canadian Cattlemen*, December 1952, 10, 11, 14, 38; January 1953, 34, 35, 38; Price, *Open Range Ranching*, 49; Yellow House Ranch Account Book, 1909–1913, GWL; Hunter, *Trail Drivers of Texas*, 189.

30. George M. Slaughter to C. C. Slaughter, April 26, 1903, George Slaughter Papers, Southwest Collection, Texas Tech University; Littlefield to Lizzie Dowell, May 31, 1903, June 14, 1906 (quotation), LL; J. Phelps White obituary, *Roswell Record*, October 22, 1934; Iverson, "White and Allied Families," 57–59; Fleming and Huffman, *Roundup on the Pecos*, 73; "Accounts Ledger Traces Yellowhouse Operation," *Lamb County Leader*, June 27, 1963. Phelps intended to make the couple's home at the Yellow House headquarters, but the 1904 prairie fire caused them to settle in Roswell.

31. *Austin Statesman*, March 7, 12, 1904 (first quotation); Littlefield to Lizzie Dowell, December 4, 1903 (second quotation), LL; Love, "History of the Cattle Industry," 17.

32. The story of that day has been so garbled since its first report that three versions agree only on the central character (see "Fire Chased Ranch Manager Out West," *Austin Statesman*, April 1, 1904; Bonney, *Looking Over My Shoulder*, 137; and Stu Pritchard, "Prairie Fire on the Yellowhouse in 1904," *Vision Magazine* [Roswell, N.Mex.], December 3, 2010). The account related here is based on George Littlefield White's telling of his father's experience that day in "Early Ranching by Maj. Littlefield and J. P. White," *Lamb County Leader*, August 18, 1938. The only entry in Yellow House account books related to the fire is $7.00 for medicine (Yellow House Ranch Account Book, Four Lakes Ranch Account Book, 1909–1915, GWL).

33. George M. Slaughter to C. C. Slaughter, April 29, 1904, George Slaughter Papers; David Joe Murrah, "A Cattle Kingdom on Texas' Last Frontier: C. C. Slaughter's Lazy S Ranch" (master's thesis, Texas Tech University, 1970), 96–97. To help their neighbor, the Slaughters afforded pasture for some 1,500 LFD cattle left without grazing (Hiley T. Boyd Jr. to DBG, interview, May 19, 1969, Southwest Collection, Texas Tech University).

34. Littlefield to Lizzie Dowell, March 18, 1905, March 29, 1906 (quotation), LL; George Slaughter to C. C. Slaughter, July 1, 1904, February 28, 1905, George Slaughter Papers; Rickard, "Cattle Ranch Industry of the South Plains," 63–66, 70–72, 147. Three months after the 1904 fire, Phelps sold five thousand two-year-old heifers for seventy-five thousand dollars, relieving pressure to find a place for them until the grass recovered (*Roswell Record*, June 30, 1904). Application of the pesticide, called dipping, required cattle to pass singly through a narrow trough so filled with the solution that only the animal's head remained above the liquid (*Roswell Record*, August 10, 1905).

35. Littlefield to Lizzie Dowell, February 27, 1906, March 18, 1905, June 21, 1906, LL.

CHAPTER 14. I'LL DO THE REST

1. Littlefield to T. M. Harwood, May 24, 1894, Thomas M. Harwood, University of Texas Board of Regents Records (hereafter BOR).

2. Ford Dixon, "Roberts, Oran Milo," *Handbook of Texas Online*; John Boles, "Robert Lewis Dabney," *Dictionary of Virginia Biography* online, Encyclopedia of Virginia, http://www.encyclopediavirginia.org/Dabney_Robert_Lewis_1820-1898.

3. Littlefield to Harwood, May 24, 1894, Thomas M. Harwood, BOR; Will White to JEH, interview, September 13, 1936.

4. Littlefield to Frank B. Chilton, December 10, 1909, Frank B. Chilton Papers, Texas Collection, Baylor University. For a succinct Southern view of the war's causes, see John H. Reagan, "Causes of the Civil War," in *Unveiling and Dedication of Monument to Hood's Texas Brigade on the Capitol Grounds at Austin Texas, Thursday, October Twenty-Seven, Nineteen Hundred and Ten and Minutes of the Thirty-Ninth Annual Reunion of Hood's Texas Brigade Association Held in Senate Chamber at Austin Texas, October Twenty-Six and Twenty-Seven, Nineteen Hundred and Ten, Together with a Short Monument and Brigade Association History and Confederate Scrap Book*, comp. Frank B. Chilton (Houston: F. B. Chilton, 1911), 317–20.

5. Harral to JEH, interview, June 13, 1939 (quotation); Littlefield to John White, April 14, 1861, BL; Foster, *Ghosts of the Confederacy*, 4–8, 115–19; Caroline E. Janney, "The Lost Cause," Encyclopedia of Virginia, http://www.encyclopediavirginia.org/Lost_Cause_The. Considering themselves to have been in the right, Confederate veterans bristled at being called "rebels" (Chilton, *Unveiling and Dedication*, 98).

6. Littlefield, "Autobiography," 1919.

7. Foster, *Ghosts of the Confederacy*, 115–31.

8. Thomas Watt Gregory quoted in Thomas Cary Johnson, *Life and Letters of Robert Lewis Dabney* (Richmond, Va.: Presbyterian Committee of Publication, 1903), 461 (quotation); Foster, *Ghosts of the Confederacy*, 72; Boles, "Robert Lewis Dabney"; Evan Anders, "Gregory, Thomas Watt," *Handbook of Texas Online*. Young professor Thomas Ulvan Taylor, who took walks with his senior, recalled Dabney saying he thought he had mellowed, even to the point that "I have

become so liberal that I think *some* Yankees may go to heaven" (Taylor, *Fifty Years on Forty Acres*, 83, 84 [quotation]).

9. *Louisville Courier-Journal* cited in Johnson, *Life and Letters of Robert Lewis Dabney*, 488 (quotation); Jeffrey David Ray, "The Education of Robert Lewis Dabney" (PhD diss., University of Southern Mississippi, 2006), 189; Littlefield to Harwood, May 24, 1894; Harwood to Dabney, March 1, 1894, Harwood, BOR; Boles, "Robert Lewis Dabney." The regents' minutes are silent regarding Dabney's dismissal (see BOR Minutes, January 16–17, April 30 May 1, 1894, University of Texas System, Meetings Archive, https://www.utsystem.edu/board-of-regents/meetings/meetings-archive; *Austin Statesman*, January 15, 1890).

10. Quoted in Ray, "The Education of Robert Lewis Dabney," 190–91. Regent Thomas D. Wooten expressed concern, too, about overbearing religious influence on the school. He worried about it coming from a proposed Episcopal women's residence (Thomas D. Wooten to Harwood, January 10, 1894, Harwood, BOR).

11. Littlefield to Frank B. Chilton, September 30, 1907, quoted in Harold B. Simpson, *Hood's Texas Brigade in Reunion and Memory* (Hillsboro, Tex.: Hill Junior College Press, 1974), 175; H. P. N. Gammel, *The Laws of Texas, 1822–1897*, 10 vols. (Austin: Gammel, 1898), vol. 9, 26.

12. *Dallas Morning News*, October 29, 1890; *Austin Statesman*, December 3, 1891 (quotation); Richard B. McCaslin, "How the Hood's Texas Brigade Monument Came to Be," ms. in possession of the author; Amelia W. Williams, "Alamo Monuments," *Handbook of Texas Online*.

13. Foster, *Ghosts of the Confederacy*, 128–29; Senate Concurrent Resolution No. 22, Twenty-Fifth Texas Legislature, April 16, 1897, in Gammel, *Laws*, 10:270; *Austin Statesman*, June 2, 1898.

14. *Austin Statesman*, June 2, 1898 (two articles); Henry F. Pringle, *Theodore Roosevelt: A Biography* (1931; repr., New York: Harcourt, Brace, 1956), 132–37.

15. Just how novel the technology of the modern Driskill was for Rangers familiar only with the affordances of small towns J. A. Holman told years later. A bellboy showed him and several comrades into their room, equipped with steam heat and "a large electric light with globe" hanging from the ceiling, then departed without instructing them in the operation of either. First, "they all tried to figure out why the room was so 'dratted' warm without a stove. They finally gave that question up, he said, and proceeded to retire." Then, "when all were abed, one of the Rangers asked another to 'blow' out the light. This was attempted repeatedly, in vain. Finally one of them said: 'Oh, well, let the d—n thing burn.' And it did, all night" (*Austin Statesman*, January 6, 1920).

16. "Texas Rangers Reunion at Austin," *Confederate Veteran*, 6:372–73 (quotation); Austin *Statesman*, June 2, 1898.

17. *Austin Statesman*, June 2, 1898, October 6, 1899 (quotation); Henry W. Graber, *The Life Record of H. W. Graber: A Terry Texas Ranger, 1861–1865: Sixty-Two Years in Texas* (H. W. Graber, 1916), 401–21; W. W. Graham to J. G. Booth, May 18, 1898, Weems Papers.

18. "Camp Mabry Fighters," *Austin Statesman*, June 2, 1898; "With the Terry Rangers," *Austin Statesman*, July 2, 3, 1898.

19. Hood Camp, Minutes, March 9, 1892, January 2, April 8, 1893; Pompeo Coppini, *From Dawn to Sunset* (San Antonio, Tex.: Naylor, 1949), 70–72.

20. Coppini, *Dawn to Sunset*, 80–81, 90 (quotation), 99; Cadwell Walton Raines, *Year Book for Texas*, 2 vols. (Austin: Gammel-Statesman, 1903), vol. 2, 80–81; Gammel, *Laws*, 10:228, 11:661–62; Hood Camp, Minutes, March 9, 1892, 109, January 2, 1893 112; Caroline Remy, Jean L. Levering, and Eldon S. Branda, Kendall Curlee, rev., "Coppini, Pompeo Luigi," *Handbook of Texas Online*; Kelly McMichael, *Sacred Memories: The Civil War Monument Movement in Texas* (Denton: Texas State Historical Association, ca. 2009), 15.

21. Coppini, *Dawn to Sunset*, 80.

22. Raines, "History and Description of the Monument in the Capitol Grounds to the Confederate Dead," *Year Book*, 2: 81; Hood Camp Minute Book, January 29, March 29, April 14, 1903.

23. Littlefield to George T. McGehee, Statement, [1903], Weems Papers; clippings in Confederate Veterans Reunion Scrapbook, Christopher Columbus Slaughter Papers, Southwest Collection, Texas Tech University; Martha Ann Hartzog to DBG, March 10, 2014; Murrah, *Slaughter*, 122–23; Cathy Wright to DBG, September 19, 2016. For the painting of Benjamin Franklin Terry, Littlefield was the agent in behalf of the Terry Ranger Association. Alice Littlefield donated the John Reagan portrait.

24. Littlefield to Frank Rainey, April 18, 1911, LLPB.

25. For Cohen, see John and Deborah Powers, *Texas Painters, Sculptors and Graphic Artists: A Biographical Dictionary of Artists in Texas before 1942* (Austin: Woodmont Books, 2000), 99; *Charleston Mercury*, April 5, 1861. The paintings are housed in the Littlefield Home at the University of Texas in Austin.

26. Littlefield to George T. McGehee, ca. 1901, Weems Papers.

27. *Austin Statesman*, December 17, 1903; Proceedings of the Terry's Texas Rangers Association, Extract, November 16, 1904, Terry's Texas Rangers Association, GWL; Littlefield chairman, et al., to W. R. Davis and Members of Terry Rangers Association, Report, November 14, 1905; Geo. W. Littlefield Statement, [1907], Weems Papers.

28. Coppini, *Dawn to Sunset*, 124; Raines, "History and Description," *Year Book*, 81.

29. Vernon Loggins, *Two Romantics and Their Ideal Life: Elisabet Ney, Sculptor, Edmund Montgomery, Philosopher* (New York: Odyssey Press, 1946), 241, 270, 295–304; Emily Fourmy Cutrer, *The Art of the Woman: The Life and Work of Elisabet Ney* (1988; repr., College Station: Texas A&M University Press, 2016), 126–27, 157, 184–86.

30. Dowell, [Littlefield Reminiscence].

31. Cutrer, *Art of the Woman*, 151–52, 197–99.

32. Coppini to D. C. McCaleb, May 3, 1911 (first quotation), General Correspondence, Coppini-Tauch Papers, BCAH; *Austin Statesman*, November 16, 17, 1904, April 14, May 10, 12, 21 (second quotation), 1905. Coppini told McCaleb (May 3, 1911) that the Terry Ranger monument was his own conception "and God only know if I didn't have all I can do to hold fast to it!" In a December 22, 1940, feature story headed "'Terry Texas Rangers' Statue at Capitol Gains World Fame," the *Statesman* reported that Baedeker travel guides included it as "one of the outstanding features of Austin."

33. *Austin Statesman*, July 18, 1905, March 4, July 18, November 7, 18, 1906, March 24, 27, June 27, 1907.

34. Ibid., June 23, 22, 1907.

35. White to Horne, interview, September 13, 1936.

36. Margaret C. Berry, *The University of Texas: A Pictorial Account of Its First Century* (Austin: University of Texas Press, 1980), 34–36, 38; Sam Beall Southwell, "A Social and Literary History of Austin From 1881 to 1896" (master's thesis, University of Texas, 1949), 18.

37. *Austin Statesman*, December 9, 1897 (first, third, and fourth quotations), June 10, 1899; *Ranger* (University of Texas), December 8, 1897 (second quotation), November 25, 1898, June 10, 1899.

38. *Austin Statesman*, November 16, 1897, January 27, May 22, June 26, 1898, June 1, 1898; BOR, Minutes, January 18, May 16, September 29, 1898. Following a variety of benefit events, the way was constructed in 1899.

39. *Austin Statesman*, March 31, 1896, March 1, 1897, June 26, 1898, June 25, 1899, October 12 (first quotation), 13, 1902, January 3, July 10, 12, 1904, July 29, 1905 (second quotation); Barkley, *History of Travis County and Austin*, 245–47, 250–51, 331; Humphrey, *Austin*, 150–53; Overbeck, *Wooldridge*, 40; Stuart A. MacCorkle, *Austin's Three Forms of Government* (San Antonio: Naylor, 1973), 26.

40. John W. Brady to JEH, interview, January 7, 1938; Edward Crane to Roy Bedichek, November 15, 1943, Littlefield Book, JEHC; Thomas W. Cutrer, "McCall, John Dodd," *Handbook of Texas Online*.

41. George T. Littlefield to JEH, interview, March 4, 1937.

42. *Austin Statesman*, March 25, 26 (first quotations, last quotation), March 27 (next to the last quotation), 1903; Calvert, Cantrell, and De León, *History of Texas*, 282–83.

43. *Austin Statesman*, February 17, April 21, 1903; MacCorkle, *Austin's Three Forms of Government*, 15–16, 23–29.

44. *Austin Statesman*, November 21, December 31 (second quotation), 30 (first quotation), 1905.

45. Bruce Mercer to DBG, September 7, 18, 2018; Sam Stimson to DDG, October 2, 2018; Daniell, *Texas*, 142; Daniell, *Types of Successful Men*, 352.

46. *Austin Statesman*, June 26 (first quotation), 27 (second and third quotations), 1907; Hamby to Chilton, October 1, 1907, Chilton Papers.

47. *Austin Statesman*, June 30, 1907; Weems "To the Terry Texas Rangers Association," ca. 1906, Weems Papers, described in Dorothy Sloan Rare Books Auction Catalog 23, 2013, http://www.dsloan.com/Auctions/A23/item-terrys_texas_rangers.html.

CHAPTER 15. SYNONYMOUS WITH AUSTIN'S ASPIRATIONS AND AMBITIONS

1. *Austin Statesman*, December 9, 1905, December 27, 1906, January 2, 1910 (quotation), June 22, 1919; S. E. Cole to JEH, interview, January 22, 1939; Humphrey, *Austin*, 112–21; Barclay, *History of Austin and Travis County*, 142–43; United States Bureau of Labor, Bulletin, quoted in *Austin Statesman*, July 26, 1906.

2. *Austin Statesman*, June 25, 27, 1906; Carl Widen to DBG, interview, June 8, 1971; Ed Cravens to DBG, interview, January 29, 1970; Gideon, *Austin and the Austin National Bank*, 6.

3. *Austin Statesman*, June 27, 1906 (quotation), June 4, 1905, September 13, 1907; American National Bank, Statement of Condition, January 29, 1906, Dowell File, HL.

4. Carlson, *Monetary and Banking History of Texas*, 54–55; *Austin Statesman*, August 10, 25, 29, 1905, May 17, June 24, 1906, June 19, September 13, 1907. In its first fifteen years, the American National Bank paid two hundred thousand dollars in dividends. Insight into Littlefield's leadership and accommodation of legislative changes in banking operations comes from sources outside the bank. The bank's records burned in 1919, the year after he relinquished the presidency.

5. American National Bank, Statement, January 29, 1906, Littlefield File, JEHC.

6. Roger Courtland Roberdeau, Texas Death Certificate, March 1, 1938, Ancestry.com; Roger C. Roberdeau, Texas Muster Roll Index Card, Texas State Archives; U.S. Spanish American War Compiled Military Service Records, NARA; Galveston City Directory, 1905; Joseph Benjamin Polley, *Hood's Texas Brigade: Its Marches, Its Battles, Its Achievements* (New York: Neale, 1910), 333; *Austin Statesman*, June 10, 1898, November 4, 1905, February 27, 1938; *Dallas Morning News*, November 12, 1905; Ellison to DBG, interview, fall 1963.

7. *Austin Statesman*, December 3, 1891, April 14, 1943; Daniell, *Texas*, 218–19; Davis and Grobe, *New Encyclopedia of Texas*, 1:354; Cutrer, *God of Battles*, 377; Littlefield, "Autobiography," 1919; Morrison and Formby, *Directory of the City of Austin, 1903–1904*, 286.

8. Alfred Ellison to DBG, interview, fall 1963; *Austin Statesman*, June 22, 1919.

9. Warren W. Moore to JEH, interview, January 8, 1938; George T. Littlefield to JEH, interview, March 4, 1937; Sam Key Jr. to DBG, interview, August 31, 1964; John W. Brady to JEH, interview, January 7, 1938; Littlefield to Cass G. Ellis, January 26, 1905 (quotation); C. G. Ellis to Littlefield, January 29, 1905; Statement of Facts, filed May 10, 1905, in Littlefield v. Amanda M. Ellis Executrix, Case 22,578, Travis County District Court. See also Littlefield to Charles G. Caldwell, August 15, 1910, LLPB. Littlefield and the Ellis family reestablished relations so warm that Leigh Ellis Jr. served as an active pallbearer at Littlefield's funeral (*Austin Statesman*, November 11, 1920).

10. Littlefield to W. L. McGaughey, September 28, 1903; Littlefield and John D. McGaughey, Memorandum of Agreement, July 30, 1910; Littlefield to John D. McGaughey, September 28, 1903; John McGaughey to R. C. Roberdeau, June 16, 1915, John D. McGaughey Papers, BCAH.

11. Compiled from Ed Cravens to DBG, interview, January 29, 1970.

12. Thornton Hardie Bowman to JEH, interview, January 8, 1938 (first quotation); Arthur P. Duggan to Robert C. Rawlings, June 27, 1913 (second quotation), LLSWC.

13. Dudley H. Snyder to Littlefield, August 19, 1898 (first quotation), Snyder to Seth Mabry, August 18, October 15, 1898; Orlando C. and Annie A. Lane to Littlefield and E. J. Olive, Quit Claim, April 26, 1899, Land documents, GWL; Snyder to Littlefield, July 19, 1900 (second quotation); W. N. Snyder to Littlefield, March 22, 1887, Letterpress Book B, Dudley Hiram Snyder Papers, BCAH; *Austin Statesman*, February 5, 1885.

14. *Austin Statesman*, July 5, 1902, January 25, 1906. The loss ratio for profitable property and casualty insurance companies ranged between 40 and 60 percent in 2016 ("Loss ratio," Wikipedia).

15. Littlefield to George Findlay, September 29, 1902, Capitol Freehold Land and Investment Company Records; Littlefield and S. E. Cole with J. W. Magill, Agreement, March 27, 1909, Harland and Stratton Farms Contracts File, GWL; J. Strobel, *The Old Plantations and Their Owners of Brazoria County, Texas* (Houston: Union National Bank, 1930), 17–18; S. E. Cole to JEH, interview, January 22, 1939. Littlefield speculated profitably in the sugar business as late as 1917 (Littlefield, Income Tax Return, 1917, GWL).

16. *Austin Statesman*, June 22, 1907; Eastern Railway Company of New Mexico, the Pecos and Northern Texas Railway Company, et al., v. George W. Littlefield, J. P. White, and Thomas D. White, Case 237 U.S. 140, Decided April 5, 1915, http://caselaw.lp.findlaw.com/scripts/getcase .pl?court=us&vol=237&invol=140.

17. *Austin Statesman*, January 26, February 2, 1906, November 1, 1907, November 26, 1908; James W. McClendon to DBG, interview, March 26, 1970; Capital Bank and Trust Company, Minute Books, 1906–1909; Central Bank and Trust Company, Minute Books, 1909–1911, GWL; Overbeck, *Wooldridge*, 42; *Texas Bankers' Journal*, December 1908, 9. To distinguish the Capital Bank under Littlefield from its predecessor, the board renamed it the Central Bank and Trust Company.

18. Release of Vendor's Lien, October 20, 1908, Lamb County Deed Book 4, 270–79; David B. Gracy II, "A Preliminary Survey of Land Colonization in the Panhandle-Plains of Texas," *Museum Journal* 11 (1969): 67 and Table 1; David B. Gracy II, "Selling the Future: A Biography of William Pulver Soash," *Panhandle-Plains Historical Review* 49 (1977): 13–18; Mardema Ogletree and Lamb County History Book Committee, comps., *The Heritage of Lamb County, Texas* (Dallas: Curtis Media, 1992), 60–61, 72–73; Murrah, *Slaughter*, 113–16.

19. C. C. Slaughter, Speech, [1907], C. C. Slaughter Papers.

20. *Austin Statesman*, October 2, 1907; *San Antonio Express*, December 26, 1908; Cotner, *Hogg*, 524; Thomas B. Duggan Jr. to Alice Gracy, Interview, November 24, 1943.

21. Soash to Laura V. Hamner, interview, November 15, 1935 (quotation), Earl Vandale Collection. See also the slightly different Soash to Hamner interview of the same date in the Soash Papers, Southwest Collection, Texas Tech University.

22. Song quoted in Gracy, "Selling the Future," 9–13; David B. Gracy II, *Littlefield Lands: Colonization on the Texas Plains, 1912–1920* (Austin: University of Texas Press, 1968), 8; *San Antonio Express*, December 26, 1908.

23. Littlefield to Chilton, September 20, 1907, Littlefield File, Chilton Papers; McCaslin, "How the Hood's Brigade Monument Came to Be."

24. Hamby to Chilton, October 1, 1907 (first quotation), July 13, 1908, March 27, July 19, October 14 (second quotation), 1909, January 8, March 10, 21, June 28, November 9, 1910, Hamby File; Littlefield to Chilton, September 21, 1909, Littlefield File, Chilton Papers; McCaslin, "How the Hood's Brigade Monument Came to Be."

25. *Austin Statesman*, June 7, 1882, December 3, 1891, October 21, November 5, 1905.

26. Hamby to Chilton, July 13, 1908, March 27, April 1, July 19, October 14, 1909, January 8, 1910, Hamby File; Littlefield to Chilton, July 13, 1908, September 21, 1909, Littlefield File,

Chilton Papers; *Austin Statesman*, June 7, 1882, December 3, 1891; McCaslin, "How the Hood's Brigade Monument Came to Be"; Chilton, *Unveiling and Dedication*, 109.

27. Hamby to Chilton, March 16, 18, 21, 1910, Hamby File, Chilton Papers; Chilton, *Unveiling and Dedication*, 115.

28. Hamby to Chilton, March 18, April 25 (quotation), 1910, Hamby File, Chilton Papers; Coppini, *Dawn to Sunset*, 188.

29. Coppini, *From Dawn to Sunset*, 189 (quotation); *Austin Statesman*, October 28, 1910.

30. Littlefield to Chilton, June 5, 1909, Littlefield File, Chilton Papers (quotation); Chilton, *Unveiling and Dedication*, 31; Simpson, *Hood's Texas Brigade in Reunion and Memory*, 188.

31. Chilton, *Unveiling and Dedication*, 41, 47, 50.

32. Program of Ceremonies in the Celebration of the Centennial of the Birth of Jefferson Davis and the Dedication of the Confederate Woman's Home, Confederate Woman's Home Folder, Austin History Center; Barbara Stocklin-Steely, "Confederate Woman's Home," *Handbook of Texas Online*; *Austin Statesman*, January 12, June 4, 1908, December 15, 1910; Littlefield to Mrs. A. R. Howard, December 30, 1909, LLPB; Barbara Ann Stocklin, "The Texas Confederate Woman's Home: A Case Study in Historic Preservation and Neighborhood Conservation Planning" (master's thesis, University of Texas, 1991), 45–58. Littlefield took his advisory board duty seriously. He and Hamby in 1909 sought unsuccessfully to secure state contribution to building upkeep that sentiment indicated soon would become state property (*Austin Statesman*, February 18, 1909).

33. *Austin Statesman*, December 6, 1907 (first quotation), June 4, 1908 (second quotation); Andrea Ivie Webb, "Daffan, Katie Litty," *Handbook of Texas Online*; "Miss Katie: Ennis' First Lady," *Ennis Daily News*, http://www.ennisdailynews.com/sports/archive-1575/; "Presidents," Texas Division, United Daughters of the Confederacy, http://www.txude.org/pastpresidents .html; Littlefield to Mrs. A. R. Howard, April 7, 1910, LLPB. Daffan had been among Littlefield's UDC correspondents about the scholarship.

34. David B. Gracy II, *The State Library and Archives of Texas: A History, 1835–1962* (Austin: University of Texas Press, 2010), 14–22, 165; Key to DBG, interview, January 26, 1970; Littlefield to W. A. Lydiatt, January 5, 1910, LLPB; Texas Library and Historical Commission, Minutes, 1909–1910, Texas State Library and Archives Commission, Records, Texas State Library and Archives Commission; *Austin Statesman*, March 23, 1909. The connection between Campbell and Littlefield is obscure. Countering Campbell's prohibitionist stance for Littlefield may have been the governor's early and lifelong identification with Governor Hogg, his support of education, or simply his sympathy for Confederate veteran initiatives including state assumption of responsibility for the Confederate Women's Home and erection of the Hood's Texas Brigade Monument on the capitol grounds (Janet Schmelzer, *Our Fighting Governor: The Life of Thomas M. Campbell and the Politics of Progressive Reform in Texas* [College Station: Texas A&M University Press, 2014], 22–33, 86–97, 104).

35. Karen L. Cox, *Dixie's Daughters: The United Daughters of the Confederacy and Preservation of Confederate Culture* (Gainesville: University Press of Florida, 2003), 16–26.

36. Littlefield to Valery Austin, January 5, 1910, LLPB; *Austin Statesman*, April 9, September 20, 1908.

37. Littlefield to Valery Austin, December 18, 1909; Littlefield to Kate Daffan, November 2, 1909; Littlefield to Mrs. A. R. Howard, January 5, 1910 (first quotation), LLPB; *Austin Statesman*, April 12, 1908.

38. This quotation combines words from Littlefield's letters to Mrs. A. R. Howard, January 8, 1910, and Valery Austin, June 11, 1910, LLPB.

39. *Austin Statesman*, April 9, September 20 (quotation), 1908. Committee members included university president David Houston, educator and journalist Clarence N. Ousley, Fannie Bruner Campbell, the governor's wife, and Molly Taylor Reagan, the Texas senator's wife. After teaching high school Latin, Tanner taught college Latin and government before working his last years as

a Dallas's Federal Reserve Bank economist. His 1913 master's thesis on Roman government and 1937 doctoral dissertation on congressional reapportionment represented the extent of his history work (*Dallas Morning News*, February 4, 1948; Kristine L. Toma to DBG, January 26, 2017).

40. Littlefield to George T. Littlefield, July 1, 1910 (first quotation), George T. Littlefield Papers, in family possession; *Austin Statesman*, June 20, 1909, February 16, 1910 (second quotation), August 22, 1912; Whitlock, *Cowboy Life*, 139; W. W. Watts with Littlefield, Agreement, September 25, 1908, GWL.

41. *Austin Statesman*, February 16, 1910; Statement of Assets of G. W. Littlefield, July 22, 1910; Littlefield to B. F. Edwards, March 4, 1910, LLPD, Nellie W. Spikes and Temple Ann Ellis, *Through the Years: A History of Crosby County, Texas* (San Antonio: Naylor, 1952), 108–9.

42. Littlefield to O. Paget, January 13, 1910 (second quotation), LLPB, J. F. Onion to Otto Wahrmund, October 7, 1903, 2:1180–81; A. B. Langermann to Otto Koehler, November 24, 1905, 2:1050–51 (first quotation); Littlefield to San Antonio Brewing Association, May 8, 1907, 2:1060; San Antonio Brewing Association to Rayner, May 17, 1907, 2:1062, in *Breweries and Texas Politics*, 2 vols. (San Antonio: Passing Show, 1916).

43. Rayner to Otto Wahrmund, May 14 (first quotation), 17 (second quotation), 1907, *Breweries and Texas Politics*, 2:1061; Gregg Cantrell, *Kenneth and John B. Rayner and the Limits of Southern Dissent* (Urbana: University of Illinois Press, 1993), 192–93, 252–64; Campbell, *Texas*, 319–25; Alwyn Barr, *Reconstruction to Reform: Texas Politics, 1876–1906* (Austin: University of Texas Press, 1971), 230–32; *Austin Statesman*, February 21, 1907, May 16, 1909; James W. Markham, "State Colored Orphans' Home," *Handbook of Texas Online*; Calvert, Cantrell, and De León, *History of Texas*, 281.

44. *Austin Statesman*, June 1, 1907 (second quotation), June 2 (first and third quotations), 3, 1907; Sybal Hazel, "Statewide Prohibition Campaigns in Texas" (master's thesis, Texas Technological College, 1942), 55–99.

45. Brett J. Derbes, "Samuel Huston College"; Rose V. Batson and William H. Dunn, "St. Edward's University" and "Tillotson College" *Handbook of Texas Online*; Humphrey, *Austin*, 84, 161 (quotations); "City Population History from 1850–2000."

46. *Austin Statesman*, December 9, 1905, January 12, June 3, 1906; Williamson, *Austin, Texas*, 138.

47. *Austin Statesman*, June 3, 1906.

48. Ibid., July 18, 1903, January 12, 1906 (first quotation), August 3 (second quotation), September 14 (third and fifth quotations), 19, October 5, 10 (fourth quotation), 1909, January 2, 27, 1910, January 8, 22, June 1, 25, July 30, August 7, 1911, June 6 (sixth quotation), 21, July 21, 1912; To Whom It May Concern, November 17, 1911, LLPB. Architect Page achieved Littlefield's call for his Littlefield Building to stand at least twenty years without equal. Only in 1929 did the sixteen-story Norwood Building eclipse it in height and in accommodations, being the first office tower in the South to be air conditioned throughout (see *Austin and its Architecture* [Austin: Austin Chapter, American Institute of Architects, 1976], 5; "Making History," Norwood Tower, http://norwoodtower.com/property/history/).

49. *Austin Statesman*, September 8, 1910, December 31, 1911; *Texas Bankers' Journal*, September 1911, 20.

50. *Austin Statesman*, April 17, 1910, April 14 (quotation), June 16, 25, 1911; Clipping, 1911, Littlefield Scrapbook; *American National Bank, Austin, Texas* (Austin: American National Bank, [1911]), n.p. (cited hereafter as Bank Opening Day Booklet); *Texas Bankers' Journal*, September 1911, 34. Arbitration with the construction company delayed the building's acceptance until 1912 (Littlefield to James E. Lacy, November 25, 1911, LLPB; Original Petition, February 14, 1912, C. H. Page and Brother vs. George W. Littlefield, Case 28741, Travis County District Court).

51. Bennett H. Young to Littlefield, November 14, 1916 (quotation), Bennett Young Letters, GWL; Ruth Key to DBG, interview, ca. June 1964; Bank Opening Day Booklet; Pearl Cashell Jackson, *Austin Yesterday and Today: A Glance at Her History, A Word about Her Enterprises, A*

Description of Her Big Banking Establishment (Austin: Pearl Cashell Jackson, 1915); Jesse Hill, Photographs in American National Bank Opening Day Booklet in possession of Patsy Hill Rahn; Russell Tether Fine Arts Associates, "The Littlefield Murals" (2010), draft in possession of the author. For a biography and discussion of Hennings's work, see Vicki Heltunen, "E. Martin Hennings: Taos Artist," *Color, Pattern and Plane: E. Martin Hennings in Taos* (Orange, Tex.: Stark Museum of Art, 1986), http://www.tfaoi.com/aa/4aa/4aa40.htm. For a full discussion of the murals, see appendix C.

52. Littlefield to Coppini, March 23, 1910 (first quotation), Coppini to Littlefield, March 25, 1910 (third quotation), Coppini-Tauch Papers; Carl Widen to DBG, interview, December 16, 1968 (second quotation).

53. Littlefield to Coppini, February 16, 1911, Correspondence, General, Coppini-Tauch Papers; *Austin Statesman*, April 14, 1911; Littlefield to American Construction Co., November 11, 1910; Littlefield to H. Daniel Webster, April 14, 1911, LLPB; H. Daniel Webster, Obituaries, March 21, 1912, two clippings.

54. *Texas Bankers' Journal* 1, no. 1 (September 1911): 33; *Austin Statesman*, June 25, August 13, 1911. Typical of a reception of the time, men received cigars, and women were given solid silver demitasse spoons (Carl Widen and Alfred Ellison to DBG, interview, June 8, 1971).

55. Contrast Littlefield's Western art with, for example, Frederic Remington's. Beginning with photographs, Littlefield's created a historical record documenting actual scenes and individuals. Fashioned from his knowledge of the sorts of actions that occurred in and individuals who lived, worked, and fought in the West, Remington's was meant to create a personal and aesthetic impression of Western places, events, and individuals. See Ben Merchant Vorpahl, *Frederic Remington and the West: With the Eye of the Mind* (Austin: University of Texas Press, 1978), xiii–xvii, 268–69. See, for example, Remington's *A Dash for the Timber*, *The Cowboy*, and *Fight for the Waterhole*.

56. *Austin Statesman*, June 25, 1911; Jackson, *Austin Yesterday and Today*.

CHAPTER 16. THE TRUE HISTORY

1. H. Y. Benedict and John A. Lomax, *The Book of Texas* (Garden City, N.J.: Doubleday, Page, 1916), 368.

2. Helen Hargrave, comp., *List of Gifts, 1881–1932, to the University of Texas or for the Benefit of Its Students* (Austin: University of Texas, 1933), 46–47; George T. Morgan Jr., "Kirby, John Henry," *Handbook of Texas Online*.

3. *University of Texas Catalog, 1891–92*, 96–99. See also BOR, Minutes, June 12, 1911, 156.

4. Littlefield to Colquitt, December 31, 1908, cited in George P. Huckaby, "Oscar Branch Colquitt: A Political Biography" (PhD diss., University of Texas, 1946), 199; BOR Minutes, April 13, 1890; *University of Texas Catalog, 1891–92*, 96–99; Littlefield to H. D. Siegfreed, November 8, 1909; Littlefield to J. H. Pardue, November 26, 1909, LLPB; *Austin Statesman*, October 20, 1904, November 9, 13, 15, 1910; *Texan* [University of Texas student newspaper], November 30, 1910; D. A. Penick, "Building the Y. M. C. A.," *Alcalde* 8, no. 5 (December 1920): 393–94; O. B. Colquitt to JEH, interview, January 18, 1938, quoted in Haley, *Littlefield*, 219–20.

5. Littlefield to Lizzie Dowell, January 27, 1896, October 28, 1897 (quotation), September 30, 1898, July 11, 1899, LL; BOR, Minutes, January 9, 1911, 83; Texas BBA Timeline, http://bba100.mccombs.utexas.edu/our-legacy/bba-timeline/. Two more years would pass before the first business professor was hired.

6. Littlefield to O. B. Colquitt, November 15, 1910, LLPB (quotation); *Austin Statesman*, January 10, 1911.

7. Robert E. Vinson, "The University of Texas," in Davis, *New Encyclopedia of Texas*, 1:10 (quotation); Vinson, "University Crosses the Bar," 284.

8. *Austin Statesman*, November 5, 1910; Littlefield to Frank Rainey, April 18, 1911 (quotation), LLPB. Emphasis mine.

9. George W. Brackenridge to Alexander W. Terrell, March 4, 1911, cited in Sibley, *Brackenridge*, 199 (quotations); Colquitt to JEH, interview, January 18, 1938, cited in Haley, *Littlefield*, 219–20; Richard A. Holland, "George W. Brackenridge, George W. Littlefield, and the Shadow of the Past," in Richard A. Holland, *The Texas Book: Profiles, History, and Reminiscences of the University* (Austin: University of Texas Press, 2006), 85.

10. Maurice Dowell quoted in Basil Young Neal, "George W. Brackenridge: Citizen and Philanthropist" (master's thesis, University of Texas, 1939), 11–12; Vinson, "University Crosses the Bar," 283. Actually, Brackenridge traded in Texas cotton along the Rio Grande before war's end (Sibley, *Brackenridge*, 37–71).

11. Colquitt to JEH, interview, January 18, 1938; J. W. Calhoun to JEH, n.d., both cited in Haley, *Littlefield*, 219–20; *Austin Statesman*, November 15, 1910; BOR, Minutes, January 9, 1911, 81.

12. BOR, Minutes, June 13, 1910, 65 (first and second quotations); Sibley, *Brackenridge*, 33–54; R. R. Smith quoted in Haley, *Littlefield*, 218–19. Brackenridge told the story in explaining a deed drawn a half century later in which he included a clause specifying that if the recipient failed to abide by certain restrictions, the property was to revert to the people of Jackson County in appreciation of "the good judgment . . . in not drawing that rope taut and not driving the horse out from under me." To ensure that he left no record of his life during the war, he destroyed his personal papers (Sibley, *Brackenridge*, 6–7, 54).

13. Sibley, *Brackenridge*, 244–46; *Austin Statesman*, February 28, 1911. Though Littlefield was the last Confederate regent, he was hardly the last regent sympathetic to the Confederate cause. The new chairman, Clarence Ousley, considered himself to be "Confederate in every fiber of his being" (*Proceedings of the Tenth Annual Convention of the Texas Division United Daughters of the Confederacy . . . 1905*, 53, quoted in Bailey, "Free Speech and the 'Lost Cause,'" 468–69).

14. *Texan*, November 30, 1910 (first quotation); *Austin Statesman*, November 27, 1910 (second quotation); William James Battle to Mansula (?), January 28, 1911, Battle Family Papers, Southern Historical Collection, Wilson Library, University of North Carolina at Chapel Hill.

15. BOR, Minutes, April 12, 1913, 293.

16. Sibley, *Brackenridge*, 197–99.

17. BOR, Minutes, October 22, 1910, 69, January 27, 1911, 97, October 17, 1911, 187–88, November 11, 1912 (including Littlefield's Land Committee Report), 282, April 12, 1913, 293, June 9, 1913, 296; *Austin Statesman*, November 12, 22 (quotation), 1912, October 11, 1913; Littlefield to E. C. Barker, September 10, 1912, LLPB; Sibley, *Brackenridge*, 187–90; Humphrey, *Austin*, 164.

18. BOR, Minutes, April 6, 1911, 111, 114–16, September 20, 1911, 175–76, April 12, 1913, 288; Littlefield to Clarence Ousley, February 10 (first quotation), 14 (second quotation), March 24, 29, 1911; Littlefield to George W. Brackenridge, February 23, 1911; Littlefield to Fred W. Cook, February 23, 1911, LLPB; *Austin Statesman*, May 29, 1910. In the same meeting, maybe in a quid pro quo, the board transferred scholarship and fellowship funds from Brackenridge's to Littlefield's bank (BOR, Minutes, April 7, 1911, 117).

19. BOR, Minutes, November 11, 1912, pps. 281, 285–86, April 12, 1913, 293, June 9, 1913, 300, 305–6, September 20, 1913, 323.

20. Littlefield to Mrs. W. M. Bateman, enclosure in Littlefield to Coppini, April 3, 1909 (quotation); Littlefield to Coppini, February 16, 20, 1911, Coppini Papers; Coppini, *Dawn to Sunset*, 181. Coppini was not the first to propose establishment of an art school at the university and to advance the idea while sculpting busts (see Cutrer, *Art of the Woman*, 146–50, 177).

21. Littlefield to Frank Rainey, April 15, 1911 (quotation), LLPB; Eugene Campbell Barker to Sidney E. Mezes, April 12, 1911; Littlefield to Barker, April 15, 1911; Barker to Littlefield, April 17, 1911, Eugene Campbell Barker Papers, BCAH; Paul Walter Schroeder worded his characterization of Littlefield nicely when he wrote: "A self-educated man, he respected and believed in education, yet he was not devoted to the cause of scholarship *per se*" ("The Littlefield Fund for Southern History," *Library Chronicle* 6 [Spring 1957]: 4).

22. Littlefield to Dr. Frank Rainey, April 18, 1911 (quotation), LLPB; William C. Pool, *Eugene C. Barker: Historian* (Austin: Texas State Historical Association, 1971), 55–58; *New York Times*, February 28, 1911. In "The Best History Money Can Buy: Eugene Campbell Barker, George Washington Littlefield, and the Quest for a Suitable Past," *Gulf South Historical Review* 20 (2014): 37, Fred A. Bailey, a critic of Littlefield's condemnation of Elson's work, nevertheless shares this view of the Barker-Littlefield relationship. Born eleven years after the war, Barker earned B.A. and M.A. degrees in history from the university. After receiving a University of Pennsylvania history doctorate, he joined UT's history faculty. The death of George Pierce Garrison in 1910 elevated Barker to department chair and Texas State Historical Association director and editor of its quarterly (Pool, *Barker*, 15–44, 60–65).

23. Littlefield to Rainey, April 18, 1911, LLPB; BOR, Minutes, May 31, 138, June 12, 1911, 151 (second quotation); Bailey, "The Best History Money Can Buy," 37–38. To President Mezes, before he even received Littlefield's inquiry, Barker wrote that "Elson did not specifically refer to the Civil War as 'the slaveholders war,' [and] did not state in so many words that decent plantation owners and farmers of the South organized harems from their female slaves" (Pool, *Barker*, 56).

24. *Austin Statesman*, June 5 (first quotation), July 23, 1911; BOR, Minutes, June 12, 1911, 150, September 20, 1911, 176; Littlefield to R. M. Johnson, June 14, 1911 (second quotation), Oscar B. Colquitt Papers.

25. *Austin Statesman*, March 4, 1911.

26. *Austin Statesman*, March 3, 4 (first quotation), 9, 1911; Littlefield to Ousley, March 6, 1911 (second and third quotations), LLPB; BOR, Minutes, April 6, 1911, 112.

27. Penick, "Building the Y.M.C.A.," 107 (quotations); *Austin Statesman*, July 3, 1912.

28. Littlefield to I. J. Fariss, July 15, 1911 (first quotation), LLPB; *Austin Statesman*, November 23, 1906; Robert Adger Law, "Vinson, Robert Ernest," *Handbook of Texas Online*; Rogan, "Converts Cattle" (second quotation); Penick, "Building the Y.M.C.A.," 107–12. Littlefield was not alone in his assessment. President Mezes included in his report to the regents' March 29, 1912, meeting that the beneficial work of the organization was patent (BOR, Minutes, March 29, 1912, 232).

29. BOR, Minutes, June 12, 1911, 156 (all quotations).

30. BOR, Minutes, June 12, 1911, pp. 165–66, 169 (quotations); *Texan*, July 1, 1911; Berry, *University of Texas*, 65–66; Jim Nicar, "How to Celebrate Texas Independence Day," UT History Corner, March 1, 2014, https://jimnicar.com/2014/03/01/how-to-celebrate-texas-independence-day/; Jim Nicar, "The Dreaded Scourge of 'Follicular Ticsiphobia,'" UT History Corner, April 30, 2015, https://jimnicar.com/2015/04/30/the-dreaded-scourge-of-follicular-ticsiphobia/; Jim Nicar, "Remembering Old B. Hall at 152," UT History Corner, December 1, 2015, https://jimnicar.com/2015/12/01/remembering-old-b-hall-at-125/.

31. Julia Cauble Smith, "Santa Rita Oil Well"; Charles D. Vertrees, "Permian Basin," *Handbook of Texas Online*.

32. Littlefield to Ousley, October 5 (quotation); Littlefield to W. H. Stark, October 7, 1911, LLPB; BOR, Minutes, October 17, 1911, 187.

33. Littlefield to Ousley, October 5, 1911 (quotation), LLPB; BOR, Minutes, October 17, 1911, 185, 187–88.

34. Penick, "Building the Y.M.C.A.," 110–13; *Austin Statesman*, July 3, 1912; Rogan, "Converts Cattle."

35. Littlefield to E. C. Barker, September 10, 1912 (quotations), LLPB; Barker to Littlefield, September 9, December 5, 1912, Barker Papers; *Austin Statesman*, November 3, 1912.

36. Pool, *Barker*, 145–48; Don E. Carleton and Katherine J. Adams, "'A Work Peculiarly Our Own': Origins of the Barker Texas History Center, 1883–1950," *Southwestern Historical Quarterly* 86 (October 1982): 199–209; Richard B. McCaslin, *At the Heart of Texas: One Hundred Years of the Texas State Historical Association, 1897–1977* (Austin: Texas State Historical Association,

2007), 46; Gracy, *The State Library and Archives of Texas*, 19; Gracy and Knowles, "State Archives"; Bailey, "Best History Money Can Buy," 34; *Austin Statesman*, June 4, 1911.

37. Barker to Littlefield, December 5, 1912, Dean H. Y. Benedict to Barker, December 6, 1912, Barker Papers.

38. Barker to Thwaites, December 17; Thwaites to Barker, December 20, 1912, quoted in Bailey, "The Best History Money Can Buy," 40–41; William Beer to Barker, December 21, 1912; R. D. W. Connor to Barker, December 17, 1912, Littlefield Papers Holdings File, BCAH; Barker to Littlefield, March 13, 1913, January 5, 1916, Barker Papers; Schroeder, "The Littlefield Fund for Southern History," 6–7.

39. Barker to Littlefield, March 13, 1913 (first quotation); Littlefield to Barker, April 30, 1913, Barker Papers; Barker to Littlefield, April 28, 1913 (third quotation), Littlefield Papers Holdings File; *Austin Statesman*, April 28, 1913 (second quotation); BOR, Minutes, April 13, May 31, June 9, 1913.

40. *Austin Statesman*, March 18, 21, April 27 (first quotation), June 11 (second and third quotations), 1913; BOR, Minutes, October 28, 1912, 273; Berry, *University of Texas*, 57, 69, 115–16.

41. *Austin Statesman*, March 21, April 13, 20, 27, June 10, 25, 29 (quotation), July 9, 10, 11, 14, September 22, 1913; Huckaby, "Colquitt," 345–59.

42. *Austin Statesman*, August 23, September 13, 1913, February 25, 1914; Littlefield to Colquitt, January 7, 1915, Colquitt Papers; Huckaby, "Colquitt," 359–63.

43. Barker to Littlefield, March 24, 1914, Barker Papers.

44. Littlefield to Clarence Ousley, April 24, 1914, Littlefield Papers.

45. Ibid. (first quotation); Littlefield to Matilda LeGrand Weeden [Mrs. E. C.] Barker, May 4, 1914 (second quotation); Barker to Professor E. P. Cheyney, April 11, 1914 (third quotation), Barker Papers.

46. Littlefield to James H. Parramore, July 9, 1913, LLPB.

47. Ibid.

48. Littlefield clearly was pleased with the result and with having sent Winkler to ensure it (Littlefield to Barker, July 26, 1916, Barker Papers).

49. Littlefield to Barker, December 5, 1916 (first quotation), Barker Papers; Ernest William Winkler to JEH, interview, January 14, 1939, quoted in Haley, *Littlefield*, 266; Schroeder, "The Littlefield Fund," 9–10, 11–12 (second quotation); "News Item," *Southwestern Historical Quarterly* 20 (October 1916): 204–5; C. W. Ramsdell to Littlefield, February 9, 1920; Littlefield to Barker, October 18, 1916; *Nacogdoches Sentinel*, July 31, 1925, Littlefield Scrapbook, GWL.

CHAPTER 17. WATCHMAN ON THE TOWER

1. BOR, Minutes, October 27, 1914, 421 (first quotation); Littlefield to Lizzie Dowell, March 30, July 12, November 4 (second and third quotations), 1912, July 2, 1913, February 28, 1914, LL; Littlefield to H. T. Kimbro, October 25, 1912, LLPB; Ruth Key to DBG, interview, November 13, 1964; Harless and Dobbins to DBG, interview, August 14, 1970; *Austin Statesman*, October 28, 1914.

2. *Austin Statesman*, July 12, 1912 (quotations), August 1, 1914; Littlefield to Phelps White, October 3, 1911, JPW.

3. Littlefield to Arthur P. Duggan, September 25, 1914, LLSWC; Littlefield to M. G. Abernathy, October 25, 1912, Littlefield to H. T. Kimbro, October 25, 1912, LLPB; Gracy, *Littlefield Lands*, 31–32.

4. Littlefield to Victor Harral, November 3, 1909, LLPB; Littlefield to Phelps White, October 3, 1911, JPW. The earliest surviving letter regarding sale of the entire ranch is dated October 1909, LLPB.

5. Littlefield to Blair Townsite Real Estate Company, October 20, 1909, Littlefield to H. C. Banke Jr., October 21, 1909; Littlefield to J. H. Pardue, November 26, December 9, 1909; Littlefield to M. G. Abernathy, February 19, 1910; Littlefield to Hockney Land Company, February

23, 1910, LLPB; *Los Angeles Times*, August 12, 1905, March 9, 1910; *New York Times*, October 3, 1906; Gracy, *Littlefield Lands*, 9.

6. Littlefield to Banke, October 21, 1909, LLPB; Map of Littlefield's Subdivision of State Capitol Leagues 657–87, Lamb County Deed Records, Book 11, 4; Gracy, *Littlefield Lands*, 9; Mardema Ogletree and Lamb County History Book Committee, comps., *The Heritage of Lamb County, Texas* (Dallas. Curtis Media, 1992), 37.

7. Littlefield to J. H. Pardue, November 9 (quotation), November 26, December 9, 1909, Littlefield to H. C. Banke Jr., October 21, 1909, Littlefield to Earnest Haiders, December 16, 1909, Littlefield to M. G. Abernathy, February 19, 1910, LLPB; Littlefield to J. H. Mook, draft contract, July 8, 1909, GWL; Arthur Duggan to Littlefield, February 11, March 17, 1914, Littlefield to Duggan, October 24, 1914, LLSWC; C. J. Duggan, "Oil Development Begins in Lamb County This Year," *Lamb County Leader*, August 18, 1938; *Lamb County Leader*, June 27, 1963. Orville R. Watkins wrote that old-timers remember the well coming to its end when the gas caught fire ("History of Hockley County" [master's thesis, Texas Tech University 1941], 78).

8. Littlefield to Arthur P. Duggan, March 1, 1910, June 25, 1912; Littlefield to H. T. Kimbro, June 1, September 16, October 25, 1912; Littlefield to C. A. Morse, June 7, 1912; Littlefield to H. A. Halbert, September 24, 1912, LLPB; Gracy, *Littlefield Lands*, 9–11, 13–17.

9. Littlefield to C. A. Morse, October 7, 1912 (quotation); Littlefield to E. P. Ripley, October 29, 1912, LLPB; S. S. McKay, "Roundup, TX"; H. Allen Anderson, "Lariat, TX"; and Mark Odintz, "Bainer, TX," *Handbook of Texas Online*; *Atchison, Topeka and Santa Fe Railway System and Connecting Lines, Corrected to June 20, 1914*, timetable (Atchison, Topeka, and Santa Fe Railway, 1914), 2 and Table 81. In time, Afton became Shallowater. The other Santa Fe towns failed.

10. Duggan to Littlefield, October 30, 1912 (quotation); Phelps White to Littlefield, November 3, 1912, LLSWC.

11. Alice Gracy to DBG, interview, January 28, 1965 (quotation); Gracy, *Littlefield Lands*, 13; *Santa Fe Railway* Timetable, June 1914, 2. For good measure, two streets were named for Santa Fe officials. At least two towns developed later, Anton and Amherst, were named by the railroad (Rachel Jenkins, "Anton, TX"; William R. Hunt, "Amherst, TX [Lamb County]," *Handbook of Texas Online*).

12. Littlefield to Duggan, November 20, 1912 (first and second quotations); Littlefield to Phelps White, July 14, 1913 (third quotation); Littlefield to Duggan, June ?, 16, 20?, 1913, LLSWC; Gracy, *Littlefield Lands*, 17–20, 31–32, 111, 118. The U.S. Post Office confirmed the name when it awarded Littlefield a post office in December, 1912 (Duggan to Littlefield, December 21, 1912, LLSWC).

13. Duggan to Littlefield, April 2, 1913 (first quotation); Littlefield to Duggan, December 8, 1912 (second quotation), January 21, March 8, April 10, December 19, 1913; Duggan to Littlefield, February 24, April 2, 1913, LLSWC; Gracy, *Littlefield Lands*, 26–27, 68–69; William R. Hunt, "Littlefield, TX," *Handbook of Texas Online*.

14. C. Grover Pipkin to Littlefield, April 13, 1914 (first quotation); Littlefield to Pipkin, April 15, 1914 (second quotation); Littlefield to Duggan, April 10, 1914; Duggan to Littlefield, April 18, 1914, LLSWC; Gracy, *Littlefield Lands*, 37.

15. Duggan to Rawlings, October 21, 1913, LLSWC.

16. Duggan to E. D. Wesmuth, December 23, 1913, Sales Folder 1, LLSWC.

17. Gracy, "Selling the Future," 2–7, 20–42.

18. Littlefield to Lizzie Dowell, November 7, 1891 (quotation), LL; Merle Weir, "Velasco, TX"; Jackie McElhaney and Michael V. Hazel, "Dallas, TX"; Janet Schmelzer, "Fort Worth, TX"; John Edward Weems, "Galveston Hurricane of 1900," *Handbook of Texas Online*.

19. Littlefield to Duggan, July 21, 1913, April 22 (third quotation), May 2, 11, June 6 (first quotation), July 5, October 15?, October 15 (second quotation), 1914, LLSWC.

20. Littlefield to Duggan, May 5, 1914, LLSWC.

21. *Austin Statesman*, December 19, 1913 (first quotation), October 2, 1914 (second quotation).

22. Ibid., October 2, 1914. The paper quoted a large taxpayer who agreed with the Major but anonymously. Whatever caused Littlefield's strong feelings against Wooldridge must have been more than the mayor's opposition the previous week to paving Twenty-Fourth Street in front of Littlefield's home. The city council ordered the work despite Wooldridge's objection to the paving material being used (ibid., September 25, 1914).

23. Humphrey, *Austin*, 159; "City Population History from 1850–2000"; Littlefield to Duggan, October 15?, 1914, LLSWC.

24. *Austin Statesman*, June 11, 1911, January 22, 1914, April 25, 1915.

25. Carlson, *Banking History of Texas*, 55.

26. *Austin Statesman*, July 1, 1913, January 1, 1915, Benedict and Lomax, *Book of Texas*, 299. On two pages, Benedict and Lomax included photographs of nine prominent Texans, including George Brackenridge. Littlefield's portrait was given a full page (facing page 31). The reason for this prominence is unexplained. John Henry Houghton's death in 1910 left Littlefield the lone surviving founder (*Austin Statesman*, October 2, 1910).

27. Littlefield to H. G. Seeligson, October 31, 1912, LLPB.

28. Littlefield to H. N. Key, October 26, 1909 (first quotation), October 30, 1909 (second quotation), LLPB. Harry Key's brother, James Richard Key, married the Major's niece, Lula Alice Harral. They were the parents of Ruth Key (Lane, *Key and Allied Families*, 142–44; James R. Key Household, U.S. Census, Population, 1910, Lampasas, Tex., Ancestry.com).

29. Littlefield to Colquitt, May 27 (quotation), June 2, 1911, Colquitt Papers.

30. Littlefield to Charles G. Caldwell, August 15 (first quotation), August 13 (second quotation), 1910, LLPB.

31. Littlefield to Duggan, September 17, 24 (quotation), 1914, LLSWC.

32. Littlefield to Duggan, September 25 (first quotation), 24 (second and third quotations), 1914, LLSWC.

33. Littlefield to Duggan, September 24 (first quotation), October 17? (second quotation), 1914, LLSWC; Littlefield to Phelps White, October 28, 1914, JPW; J. Phelps White III to DBG, interview, June 29, 2017; Thomas David White, Tombstone, Masonic Cemetery, Gonzales, Tex.; Estate of Thomas White in John Ben Robertson Papers, Austin History Center.

34. Littlefield to Phelps White, October 24, 1914 (first quotation), 28 (second quotation), JPW; Littlefield to Duggan, September 25, October 17(?), 1914, LLSWC; J. P. White, T. D. White, and George Littlefield, Agreement, October 9, 1914, Lamb County Deed Records, vol. 9, 386; Phelps White III to DBG, interview, June 29, 2017.

35. Littlefield to Duggan, October 24, 1914, LLSWC.

36. Ralph W. Steen, "The Political Career of James E. Ferguson, 1914–1917" (master's thesis, University of Texas, 1929), 5 (first quotation), 7–8, 10, 43; Carol O'Keefe Wilson, *In the Shadow: The True Story of Ma and Pa Ferguson* (Denton: University of North Texas Press, 2014), 29 (second and third quotations).

37. James E. Ferguson to JEH, interview, January 6, 1938; *Austin Statesman*, June 13, 1914; Campbell, *Gone to Texas*, 348–50.

38. Dudley K. Woodward to JEH, interview, January 14, 1939.

CHAPTER 18. IN A MAN'S SIZED WORLD

1. *Austin Statesman*, June 22, 1915 (first quotation); Littlefield to Lizzie Dowell, August 7, 1911 (second quotation), LL; *University of Texas Magazine* 32, no. 10 (June 1917): n.p. (third quotation); Wilson, *In the Governor's Shadow*, 45.

2. BOR, Minutes, April 30, 1915, 432, 435, 441; Sibley, *Brackenridge*, 109–10, 207, 210–11.

3. *Austin Statesman*, March 24, April 15, 16, 1915; clipping, n.d., Littlefield Scrapbook.

4. Ibid., April 17, 1915.

5. Ibid., May 7, June 27, July 20 (quotation), July 30, 1915; Humphrey, *Austin*, 140–42.

6. Ibid., August 4, December 22, 1915; H. C. Ramsey v. George W. Littlefield, Case 32349, Travis County District Court, and Civil Minute Book 27, 617–19.

7. *Austin Statesman*, September 17 (quotation), 19, 20, 1915, April 26, 1916.

8. BOR, Minutes, October 26, 1915, 495.

9. Duggan to Littlefield, May 8, 1914, LLSWC; Gracy, *Littlefield Lands*, 62–63.

10. Littlefield to Duggan, September 18, September 29 (first quotation), October 24, 30 (third quotation), December 20 (second quotation), 1914, LLSWC.

11. Littlefield to Duggan, November 28, 1914, October 30, 1915, LLSWC; Gracy, *Littlefield Lands*, 41.

12. Littlefield, William R. Hamby, E. P. Wilmot, and John H. Robinson to E. M. House, October 13, 1914 (first quotation), E. M. House Papers, Sterling Memorial Library, Yale University; Littlefield to Duggan, October 15?, 1914 (second quotation), LLSWC. The American National Bank's contribution to resolving the crisis was to participate in forming a corporation to build and operate a cotton mill in Austin. The initiative designed to benefit the city's economy as well as the cotton growers never came to fruition (*Austin American-Statesman*, October 12, 1914)

13. Littlefield to Bennett Young, August 15, 1914, South File, in possession of the author; Young to Littlefield, June 10, 1915, March 13, 1916, Bennett Young Letters (hereafter BYL), GWL.

14. Young to Littlefield, March 13, 1916 (quotations); Young to J. A. Hayes, November 15, 1916, BYL; Roy Hays, "Is The Lincoln Birthplace Cabin Authentic?" *Abraham Lincoln Quarterly* 5, no. 3 (September 1948): 151, 153, 160, http://quod.lib.umich.edu/a/alajournals/0599998.0005.003; Jefferson Davis State Historic Site, Kentucky State Parks, http://parks.ky.gov/parks/historicsites /jefferson-davis/history.aspx; Oscar A. Kinchen, *General Bennett H. Young: Confederate Raider and A Man of Many Adventures* (West Hanover, Mass.: Christopher Publishing House, 1981), 112–13.

15. *Austin Statesman*, October 1, 1916 (quotations); Young to Littlefield, October 19, 1916; Young to J. A. Hayes, November 15, 1916, BYL; Kinchen, *Young*, 103.

16. Littlefield to Phelps, September 29, 1916, JPW.

17. Young to Littlefield, September 27, 29 (quotation), 1916, BYL.

18. Young to Littlefield, March 13, October 4, 19 (third quotation, emphasis mine), 1916, May 31, 1918 (first quotation), Young Letters, GWL; *Dallas Democrat*, November 11, 1916 (second quotation).

19. Young to Littlefield, November 6 (quotation), 9, 20, 30, December 16, 1916, BYL.

20. *Austin American*, November 10, 1916; clipping, n.d. (quotation), BYL; Littlefield to Young, September 18, 30, 1917, LLPB; Littlefield to Wroe, November 7, 1919, Wroe Papers, GLC; Littlefield to Samuel A. King, March 17, 1917, Samuel Alexander King Papers, Austin Seminary Archives, Austin Presbyterian Theological Seminary.

21. Young to Littlefield, January 24, 29, February 15, April 9, May 14, 19, 30, July 28, August 7, September 6, 1917, March 2, 1918 (quotation), January 21, 1919, BYL; Littlefield to Samuel A. King, March 17, 1917, Littlefield Biographical File, BCAH; Kinchen, *Young*, 147–52; Jefferson Davis State Historic Site, Wikipedia.

22. *Dallas News*, November 25, 1914, quoted in Steen, "Ferguson," 7, 45, 78, 95–96; *Austin Statesman*, February 8, 1915; Wilson, *In the Governor's Shadow*, 27–30. Steen based his recounting of events upon both the contemporary *Dallas News* and testimony given in the *Proceedings of the High Court of Impeachment*.

23. Ouida Ferguson Nalle, *The Fergusons of Texas, or "Two Governors for the Price of One"* (San Antonio: Naylor, 1946), 66, 67 (quotation); Benedict and Lomax, *Book of Texas*, 372–73; U.S. Department of Commerce and Labor, *Statistical Abstract of the United States, 1910, Thirty-Third Number* (Washington, D.C.: Government Printing Office, 1911), 97–98.

24. Lewis L. Gould, *Progressives and Prohibitionists: Texas Democrats in the Wilson Era* (Austin: University of Texas Press, 1973), 186, 187 (quotation); Nalle, *The Fergusons*, 81. The actual average cost to attend the university between 1913 and 1916 was $227, half the cost

to attend the University of Virginia (Eugene C. Barker, *Ferguson's War on the University of Texas: A Chronological Outline, January 12, 1915, to July 31, 1917, Inclusive* (Austin: Ex-Students Association, 1917).

25. Nalle, *The Fergusons*, 34, 83 (quotation); Wilson, *In the Governor's Shadow*, 7–8.

26. Gracy, *History of the State Library and Archives of Texas*, 29–31, 30 (quotation).

27. Ibid., 31 (quotation), 32; John R. Lundberg, "The Great Texas 'Bear Fight': Progressivism and the Impeachment of James E. Ferguson," in *Impeached: The Removal of Texas Governor James E. Ferguson*, ed. Jessica Brannon-Wranosky and Bruce A. Glasrud (College Station: Texas A&M University Press, 2017), 13–52.

28. James C. Martin, "Battle, William James," *Handbook of Texas Online*; Gould, *Progressives and Prohibitionists*, 190.

29. Ferguson quoted in Gould, *Progressives and Prohibitionists*, 190.

30. BOR, Minutes, October 26, 1915, 503; *Dallas News*, June 14, 1917; *Austin Statesman*, June 3, 1917; Gould, *Progressives and Prohibitionists*, 191 (quotation); Steen, "Ferguson," 113–15, 121.

31. Ferguson quoted in Gould, *Progressives and Prohibitionists*, 190 (first quotation), 191 (second quotation); *Austin Statesman*, December 14, 1910, July 31, September 15, 1914; *Dallas News*, June 14, 1917.

32. *Austin Statesman*, June 14, 1917; *The Cactus* (Kansas City, Mo.: Union Bank Note Company, 1916), 6.

33. *Dallas News*, June 14, 1917 (first and fourth quotations); Wilson, *In the Governor's Shadow*, 74 (second quotation), 75–76; Steen, "Ferguson," 115–16; Gould, *Progressives and Prohibitionists*, 192–93, 194 (third quotation); BOR, Minutes, November 16, 1914, 430, April 26, 1916, 533; Law, "Vinson, Robert Ernest," *Handbook of Texas Online*. When brought to a vote, Littlefield's motion regarding appointments failed (BOR, Minutes, April 30, 1915, 433).

34. *Austin Statesman*, October 11 (second quotation), 12, December 17, 1916, June 14, 1917 (first quotation); BOR, Minutes, October 10, 1916, 1; Littlefield to Ousley, January 4, 1913 (third quotation), LLPB; *Dallas News*, October 12, 1916; Gould, *Progressives and Prohibitionists*, 195–96; Steen, "Ferguson," 119; Lundberg, "Great Texas 'Bear Fight,'" 22–27; John A. Lomax, *Will Hogg, Texan* (Austin: University of Texas Press, 1956), ix, 46–48 (fourth quotation).

35. BOR, Minutes, October 24, 1916, 12; Lundberg, "Great Texas 'Bear Fight,'" 24; Gould, *Progressives and Prohibitionists*, 122–24; "Mayes, William Harding," *Handbook of Texas Online*.

36. BOR, Minutes, October 24, 1916, 13, 19.

37. BOR, Minutes, November 1914, 422, April 24, 1917, 36; Gould, *Progressives and Prohibitionists*, 197–98; Lundberg, "Great Texas 'Bear Fight,'" 26–27; *Dallas News*, August 18, 1917; Daniell, *Texas*, 415–17; Clinton P. Hartmann, "Kelly, Charles Edgar"; Chester R. Burns, "Fly, Ashley Wilson," *Handbook of Texas Online*; "Wilbur Price Allen," *New Encyclopedia of Texas*, 1:398.

38. No wonder the governor considered the Ex-Students Association central committee to be principal to the political opponents he meant to root out. One historian termed it "one of the most remarkable vigilance committees in any academic history" (Barker quoted in Haley, *Littlefield*, 233).

39. *Austin Statesman*, June 14, 1917 (quotation); *Dallas News*, March 20, 1917; Lundberg, "Great Texas 'Bear Fight,'" 27; Sibley, *Brackenridge*, 230; Gould, *Progressives and Prohibitionists*, 198–200.

40. *Dallas News*, May 27 (first quotation), 28 (second quotation), 1917; Steen, "Ferguson," 127. Students repudiated this attack on fraternities as a means of dividing the student body (Barker, *Ferguson's War*, 27).

41. *Austin Statesman*, June 14, 1917; *Dallas News*, May 31, June 14, 1917. Versions of the quotation are in each paper.

42. *Austin Statesman*, June 30, 1912, September 9, 30, 1915, May 28, 1917; *Dallas News*, January 27, 1917; Littlefield to Wilbur P. Allen, July 5, 1917, LLPB. Allen named one fund for his

father-in-law and American National Bank founding director, John Houghton (*Austin Statesman*, September 9, 1915; Daniell, *Texas*, 417).

43. Haley, *Littlefield*, 239 (first quotation); *Dallas News*, June 1 (second quotation), 2, 14, 1917; *Austin Statesman*, May 31, 1917; BOR, Minutes, May 31, June 1, 42, 49–51; Steen, "Ferguson," 129; Lomax, "Ferguson and The University," 16.

44. *Austin Statesman*, June 3 (first quotation), 1917, *Dallas News*, May 30, June 3 (second quotation), 1917.

45. Vinson, "University Crosses the Bar," 286–87 (quotation); *Dallas News*, June 6, 7, 15, 1917; *Austin Statesman*, June 14, 1917; State of Texas, Senate, *Record of Proceedings of the High Court of Impeachment in the Trial of Hon. James E. Ferguson, Governor* (Austin: A. C. Baldwin and Sons, 1917), 206. Lomax stated that Allen sat quietly while Littlefield took the lead and that "Dr. Vinson dramatically and emphatically refused to resign. Major Littlefield urged this course as the only possible way to save the University from ruin. Again, vehemently, President Vinson refused. The talk between the two men became acrimonious." But Lomax also wrote that Vinson told him that "Major Littlefield has been cruelly misunderstood. . . . All of the Major's actions towards you and the other members of the faculty were motivated entirely by his desire to save me to the University" (Lomax, "Ferguson and The University," 16 [second quotation], 22 [first quotation], 23). Though Ex-Students leader John W. Brady concurred in Lomax's recollection (Woodward to JEH, interview, January 7, 1938, cited in Haley, *Littlefield*, 243), I have relied upon President Vinson's recollection, which is corroborated by testimony in the *Record of Proceedings*, 206–8.

46. *Austin Statesman*, June 14 (first and fourth quotations), 1917; Littlefield to Phelps White, June 4 (second quotation), 1917, JPW; Woodward to JEH, interview, January 14, 1939 (third quotation).

47. Littlefield to Ferguson, June 22, 1917, LLPB.

48. Vinson, "University Crosses the Bar," 286 (quotation); *Austin Statesman*, June 6, 1917.

49. Lomax, "Ferguson and the University," 17–18 (first quotation); Vinson, "University Crosses the Bar," 283 (second quotation), 286–88 (third quotation); *Austin Statesman*, June 6, 1917; Sibley, *Brackenridge*, 231, 234–35. Brackenridge's biographer called Brackenridge's challenge "wicked humor."

50. Vinson, "University Crosses the Bar," 288.

51. BOR, Minutes, July 12, 1917, 98, 103–4, September 14, 1917, 106–8; Lomax, "Ferguson and the University," 13, 28 (quotation); *Austin Statesman*, September 15, 1917.

52. BOR, Minutes, July 12, 1917, 73, 97 (first quotation); Helen Knox to Anna Pennybacker, August 5, 1917 (second quotation), Mrs. Percy V. [Anna] Pennybacker Papers, BCAH; Kay Reed Arnold, "'Think of the Lives That Might Be Saved': James Ferguson, Women's War Work, and the University of Texas," in Brannon-Wranosky and Glasrud, *Impeached*, 59, 66, 67 (third quotation); Kelley M. King, *Call Her A Citizen: Progressive-Era Activist and Educator Anna Pennybacker* (College Station: Texas A&M University Press, 2010), 63, 75–104, 141–42.

53. Littlefield to Ross L. Malone, August 25 (first, third, and fourth quotations), 15 (second quotation), September 5, 1917, Ross L. Malone Letterbook, 1917–1919, GWL; *Austin Statesman*, August 10, 1917; George T. Littlefield to JEH, interview, March 4, 1937.

54. *Austin Statesman*, September 27, 1917, Littlefield Scrapbook; Harry Yandell Benedict, comp., *A Source Book Relating to the History of the University of Texas: Legislative, Legal, Bibliographical, and Statistical* (Austin: University of Texas, 1917), 557.

55. Littlefield to Malone, August 15, 1917 (quotation), Ross L. Malone Letterbook, 1917–1919, GWL; BOR, Minutes, October 23, 1917, 111; *Austin Statesman*, September 26, 1917.

56. Vinson, "University Crosses the Bar," 288; Sibley, *Brackenridge*, 235–36.

57. *Austin Statesman*, June 3, 1917.

58. Mildred F. Littlefield to Pat H. Boone, November 3, 1919, Pat H. Boone Jr., Papers, in possession of Pat H. Boone IV.

CHAPTER 19. TO ACCOMPLISH WHAT
OUGHT TO BE ACCOMPLISHED

1. Phelps White to Littlefield, September 8, 1914, J. P. White file, GWL.

2. Statement of Assets of G. W. Littlefield, July 22, 1910, LLPR. His estimate should have been higher, as subsequent sale of the Four Lakes Ranch and its stock showed that he considerably underestimated its value.

3. *Austin Statesman*, June 20, 1909, February 16, 1910; Walker White to DBG, interview, June 2, 1971 (quotation); J. P. White Jr. to DBG, interview, November 5, 1966; J. P. White to C. L. Ballard, G. B. Armstrong, and S. F. Baker, Contract of Sale [Four Lakes Ranch], August 25, 1915, GWL; Robinson, "History of Roosevelt County," 69.

4. Will White to Horne, interview, September 9, 1936; Littlefield to J. W. White, Deed, June 14, 1916, Roscoe Runge Papers, Texas State Archives; G. Newton to Littlefield, February 17, 1920, Income Tax, GWL; Littlefield to Duggan, October 25, 1915, February 5, 10, 18, 1916, LLSWC; *San Antonio Express*, April 2, 1906; *Austin Statesman*, September 26, 1915 (quotation).

5. Ruth Key to DBG, interview, May 6, 20, 1965; Littlefield to Duggan, July 14, 1913, January 7, February 17, September 6, 1916, LLSWC.

6. Littlefield to Phelps White, June 2, 6 (quotation), September 29, 1916, Littlefield Letters, JPW; Littlefield to Duggan, January 7, February 15, 17, March 24, 1916, LLSWC; Littlefield to Lizzie Dowell, April 19, 1918, LL; Littlefield to Robert B. Van Cortlandt, June 9, 1917, LLPB; *Austin Statesman*, July 30, August 25, 1915, October 10, 1918, February 13, 1920.

7. At 200 North Lea, the structure houses the museum and offices of the Historical Society for Southeast New Mexico.

8. Littlefield to Phelps, September 28, 29 (first quotation), 1916, January 24, 1917, Littlefield Letters, JPW; Littlefield to Duggan, May 25, 1916, LLSWC; Phelps White to Littlefield, February 14, 1913 (second quotation), February 14, 1913, March 21 (fourth quotation), 1917; Will White to Phelps White, September 9 (third quotation), 1916, J. P. White letters, GWL.

9. Phelps White to Littlefield, March 21, 1917, August 16, 1919, Littlefield Letters, JPW; Littlefield to Lizzie Dowell, January 24, 1918, LL; Yellow House Ranch Checks, 1916, GWL.

10. Littlefield to Duggan, February 28, 1917, LLSWC.

11. Ibid., October 16, 1917, LLSWC; James D. Draraford (?) to Littlefield, April 5, 1918; Ross L. Malone to Thomas W. Gregory, November 8, 1920, Income Tax, GWL.

12. J. C. Whicker to Arthur Duggan, December 11, 17, 1917 (first quotation); Duggan to Whicker, December 17, 1917, Whicker Folder 5; Littlefield to Duggan, October 16, 1917; Littlefield to Phelps White, November 3, 1917 (second quotation), LLSWC; Littlefield to J. H. Pardue, September 21, 1917; Littlefield to J. D. Parramore, October 8, 1917, LLPB; Gracy, *Littlefield Lands*, 92–93, 96.

13. *Austin Statesman*, January 1, December 4, 1916; Littlefield to H. A. Wroe, November 26 (quotation), December 8, 1919, Wroe Papers, GLC.

14. *Austin Statesman*, April 16, 1916 (quotations), February 22, March 31, October 10, 18, November 13, 1918; Littlefield to Lizzie Dowell, April 19, 1918, LL.

15. *Austin Evening Statesman*, October 18, 1916, June 3, June 24, October 4, 1917; *Dallas News*, June 1, 1917; Littlefield to H. D. Craig, October 9, 1917; Littlefield to Lawrence M. Cathles, December 29, 1917, LLPB; "Liberty Bond," Wikipedia.

16. *Austin Statesman*, November 16, 1915 (quotation), June 24, October 4, 1917; *Austin Evening Statesman*, October 18, 1916; Littlefield to H. D. Craig, October 9, 1917; Littlefield to Lawrence M. Cathles, December 29, 1917, LLPB.

17. *Austin Statesman*, November 16, 1915; John Higham, *Strangers in the Land: Patterns of American Nativism, 1860–1925* (1955; repr., New Brunswick, N.J.: Rutgers University Press, 1992), 197–200, 205, 208; Leroy G. Dorsey, *We Are All Americans, Pure and Simple: Theodore Roosevelt and the Myth of Americanism* (Tuscaloosa: University of Alabama Press, 2007), 126–29, 135–36; "American Defense Society," Wikipedia.

18. BOR, Minutes, April 24, 1917, 34–40.

19. Ibid., June 11, 1917, 55; *Austin Statesman*, May 16, 1917.

20. BOR, Minutes, June 11, 55, September 14, 106, April 8, 1918, 139–40, 151, 205; *Austin Statesman*, September 21, 25, November 13 (quotation), 1918; Jim Nicar, "A Flag Full of Stars," UT History Corner, May 29, 2016, https://jimnicar.com/2016/05/29/a-flag-full-of-stars/; Berry, *University of Texas*, 212.

21. *Austin Statesman*, March 3, 1918 (first quotation); Frederic F. Norcross, *John H. Wrenn and His Library: Notes and Memories* (Chicago: Privately Printed, 1933), 13, 17–18; Vinson, "University Crosses the Bar," 284 (fourth quotation), 289 (second and third quotations).

22. Vinson, "University Crosses the Bar," 284 (first quotation), 289 (second quotation), 288–91.

23. Ibid., 289–90.

24. *Austin Statesman*, February 26, 1918 (first quotation); clipping, Littlefield Scrapbook (second quotation); Norcross, *Wrenn and His Library*, 19–20.

25. *Austin Statesman*, March 3, 1918 (quotations); BOR, Minutes, April 8, 1918, 151. The Wrenn Library turned out to have within it a hundred-piece collection that added a value beyond what anyone knew, except bibliographer Thomas James Wise, Wrenn's agent in amassing his collection. Wise sold Wrenn a complete set of his forgeries of first editions, which included those for which Griffith searched. See Harold B. Wrenn, comp., Thomas J. Wise, ed., *A Catalogue of the Library of the Late John Henry Wrenn*, 5 vols. (Austin: University of Texas, 1920); and John Carter, *Thomas J. Wise and His Forgeries* (Boston: The Atlantic, 1945). In 2018 the Wrenn Library is housed in the university's Humanities Research Center.

26. *Austin Statesman*, April 8, 1918; Wrenn and Wise, *Catalogue* 1:ix; Sarah L. C. Clapp and Fannie E. Ratchford, "Griffith, Reginald Harvey," *Handbook of Texas Online*. Observed Sibley, "The university crowd did indeed try to make Brackenridge play the game of Keep-Up-With-Littlefield." He declined. While "he was willing to be the stalking horse if that would bring more money to the cause," he "was hardly in a position to match dollars" with his rival (*Brackenridge*, 201–2).

27. BOR, Minutes, June 10, 1918, 205. The loan yielded a nice 6 percent interest (see Littlefield to Lizzie Dowell, December 7, 1917, LL). Reporting to the regents' October 1917 meeting that he had met with Littlefield about expenditures for preparing the Old Blind Institute facility (today's Little Campus) for military use, Vinson signaled that he had laid the predicate for the request (BOR, Minutes, October 23, 1917, 116, April 8, 1918, 152). The school opened in March 1918.

28. Thomas H. White, "Radio During World War One (1914–1919)," United States Early Radio History, http://earlyradiohistory.us/sec013.htm; Mildred Wagner, "A Study of the Changes Made in the Housing and Food Service on the Campus of the University of Texas during World War I and World War II" (master's thesis, University of Texas, 1944), 56–57; "Radio," *Handbook of Texas Online*; *Austin Statesman*, December 10, 1917; "University of Texas Founding of Radio Stations at UT by Professor S. Leroy Brown, 1915," History of the University of Texas Department of Physics, https://web2.ph.utexas.edu/utphysicshistory/PhysicsandKUT.html.

29. *Austin Statesman*, June 13, September 21, November 13 (quotation), 1918; Wagner, "Study of Changes," 56–57.

30. *The Cactus, 1919* (Austin: University of Texas Students 1919), 106; *Austin Statesman*, September 25, 1918.

31. BOR, Minutes, July 21, 1919, 308–11.

32. Ibid., 312; Jim Nicar, "The Great South Mall Controversy," UT History Corner, August 10, 2015, https://jimnicar.com/2015/08/10/the-great-south-mall-controversy/.

33. Coppini, *From Dawn to Sunset*, 180–81, 208–9, 250–51; George Washington Littlefield, Will, July 1, 1918, 3–4.

34. Littlefield to Coppini, July 23, 1919 (first quotation); Coppini to Littlefield, July 30, 1919 (second quotation); Coppini to Vinson, September 3, 1919 (third quotation); Littlefield Memorial Fountain, General Correspondence, Coppini-Tauch Papers.

35. Littlefield, Will, July 1, 1918.

36. Littlefield confirmed the fifty-thousand-dollar increase only in his will's second codicil, signed on November 9, 1920. Littlefield to Coppini, July 30, 1919, General Correspondence, Littlefield Memorial Fountain, Coppini-Tauch Papers. The timing and other details of the meeting recounted in Coppini's *From Dawn to Sunset* do not correspond with facts documented in Coppini's correspondence. I have incorporated the story because something similar did occur, as the half million-dollar figure common to other accounts testifies (Coppini, *Dawn to Sunset*, 250–51).

37. Coppini to Vinson, September 3, 1919 (first quotation); Vinson to Coppini, October 6, 1919 (second quotation), Littlefield Memorial Fountain, General Correspondence, Coppini-Tauch Papers; Coppini, *Dawn to Sunset*, 254.

38. Vinson, "University Crosses the Bar," 291.

39. Littlefield to Wroe, November 1 (quotations), 5, 1919, February 8, 1920, Wroe Papers, GLC.

40. Littlefield to Wroe, December 8, 1919, Wroe Papers, GLC.

41. Wroe to Coppini, September 13, 19, 1919; Coppini to Vinson, September 17, 1919; Coppini to Littlefield, December 26, 1919, February 3, 1920; Vinson to Coppini, September 20, 1919, Littlefield Memorial Fountain, General Correspondence, Coppini-Tauch Papers; *Austin Statesman*, March 2, 10, July 27, 1919.

42. Littlefield, to H. A. Wroe, October 21 (first quotation), November 26, 28, December 9, 1919, Wroe Papers, GLC; Littlefield to Ed Rhodes L. Wroe, January 15, 1920 (second quotation) (in possession of Susan Wroe Perry); H. A. Wroe to Coppini, September 13, 1919, Vinson to Coppini, September 20, 1919, Littlefield Memorial Fountain, General Correspondence, Coppini-Tauch Papers; Littlefield to Lizzie Dowell, December 21, 1898, January 25, 1899, April 19, 1918, January 25, 1919, LL; Littlefield to Malone, July 6, 18, September 14, 18, 1918; Malone to J. P. White, August 28, 1918, Malone Papers, GWL; BOR, Minutes, October 22, 1918, 209. Littlefield spent a major portion of 1918 away from home in search of relief.

43. Coppini to Littlefield, February 3 (first quotation), March 19, 1920, Littlefield Memorial Fountain, General Correspondence, Coppini-Tauch Papers; Coppini, *From Dawn to Sunset*, 260, 261 (second quotation). The date Coppini finally gained the Major's attention and thus entry to the house is uncertain because Coppini gave conflicting times (254, 260).

44. Hardly had Coppini been "forced" into anything. Coppini not only forgot "the lucky strike" but also wrote Littlefield on December 22, 1919 that "we must give up the Arch idea, as it would be a sin to sacrifice any sum of money for some thing that could not be either a credit to you or to me" (Littlefield Memorial Fountain, General Correspondence, Coppini-Tauch Papers). Coppini, *From Dawn to Sunset*, 254–55.

45. Coppini, *From Dawn to Sunset*, 255 (quotations). Littlefield must have recognized the faculty sentiment. To a lost letter from Wroe he responded that "you should say but little of my Soldier life" (Littlefield to Wroe, November 5, 1919, Wroe Papers, GLC). Coppini always believed that his inspiration to add the World War component saved the memorial entrance project. Coppini to Wroe, September 12, 1931, UT President's Office Records, Littlefield Memorial 1931–32, BCAH (quotation); Nicar, "The Great South Mall Controversy."

46. Coppini, *From Dawn to Sunset*, 255–56; Coppini to Wroe, September 12, 1931, Littlefield Memorial, 1931–32, UT President's Office Records, BCAH.

47. The account here allows Coppini the veracity of his memory but sets the conversation in March, not April. See *From Dawn to Sunset*, 254–56, 260–62.

48. Dowell, [George Littlefield Reminiscence].

49. Vinson, "University Crosses the Bar," 291–92; Coppini to Wroe, September 12, 1931, Littlefield Memorial, 1931–32, UT President's Office Records. Paragraphing is mine.

50. H. A. Wroe, Robert E. Vinson, and W. C. Hogg, Trustees, with Pompeo Coppini, Agreement, April 20, 1920; Vinson to Albert S. Burleson, November 8, 1920, Littlefield Memorial Fountain, General Correspondence, Coppini-Tauch Papers.

51. Littlefield to H. J. L. Stark, January 24, 1920, GWL; Littlefield to Wroe, November 28, 1919, Wroe Papers, GLC; James A. Clark with Weldon Hart, *The Tactful Texan: A Biography of Governor Will Hobby* (New York: Random House, 1958), 80, 110. Ever active in supporting his candidates, Littlefield had taken prominent roles in Hobby's successful 1918 election campaign and inauguration.

52. *Austin Statesman*, February 13, March 6, 24, 26, April 15, 18, 1920.

53. Ogletree and Lamb County History Book Committee, *Lamb County Heritage*, 166; Boone, "Oral History."

54. Littlefield to Pat Boone, June 7 (first quotation), July 17, July 28 (third quotation), October 20, December 11 (second quotation), 1919, October 20, 1920 (fourth quotation), Boone Family Papers; Boone, "Oral History"; Pat Boone IV to DBG, interview, August 18, 2018.

55. *Austin Statesman*, October 31, 1917, November 20, 1918, November 6, 1919, October 10, 12, 13, 1920; Ruth Key to DBG, interview, January 26, 1970.

56. "The Blue and the Gray (song)," Wikipedia. The title was given to several sets of distinctly different lyrics. Uncertain as to which the girl sang, I chose the Dresser version that mentions Chickamauga, which was so memorable to Littlefield.

57. Ruth Key to DBG, interview, January 26, 1970.

58. *Austin Statesman*, November 10, 1920.

59. Ibid., October 14, 1928.

CHAPTER 20. AS EVER YOURS

1. *Austin Statesman*, November 12, 13, 1920. Only one other figure has lain in repose on campus—popular president Harry Yandell Benedict, who died in office (Harry Yandell Benedict, Tenth President, 1927–1937, https://president.utexas.edu/past-presidents/harry-yandell-benedict).

2. *Austin Statesman*, November 13, 20, 1920.

3. Sibley, *Brackenridge*, 238–41; Berry, *University of Texas*, 69.

4. BOR, Minutes, October 28, 1912, 273, November 16, 1914, 428, October 28, 1919, 315, October 26, 1920, 409.

5. Ibid., June 9, 1913, 321, February 24, 341, 349, 365 (quotation).

6. Ibid., October 26, 1915, 514, 515.

7. Ibid., October 26, 1915, 498, April 26, 1916, 571, June 12, 1916, 601, April 24, 1917, 40; "Cavanaugh Tract," University of Texas, President's Office Records, BCAH. Vinson thought Littlefield's opposition to the move began with listening to Mezes's remarks on the unacceptable crowding of the historic campus (Vinson to JEH, January 16, 1944, Littlefield, Papers and Correspondence Re: Book, JEHC).

8. Sibley, *Brackenridge*, 244–45; *Austin Statesman*, November 15, 1920.

9. Littlefield, Will, July 1, 1918; Dowell, [George Littlefield Reminiscence]. For a contemporary history and description of the dormitory, see Battle, "The Alice Littlefield Memorial Dormitory," 136–40.

10. In a community property state, half of the total belonged to Alice. But in tandem on the same days in 1918, 1919, and 1920, George and Alice executed wills and codicils whose principal provisions were identical.

11. "For the Study of the South," *Texas Quarterly* 1 (Spring 1958): 163.

12. Littlefield, Will, July 1, 1918, First Codicil, October 14, 1919, Second Codicil, November 9, 1920; H. A. Wroe, J. P. White, Whitfield Harral, Inventory and Appraisal of Estate of George W. Littlefield, February 1921, copy in possession of the author. The Littlefield Fund has supported both a ten-volume *History of the South, 1607–1980*, published by Louisiana State University Press, and a sixteen-volume *Littlefield History of the Civil War Era* from the University of North Carolina Press. For a recent history and contribution of the Littlefield Fund, see David B. Gracy II, "'It Is but Just to the Cause': George W. Littlefield, Patriotic Memory, and the Littlefield Fund for Southern History," unpublished ms. in possession of the author.

13. Sibley, *Brackenridge*, 245–46, 247 (quotation); *Austin Statesman*, January 25, 1921.

14. Sibley, *Brackenridge*, 249–53. See *Memorial of the Chamber of Commerce of Austin and of Certain Ex-Students of the University of Texas Concerning Proposed Abandonment of the Present University Site and Plant* (Austin, Tex.: Tobin, 1921) for the initial argument in behalf of the move. Through the years, legends using Littlefield's name and proclivities have been invented and perpetuated. One of the most fanciful is that he caused all university buildings to face south (which even then they didn't). When asked about it, UT historian Margaret Berry replied: "Oh, well, let sleeping dogs lie. That's too good to change" (*Daily Texan*, February 3, 1978).

15. Ruth Key to DBG, interview, November 1, 1964; Littlefield, Will, July 1, 1918; Drawing of monuments, GWL; *Austin Statesman*, February 20, 1921; Austin City Cemetery Assn. to Littlefield, July 17, 1899; Deed, Travis County Deeds, vol. 159, 140.

16. Key replaced Selma Lindblad, Alice's beloved housekeeper, nurse, and comfort who died of the Spanish flu in 1919 and became the first to be buried at the family plot.

17. Bonilee Garrett, Newton Key, and Ruth Wise to DBG, interview, September 18, 2004; Alice Gracy to Sharon Wallace, interview, June 17, 1982; "Christmas Trees That Live," *Texas Star Sunday Magazine, Houston Post*, December 12, 1971.

18. Alice Daniel to Haley, interview, July 18, 1939 (quotations); Garrett, Key, and Wise to DBG, interview, September 18, 2004; Mrs. Sully Roberdeau to JEH, interview, January 12, 1939; Buford, "My Life," 4.

19. "Mrs. Littlefield Dead," *Alcalde*, February 1935 (quotation); Ruth Key to Alice Gracy, interview, November 29, December 5, 1943; Alice Gracy to Sharon Wallace, interview, June 17, 1982; Max Bickler to DBG, interview, May 16, 1968; Littlefield, "Autobiography," 1919; Taylor, "Major George W. Littlefield," 577. In 1997, seventy years after Alice Littlefield Dormitory opened, a portrait of Alice Littlefield was hung in the lobby. Based on a carte de visite of Alice in her thirties (fig. 14), it was painted by niece Sarah Harral Duggan, who grew up in the Littlefield home and was so devoted to Aunt Alice that she named her only daughter for her.

20. *Austin American-Statesman*, June 15, August 25, September 10 (quotation), November 26, 1924.

21. *Austin American-Statesman*, November 8, 1929, January 15, February 14, 1930, April 29, 1933.

22. BOR, Minutes, June 9, 1919, 284, July 7, 1919, 306, July 21, 312; Littlefield to Wroe, January 15, 21, 1920, Wroe Papers, GLC; Littlefield, Will, Codicil 2, Item 10.

23. Williamson, "Littlefield House," 16; *Daily Texan*, December 13, 1955, March 1, 1978; *Austin Centennial Weekly* [Official Program of the University of Texas Centennial Exposition], August 2, 1936; *Austin American*, August 26, 1952, September 29, November 27, 1957; *Texas Times*, September–October 1970, "Ghost Stories, Littlefield Style," *Images*, February 18, 1980; *Dallas Morning News*, August 2, 1970; Jim Nicar, "The Alumni Center Turns 50!," UT History Corner, April 10, 2015, https://jimnicar.com/2015/04/10/the-alumni-center-turns-50/.

24. Ruth Key to DBG, interview, January 26, 1970.

25. Lomax, "Review of *George W. Littlefield*," 439–45, 442 (quotation); Campbell J. Duggan to DBG, interview, July 17, 1964; E. C. Barker to Haley, January 15, 1944, Littlefield Wallet 1, Papers and Correspondence Re: Book, JEH; Boone, "Oral History."

26. Nathan did not know his age with certainty, but the ages he gave census takers and others suggest he was born in 1832, give or take a year. In 1936 the Whites inscribed 105 on his tombstone, all the while saying he was ten years older than Littlefield, which would have meant he was 104 when he died (David B. Gracy II, "'I Ain't Never Gwuine to Leave Him': The Life of Nathan Stokes, 1832–1936").

27. *New York Times*, February 3, 1936; *Austin Statesman*, February 3, 1936. The *Times* misspelled the name as "Stockes." The monument never materialized.

28. Littlefield to J. M. Murphy, January 23, 1915 (first quotation), in possession of the author, courtesy E. R. L. Wroe; Littlefield to Lizzie Dowell, February 18, 1916 (second quotation), LL; Littlefield, Will, July 1, 1918, First Codicil, October 14, 1919, Second Codicil, November 9, 1919; Ruth Key to Alice Gracy, interview, November 29, 1943; Bootie, "Oral History." Littlefield communicated with several heirs regarding properties that could constitute part of their inheritance (Littlefield to Duggan, August 2, 1919, George W. Littlefield File, ADG).

29. *Austin American-Statesman*, January 10, 1924.

30. *Austin Statesman*, August 1, 1957, February 11, 1960, August 5, 1973, November 2, 1978, July 29, 1979; *Daily Texan*, February 6, 1975. For information on the murals, see appendix C.

31. Unidentified clipping, 1924, Littlefield Scrapbook; J. T. Scott to J. R. Key, April 17, 1935; J. R. Parten to Key, April 22, 1935; K. H. Aynesworth to Key, April 18, 1935; Arthur P. Duggan to J. R. Key, April 11, 1935, J. R. Key Initiative, Alice P. Tillar Papers, DBG; Littlefield Gifts to the University of Texas, n.d., UT Board of Regents Records; *Dallas Morning News*, January 22, 1928; *Austin American*, July 19, 1936.

32. "George Washington Littlefield," University of Texas, Littlefield Society, https://giving.utexas.edu/2010/04/14/george-washington-littlefield/ (quotation); Development Guide: President's Associates, https://giving.utexas.edu/devguide/presidents-associates/; Lee Bash to DBG, email, August 1, 1918; Gregory L. Fenves to Dear Longhorns, email, August 19, 2017; Victoria Davis, "A Monumental Decision," *Life and Letters*, Spring 2017, 25–30, http://lifeandletters.la.utexas.edu/2017/05/a-monumental-decision-what-to-do-about-jefferson-davis-and-the-challenges-of-commemoration/; *Austin American-Statesman*, August 20, 2017; *Daily Texan*, September 14, 2017. The Davis statue had been carelessly divorced from Coppini's thoughtful design arranging the six statues to symbolize the unification of North and South in winning World War I and thereby saving democracy.

33. Littlefield to H. J. L. Stark, March 24, 1920 (quotation), GWL; Edmunds Travis to DBG, interview, June 9, 1971.

34. Littlefield to Shelton Dowell, April 5, 1875; Littlefield to Maurice Dowell, December 29, 1904, September 11, 1894, LL.

APPENDIX B

1. Daniell, *Texas*, 138; Daniell, *Types of Successful Men*, 348–49; and Posey, "A Story of Terry's Texas Rangers."

2. This account is based on Chickamauga troop movement authority David A. Powell to DBG, November 15, 20, 23, 25, 2014; Robert L. Carter to DBG, interview, May 14, 2016; David A. Powell, *Failure in the Saddle: Nathan Bedford Forrest, Joseph Wheeler, and the Confederate Cavalry in the Chickamauga Campaign* (New York: Savas Beatie, 2010), 158–73, 273–77; David A. Powell, *Maps of Chickamauga: An Atlas of the Chickamauga Campaign, Including the Tullahoma Operations, June 22–September 23, 1863* (New York: Savas Beatie, 2009), 250–53; A. F. Shaw, "My Experiences, The War of the 60s Briefly Told," *Walker County (Georgia) Messenger*, April 3, 1902, Fourth Georgia Cavalry File, Chickamauga-Chattanooga National Military Park; Bunting Letter, September 29, 1863, in Cutrer, *God of Battles*, 197–99; "Report of Maj. Gen. Joseph Wheeler, October 30, 1863," in *Official Records*, 30, pt. 2, 519–21; Frank Batchelor to My Dear Wife, October 18, 1863, in Rugeley, *Batchelor-Turner Letters*, 72; Chickamauga and Chattanooga National Park Commission, *Atlas of the Battlefields of Chickamauga, Chattanooga and Vicinity* (Washington: Government Printing Office, 1901), Plates 7 and 8, https://www.loc.gov/resource/g3924cm.gcw0162000/? sp=13 and . . . =14; Cozzens, *This Terrible Sound*, 90, 288–90, 392–94, 463–66.

APPENDIX C

1. Kenyon Cox, "Mural Painting in France and America," *Concerning Painting: Considerations Theoretical and Historical* (1917), 258; and Edwin H. Blashfield, *Mural Painting in America: The Scammon Lectures Delivered Before the Art Institute of Chicago, March 1912* (1913), 6, quoted in Russell Tether Fine Arts Associates, "The Littlefield Murals."

2. *Texas Bankers' Journal* 1, no. 1 (September 1911): 34; *American National Bank, Austin, Texas* (Austin: American National Bank, 1911); Pearl Cashell Jackson, *Austin Yesterday and Today: A Glance at Her History, a Word about Her Enterprises, a Description of Her Big Banking Establishment* (Austin: Pearl Cashell Jackson, 1915).

3. They were either not kept by him, lost in a 1919 fire that destroyed bank records, or destroyed with other documentation as trash when the bank moved out of the Littlefield Building in 1954.

4. Littlefield to Webster, April 14, 1911, LLPB.

5. *Austin Statesman*, August 6, 1911, February 11, 1960; Carl Widen and Alfred Ellison to DBG, interview, June 8, 1971.

BIBLIOGRAPHY

ARCHIVAL SOURCES

Austin History Center, Austin, Tex.
   Confederate Woman's Home. Folder.
   Driskill, Jesse Lincoln. File.
   Johnson, John O. File.
   Niles-Graham-Pease. Collection.
   Robertson, John Ben. Papers.

American National Bank, Austin, Tex. No records exist for the twenty-eight years that Littlefield directed the bank's affairs. The bank's records burned in 1919, forcing me to rely primarily on newspaper accounts for developments in the bank.

Austin Presbyterian Theological Seminary Archives, Austin, Tex.
   King, Samuel Alexander. Papers.

Baker Library. Harvard Business School, Cambridge, Mass.
   R. G. Dun and Co. Credit Report Volumes.

Boone, Pat H., Jr., Family Papers. In possession of Pat H. Boone IV.
   Boone, Mildred F. Letters.
   Littlefield, George W. Letters.

Brazoria County, Angleton, Tex.
   District Court, Divorce Case 2349.

Caldwell County, Lockhart, Tex.
   Deeds.
   Promissory Notes.

Carroll County, Huntington, Tenn.
   Commissioners Court. Minute Books.
   Tax List, Records, 1783–1895. Accessed on Ancestry.com.

Chaves County, Roswell, N.Mex.
   County Clerk.
       Deeds.
       Miscellaneous Book.
   District Clerk. Case Files.

Chilton, Frank Bowden. Papers. Texas Collection, Baylor University, Waco, Tex.

Dolph Briscoe Center for American History, University of Texas at Austin (BCAH)
> Barker, Eugene C. Papers.
> Bunting, Robert Franklin. Papers.
> Calhoun, John William. Papers.
> Colquitt, Oscar B. Papers.
> Coppini-Tauch. Papers.
> Gracy-Littlefield Collection (GLC).
>> Littlefield, Alice. Papers (ALP).
>> Littlefield, George. Papers.
>> Wroe, H. A. Papers.
> Gunter, Jot. Papers.
> Hill, John W. Papers.
> Littlefield, George Washington. Papers (GWL).
> The papers are sadly incomplete because quantities were destroyed when the American National Bank moved out of its Littlefield Building home in 1954. Particularly notable by its absence is documentation of Littlefield's political and Confederate veteran activity.
> *Littlefield Letterpress Book* (LLPB). Two books exist, covering the years 1909–13 and 1917–18, respectively. The dates of documents cited establish the particular book. These two books survive because a passerby took them from a pile of papers the American National Bank was having hauled off as part of its move out of its Littlefield Building Home.
> *Littlefield Letters* (LL). Transcriptions of Dowell Family letters, most written by George Littlefield, loaned by Maurice H. Dowell to the University of Texas in 1937 for transcription. Dowell subsequently disbursed the originals between the Dolph Briscoe Center for American History and the Texas State Archives (which holds the largest group). Having satisfied myself of the accuracy of the transcriptions, I have utilized the Littlefield Letters transcriptions for convenience.
> *Littlefield Papers Holdings Record.*
> *Littlefield Scrapbook.* Newspaper articles clipped by the university and later designated "Littlefield Scrapbook."
> McGaughey, John D. Papers.
> Pennybacker, Mrs. Percy V. [Anna]. Papers.
> Pierce, Abel Head "Shanghai." Papers.
> Snyder, Dudley Hiram. Papers.
> Spencer, C. B. Collection.
> Stout. Samuel H. Collection.
> Texas and Southwestern Cattle Raisers Association. Records.
> United Daughters of the Confederacy. Papers.
> University of Texas. Board of Regents (BOR). Records.
> University of Texas, President's Office. Records.
> Vandale, Earl. Collection.

Dowell, Greensville. Autobiography. Typescript. Texas State Archives and the Dolph Briscoe Center for American History. The original autobiography, titled "Truth Is Stranger Than Fiction," is housed at and is online from the Blocker History of Medicine Collection, University of Texas Medical Branch, Galveston.

Dowell-Littlefield Collection, Houston Metropolitan Research Center, Houston, Tex.
> Dowell, Maurice Hood. ["George Littlefield Reminiscence"].
> Dowell Family. Papers. Largely letters from George W. Littlefield.

Elbert County, Elberton, Ga.
> Will Book, 1825–1829.

Gibson County, Tenn.
Early Tax List Records, 1783–1895. Available on Ancestry.com.

Gonzales County, Gonzales, Tex.
County Clerk.
Brand Books.
Characters and Devices Book.
Deeds.
Probate Records.
District Court.
Journal Book.

Gracy, Alice Duggan. Papers (ADG). In possession of the author.
Littlefield, Nance, White. Genealogy files.
Littlefield, George W. File.

Gracy, David B. II. Papers and Collection (DBG). In possession of the author.
Littlefield, George Washington. Civil War Letters (LCWL). Typescripts of lost originals.
Maxwell, Norma. Littlefield Genealogy Documentation.

Harris County, Houston, Tex.
Marriage License Records.

Hays County, San Marcos, Tex.
Deed Book.

Hill, Jesse (Mrs. Hamlin). Photographs. In possession of Patsy Hill Rahn.

Kansas Historical Society, Topeka, Kans.
Grand Central Hotel. Register.

Lamb County, Littlefield, Tex.
Deed Records.

Lindstrom, Betsy Anne Springfield. Papers (BL). In possession of Betsy Lindstrom.
Satterwhite Family Bible.
White Family Genealogy.
White, John H. Jr. Family Papers.

Littlefield, George Theodore. Papers. In family possession.

Mississippi Department of Archives and History, Jackson, Miss.
Mississippi State Census. 1841. Available on Ancestry.com.
Panola County. Combined Tax Rolls. 1840s. Available on Ancestry.com.

Mason County, Mason, Tex.
Brand Book.
Deed Book.

National Archives and Records Administration, Washington, D.C.
Eighth Texas Cavalry. Muster Rolls. Compiled Military Service Records, Confederate.
Spanish-American War. Compiled Military Service Records. Available on Ancestry.com.

Nita Stewart Haley Library, Midland, Tex.
Haley, J. Evetts. Collection.
Texas Confederate Museum. Collection.

Oldham County, Vega, Tex.
Deed Book.
Bill of Sale Book.

Panhandle-Plains Historical Museum, Canyon, Tex.
    XIT Ranch. Records.

Panola County, Sardis, Miss.
    Chancery Clerk.
            Circuit Court. Minutes.
            Deed Books.
            Probate Court. Minutes.
            Will Books.

South Carolina Department of Archives and History, Columbia, S.C.
    Union County. General Sessions Court. Records. Compiled in Ann Littlefield Coleman to
        David B. Gracy, September 26, 2012.

Southern Historical Collection, Wilson Library, University of North Carolina, Chapel Hill.
    Battle Family. Papers.

Southwest Collection, Texas Tech University, Lubbock.
    Harris, Harve H. Papers.
    Littlefield Lands Company. Records.
    Slaughter, Christopher Columbus. Papers.
    Slaughter, George M. Papers.

Sterling Memorial Library, Yale University, New Haven, Conn.
    House, E. M. Papers.

Texas State Archives, Austin.
    Confederate Muster Roll 1411.
    Dowell, Maurice H. Family Papers.
    1867 Voter Registration Lists. Available on Ancestry.com.
    Runge, Roscoe. Papers.
    Texas Bonds and Oaths of Office. Available on Ancestry.com.
    Texas Library and Historical Commission. Records.
    Texas Muster Roll Index Cards. Available on Ancestry.com.

Travis County, Austin, Tex.
    County Clerk.
            Deed Book.
            Marks and Brands Book.
    District Court.
            Case Files.

Union County, Union, S.C.
    Probate Court.
            Will Books.

Weems, B. F. Papers. Copies in possession of Paul Robert Scott and the author.

White, John Henry III. Papers. In possession of Betsy Lindstrom.

White, James Phelps. Papers. In possession of J. Phelps White III.

Wroe, William A. Littlefield Collection. In possession of William A. Wroe.

ORAL HISTORY INTERVIEWS

Bancroft, H. H., researcher, and C. W. Littlefield. "Remarks on Cattle and Agriculture." Austin, Tex., January 1885. Bancroft Library, University of California, Berkeley.

Basford, Lloyd. Interview by David B. Gracy II. Austin, Tex., December 14, 1970.

Bell, Wayne. Discussion of the Littlefield Home with Alice Duggan Gracy. Austin, Tex., 1964. Recorded by and in possession of the author.

Bickler, Max. Interview by David B. Gracy II. Austin, Tex., May 16, 1968. Southwest Collection, Special Collections Library, Texas Tech University, Lubbock.

Boone, Pat H., III. "An Oral History: The Pat H. Boone Family, the William P. Littlefield Family, the Kenna, N.Mex. Ranch." In possession of Pat H. Boone IV.

Bouldin, Joe G. Interview by J. Evetts Haley. Gonzales, Tex., May 18, 1935. Nita Stewart Haley Memorial Library, Midland, Tex.

Bowman, Thomas H. Interviews by J. Evetts Haley. Austin, Tex., January 8–9, 1938. Nita Stewart Haley Memorial Library, Midland, Tex.

Boyd, Hiley T., Jr. Interview by David B. Gracy II. May 19, 1969. Southwest Collection, Special Collections Library, Texas Tech University, Lubbock.

Brady, John, W. Interview by J. Evetts Haley. January 7, 1938. Nita Stewart Haley Memorial Library, Midland, Tex.

Brazeal, Mrs. J. E. Interview by David B. Gracy II. El Paso, Tex., September 13, 1966.

Carroll, Horace Bailey. Interviews by David B. Gracy II. Austin, Tex., February 2, 11, 1965.

Cole, S. E. Interview by J. Evetts Haley. January 22, 1939. Nita Stewart Haley Memorial Library, Midland, Tex.

Cravens, Ed. Interview by David B. Gracy II. Austin, Tex., January 29, 1970.

Daniel, Alice. Interview by J. Evetts Haley. Austin, Tex., July 18, 1939. Nita Stewart Haley Memorial Library, Midland, Tex.

Dingus, Georgia. Interview by David B. Gracy II. Austin, Tex., November 23, 1969.

Dowell, Maurice Hood. Interviews by J. Evetts Haley. Austin, Tex., March 24, 1937; Gonzales, Tex., January 12, 1939. Nita Stewart Haley Memorial Library, Midland, Tex.

Duggan, Campbell Jackson. Interviews by David B. Gracy II. Dallas, Tex., July 17, 1964, and undated.

Duggan, Sarah Harral. Interviews by Alice Duggan Gracy. Austin, Tex., September 19–20, 1962.

Duggan, Thomas B. Interview by Alice Duggan Gracy. Lubbock, Tex., November 24, 1943.

Dunn, Henry E. Interview by David B. Gracy II. Austin, Tex., December 31, 1963.

Ellison, Alfred. Interview by David B. Gracy II. Austin, Tex., fall 1963.

Ellison, Alfred, with Carl Widen. Interview by David B. Gracy II. Austin, Tex., June 8, 1971.

Evans, Grace Margaret. Interview by David B. Gracy II. Santa Fe, N.Mex., July 25, 1970.

Ferguson, James E. Interview by J. Evetts Haley. Austin, Tex., January 6, 1938. Nita Stewart Haley Memorial Library, Midland, Tex.

Garrett, Bonilee Key. Interview by David B. Gracy II. Lampasas, Tex., April 10, 2014.

Goldsmith, M. M. Interview by David B. Gracy II. Austin, Tex., January 4, 2010.

Gracy, Alice Duggan. Interviews by David B. Gracy II. Austin, Tex. January 4, 2010, and undated.

Haley, James Evetts. Interview by David B. Gracy II. Canyon, Tex., January 7, 1960.

Harless, Jennie Walker, and Pearl Walker Dobbins. Interview by David B. Gracy II. Gonzales, Tex., August 14, 1970.

Harral, Edgar. Interview by J. Evetts Haley. Roswell, N.Mex., June 13, 1939. Nita Stewart Haley Memorial Library, Midland, Tex.

Harral, Victor. Interview by Alice Duggan Gracy. January 19, 1944.

Hart, J. D., and Bob Beverley. Interview by Brockman Horne. Lovington and Monument, N.Mex., June 24, 1937. Nita Stewart Haley Memorial Library, Midland, Tex.

Holden, William Curry. Interview by David B. Gracy II. Lubbock, Tex., January 27, 1967.

Holman, Mrs. Berkeley. Interview by David B. Gracy II. Austin, Tex., January 30, 1970.

Hunter, Jefferson Davis. "Memoirs of a West Texas Cowboy." Interviewed by and filed under Cornelia Hunter. In Manuscript-Interview Collection, Panhandle-Plains Historical Museum, Canyon, Tex.

Key, Ruth. Interviews by Alice Duggan Gracy. Austin, Tex., November 29, December 5, 1943

———. Interviews by David B. Gracy II. Austin, Tex., March 7, June ?, October 30, November 1, 13, 15, 1964; May 6, 20, 1965; January 26, 1970.

Key, Sam, Jr. Interview by David B. Gracy II. Austin, Tex., August 31, 1964.

Littlefield, George T. Interview by J. Evetts Haley. Elida, N.Mex., March 4, 1937. Nita Stewart Haley Memorial Library, Midland, Tex.

Long, Walter. Interview by David B. Gracy II. Austin, Tex., May 18, 1968. Southwest Collection, Special Collections Library, Texas Tech University, Lubbock.

McClure, Harrison. Interviews by J. Evetts Haley. Gonzales, Tex., September 22, 1935, March 25, 1937, January 14, 1938. Nita Stewart Haley Memorial Library, Midland, Tex.

McCrummen, Elizabeth. Interview by David B. Gracy II. Austin, Tex., January 30, 1970.

Roberdeau, Mrs. Sully. Interview by J. Evetts Haley. Austin, Tex., January 12, 1939. Nita Stewart Haley Memorial Library, Midland, Tex.

Roberts, Jim W. Interview by J. Evetts Haley. New Mexico, June 24, 1937. Nita Stewart Haley Memorial Library, Midland, Tex.

Satterwhite, Alf. Interview by J. Evetts Haley. January 14, 1938. Nita Stewart Haley Memorial Library, Midland, Tex.

Taylor, T. U. Interview by J. Evetts Haley. Austin, Tex., January 6, 1938. Nita Stewart Haley Memorial Library, Midland, Tex.

Terry, Morris. Interview by David B. Gracy II. On the road between Como and Longtown, Miss., October 12, 2011.

Tipps, Mr. and Mrs. J. R. Interview by David B. Gracy II. Four Lakes Ranch Headquarters, N.Mex., October 31, 1968. Southwest Collection, Special Collections Library, Texas Tech University, Lubbock.

Travis, Edmunds. Interview by David B. Gracy II. Austin, Tex., June 9, 1971.

Walker, Charles. Interview by J. Evetts Haley. Roswell, N.Mex., March 5, 1937. Nita Stewart Haley Memorial Library, Midland, Tex.

Walker, Charlie W. and Walter W. Interview by J. Evetts Haley. Dunlap, N.Mex., August 5, 7, 1937. Nita Stewart Haley Memorial Library, Midland, Tex.

Walker, Mrs. R. H. [Ida White]. Interview by J. Evetts Haley. Gonzales, Tex., March 29, 1937. Nita Stewart Haley Memorial Library, Midland, Tex.

Wallace, Sharon. Discussion of the Littlefield home with Alice Duggan Gracy. Austin, Tex., June 17, 1982. Winedale Historical Center Collection, Alexander Architectural Archives, University of Texas, Austin.

Wise, Ruth Gracy. Interview by David B. Gracy II. Lampasas, Tex., April 10, 2014.

White, George Littlefield. Interview by David B. Gracy II. Littlefield, Tex., February 29, 1964.

White, James Phelps. Interviews by J. Evetts Haley. Roswell, N.Mex., January 15, 1927, March 2, 1933. Nita Stewart Haley Memorial Library, Midland, Tex.

White, John Wilburn "Will." Interview by J. Evetts Haley. Mason, Tex., October 18, 1935. Nita Stewart Haley Memorial Library, Midland, Tex.

———. Interviews by Brockman Horne. Mason, Tex., September 9, 13, 1936. Nita Stewart Haley Memorial Library, Midland, Tex.

White, Lou. Interview by David B. Gracy II. Roswell, N.Mex., November 5, 1966.

White, Walton Walker. Interview by David B. Gracy II. Mill Creek Ranch, Mason County, Tex., June 2, 1971.

Widen, Carl, and Alfred Ellison. Interview by David B. Gracy II. Austin, Tex., June 8, 1971.

Woodward, Dudley K. Interview by J. Evetts Haley. Dallas, Tex., January 14, 1939. Nita Stewart Haley Memorial Library, Midland, Tex.

Wroe, Ed Rhodes Littlefield Jr. Interview by David B. Gracy II. Austin, Tex., October 28, 2006.

Wroe, William Augustus. Interview by David B. Gracy II. Austin, Tex., January 29, 1970.

MAPS

County Map of Arizona and New Mexico. 1871.

Jones, Charles H,, Theodore F. Hamilton, and J. David Williams, comps. and eds. *The Peoples' Pictorial Atlas: Being a Complete and Popular Account of All the Countries of the World, in Their Geographical, Statistical, Topographical and Commercial Aspects, with 52 Maps.* New York: J. David Williams, 1873.

[LIT Ranch]. "Map of the L.I.T. Ranche Situated in the Panhandle of Texas, the Property of the Prairie Cattle Co. L'd, 1898." Archives, Panhandle-Plains Historical Museum, Canyon, Tex.

Rand, McNally and Co's. Indexed County and Township Pocket Map and Shippers' Guide of New Mexico. Chicago: Rand, McNally, 1891.

Territory of New Mexico. Washington, D.C.: General Land Office, 1907.

Twichell, W. D. "Map of Geo. W. Littlefield's Ranch Located on State Capitol Leagues 657–736 Situated in Lamb and Hockley Counties Texas." 1912. Copy in possession of the author.

———. "Littlefield, Lamb County, Texas."

U.S. Geological Survey. "Mescalero Point Quadrangle." New Mexico. 2013.

NEWSPAPERS

Austin American
Austin American-Statesman
Austin Record
Austin Statesman
Charleston Mercury
Clarendon News
Dallas Democrat
Dallas Morning News
Dodge City Times
Ennis Daily News
Ford County Globe (Dodge City)
Fort Griffin Echo
Fort Worth Gazette
Gonzales Inquirer
Houston Chronicle
Houston Post
Lamb County Leader (Littlefield, Tex.)
Los Angeles Times
New York Times
Ranger (University of Texas student publication)
San Antonio Express
Southwestern Index (Gonzales, Tex.)
Texan (University of Texas student newspaper)
University of Texas Magazine (University of Texas student publication)

PRIMARY SOURCE PUBLICATIONS

"Accounts Ledger Traces Yellowhouse Operation." *Lamb County Leader* (Littlefield, Tex.), June 27, 1963.

Alexander, W. H. "History of Panola County." *Southern Reporter*, November 7, 1963.

American National Bank, Austin, Texas. Austin: American National Bank, 1911.

Atchison, Topeka and Santa Fe Railway System and Connecting Lines, Corrected to June 20, 1914. Timetable. Atchison, Topeka, and Santa Fe Railway, 1914.

Baylor University. *Catalogue of the Trustees, Faculty and Students of Baylor University, Female Department, Independence, Texas, for the Year 1857.* Independence, Tex.: Baylor University, 1857.

———. *Sixth Catalogue of the Trustees, Faculty and Students of Baylor University, Independence, December, 1857.* Independence, Tex.: Baylor University, 1857.

Barker, Eugene C. *Ferguson's War on the University of Texas: A Chronological Outline, January 12, 1915, to July 31, 1917, Inclusive.* Austin: Ex-Students Association, 1917.

Benedict, Harry Yandell, comp. *A Source Book Relating to the History of the University of Texas: Legislative, Legal, Bibliographical, and Statistical.* Austin: University of Texas, 1917.

Benedict, Harry Yandell, and John A. Lomax. *The Book of Texas.* Garden City, N.J.: Doubleday, Page, 1916.

Benson [Henson], Mack. "Finally at Rest." *Austin Statesman*, March 18, 1893.

Breweries and Texas Politics. 2 vols. San Antonio: Passing Show, 1916.

Brisbin, James S. *The Beef Bonanza, or, How to Get Rich on the Plains, Being a Description of Cattle-Growing, Sheep-Farming, Horse-Raising, and Dairying in the West.* Philadelphia: J. B. Lippincott, 1881.

Buford, Christine Littlefield. "My Life." Ms. in possession of Nancy Buford.

Campbell, R. A., S. A. Mitchell, and H. F. Walling. *Mitchell's New General Atlas.* Philadelphia: Samuel Augustus Mitchell Jr., 1870.

Cattle Sanitary Board of New Mexico. *Brand Book of the Territory of New Mexico.* [Las Vegas?]: Cattle Sanitary Board, [1907?]. Available at: https://babel.hathitrust.org/cgi/pt?id=mdp .39015011391987;view=1up;seq=5.

Chickamauga and Chattanooga National Park Commission. *Atlas of the Battlefields of Chickamauga, Chattanooga and Vicinity.* Washington, D.C.: Government Printing Office, 1901.

Chilton, Frank B., comp. *Unveiling and Dedication of Monument to Hood's Texas Brigade on the Capitol Grounds at Austin Texas, Thursday, October Twenty-Seven, Nineteen Hundred and Ten and Minutes of the Thirty-Ninth Annual Reunion of Hood's Texas Brigade Association Held in Senate Chamber at Austin Texas, October Twenty-Six And Twenty-Seven, Nineteen Hundred and Ten, Together with a Short Monument and Brigade Association History and Confederate Scrap Book.* Houston: F. B. Chilton, 1911.

"Civil War Letter." *Quarterly of the South Texas Genealogical Society* 1, no. 4 (June 1967): 60.

Coppini, Pompeo. *From Dawn to Sunset.* San Antonio: Naylor Company, 1949.

Confederate Gray Book: John B. Hood Camp, United Confederate Veterans, #103, Austin, Texas. ca. 1913.

Cutrer, Thomas W., ed. *Longstreet's Aide: The Civil War Letters of Major Thomas J. Goree.* Charlottesville: University Press of Virginia, 1995.

———, ed. *Our Trust Is in the God of Battles: The Civil War Letters of Robert Franklin Bunting, Chaplain, Terry's Texas Rangers, C.S.A.* Knoxville: University of Tennessee Press, 2006.

Daniell, Lewis E. *Types of Successful Men of Texas.* Austin: L. E. Daniell, [1890].

———. *Texas, the Country and Its Men: Historical, Biographical, Descriptive.* Austin, ca. 1918.

Dorothy Sloan Rare Books. Auction Catalog 23. 2013. http://www.dsloan.com/Auctions/A23 /item-terrys_texas_rangers.html.

Dowell, John Henry White. "Land Titles of Texas." *Gonzales Inquirer*, December 30, 1913– March 21, 1914.

Eastern Railway Company of New Mexico, the Pecos and Northern Texas Railway Company, et al, v. George W, Littlefield, J. P. White, and Thomas D. White, Composing the Firm of Littlefield Cattle Company, Case 237 U.S. 140, Decided April 5, 1915. Available on Findlaw, http://caselaw.lp.findlaw.com/scripts/getcase.pl?court=us&vol=237&invol=140.

Edwards and Church's General Directory of the City of Austin for 1883–4. Austin: Edwards and Church or E.W. Swindells, [1883?].

Ellison, J. F., Jr. "Sketch of Col. J. F. Ellison." In Hunter, *Trail Drivers of Texas.*

Galveston City Directory, 1905.

Gammel, H. P. N. *The Laws of Texas, 1822–1897.* 10 vols. Austin: Gammel, 1898.

General Register of the Students and Former Students of the University of Texas, 1917. Austin: Ex-Students Association, 1917.

Giles, L. B. "Terry's Texas Rangers." In Thomas W. Cutrer, *Terry Texas Ranger Trilogy: J. K. P. Blackburn, L. B. Giles and E. S. Dodd.* Austin: State House Press, 1996.

Giles, Val C. "A Brave Old Black Confederate." *Austin Statesman,* December 31, 1901.

[Gilmer, George Rockingham]. *Sketches of Some of the First Settlers of Upper Georgia, of the Cherokees, and of the Author.* New York: D. Appleton, 1855.

Gordon, Clarence W. "Report on Cattle, Sheep, and Swine, Supplementary to Enumeration of Live Stock on Farms in 1880." Part 3. *Tenth Census, 1880: Report on the Production of Agriculture.* Washington, D.C.: Government Printing Office, 1883.

Graber, H. W. *A Terry Texas Ranger: The Life Record of H. W. Graber.* Austin: State House Press, 1987.

Hinkle, James F. *Early Days of a Cowboy on the Pecos.* 1937; Santa Fe: Stagecoach Press, 1965.

Hornaday, William T. *Extermination of the American Bison.* Washington, D.C.: Government Printing Office, 1889.

Jackson, Pearl Cashell. *Austin Yesterday and Today: A Glance at Her History, A Word about Her Enterprises, a Description of Her Big Banking Establishment.* Austin: Pearl Cashell Jackson, 1915.

Jackson, W. H., and S. A. Long. *Texas Stock Directory, or Book of Marks and Brands.* San Antonio: Herald Office, 1865.

Johnson, Thomas Cary. *Life and Letters of Robert Lewis Dabney.* Richmond, Va.: Presbyterian Committee of Publication, 1903.

Lomax, John A. "Governor Ferguson and The University of Texas." *Southwest Review* 28 (Autumn 1942), 11–29.

———. "Review of *George W. Littlefield: Texan* by J. Evetts Haley." *Southwest Review* 29 (Spring 1944): 439–45.

Littlefield, George T. "History of the Littlefield Ranch Began in 1884." *Portales Tribune,* April 1, 1938.

MacDonald, James. *Food from the Far West, or, American Agriculture with Special Reference to the Beef Production and Importation of Dead Meat from America to Great Britain.* London: William P. Nimmo, 1878.

Memorial of the Chamber of Commerce of Austin and of Certain Ex-Students of the University of Texas Concerning Proposed Abandonment of the Present University Site and Plant. Austin: Tobin, 1921.

Morrison and Fourmy's General Directory of the City of Austin, 1885–86. Galveston: Morrison and Fourmy, 1885.

Morrison and Fourmy's General Directory of the City of Austin, 1887–88. Galveston: Morrison and Fourmy, 1887.

Morrison and Fourmy, *Directory of the City of Austin, 1903–1904.*

Nimmo, Joseph, Jr. *Report in Regard to the Range and Ranch Cattle Business of the United States.* 1885; New York: Arno Press, 1972.

O'Keefe, Rufus W. *Cowboy Life: Reminiscences of an Early Life, Early Boyhood and Experiences as a Cowboy on the Range, on the Trail, as Manager of a Ranch and Then Owner and Operator in Cattle.* San Antonio: Naylor, 1936.

"Passing of a Lifelong Friend [John Wilburn White]." *Frontier Times* 17, no. 5 (February 1940): 230.

Penick, D. A. "Building the Y. M. C. A." *Alcalde* 8, no. 5 (December 1920): 105–14.

Posey, Mrs. Samuel. "A Story of Terry's Texas Rangers." *Confederate Veteran* 32 (April 1924): 137–38.

Price, Eugene H. *Open Range Ranching on the South Plains in the 1890s.* Clarendon, Tex.: Clarendon Press, 1967.

Raines, Cadwell Walton *Year Book for Texas.* 2 vols. Austin: Gammel Statesman, 1903.

"Rancher [Will H. Johnson] Remembers Early Centexas Days." *Austin American-Statesman,* June 5, 1966.

Reese, Annie. "Famed Letter." *Gonzales Inquirer,* June 4, 1953.

Rock, James L., and W. I. Smith. *Southern and Western Texas Guide for 1878.* Saint Louis, Mo.: A. H. Granger, 1878.

Rogan, Octavia F. "Converts Cattle into Gold to give Nation True History of War." *San Antonio Express,* June 4, 1916.

Rugeley, Helen J. H., comp. *Batchelor-Turner Letters, 1861–1864.* Austin: Privately printed, 1961.

Shaw, A. F. "My Experiences, The War of the 60s Briefly Told." *Walker County* [Ga.] *Messenger,* April 3, 1902. In Fourth Georgia Cavalry file, Chickamauga-Chattanooga National Military Park.

Shinkle, James D. *Reminiscences of Roswell Pioneers.* Roswell, N.Mex.: Hall-Poorbaugh Press, 1966.

Siringo, Charles A. *A Texas Cowboy.* 1886; New York: Signat, 1951.

State of Texas. Senate. *Record of Proceedings of the High Court of Impeachment in the Trial of Hon. James E. Ferguson, Governor.* Austin: A. C. Baldwin and Sons, 1917.

Stewart, A. A., comp. *Type Cases and Composing-Room Furniture: A Primer of Information about Type Cases, Work Stands, Cabinets, Case Racks, Galley Racks, Standing Galleys, &c.* 1918. Available on Project Gutenberg, https://www.gutenberg.org/files/31704/31704-h/31704-h .htm#STRUCTURE_OF_TYPE_CASES).

Taylor, Thomas Ulvan. *Fifty Years on the Forty Acres.* Austin: Alec, 1938.

———. "Major George W. Littlefield." *Frontier Times* 13 (September 1936): 574–77.

The Texas Almanac for 1868. Galveston, 1868.

The Texas Almanac for 1869, and Emigrant's Guide to Texas. Galveston, 1869.

Texas Division, United Daughters of the Confederacy. "Presidents." http://www.txudc.org /pastpresidents.html.

Texas Live Stock Association. *Proceedings of the Second Annual Session of the Texas Live Stock Association.* 1883.

———. *Proceedings of the Fourth Annual Session of the Texas Live Stock Association, Held at Austin, Texas, January 12, 13, 14, 1886.* Austin: Warner and Draughon, 1886.

"Uncle Nathan Talks of Major Littlefield." *Austin American-Statesman Magazine,* October 14, 1928.

U.S. Department of Commerce and Labor. *Statistical Abstract of the United States, 1910, Thirty-third Number.* Washington, D.C.: Government Printing Office, 1911.

University of Texas, Littlefield Society. "George Washington Littlefield." https://giving.utexas .edu/2010/04/14/george-washington-littlefield/.

The War of the Rebellion: A Compilation of the Official Records of the Union and Confederate Armies. 128 vols.; Washington: Government Printing Office, 1880–1901.

White, George Littlefield. "Early Ranching by Maj. Littlefield and J. P. White." *Lamb County Leader.*

Whitlock, Vivian H. *Cowboy Life on the Llano Estacado.* Norman: University of Oklahoma Press, 1970.

Wilson, Mrs. Augustus, ed. and comp. *The Opening Session of the First National Cattle Growers' Convention Held at St. Louis, Missouri, 1885 [1884] Extracted from Parsons' Memorial and Historical Library Magazine.* Bryan, Tex.: Fred White Jr., Bookseller, 1970.

Young, Stark. *The Pavilion: of People and Times Remembered, of Stories and Places.* New York: Charles Scribner's Sons, 1951.

SECONDARY SOURCES

Books

A Century of Texas Cattle Brands. Fort Worth. Fair Publishing, 1936.

Ackman, Jo Toland, and Glen Sachtleben. *Gonzales Drovers, Brands, Cattle and Mon.* 1996.

Adams, Ramon F. *The Cowman and His Philosophy.* Austin: Encino Press, 1967.

Akers, Monte. *A History of the Driskill Hotel: The Grande Dame of Austin.* Austin: Austin History Center Association, 2017.

Allen, Lewis F. *American Cattle: Their History, Breeding and Management.* New York: D. D. T. Moore, 1871.

American Institute of Architects, Austin Chapter, and Women's Architectural League. *Austin and Its Architecture.* Austin: Austin Chapter, American Institute of Architects, 1976.

Barkley, Mary Starr. *History of Travis County and Austin, 1839–1899.* Waco: Texian Press, 1903.

Barr, Alwyn. *Reconstruction to Reform: Texas Politics, 1876–1906.* Austin: University of Texas Press, 1971.

Berry, Margaret C. *The University of Texas: A Pictorial Account of Its First Century.* Austin: University of Texas Press, 1980.

Bierschwale, Margaret. *A History of Mason County, Texas, through 1964.* Mason, Tex.: Mason Historical Commission, 1998.

Billington, Monroe Lee. *The American South: A Brief History.* New York: Scribner, 1971.

Billington, Ray Allen. *Westward Expansion: A History of the American Frontier.* New York: Macmillan, 1960.

Brannon-Wranosky, Jessica, and Bruce A. Glasrud, eds. *Impeached: The Removal of Texas Governor James E. Ferguson.* College Station: Texas A&M University Press, 2017.

Calvert, Robert A, Gregg Cantrell, and Arnoldo De León. *The History of Texas.* 3rd ed. Wheeling, Ill.: Harlan Davidson, 2002.

Campbell, Randolph B. *Gone to Texas: A History of the Lone Star State.* New York: Oxford University Press, 2003.

Cantrell, Gregg. *Kenneth and John B. Rayner and the Limits of Southern Dissent.* Urbana: University of Illinois Press, 1993.

Carlson, Avery Luvere. *A Monetary and Banking History of Texas from the Mexican Regime to the Present Day, 1821–1929.* Fort Worth: Fort Worth National Bank, 1930.

Carrington, Evelyn M., American Association of University Women, and Austin Branch. *Women in Early Texas.* Austin: Jenkins Publishing, 1975.

Carter, John. *Thomas J. Wise and His Forgeries.* Boston: The Atlantic, 1945.

Cauley, Troy J. *Early Business Methods in the Texas Cattle Industry.* 1932.

Chaves County Historical Society. *Roundup on the Pecos.* Edited by Elvis E. Fleming and Minor S. Huffman. Roswell, N.Mex.: Chaves County Historical Society, 1978.

Chesley, Hervey E. *Adventuring with the Old-Timers: Trails Travelled—Tales Told.* Midland, Tex.: Nita Stewart Haley Memorial Library, 1979.

Clark, James A., and Weldon Hart. *The Tactful Texan: A Biography of Gov. Will Hobby.* New York: Random House, 1958.

Clarke, Mary Whatley. *A Century of Cow Business: A History of the Texas and Southwestern Cattle Raisers Association.* Fort Worth: Texas and Southwestern Cattle Raisers Association, 1976.

Coan, Charles F. *A History of New Mexico.* Chicago: American Historical Society, 1925.

Cotner, Robert Crawford. *James Stephen Hogg: A Biography.* Austin: University of Texas Press, 1990.

———. *The Texas State Capitol.* Austin: Pemberton Press, 1968.

Cutrer, Emily Fourmy. *The Art of the Woman: The Life and Work of Elisabet Ney.* 1988; Reprint, College Station: Texas A&M University Press, 2016.

Coulter, E. Merton. *Old Petersburg and the Broad River Valley of Georgia: Their Rise and Decline.* Athens: University of Georgia Press, 1965.

Cox, Karen L. *Dixie's Daughters: The United Daughters of the Confederacy and the Preservation of Confederate Culture.* Gainesville: University Press of Florida, 2013.

Cozzens, Peter. *This Terrible Sound: The Battle of Chickamauga.* Urbana: University of Illinois Press, 1996.

Cunningham, O. Edward. *Shiloh and the Western Campaign of 1862.* Edited by Gary D. Joiner and Timothy B. Smith. New York: Savas Beatie, 2007.

Dale, Edward Everett. *The Range Cattle Industry: Ranching on the Great Plains from 1865 to 1925.* Norman: University of Oklahoma Press, 1960.

Davis, Ellis Arthur, and Edwin H. Grobe, eds. *The New Encyclopedia of Texas.* Dallas: Texas Development Bureau, 1929.

Dearen, Patrick. *A Cowboy of the Pecos.* Plano, Tex.: Republic of Texas Press, 1997.

Dick, Everett. *The Lure of the Land: A Social History of the Public Lands from the Articles of Confederation to the New Deal.* Lincoln: University of Nebraska Press, 1970.

Dobie, J. Frank. *Cow People.* Boston: Little, Brown, 1964.

———. *The Longhorns.* Boston: Little, Brown, 1941.

Dolce, Ann Johnston. *John H. Robinson: A Pioneer Austin Family, 1817–2010.* 2010.

Dorsey, Leroy G. *We Are All Americans, Pure and Simple: Theodore Roosevelt and the Myth of Americanism.* Tuscaloosa: University of Alabama Press, 2007.

Dunmire, William W. *New Mexico's Spanish Livestock Heritage: Four Centuries of Animals, Land, and People.* Albuquerque: University of New Mexico Press, 2013.

Dykstra, Robert R. *The Cattle Towns.* New York: Alfred A. Knopf, 1971.

Eckhardt, Carl J. *The Promise of Greatness: Early Experiences at the University of Texas.* 1978.

Emmett, Chris. *Shanghai Pierce: A Fair Likeness.* Norman: University of Oklahoma Press, 1953.

Ericson, Joe E. *Banks and Bankers in Early Texas, 1835–1875.* New Orleans: Polyanthos, 1976.

Fleming, Elvis E. *Captain Joseph C. Lea: From Confederate Guerrilla to New Mexico Patriarch.* Las Cruces, N.Mex.: Yucca Free Press, 2002.

Foster, Gaines M. *Ghosts of the Confederacy: Defeat, the Lost Cause, and the Emergence of the New South, 1865 to 1913.* New York: Oxford University Press, 1987.

Frantz, Joe B. *The Driskill Hotel.* Austin: Encino Press, 1977.

Frenzel, Paul. *Historic Homes of Gonzales.* Gonzales, Texas: Reese's Printing, 1999.

Gatton, T. Harry. *The Texas Bankers Association: The First Century, 1885–1985.* Austin: Texas Bankers Association, 1964.

General Register of the Students and Former Students of the University of Texas, 1917. Austin: Ex-Students Association, 1917.

Gideon, Samuel E. *Austin and the Austin National Bank, 1890–1940.* Austin: Austin National Bank, 1984.

Gonzales County Historical Commission. *The History of Gonzales County, Texas.* Dallas: Curtis Media, 1986.

Gould, Lewis Ludlow. *Progressives and Prohibitionists: Texas Democrats in the Wilson Era.* Austin: University of Texas Press, 1973.

Gracy, David B., II. *Littlefield Lands: Colonization on the Texas Plains, 1912–1920.* Austin: University of Texas Press, 1968.

———. *The State Library and Archives of Texas: A History, 1835–1962.* Austin: University of Texas Press, 2010

Grant, Joseph M., and Lawrence L. Crum. *The Development of State-Chartered Banking in Texas: From Predecessor Systems until 1970.* Austin: University of Texas Bureau of Business Research, 1978.

Gressley, Gene M. *Bankers and Cattlemen.* New York: Alfred A. Knopf, 1966.

Gwynne, S. C. *Empire of the Summer Moon: Quanah Parker and the Rise and Fall of the Comanches, the Most Powerful Indian Tribe in American History.* New York: Scribner, 2010.

Haley, J. Evetts. *Charles Goodnight*. 1936; Norman: University of Oklahoma Press, 1981.

————. *George W. Littlefield, Texan*. Norman: University of Oklahoma Press, 1943.

————. *The XIT Ranch of Texas, and the Early Days of the Llano Estacado*. Chicago: Lakeside Press, 1929. Reprint, Norman: University of Oklahoma Press, 1954.

Hardy, Dermot H., and Ingham S. Roberts. *Historical Review of South-East Texas, and the Founders, Leaders, and Representative Men of Its Commerce, Industry, and Civic Affairs*. Chicago: Lewis Publishing, 1910.

Hargrave, Helen, comp. *List of Gifts, 1881–1932, to the University of Texas or for the Benefit of Its Students*. Austin: University of Texas, 1933.

Harper, Minnie Timms, and George Dewey Harper. *Old Ranches*. Dallas: Dealey and Lowe, 1936.

Hendrix, John. *If I Can Do It Horseback: A Cow-Country Sketchbook*. Austin: University of Texas Press, 1964.

Henry, Jeanne Hand, comp. *1819–1849 Abstradex of Annual Returns: Mississippi Free and Accepted Masons, with 1801, 1816, and 1817 Petitioners and First Returns through 1851*. New Market, Ala.: Southern Genealogical Services, 1969.

Henry, O. *Roads of Destiny*. Garden City: Doubleday, Page, 1920.

Henry, Robert Selph. *"First with the Most" Forrest*. Indianapolis: Bobbs-Merrill, 1944.

Higham, John. *Strangers in the Land: Patterns of American Nativism, 1860–1925*. New Brunswick, N.J.: Rutgers University Press, 1992.

Hinshaw, Gil. *New Mexico's Last Frontier*. Hobbs, N.Mex.: Hobbs Daily News-Sun, 1976.

History of the Cattlemen of Texas: A Brief Resume of the Live Stock Industry of the Southwest and a Biographical Sketch of Many of the Important Characters Whose Lives Are Interwoven Therein. 1914; reprint, Austin: Texas State Historical Association, 1991.

Holden, William Curry. *Alkali Trails; or, Social and Economic Movements of the Texas Frontier, 1846–1900*. Dallas: Southwest Press, 1930.

Holland, Richard A. *The Texas Book: Profiles, History, and Reminiscences of the University*. Austin: University of Texas Press, 2006.

Horn, Stanley F. *The Army of Tennessee*. 1941; reprint, Norman: University of Oklahoma Press, 1955.

Hornaday, William Temple. *The Extermination of the American Bison*. Washington, D.C.: Government Printing Office, 1889.

Humphrey, David C. *Austin: An Illustrated History*. Northridge, Calif.: Windsor, 1985.

Hunter, J. Marvin, and George W. Saunders. *The Trail Drivers of Texas*. 1924; Austin: University of Texas Press, 1992.

Iverson, Patricia Garrett. *White and Allied Families: Of Virginia, Elbert County, GA, North Mississippi and Beyond*. Roundup, Mont.: P. G. Iverson, 2007.

Josephson, Matthew. *The Robber Barons: The Great American Capitalists, 1861–1901*. 1934; reprint, New Brunswick, New Jersey: Transaction Publishers, 2011.

Johnson, Frank W., Eugene C. Barker, and Ernest William Winkler. *A History of Texas and Texans*. Chicago; New York: American Historical Society, 1916.

Johnston, William Preston. *The Life of General Albert Sidney Johnston: Embracing His Services in the Armies of the United States, the Republic of Texas, and the Confederate States*. New York: D. Appleton, 1878.

Keleher, William A. *The Fabulous Frontier: Twelve New Mexico Items*. Rev. ed. Albuquerque: University of New Mexico Press, 1962.

Kinchen, Oscar Arvle. *General Bennett H. Young, Confederate Raider and A Man of Many Adventures*. West Hanover, Mass.: Christopher Publishing House, 1981.

King, Kelley M. *Call Her a Citizen: Progressive-Era Activist and Educator Anna Pennybacker*. College Station: Texas A&M University Press, 2010.

Lamar, Howard Roberts. *Charlie Siringo's West: An Interpretive Biography*. Albuquerque: University of New Mexico Press, 2005.

Lane, Janie Warren Hollingsworth. *Key and Allied Families.* Macon, Ga.: J. W. Burke, 1931.

Larson, Carole. *The Forgotten Frontier: The Story of Southeastern New Mexico.* Albuquerque: University of New Mexico Press, 1993.

Lipsey, John Johnson, and Edith Powell. *The Lives of James John Hagerman: Builder of the Colorado Midland Railway.* Denver: Golden Bell Press, 1968.

Loggins, Vernon, *Two Romantics and Their Ideal Life: Elisabet Ney, Sculptor, Edmund Montgomery, Philosopher,* New York: Odyssey Press, 1946.

Lomax, John Avery. *Will Hogg, Texan.* Austin: University of Texas Press, 1956.

Ludwig, Wayne. *The Old Chisholm Trail: From Cow Path to Tourist Stop.* College Station: Texas A&M University Press, 2018.

MacCorkle, Stuart A. *Austin's Three Forms of Government.* San Antonio: Naylor, 1973.

Massey, Sara R., ed. *Black Cowboys of Texas.* College Station: Texas A&M University Press, 2000.

Matthews, Charles R. *Higher Education in Texas: Its Beginnings to 1970.* Denton: University of North Texas Press, 2018.

Mauldin, Lynn C. *Lea County, New Mexico: A Pictorial History.* Virginia Beach: Donning, 1997.

McAdams, Ina May Ogletree. *Texas Women of Distinction: A Biographical History.* Austin: McAdams Publishers, 1962.

McCallum, Henry D., and Frances T. McCallum. *The Wire That Fenced the West.* Norman: University of Oklahoma Press, 1965.

McCarty, John L. *Maverick Town: The Story of Old Tascosa.* Norman: University of Oklahoma Press, 1988.

McCaslin, Richard B. *At the Heart of Texas: One Hundred Years of the Texas State Historical Association, 1897–1997.* Austin: Texas State Historical Association, 2007.

McMichael, Kelly. *Sacred Memories: The Civil War Monument Movement in Texas.* Denton: Texas State Historical Association, 2009.

Merlan, Thomas W. *Historic Homesteads and Ranches in New Mexico: A Historic Context.* Santa Fe: New Mexico Office of Cultural Affairs, Historic Preservation Division, 2010.

Miller, Michael C. *Austin's First Cookbook: Our Home Recipes, Remedies and Rules of Thumb.* Austin: American Palate, 2015.

Murrah, David J. *C. C. Slaughter: Rancher, Banker, Baptist.* Austin: University of Texas Press, 1981.

Murrah, Jeffrey D. *None but Texians: A History of Terry's Texas Rangers.* Austin: Eakin Press, 2001.

National Live Stock Association. *Prose and Poetry of the Live Stock Industry of the United States, with Outlines of the Origin and Ancient History of Our Live Stock Animals.* 1904; reprint, New York: Antiquarian Press, 1959.

Nolan, Frederick W. *Tascosa: Its Life and Gaudy Times.* Lubbock: Texas Tech University Press, 2007.

Norcross, Frederic F. *John H. Wrenn and His Library: Notes and Memories.* Chicago: Privately printed, 1933.

Nordyke, Lewis. *Cattle Empire: The Fabulous Story of the 3,000,000 Acre XIT.* New York: William Morrow, 1949.

Ogletree, Mardema, comp. *The Heritage of Lamb County, Texas.* Dallas: Curtis Media, 1992.

Overbeck, Ruth Ann. *Alexander Penn Wooldridge.* Austin: Von Boeckmann-Jones, 1963.

Paddock, B. B., ed. *A History of Central and Western Texas.* Chicago: Lewis Publishing, 1911.

Pearce, William Martin. *The Matador Land and Cattle Company.* Norman: University of Oklahoma Press, 1964.

Poe, Sophie A., and Eugene Cunningham. *Buckboard Days.* Caldwell, Idaho: Caxton Printers, 1936.

Polley, Joseph Benjamin. *Hood's Texas Brigade: Its Marches, Its Battles, Its Achievements.* New York: Neale , 1910.

Pool, William C. *Eugene C. Barker, Historian*. Austin: Texas State Historical Association, 1971.

Powers, John F., Deborah Daniels Powers, and Ron Tyler. *Texas Painters, Sculptors and Graphic Artists: A Biographical Dictionary of Artists in Texas before 1942*. Austin: Woodmont Books, 2000.

Price, B. Byron. *The Chuck Wagon Cookbook: Recipes from the Ranch and Range for Today's Kitchen*. Norman: University of Oklahoma Press, 2004.

Pringle, Henry Fowles. *Theodore Roosevelt: A Biography*. New York: Harcourt Brace, 1956.

Randall, J. G., and David Donald. *The Civil War and Reconstruction*. 2nd ed. Boston: D.C. Heath 1961.

Ratner, Sidney. *New Light on the History of Great American Fortunes: American Millionaires of 1892 and 1902*. New York: Augustus M. Kelley, 1953.

Richardson, Rupert Norval. *The Comanche Barrier to South Plains Settlement: A Century and a Half of Savage Resistance to the Advancing White Frontier*. Glendale, Calif.: Arthur H. Clark, 1933.

Ritchhart, Delbert A. *Breathing Life into Family Ancestors: About the Ritchhart, Dean, Bush, O'Malley, Schmidt, McConnell and Other Associated Families*. Bloomington, Ind.: Author-House, 2011.

Robertson, Pauline Durrett, and R. L. Robertson. *Cowman's Country: Fifty Frontier Ranches in the Texas Panhandle, 1876–1887*. Amarillo: Paramount Publishing, 1981.

Rosenburg, R. B. *Living Monuments: Confederate Soldiers' Homes in the New South*. Chapel Hill: University of North Carolina Press, 1993.

Sanders, Alvin Howard. *The Cattle of the World: Their Place in the Human Scheme—Wild Types and Modern Breeds in Many Lands*. Washington, D.C.: National Geographic Society, 1926.

———. *The Story of the Herefords: An Account of the Origin and Development of the Breed in Herefordshire, a Sketch of Its Early Introduction into the United States and Canada, and Subsequent Rise to Popularity in the Western Cattle Trade, with Sundry Notes on the Management of Breeding Herds*. Chicago: Breeder's Gazette, 1914.

Sandoz, Mari. *The Cattlemen*. Lincoln: University of Nebraska Press, 2010.

Scarborough, William Kauffman. *The Overseer: Plantation Management in the Old South*. Baton Rouge: Louisiana State University Press, 1966.

Schmelzer, Janet. *Our Fighting Governor: The Life of Thomas M. Campbell and the Politics of Progressive Reform in Texas*. College Station: Texas A&M University Press, 2014.

Schofield, Donald F. *Indians, Cattle, Ships, and Oil: The Story of W. M. D. Lee*. Austin: University of Texas Press, 1985.

Scott, Anne Firor. *The Southern Lady: From Pedestal to Politics, 1830–1930*. Chicago: University of Chicago Press, 1970.

Sheffy, Lester Fields. *The Francklyn Land and Cattle Company: A Panhandle Enterprise*. Austin: University of Texas Press, 1981.

Shinkle, James D. *Fifty Years of Roswell History, 1867–1917*. Roswell, N.Mex.: Hall-Poorbaugh, 1964.

Sibley, Marilyn McAdams. *George W. Brackenridge: Maverick Philanthropist*. Austin: University Texas Press, 1973.

Simpson, Harold B. *Hood's Texas Brigade in Reunion and Memory*. Hillsboro, Tex.: Hill Junior College Press, 1974.

Skaggs, Jimmy M. *The Cattle-Trailing Industry: Between Supply and Demand, 1866–1890*. Lawrence: University Press of Kansas, 1973.

———. *Prime Cut: Livestock Raising and Meatpacking in the United States, 1607–1983*. College Station: Texas A&M University Press, 1986.

Smith, Timothy B. *Shiloh: Conquer or Perish*. Lawrence: University Press of Kansas, 2014.

Spikes, Nellie Witt, and Temple Ann Ellis. *Through the Years: A History of Crosby County, Texas*. San Antonio: Naylor, 1952.

Spratt, John S. *The Road to Spindletop: Economic Change in Texas, 1875–1901.* Austin; University of Texas Press, 1970.

Stampp, Kenneth M. *The Peculiar Institution: Slavery in the Ante-Bellum South.* New York; Vintage, 1956.

Steen, Ralph Wright. *The Ferguson War on the University of Texas.* Austin: Southwestern Social Science Association, 1955.

Strobel, J. *The Old Plantations and Their Owners of Brazoria County, Texas.* Houston: Union National Bank, 1930.

Tatum, New Mexico. *Golden Jubilee Souvenir.* Tatum, 1959.

Texas Legislative Council. *The Texas Capitol: Symbol of Accomplishment.* Austin: Texas Legislative Council, 1982.

Texas State Historical Association. *Handbook of Texas Online.* https://tshaonline.org/handbook.

Tye, Larry. *Rising from the Rails: Pullman Porters and the Making of the Black Middle Class.* 2004; reprint, New York: Henry Holt , 2005.

Utley, Robert M. *Billy the Kid: A Short and Violent Life.* Lincoln: University of Nebraska Press, 1989.

Vorpahl, Ben Merchant. *Frederic Remington and the West: With the Eye of the Mind.* Austin: University of Texas Press, 1978.

Webb, Walter Prescott. *The Great Plains.* Boston: Houghton Mifflin, 1936.

Westphall, Victor. *The Public Domain in New Mexico, 1854–1891.* Albuquerque: University of New Mexico Press, 1965.

White, Richard. *Republic for Which It Stands: The United States during Reconstruction and the Gilded Age, 1865–1896.* New York: Oxford University Press, 2017.

Williams, Rusty. *My Old Confederate Home: A Respectable Place for Civil War Veterans.* Lexington: University Press of Kentucky, 2010.

Williamson, Roxanne Kuter. *Austin, Texas: An American Architectural History.* San Antonio: Trinity University Press, 1973.

Wilson, Carol O'Keefe. *In the Governor's Shadow: The True Story of Ma and Pa Ferguson.* Denton: University of North Texas Press, 2014.

Wooten, Dudley G. *A Comprehensive History of Texas, 1685 to 1897.* 2 vols. Dallas: W. G. Scariff, 1898.

Worcester, Don. *The Chisholm Trail: High Road of the Cattle Kingdom.* Lincoln: University of Nebraska Press, 1980.

Wortham, Louis J. *History of Texas from Wilderness to Commonwealth.* Fort Worth: Wortham-Molyneaux, 1924.

Wrenn, Harold Brent, and Thomas James Wise, eds. *A Catalogue of the Library of the Late John Henry Wrenn.* Austin: University of Texas, 1920.

Wunder, John R. *At Home on the Range: Essays on the History of Western Social and Domestic Life.* Westport, Conn.: Greenwood Press, 1985.

Wyatt-Brown, Bertram. *Southern Honor Ethics and Behavior in the Old South.* Oxford: Oxford University Press, 2007.

Articles and Chapters

Bailey, Fred Arthur. "The Textbooks of the 'Lost Cause': Censorship and the Creation of Southern State Histories." *Georgia Historical Quarterly* 35 (Fall 1991): 507–33.

———. "Free Speech and the 'Lost Cause' in Texas: A Study of Social Control in the New South." *Southwestern Historical Quarterly* 97 (January 1994): 253–77.

———. "The Best History Money Can Buy: Eugene Campbell Barker, George Washington Littlefield, and the Quest for a Suitable Past." *Gulf South Historical Review* 20 (2014): 24–48.

Battle, William J. "Littlefield Memorial Dormitory." *Alcalde* 16 (January 1928): 136.

Baydo, Gerald. "Cattle Ranching in the Pecos Valley of New Mexico." *Rocky Mountain Social Science Journal* 8 (1971): 85–96.

Buenger, Walter J. "Texas Identity: Alternatives to the Terrible Triplets." In *This Corner of Canaan: Essays on Texas in Honor of Randolph B. Campbell*, edited by Richard B. McCaslin, Donald E. Chipman, and Andrew J. Torget, 3–35. Denton: University of North Texas Press, 2013.

Carleton, Don E., and Katherine J. Adams, "'A Work Peculiarly Our Own': Origins of the Barker Texas History Center, 1883–1950." *Southwestern Historical Quarterly* 86 (October 1982): 197–230.

Cauley, T. J. "Early Business Methods in the Texas Cattle Industry." *Journal of Economic and Business History* 4 (May 1932): 461–86.

Dawson, A. G. "Texas' Great Cattle Industry." *Texas Almanac and State Industrial Guide for 1904*. Galveston: A. H. Belo, 1904.

"Gonzales College." *Yesterdays* 16 (September 1981): 15–16; (March 1982): 84–87.

Gracy, David B., II. "Business and Books." *Texas Libraries* 35 (Summer 1973): 83–90.

———. "A Cowman's-Eye View of the Information Ecology of the Texas Cattle Industry from the Civil War to World War I." *Information and Culture* 51 (2016): 164–91.

———. "Cows Have Calves: The Hesitant Beginning and Remarkable Career of Cowboy, Cattleman, Rancher George Washington Littlefield." *West Texas Historical Review* 89 (2013): 8–26.

———. "The Dowell Family Papers: The Splintering of an Archival Treasure." *Southwestern Historical Quarterly* 107 (January 2014): 285–97.

———. "The Duty of Such As Myself: George W. Littlefield's Ranching and Confederate Art." *Panhandle-Plains Historical Review* 83 (2011): 13–32.

———. "George Washington Littlefield: Portrait of a Cattleman." *Southwestern Historical Quarterly* 68 (October 1964): 237–25.

———. "A Man of Large Heart: George W. Littlefield and the Davis Obelisk." *United Daughters of the Confederacy Magazine* 46, no. 3 (March 1983): 19–21.

———. "Mildred Satterwhite Littlefield (1811–1880)." In *Women in Early Texas*, edited by Evelyn M. Carrington. Austin: Jenkins Publishing, 1975.

———. "A Preliminary Survey of Land Colonization in the Panhandle-Plains of Texas." *Museum Journal* 11 (1969): 53–79.

———. "Selling the Future: A Biography of William Pulver Soash." *Panhandle-Plains Historical Review* 49 (1977): 1–75.

———. "With Danger and Honor: George W. Littlefield." *Texana* 1 (Winter–Spring 1963): 1–19, 120–52.

Gracy, David B., II, and Adam D. Knowles. "State Archives." In *Encyclopedia of Library and Information Sciences*. 3rd ed. 2011. http://www.tandfonline.com/doi/abs/10.1081/E-ELIS3-120044426#.UvhB3rTEY7c.

Havins, T. R. "The Passing of the Longhorn." *Southwestern Historical Quarterly* 56 (July 1952): 51–58.

Hays, Roy. "Is The Lincoln Birthplace Cabin Authentic?" *Abraham Lincoln Quarterly* 5, no. 3 (September 1948): 151, 153, 160. http://quod.lib.umich.edu/a/alajournals/0599998.0005.003.

Heltunen, Vicki. "E. Martin Hennings: Taos Artist." *Color, Pattern and Plane: E. Martin Hennings in Taos*. Orange, Tex.: Stark Museum of Art, 1986. tfaoi.com/aa/4aa/4aa40.htm.

Hendrix, John M. "Perpetuating the Epoch of Cattle." *Cattleman* 23 (June 1936): 27–28.

Hinton, Harwood P. "John Simpson Chisum." *New Mexico Historical Review* 32 (January 1957): 53–65.

Hoskins, B. B., and Jack Blackwell, "Gonzales: One Hundred and Ten Years a Cow-Country." *The Cattleman* 26, no. 5 (October 1939): 23–28.

Kielman, Chester V. "The Texas and Southwestern Cattle Raisers Association Minute Book." *Southwestern Historical Quarterly* 71 (July 1967): 91–108.

Lipp, George A. "Passing of the Western Cattle Ranchers." *Overland Monthly* 68 (February 1914): 131–38.

Love, Clara M. "History of the Cattle Industry in the Southwest." *Southwestern Historical Quarterly* 19 (April 1916): 370–89; 20 (July 1916): 1–18.

Nicar, Jim. "The Alumni Center Turns 50!" UT History Corner. April 10, 2015. https://jimnicar.com/2015/04/10/the-alumni-center-turns-50/.

———. "The Dreaded Scourge of 'Follicular Hesiphobia.'" UT History Corner. April 30, 2015. https://jimnicar.com/2015/04/30/the-dreaded-scourge-of-follicular-hesiphobia/.

———. "A Flag Full of Stars." UT History Corner. May 29, 2016. https://jimnicar.com/2016/05/29/a-flag-full-of-stars/.

———. "The Great South Mall Controversy." UT History Corner. August 10, 2015. https://jimnicar.com/2015/08/10/the-great-south-mall-controversy/.

———. "How to Celebrate Texas Independence Day," UT History Corner. March 1, 2014. https://jimnicar.com/2014/03/01/how-to-celebrate-texas-independence-day/.

———. "Remembering Old B. Hall at 152." UT History Corner. December 1, 2015. https://jimnicar.com/2015/12/01/remembering-old-b-hall-at-125/.

O'Quinn, Trueman. "O. Henry in Austin." *Southwestern Historical Quarterly* 43 (October 1939): 143–57.

Rippy, J. Fred. "British Investments in Texas Lands and Livestock." *Southwestern Historical Quarterly* 58 (January 1955): 331–41.

Saunders, George W. "More Lore of Cattle Trails." *Frontier Times* 4 (October 1926).

Schroeder, Paul Walter. "The Littlefield Fund for Southern History." *Library Chronicle of the University of Texas* 6 (Spring 1957): 3–23.

Scott, Valerie Weeks. "The Range Cattle Industry: Its Effect on Western Land Law." *Montana Law Review* 28 (Spring 1967): 155–83.

Skaggs, Jimmy M. "John Thomas Lytle: Cattle Baron." *Southwestern Historical Quarterly* 71 (July 1967): 46–60.

———. "Northward across the Plains: The Western Cattle Trail." *Great Plains Journal* 12 (Fall 1972): 52–68.

"The Story of Austin's Railroads." In *Along the Granite and Iron Route: A Guide to the Hill Country's Historic Excursion Railroad.* Cedar Park, Tex.: Austin Steam Train Association, 2011.

Vinson, Robert E. "The University Crosses the Bar." *Southwestern Historical Quarterly* 43 (January 1940): 281–94.

Wallis, George A. "Major George W. Littlefield and the Yellow House: A Texas Ranger Who Made $6,000,000 in Ranching." *True West* 11, no. 4 (March–April 1964): 9–10.

Watt, Margaret V. "McCord's Ranch: A Chronicle of Sounding Lake." *Canadian Cattlemen*, December 1952.

Theses and Dissertations

Bailey, Lelia. "Economic History of Texas' Institution for the Blind." Master's thesis, University of Texas, 1922.

Dixon, Frederick Kemp. "A History of Gonzales County in the Nineteenth Century." Master's thesis, University of Texas, 1964.

Eilers, Kathryn Burford. "A History of Mason County, Texas." Master's thesis, University of Texas, 1939.

Felgar, Robert Pattison. "Texas in the War for Southern Independence, 1861–1865." PhD diss., University of Texas, 1935.

Fowler, Lula Mae. "A History of Panola County, 1836–1860." Master's thesis, University of Mississippi, 1960.

Gracy, David B., II. "George Washington Littlefield: A Biography in Business." PhD diss., Texas Tech University, 1971.

Haley, James Evetts. "A Survey of Texas Cattle Drives to the North, 1866–1895." Master's thesis, University of Texas, 1926.

Hazel, Sybal. "Statewide Prohibition Campaigns in Texas." Master's thesis, Texas Technological College, 1942.

Huckaby, George P. "Oscar Branch Colquitt: A Political Biography." PhD diss., University of Texas, 1946.

McArthur, Daniel Evander. "The Cattle Industry of Texas, 1685–1918." Master's thesis, University of Texas, 1918.

Murrah, David Joe. "A Cattle Kingdom on Texas' Last Frontier: C. C. Slaughter's Lazy S Ranch." Master's thesis, Texas Tech University, 1970.

Neal, Basil Young. "George W. Brackenridge: Citizen and Philanthropist." Master's thesis, University of Texas, 1939.

O'Hare, Lowell. "Social and Economic History of Roosevelt County to 1925." Master's thesis, Texas Technological College, 1949.

Ray, Jeffrey David. "The Education of Robert Lewis Dabney." PhD diss., University of Southern Mississippi, 2006.

Rickard, John Allison. "The Cattle Ranch Industry of the Texas South Plains." Master's thesis: University of Texas, 1927.

Robinson, Mary Lee. "History of Roosevelt County, New Mexico." Master's thesis, University of Texas, 1947.

Scott, Paul Robert. "Eighth Texas Cavalry Regiment, CSA." Master's thesis, University of Texas at Arlington, 1977.

Southwell, Sam Beall. "A Social and Literary History of Austin from 1881 to 1896." Master's thesis, University of Texas, 1949.

Steen, Ralph W. "The Political Career of James E. Ferguson, 1914–1917." Master's thesis, University of Texas, 1929.

Stocklin, Barbara Ann. "The Texas Confederate Woman's Home: A Case Study in Historic Preservation and Neighborhood Conservation Planning." Master's thesis, University of Texas, 1991.

True, Clyde Allen. "Development of the Cattle Industry in the Southwest." Master's thesis, Texas Christian University, 1928.

Wagner, Mildred. "A Study of the Changes Made in the Housing and Food Service on the Campus of the University of Texas during World War I and World War II." Master's thesis, University of Texas, 1944.

Watkins, Orville R. "History of Hockley County." Master's thesis, Texas Technological College, 1941.

Unpublished [in possession of the author except as noted]

Gracy, David B., II. "Alice P. Tillar Littlefield: Her Life."

———. "'I Ain't Never Gwuine to Leave Him': The Life of Nathan Stokes, 1832–1936."

———. "'It Is but Just to the Cause': George W. Littlefield, Patriotic Memory, and the Littlefield Fund for Southern History."

Jones, Andrew. "Thomas Walker Jones and the Skirmish at Mossy Creek, TN."

Kirch, Lisa. "The Saga of the Littlefield Fountain."

McCaslin, Richard B. "How the Hood's Texas Brigade Monument Came to Be."

Russell Tether Fine Arts Associates. "The Littlefield Murals." 2010 draft.

Satterwhite, D. M. "Satterwhite Family History with Ancestors Names."

Smith, Wayne. "Littlefield Home." 1965.

Taylor, Jayne. "'Bud' Wilkinson." Archives, Historical Society for Southeast New Mexico, Roswell.

Williamson, Roxanne Kuter. "The Littlefield House." Paper for Arc. 382, December 17, 1965.

INDEX

Page numbers in italics indicate figures or maps.

435